SELF-
DIRECTION
FOR
LIFELONG
LEARNING

Philip C. Candy

Foreword by Stephen D. Brookfield

SELF-DIRECTION FOR LIFELONG LEARNING

A Comprehensive Guide to Theory and Practice

Jossey-Bass Publishers

San Francisco • Oxford • 1991

SELF-DIRECTION FOR LIFELONG LEARNING
A Comprehensive Guide to Theory and Practice
by Philip C. Candy

Copyright © 1991 by: Jossey-Bass Inc., Publishers
350 Sansome Street
San Francisco, California 94104
&
Jossey-Bass Limited
Headington Hill Hall
Oxford OX3 0BW

Library of Congress Cataloging-in-Publication Data

Candy, Philip C.
Self-direction for lifelong learning : a comprehensive guide to
theory and practice / Philip C. Candy.
p.   cm. — (The Jossey-Bass higher and adult education series)
Includes bibliographical references and index.
ISBN 1-55542-303-5
1. Adult learning.   I. Title.   II. Series.
LC5225.L42C36   1991
374—dc20   90-47291
                                                                CIP

Manufactured in the United States of America

The paper in this book meets the guidelines for
permanence and durability of the Committee on
Production Guidelines for Book Longevity of
the Council on Library Resources.

Part of Chapter Eight is adapted with permission from Philip C. Candy's article
"Constructivism and the Study of Self-Direction in Adult Learning." *Studies in
the Education of Adults*, 1989, *21* (2), 95–116.

Part of Chapter Twelve is adapted with permission from Philip C. Candy's chapter
"On the Attainment of Subject-Matter Autonomy." In D. J. Boud (ed.), *Developing Student Autonomy in Learning*. (2nd ed.) London: Kogan Page, 1988.

Credits continued on page 548.

JACKET DESIGN BY WILLI BAUM

FIRST EDITION

Code 9104

The Jossey-Bass
Higher and Adult Education Series

Consulting Editor
Adult and Continuing Education

Alan B. Knox
University of Wisconsin, Madison

CONTENTS

FOREWORD

Self-directed learning has taken the adult educational world by storm in the last two decades. In dissertations and theses, in the pages of professional journals, and in various monographs and books, the idea of self-directed learning has been defined, debated, reviled, and revered. Yet despite the thousands of printed pages devoted to the idea, no single piece of work has emerged that could justifiably lay claim to being the definitive scholarly treatment of the topic.

Candy's book does, in my opinion, stand as the definitive text in this area. I have admired Phil's work for several years, ever since I came across his monograph *Mirrors of the Mind. Mirrors of the Mind* was an intriguing piece of writing, which received my ultimate personal tribute as a reader by prompting me to deface practically every page with penciled comments. The monograph gave notice that here was a voice in adult education possessing the rare combination of scholarly credibility and literary grace, yet one informed by the solid experience of the practitioner.

Self-Direction for Lifelong Learning realizes the promise of *Mirrors of the Mind* and does much more. It is packed with provocative ideas, so much so that I will need to own two copies of this book — one for my penciled comments in the margin and one that will remain undefaced, for reference purposes. The range of the literature covered is astonishing. I can think of no other book that reviews so much material on self-directed learning drawn from so many diverse sources. Geographically and academically, the scope of Candy's analysis is very wide — works from North America, Australasia, and Europe are cited throughout, including discussions on interpretations of self-direction drawn from very different academic traditions.

Yet, despite the density of references cited, the prose does not drag. Candy writes clearly, interestingly, and accessibly. His style is a model for anyone trying to communicate central ideas and points of debate embedded in thousands of academic sources. And he also writes provocatively; he casts a fair but critical eye on the research conducted in the field and on the claims made for the idea of self-direction. Self-direction is often thought of as a grasp of decontextualized tools and techniques that can be applied in any setting for any educational purpose. This book reminds us that there are four very different paradigms for self-direction and that at the heart of the concept is the very complex idea of autonomy.

So for all these reasons, I am very pleased to commend *Self-Direction for Lifelong Learning* to everyone interested in the idea of self-direction in learning. As you read through these pages, you will be intrigued by the ideas you encounter, impressed by the breadth and depth of the knowledge revealed, challenged by the opinions expressed, and provoked by the critical questions raised. In short, if you read the book with an open mind, you will never be bored, and you will almost certainly change the way you think about self-directed learning.

February 1991   Stephen D. Brookfield
                                                                Columbia University

PREFACE

Cease not to learne until thou cease to live.
                    —*du Faur, 1608*

Rapid social change and technological changes have become so commonplace that their ability to shock has diminished. Developments that yesterday were in the realm of science fiction are now taken for granted. Throughout this bewildering maelstrom, however, one thing has remained more or less constant: the limitations to people's ability to cope with change. The effect has been not only to throw into sharp relief our human frailty, but even more to highlight the apparent inadequacy of educational systems to cope with people's hunger for new skills and information. One response to this demand has been to emphasize the need for "self-directing individuals" who are capable both of carrying on their education and of learning for themselves without the cumbersome apparatus of educational institutions. Into the bargain, it has been asserted that creating "self-directed learners" will improve the quality of democratic participation, and ultimately the quality of life, because self-directed learners must inevitably become more self-determining citizens.

In recent years, the notion of self-direction has accordingly attained something of a cult status in the literature of adult education. It has been claimed as a central construct in the theory and practice of educational endeavors of almost every imaginable form and ideological hue and has influenced much recent discourse about both the form and the function of educational programs. One side effect of this pervasive movement has been that the study of self-direction has been included in the syllabus of many programs for the professional development of adult educators and of teachers in the field of higher education. A corollary has been the dramatic increase in the literature that has appeared on the subject.

Despite its meteoric rise to prominence, however, there is still no comprehensive study of the phenomenon of self-direction, nor is there any authoritative guide to the expanding body of literature in the field. As a consequence, research and practice have continued unabated — often in divergent directions — without the benefit of any systematic synthesis or overview, and educators have been forced to rely on a great number of books and other resources, many of which are perceived to be inadequate because they are narrow in focus, out of date, or atheoretical.

Although self-direction has recently been "captured" by adult education, it has in fact been a recurrent concern of educators in all ages, in most cultures, and for all levels. In classical Rome, for instance, the role of the teacher was conceived of as "trivial," in the sense that it was a teacher's duty to impart the trivium, so that learners could get on with the important business of self-education. Then again during the nineteenth century, self-direction enjoyed a surge in popularity as everyone from artisan to aristocrat embarked on programs of self-improvement and cultural advancement. Likewise, the development of self-direction has been hailed as the primary function of elementary, secondary, higher, and adult education in various systems and cultures — although principally those emphasizing competitive individual effort and geared to technologically advanced economic systems. Perhaps surprisingly, however, even in Eastern Europe self-direction is held to be a major element in education at all levels from kindergarten to university, and in a variety of settings from evening colleges to on-the-job training and programs of "social and cultural awareness."

In addition to this stress on self-direction as a goal or outcome of education, methods that emphasize the self-responsibility of the learner have also become prominent in many aspects of education and training. This, in turn, has spawned a burgeoning case-study literature focusing on educational strategies that are, or are intended to be, learner-centered and self-directed or -controlled. In short, self-direction is an enduring concern, both as a process and as a product of education. In recent years, however, it has been elevated to the status of an article of faith, a banner under which educators of remarkably divergent perspectives have rallied. However, despite the attention that has been lavished on the domain of self-direction by theorists and practitioners alike, there is still no robust theoretical framework, no universally accepted method for enhancing learners' capacity for self-directed learning, and no existing conspectus of the entire field.

Self-Direction for Lifelong Learning will contribute to filling that void. Put simply, the purpose of the book is to present a comprehensive survey and analysis of the concept of self-direction in learning, to trace its ideological roots, to examine its history, to explore its manifestations in various fields of education, and to provide some specific insights into strategies that may be used to induce or develop self-direction in learners. Basically, then, the book is about the development and exercise of self-directedness in learning, especially in adulthood. It celebrates individuality but at the same time recognizes the essentially social nature of learning and of human existence. It attempts to reconcile and integrate ideas and practices — some very familiar and some quite novel — derived from many parts of the world, many domains and contexts of learning, and many historical periods. It is a tapestry woven from threads provided largely by others.

But a tapestry requires two sets of threads: a warp and a weft. In this book, the second set of threads comes from constructivism, a branch of philosophy concerned with how people individually make sense of their worlds and how they create personal systems of meaning that guide them throughout their lives. In many ways, constructivism is closely related to self-direction, though few authors seem to have explicitly acknowledged the parallels. Thus, there are really two themes run-

ning through this book, each clarifying and illustrating the other:
The familiar threads from the literature of self-direction help
to explicate aspects of constructivism, just as notions from constructivism illuminate neglected or underdeveloped dimensions
of self-direction.

Two and a half thousand years ago, the noted Athenian
statesman Themistocles observed that "a piece of tapestry . . .
when spread open, displays its figures; but when it is folded up,
they are hidden and lost" (Plutarch, 1878 [first century A.D.],
p. 95). The same is true of this book; it is only when one stands
back and views the whole that the familiar and unfamiliar threads
merge to create a recognizable picture: the noble vision of individuals pursuing their own education and personal fulfillment
within their societal context.

Overview of the Contents

This book is not intended as a "how-to" manual, nor is
it loaded with practical tips or simple advice on bridging the
gap between theory and practice. By the same token, however,
it is not just an abstract theoretical book of no relevance to practicing adult educators. On the contrary, there are many implications in it for practice, and it is hoped that practitioners who
take time to reflect on the theory and research presented and
discussed here will find this a thought-provoking and useful addition to their armamentarium of strategies to induce or develop
self-direction in learners.

Because the book is intended for researchers as well as practitioners, I have taken care to provide comprehensive references,
which will also serve as a jumping-off point for further reading.
For the same reason, I have included one whole section (Part
Two) that reviews and critiques past research traditions and
another (Part Three) that offers an alternative theoretical framework on which my recommendations for practice (presented in
Part Four) are largely based. Readers whose interests are primarily practical should read Chapter One and then Chapters Eleven
to Fourteen. Because these were not intended to stand alone,
however, I hope that such readers will take the time to explore

the rest of the book, as well, to see how my views of self-direction differ from certain others. At the least, it would be useful to read the introductions to each of the five parts, which taken together outline the main argument of *Self-Direction for Lifelong Learning*. Part One, comprising Chapters One to Three, maps out the terrain covered by the book and acts as an introduction to many of the issues and arguments that are more fully explored later. It provides a discussion and analysis not only of the current state of thinking about self-direction and how we got there but also of some of the possible pitfalls and problems in thinking and writing about the field.

Chapter One begins with some important but often ignored distinctions. The term *self-direction* has been applied to at least four distinct phenomena, and I argue that this terminological imprecision is both a cause and an effect of conceptual confusion. Once the four usages are teased apart, it becomes easier to analyze the literature of self-direction and to look for gaps in what has been studied and written about.

In Chapter Two I seek to explain why interest in self-direction — an enduring feature of education — has intensified in recent years. I further attempt to identify some of the social and educational challenges, features, and factors that have conspired to thrust self-direction into such prominence, especially but not exclusively in the field of adult education.

Because self-direction is such an attractive concept and seems to capture the current zeitgeist so well, it is easy to accept it uncritically, but Chapter Three cautions against uncritical advocacy. Although acknowledging its great promise, I explore a number of significant limitations.

Part Two comprises Chapters Four through Seven and contains a more careful analysis of the four principal domains of self-direction: self-direction as personal autonomy, as the willingness and ability to manage one's overall learning endeavors, as the independent pursuit of learning without formal institutional support or affiliation, and as learner-control of instruction.

Over the years, each of these domains has been extensively studied, and accordingly it is possible in a work such as this one to give only a *sense* of the major lines of research. Furthermore, since I am seeking to offer some new ways of thinking about, studying, and promoting self-direction in learning, I have not dealt with some of the past traditions as extensively or perhaps even as sympathetically as their supporters and practitioners would like. It is, however, important to acknowledge the enormous debt of gratitude that I, and other researchers, owe to those who have gone before.

Chapter Four examines personal autonomy as a valued philosophical ideal. I show that personal autonomy — like self-direction in learning — is a variable concept, that it has several distinct but interrelated components (moral, intellectual, and emotional), and that its development represents one of the principal goals of all education in all settings and in all ages.

Chapter Five serves as a bridge between the issues of personal autonomy as an overall disposition or quality and the exercise of autonomy in learning. It reviews literature that relates to the self-directed learner and attempts to distill from it both a useful profile of the self-directed learner and some guidelines on how given abilities and orientations may be developed or enhanced through educational interventions.

Chapter Six tackles the vast subject of adult independent learning outside formal settings and contexts. Arguably the most truly "adult" form of educational endeavor, autodidaxy has been extensively documented (Caffarella and O'Donnell, 1987), although it is averred in this chapter that the heuristic nature of such learning has been inadequately explored, as have the personal purposes, intentions, and understandings of the learners themselves.

Chapter Seven examines the incidence of self-direction within formal instructional contexts and reviews the extensive literature on the dimensions over which learners can exercise control in formal settings. I argue that the transition from teacher-control to learner-control is fraught with tensions for teacher and learner alike and that there are very real though hidden difficulties in surrendering control entirely to learners — even where such a goal is appropriate.

Chapters Eight to Ten, which constitute Part Three, adopt a different theoretical perspective from that on which most thinking and writing about self-direction has rested. As a result, Part Three should act as a catalyst for both theorists and practitioners with an interest in this vital subject.

In Chapter Eight, I maintain that learning consists of the construction of personal meaning and the assimilation of new information, attitudes, and skills into the existing framework of personally meaningful constructs. Since no two people will have identical systems of meaning, the adoption of this approach has important implications for how we view knowledge and also how people's skills as learners can be enhanced.

Chapter Nine approaches the question of how learners orient themselves to new learning tasks, how they make sense of the bewildering array of stimuli that constantly assail them, and how all learning is in one psychological sense self-directed, while much of it is at the same time a social activity — the appropriation of socially constructed meaning systems.

Chapter Ten emphasizes that in learning, as in other aspects of life, autonomy is not a single, once-and-for-all attainment but varies according to situations. In perfect consistency with common sense and everyday experience, a person may be quite independent and autonomous in some domains of learning yet opt to be dependent and to accept direction from others when learning something entirely new. Thus, self-directedness is a product of the interaction between a person and a situation rather than a quality that inheres in either the person or the situation independently.

Part Four, which comprises three chapters, examines ways of increasing learners' self-directedness in a variety of contexts. I propose that the learner's capacity for self-direction in any given situation has three primary facets. The first is the broad self-management competencies that are the basic building blocks of all independent learning; these include research skills, time management, goal setting, critical thinking, and so on. The second facet, frequently overlooked, is sufficient familiarity with the subject matter to be able to engage in truly self-directed learning. The third and arguably the most elusive is the attainment of a sense of learning competence — the quiet assurance that one is able to exercise control effectively in a certain situation. These three areas of prerequisite achievement are discussed in Chapters Eleven, Twelve, and Thirteen respectively.

The final part of the book, Part Five, provides a new and, it is to be hoped, more comprehensive way of thinking about and studying self-direction in learning. Not only does it synthesize the main themes and issues of the entire book but it draws some parallels between the activities and characteristics of self-directed learning and of research motivated by curiosity.

Chapter Fourteen draws together the main arguments presented in the book and offers a three-part model of ways in which adult educators can enhance people's self-directedness in learning. The development of personal autonomy is a critical goal for education in general — not only adult education — but I suggest that it is not necessarily furthered by the application of learning methods that emphasize learner-control. I show that our frequently simplistic notions about how adults learn must give way to a more complex and sophisticated understanding and that there are important constraints on the extent to which people can or should strive to be self-directed, particularly in learning formal or technical bodies of knowledge, as opposed to acquiring greater self-knowledge. This chapter again stresses the highly situation-dependent nature of self-directedness in learning.

Chapter Fifteen is addressed specifically, but not exclusively, to researchers. It discusses briefly major paradigms in educational research and posits that research into self-direction — along with much of the rest of education — has been dominated by the positivist/empiricist paradigm. Because of a fundamental incompatibility between the assumptions underlying positivism and those underlying "self-direction," research into self-direction has not been well served by that particular approach, and I accordingly urge the adoption of an interpretive paradigm, which promises to redirect and reinvigorate research in that vital domain. This final chapter contains some suggestions for research topics in and approaches to studying self-direction from an interpretive point of view.

Acknowledgments

It is difficult to single out or specify all the people and points of view that have influenced my thinking about self-directed learning. The ideas in this book have diverse sources; of some of them probably even I am unaware. I am conscious, however, that, like all authors, I owe a great debt of gratitude to the thinkers and scholars whose work is cited in the text and whose ideas have contributed so richly to my own insights.

Because I have drawn extensively on a great many references, I have been confronted with the problem of how to reconcile varying spellings and forms of expression, both from different continents and from different historical periods. In the event, I have followed these guidelines. For the most part, I have settled on American rather than British conventions of spelling. Because the book focuses on adult learners — often in everyday settings — I have sometimes substituted the word *learner* for *student*. Also, I have occasionally taken the liberty of recasting direct quotations to eliminate gender bias. At other times, however, where the "tone" of the quotation would have been adversely affected, I have used the author's original wording. In either case, I have avoided distorting the quotation in any material way and hope that I have not offended the sensibilities either of readers or of the authors cited.

Like many other books, this one started life as an academic dissertation, and I am therefore particularly indebted to the committee members at the University of British Columbia who helped me — both academically and personally — to give shape to what I wanted to learn and later to say. I am grateful to Roger Boshier, Gaalen Erickson, Jean Hills, and Daniel Pratt for a multitude of kindnesses and for diverse kinds of intellectual stimuli. As so often happens, especially in adult education, my greatest obligation is however to fellow students who not only pointed out references or perspectives that would otherwise have escaped me but also provided the sort of camaraderie so often associated with desperate situations such as graduate study! I would like to acknowledge, with thanks, the encouragement of Paula Brook, Shauna Butterwick, Carmel Chambers, Maurice Gibbons, Nand Kishor, Mikaela Latieff, Michael Law, Jane Munro, and Joyce Stalker.

I have other, more recent, debts of gratitude too. I would like to acknowledge the support of David Boud of the University of New South Wales, Stephen Brookfield of Columbia University,

Peter Freebody of the University of New England, Dai Houn-sell of the University of Edinburgh, Clive Millar of the University of Cape Town, and Robert Smith of Northern Illinois University, each of whom, in his own way, has encouraged me to commit my ideas to paper.

My former colleagues at the University of New England were supportive of my endeavors. Grant Harman in particular encouraged me to accept the challenge of producing a book, and Glenn Swafford was unfailingly supportive, acting as a sounding board, reading drafts of various chapters, and spurring me on whenever my enthusiasm flagged (which, as any author will tell you, happens often). I am also thankful to Robyn Daniel, Evelyn McCann, Kathleen Santleben, and Cindy Strahle, who turned my hieroglyphics into text and cheerfully revised successive drafts as I reread them or received feedback from others.

I am grateful to my three mentors at Jossey-Bass — Susan Abel, Lynn Luckow, and series editor Alan Knox. Each of these people has an extraordinary talent for helping an author to shape ideas for the widest possible readership, without depriving the author of a sense of ownership. I am also indebted to the three anonymous reviewers whose extensive comments and detailed feedback not only have sharpened my own understanding but have undoubtedly improved the text.

Finally, however, and most important, I must pay tribute to my wife, Mary-Anne, without whose support, encouragement, forbearance, and patience this book would never have materialized.

Despite my indebtedness to all these people, I must bear the final responsibility for this book. I hope only that it may contribute to advancing that greatest of all human adventures — learning about ourselves.

Brisbane, Australia   Philip C. Candy
February 1991

THE AUTHOR

Philip C. Candy is associate professor and director of the Academic Staff Development Unit at the Queensland University of Technology in Brisbane, Australia. He received his B.Com. degree (1972) from the University of Melbourne in accounting, economics, and commercial law; his B.A. degree (1977), also from the University of Melbourne, in history and geography; his M.Ed. degree (1979) from the University of Manchester in adult education; and his Ed.D. degree (1987) from the University of British Columbia in adult education. He also holds a postgraduate diploma in education (1977) from the University of Adelaide and a postgraduate diploma in adult education (1981) from the University of New England, Australia. In 1985, he received the Coolie Verner Memorial Award for his studies at the University of British Columbia.

In his research, Candy has investigated primarily the theoretical and conceptual aspects of adult education and constructivist approaches to research and teaching. He has published a number of papers, a monograph entitled *Mirrors of the Mind: Personal Construct Theory in the Training of Adult Educators* (1981), and chapters in books on adult teaching and learning.

Before taking up his present appointment, Candy was a faculty member in the Department of Administrative and Higher Education Studies at the University of New England, Australia, and before that he taught at a four-year college in Adelaide, South Australia. He has worked extensively throughout Asia and Southeast Asia as a consultant, principally on distance education and learning-to-learn.

SELF-
DIRECTION
FOR
LIFELONG
LEARNING

Part 1

The Scope
and Meaning
of Self-Directed
Learning

Knowledge lies everywhere to hand for those who observe and think.

—Holyoake, 1892, vol. 1, p. 4

In 1852, Cardinal John Henry Newman addressed his now-famous *Discourses on the Scope and Nature of University Education* to the Catholics of Dublin. Unlike many of his contemporaries, and indeed unlike many present-day advocates of self-education, Newman was aware that those who are entirely self-taught are at a considerable disadvantage because of "their imperfect grounding, the breaks, deficiencies, and irregularities of their knowledge, the eccentricity of opinion and the confusion of principle which they exhibit" (p. 237). He goes on to adumbrate these disadvantages: "They will be too often ignorant of what everyone knows and takes for granted, of that multitude of small truths, which fall upon the mind like dust, impalpable and ever accumulating; they may be unable to converse, they may argue perversely, they may pride themselves on their worst paradoxes or their grossest truisms, they may be full of their own mode of viewing things, unwilling to be put out of their way, slow to enter into the minds of others . . ." (pp. 237–238).

1

However, despite these disadvantages, he argued that such people were preferable to the products of the university system as it was then emerging. Whatever the drawbacks of self-education, Newman argued, the self-taught were still likely "to have more thought, more mind, more philosophy, more true enlargement than those earnest but ill-used persons, who are forced to load their minds with a score of subjects against an examination, who have too much in their hands to indulge themselves in thinking or investigation, who devour premiss and conclusion together with indiscriminate greediness, who hold whole sciences on faith, and commit demonstrations to memory, and who too often, as might be expected, when their period of education is passed, throw up all they have learned in disgust, having gained nothing really by their anxious labours, except perhaps the habit of application" (p. 238).

If the university system produced people like this — and these are the ones whom Newman described as "the better specimen of the fruit of that ambitious system" — then he argued that it would be preferable for people to undertake their own education: "Self-education in any shape, in the most restricted sense, is preferable to a system of teaching which, proposing so much, really does so little for the mind" (p. 237).

Since the 1960s, but particularly in recent years, self-direction in learning has become a major object of scholarly study and inquiry. Yet, as Long (1988) points out, "despite the favorable conditions suggested by the popularity of the topic, adult self-directed learning remains weakly conceptualized, ill-defined, inadequately studied and tentatively comprehended" (p. 1).

The purpose of Part One is to introduce the study of self-direction in learning. In Chapter One, it is suggested that the term *self-direction* has been applied to a range of phenomena that, although they may be related, are not interchangeable. It is suggested that drawing distinctions between these various usages will lead to greater precision in thinking about and studying self-directed learning and that this, in turn, should beneficially affect adult education practice.

Chapter Two identifies several strands or themes that have flowed together to push self-direction to prominence as an area of educational interest. However, it also includes a historical introduction that shows that the practice of self-directed inquiry, and even of attempts to facilitate such activities, is quite ancient.

Chapter Three seeks to present a balanced view of self-directed learning. Like Newman, who is quoted earlier, I take the position that self-directed learning is preferable to the worst excesses of the system of instruction. But also like Newman, I recognize that self-direction can never, and should never, replace the position of the teacher in every learning situation, and that attempts to induce people to be more self-directed must be based on a deeper and more comprehensive understanding of the nature of learning, of knowledge, and of society than has prevailed up to the present.

The practical implications of this first part are really threefold. First, it should help us to tease apart the various meanings of self-direction and to ask whether or not they are really related to one another, and, if so, how. Second, it will allow adult educators to see that there are a number of both theoretical and practical reasons why self-direction is often promoted, and to consider how different pressures lead to different views of what self-direction should or might achieve. Third, it emphasizes that great caution is required when considering self-direction in learning, because there are hidden drawbacks and problems that may arise from the inappropriate or indiscriminate advocacy and use of self-directed methods of learning.

One

What Is Self-Directed Learning?

In 1830 George Craik wrote: "The truth is, that even those who enjoy to the greatest extent the advantages of what is called a regular education must be their own instructors as to the greater portion of what they acquire, if they are ever to advance beyond the elements of learning. What they learn at schools and colleges is comparatively of small value, unless their own after-reading and study improve those advantages" (1866, p. 61). When he wrote these words, Craik can scarcely have anticipated the impact that self-direction in learning would ultimately have on education in general and on the education of adults in particular. Although self-direction has been, as I will show in this book, a recurring preoccupation of educators throughout the ages, it seems particularly to have dominated the thinking, and hence to have captured the imagination, of many adult educators in recent years.

Whenever people speak or write about self-direction in learning, the images that they have in mind or that they conjure up in the minds of others may be quite varied. For some, self-directed learning is a solitary activity, carried out in a library or at least in the privacy of one's own home or office. Others call to mind a picture of a number of students individually pursuing inquiry projects and presenting evidence of their learning to be assessed and evaluated. For some, the self-directed learner will be somewhat isolated, perhaps living in a lonely and remote location and learning from radio, television, or materials received through the mail; for others, self-direction can occur amid the bustle and turmoil of a formal course, with the full resources of a major university, college, or training department to call on. There are those who believe that self-direction is either the expression of or the route to realize and attain the innermost personhood of the learner, while others do not attribute to it such profound importance, and use the term to refer simply to independent academic or intellectual pursuits.

Perhaps because of this range of connotations, self-direction is a concept that has attracted the loyalties of adult educators across a diverse spectrum. For instance, self-direction has been advocated both because it contributes to the development of the "whole person," and on the instrumental grounds that it allows people to be more responsive to the rapidly changing demands of a market-oriented workplace. Similarly, it is supported by those who espouse the "rugged individualism" of the United States, and what has traditionally been seen as the more conservative and conformist social system of the Soviet Union. It is envisaged by some as a useful adjunct to the traditional education system, and by others as a radical alternative to school-based learning.

Overall, it is clear that self-direction is indeed a versatile concept. However, it seems likely that any term that can be used by such a diverse range of authors might also mask a certain conceptual confusion. It is the purpose of this chapter to identify and distinguish some of the various uses and meanings of the term *self-direction* and to provide a framework for the discussion that follows. In this chapter, self-direction as an outcome of learning will be distinguished from self-direction as a process of learning. It will also be shown that self-direction as an outcome further breaks down into a psychological and philosophical characteristic of people, and that self-direction as a process needs to distinguish learning in formal instructional settings from learning in natural or everyday contexts.

Goal and Process

The first major distinction to be examined is that between self-direction as a goal and as a process. For many authors, self-direction is seen simply as a method of organizing instruction. Thus, in 1967 MacNeil undertook "A Comparative Study of Two Instructional Methods Employed in Teaching Nutrition: Lecture-Discussion and Self-Directed Study." Three years later, in 1970, Himmel presented a dissertation entitled "A Critical Review and Analysis of Self-Directed Learning Methods Utilized in the Teaching of Undergraduate Psychology Courses." Redditt's (1973) doctoral dissertation reported "A Quasi-Experimental Comparison of a Group Lecture Method and a Self-Directed Method in Teaching Basic Electricity at the College Level," and in 1978 Harrison wrote an article that counseled on "How to Design and Conduct Self-Directed Learning Experiences"!

For others, self-direction is not so much a method of teaching as a characteristic of learners. Thus, when Skager (1984) writes of *Organizing Schools to Encourage Self-Direction in Learners,* Sizemore (1979) identifies "Forces Which Affect Self-Direction and Self-Responsibility of Students," and Cheren (1983) presents a model for "Helping Learners Achieve Greater Self-Direction," it is clear that they are referring to a personal quality or characteristic of learners. In fact, self-direction is increasingly viewed not simply as an attribute that people either have or do not have, but as a quality that may be present in varying degrees. Kasworm (1983b) presents a model of increasing self-directedness in her article on "Self-Directed Learning and Lifespan Development" and, since the appearance of Guglielmino's Self-Directed Learning Readiness Scale (1977), there has been a succession of studies based on the questionable notion that self-direction is a measurable attribute, distributed throughout the adult population (Bayha, 1983; Box, 1982; Brockett, 1982, 1983a, 1985b; Curry, 1983; Mourad, 1979; Sabbaghian, 1979; Savoie,1979; Skaggs, 1981; Torrance and Mourad, 1978). In practice, this means that educators can adapt their strategies to different levels of self-directedness that learners exhibit in various situations, and moreover that they might, at the request of the learner, try to help the learner to increase or improve his or her ability to be self-directing.

In itself, the use of the same term for these two phenomena is not particularly problematic; it is usually possible to tell from the context whether the author has in mind self-directedness as an activity or as an outcome. It does have less desirable consequences, however, where it is implicitly assumed that there is a necessary connection between one concept and the other. In other words, many people seem to believe that participation in "self-directed learning" will inevitably lead to the development of "self-directedness" in some wider sense. Mezirow states explicitly what many adult education theorists seem to believe tacitly: "It is almost universally recognized, at least in theory, that central to the adult educator's function is a *goal and method of self-directed learning.* Enhancing the learner's ability for self-direction in learning as a foundation for a distinctive philosophy of adult education has breadth and power. It represents the mode of learning characteristic of adulthood" (1981, p. 21).

It seems to me that this quotation embodies an error in thinking to which Hamm alluded in his "Critique of Self-Education," namely that of "mistaking the means for the end . . . making no distinction between the characteristics of an ideal end product and the characteristics of the process that is supposed to lead to such a product" (Hamm, 1982, p. 102).

It may well prove to be the case that self-direction as a philosophical ideal is actually promoted by self-directed methods of learning. This is a plausible assumption, but it is little more than that. I will explore the connections between these two ideas later in the book, especially in Chapter Three. For the moment, however, I will draw a distinction between the "method" and the "goal."

The "Method" of Self-Directed Learning

Having separated self-direction as a method from self-direction as a goal of education, the question that presents itself is this: Is there only one type of self-direction in learning, or does the "method" itself subdivide? Many people think and write about self-directed learning as if it were a single entity. It is presented as an alternative to other modes of conducting education and, as such, is viewed as "a method" like other methods: An educational experience is either self-directed, or it is directed by someone else, called a teacher.

Although some authors write as if the teacher's responsibilities and those of the learner are simple, mutually exclusive domains that can be distinguished from one another on the basis of objective criteria, others acknowledge that control over the teaching/learning situation is more like a continuum than a dichotomy. It is perhaps useful to think of teachers and learners as occupying positions on a continuum extending from teacher-control at one extreme to learner-control at the other, where the deliberate surrendering of certain prerogatives by the teacher is accompanied by the concomitant acceptance of responsibility by the learner or learners. In the sense that there can be a dynamically changing equilibrium in this arrangement, it is reminiscent of the famous image of the teacher on one end of a log, with the learner on the other end.

Diagrammatically, the situation may be portrayed as a continuum, where each diminution in the teacher's control may be compensated for by a corresponding increase in the learner's, so that it resembles a sliding scale from complete teacher-control at one extreme to total learner-control at the other (see Figure 1.1). Both Gibbons and Phillips (1982, p. 76) and Millar, Morphet, and Saddington (1986, p. 437) utilize such diagrams to express the gradual shift in control from one party to the other. To describe this continuum, the term *learner-controlled instruction* will be used.

Figure 1.1. A Hypothetical Learner-Control Continuum.

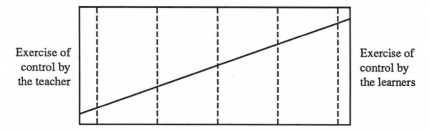

Exercise of control by the teacher   Exercise of control by the learners

Source: Adapted from Millar, Morphet, and Saddington, 1986, p. 437. Reprinted with permission.

Although the term *learner-control* was reasonably common-place in the 1960s (for example, Campbell and Chapman, 1967; Mager and McCann, 1961), it suffered a decline in usage, presumably because of its unfashionable "behavioristic" connotations. However, it was rehabilitated by Snow in 1980 and, for the present purposes, has the advantage that it is logically possible to speak of learner-control as "both a dimension along which instructional treatments differ, and a dimension characteristic of individual differences among learners." Thus, as Snow points out, "it is perhaps the first instance of an aptitude and treatment variable being potentially definable in common terms" (1980, pp. 157–158). As so often happens in education, the term *learner-control* has again been coopted in recent years, this time by those concerned with computer-based education (for example, Gay, 1986; Judd, 1975), but no such specialized meaning is intended here.

If learner-control is conceived of as a range or continuum (or more likely a series of continuums, for it is possible to exert differing degrees of control over various dimensions), then one end of the range will involve a great degree of learner-control over valued instructional functions. Various instructional strategies could be placed at intervals along this continuum, to imply the differing balance of teacher-control and learner-control (see Figure 1.2).

At the far left of the continuum might come indoctrination (a), with almost total teacher-control and little room for learner-control at all. Then might come, in sequence, lectures (b),

**Figure 1.2. A Hypothetical Learner-Control Continuum
Showing Different Instructional Strategies.**

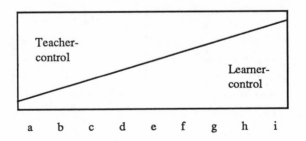

lessons (c), programmed instruction (d), individualized instruction (e), personalized instruction (f), interactive computer-managed learning (g), discovery learning (h), and so on, until finally the point is reached where learners have accepted almost all control over valued instructional functions. This point, at the far right-hand edge of the continuum (i), is called here *independent study*.

Like *self-directed learning, independent study* is a catchall for all manner of educational practices having some bearing on the notion of learner-control. In surveying usages of the term, and attempting to distill out of them common themes, Moore (1973, p. 663) identified at least four distinct meanings commonly encountered for the term *independent study:* correspondence courses; individualized, programmed instruction in a school setting; supervised reading programs in schools; and out-of-school, part-time degree programs for adults.

In addition to these other applications, the term *independent study* has been used since the 1920s in higher education in the United States to refer to "teaching and learning which focuses on the individual instead of the group, which emphasizes the person-to-person relationship between teacher and student" and "the pursuit of special topics by individual students under the guidance of faculty advisers apart from organized courses" (Bonthius, Davis, and Drushal, 1957, pp. 3–8). For a long time, such practices were restricted to "superior" or "honors" students (Felder, 1963, 1964; Stein, 1954; Umstattd, 1935), yet by 1960, Hatch and Bennet were able to state that "of late, there has been much experimentation with independent study quite outside of 'honors' programs. In addition, there are other programs or practices that advance the purpose of independent study, but are not always identified with it. Included are Socratic, problem and case methods of instruction, student research and administrative and curricular practices that introduce greater flexibility into academic programs and so provide an opportunity for independent study" (p. 1).

Thirteen years later, in 1973, Dressel and Thompson published another major survey in which they defined *independent study* as "the student's self-directed pursuit of academic competence

in as autonomous a manner as he is able to exercise at any particular time" (p. 1). Aside from importing yet another term into
the field *(autonomous),* this definition also introduced the notion
that independent study might be a situationally variable construct, depending on the individual student's capability to act
"independently" in a particular situation. The part of the term
that has caused much of the confusion is *independent,* and it was
this that prompted Percy and Ramsden (1980) to observe that
"talk of student 'independence' needs to begin from the question: of what is the student to be independent? In theory, at
least, he might be independent of teachers, of fellow students,
of prescribed course content or methods of learning, of special-
isms and publicly acknowledged categorizations of knowledge,
of limitations on sequence or pace of learning, of assessment,
even of academic conventions in the use of evidence and sources.
When a student simply works on his own on individually set
tasks, when he has some control over the pace or mode of learning, or some choice of options, it may be more realistic to talk
of 'individualized' study" (pp. 5–6).

This quotation clearly acknowledges the notion of varying levels of independence, a point also recognized by Passmore
and others (1963) in their survey of teaching in Australian
universities:

> We need . . . to begin by distinguishing a number of different
> levels of independence. At one extreme, the student is thought
> of as, in general, doing no work whatever beyond attending lec-
> tures, taking part in practical classes, reading his textbook, prepar-
> ing for examinations. At this level, he is regarded as doing "in-
> dependent work" if he so much as opens his mouth in a discussion
> class, works at a set assignment, or reads any book or periodical
> except a set text. Thus in some departments the introduction of
> a "tutorial" of any sort — even a "tutorial" which is basically a class
> for the working out of exercises — the setting of any sort of as-
> signment, the recommendation of any reading whatsoever, is
> thought of as the encouragement of independent work. At the
> opposite end of the scale, "independent" work is defined as con-
> sisting in the tackling by the student of problems he has thought
> up by himself, by methods he chooses to employ, with the teacher
> acting only as a supervisor. So when departments describe as

> making provision for independent work or say that they cannot possibly do so, they may be thinking of independent work at different levels [p. 216].

For many, the term *independent study* has special connotations relating to a physical separation of teachers and learners as in distance education (for example, Wedemeyer, 1975, p. 57). In the present context, however, no such significance is attached to it. Admittedly, it is hard to imagine an instance of independent study that would be carried out in a contiguous or face-to-face mode, but the separation of the learner from the teacher is not necessary. Instead, it is more a function of independence in the form of "freedom in the self-determination of goals and activities" and of "learning programs which are carried on to the greatest extent possible at the convenience of the learner" (Wedemeyer, 1971, p. 550).

Overall, the definition that has been found most appropriate for the present situation is that proposed by Forster (1972) in her philosophical and historical analysis of independent study: "Independent study is a process, a method and a philosophy of education: (1) in which a student acquires knowledge by his or her own efforts and develops the ability for inquiry and critical evaluation; (2) it includes freedom of choice in determining those objectives, *within the limits of a given project or program and with the aid of a faculty adviser;* (3) it requires freedom of process to carry out the objectives; (4) it places increased educational responsibility on the student for the achieving of objectives and for the value of the goals" (p. ii; emphasis added).

Independent study then, is characterized by a high degree of learner-control over many instructional elements, including the setting of objectives, choices about pacing, content and methodology, and assessment of learning outcomes. Because of this, it bears a strong resemblance to the sort of self-directed learning that takes place outside formal institutional settings, which I will refer to as *autodidaxy*. In the final analysis, however, as indicated by the emphasis in the preceding quotation, it is a method of conducting instruction that, I believe, differs in several important respects from autodidaxy.

In order to test this, it is necessary to look in more detail at the similarities and differences between the instructional domain and the self-instructional domain.

One Education or Two? In his autobiography, the prolific writer and noted historian Edward Gibbon stated that "every man who rises above the common level has received two educations: the first from his teachers; the second, more personal and important, from himself" ([1796] 1907, p. 65). This quotation is interesting at two levels. First, it emphasizes the value that Gibbon placed on "self-directed learning" or, as it was often called in his time, "self-education." In this sense, he was expressing a common (though by no means universal) belief in the ennobling power of education generally, and of self-education in particular (Houle, 1961, p. 111). Second, and more important for the present purpose, Gibbon distinguishes "the education obtained from his teachers" from that which he "received from himself." Are these really two educations, or are they just different aspects of one? This question is not as trivial as it may appear; indeed the answer has important implications for how self-direction is to be construed in this book.

In recent years, the notion of lifelong education has provided a unifying conceptual framework for much thinking and writing about educational issues generally. Despite Yeaxlee's use of the term *lifelong education* as early as 1929, it has only entered the educational lexicon in the past two decades. From the late 1960s onward, there has been a series of publications, most of them emanating from Unesco, dealing with the concept itself and its implications for education worldwide (Cropley, 1977, 1979, 1980; Dave, 1973, 1976; Duke, 1976; J. B. Ingram, 1979; Jessup, 1969; Lengrand, 1970; Parkyn, 1973; Skager and Dave, 1977; Wain, 1987). Other terms have been coined that describe similar educational reforms—for instance, *permanent education* by the Council of Europe and *recurrent education* by the Organization for Economic Co-operation and Development (OECD). According to the definition adopted by the Unesco Institute of Education, lifelong education should have the following characteristics:

1. Last the whole life of each individual
2. Lead to the systematic acquisition, renewal, upgrading and completion of knowledge, skills and attitudes made necessary by the constantly changing conditions in which people now live
3. Have, as its ultimate goal, promotion of the self-fulfillment of each individual
4. *Be dependent for its successful implementation on people's increasing ability and motivation to engage in self-directed learning activities*
5. Acknowledge the contribution of all available educational influences, including formal, non-formal and informal [Cropley, 1979, p. 3; emphasis added]

The relationship between self-directed learning and lifelong education is a reciprocal one. On the one hand, self-directed learning is one of the most common ways in which adults pursue learning throughout their life span, as well as being a way in which people supplement (and at times substitute for) learning received in formal settings. On the other hand, lifelong learning takes, as one of its principal aims, equipping people with skills and competencies required to continue their own "self-education" beyond the end of formal schooling. In this sense, self-directed learning is viewed simultaneously as a means and an end of lifelong education.

Thus, the lifelong project of self-development and self-actualization — as Jankovic and others put it, "the beautiful and arduous task of becoming a person" (1979, p. 1) — is consistent with, and facilitated by, a system of lifelong education (Skager, 1984, p. 8), and accordingly there can only be one education. In this view, learner-controlled instruction would be contiguous with self-directed learning outside formal institutional settings *(autodidaxy)*. Indeed the indiscriminate application of the term *self-direction* to both phenomena has done much to blur the distinction.

It is easy to see how the confusion might have arisen. Both phenomena share a number of similarities: stress on the primacy of the learner's purposes; independence of effort on the part of the learner; support or assistance rendered, rather than direct instruction. Moreover, one can see why, even at a subliminal level, educationists might want to stress the similarities. Autodidaxy is taken to be the paradigmatic case of autonomy in learning; autonomy, in turn, is a central notion within adult education. Autodidacts are known to be single-minded in their commitment to learning tasks, and often achieve high levels of expertise in their chosen areas of inquiry. All in all, it is argued, if adult educators were able to encourage learners into autodidaxy, or even to be able to "define" them as autodidacts, then such major instructional issues as motivation, relevance, meaningfulness, independence, and so on would be taken care of, ipso facto. As I will demonstrate later, it is not as simple as this, primarily because autodidaxy is not a method of instruction that can be called on by an educator. To understand why, let me explore the relationship in more depth.

In the same way that instructional situations may be portrayed as falling along a continuum from almost total teacher-control at one extreme to virtual learner-control at the other, self-instructional situations are also distinguished from one another by the level of assistance sought. Thus, although the initiative for a learning project rests firmly and indisputably with the learner, it is possible that the autodidact might make extensive use of a "guide" or "helper" (or perhaps even more than one) to assist with a range of factors from emotional encouragement, to the location and utilization of specific resources, to management of the learning process itself (Danis and Tremblay, 1985b, p. 286). This, too, may be portrayed diagrammatically (see Figure 1.3).

From the point of view of an outside observer, such as a researcher, it might be difficult, if not impossible, to dis-

Figure 1.3. A Hypothetical Continuum of
Autodidaxy Showing Differing Levels of Assistance.

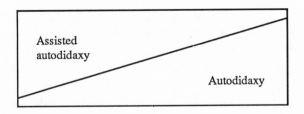

tinguish a situation of assisted autodidaxy from one of independent study. It is as if the two phenomena (that is, the independent study part of the instructional domain and the assisted autodidaxy part of the autodidactic continuum) were interchangeable. This point might best be understood by superimposing the self-instructional domain (Figure 1.3) onto the instructional domain (Figure 1.2) to reflect the simple notion that there exists a single continuum from a high degree of teacher-control to "pure" autonomous learning or autodidaxy, with an area of overlap (the shaded area) in between (see Figure 1.4).

**Figure 1.4. The Relationships Between Autodidaxy
and Learner-Control of Instruction.**

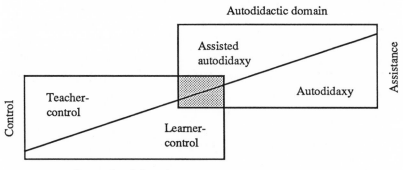

The area of overlap represents the apparent intersection of domains where, from the point of view of an outside observer, it is impossible to discern whether the primary orientation is one of "instruction" or of "self-instruction" (autodidaxy). However, it is argued here that the notion of a single continuum is misleading. Independent study and assisted autodidaxy, despite their external similarity, are not the same. Even if the difference cannot be detected readily by an outside observer, it is still important to the respective participants, because the quality of their interaction is partly dependent on their subjective interpretations of the situation.

What, then, is the difference? It seems to depend on the notion of "ownership." In the earlier learner-control diagram

(Figure 1.2), it can be seen that there is still a residue, albeit small, of teacher-control. Even though the instructor might have all but vanished, "The image of hierarchial power does not automatically disappear from the learner's mind" (Chené, 1983, p. 44). The "ghost" of the instructor lingers on, subtly influencing the learner's choices, and even the criteria used to make those choices. Whether symbolically or otherwise, the instructor maintains some degree of control (and hence ownership) over the instructional transaction and, in the final analysis, independent study is still a technique of instruction.

In the autodidactic domain, on the other hand, the learner is frequently not conscious of being a learner, much less a student, and hence the image of an instructor is not present to begin with (Thomas, 1967). Both ownership and control are vested in the learner from the outset, and the only question is the amount and type of assistance obtained. One way of envisaging this is to imagine these two continuums rotated along their axes through 90°, so that they are viewed "edge on" or in elevation, instead of from above (see Figure 1.5).

**Figure 1.5. Learner-Control and
Autodidaxy as "Laminated" Domains.**

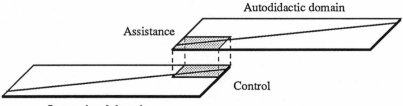

Viewed in this way, it can be seen that they are not continuous at all, but are laminated or layered. One part is concerned with who has control, the other with the assistance obtained by the learner. A researcher or other outside observer may be unable to distinguish one situation from the other. Only the participants can be certain about whether "ownership" has been transferred to the learner or not, and even they may be unclear, leading as discussed in Chapter Fourteen to the potential for mismatched expectations.

There are three reasons why it is important to distinguish these two domains from one another: First, confusing autodidaxy with methods of instruction may have serious repercussions for theory building in adult education; second, learners and those assisting them may behave differently in the two situations, and this will influence learning outcomes; and third, if there are qualitative differences between the two, then the transition from one plane or level to the other is a matter of great practical and theoretical significance.

I will return to this later in the book because the issue of ownership — particularly ownership of the questions that guide a learning endeavor — is actually vital to an understanding both of the operational limits of self-direction in learning and also to attempts to foster the capability for it (Hynes, 1986, p. 38). Also, as I will show, the issue of ownership has inescapable ramifications for the type of research that can be carried out into "self-directed learning," because it implies the need somehow to enter into the "mind-set" of the learner and his or her assistants to be able to distinguish one phenomenon from the other.

Self-Direction as a Goal of Adult Education

I began this chapter by drawing a distinction between self-direction as a process or method of education and self-direction as a goal or outcome. I have also argued that the method of self-direction in learning further subdivides into the two domains, which I have labeled *learner-control* and *autodidaxy*. It is now appropriate to return to self-direction as a goal of education.

The development of self-directed individuals — that is, people who exhibit the qualities of moral, emotional, and intellectual autonomy — is the long-term goal of most, if not all, educational endeavors. As such, it has a long and distinguished history in the philosophy of education (Crittenden, 1978; Dearden, 1972, 1975; Gibbs, 1979; H. A. Lewis, 1978; Strike, 1982; White, 1982) and is not the exclusive prerogative of adult education. Most government policies on education, and many institutional policies and mission statements as well, stress the development of independence, autonomy, and the ability to control their own affairs as major objectives for learners of all ages. Indeed, the rapid rate of political, social, and technological change with which we are currently confronted has increased, rather than diminished, the need for self-directed citizens. The bewildering complexity of society highlights not only the need for constant adaptive change, but for individuals who can, and do, responsibly exercise and fulfill their democratic rights and obligations.

Given the widespread acceptance of autonomy as a valued social and cultural ideal, combined, as I will show later, with a concept of adulthood as being largely defined in terms of autonomous thought and action, it is not surprising that the enhancement and development of self-directedness has been adopted as a major goal of adult education (Strong, 1977, p. i). What is surprising, however, is the way this broad goal is often superseded by the narrower objective of producing self-directed learners.

This is not to deny the importance or utility of self-direction in learning, but simply to recognize that "we cannot conceive of self-direction solely in terms of a command of self-instructional techniques" (Brookfield, 1985c, p. 29). This point is made forcefully by Bagnall (1987), who writes that "there is frequently evidenced a failure to recognise a crucial dichotomy in the meaning of 'self-direction.' . . . The distinction involved here is that between what I am terming *self-management* (the variable quality of being self-directing *within* one's field of constraints to free actions) and what I am terming *self-determination* (the variable quality of being self-directing to the extent that one is in control of one's destiny). Whereas self-determination would seem, rationally, to be the quality which is being advocated and desired, it is arguably self-management which, in many cases, is articulated, elaborated and (proudly) attained" (p. 91).

Intuitively, it would seem logical that self-management is a subset of the broader domain of self-determination (or, as I will call it in this book, *personal autonomy*). This means that a person who is autonomous would be both willing and able to exert a degree of control over aspects of his or her learning situation, and likewise that the acceptance and exercise of such responsibility would be taken to indicate high levels of personal autonomy. The connection, however, is not so straightforward.

As Brookfield puts it, it may be "possible to be a superb technician of self-directed learning in terms of one's command of goal setting, instructional design or evaluative procedures, and yet to exercise no critical questioning of the validity or worth of one's intellectual pursuit as compared with competing, alternative possibilities" (1985c, p. 29). In putting the matter like this, Brookfield highlights the fact that increasing the capacity for self-management may not address really crucial questions such as the social, political, moral, or ideological dimensions of learning. Similarly, if a person is self-determining in the broader sense, this does not mean that he or she will also be self-managing in the narrower context: "A highly self-determining learner may — through the well informed delegation of control to others — be minimally self-managing" (Bagnall, 1987, p. 94).

This apparent paradox is really very important. Simply because a learner exercises control over dimensions of the teaching/learning situation does not mean that he or she is capable of exercising personal autonomy in the broader sense, and indeed — as I will discuss in Chapter Ten — the extent to which people are, or can be, self-determining is itself largely situation-specific. Conversely, the fact that a learner does not choose to exercise control in a particular educational setting cannot be taken as evidence that he or she lacks personal autonomy in the broader sense. Indeed, in their collection of materials on independence in learning, the Nuffield Foundation Group for Research and Innovation in Higher Education advocates the use of the term *autonomy* to describe situations in which the learner is able "to choose between dependence and independence as he (or she) perceives the need" (Nuffield Foundation, 1975, p. ii). As I have observed elsewhere, "anyone who is unfamiliar with a subject or topic may well choose to submit to being taught, at least at the beginning. This does not necessarily imply any pathological lack of [personal autonomy], but rather an acknowledgement that the best way to master the rudiments of a new area is to be taught by an expert" (Candy, 1987, p. 173).

In short, self-direction as a goal, like self-direction as a method, has two dimensions, and although there is an intuitive link between the two, for clarity in argument it is essential to distinguish personal autonomy from self-management of learning. From the practitioner's point of view, it is necessary to decide whether the aim is to produce self-managing learners or self-determining people and, in either case, to question whether the best way to achieve it is by giving learners more of a say in the learning situation.

Before leaving this issue of self-direction as a goal of adult education, it is necessary to acknowledge both the limitations and the strengths that are derived from membership of social groups. As I stress and reiterate throughout this book, adult education is distinguished by the extent to which it arises naturally as a result of, and takes place within, social contexts. Even truly independent and solitary learning activities are commonly the result of the learner's membership in some group or society, and although the learning process itself may be largely solitary, its intention and justification is social.

The challenge for adult educators is to assist people to reach their full potential, to maximize their opportunities, and to accomplish their individual goals. However, all this must be achieved within a social context. Whether at the level of the group, the community, the society, or humankind generally, learning in its fullest sense is a social activity, and the attainment of full personal autonomy — both in learning and outside it — must recognize this interdependence.

Summary

Self-direction has become, for many, a battle flag under which adult educators of remarkably diverse persuasions have rallied. The fact that one concept can unite such disparate interest groups, however, may be less an indication of its inherent power than that it is really several concepts, whose differences are submerged and obscured by the use of a single term.

It has been argued in this chapter that the term *self-direction* actually embraces dimensions of process and product, and that it refers to four distinct (but related) phenomena: "self-direction" as a personal attribute (personal autonomy); "self-direction" as the willingness and capacity to conduct one's own education (self-management); "self-direction" as a mode of organizing instruction in formal settings (learner-control); and "self-direction" as the individual, noninstitutional pursuit of learning opportunities in the "natural societal setting" (autodidaxy).

In this book, this four-way distinction will be maintained and the relationship between and among the concepts will be explored. However, before doing so, I would like to consider why self-direction in learning has become such an attractive and vital concept, especially in recent years. Accordingly, it is to this theme that I will now turn.

Two

The Growth of Interest in Self-Directed Learning

As mentioned in Chapter One, in recent years "self-direction" has become a major — perhaps the major — growth industry in adult education teaching and research (Brookfield, 1984a, p. 59). In the domain of teaching, the literature of adult education has reverberated with the call for adult educators to surrender to learners some measure of control over the instructional situation. This demand comes in many guises, including open education, self-directed learning, individualized instruction, discovery learning, student-centered instruction, metalearning, learning-to-learn, and independent study. At first sight, perhaps, there seems little to unify such diverse themes, which — to use Griffin's (1977) phrase — tend to look more like a "mishmash" than a "movement." However, closer inspection reveals that, although these terms are by no means synonymous, they do seem to constitute a constellation of ideas and practices. Collectively they represent an ideology "in which many more initiatives have passed over to the [learners], who are now expected to be much more independent, self-directed or, in a word, autonomous" (Dearden, 1972, p. 449).

In the field of research, too, although the practice of learning for oneself is very ancient, scholarly attention to the subject is comparatively recent. It is usually possible to identify, in hindsight, the shadowy intimations and precursors of later developments, and in the case of self-directed learning, there are plenty of allusions, back to Socrates and even earlier, of the importance of self-education. However, for practical purposes the serious study of self-direction in adult learning can be traced back to the appearance in 1961 of Houle's book *The Inquiring Mind.* In a brief, lucid, and scholarly essay, Houle sketched in outline the learning motives and activities of twenty-two continuing learners, who chose to pursue their learning at length and in depth, without institutional support or affiliation. He signaled that this was an important topic for adult education that he believed to be worthy of "further investigation" (p. x).

Tough, who is usually credited with having "sparked the revolution," traces the origin of his own interest to a time in January 1963, "when he received an assignment in a graduate course taught by Professor Cyril O. Houle at the University of Chicago" (1967, p. 1). Tough saw the potential for a study such as Houle's to be undertaken on a much wider scale, and his doctorate concerned "The Teaching Tasks Performed by Adult Self-Teachers" (1966). At around the time that Houle and Tough were beginning their studies of autodidaxy, Verner suggested — almost in passing — that "research into self-direction might be a fruitful area of investigation for adult educators" (Verner, 1964, p. 31). The following year, Johnstone and Rivera released their massive survey of adult education activity in the United States, in which they stated that, with an estimated nine million adults active in learning on their own, "self-instruction is probably the most overlooked avenue of activity in the whole field of adult education" (1965, p. 37). As Brookfield (1984a) wryly observes, "These authors' intimations of promise, of a veritable publications bonanza for graduate students and professors who might mine this research vein, have been well justified" (p. 60).

Tough's contributions to the study of autodidaxy can hardly be overestimated, and he has been one of the mainstays of research in the field. He published two monographs in the late 1960s and the first edition of his now-famous book *The Adult's Learning Projects* in 1971. He in turn managed to inspire successive generations of graduate students so that in a series of "begats" of truly biblical proportions, there are now many hundreds of masters' and doctoral theses and dissertations, journal articles, research reports, and conference papers on various aspects of self-directed learning in adulthood. Almost every book published in English on adult learning in the past decade has dealt somewhere or other with the question of adult self-direction; it is impossible to attend an adult education conference without seeing at least several papers dealing with the topic, and the Commission of Professors of Adult Education has established a special task force on self-directed learning.

Clearly, there have always been some educational philosophers for whom individual autonomy is paramount, but what is particularly striking about this sudden upsurge of interest in, and support for, the concept of autonomy is that it is shared by theorists and others, who, in other respects, represent quite incommensurable paradigms in education (Crittenden, 1978, p. 105). Dearden (1972) suggests that "this shift in emphasis, which is still very recent indeed as a marked phenomenon, is connected with wider social changes" (p. 449). In this chapter, it is intended to examine some of these "wider social changes" and to identify other major reasons that may help to explain why self-direction in learning has achieved so much prominence recently. Before doing so, however, it is worth examining the historical antecedents of the modern-day interests in self-directed learning.

Historical Background

For the person interested in adult learning, nineteenth-century Britain would have been a fascinating social laboratory. Newspapers began to proliferate; public libraries sprang up in towns and villages throughout the country; labor unions coalesced out of friendly societies; adult Sunday schools were established, especially by many nonconformist denominations; mechanics institutes, and scientific and literary societies flourished; and universities made their first tentative forays into extramural and extension work (Harrison, 1961; Hudson, 1851;

Johnson, 1979; T. Kelly, 1970; Pole, 1816; Stephens and Roderick, 1983).

Across the Atlantic, a similar phenomenon was manifest. With the westward expansion came the spread of literacy. Fired by ideals of democracy and social progress, and fanned by the egalitarianism of the New World, the flames of learning spread rapidly, lapping at the old bastions of privilege. As in Britain, mechanics institutes and lyceums, reading societies and circulating libraries, adult Sunday schools and evening colleges sprang up and took learning to the people, so that "by the 1850's institutions for self-culture blanketed the northern and western states" of America (Cawelti, 1965, p. 83).

Perhaps, however, it would be more accurate to say that people took themselves to learning, rather than the other way round, for nineteenth-century adult education is dominated by two motifs: universality and self-improvement.

As to universality, although no educational movement has yet succeeded entirely in reaching people of all classes, categories, positions, and locations, in many senses the late eighteenth and early nineteenth century in both Britain and America approximated the ideal of a learning society (Husén, 1974; Hutchins, 1968). The principles of both lifelong and lifewide education were very much in evidence. No major distinction was made between the education of children and that of adults as a goal, and the mixing together of children and adults in the same classroom was widely practiced, despite the fact that "it is particularly unpleasant to persons of mature age to expose their ignorance and awkwardness before children" (Pole, 1816, p. 34). Learning was undertaken in a variety of situations, "not only in schoolrooms, but in kitchens, manses, churches, meeting houses, sheds erected in the fields and shops erected in the towns, [and] pupils were taught by anyone and everyone, not only by schoolmasters, but by parents, tutors, clergymen, lay readers, precentors, physicians, lawyers, artisans and shopkeepers . . ." (Cremin, 1970, p. 192). In fact, "typically . . . educational pursuits were not separated out and labelled 'school' or 'institute' or even 'rational recreation.' They did not typically occur in purpose-built premises or places appropriated for one purpose.

The typical forms were improvised, haphazard and therefore ephemeral. . . . Educational forms were closely related to other activities or inserted within them, temporally and spatially" (Johnson, 1979, p. 79).

This multiplicity of forms and processes of adult education both contributed to, and derived from, the prevailing ethos of self-improvement and self-help (Houle, 1961, p. 11). Samuel Smiles's legendary book *Self Help,* first published in 1859 in London, captured perfectly the fashionable notion that the self-generated growth of the individual lay at the heart both of personal and societal progress and development. In America, *self-culture* was the preferred term and, over a period of fifty years, authors such as Channing (1883), Clarke (1880), Fowler (1851), and Whipple (1888) unleashed their considerable rhetorical skills in propounding and defending the virtues of self-improvement, not merely for social advancement or economic mobility, but for intellectual and spiritual fulfillment: "There are two powers of the human soul which make self-culture possible—the self-searching and the self-forming power. We have first the facility of turning the mind on itself; of recalling its past, and watching its present operations; . . . we are able to discern not only what we already are, but what we may become. . . . We have a still nobler power, that of acting on, determining, and forming ourselves. This is a fearful as well as glorious endowment, for it is the ground of human responsibility. We have the power not only of training our powers, but of guiding and impelling them; not only of watching our passions, but of controlling them; not only of seeing our faculties grow, but of applying to them means and influences to aid their growth" (Channing, 1883, pp. 14–15).

The combination of these two great nineteenth-century forces—the seemingly limitless possibilities for undertaking learning, and the near-universal push for self-improvement—created in England, Canada, America, Australia, New Zealand, and elsewhere an unparalleled climate for self-directed learning (or, as it was then called, self-education). Not unexpectedly, any movement that enjoyed such widespread acceptance inevitably rested on a diversity of motives and intents: "There were workers and farmers seeking to increase their skills or to become more successful economically; there were philanthropists who felt a moral duty to extend some of the cultural benefits they enjoyed to the less fortunate; there were businessmen needing a better trained and more docile labor force; and determined aristocrats who hoped that education would teach the rising classes to respect the leadership of their social superiors. Finally, there were those who dreamed of a society in which all people would have the opportunity to develop their spiritual and creative potential" (Cawelti, 1965, pp. 83–84).

Such a varied range of motives called forth an equally varied spectrum of opposition to self-education. For every clergyman who wanted people to be able to read the scriptures for themselves, there was another who feared that his authority as God's spokesman would be undermined by the ability of members of the congregation to read; for every politician who believed that a better informed, better read, more thoughtful populace would lead to a fuller exercise of democratic rights, there were others who feared the erosion of their power for the same reason; for each radical spokesman who argued that education was "not a charity, but a right" (Lovett, 1920, p. 142), there was a conservative who wanted to keep the lower orders in their place; for each advocate of literacy as opening the gates of paradise and allowing people to "converse with Herodotus and Livy, Demosthenes and Cicero, Homer and Virgil [and] with Paul and Moses . . . ," there were yet others who warned against the evil influence of "light literature and works of fiction [that] not only enfeeble the mind but pervert the taste and corrupt the imagination" (Ryerson, 1849, p. 182). And against those who saw self-education as the key to a better and more enlightened society, where work and leisure were intertwined (Channing, 1883, p. 32; Maurice, [1855] 1968, p. 61), were set patrician traditionalists who rejected the self-educated and self-made man in favor of the traditional ideal of a cultivated class that represented "the natural repository of the manners, tastes, tone, and to a certain extent, of the principles of a country" (Cooper, 1956, p. 89).

While many of the preceding arguments both for and against self-education sound quaint and anachronistic to modern readers, they nevertheless have their faint echo in the literature of contemporary adult education. However, in recent years, the emphasis has shifted away from the discussion of motives and purposes, and more toward technical aspects: the professionalization of education and formalization of structures and processes of learning. As a consequence the debate about self-direction in learning has largely shifted from a concentration on the independent pursuit of learning opportunities (autodidaxy) to methodological and other issues surrounding the involvement of learners in determining the form and focus of instruction (learner-control). In this chapter, I will examine and discuss some of the forces that, together, have pushed "self-directed learning" into the limelight as a major educational issue. Before doing so, however, it is necessary to point out that whatever prominence autodidaxy may have enjoyed in the nineteenth century, or for that matter in recent decades, it is by no means a new idea. In fact, it may be argued that learning for oneself is the prototype of all learning.

Craik, in his book *The Pursuit of Knowledge Under Difficulties* (first published in 1830 under the auspices of the Society for the Diffusion of Useful Knowledge), makes the point forcefully:

> Originally, all human knowledge was nothing more than the knowledge of a comparatively small number of such simple facts as those from which Galileo deduced the use of the pendulum for the measurement of time, and Newton the explanation of the system of the heavens. All the rest of our knowledge, and these first rudiments of it also, a succession of individuals have gradually discovered, each his own portion, by their own efforts, and without having any teacher to instruct them. In other words, everything that is actually known has been found out and learned by some person or other, without the aid of an instuctor. There is no species of learning, therefore, which self-education may not overtake; for there is none which it has not actually overtaken. All discoverers (and the whole of human knowledge that has not been divinely revealed is the creation of discovery) have been self-taught, at least in regard to that which they have discovered . . . [1866, p. 13].

Certainly, there is considerable historical evidence of the extent and significance of autodidactic learning through the ages.

In addition to the many biographies and autobiographies that recount the self-educational efforts of individual people throughout history, there has been some scholarly attention to the issue. For instance, Newsom (1977) discussed the prevalence of what he terms *lifelong learning* in sixteenth-century London, Long and Ashford (1976) adduce evidence of its extent in Colonial America, and Bouwman (1982), Craik (1866), Houle (1961, 1984), Kulich (1978), McClintock (1982), and Tough (1967) all attest to the historicity of the phenomenon.

Of even greater interest in the present context are the attempts that have been made deliberately to develop people's capability or capacity for autodidactic learning. The fact that people can, and do, undertake learning on their own, without institutional support or affiliation, is indeed interesting but hardly surprising. What does come as something of a shock, however, is to discover that attempts to foster and facilitate such learning are also quite ancient. According to McClintock (1982), "study" or "self-set learning" is both the oldest and most noble form of inquiry, and the supremacy of teaching or instruction is of comparatively recent origin.

From this very brief historical introduction, then, several generalizations are clear. First, autodidactic learning is ancient; in fact it predates learning from teachers, for the very first teachers had, of necessity, to learn things for themselves. Second, autodidactic learning is an extremely diverse phenomenon, occurring in a range of settings and for a multiplicity of reasons. Of these, however, two categories stand out. Some independent learning is a supplement to formal education, and those who use such self-directed inquiry are often well educated, utilizing their knowledge and powers of discernment to further enhance their educational advantage. Other independent learning is a substitute for regular formal education, and thus traditionalists look down on it as an inferior form of education. These two archetypes are captured in the phrases "autodidacts as the aristocrats of culture" and "autodidacts as the orphans of culture," and this ambivalence toward self-directed learners is still evident today in the mixed response to the notion of the "self-taught" expert. Third, although the capability for autodidactic

learning is present in everyone to some degree, it can be enhanced through certain approaches to education and, until relatively recent times, this was taken to be the primary objective
of teaching. However, "as passionate causes wracked human
affairs, . . . people found it hard to maintain restraint, they
ceased to be willing merely to help in the self development of
their fellows; they discovered themselves burdened, alas, with
paternal responsibility for ensuring that their wards would not
falter and miss the mark. . . . Pressures — religious, political, social, economic, humanitarian pressures — began to mount upon
the schools, and it soon became a mere matter of time before
schools would be held accountable for the people they produced"
(McClintock, 1982, p. 60). Against this historical background,
what has happened to make self-direction such a topic of contemporary interest?

Even a cursory perusal of the literature reveals that there
are many convergent factors that contribute to the recent popularity of self-direction as a field of both practice and scholarly
inquiry. Six in particular will be examined: the democratic ideal,
the ideology of individualism, the concept of egalitarianism, subjective or relativistic epistemology, the emphasis on humanistic education, and the construct of adulthood and adult education's search for an identity.

The Democratic Ideal

One of the driving forces behind the ideology of autonomous learning is the democratic ideal. According to Gibbs
(1979), "Autonomy . . . is part of an individualistic, anti-authoritarian ideology which is very deep rooted in Western capitalist
democracies . . . and it is naturally the conception usually proposed and expounded by our philosophers" (p. 121). It seems
to me that there are three distinct components in the relationship between the democratic ideal and autonomous learning:
the democracy of the soul, democracy of the teaching/learning
transaction, and preparing for democratic responsibilities.

The Democracy of the Soul. In his paper on "Autonomy
and Authority in Education," Gibbs (1979) defines the essential

characteristics of autonomy as intellectual self–determination, fortitude, and temperance. These personal qualities, he argues, are precisely the cardinal virtues that Plato delineated in *The Republic*. Gibbs goes on to demonstrate the parallels that Plato drew between the individual soul and the city, where the proper task of education was to establish within the soul something analogous to the constitutional government of the city. Thus, as the city was to be self-regulating, so the individual learner should likewise be autonomous in the conduct of his or her affairs — including learning. This philosophical basis for the development of self-direction is discussed in detail in Chapter Four.

Democracy in the Teaching/Learning Transaction. As Naisbitt (1984) points out, there is (at least in America) a trend from representative to participatory democracy, brought about by the increasingly widespread belief that "people whose lives are affected by a decision must be a part of the process of arriving at that decision" (p. 159). The same point is made by Botkin, Elmandjra, and Malitza (1979) in their authoritative report to the Club of Rome. This trend toward participatory democracy is clearly one of the "wider social changes" contributing to increased interest in autonomy.

As people become more accustomed to, and skilled at, informed participation and "choosing" in these aspects of their lives, they have made increasing demands for similar power sharing in relation to their education. These demands go far beyond so-called "participatory learning methods," and extend into all aspects of the educative process, from the assessment of needs through the design of programs to the evaluation of learning outcomes. Thus the democratic ideal has influenced the conduct of education — especially the education of adults — and both teachers and learners alike have felt obliged to shift the locus of responsibility for certain instructional functions from the teachers to the taught. As I discuss in Chapter Seven, this is not always a congenial or a sucessful strategy, but it derives substantially from a widespread (if misplaced) emphasis on how democratic principles should translate into the domain of education.

Preparing for Democratic Responsibilities. A third link between the democratic ideal and the conduct of adult education activities is to be found in the notion that education should enhance people's ability to participate fully in the democratic processes in society at large. In his book on *Educative Democracy,* Garforth (1980) writes: "Without an educated electorate democracy is impossible, for it requires of its citizens an alert, informed, critical interest and, as far as possible, participation in the processes of government" (p. 36).

This aim of preparing people to participate in democracy may be pursued in two main ways: One is by conducting courses and programs on critical thinking, social literacy, and the democratic process, and the other is indirectly or "concomitantly" (Dittman, 1976) through the way in which the education is itself conducted.

If the society were fully and genuinely democratic, and people were able to assert their democratic rights, then there would be a congruence between the educational ideal and the social reality. However, the democratic ideal is just that, an ideal, and it is often the case that, in their everyday lives, people do not have the opportunity to influence the circumstances of their lives as presumed. Accordingly, adult educators are confronted with a difficult decision. Should they adopt an ideological stance, and encourage the development of autonomous learners in the full knowledge that many people will be denied the opportunity to exert their autonomy fully outside the classroom or meeting? Or should they adopt a pragmatic approach and concentrate on the development of "coping mechanisms?" Ingleby (1974) neatly captures the spirit of this dilemma when he comments that many of those individuals involved in the "people professions" may experience some discomfort as they realize that their role is to help people to lead better and more fulfilling lives within a sociopolitical system that "systematically limits the quality of their clients' lives." This leads into the vexed and complex question of collective as opposed to individual action for social improvement and, as I will discuss later in this book, highlights the fact that self-direction, when taken to its logical conclusion, envisages a different social order from that with which we are familiar. Adult educators need to think through the long-term implications of promoting self-direction in particular instructional settings.

The Ideology of Individualism

The second of the "wider social changes" with which I will deal is the increased emphasis on the ideology of individualism. Although it has always been with us in our culture in one form or another, its influence has fluctuated through historical epochs (Riesman, 1950). At present, it represents a dominant value; thus Faure and his colleagues in the International Commission on the Development of Education state as one of the key principles for the conduct of education worldwide: "The new educational ethos makes the individual the master and creator of his own cultural progress. Self-learning, especially assisted self-learning, has irreplaceable value in any educational system" (1972, p. 209).

Keddie points out that "the notion of individuality as a desirable personality goal is not universal, but is cultural specific and tends to be found in those cultures [such as ours] where high status is obtained by competitive individual achievement . . ." (Keddie, 1980, p. 54). However, even among those cultures that value "competitive individual achievement," there are differences in the meaning ascribed to individualism. In the United Kingdom, for instance, individualism tends to wear a mask of "genteel anarchy" that is related, very often, to a "sincere wish to revise and purify democratic ideals, not to challenge and overturn them completely" (Gibbs, 1979, p. 131). In the United States, on the other hand (which has spawned by far the lion's share of literature pertaining to self-direction in adult education), the ideology of individualism is much more strident and provocative (Bellah and others, 1985; Rosenblatt, 1984; Spence, 1985). Moreover, there is even a class dimension to individualism. "Nor is it valued equally by all groups within our society. The force of the research which has attempted to distinguish between middle and working class cultures has stressed that while the middle class . . . are oriented towards the value of individual achieve-

ment, working class culture places emphasis on collective values . . . " (Keddie, 1980, pp. 54–55).

This point is confirmed by Brookfield (1984a), who, in
his critical review of research into self-directed learning, laments
both the middle-class bias of most studies and their failure to
deal adequately with the social setting and support mechanisms,
particularly of working-class learners and those of low educational attainment. Thus, although the notion of individualism
is cited in support of the development of autonomy, it means
rather different things even as between major English-speaking
countries, and this in turn may have implications for the qualities that are valued in the autonomous learner and for how such
qualities are developed, in collaborative or competitive settings.

One of the themes in this book is that learning is nearly
always a social activity, and there are limits to how much individual activity and emphasis should be pursued in the instructional situation.

The Concept of Egalitarianism

Yet another wellspring for the ideology of autonomy is
the notion of egalitarianism. The broad area of egalitarianism
in adult education is a conceptual and terminological minefield,
concerned as it is with issues of equity (fairness and justice) as
well as equality — of opportunity, of participation, and of outcomes (Stalker-Costin, 1985). In this chapter, my focus is on
the more restricted issue of equality in the relationships between
teachers and learners, and among learners. I will also deal with
the development of learner autonomy as a goal or outcome of
adopting an egalitarian perspective.

There are two broad categories of reasons why adult educators might choose to treat learners as equals. In the first case,
the adult learner is seen to be as autonomous as the teacher,
capable of making informed choices, and both the content of
the curriculum and the instructional process itself are shaped
by the needs and preferences of the learners. The adoption of
egalitarianism leads to the educator's accepting and respecting
the learners as absolute equals and to the conclusion that there

is "no relevant difference between those qualified to teach and those still under instruction" (Flew, 1976, p. 1).

The second wellspring of egalitarianism, often based on the pragmatic threat that "adult students can vote with their feet," leads to "the belief by organisers and teachers that they ought not to impose their own educational and curricular values if they can avoid doing so" (Lawson, 1979, p. 19). In the sphere of adult education, this trend also manifests itself in the emphasis on "needs and interests"–based curricula (Brookfield, 1985a; Candy, 1983), whereby the major part of adult education is "engaged in helping people meet their individual needs as they are interpreted by individuals themselves" (Essert, 1951, p. 8).

Turning now to the question of egalitarianism among learners, if one adopts egalitarianism as a goal rather than as a presupposition, then one is committed to one of two positions: either equality of opportunity for access to education, or alternatively equality of educational outcomes — in this case, the attainment of autonomy.

It is widely assumed that self-directed or autonomous learning is freely available to anyone, and that accordingly it is a truly egalitarian form of education. Although this is broadly true, as discussed in Chapters Three and Fourteen there are certain subtle limitations on people's ability to learn things for themselves if they lack the required formal background and/or access to particular facilities and resources. With respect to equality of outcomes, many authors have pointed out the virtual impossibility of all people attaining comparable levels of autonomy (see, for example, Boud, 1981; Holmberg, 1984). Thus, the committed egalitarian must encourage the opportunity for the development of autonomy in education, but at the same time is confronted with the paradox that the less accustomed learners are to thinking and acting autonomously, the more encouragement, direction, and support they are likely to require in their first tentative steps toward autonomy. Accordingly, the development of autonomy as a goal is not necessarily best achieved by the use of autonomy as a method, and adult educators may find that equality is not inconsistent with direct instruction in some subject areas.

Subjective or Relativistic Epistemology

Closely related to, and often quite inseparable from, the idea of egalitarianism is the "democratization of knowledge," where the creation, distribution, and interpretation of knowledge are seen as social processes involving everyone (Lawson, 1982, p. 36). Clearly, this trend is "reacting to the excesses of the mechanistic, positivist account of knowledge" (Crittenden, 1978, p. 111), and is in turn part of a larger backlash against positivism generally (Manicas and Secord, 1983).

In opposition to the so-called "received view" of objective knowledge there are two alternative paradigms. The first might be called *radical subjectivism,* which holds that each person is entirely the author of his or her own knowledge and worldview. This position, however, leads to a denial of the influence of socializing variables in people's lives and of the intersubjectively validated nature of such knowledge, and, as Crittenden (1978) points out, "There are probably very few serious defenders of the complete subjectivism that intellectual autonomy in the strict sense entails" (p. 108).

A second, and perhaps "softer," interpretation is the relativistic view of knowledge, which is propounded by theorists such as Rathbone (1971) and Barth (1972) under the rubric of *open education.* Among their tenets are the following:

- Knowledge is idiosyncratically formed, individually conceived, fundamentally individualistic. Theoretically, no two people's knowledge can be the same, unless their experience is identical.
- Because knowledge is basically idiosyncratic, it is most difficult to judge whether one person's knowledge is "better" than another's.
- Knowledge does not exist outside of individual knowers; it is not a thing apart. . . .
- Knowledge is not inherently ordered or structured, nor does it automatically subdivide into academic "disciplines." These categories are artificial, not natural. . . .
- People do not make their cognitive way up any universal ladder; ladders are linear, restricting, and conforming. On the contrary, the learner envisioned by open education faces a

world of potential but unpredetermined knowledge that will
admit to a plurality of interpretations [Rathbone, 1971, pp.
102–103].

Given these beliefs about the nature of knowledge and
the autonomy of the person as learner and moral agent, it is
not surprising that the ideal teacher-student relationship bears
no resemblance to that of master and apprentice. Terms like *facilitator, resource person,* and *animateur* have replaced *trainer, instructor,*
and *teacher* in much of the adult education literature. There are,
however, two paradoxes confronted by the supporters of a relativistic epistemology.

The first is that they cannot simultaneously hold the view
that all knowledge claims are equally valid, and that alternative interpretations to their own are wrong. Hence, in advocating (as they are bound to do) the value of autonomous learning, they are also obliged to recognize that nonautonomous
learning is equally legitimate (for, after all, there are no absolute tests of truth, goodness, or appropriateness). Thus, the very
values for which they are striving in education are seen to be
no more than a matter of private taste.

A second, and in some senses more crucial, problem is
the epistemological issue of reconciling learning with autonomy
at all. In order for someone to claim to have learned something
of social value or to have acquired some skill, he or she must,
sooner or later, subject this newly acquired insight or behavior
to the critical scrutiny of others. As soon as this occurs, the
learner is acknowledging the essential importance of norms, and
yet "autonomy can be defined as one's ability to be free in regard
to established rules or norms, to set the goals of one's own action and to judge its value" (Chené, 1983, p. 39). As discussed
in Chapter Twelve, many domains of knowledge carry with them
standards "which, at least at the beginning of the learning process
[are] outside of the self," and hence "we find it difficult to say
that learners have autonomy in regard to what they are learning if they have not already learned it" (Chené, 1983, p. 45).
This objection depends on a very narrow and technical definition of autonomy, however, and does not seriously threaten the

commonsense interpretation of the phrase "autonomous (or self-directed) learning."

Humanistic Education

Despite the fact that self-directed learning has found its way into the consciousness, and hence into the vocabulary, of adult educators throughout the world, nowhere has it been embraced as wholeheartedly as in North America. The reason for this would seem to lie in its congruence with the aims of humanistic education, which has also taken root very firmly particularly in the United States.

Although humanism has been a movement in European philosophy since at least the fourteenth century, modern-day educational humanism owes its origins to psychology rather than to philosophy. Humanistic psychologists, in a reaction to the psychoanalytic preoccupation with studying the mentally ill, chose instead to focus on normal healthy, even exceptional people. Instead of dealing with disease, disorder, and disintegration, humanistic psychologists tried to understand what it means to be fully human, in all its richness and complexity. In doing so, they adopted a predominantly positive and optimistic view of people, seeing them as basically good. Moreover, unlike psychoanalytic researchers who studied people in laboratories, asylums, and clinics, humanistic psychologists undertook their research in real-life settings. As a result, they formulated a more complete, comprehensive, and compassionate view of individual human performance.

Probably the best-known proponent of humanistic psychology in the United States is Abraham Maslow. In his various books and articles — including *Toward a Psychology of Being* (1968), *Motivation and Personality* (1970), and *The Farther Reaches of Human Nature* (1971) — he mapped out a comprehensive and compelling vision of people as self-actualizing beings, striving toward health, individual identity and integrity, and autonomy. Maslow based his early study on a survey of people whom he deemed to be "self-actualizers," and he identified a number of characteristics that they all seemed to possess. These attributes

include acceptance of self and others; spontaneity and natural-
ness; autonomy and independence; freshness of perception;
genuineness in relationships with others; creativity; positive self-
concept; and "without one single exception, involvement in a
cause outside their own skin, in something outside of themselves"
(1971, p. 43).

This vision of people has many aspects in common with
the archetype of the self-directed individual, and indeed humanistic psychology has informed much educational practice.
For instance, Carl Rogers, a contemporary of Maslow, adopted
a very similar value position, although he concentrated instead
on the role of the therapist or, in the teaching situation, of the
educator. In Rogers's view, the optimal relationship would be
a client-centered one, with the educator or therapist adopting
a nonjudgmental, facilitative role to help the client or learner
achieve self-fulfillment or self-actualization. Like Maslow, Rogers believed that people are born with a natural tendency toward
exploration, growth, and higher achievement. The corollary of
this is that educators need to intervene as little as possible in
the natural development of the person.

The noble aim of helping people to grow and to reach
their full potential has captured the imagination of many educators and has accordingly animated many educational programs
and activities. Clearly, both Maslow and Rogers (along with
others such as Combs, Knowles, and May) have been enormously influential in shaping the thinking of North American
adult educators (Brookfield, 1985, p. 19). This is probably because both their underlying values and their recommendations
for practice resonate with certain philosophical convictions deeply
held by many educators (Tennant, 1988, pp. 8–9). Elias and
Merriam (1980), in their review of *Philosophical Foundations of
Adult Education,* put it this way: "Principles from humanistic
philosophy and psychology have permeated the field of adult
education. . . . One of the reasons for this popularity . . . is humanism's compatibility with democratic values. . . . A second
reason for humanism's hold in adult education is that unlike
other levels of education, nearly all adult education is voluntary. Educational activities must meet the needs of adult learners

in order to survive. [Third] . . . humanistic adult education takes into account adult development. . . . The notion of growth, development and change is integral to much of the psychological literature on adult development" (pp. 135–136).

It is evident, therefore, that self-directed learning draws a lot of its popular support from the same philosophical heartland as humanistic education, and moreover that it is based at least partly on similar tenets. In his essay "Humanistic Psychology and the Self-Directed Learner," Tennant (1988) identifies both conceptual and methodological points of convergence between humanism and self-direction, but perhaps the most significant similarity is their respective emphasis on the essential aloneness of the individual. Whereas early humanists strove to harmonize their ideas with Christian values and beliefs, including a personal relationship with God, and with other people, modern-day advocates have often adopted a different stance, arguing first that the concept of God is inconsistent with advanced thought and human freedom and second that principles and values should be derived entirely from within the individual. In an essay on existential psychology, for instance, Maslow (1969) writes of "the total collapse of all sources of values outside the individual," with the consequent recognition that "there is no place else to turn but inward, to the self, as the focus of values" (pp. 50–51).

The corollary of this in the field of self-direction has been that many adult educators have lost sight of the interdependent and socially determined nature of much adult learning. By placing emphasis on the uniqueness and individuality of each person, and stressing subjective experience as the primary or even the only meaningful criterion of truth, they have inadvertently caused people to "become more detached from the need to fulfill the expectations of their culture, and [to] become less involved in the structure of society" (Barshinger, 1973, p. 166).

The Construct of Adulthood

A sixth factor that has tended to increase the emphasis on self-direction in adult education is the development of the concept of adulthood. Although each of the other five considerations has its place in helping to understand the significance of self-direction in adult learning, probably the most compelling factor is that it exemplifies and embodies many of the critical elements of adulthood, and of adults as learners.

Throughout its history, but more particularly in the past two decades, attempts have been made by scholars and theorists to identify, analyze, define, map, or otherwise delineate the essential characteristics as well as the boundaries of the field of adult education (for example, Lindeman, 1926b; Bryson, 1936; Jensen, Liveright, and Hallenbeck, 1964; Schroeder, 1970; Champion, 1975; Campbell, 1977; Little, 1979; Boyd, Apps, and Associates, 1980; Rubenson, 1982; Tight, 1983; Sinnett, 1985). A number of these attempts are the result of "professors of adult education nervously trying to stake out a territory separable from other territories, both within educational studies in particular, and the social sciences and humanities in general" (Welton, 1987, p. 50).

In these general reviews, several features are commonly mentioned that supposedly differentiate adult education from other sectors of education: It has an extremely diffuse and nebulous mandate; it is distinguished by an ethos of voluntarism among both teachers and learners; it is often treated as peripheral or marginal to mainstream educational efforts (including what Ranger, 1985, describes as its "nocturnal ritual"); it has something of a social activist tradition, which places it somewhere "between a social movement and a profession" (Selman and Kulich, 1980); it claims to place a higher emphasis on meeting the "needs" of learners than other sectors of education do; and many of its activities are characterized by what Bernstein has called weak classification and weak framing (Bernard and Papagiannis, 1983; Stalker-Costin, 1986). Although there is clearly more than a grain of truth to these self-characterizations, many of these claims are ideological rather than empirical, part of the folklore that adult education has developed to justify and distinguish itself.

According to Welton (1987), various attempts to provide a theoretical framework for adult education have been based on a "shaky and porous foundation," namely, that of seeking to develop its own epistemological basis from within itself. Welton goes on to examine critically the three "modalities" within this episteme: first, the claim that adult education is distinctive because there are forms of knowledge that are "adult" (the "adult knowledge" modality); second, because adult educators seek to meet the needs of their clients through flexible and responsive provision and open access (the "needs, access, and provision" modality); and third, because of something special and unique about the methods of teaching that are employed with adults (the "methodological" modality).

It seems to me that autodidaxy strikes a responsive chord on each of these three heads: It deals with subject matter that is highly relevant to the learner's present life role and/or self-concept, it is highly flexible and occurs in virtually every life situation and potential learning context in which adults find themselves, and it is apparently unique to adults — the myth persists that children must be taught, whereas adults can learn for themselves (Joblin, 1988). It must be observed that these features do not have to be demonstrably true; they only need to be perceived to be true for them to function as tacit justifications for the promotion of self-direction by adult educators.

More important than, and in fact critical to, each of these three modalities is the notion of adulthood itself. Accordingly, over the years, the construct of adulthood has received a good deal of attention from adult education theorists. For instance, in 1964 in a paper on the "Definition of Terms," Verner wrote that " . . . the precise meaning of the term *adult* is actually quite vague — particularly when it is used to identify the clientele of adult education. The notions of who is an adult vary from 'those past school age' through 'grownups' to 'mature individuals' — perceptions so indefinite as to be all but meaningless. Attempts to arrive at a precise identification of an adult tend to fall into the categories of age, psychological maturity, and social role" (Verner, 1964, p. 28).

Subsequent research has tended to emphasize one or other of these same three categories: age, social role, or psychological maturity. However, despite more than two decades of further research and inquiry (Bova and Phillips, 1985), there are still few, if any, satisfactory and comprehensive conceptualizations of adulthood. Perhaps this is because adulthood is a residual concept, what is left after defining other stages in the human life cycle (Jordan, 1978). Perhaps it is simply because adulthood is such a broad, amorphous, and diffuse phenomenon.

Despite Paterson's (1979) assertion that "adults are adults, in the last analysis, because they are older than children" (p. 10), age has proved to be an unsatisfactory criterion for determining the threshold of adulthood. Studies have variously cited sixteen, eighteen, or twenty-one as the "magic age," based on laws that permit one to vote, drink, drive, or be drafted into the armed services (Bova and Phillips, 1985, p. 38). Yet, it is not difficult to think of instances in which age alone is a poor indicator of adult status: the eldest child who, orphaned at age fifteen, becomes responsible for her or his younger brothers and sisters or, at the other extreme, the twenty-five-year-old student who, still living at home, is protected from life's vicissitudes by his or her doting parents.

According to H. M. Kallen (1962), "Adulthood, even if determinate biologically, is culturally a variable" (p. 38). In our society, it is true that our ability to recognize ourselves and others as adult is based, at least in part, on developing independence, along with the adoption of responsibilities (such as worker, spouse, parent, citizen and so on). However, definitions of adulthood based on social roles have a disconcerting tendency toward circularity: "The adult . . . can be distinguished from a child or adolescent by his or her acceptance of the social roles and functions that define adulthood" (Darkenwald and Merriam, 1982, p. 77).

The third class of definitions, namely, those concerned with psychological maturity, are potentially the most promising for the present purpose. Some of these definitions portray adulthood as the development or acquisition of an interrelated set of psychological characteristics, usually including independence, autonomy, or freedom from the influence of others. Other definitions, such as those of Maslow or Rogers, "stress the idea that adulthood is a *process* rather than a *condition*, a process in

which men and women continually strive toward self-actualization and self-fulfillment" (Darkenwald and Merriam, 1982,
p. 40). Whether viewed as a process or a condition, however,
the common element is the achievement of autonomy (Birren
and Hedlund, 1984).

This fact has profound significance for adult education.
Darkenwald and Merriam (1982) claim that the mission of adult
education "is not preparatory, so much as it is one of assistance — helping adults to realize their potential, make good decisions and in general, better carry out the duties and responsibilities inherent in the adult role" (p. 77). Thus, it would appear
that one of the primary tasks of adult education is to develop
and to permit the exercise both of individuality (Hostler, 1981)
and autonomy: "While the fostering of mental autonomy is an
important objective in the education of children, it is of special
importance in the education of adults. In deeming someone to
be an 'adult,' we are ascribing to him various rights and responsibilities in virtue of certain distinctive moral and personal qualities which we presume him to have . . . the qualities of impar-
tiality, objectivity and balance, at least in some minimum degree,
and the ability to draw on his experience with some measure
of sense and skill . . . The project of fostering mental autonomy
is the project of helping adults to be adult" (Paterson, 1979,
pp. 120–121).

Thus it appears that autonomy, and the ability to think
and act autonomously, are central to our conception of adulthood. Adulthood, in turn, occupies a place of honor as a unique
distinctive foundation for the work of adult educators. Accordingly, any educational approach such as self-directed learning —
either autodidaxy or learner-control — that exemplifies and builds
on autonomy in learning is held to be uniquely relevant to the
education of adults.

Summary and Conclusion

Out of this review of reasons for the recent upsurge of
interest in self-direction, it is possible to distill several tentative
conclusions and some observations. The first is that "self-
direction" in the broadest sense seems to have captured the spirit

the times — that is, to embody a number of contemporary issues that have flowed together. These include the democratic ideal, the ideology of individualism, the concept of egalitarianism, the subjective or relativistic epistemology, the principles of humanistic education, and the construct of adulthood (Candy, 1985, pp. 60–65), all within a turbulent time of rapid and pervasive changes that has resulted in an unprecedented questioning of the forms and functions of conventional educational approaches: "The world we live in demands self-starting, self-directing citizens capable of independent action. The world is changing so fast we cannot hope to teach each person what he/she will need to know in twenty years. Our only hope to meet the demands of the future is the production of intelligent, independent people" (Combs, 1972, p. 59).

Second, as discussed in the previous chapter, there is a good deal of "slippage" in the literature between the concepts of autodidaxy, learner-control, self-management, and self-determination. Implicitly, there is held to be a connection between the way formal education is arranged and conducted, the propensity of people to indulge in learning activities in everyday settings, the ability and willingness to accept responsibility for certain functions in the instructional setting, and the development of autonomous and "fully functioning" adult citizens. It appears however that little empirical connection has yet been established between these various aspects of "self-direction," and that greater circumspection is therefore required.

Third, it is apparent that self-direction in learning is not a single undifferentiated phenomenon, and likewise that its rise to prominence has been promoted by a coalition of different — at times even contradictory — forces. In many cases, people of quite radically opposed ideological positions have been advocating the need for self-direction in learning. This diversity is reflected in the range of different meanings attributed to the term *self-direction* as discussed in Chapter One, and in the range of different factors that have contributed to supporting the development of self-directed learning.

One of the central messages of this chapter is that if self-direction is valued in an organization — if it is mentioned in mission statements, discussed at staff meetings, and emphasized as a desirable feature for students or employees—perhaps it is worth considering what beliefs and values lie behind the support for it. Based on some of the issues discussed in this chapter, it should be possible to analyze whether this is a deeply held conviction or simply a matter of convenience and to consider whether the rest of the organization has values, systems, structures, and activities that support the development and exercise of autonomy.

To assist in the process of exploring one's own beliefs and investigating the seriousness of an organization's commitment to the idea, some of the claims that have been advanced for self-direction in learning are examined in the next chapter, along with some cautionary observations about its limits.

Three

Promise and Limitations for Education and Training

Given the many facets and components of self-direction in learning, and the range of ideological perspectives that influence its advocacy and use, it is hardly surprising to find that self-direction is said to offer many advantages over conventional educational approaches. In fact, in their more euphoric moments, advocates of self-direction have made some extravagant claims. They have alleged that self-direction in learning will solve forever the problem of motivation; that it will overcome difficulties of dealing with rapid obsolescence of knowledge; that it will render irrelevant the issue of nonparticipation in adult education; and ultimately that it will form the cornerstone of a learning society, dedicated to the pursuit of knowledge for its own sake.

Appealing as these visions are, however, there are also limitations—both practical and theoretical—as to what self-direction can realistically achieve. Accordingly, this chapter has two, almost opposing, purposes. If you are in favor of self-education and would like to be able to marshal some arguments to support your point of view, you will find some definite advantages and positive features mentioned here. Alternatively, if you are skeptical about the many claims made for self-direction as something like a "miracle cure" in education, you will find

listed here some of the limitations of the concept and its practice. And if you simply have an open mind, this chapter will
show you two things: first that the decision to support self-
direction is at least partly an ideological decision, based on a
particular value system, and second that it is no panacea for
all the many problems and complexities that have confronted
education since it emerged as a formal social process.

The distinction has already been raised in Chapter One
between self-direction in formal instructional settings (learner-
control) and outside them in everyday learning contexts (autodidaxy). Since these phenomena are educationally distinct,
self-direction in these two environments will be treated separately, before I draw some overall conclusions about the promise
and limitations of self-direction in learning.

The Promise of Learner-Control

Throughout the history of education — including of adult
education — the involvement of learners in planning, implementing, and evaluating their own learning has had a continuing presence. However, its prominence and popularity have ebbed and
flowed in line with changing societal values and educational philosophies. "There was the equivalent of a high tide for self-directed
learning activities in the heydey of the progressive education
movement which reached a crest in the 1930s and early 1940s.
It receded drastically as soon as the Russian Sputnik orbited in
1957. Another high tide for student participation in decision-making came during the period of college campus 'unrest' . . . in the
late 1960s" (Della-Dora and Blanchard, 1979, p. 11).

Each time support for increased learner-control has advanced, a range of justifications have been put forward by its
advocates. The following are recurring claims made in support
of increased learner-control, especially for adult learners: It
responds to the apparent inflexibility of conventional education
in the face of rapid change; it recognizes the way in which people generally, and adults in particular, habitually learn; it reflects
the primacy of learning over teaching; it accommodates individual differences in learning; it leads to enhanced learning

outcomes through increased motivation; it models democratic principles and develops skills of democratic participation; it inculcates habits of curiosity and self-initiated inquiry; and it encourages the development of self-determining individuals, capable both of undertaking learning on their own outside formal instructional settings and of giving meaning and direction to their lives. Each of these claims will be examined before turning to an assessment of some of the limitations inherent in the notion of learner-control.

Learner-Control Responds to the Inflexibility of Conventional Education. The rapid rate of social and technological change with which we are confronted daily has challenged conventional educational providers to become more flexible, responsive, and "relevant." At the margins, in experimental programs and in some areas where change has led to profound problems such as mass unemployment or extreme racial tensions, educational providers have responded to these calls. But in most mainstream institutions — in schools, colleges, universities, training departments, and even in adult education organizations — it is still very much a matter of "business as usual," and there is little more than a cursory nod in the direction of equipping people for a rapidly changing and uncertain future.

Interestingly, educational theorists of remarkably diverse ideological orientations have suggested that self-directed learning may be a panacea for an ailing educational system. On the one hand, there are the pragmatic instrumentalists — latter-day descendants of the nineteenth-century "businessmen seeking a better trained and more docile labor force" (Cawelti, 1965, p. 84) — who support self-directed learning as a method of "keeping up" with recent developments and advances in various occupational domains (Ravid, 1987). On the other hand, there are the proponents of lifelong and recurrent education, visionaries and idealists who acknowledge the inability of formal education institutions to prepare people with skills and knowledge to serve them in five, ten, fifteen, or fifty years. Such people call for self-directed learning that is linked with, and responsive to, the changing circumstances of people's lives.

Practitioners can take advantage of this feature of learner-controlled instruction by allowing learners to devise and follow their own programs. Inquiry projects, self-set studies, and free-ranging discussions can all allow the program or course of study to unfold in line with changing circumstances and altered priorities.

Learner-Control Recognizes the Way Adults Actually Learn. As discussed in Chapter Six, considerable research has now established that up to 98 percent of the adult population is regularly involved in independently undertaking self-initiated learning activities outside formal educational institutions (Brookfield, 1982b; Caffarella and O'Donnell, 1986; Mocker and Spear, 1982; Tough, 1978, 1979a). Since this propensity appears to be so widespread, and has been shown to occur across the spectrum of social, cultural, and educational backgrounds of adults in various parts of the world, it may be said to be a universal characteristic, and a natural indication of humanity's learning nature. One of the alleged strengths of learner-controlled instruction, therefore, is that it harnesses the innate predisposition to learn, and rather like a hydroelectric turbine, converts this enormous potential into directed learning efforts. It is argued that failing to recognize and make use of this vast storehouse of learning potential is an affront to adult learners, besides threatening to make formalized adult education redundant through an unwillingness to adapt to the realities of people's learning needs and preferred learning styles.

In practice, this means that adult educators should place minimal restrictions on learners, allowing them to achieve objectives of their own choosing through approaches that seem most appropriate or convenient to them. Even where the objectives are specified beforehand, the principle of learner-control means that learners may safely be permitted to select for themselves how they will achieve and demonstrate mastery of the subject matter.

Learner-Control Reflects the Primacy of Learning over Teaching and Allows for Different Learning Styles. As I have discussed in Chapter Two, there are logical grounds for arguing that self-directed learning is the prototype of all learning. Extending this principle, some even go so far as to claim that teaching is a deliberate or intentional interference with the on-going process of learning. McClintock (1982), for instance, writes that traditionally the teacher did not make the choices that guided the learner: "Instead there seemed to be an inward, almost inborn power of judgment in every individual — as it directed the person would attend. To those who thus recognized each person's autonomy of judgment, education could only coincidentally be a process of teaching and learning; more essentially, it had to be a zig-zag process of trial and error, of studious, self-directed effort by which an inchoate, infantile power of judgment slowly gave itself form, character, perhaps even a transcendent purpose. This effort was study in its most general sense" (p. 52).

If, therefore, teaching is seen as artificially superimposed onto the innate drive towards learning possessed by all people, a return to self-directed learning is no more than removing the burdensome and cumbersome apparatus of teaching from a natural disposition to learn.

Related to this idea of what Rogers (1969) called "freedom to learn" is the perspective that individual learners have their own "native" or "natural" styles of learning, which emerge when the yoke of "other-direction" is lifted. Accordingly, learner-control is often advocated because it permits the spontaneous assertion of learners' natural (and therefore presumably best for them) approach to learning tasks. Approaches to teaching that acknowledge the inherent autonomy of learners, and that seek to give them control over certain aspects of the teaching situation, explicitly allow for individual differences among learners, so that the person who prefers a more active experimental orientation may select that, while a more reflective or passive orientation could be chosen by another learner. For the instructor, this means providing a range of resources and facilitating learners in their selection and use of their chosen approach to the material to be learned.

Learner-Control Leads to Enhanced Learning Through Increased Motivation. It is widely recognized that people are more likely to be committed to activities and ideas they have had some hand in developing and shaping; indeed, they may feel opposed, simply on principle, to being subjected to situations over which they feel they have little, if any, control. Accordingly, one of the most commonly advanced justifications for increasing learner-control is that it leads to increased satisfaction (Southern, 1971) and to heightened motivation to learn (Johnson, 1974; Patton, 1955). In their early experimental work on learner-control, Mager and McCann (1961) began with the tentative hypothesis that "learner motivation in an instructional situation is a direct function of the amount of apparent control the learner can exert over the situation" (p. 5). This is particularly true of adults, who, as Knowles (1984, p. 56) points out, have a self-concept of self-directedness that is violated when their autonomy is disregarded.

Some people argue that increased learner-control can only act to increase motivation once learners have made a decision to participate: "If the student will not try to learn, more freedom probably not only will not help, it may even detract. . . . But if a student wants to learn, he would surely want also to direct his own study effectively given the chance. For many students, greater freedom and responsibility in itself may increase motivation to learn" (Campbell, 1964, p. 350). Others, however, adopt the point of view that, even if the subject of inquiry is not one in which the learner is inherently interested, the "method of work" can create the necessary orientation. Elton (1973) writes:

> To motivate a student to study is not in itself an ultimate educational aim, but rather an interim one and a means towards ultimate ones, a kind of needle's eye through which a student must pass before he or she is likely to achieve really worthwhile objectives. Much discussion in educational circles centers on how to get the student through this eye, and three specific means are generally distinguished:
>
> 1. Intrinsically, through interest in the subject
> 2. Extrinsically, through examination pressure
> 3. Extrinsically, through rewards
>
> However, there is another one, which is far less frequently recognized:
>
> 4. Intrinsically, through interest in the method of work [pp. 75–76]

In short, whether they focus on the content or the process of learning, learner-controlled modes of instruction have the dual benefits of avoiding the imposition on learners of unwelcome direction and fostering motivation in learners who have been responsible for selecting or shaping their own direction. Once the educator is freed of the role of "motivating" unwilling students, he or she is able to spend more time assisting learners with their own projects by helping them to define goals, locate resources, and clarify their understandings, often on a one-to-one or small-group basis.

Learner-Control Models Democratic Principles and Behavior. Adult education has long been associated with the activist tradition (Jarvis, 1987b, pp. 305–308; Selman and Kulich, 1980; Welton, 1987) of social emancipation (Johnson, 1979) and personal empowerment (Freire, 1972). The use of self-directed and learner-controlled methods not only models such changed power relationships, but equips learners with the skills and expectations to deal with potentially oppressive situations encountered elsewhere in their daily lives.

In particular, one of the distinctive features of adult education is the equality of teachers and learners. In our political system, for instance, we expect each person's vote in the democratic structure to be exactly equal to every other person's vote. Extending this idea to education, if the process of education is to be truly democratic, each person (teacher or learner) should have the same weight in deciding the direction of an educational event or experience. The principle of learner-control gives equal respect to the needs of each individual learner as to the expertise of the teacher or trainer.

What this implies in practice is that the educator avoids, as far as possible, imposing his or her own agendas, values, and expectations on learners, instead facilitating discussions and acting as a responsive resource as required or directed by the learners. Of course the instructor does not give up his or her special knowledge or bow to requests that are clearly inappropriate, dangerous, or grossly misdirected, but he or she must be flexible enough to react to reasonable demands and to play a full and active role as a member of the learning team.

Learner-Control in Instructional Settings Inculcates Habits of Curiosity and Self-Initiated Inquiry and Encourages the Development of Autodidacts. One of the most common and indeed most compelling arguments in favor of increasing learner-control is that as people exert influence over their own educational destiny, their willingness to do so, and their general feelings of potency and self-efficacy are enhanced (Henney, 1978, p. 130). Research carried out in the early 1960s, for instance, showed that as people were given, and accepted, increased responsibility for valued instructional functions, there was a concomitant rise in their curiosity and information-seeking behavior.

For instance, Gruber and Weitman (1962) demonstrated that increased learner-control resulted in increased curiosity about the subject matter, "as measured by the rise in questioning behaviors" (p. 23), and in turn, "curiosity may be said to have a 'gatekeeper' function in the educational system" (Hovey, Gruber, and Terrell, 1963, p. 351). Later, other researchers, suggested that "giving learners more control gave them a taste for more control, as well as greater interest in the topic" (Campbell and Chapman, 1967, p. 130), and that "certain competencies for self-directedness in learning . . . can be fostered in part of a formal learning situation" (p. 123). More recently, Caffarella (1983) undertook a study in which she explored respondents' satisfaction with the use of learning contracts in a graduate course in education. On the basis of this research, she concluded that "using a learning contract is both valuable and worthwhile and thus its use should be continued in graduate level courses," and furthermore that "these students did agree that they had increased their competencies as self-directed learners as a result of using the learning contract" (pp. 13, 25).

Of course, the creation of people who are willing and able to exert control in learning situations is not an end in itself, but rather a means to an end (Elton, 1973, p. 75). The argument is that learner-control and autodidaxy are linked, and that "the pupil's potential aptitude for successful self-education [as an adult] will depend upon the extent to which he or she has been exposed to situations of responsibility and autonomy in the school years" (Marbeau, 1976, p. 15). Self-education beyond formal schooling is itself taken to be a worthwhile policy objective. For instance, Gardner (1963), in his wide-ranging social analysis, offered the view that the ultimate aim of instruction is "to shift to the individual the burden of his own education" (p. 12), and Combs (1972) claims that "the goals of modern education cannot be achieved without self-direction . . . The world we live in demands self-starting, self-directing citizens capable of independent action." Kidd (1973), one of the leading figures in adult education, wrote in his book *How Adults Learn* that "it has often been said that the purpose of adult education, or of any kind of education, is to make of the subject a continuing 'inner-directed' self-operating learner," and Dressel and Thompson (1973), who surveyed independent study in American higher education, write that it "comes close to being, if it is not indeed, the major goal of all education" (p. vii).

These comments have been echoed and reiterated down the years by all manner of influential thinkers: the Commission of Non-Traditional Study, the Club of Rome, the Unesco Institute of Education, and numberless educators, futurists, and scholars. Repeatedly, the ability to pursue one's own education after the end of formal schooling, and to broaden one's own social and cultural participation through self-initiated learning endeavors, has been endorsed not only as the true purpose of education, but also the path to social equality and participative democracy.

In short, the argument runs that methods of instruction that emphasize and encourage self-direction in learning will arouse curiosity, enhance people's self-concept as learners, and increase information-seeking behaviors. This in turn will carry over to the independent pursuit of learning opportunities both beyond and outside formal instructional settings, and this, in turn, is a basic building block of the "learning society" (Butler, 1989; Husén, 1974; Knowles, 1983b; Unesco, 1990), whereby "every citizen should have the means of learning, training and cultivating himself freely available to him, under all circumstances, so that he will be in a fundamentally different position in relation to his own education. Responsibility will replace obligation" (Faure and others, 1972, p. 163).

This connection between self-direction in educational settings and the development of a mature and enriching society
is indeed an impressive claim, and one that, if it is correct, is
worthy of the utmost effort of every person entrusted with the
education of others (Ebersole, 1979). Practitioners need to encourage learners to take up their interests by pursuing questions and topics they find particularly intriguing, by helping them
to identify and utilize learning resources in the community
(Heffernan, Macy, and Vickers, 1976) and by themselves modeling self-directed coninuing learning, as discussed in Chapter
Seven.

The Limitations of Learner-Control

When they are assembled in one place like this, the arguments in favor of learner-control seem very persuasive. They
are very much in line with the liberal/democratic tradition,
and posit self-direction as a valuable — perhaps indispensable —
component in the search for a more just, equitable, and satisfactory educational system and ultimately society. Accordingly, it is difficult to write about reservations and limitations
without seeming unduly negative toward either self-direction,
or the broader values that underlie it. However, there are
many unexamined conceptual as well as practical limitations
to learner-control in learning, and it is necessary to sound a
note of warning about uncritical endorsement or advocacy of
the concept.

Many of these reservations may usefully be discussed under the same headings as those used in listing advantages and
promises, and accordingly, this part of the chapter will employ
the same structure as the last section. Before turning to this,
however, one overarching comment must be registered: Learner-
controlled instruction will never entirely eclipse learning that
is planned and mediated by another. This is not to be construed
as a reactionary defense of inappropriate forms of didacticism,
but rather as a recognition of the limits of learning for oneself:
"Ultimately the goal of all adult education is the independent
pursuit of learning. But, desirable as the constant growth of independence may be, it still remains that some kinds of learning

will always have to be done in the society of fellow students. Some kinds of learning will always depend upon the guidance of a leader or teacher" (Bryson, 1936, p. 98).

Learner-Control and the Inflexibility of Conventional Education. When authors advocate the use of learner-control by pointing out the shortcomings of the formal educational system, they conventionally portray the latter as a ponderous monolith, hopelessly bogged down in bureaucracy and incapable of a swift and appropriate response to changing circumstances.

Although this caricature may be a fair criticism of some centralized and highly authoritarian educational systems, at the level of individual institutions and individual instructors, it is possible for programs and courses to be highly responsive to local conditions and changing circumstances. Moreover, although the individual learner may be unencumbered by the apparatus of formal education, the same phenomenon of rapid and pervasive change that bedevils educators also confronts the self-educator. Accordingly, despite the idealized image of the self-directed learner lightly and easily pursuing his or her own interests, the very complexity and rapidity of change — both societal and occupational — may baffle and perplex the individual learner, leaving him or her confused, anxious, and far from confident about how best to proceed or what to learn.

Thus, the apparent flexibility and freedom offered by learner-control may be more illusory than real, especially in those complex areas characterized by rapid change. Instructors and other practitioners need not resort to learner-controlled methods of instruction in order to cope with rapid change. By keeping up with reading in their fields, providing learners with opportunities to ask questions and undertake relevant projects, making use of invited speakers, and drawing teaching resources from newspapers, journals, documentary films, and the like, it is possible for educators to build in needed flexibility even in formally structured courses.

Learner-Control and How Adults Actually Learn. The assertion that self-direction mirrors the natural learning preferences of adults has pervaded much recent writing on learner-control in adult education. Many authors, including Tough in his book *The Adult's Learning Projects* (rev. ed., 1979a), begin from the premise that adult education must adapt itself to the "natural" learning styles of these self-directed adult learners. Such a recommendation certainly seems intuitively appealing, but it has several significant flaws.

The first is the assumption that all adults are self-directing. Knowles (1980), for instance, defines adulthood explicitly in terms of self directedness: "Something dramatic happens to their self-concepts when people define themselves as adults. . . . Their chief sources of self-fulfillment are now their performances as workers, spouses, parents and citizens. . . . Their self-concept becomes that of a self-directing personality. . . . In fact, the psychological definition of adulthood is the point at which individuals perceive themselves to be essentially self-directing. And at this point, people also develop a deep psychological need to be perceived by others as being self-directing" (pp. 45–46). As Collard (1985) observes: "The first thing one notes is that his argument is tautological: that is, the terms 'adult' and 'self-directing' are used to define each other. An abbreviated form of the above would read 'adults are self-directing people therefore self-directing people are adults.' Yet is this the case? Would it be possible for someone to perceive themselves as adult, and yet as other than self-directed? Could there be self-directed children?" (pp. 3–4).

Thus it appears that the concepts of adulthood and self-direction, both of which are central constructs in adult education, are not merely closely related but, at least in the way Knowles uses them, are defined in terms of each other.

A second, related problem is the assumption that all adults are necessarily self-directing with respect to their learning. Yet, in the literature, there is much to suggest that many adult learners feel far from self-directing (Pratt, 1988): We have evidence of "cue-seeking" behavior (Entwistle, Hanley, and Hounsell, 1979) and of "syllabus-bound" students (Parlett, 1970); of external locus of control (Lefcourt, 1976; Rotter, 1966); of low self-efficacy (Bandura, 1981); of field dependence (Theil, 1984a, 1984b; Theil and Tzuk, 1985; Witkin, Moore, Goodenough, and Cox, 1977); of fragile or imperfectly developed self-concept (Powell, 1976); of learned helplessness (Even, 1984, 1985; Perry and Dickens, 1984; Roth, 1980; Seligman, 1975); and generally of docile, passive, and acquiescent learners who prefer, or could be held to prefer, other-direction to self-direction. Indeed, Carl Rogers, the doyen of student centeredness, has observed that only a third or a quarter of learners are self-directing individuals, the majority being people who "do just what they are supposed to do" (Rogers, 1969, cited by Moore, 1972, p. 85). Moreover, even if the incidence of "self-directed learning" outside formal instructional settings is as widespread as claimed, this does not necessarily mean that people want, or feel able, to exert control over the teaching situation (Tremblay and Danis, 1984; Taylor, 1980).

As early as 1951, Wispe reported a study that distinguished those learners wanting more permissiveness from those wanting more direction. In a match/mismatch experiment, some members of the "want-more-permissiveness" group were placed in the structured teaching situation, and some members of the "want-more-direction" group were given more freedom. Thus, in both cases, some learners were denied exactly what they wanted, and accordingly may have felt quite frustrated. Wispe (1951) writes: "Realizing the importance of these student classroom needs, what must have been the effects of their frustrations? The want-more-direction students said on the questionnaires that the instructors 'never lectured,' were 'poorly prepared' and 'couldn't even answer a question in a straight-forward manner.' To the want-more-permissiveness students, the instructors 'lectured too much,' 'discouraged viewpoints other than his own,' and 'identified with the head of the course.' Every indication is that the frustration in both groups was very intense; but it was especially so in the want-more-direction group. This group, particularly the sub-group wanting more direction, but being permissively treated, held the lowest opinions of sections and instructors . . . " (p. 174).

Linked to this is the point that, even if learners do see themselves as autonomous, and would like, ultimately, to take responsibility for directing their own inquiries, they may (as discussed in Chapter Twelve) lack the necessary knowledge of the subject matter to make a beginning. Thus, the truly autonomous person may intentionally make a "strategic suspension" of his or her independence, in order to be taught. Just as many researchers on self-directed learning point out that adult learners may opt to undertake their learning projects specifically to avoid the constraints and restrictions imposed by formal providers, so those people who deliberately inquire into, seek out, enroll in, and pay for planned programs of instruction may have very specific expectations about the type and degree of direction they are likely to receive.

To ignore these legitimate expectations, and instead to force learners into a self-directed or learner-controlled mode for which they may feel unprepared seems to me every bit as unethical as denying freedom when it is demanded. This places a very heavy burden of responsibility on the adult educator, for he or she must be able to discern those situations where the learner is simply being "lazy" or overdependent from those where there is a legitimate and defensible reason for relying heavily on the expertise of the instructor. Two courses of action seem appropriate; the first is to determine what learners already know and what their expectations are with regard to guidance and direction at the start of instruction, and the second is to be open and honest with learners about the intention of sharing responsibility with them (Pratt, 1988). If Figure 1.1 is taken as a guide, the instructor may well announce his or her intention of moving toward the independent study end of the continuum, and negotiate with the learners the progressive devolution of responsibility this entails. At the start, this may involve direct instruction, clearly specified objectives, agreed curriculum goals, and clear marker events including assessment tasks. Gradually this could give way to more collaborative modes of teaching and learning, negotiated contracts, and various forms of peer and self-assessment.

Learner-Control and Individual Differences in Learning Styles. Any person who has taught adults for any length of time, or indeed who has participated in courses of adult education, does not need to be reminded that individuals differ from one another in significant ways that affect both their approaches to learning and their learning outcomes. Obviously, physical characteristics, personality, family background, intellectual ability, life experiences, and personal goals form a unique pattern for each individual, which in turn influences the way the individual interacts with the larger environment and obtains information from it. Less obviously, but no less significantly, individuals also differ from each other "in the way in which they carry out the organizing process referred to . . . as 'cognition'" (Cropley, 1977, p. 84). During the 1970s, much research effort was directed toward identifying significant, stable dimensions along which learners were found to differ from one another (Candy, 1980; Kolb, 1976a; Messick and Associates, 1976; Wang, 1980).

One corollary of recognizing these "systematic and idiosyncratic qualitative individual differences" between learners was the movement towards individualization (Keller, 1968) or even personalization of teaching methods and systems (Hill, 1971; Nunney, 1975; Wallace, 1977). An alternative approach to such differences has been to give increased control to learners. However, the question is whether handing over control of certain valued instructional functions really does allow for these different learning styles as claimed.

At one level, learner-control clearly allows for individual differences—indeed it is predicated on the existence of such differences—but there is little if any evidence to suggest that it reduces inherent inequalities by compensating for such differences (Snow, 1980, p. 151). If an educational approach is to accommodate individual differences in the strict sense, this means that it should obliterate any contingent relationship between aptitude and learning outcome in one of two ways: either by compensating for the effects of aptitude differences or by directly training away such differences in the process of instruction. However, Snow goes on to observe that "no known training program has been shown consistently to erase the individual differences in aptitude . . . [and] learner-control cannot be expected to overcome the persistent fact that individual characteristics will determine to a significant extent what and how much that individual will learn in a given instructional setting" (pp. 151–152).

Research evidence has consistently demonstrated that not all learners necessarily benefit from learner-control, and that some — especially the less able academically — are actually disadvantaged by it. It appears that increasing learner-control, although it might allow for individual differences, does not compensate for them. Thus, giving freedom of action to those able to deal with it may well increase their natural advantages, while placing those lacking self-confidence at even greater relative disadvantage. McClintock (1982) writes: "Perhaps self-set study is an education designed to perpetuate privilege and to create elites. By this means, the rich may get richer, the powerful more powerful, the cultured more cultured, while the common man gets more common yet . . . " (p. 51).

A second problem is the widespread assumption in the literature that, on the whole, "all [learners] should want or, under certain specifiable conditions, would want, more autonomy" (Dearden, 1972, p. 449). Very frequently, programs that seek to increase learner control do so from an ideological point of view (Candy, 1985), and learners who actually want or need more direction are not very well looked after: What the teacher, trainer, or facilitator is really saying is that it would be "good" for learners to exert more control, irrespective of what the learners themselves might think. It seems ironic that individual differences in learning style can be enlisted as a justification for increasing learner-control, yet it appears, as Dearden points out, that there is no room for individual differences in respect to people's willingness to be self-directing. This point is discussed again in Chapter Thirteen.

Problems may arise, however, even in those situations where learners are willing to accept responsibility for their own learning. Snow (1980) points out that "the idea that learner-control can accommodate individual differences rests on two assumptions. One is that all learners know what is best for themselves at any given moment in an instructional sequence; the other is that all are capable of acting on this knowledge" (p. 158). As it turns out, these assumptions have proved untenable for many learners. In particular, as to the assumption that "all learners know what is best for themselves at any given moment," Cross (1976) has written that "if we know that field-independents learn best and most pleasantly in independent study, are we necessarily serving them well if we offer them a steady diet of independent work? Maybe they need to learn to work cooperatively with others. 'Matching' them to their own style or preference may push them toward further field independence, and that may be maladaptive in certain social situations. Maybe we should expose them to a 'challenge match'—that is, place them in an uncongenial or conflict setting, so that they are forced to develop an area of weakness or at least some flexibility in dealing with uncomfortable situations . . . " (p. 111).

This situation may be likened to coaching tennis: If the players already have strong forehands then playing to this strength is unlikely to lead to an improvement in their backhands. And if, indeed, they have never ever been shown the backhand, this is a double advantage, for they may excel at something of which they are presently unaware. Thus, educators have an obligation to expose learners to a variety of instructional techniques and learning demands and to assist them in coping with situations with which they feel less confident.

Sometimes, the push by instructors for increased learner-control is not ideological, but pragmatic; they cannot easily cope with the enormous diversity within a group of learners, and so effectively abdicate responsibility by handing control over to the learners. However, I know from my own experience as a learner in adult education activities that I do not expect the teacher or trainer to throw up his or her hands in exasperation at the range of different learning styles, personalities, experience bases, interests, and so on within the group. Instead, I expect that person to make the most of such differences, to have the more experienced helping those with less knowledge in the group, or undertaking advanced or enrichment activities while the rest of us are struggling with the basics. Simply handing over the reins to the learners is only likely to lead to frustration and disappointment.

Finally, to adopt the stance that adult educators should modify their offerings (sequence, pacing, mode of presentation, level of content, and so on) to the demands of learners is to relegate adult education permanently to the status of a reactive field—determined entirely by the whim or preference of learners who, by definition, may not be in a position to direct their own education. Although it may be unfashionable to say so, "Unless education in the adult context is given a very different meaning, unless it is taken to involve no values whatever about what is learned, to refer to no standards of performance or achievement but to remain at the level of subjective personal insights which have no external intersubjective points of reference . . . the positive conception of a teacher has to be introduced" (Lawson, 1979, p. 26).

Learners are not the only ones who suffer from "the tyranny of self-direction" (Frewin, 1976), and educators can at least rest assured that in most subject areas there is likely to be a continuing demand for their expertise, even (or perhaps especially) if the vision of a learning society is fulfilled.

Learner-Control and Enhanced Motivation to Learn. The so-called motivation question is one of the most intractable in education. Essentially, it involves encouraging people either to learn something for which they see no purpose or, alternatively, to undergo certain experiences that lead to a desirable goal, but where the connection between the activities and the ultimate goal is unclear to the potential learner. It is often claimed that allowing learners to decide their own direction solves the motivation dilemma, because they are then pursuing a course of action that they have had a hand in determining. However, as Hamm (1982) observes: "The solution to the motivation problem is not allowing [learners] to choose what they want to do. Being motivated to do what one wants is either a tautology or not a problem. Instilling in [learners] the desire to pursue what is in their interest to pursue when they lack that interest initially is the motivational problem in education" (p. 96).

To some extent, Elton (1973) answers this criticism, when he argues that the method of instruction, as distinct from the content of instruction, can be inherently motivating: "By this, I mean that one devises learning situations in which the student feels himself involved, and in which he is active, perhaps through some form of self-study. The hope is that these situations, which in general appear to be designed in the main to achieve cognitive aims, lead to such student involvement, that he is carried over into the affective domain" (p. 76).

This is an appealing argument. It maintains that handing over control of the learning situation is an inherently motivating thing to do, and that the excitement and pleasure it engenders will carry over to an enthusiasm for the subject matter itself. If this were true, however, the many research studies that report increased enjoyment from various forms of learner-control (see, for example, Gruber, 1965; Caffarella, 1983) should also report enhanced learning outcomes, yet this is rarely the case: Wispe's (1951) pioneer study, to which I have already referred, clearly demonstrates the capacity of learners to distinguish the constructs of enjoyment and achievement in learning tasks.

Moreover, this line of reasoning is something of a two-edged sword, for if positive feelings about the process of learning are expected to spill over to the content, then there would seem to be no reason why negative attitudes might not do the same. Thus, learners with unhappy or unsuccessful experiences in learner-controlled instruction may feel inept and uncomfortable when confronted with the demand that they direct their own learning. Their feelings of frustration, anger, and disappointment, derived from being placed in an uncongenial learning situation, could "spill over" and contaminate their learning outcomes, and perhaps even lead to dropout or attrition. It would indeed be ironic if a teaching strategy designed to increase autonomy and learner satisfaction actually led to feelings of frustration, impotence, and ultimately of failure.

The implications of this for practice are twofold. First, instructors cannot "get off the hook" simply by handing over responsibility to learners; if they are to be encouraged to learn some aspects of the subject that are difficult or distasteful, then the educator must use all of his or her skills both to provide the needed instruction and to explain to learners *why* the learning is necessary in the first place. Second, practitioners must recognize that the unwanted side effects of inappropriately giving learners control may include anger or loss of confidence by the

learner. In such cases, learner-control may "backfire" by caus-
ing learners to withdraw, either psychologically or physically.

Learner-Control and the Modeling of Democratic Behavior.
Within the culture of Western democracies, few would oppose
the idea that teachers and adult learners are equal moral agents.
However, this should not be taken as evidence that they are equal
when it comes to the issue of teaching and learning, especially
where the subject matter consists of a body of knowledge that
is reasonably well codified and for which there are publicly available criteria for success.

At first sight, the argument that teachers and adult learners are equals and that they should have an equal vote in deciding what is to be taught and learned seems quite plausible.
So deeply ingrained are our notions of political equality that
we easily and unwittingly apply the same criteria to other domains of our lives. Moreover, many authors have an almost
instinctive reaction against the notion that one adult might have,
or be seen to have, power over another, and the inequality that
such a situation implies is anathema. According to Phillips
(1973), such conceptions of equality are usually based on one
or other of a number of analogies, and these do not really stand
up to critical scrutiny.

The first of these is the political analogy that claims that
in a democracy there is the principle of "one person, one vote,"
and that this should likewise apply in education. Phillips (1973)
explains the invalidity of this proposition as follows:

> If I am awaiting an operation, I shall express justifiable concern
> if I see a group which includes experienced surgeons, new doc-
> tors and students take a popular vote to determine who shall per-
> form the operation. Similarly, if my car breaks down I should
> be worried if those who happen to be on the premises at the time
> hold a popular vote to determine who shall attempt to repair my
> car. Given that certain people were elected to perform the oper-
> ation or to repair the car, I should protest on the grounds that
> they are not *qualified* to do so. If asked to expound what I mean
> by this, I should refer to the fact that the person elected is not
> a qualified surgeon or a qualified car mechanic respectively. What
> we mean by "qualified" in these contexts will be elucidated in terms
> of the skills, knowledge, expertise and standards involved in the
> field of surgery and car mechanics respectively. It is extremely

important to notice that the notion of being qualified in these fields can be understood quite independently of the popular vote. It does not derive its meaning from such a vote, but from the content and standards of the disciplines concerned . . . [p. 136].

In adult education, the authority of the adult educator (Weber, 1985) does not (for the most part) derive from a show of hands, but from having expertise in the particular subject area. And just as I would be dismayed if a surgeon or mechanic denied his or her special expertise in the name of a spurious democracy, so I would be justified in feeling cheated if, having enrolled in a course of instruction, the instructor suddenly denied that he or she had any special knowledge of the subject, and insisted that I had the ability (and indeed the responsibility) to discover things for myself, to plan my own program of inquiry, and to identify my own learning goals.

This disappointment, however, should not be construed as meaning that I accept the right of the adult educator to dictate to me in other areas, for we may well be equals in other domains of life. But I can recognize and acknowledge a lack of equality with respect to the subject being taught and learned without its detracting from my self-concept of autonomy overall. Thus, there is " . . . no analogy between the notion of democracy as used in the context of parliamentary representation, and talk of so-called democratisation in academic institutions" (Phillips, 1973, p. 137).

A second source of confusion, claims Phillips, rests on the notion of intellectual equality, and the moral right of people to be treated equally and to be listened to: "I have a right to have my say and my say should count, simply because I am a human being." Phillips (1973) states that although this proposition is far from nonsense in many realms of human affairs, it is most emphatically nonsense in the domain of education; " . . . the advocates of democratization . . . speak as if the mere fact that someone is an individual makes what he says intellectually worthwhile. This is to deny the very meaning of intellectual enquiry. Where matters of the intellect are concerned, it is fatal to confuse the statement 'I can say something' with 'I have something to say' " (p. 139). "Certainly," Phillips continues, "a teacher must think it worthwhile listening to what his pupils say, but the relationship between the teacher and what is said must be a critical one and it is in terms of intellectual criticism that a distinction appears between what is said and what is worth saying. Without such a distinction, there can be no academic standards and hence no deep inquiry into any subject" (p. 140).

There are certainly some domains of adult education where the expertise of the adult educator is in his or her knowledge of group processes, for instance, or where the subject is one (such as philosophy or religion), where each person is truly entitled to personal beliefs and there is no one "right" or "correct" answer. Yet even here it is reasonable to expect the adult educator to know (at least at the outset) more about the subject than the learners, and to accept a leadership role, rather than handing over control to the learners and expecting them to identify learning needs in an area of which, by definition, they are ignorant, or at least less competent than the instructor.

According to Phillips, a third mistaken proposition rests on the assertion that, because each adult learner is unique, each has the right to determine what is worth learning, and not to have any curriculum imposed: " . . . the confused view put forward by some advocates of democratisation, namely, that the student should be the person who determines what subject should be taught or what parts of a subject he wants to study" (p. 141). As Phillips says, to the extent that learning involves developing a critical stance in relation to the subject being studied, then a learner can assert his or her essential intellectual autonomy with respect to the subject either by accepting it or rejecting it, but such a choice must be "determined by critical standards inherent in the subject itself" (p. 141). The issue of subject matter autonomy forms the substance of Chapter Twelve.

Finally, there is a paradox relating to the notion of learners setting their own goals and making reasoned choices from among alternatives: "The democratic ideal requires knowledge and an ability to decide between a range of possibilities. When this ideal is applied to situations which involve learning, we face the paradox that by definition, what has not yet been learned is not yet known, and the potential learners can only at best dimly perceive what they want to know more about. They are not therefore fully in a position to judge and decide what they shall do and they are inevitably placed in the position of having to learn from somebody and that 'somebody' is a teacher whether he [or she] be so called or not" (Lawson, 1979, p. 26).

This is a point that has frequently been overlooked by writers on adult education. The important factor for educators is to recognize that if they are teaching a subject for which there are public criteria, rather than assisting learners to acquire greater self-awareness, there is nothing inherently undemocratic about knowing more than a novice. Of course learners must be treated with respect, and their needs and interests taken into account in devising and conducting a course or program. But inappropriate use of self-direction only belittles the educator and confuses the learner.

Learner-Control Encourages the Development of Autodidacts. There is much face validity and intuitive appeal to the proposition that giving learners control over certain functions in the instructional situation will lead to an enhanced capacity for self-directed learning outside formal instructional settings. However, despite the potentially critical relationship between the conduct of formal education and people's propensity to engage in learning in natural societal contexts, there is remarkably little research into the nexus. Skager (1979) describes as "a plausible assertion, but little more than that" the alleged connection between learner-control and autodidaxy, and goes on to observe that "no evidence links situations of responsibility and autonomy in the school years with participation in education later in life" (p. 520).

Implicit in the belief of a connection between learner-control and autodidaxy is the assumption that the use of self-directed or independent learning methods will lead to desirable social outcomes and the development of broader skills and attitudes both of critical judgment and of autonomous action (Aroskar, 1976; Dittman, 1974; Hausdorff, 1973; Rubenson and Borgström, 1981). But does the use of methods that encourage learner-control lead to more global qualities such as critical judgment, autonomous action, and self-initiated inquiry? H. A.

Lewis (1978) points out that "To approve 'autonomy' as an ideal for students is one thing: to commend 'autonomous' methods of learning is another—however autonomy is defined. If, for the purposes of argument, we gloss it as independence, it is not quite obvious that independent methods of learning promote independence—auxiliary causal relationships must be established" (p. 152).

In response to this view, however, Boud (1981) has written: "We should be careful in following this path too far. Although it may be in doubt that independent methods of learning in themselves promote independence, it is certainly unlikely that dependent teacher dominated methods would do so" (p. 23).

At the heart of this controversy is the useful distinction made by philosophers and logicians between *necessary* and *sufficient* conditions. A simple example of this distinction might be that the presence of water vapor in the atmosphere is a *necessary* but not a *sufficient* condition for precipitation to occur. With reference to the issue of autonomy, Dearden (1972) has analyzed the relationship between freedom and autonomy and argues that the absence of external constraints is a necessary but not sufficient condition for the development and exercise of autonomy. He cities the example of a prisoner who, having his freedom restored after a long period of incarceration, "exhibits only anxiety and withdrawal in the state of freedom, rather than the capacities of self-direction and choice which are characteristic of autonomy" (p. 451). He goes on to argue that "the granting of various freedoms by a parent or teacher might simply have the result that his direction is replaced by that of some other agency still external to the [learner]" (p. 451).

In summary, although the use of autonomous methods of learning may encourage the development of autonomy, the relationship is by no means automatic. It is clear that a person may be exposed to so-called autonomous methods of learning without internalizing the values of autonomy or necessarily being enabled to think and act autonomously (Campbell, 1964; Torbert, 1978). Conversely, it may be possible to develop autonomy without recourse to autonomous methods. If, for instance, autonomy is defined as the ability and willingness to approach situations with an open mind, to suspend critical judgment, and to act in accordance with rules and principles that are the product of the autonomous person's own endeavors and experience, then, paradoxically, as Dearden (1972, p. 452) argues, it might be precisely a student's upbringing and previous educational experience, with relatively little freedom, that does develop autonomy.

It seems to me that the distinction between autonomous learning as a goal (or teachable capacity) and autonomous learning as a method (or learning experience) is a crucial one for the practicing adult educator, and that it deserves careful analysis and research. It is clearly vital for adult learners, and indeed for all learners, to have the opportunity of exerting appropriate control in certain learning situations. However, this is not the best, and certainly not the only, way to encourage the development of autodidacts. Practitioners need to consider a range of other approaches that have been shown to facilitate such developments; this is a theme to which I return in Chapter Eleven.

The Promise of Autodidaxy

In the same way that learner-control has been advocated for a variety of reasons, so autodidaxy is also said to constitute a unique sector in the educational spectrum, and to offer certain advantages not available through other educational forms. Many of these assertions, however, are ideological rather than empirical; that is, they represent what people think is true, or wish were true, and not necessarily what is demonstrably the case. But although autodidaxy may offer certain advantages, little systematic attention has been devoted either to evaluating these assumptions and beliefs, or to examining its negative aspects as an educational practice. In the section that follows, therefore, several of the ostensible strengths or advantages of autodidaxy will be explored, and this will be balanced by an examination of some of the limitations of the concept, many of which are seldom discussed or examined in the literature. The following major assertions are discussed: In a democratic society, autodidaxy allows for the fullest expression of individual differences; autodidaxy is central to a fully developed concept of lifelong education; autodidaxy provides the cornerstone of moves toward a learning society; and autodidaxy, because it is freely available to everyone, offers the prospect of eliminating social inequality based on differential access to education.

Autodidaxy and the Expression of Individual Differences. As discussed elsewhere in this book, the ideology of individualism is deeply rooted in Western capitalist democracies (Gibbs, 1979; Spence, 1985) and is accordingly embodied in socially approved ideals that guide education. In 1961, for instance, a Joint Policy Commission of the National Education Association and American Association of School Administrators stated that "the basic American value, respect for the individual, has led to one of the major charges which the American people have placed on their schools: to foster that development of individual capacities which will enable each human being to become the person he or she is capable of becoming" (quoted by Dittman, 1976, p. 463). This kind of ideological commitment has led to the widespread acceptance of individualism in learning as a universal good.

An inevitable corollary of this individualistic orientation is the emphasis on people's ability to pursue learning opportunities as determined by their particular needs and interests. Clearly, one of the most individualistic forms of learning is that in which people undertake their own learning projects, in their own time and at their own pace, without any of the restrictions implied by formal courses or even institutional requirements. In fact, it is the highly individualistic nature of autodidactic activities, combined with an abiding preoccupation with acknowledging individual differences, that has helped to create such intense interest in and support for self-directed learning. Those who advocate autodidaxy as a valued strategy for promoting learning often refer to its highly individualistic focus as both a defining characteristic and advantage.

Autodidaxy manages to accommodate many of the significant individual differences that confront and often vex educators who try to teach groups. Differences in personality, age, motivation, previous educational attainment, socioeconomic status, preferred learning style, cognitive processing, and so on are all accounted for by the highly idiosyncratic way in which self-directed learners go about their learning tasks. However, because autodidaxy is not a method of instruction, the most that educators can hope to achieve is to encourage such learning as a lifelong pursuit. As discussed in Chapter Fourteen, this involves both removing impediments to people's self-education and providing resources, facilities, and skills necessary to pursue learning goals.

Autodidaxy and the Concept of Lifelong Education. In recent years, a number of theorists have attempted to develop a theoretical basis for autodidaxy. Three of these (Gibbons and others, 1980; Moore, 1973b, 1977; and Penland, 1981) have based their work on empirical research in the form of grounded theory building. A fourth (Boyd, Apps, and Associates, 1981) comprises an attempt to derive from within the literature a theoretical framework for what they have called the "individual transactional mode" in adult education.

Other theorists, instead of attempting to develop a theoretical basis for autodidaxy from within itself, have sought to place the phenomenon within a broader theoretical framework, such as that afforded by lifelong education (Brockett, 1983b; Clark, 1973; Council of Europe, 1975; Gibbons and Phillips, 1982; Rubenson and Borgström, 1981; Savićević, 1985; Skager, 1978, 1979, 1984; Unesco, 1990). This has proved difficult, not least because lifelong education itself is a notoriously nebulous and fluid construct.

In 1972, lifelong education was proposed by the International Commission on the Development of Education (Faure and others, 1972) "as the master concept for educational policies in the years to come for both developed and developing countries" (p. 182). According to one of its chief proponents, Dave (1973), the director of the Unesco Institute for Education, "It is a very comprehensive idea which includes formal as well as nonformal learning extended throughout the lifespan of an individual to attain the fullest possible development in personal, social and professional life. It includes all desired learning that occurs in a planned or incidental way in the home, educational institutions, community and place of work. Lifelong education encompasses all stages and aspects of education in an integrated and articulated manner" (p. 30).

As Rubenson and Borgström (1981, pp. 116–117) point out, the Unesco Institute of Education has consistently emphasized the importance of the individual learner and has argued that one of the major goals of lifelong education should be to develop learners capable of self-directed learning. The Institute has dealt with this concept in a comparative evaluation of school curricula (Skager and Dave, 1977; J. B. Ingram, 1979) and in more general analyses, often in the form of speculations of a normative character (for example, Cropley, 1980). One of the most interesting aspects of this work has been the attempt to operationalize what self-directed learning would mean for both the content and the process of school education. Skager and Dave (1977) list the following five criteria:

1. Participation in the planning, execution and evaluation of learning: learners are involved in planning both school and out-of-school activities
2. Individualisation of learning: organisational facilities are provided for making individualised teaching and learning practicable
3. Development of self-learning skills: opportunity is provided for use of a variety of learning sources, media and materials
4. Development of inter-learning of skills: learners share responsibility in the teaching/learning process
5. Development of self-evaluation and co-operative evaluation skills: group or individual work is evaluated co-operatively [p. 53]

Lifelong education differs from the conventional or traditional model of education in two major respects. The first is "the conviction that all individuals ought to have organised and systematic opportunities for instruction, study and learning at any time throughout their lives" (Cropley, 1977, p. 21), not simply from five to sixteen, or six to twenty-one, and that artificial barriers to, and between, levels of education should, as far as possible, be eradicated. This is referred to as *vertical integration*.

The second difference is the acknowledgment that people learn in a wide variety of contexts and settings, and that at any given stage of life—whether they are enrolled in formal educational activities or not—people are learning: from friends and family; from libraries; at work; in clubs and societies; in churches and other religious bodies; from radio, television, newspapers, and so on. This is defined as *horizontal integration* or "lifewide education" (Cropley, 1979, p. 15). Knapper and Cropley (1980) put the issue in perspective when they comment that, "in a sense, learning is far too important to be left solely to professional educators in direct teaching situations. Rather, educators would be better employed devising some means to foster self-directed learning and help it to take place productively and efficiently" (p. 3).

It can be seen that the phenomenon of autodidaxy fits into both the horizontal and vertical dimensions of lifelong education: It is at once one of the most common ways adults pursue learning throughout their lifespan, as well as being a way people everywhere supplement (and at times substitute for) the types of learning received in formal settings (Savićević, 1985, p. 293). It is in this respect that autodidaxy has in the minds of many become almost synonymous with lifelong education.

Those engaged as adult educators can encourage both horizontal and vertical dimensions of self-directed learning. They can create networks of contacts throughout the society and provide referrals and introductions for learners wishing to pursue their interests more extensively (Perkins, 1985). They can also form liaisons with other educators—including school teachers, university professors, and training personnel—to reinforce the interconnectedness of learning opportunities and skills throughout the life span.

Autodidaxy Provides the Cornerstone of Moves for a Learning Society. In recent years, the concept of a "learning society" has provided a unifying model within which a diverse range of educative activities may be accommodated. Although the term itself is fairly recent, the concept of a society in which learning is both continuous and universal is not. John Stuart Mill, for instance, throughout his extensive writings, developed the notion of an "educative society" where government created—not only through formal institutions of education but also through the general social environment, industry, literature, and cultural activities—opportunities for individual as well as collective advancement.

According to Garforth (1980), Mill in turn based his vision of society on a rather idealized picture of ancient Athens, which he praised "lavishly, indeed immoderately," for a number of features, but "most of all for its educational impact on the ordinary citizens" (p. 16). Ancient Athens was perhaps the prototype of the learning society, for "in Athens, education was not a segregated activity, conducted for certain hours in certain places at a certain time in life. It was the aim of the society. The city educated the [person]. The Athenian was educated by the culture, by *paideia*" (Hutchins, 1968, p. 133).

For all its many strengths, however, Athens fell short of the ideal of the learning society in at least two significant respects. First, it disenfranchised both women and permanent resident aliens, excluding them from political life and from the benefits of education. Second, the leisure time that Athenian citizens were expected to devote to learning was only "made possible by slavery" (Hutchins, 1968, p. 133). Thus the advantages enjoyed by some were at the cost of disadvantages suffered by others. In the present context, however, where "ordinary citizen" does not simply connote "freeborn male," "machines can do for every modern [person] what slavery did for the fortunate few in Athens. The vision of the learning society . . . can be realized" (Hutchins, 1968, pp. 133–134).

What exactly is the connection between autodidaxy and the learning society? Probably the clearest statement of the link is given in a Unesco document on literacy and continuing education: "The 'learning society' . . . involves the idea that ultimately the educational process is the function of society as a whole—not just part of society such as literacy agencies, schools, colleges, and so on. *All* groups, associations, institutions and agencies have a role to play. . . . [However], if a learning society is to be effective, the opportunities provided by it must be accepted and utilized by its citizens. *Only autonomous learners can take maximum advantage of such an opportunity so the evolution of a learning society depends on the development of autonomous learning"* (Unesco, 1990, p. 6; emphasis added).

As with lifelong learning, there is a reciprocal relationship between autodidaxy and the emergence of a learning society. As indicated in the preceding quotation, "the evolution of a learning society depends on the development of autonomous learning." But the converse is also true: People's ability to behave autonomously, to fully develop mentally, physically, and spiritually, and to view education as valuable in itself (Cross, 1981, p. 177) is dependent on the emergence of "lifelong learning communities," where "any social system (family, neighborhood, organization, agency, community, state, nation, or world) can be conceptualized as a system of learning resources" (Knowles, 1983b, p. 4).

Not unreasonably, many adult educators may feel daunted by the prospect of creating a learning society. Such a task may appear impossibly large, and there is no doubt that it does require both large amounts of money and necessary political will at very high levels. There are, however, steps that individuals can take to promote the cause of the learning society (Cropley and Dave, 1978). These include joining relevant professional organizations; pushing for the development of appropriate policy statements and opportunities for access within their own organization; reading about the concepts and practices of lifelong learning and discussing these with learners; thinking actively about how to provide access to educational opportunities in their own organization and more widely in their city, region, state, or country; networking with other educators working in other sectors of educational provision, and, perhaps most important, becoming a continuing lifelong learner and user of educational opportunities (Overstreet, 1950, pp. 282–285).

Autodidaxy and the Elimination of Social Inequality. One of the most telling criticisms leveled at formal educational systems virtually worldwide is their tendency to reinforce social inequality through a subtle and complex process of "cooling out." In brief, the argument is that different forms and levels of education provide access to more or less rewarding and fulfilling life opportunities, and that access to and ability to benefit from the more desirable forms of education is mediated through a complex of interacting variables, including socioeconomic status, past educational background, location and mobility, expectations and self-concept, and even such things as accent and vocabulary.

That formal education performs this doleful function of allocating people to levels or layers in the social hierarchy seems beyond argument. For a long time, however, it was believed that adult education stood outside this distributive paradigm, and that it provided an alternative route to social mobility and societal transformation. Present work by critical theorists, however, has cast considerable doubt on this proposition. It now seems that adult education, too, despite its long tradition of social activism, appears to attract clients and offer programs that have differential payoff in terms of access to social, cultural, and economic resources (Hopper and Osborn, 1975).

As the floodwaters of criticism have risen higher, many adult education theorists have retreated to the rapidly shrinking and isolated patches of informal learning left, including that of self-directed learning. Here, in the sanctity of libraries and clubs, in the privacy of homes and offices and factories, people can at least undertake learning that compensates for the failures and setbacks of their earlier experience. It is argued that people can undertake self-directed learning as an antidote to the pernicious and socially divisive effects of formal education, that only when people are free to construct their own learning pathways will education be truly emancipatory. This is indeed a noble aim, and one toward which most if not all adult educators would strive.

The Limitations of Autodidaxy

Despite the appeal of the various arguments in favor of autodidaxy, there are, lurking in the shadows, certain limitations both to the concept and its practical outworking that are frequently ignored or glossed over by its advocates and apologists.

In offering these reservations, it should not be inferred that I am opposed to autodidaxy: On the contrary, I believe that it is a vital concern and that the very future of humankind depends in part on people's ability and willingness to undertake learning of their own choice in self-planned and self-initiated ways. However, any serious appraisal of the potential of autodidaxy needs to take account of the limitations that are imposed by the imperfections of human nature, the nature of knowledge, and social conventions and norms.

Autodidaxy and the Expression of Individual Differences. The history of educational philosophy is marked by a recurring consideration of the relative importance of the individual and of the social group in influencing the progress of teaching and learning. As discussed in Chapter Two, the pendulum swings between the extreme positions of radical individualism and social determinism, and to the extent that one view is in the ascendancy at any particular time, so educational practice (and theory) tends to reflect that preoccupation. In the past few years, sociologists have tended to the view that education has overemphasized the individual with respect to the societal context. Jarvis (1987a) for instance points out that "learning always occurs within a social context, and the learner is also to some extent a social construct, so that learning should be regarded as a social phenomenon as well as an individualistic one" (p. 15).

Because of its intensely individualistic focus, the study of autodidaxy has been significant in this emphasis on individual learning. In a brief but powerful critique of individualism in education, Hargreaves (1980) traces the triumph of individualism, represented most often by egoism and anomie (Durkheim, 1925), over organic solidarity. He writes: "The working vocabulary of teaching reflects the cult of individualism. When teachers talk about their aims, the rhetoric is replete with concepts such as 'individual development,' 'personal growth,' and a whole host of concepts — independence, autonomy, self-reliance, initiative — which can all be prefaced with the word 'individual.' Collective or corporate concepts which were once much more popular — esprit de corps, 'team spirit,' etc. . . . — are fast vanishing" (Hargreaves, 1980, pp. 193–194).

Adult educators are not exempt from this trend. As Welton (1987) laments of Canada (and the situation is probably similar in other major English-speaking nations such as Britain, Australia, New Zealand, and the United States), "Adult educators appear to have forgotten our movement tradition (mobilizing groups to make the social order more responsive to their interests). Now the intellectual dike is riddled with holes and the seas of humanistic, individualistic psychology have flooded in, engulfing us all" (p. 52).

This criticism is not directed at autodidaxy alone, but at any perspective that tends to emphasize individual over collective effort. Not unexpectedly, approaches to formal education that emphasize "independent study" are criticized for the same reason: They are socially divisive and tend to emphasize certain cultural values in preference to others. As mentioned in Chapter Two, Brookfield, for instance, laments both the middle-class bias of most studies of autodidaxy and their failure to deal adequately with the social setting and support mechanisms, particularly of working-class learners, and those of low educational attainment. Walker (1984) is critical of the emphasis on "self-directed learning" because of its gender bias towards males, and in an essay on "Individual and Cultural Determinants of Self-Directed Learning Ability," Halverson (1979) points out that "women are socialized into accepting a set of values associated with responsible behavior, friendliness, co-operativeness and acceptance of authority . . . " and that "those of a non-Western cultural background, such as Mexican Americans, blacks, and Native Americans, tend to have a value orientation based on communal values and holistic thought processes" (p. 63). She goes on to ask: "Should we design self-directed learning environments to foster learning styles and characteristics of independence, aggressiveness, and analytic thought which are rewarded in the dominant society? Should women and racial/ethnic minorities consider their cultural heritage of field sensitivity in terms of cognitive style and interpersonal relationships a barrier to achievement and self-directed learning? If not, how can women and racial/ethnic minorities gain access to society's rewards? We need to consider the costs to individuals and to society of following this path" (1979, p. 63).

It is also relevant to ponder whether individualism (and hence individual, self-directed learning) is not also influenced by considerations of class, as well as of gender and cultural background. As discussed in the previous chapter, Keddie (1980) has observed that individualism is not valued equally by all groups in society, yet with few exceptions, little scholarly attention has been focused on the sociological aspects of autodidaxy, including whether or not some forms of autodidactic endeavor either lead to, or else result from, social alienation (Entwistle, 1979, p. 190). It is clear that this educational domain demands further critical analysis from a sociological, as well as the more common psychological, perspective — a point to which I will return in Chapter Fourteen.

There may be relatively little that individual educators can do in the face of profound and deeply entrenched social inequalities, but further isolating people from one another through excessive emphasis on individualism is hardly conducive to enhancing societal structures. Those who support individuality in learning must be confident that they are not, at the same time, weakening the ability especially of the powerless or disadvantaged to work together for their collective advancement.

Autodidaxy and the Concept of Lifelong Education. Few concepts have managed to attract support across such a wide spectrum of educational opinion as lifelong education and autodidaxy. Several reasons for this suggest themselves. The first is that both are fairly fuzzy concepts that lend themselves to a mosaic of interpretations. Writing about lifelong education, Rodriguez (1972) comments that "the still highly abstract nature of the idea facilitates the emergence of an almost universal consensus in its favour. . . . Only a very few discordant voices are raised to warn against the danger of totalitarianism" (p. 27). Cross (1978) makes a similar point, in slightly different terms: "It is quite possible that lifelong learning now outranks mother-

hood, apple pie, and the flag as a universal good. Almost everyone is in favor of lifelong learning despite mounting confusion
among experts over the meaning of the term" (p.1). It appears
that this comment is also true of autodidactic or self-directed
learning; it is a construct to which people from widely differing
ideological positions can equally subscribe (for example, Dill,
Crowston, and Elton, 1965; Raiskii, 1979, p. 76).

The second reason for this widespread acceptance is that,
as discussed in Chapter One, the concepts are closely related,
and that acceptance of one therefore frequently entails endorsement of the other. As previously mentioned, autodidaxy is one
of the principal ways in which lifelong education is pursued,
and is accordingly inseparable, for many people, from their understanding of lifelong education. Moreover, lifelong education
takes, as one of its principal aims, equipping people with the
skills and competencies required to continue their own "self-
education" beyond the end of formal schooling. Autodidaxy is
thus viewed simultaneously as a means and an end of lifelong
education, and this has contributed to some confusion in writing and thinking about it.

A third reason that may help to account for the near-
universal acclaim for these two constructs is that they are commonly viewed as being value neutral, and hence "safe" for people
from either end of the political spectrum to endorse. However,
both this and the previous assertion are open to more careful
analysis and scrutiny. Like many educational ideas, lifelong education and autodidactic learning have the potential either for
liberation or repression; they may be either progressive or reactionary (Griffin, 1987, p. 285). Griffin goes on to note: "Lifelong
education policies are not neutral. . . . Why should there be an
almost total international consensus on lifelong education alongside what Gelpi calls 'a progressive reduction of self-directed
learning'? Policies for lifelong education which have the whole-
hearted backing of the state are not likely to be advancing human freedom, in that they are unlikely to advance the cause
of self-directed learning [which, if it were thoroughly applied]
would actually threaten the social order" (1987, p. 285).

If one accepts the legitimacy of the claim that education's primary role is "to teach and to learn in order to protect the established order," and to "adapt people to change in consequence of the application of science and technology" (Griffin, 1987, p. 285), then any educational innovation that successfully resists or goes against this trend is clearly a target for those in established positions of power. To the extent that autodidactic learning means "individual control of the ends, contents and methods of education," it places itself at odds with the entrenched interests of "repressive forces of our contemporary society" (Gelpi, 1979, vol. 1, p. 2), and one of two courses of action seems possible. One is to suppress or ban the practice, which is difficult enough in totalitarian countries and virtually impossible in more democratic settings. The second possibility is to coopt the practice, by making it part of the formal educational structures (Shapiro, 1984). Several authors, including Bock (1976) and Ziegler (1977), have expressed the concern that autodidaxy will be coopted by the formal educational system and that many of its distinctive attributes will be lost. Already in many parts of the Third World, there are Ministries of Nonformal Education; it is only a short step to the institutionalization of autonomous learning.

Although this scenario may seem unlikely, a Charter of Rights for independent learners has already been proposed, and one could imagine a situation in which autonomous learners could obtain some sort of certification for their competence at this mode of learning. Objectors such as Ohliger (1974), Ziegler (1977), and Illich and Verne (1976) argue not so much against the need for expanded educational opportunities throughout one's lifetime as against the excessive formalization of the system. Illich and Verne claim that the emergence of a class of "professional educators" with their penchant for systematizing and certifying all manner of learning experiences is an inevitable corollary of the "idea of education as a compulsory mediation between the individual's desire to learn and what he desires to learn" (1976, p. 13). Ohliger makes a similar point when he writes, "In the past, the field of adult education has been for many of us a haven where we could believe that spontaneous and voluntary learning was honored as the most important type of knowledge . . . [but now] we seem to be moving toward a society in which adults are increasingly told that they must consume 'official knowledge' in lifelong education" (1974, p. 54). Both sets of authors also warn against technocrats and politicians who, in the interests of developing a more productive and quiescent work force, may pervert the vision of a learning society into a "training society, ruled by educators" (Ohliger, 1974, p. 53) or, as Illich and Verne put it, into "an enormous planet-sized classroom, watched over by a few satellites" (1976, p. 20).

An alternative source of concern about the relationship between autodidaxy and lifelong education is ironically almost the antithesis of the first. This is the suggestion that, far from being swamped by the formal system, autodidaxy might one day supplant formal schooling, education, and training as the dominant (and perhaps even the only) mode of learning in society.

In their more euphoric moments, various authors have implicitly or explicitly suggested that the formal education system will be, or should be, disestablished, dismantled, or discarded in favor of networks of learning resources to serve the needs of autodidacts. A more balanced and parsimonious assessment, however, is offered by Jankovic and others (1979) in their report on the European meeting of experts on autodidaxy:

> The affirmation of the interest which the development of autodidaxy represents is not tantamount to a condemnation of the formal educational institutions.
> On the contrary, the specific contribution of school and university structures appears irreplaceable, both in terms of teaching services and the corpus of established knowledge they can provide. Autodidaxy should not be used as an excuse to cut funding to regular formal institutions.
> Briefly, autodidaxy, far from being an insurrection against the school, can only be implemented within a global strategy of educational development, and with the support and assistance of the school system, whatever the reticence and resistance it now enounters [p. 29].

V. N. Campbell (1964) observed this over twenty-five years ago: "If self-direction were to begin early in school and increase in scope as the student demonstrated his competence at it and saw that his reward was greater freedom and responsibility, by the time he was an adult, the cumulative effect on his problem-solving, decision-making, and creativeness might be impressive" (p. 358).

Autodidaxy and formal instruction have always coexisted and, as McClintock (1982, p. 55) notes, there is no reason to suppose that either one will entirely eclipse the other. There will always be a demand for instruction in forms of discipline-based knowledge, just as there will always be room for the independent pursuit of learning. The challenge for policymakers and theorists is to envisage an educational system in which these activities can both continue, each performing its legitimate share in the provision of learning opportunities. The challenge for practitioners is to recognize that autodidaxy in the full sense is an emancipatory activity, and that in advocating it, they are implicitly endorsing a view of education as a lifelong pursuit that may be manifested in all sorts of nontraditional ways.

Autodidaxy and the Development of a Learning Society. Frequently, when people think and write about a society in which learning opportunities are virtually limitless, and where the needs and interests of the individual learner are sovereign, they inadvertently ignore or gloss over two major concerns: the social nature of learning and the socially constructed nature of knowledge.

The first major reservation about autodidaxy in the context of a learning society is that it frequently implies solitary activity, yet learning is more than simply a psychological process. In recent years, considerable research has been undertaken into the experiences of learners enrolled in external studies or distance teaching awards. Such people are often typified as archetypal self-directed learners, working independently, at their own pace, at home or in the office, setting their own timetable, and generally behaving very autonomously. Much of this independence is more illusory than real, however; distance education students are frequently tied to objectives, assessment criteria, and schedules every bit as much as their on-campus counterparts (Elton, 1988; Parer, 1988), and similarly, on-campus students may suffer from social and psychological distance as much as or more than those studying by distance education (Adekanmbi, 1989; Bagnall, 1989). Moreover, one finding that has emerged repeatedly from such studies is that these supposedly self-directed learners crave contact with their teachers and with other students, and they feel that their experience of education is somehow counterfeit if it misses out on such contact.

Admittedly, self-directed learning does not have to be independent: Autodidacts may enjoy contacts that provide a rich pattern of support and stimulation, and likewise those who are given various degrees of learner-control may also work collaboratively. But it is not uncommon to find writers who seem to make the assumption that self-direction necessarily involves separation both from other learners and from the teacher or trainer. There may well be times when such independent and autonomous effort is called for, but there are distinct limits on the nature and extent of learning that can be achieved or should be attempted alone. In part this reflects the need for dialogue and discussion to clarify ideas, in part the need to hear other people articulate their ideas, and in part because knowledge itself is largely a consensually validated social artifact.

This leads to a consideration of the second major reservation, which is the nature of knowledge. Unlike the Ten Commandments, which were apparently handed down to Moses by God on tablets of stone, most knowledge that people encounter in everyday situations is a highly refined artifact, created out of intersubjective agreement among communities of knowledge users. Whether this concerns the best time to plant certain seeds, or the best and most appropriate way to express an idea, or how to behave in a particular social situation, knowledge is developed and shared by people, and it is people who, in the final analysis, are responsible for acknowledging whether some proposition or utterance is to count as knowledge or not.

Autodidaxy in the context of a learning society often carries with it the connotation of the learners creating or constructing their own understandings and deciding for themselves what they will or will not accept. This is, however, untrue. Learners require contact with others for two reasons: first to provide them with insights and understandings, and second to evaluate or validate the worth of what they claim to have learned (Chené, 1983).

Clearly there are plenty of domains of knowledge where a learner has every right to set his or her own agenda and to decide whether what has been learned is "true" or appropriate or sufficient. But the existence of a learning society would not change the fact that there are certain bodies of knowledge for which one of the most formidable obstacles for people undertaking their own education is the problem of not knowing: not knowing where to begin; not knowing how to proceed; not knowing what is valuable and valueless; not knowing when to stop; and, perhaps most difficult of all, not knowing what there is to know.

In the case of direct instruction, it may be both desirable and practical for a teacher, trainer, coach, or facilitator to consult adult learners, individually or as a group, to determine what issues they would like to see explained, discussed, or demonstrated during a course of instruction. It seems to me perfectly defensible as a tenet of adult education that adults frequently orient their learning endeavors to real-life situations of which they have some experience, and that their requests or demands for particular curricular content are both legitimate and appropriate. It must also be noted, however, that adults—especially those who have enrolled in a course and paid good money to be taught by an expert—also have a right to be given clear, explicit, and comprehensive instruction when they ask for it. This, too, is both legitimate and appropriate.

I am not advocating here the sort of overdependence that saps initiative and denies autonomy, but in those instances where there is a body of skill or knowledge to be mastered, and where the adult learner makes a request to be instructed as a legitimate introduction or shortcut, I can see no reason why the instructor should deny the learner's requests. Confronted with the limitless possibilities for learning, the immense complexity of knowledge structures in our society, and the real possibility that the learner may never have even heard of the concepts, approaches, or skills that may help him or her to meet some current or likely future situation, it is both unwieldy and, in my opinion, inappropriate to rely exclusively on self-direction. In his anthology of conundrums and paradoxes *Knots*, Scottish philosopher and poet R. D. Laing writes of adult learners:

> There is something I don't know
>   that I am supposed to know.
> I don't know *what* it is I don't know,
>   and yet am supposed to know,
> and I feel I look stupid
>   if I seem both not to know it
> and not know *what* it is I don't know.

In reality, there is no disgrace in not knowing something; it is simply a reflection of the unique pattern of one's experiences. However, our society places great stress on "saving face," and accordingly adults frequently feel compelled not to admit to their shortcomings, or to cover them up:

> Therefore I pretend to know it.
>   This is nerve-racking
>   since I don't know what I must pretend to know.
> Therefore I pretend to know everything.

Source: Laing, 1970, p. 56. Reprinted with permission.

It could be argued that advocates of self-direction, by emphasizing the constant and universal competence of learners, may deny their legitimate right to ask to be told, and hence to impose the "tyranny of self-direction" (Frewin, 1977) onto adults who, for a variety of reasons, may not know how best to tackle an unfamiliar domain.

Linked to this is the problem confronted by supporters of discovery learning, that each person need not recapitulate the entire intellectual history of whatever domain they choose to learn. However, if self-direction were always advocated, they would be condemned to do so because there is no definitive way of taking shortcuts in mastering an unfamiliar or novel branch of knowledge. As the Nuffield Foundation Group for Research and Innovation in Higher Education (1975) put it, "Autonomy is the quality of being able to choose dependence or independence as the learner sees fit" (p. ii). This issue is dealt with in greater detail in Chapter Twelve.

Adult educators who espouse the cause of a learning society (Butler, 1989) must not lose sight of the fact that most knowledge is socially constructed, and that most learning occurs in a social context. Self-direction, if pushed to extremes, may emphasize individual needs and interests to the exclusion of social cohesion, and the learning society could become a place where none of us would actually want to live.

Autodidaxy and the Elimination of Social Inequality. As mentioned earlier in this chapter, the propensity of the formal educational system to "sort" and "allocate" people to various societal roles is a phenomenon that has been extensively documented in recent years (Bourdieu, 1973, 1977; Bowles and Gintis, 1976; Connell, Ashenden, Kessler, and Dowsett, 1982; Karabel and Halsey, 1977). The formal system of schooling also reinforces and legitimizes these inequalities, through the subtle messages, or "hidden curriculum" (Snyder, 1971), embodied in both the content and process of education. It is also apparent that a vicious cycle is operating at the societal level as well, for those who have more education tend to partake of more still, while those without education tend to fall further and further behind. Moreover, the children of the well-educated, having access to an enriched home environment and often to a privileged system of schooling are more or less assured of the opportunity for higher education, better paid jobs, and more social and cultural stimulation, and thus the inequalities tend to be perpetuated, or even accentuated, generation after generation.

It is a professed intention of lifelong education as a policy goal to eradicate these invidious inequalities, and to break the cycle whereby such inequalities are perpetuated, and even exacerbated, by formal education. Some have considered the possibilities that adult education (Hoghielm and Rubenson, 1980; Thompson, 1980), particularly the nonformal (Stalker-Costin, 1985, 1986) and autodidactic (Borgström, 1985; Gelpi, 1979; Rubenson and Borgström, 1981) forms of adult education, might offer in this process. Gelpi (1979), for instance, writes that self-directed learning by individuals and groups is a danger to repressive forces and powerful elites, because it challenges their control: "Radical change in social, moral, aesthetic and political affairs is often the outcome of a process of self-directed learning in opposition to the educational message imposed from without" (p. 2). According to this perspective, if only autodidaxy could be encouraged, there would be a progressive overturning and reversal of the reproduction of inequalities via formal education.

The problem with this line of reasoning is that, as has been discussed elsewhere in this chapter, the incidence of autodidaxy already seems to be reasonably evenly distributed throughout the adult population. Even those groups conventionally classified as "hard-to-reach" or "disadvantaged" seem to undertake various forms of learning efforts, yet there has not been any appreciable improvement in their status, or ability to transform their lives. Thus, as Rubenson and Borgström (1981) note, "The link which has been presumed to exist between self-directed learning and progressive social change is more complicated than the literature on the subject usually suggests" (p. 118). In Sweden, for instance, adult education has been deliberately employed as a mechanism to enhance equality: "Previously in the educational debate, greater equality was often viewed in terms of economic equality. In the adult educational policy of the 1970s, however, the goals of adult education can be taken to refer to the creation of resources in a broader sense . . . contributing toward a further development of democracy by increasing the social and cultural awareness of citizens, and their active contribution towards social change" (Rubenson and Borgström, 1981, p. 121).

In line with this policy objective, attempts have been made to study the effects of participation in various forms of adult education on the creation of personal resources, not just economic, but social, cultural, and political resources as well (Johansson, 1970, p. 25). Rubenson and Borgström (1981), noting the apparent failure of autodidaxy to yield improved economic resources, ask: "What kind of resources are really created by this activity? Do people mainly participate in activities which only create resources in the areas where they are already strong?

If this should be the case, the redistribution effects will be quite small" (p. 125).

By 1985, Borgström was in a position to be able to offer at least a tentative answer to the question, "What kind of resources are really created by this activity?" In an extensive study of the living conditions of the Swedish people conducted by the Central Bureau of Statistics, she was able to include some questions about the leisure time pursuits and adult education (including autodidactic) activities of some 6,700 adults in Sweden aged between sixteen and seventy-four years. She established that "the group 'self-directed learners' seem to be a group that has stronger resources in cultural, political and social matters [generally]." She goes on to observe: "These results seem to give poor support to the hopes that have been attached to the function of self-directed learning to increase democracy. Different knowledge and competence is created or reinforced in different groups. In contrast to statements in the literature, this study found that self-directed learning rather contributes to the reproduction of inequalities in society. This occurs through a tracking process by which self-directed learners from the upper classes pursue activities with the best 'pay-off' in the form of cultural enrichment, occupational and political efficiency" (Borgström, 1981, pp. 13–14).

It appears, then, that autodidaxy may not hold the key to improved social equality, as commonly claimed, and that it is not simply the number, but the type of autodidactic activities that are engaged in that makes a difference to people's quality of life.

Even in those situations where autodidacts are pursuing topics that appear to have potential for increasing their personal resources, some learners could be at a disadvantage. Because they are incapable of understanding fully the "logic" of the subject, they might be restricted to superficial or reproductive strategies, and material which is only superficially understood has comparatively little power to transform people's lives or to equip them with enhanced "resources."

It might be argued (Häyrynen and Häyrynen, 1980) that people from an impoverished sociocultural environment (that is, "hard-to-reach" or "disadvantaged" adults) may experience a qualitatively different level of learning when they undertake their own projects, and they may be unable to undertake "deep-level" learning of a subject. Although it is perhaps tempting to assume that people who are self-taught are the "orphans of culture" (Jankovic and others, 1979, p. 3), and that those from economically underprivileged situations are unable to learn as well as those who have had more advantages in life, one should be careful in following this line of reasoning too far. The assumption is simplistic, and the correspondence far from absolute.

Häyrynen and Häyrynen (1980) argue that there are forms of aesthetic awareness that allow people to follow quite complex philosophical arguments, "even though they were not able to understand everything conceptually." They go on to explain that "a task involving a challenge often leads to a discovery of new abilities in oneself" (p. 12), and Tough (1979a) also comments on the same aspect when he writes of his experiences interviewing people about their learning projects: "Several times, during an exploratory interview with a family member or friend whom I thought I knew very well, I have discovered an attractive, but unsuspected, side of the person. Sometimes this impressive new aspect is a goal or interest, sometimes an earnestness or thoughtfulness, and sometimes an intelligent, aggressive striving to become a better person" (p. 19).

It is beyond the scope of this book to undertake a full sociological analysis of autodidaxy. However, the preceding comments by Häyrynen and Häyrynen as well as by Tough serve to underscore the fact that people are not always victims of their biographies, and that self-education can allow them to reconstruct their realities as well as to change their concepts of themselves. This theme will be discussed again in Chapters Eight and Thirteen. Clearly, adult educators have no mandate to stand in the way of people learning whatever they choose. But it is necessary to recognize that, unless other significant aspects of the social fabric also change, self-directed learning on its own is not necessarily going to lead to a more just and equitable society, and ironically it may have the reverse effect, if steps are not taken to discriminate positively in favor of those with various forms of disadvantage.

Conclusion

> When we look realistically at the world in which we are living today . . . we are no longer dealing primarily with the *vertical* transmission of the tried and true by the old, mature, and experienced teacher to the young, immature, and inexperienced pupil. This was the system of education developed in a stable, slowly changing culture. In a world of rapid change, vertical transmission of knowledge alone no longer serves the purposes of education.
>
> What is needed and what we are already moving toward is the inclusion of another whole dimension of learning: the *lateral* transmission, to every sentient member of society, of what has just been discovered, invented, created, manufactured, or marketed. This need for lateral transmission exists no less in the physics or genetics laboratory than it does on the assembly line with its working force of experienced and raw workers. The person who teaches another individual the new mathematics or the use of a newly invented tool is not sharing knowledge acquired years ago. He or she learned what was new yesterday, and the pupil must learn it today.
>
> The whole teaching-and-learning continuum, which once was tied in an orderly and productive way to the passing of generations and the growth of the child into an adult — this whole process has exploded in our faces [Mead, 1958, p. 23].

Although these words were written more than three decades ago, they have not lost their force, and their relevance is, if anything, greater now than it was then. Clearly, both learner-control and autodidaxy have much to offer in a world of lateral transmission of knowledge. Accordingly, to develop, enhance, and facilitate people's capacity to participate in these forms of inquiry is a defensible educational goal. However, as long as there are still forms of knowledge for which there are public criteria, it is unlikely that such learner-centered, individualistic, and self-planned forms of learning will ever entirely replace all forms of mediated instruction: "Instruction and 'study' [that is, self-directed learning] at all times coexist; they will always be present in varying proportions in all educational phenomena" (McClintock, 1982, p. 55).

It has been the purpose of this chapter to highlight some of the unique advantages, the strengths, and the promise of self-direction in learning, but to counter these with a sober assessment of their limitations and shortcomings. Only in this way can a balanced appraisal and appreciation of self-direction be attained: a foundation on which a more detailed analysis and program for action might be constructed. It has been pointed out that there is much that practicing adult educators can do, both to encourage and to enhance learner-control in instructional settings and to facilitate and model autodidaxy in everyday settings. There seems little doubt that self-direction in both these contexts has methodological and ideological strengths that are consistent with many of the values held dear by adult educators in the Western democratic system. They are, however, no panacea for all the ills that beset education and society, and they must be introduced, promoted, and pursued with a realistic awareness of the many difficulties, prejudices, and limitations that are embedded in other aspects of the social fabric.

In the next part of the book — Chapters Four to Seven — much of the existing thinking and research about self-direction in learning will be reviewed, in order to identify the dominant assumptions and methods that have influenced its evolution as a major field of study and practice in adult education.

Part 2

Four Dimensions
of Self-Direction

> The term self-directed learning is normatively and functionally
> ambiguous. As a result of various philosophical and research
> orientations as well as through overuse, misuse, and various
> definitional emphases, the term self-directed learning lacks both
> explicitness and discreteness.
>
> — *Gerstner, 1987, p. 171*

There can be little doubt that *self-direction* is an important and
powerful educational construct. The term itself resonates with
overtones of purposefulness, autonomy, potency, and self-
awareness. It conjures up a cluster of connotations that by and
large are viewed positively in our culture.

However, as previously mentioned, it is the very fuzzi-
ness of the term that has led to its use in a range of educational
settings, and that has elevated self-direction to a position of honor
in the adult education lexicon. This same imprecision has also
contributed to the tendency to apply the term somewhat indis-
criminately to a diverse range of phenomena. Thus self-direction
is portrayed both as a personal quality or attribute and as a characteristic of situations (Oddi, 1987). It is advocated as a means
to an end, and as an end in itself. There is an implicit assumption that self-direction in learning will eventually manifest itself
in self-direction in social, cultural, political, and civic affairs;
however, there is a certain circularity in this view, because the
ability and willingness to be "self-determining" in the larger
sphere of life is also taken as a prerequisite for (and argument
in favor of) "self-management" in learning (Bagnall, 1987).

The purpose of Part Two is to take four common usages of the term *self-direction* and to explore what is or might be meant by the term in each context, the relationships (if any) among the contexts, and the dominant research approaches and findings in each area.

As Gerstner (1987) so ably demonstrates, this is by no means the only way that the phenomenon of self-direction may be divided up and examined, but it does at least coincide with several major divisions and preoccupations in the literature. If there is a predominantly theoretical part of the book, this is it. This is not to say, however, that practitioners will find nothing of interest; on the contrary, a good understanding of previous practice and past research is indispensable to consideration of changing one's educational approaches. In the reviews that follow, I have tried as far as possible to portray major strands of research and practice. However, the field of self-direction is such a large and diffuse one that it would be inappropriate to pretend this coverage is exhaustive. Furthermore, since I am adopting a somewhat different theoretical position from that which underlies a good deal of this research, I might also be accused of some bias in either my selection or presentation of the "state of the art."

Clearly, the chapters that follow betray a certain theoretical orientation, but to answer in advance the claim that I have been unduly harsh in my treatment or partial in my selection, let me offer three introductory comments. First, I believe that self-directed learning is an exciting and vital field, and that it is "one of the few areas of research in adult education with an extensive research-based body of knowledge" (Garrison, 1989, p. 53). Each person who writes on this topic is indebted to those who have gone before: As Sir Isaac Newton put it, "If I see further, it is because I stand on the shoulders of giants."

Second, there are already some excellent reviews of the literature; the recent volumes by Long and his associates (1988, 1989, 1990) and by Caffarella and O'Donnell (1990) provide a much needed overview and compendium of previous research. It would seem to be redundant to replicate what they and others have already accomplished so ably.

Third, particularly in the United States, self-direction has been closely aligned with and strongly influenced by the principles of humanistic education. In my opinion, the aims of encouraging personal growth and self-actualization are noble and worthwhile, and by adopting a constructivist approach — as I do in Part Three — I do not intend to diminish the importance of this aspect of self-direction. However, self-direction is broader, both in its aims and its effects, than just individual development, and I believe that, important as this domain is, we need to consider self-direction in all its fullness. Accordingly, the following four chapters provide a basis on which, and background against which, subsequent recommendations for study and practice of self-direction in the book are based.

Chapter Four concerns self-direction as an umbrella term, a culturally influenced philosophical ideal in which individual freedom and expressive individualism are approved and sought. It is shown that a concern with self-direction as personal autonomy has a long and distinguished history in Western thought and educational practice; that such self-direction has emotional and moral as well as intellectual or cognitive aspects; and that it is a lifelong endeavor, not exclusively the preserve of any one phase or stage of the educational spectrum. Nonetheless, self-direction is a hallmark of adulthood, and adult education has a particular mandate both to acknowledge and to facilitate learners' self-directed inquiries.

Chapter Five narrows the focus from self-direction as a philosophical ideal and broad characteristic exhibited in a range of settings to a psychological attribute and specifically educational orientation. Here, it is argued that individual people may vary "in their ability, capacity and preference" (Gerstner, 1987, p. 171) to undertake intentional learning. It is however acknowledged that the capacity for and inclination toward accepting responsibility for learning can be enhanced, and this chapter therefore explores some of the personal characteristics or qualities of a successful self-directed learner and ventures some speculations about how such orientations and abilities might be deliberately strengthened.

Whereas Chapters Four and Five are concerned with self-direction as a personal attribute, Chapters Six and Seven focus on learning activities. Chapter Six reviews some of the extensive literature about adult self-directed learning outside formal settings. It is shown that the practice of intentional self-education is extremely widespread amongst adults, but that most such projects are very unpredictable and exploratory, not conforming to rigid protocols or linear trajectories. Despite the extensive research in this domain, comparatively little is known about the personal purposes, intentions, or understandings of the learners themselves, or about how these are changed, transformed, and reshaped as the learning project progresses.

Chapter Seven concerns the forms and limits of self-direction in formal instructional settings. Under the general heading of learner-control, it is argued that learners may be given varying degrees of control over a number of dimensions. Such initiatives are either partial and illusory or alternatively, deeply subversive and contrary to the historic mandate of education to preserve and transmit culture from generation to generation. In either case, there are profound difficulties confronted by teachers and learners alike. It is here, perhaps more than anywhere else, that the contradictory and paradoxical nature of "forcing people to be free" (Torbert, 1978, p. 116) is most apparent. This particular chapter also throws into sharp relief the difference between learning for self-knowledge and learning to master a body of knowledge or skill for which there are public criteria. It is clear that as one approaches the self-knowledge end of the continuum, formal educational patterns and structures are decreasingly appropriate; conversely, where the knowledge or skill to be learned is publicly verifiable, there are severe limits to the appropriateness of self-directed inquiry.

Four

Personal
Autonomy

As mentioned in Chapter One, the term *self-direction* is applied to people — as a personal attribute or characteristic — as well as to learning situations. When self-direction is used in the sense of *personal autonomy,* it may have one of two meanings: either a broad disposition toward thinking and acting autonomously in all situations (self-determination) or, more narrowly, an inclination to exert control over one's learning endeavors (self-management). It is the purpose of this chapter to analyze literature pertaining to personal autonomy in the first of these senses, to derive a working definition of it, and to examine the extent to which its attainment may be attributable to educational (particularly adult educational) interventions. The next chapter will consider the issue of self-direction or self-management specifically within learning situations.

The term *autonomy* literally means "self-rule." Originally, the term applied to the property or characteristic of cities in Ancient Greece: "The city had autonomia when its citizens were free to live according to their own laws, as opposed to being under the rule of some conquering or imperial neighbour" (Dearden, 1972, p. 448). In due course, the term was extended to smaller social groupings, and the parallel between a self-governing city-state and an individual person eventually led to the adjective *autonomous* being applied to persons as well as cities: "By analogy, the autonomous person is an independent agent, one who is in command of himself, the author of his own work, deeds and way of life, not subject to the authority of other persons or things" (Gibbs, 1979, p. 119).

As mentioned in Chapter Two, Gibbs defines the essential characteristics of autonomy as intellectual self-determination, fortitude, and temperance—precisely the same cardinal virtues Plato delineated in *The Republic*. He deals with each of the three aspects of autonomy in turn, and notes that, "just as the several elements of a self-governing nation must be unified and at peace with one another, so in a temperate soul there is 'friendship and accord' between the elements" (p. 123).

In everyday discourse, the term *autonomy* is used to denote a state of freedom, of independence, and perhaps of self-sufficiency. Many people have attempted to define what may be meant by autonomy, and its multidimensional nature is reflected in its many possible definitions. Thus, an autonomous person is one:

- Whose life has a consistency that derives from a coherent set of beliefs, values, and principles (Benn, 1976)
- Who engages in a "still-continuing process of criticism and re-evaluation" (Benn, 1976)
- Who "is obedient to a law that he prescribes to himself" (Rousseau, [1762] 1911)
- Whose thoughts and actions, being determined by himself, "cannot be explained without referring to his own activity of mind" (Dearden, 1972)
- Who demonstrates a responsiveness to his or her environment, and the ability to make creative and unique responses to situations as they arise, rather than patterned responses from his or her past (Jackins, 1965)
- Who is "capable of formulating and following a rule, pattern or policy of acting and working" (Gibbs, 1979)
- Who has independence from external authority, being free from the dictates and interference of other people (Gibbs, 1979)
- Who has mastery of himself or herself, free from disabling conflicts or lack of coordination between the elements of his or her personality
- Who, instead of taking over unquestioningly the judgments and opinions of others, scans evidence, examines assumptions and traces implications—in short, who uses his or her reason (Paterson, 1979)

Two comments with respect to the preceding list are called for. First, many of these definitions emphasize the highly individualistic, situationally variable, and psychologically complex nature of personal autonomy — features that should be, but often are not, reflected in both the research and practice concerning "self-direction" in learning. Second, although definitions such as the foregoing accord with our commonsense understandings of the concept of autonomy, if the development, enhancement, or recognition of personal autonomy is to be a central feature of the enterprise of adult education, it is essential to have a more specific idea of what an autonomous person is like: "If we cannot distinguish . . . self-actualized individuals from those who lack any distinctive human excellences, then we can have no hope of finding reliable ways of liberating the former from within the latter, nor of developing (Rogerian) men from whom creative products and creative living emerge. . . . We will be unable to assist ourselves or others in enlarging the scope of choice and autonomy or in moving towards what we think of as the most distinctive and desirable forms of human activity" (Krimerman, 1972, pp. 333–334).

Accordingly, the next part of this chapter will review literature on personal autonomy and will include an operational definition of what might usefully be meant by the term.

The Concept of Personal Autonomy

In discussing the sort of evidence one might search for to ascertain whether or not a person is autonomous, Gibbs (1979) distinguishes two approaches to autonomy: those that concentrate on its intellectual dimensions and those that regard it more as a moral quality. In one view, autonomy is "equated with critical intelligence, independence of thought and judgement, discernment, [and] . . . a readiness to think things out for oneself free from bias and prejudice . . . " This conception of autonomy, Gibbs writes, "is probably the most familiar, for it is part of an individualistic, anti-authoritarian ideology which is very deep-rooted in Western capitalist democracies . . . " (p. 121).

The other conception envisages autonomy as "fundamentally a moral virtue or a disposition of character rather than intellect: self-mastery or self-discipline, having command of one's own feelings and inclinations . . . [where] self-mastery is conceived as something like what used to be called fortitude, or . . . temperance, or a combination of the two . . . " (pp. 121–122).

Crittenden (1978) identifies not two, but three overlapping components or dimensions to autonomy: intellectual, moral, and emotional autonomy. According to him, "Intellectual autonomy would require in the first place that a person not accept any of his important beliefs primarily on the authority of others, but on his own experience, his own reflection on evidence and argument, his own sense of what is true and right. . . . Moral autonomy . . . in addition to independence of thought in determining and applying criteria of moral judgment . . . also includes the executive capacities for carrying into practice what one decides should be done. The possession of these capacities is commonly described by such terms as tenacity, resoluteness, strength of will, self-mastery. [Emotional autonomy] implies not simply that a person would exercise self-mastery in the face of strong emotional involvement, but that he or she would remain emotionally detached in relationships with other persons and things" (p. 108).

Although we might question the assertion that emotional detachment in personal relationships is a valued aspect of autonomy, this tripartite definition does emphasize the often-ignored moral dimension — the fact that autonomy is not simply a matter of being "master of one's own destiny," but of being so within a framework of culturally sanctioned and socially agreed norms. In discussing educational attempts to develop autonomy, Dearden (1972) stresses the central importance of this moral element: "Without morality, for instance, the more autonomous an agent is, the worse he is likely to be. Great criminals are markedly autonomous men. . . . The rise of autonomy to prominence in education certainly does not mark the eclipse of such other values as those of morality and truth" (p. 461).

The development of autonomy in this full sense is neither the exclusive preserve of adult education, nor is it some luxurious accessory; it is fundamental to a fully developed curriculum in our society. In fact, in her doctoral dissertation, Partridge (1979) argued that the development of personal autonomy is a sufficiently important goal that ironically it justifies the compulsory imposition of liberal education on children, and the violation of the prima facie right to noninterference. She claims that three conditions distinguish the autonomous person: freedom of choice, rational reflection, and strength of will.

The first of Partridge's criteria, freedom of choice, concerns "freely chosen acts . . . for which the agent has causally operative reasons as opposed to rationalizations" (p. 65) for acting in a particular way. "We do not attribute the exercise of autonomy to anyone whose freedom is constrained either outwardly or inwardly" (p. 65). Outward freedom implies the absence of physical constraints (such as violence or threat of violence) and psychological constraints (including, but not limited to, hypnosis and other forms of psychological manipulation). Inward freedom, which has been dealt with at length by Peters (1973, pp. 123–124), includes the absence of acute deprivation, hysteria, paranoia, obsessions and delusions, psychopathy, and various forms of compulsions such as kleptomania.

Partridge's second criterion for identifying autonomous people is rational reflection, and she goes on to define what is meant by this term: "In saying that rational reflection is a necessary condition of autonomy, we are saying two things: firstly that one must have reasons for one's behaviour; and secondly that one's reasons must be good ones" (p. 69). "Reasons" are defined as "considerations which the actor takes into account in holding certain beliefs, proving certain points etc." (p. 69). Partridge (1979) states that this criterion does not mean that one has to consciously review one's reasons for doing everything, "but [that] very likely one could supply the reasons if asked to do so . . . " (p. 69).

Being able to supply reasons is one thing, but being able to show that they are good is more difficult, and Partridge lists four criteria for deciding if reasons are good or not: (1) they must be deliberated on (2) using nonarbitrary criteria (3) in as objective a way as possible (which implies the ability and willingness to change one's mind or alter one's belief in the light of new evidence or changed circumstances) (4) using relevant and adequate evidence. She goes on to say that "we do not require that one's beliefs be true or one's reasons wholly accurate before we attribute the possession or exercise of autonomy. . . . Neither false belief nor errors in judgement necessarily constitute a threat to autonomy . . . " (pp. 73–74).

The third of Partridge's criteria for judging autonomy sounds somewhat quaint; it is strength of will. Where there is no strength of will to carry through with the choices one has made, according to Partridge, there can be no autonomy. This does not mean that a strong-willed person will not experience conflicts or indecision; indeed, the more one engages in rational reflection, the greater may be the conflict one experiences. What it does imply, however, is that the strong-willed person, having systematically organized his or her priorities into some sort of hierarchical structure, is more likely to resolve conflicts and dilemmas and arrive at a new state of equilibrium. The weak-willed person, on the other hand, is more likely to be swayed by whims and impulses, to be immobilized by indecision, and to act anomically rather than autonomously (pp. 74–75). According to Peters (1973), "The strong-willed [person] . . . sticks to his [or her] principles in the face of ridicule, ostracism, punishment, and bribes" (p. 125).

Each of these authors is increasingly specific as to the type of behavior that an autonomous person might be expected to exhibit. Krimerman (1972) goes even further. He concerns himself with autonomously selected beliefs and desires, which may be thought of as approximately equivalent to Partridge's criteria of rational reflection and strength of will, respectively. In discussing how to decide whether or not a person's beliefs in proposition (P) are autonomously, as opposed to nonreflectively, held, he offers the following guidelines. The person:

> Has the ability to explain P to others using words and in circumstances substantially unlike those in which P was first encountered
>
> Has tested and evaluated P against alternatives, even when there are no extraneous rewards (social, psychological or physiological) for doing so

Is willing to relinquish or decrease belief in P when relevant coun-
terevidence is presented

Is not angered, threatened or incapacitated when objections or
alternatives to P are presented

Likewise, the following are among the considerations that
might be used to test whether a person's desire for a goal (G)
is autonomous. The person:

Has the ability to explain (in terms and circumstances different
from those in which the goal was first encountered) what G
consists of, how it differs from other goals, and how it might
be achieved

Has personally experimented with alternative goals without the
threat of sanctions, or hope of rewards, for such experimentation

Is willing to curtail or eliminate the pursuit of G when autonomously held beliefs concerning G alter, or when it becomes
apparent that attainment of G is incompatible with other, more
highly valued goals

Is not angered, incapacitated or threatened when exposed to criticisms of the value of G, or when temporarily prevented from
pursuing or attaining G [Krimerman, 1972, pp. 334–336,
passim]

Dearden (1975), another philosopher of education who
has devoted considerable attention to the links between education and autonomy, suggests that autonomous individuals would
characteristically:

Wonder and ask, with a sense of the right to ask, what the justification is for various things which it would be quite natural
to take for granted

Refuse agreement or compliance with what others put to them,
when this seems critically unacceptable

Define what [they] really want, or what is really in [their] interests,
as distinct from what may be conveniently so regarded

Conceive of goals, policies and plans of their own, and form purposes and intentions of [their] own, independently of any pressure to do so from others

Choose amongst alternatives in ways which could exhibit that
choice as the deliberate outcome of [their] own ideas or purposes

Form [their] own opinions on a variety of topics that interest them

Govern [their] actions and attitudes in the light of the previous
sorts of activity [p. 7]

Behavior such as this implies an intentional control of one's life, and accordingly, "a person could not be to any marked degree autonomous, without this being an important part of his self-concept" (Dearden, 1972, p. 460). With respect to all these criteria for judging an autonomous person, Dearden (1975) concludes: "To be autonomous therefore, is very much a matter of degree. . . . Unlike being six feet tall, married or a British citizen, whether a person is autonomous or not is something we will quite often rightly refuse to say. And our hesitation will be related to at least three dimensions of variability: the extent to which he or she shows initiative in forming [personal] judgements . . . , the firmness with which he or she then adheres to those judgements, and finally the depth of ramifying reflection which lies behind the criteria which are employed in making those judgements" (p. 9).

Krimerman (1972) concurs with this judgment that autonomy is a matter of degree, and even goes so far as to suggest that any given act might be assessed using various criteria and might be rated along a scale according to how many of the criteria were satisfied, from "unequivocally or paradigmatically autonomous" to "an ideal case of non-autonomous behavior" (p. 336). Even though one might blanch at the practical, not to mention the ethical, difficulties of attempting to classify people's activities along a continuum of personal autonomy, nonetheless the notion that autonomy is a "matter of degree" is a useful one. To the extent that autonomy is regarded as a developable capacity, the notion may have important implications. It would perhaps allow educational practitioners to identify and, with learners, to work on areas of perceived weakness — that is, aspects of their lives where they believed it both possible and desirable to think and act more autonomously.

Toward a Definition of Autonomy. As a result of the foregoing discussion, it is now possible to conclude that an individual may be judged to be autonomous to the extent that he or she:

1. Conceives of goals, policies, and plans, and forms purposes and intentions of his or her own, independently of any pressure to do so from others

2. Exercises freedom of choice in thought or action, without inward or outward constraints or restrictions on his or her capacities to act or to reason
3. Uses the capacity for rational reflection, judging among alternatives:
   a. On the basis of morally defensible, nonarbitrary beliefs as to what is true or right, derived from personal experience and/or reflection
   b. As objectively as possible
   c. Using relevant and adequate evidence
4. Has the will and the capacity fearlessly and resolutely to carry into practice, and through to completion, plans of actions arrived at through (1), (2), and (3) above, without having to depend on others for encouragement and reassurance, and regardless of opposition
5. Exercises self-mastery in the face of strong emotional involvements, reversals, challenges, and setbacks, and remains emotionally detached as far as possible
6. Has a concept of himself or herself as autonomous

Perhaps the most controversial of these criteria, especially within adult education, is the fourth, which suggests that autonomous people are emotionally self-contained and do not need, enjoy, or respond to social interaction. As with so many other issues, this question of independence is a matter of degree. The person who depends too heavily on the approval and regard of others is as undesirable as the uncaring individualist who is impervious to the opinions of others. Autonomy should not be endorsed or promoted as a goal to the detriment of social interdependence.

Clearly, a list such as this may provide a profile of an "ideal" or prototypic autonomous person, and might even serve as a checklist for designing learning activities to encourage personal autonomy. For instance, in a program based on contract learning, the learner could be asked to develop objectives, and criteria, and then to defend these in a reasoned debate either with the facilitator or with other learners. Group discussions could be characterized by learners' arguing for points of view on the basis of their prior reading and analysis of case materials and they could then be called on to compare and contrast different points of view, citing evidence in support of their final position. Learners could be required to make presentations to their peers, some of whom may be encouraged to take up contrary positions to test the strength and depth of the learners' understanding and conviction. Even an education designed to develop such manifestations of autonomy, however, is not guaranteed to succeed, and even if a person seemed on the face of it to behave in accordance with these characteristics, it is still not easy to be clear whether or not he or she actually is autonomous. There are two reasons for this: First, there are many threats to autonomy that are not evident to an observer (and sometimes not even known to the subject himself or herself), and second, autonomy is situationally variable. These considerations will be dealt with in turn.

Threats to Autonomy

In the original political context, autonomy was contrasted on the one hand with "heteronomy" (meaning domination and rule by others) and, on the other hand, with "anarchy" (meaning chaos and disorder occasioned by absence of government). These two situations have their parallel in the case of the individual people who may lack autonomy either because they are under the jurisdiction or influence of another, or alternatively because of discord and disharmony within themselves.

The situation of being under the control or influence of others is by no means easy to identify, and it is this difficulty that perhaps causes many educators to mistake the absence of overt or apparent constraint for autonomy. At one level, it is often assumed that as long as people are not physically and psychologically threatened, they will behave autonomously. Clearly, if someone hands over his or her possessions at the point of a gun or, in less dramatic circumstances, enrolls in a course because of threatened retrenchment, he or she is not acting autonomously. However, these are by no means the only types of pressure to which people are subject, and it is seriously questioned whether we can ever be entirely free from external pressures and considerations in living our lives. The fact of being part of a social community implies the acceptance of certain rules, such as those governing the use of language and standards of behavior.

While freedom may be necessary to the exercise of autonomy, and even to its development (although Dearden, 1972, p. 452, argues this is not necessarily so), the absence of external constraints in a particular context is not, in itself, a sufficient condition for autonomy. Certain other factors must be present. For instance, "a long term prisoner might gain his freedom, but have been so incapacitated for ordinary life by the institutional life of the prison that he exhibits only anxiety and withdrawal in this state of freedom, rather than the capacities of self-direction and choice which are characteristic of autonomy" (Dearden, 1972, p. 451).

This is frequently overlooked by adult educators who advocate certain freedoms in the instructional setting in the mistaken belief that this will inevitably lead to the exercise of autonomy. This issue will be dealt with later in the book, and especially in Chapter Eleven, in considering whether or not it is logically possible for adult educators to give learners autonomy, to assist them to develop autonomy, or merely to create circumstances within which they might exercise autonomy.

But even supposing that people were ostensibly free to think and act as they like, this would still not guarantee that they would behave autonomously. A person would not be regarded as autonomous if, for instance, he or she were merely following some anomic whim or falling under the influence of some propaganda, advertising claim, opportunity, or point of view that had been encountered. What is required is a stable set of personal beliefs (or "rules") that guide and give consistency (but not rigidity) to the person's actions.

It will be recalled that, in the political domain, autonomia referred to "self-rule," and the notion of rules or laws is one of the features that was carried over when autonomy was transplanted from the political to the personal domain. Accordingly, the existence, development, and status of personal rules, laws, or norms of behavior or judgment are central to discussions of personal autonomy. One position holds that the fully autonomous person is, in every respect, the author of his or her own destiny, and that the criteria used to make personal decisions are in themselves the product of his or her own inquiries, analysis, and reflection.

Perhaps one of the most outstanding examples of this is the French philosopher Descartes, who "learned to believe nothing very firmly concerning what I had been persuaded to believe only by example and custom." Thus, writes Descartes ([1637] 1981), "I gradually freed myself from many errors that can darken our natural light and render us less able to listen to reason" (p. 6). Husserl (1960), taking the Cartesian *Meditations* as a model for anyone wanting to achieve a bedrock of self-understanding, emphasizes the need to begin with an absolute lack of knowledge: "The mediator executes this regress by the famous and very remarkable method of doubt. Aiming with radical consistency at absolute knowledge, he refuses to let himself accept anything as existent unless it is secured against every conceivable possibility of becoming doubtful. Everything that is certain in his natural experiencing and thinking life, he therefore subjects to methodical criticism with respect to the conceivability of a doubt about it; and, by excluding everything that leaves open any possibility of doubt, he seeks to obtain a stock of things that are absolutely evident" (p. 1).

Most people do not, however, have the patience, the persistence, or the predisposition to doubt everything they encounter, and an alternative point of view acknowledges that it is impossible for a person to achieve the maturity of adulthood without innumerable encounters with the environment and with other people — encounters that inevitably shape values or conceptions of right and wrong, good and bad, worthwhile and worthless. Few, perhaps, would agree with Skinner's (1971) rather pessimistic observation that "as we learn more about the effects of environment, we have less reason to attribute any part of human behavior to an autonomous controlling agent" (p. 96). However, there is no denying that in view of the pervasive and profound influence of early conditioning, it is unlikely, if not impossible, for anyone to escape entirely the influence of others in forming personally relevant rules (Simons, 1986). This is not to say, however, that people must always be passive victims of their biographies, condemned forever to an acceptance of values and rules uncritically internalized at an early age. An autonomous person is able to assent to rules, or modify or reject them, if they are found wanting.

Irrespective of whether rules are autonomously derived, as in the first case, or critically assented to, as in the second, there still arises the question of what criteria people bring to bear in determining the value, legitimacy, or appropriateness of their "first-order" rules. What is called for is a superordinate or "second-order" value system by which to judge the "first-order" rules. However, these "second-order" criteria also have to be subjected to some sort of scrutiny, or else to be derived autonomously and, in either case, they too need to be critically evaluated according to yet another higher-order set of criteria. This line of reasoning is followed backward in an infinite regress, until the point is reached of the autonomous person making some "criterionless choices." At this point, as Phillips (1975) indicates, for all practical purposes, it becomes impossible for an outside observer such as a researcher to distinguish the Autonomous Person (AP) making "criterionless choices" from the Person Lacking in Autonomy (PLIA), whose behavior is based on following rules that have been internalized without being subjected to critical reflection. Such a picture runs counter to the usual notion of the autonomous person as one who makes decisions on the basis of carefully considered values and beliefs.

This issue about the third-person perspective has already been mentioned in Chapter One. In the same way that it is impossible for an outside observer to be able to say with certainty whether a learner is engaging in independent study or autodidaxy, as Dearden (1972) notes, it is also impossible to distinguish the situation of the truly autonomous person from the one where "direction appears to be that of the person himself or herself, but really it is father, teacher, or nanny who is speaking from out of the past" (p. 450). This latter situation roughly corresponds with Riesman's (1950) concept of "inner-directedness," which turns out to be a special case of "other-directedness," except that the influence of the "other" has been internalized at some early stage.

It can be seen that autonomy is a difficult concept to operationalize, and that it is not easy for an outside observer to be clear whether any given pattern of behavior is autonomous or not. This is because autonomy cannot be detected solely from behavior, but must also be understood in terms of the actor's (for instance a learner's) own intentions and understandings. Behavior that may, on the surface of it, seem to be autonomous, may in fact be determined by some "script" or "program" implanted in the person at an earlier time. In an attempt to get around this problem, Benn (1976) acknowledges the pervasive effect of socializing influences, but goes on to write: "Within this conception of a socialized individual, there is room to distinguish one who simply accepts the roles society thrusts on him or her, uncritically internalizing the received mores, from someone committed to a critical and creative conscious search for coherence . . . " (p. 126).

However, even this generalized definition is of limited use to a researcher or observer, unless he or she is somehow able to have access to the perspective of the person being observed. This is because coherence, like autonomy in behavior, is not inherent in the act itself, but is attributed to the act by an individual actor. This issue will be considered again in Chapters Eight, Nine, and Fifteen.

Personal Autonomy as Situationally Variable

A second reservation about the definition of autonomy presented earlier in this chapter is its failure to account for situational variability. Much of the research into personal autonomy has been based on the notion that it is a context-free disposition; once people "become" autonomous, they will behave autonomously in whatever situation they find themselves. In terms of the argument put forward in this book, there are two flaws with this line of reasoning. The first is that autonomy is more akin to a process than a product. That is, one does not "become" autonomous in any final or absolute sense; rather one is able to think and act autonomously in certain circumstances. The second flaw is that, although some people manifest more self-assurance or clarity of purpose across a range of situations than others, it is impossible to judge whether or not a person is autonomous without specifying the context within which this autonomy will, or might, manifest itself.

In other words, autonomy is not simply a personal quality or characteristic, but is a relation involving the interplay of personal and situational variables. Accordingly, any person could vary in the degree of autonomy he or she exhibits from situation to situation. For instance, a person who may be autonomous with respect to career or family may lack autonomy (that is, be dependent) when it comes to learning; alternatively, a person who is autonomous with respect to learning how to sail a boat might prove to be dependent when it comes to learning calculus or Spanish. This reservation about personal autonomy has already been alluded to in Chapter Three and will be considered at greater length in Chapter Ten.

The Development of Autonomy

As I mentioned at the start of the book there is a widespread belief that permitting or encouraging "self-direction" in learning will lead to the development of personal autonomy as an educational outcome. It is the purpose of this section of the chapter to examine evidence concerning whether or not personal autonomy is attained as part of a natural developmental process, or whether it is susceptible to educational interventions and, if so, what sort. This is important because of the reciprocal relationship that is assumed to exist between personal autonomy and autonomy in learning.

In the discussion that follows, three alternative points of view are put forward. These are first, that autonomy is a trait, or innate disposition; second, that it is acquired through noneducational processes of socialization and maturation; and third, that it is learned at least partly through educational experiences. Each of these will be dealt with and its educational implications considered in turn.

Autonomy as an Innate Disposition. In the first case, which is sometimes called *nativism,* autonomy is seen as a condition of freedom from the dictates and interference of other people, and is thus the situation in which children are born. One of the best-known contemporary advocates of this position is Carl Rogers (1969), who writes of the child, "Unlike many of us, he knows what he likes and dislikes, and the origin of those value choices lies strictly within himself" (p. 243). Rousseau is another famous advocate of the essential goodness and autonomy of the "natural child," as typified by the spontaneous, uninhibited, and free behavior of Emile. So, too, is A. S. Neill, father of the famous experiment in free education at Summerhill.

One corollary of viewing autonomy in this way is that education should interfere as little as possible with the learner's natural inclinations and interests, because these represent the outworking of the person's autonomous preferences. For those who regard autonomy as an innate quality of childhood, one that is diminished or even extinguished by the processes of socialization, education should consist of liberating the real self from within the social self (Strike, 1982, p. 151). Teachers should limit themselves to supplying resources required by the student's natural inclinations and, since liberty is the removal of restraint, autonomy is facilitated by having minimal intervention by the teacher. According to Dearden (1975), it is difficult to know what method of education is appropriate to such innately autonomous people: "The only appropriate method would seem to be that of personal discovery. But if this method were taken quite literally, its effectiveness for most individuals would be limited, and it would make impossible the cumulative achievement of knowledge and skill from one generation to another. Nor would it be possible to apply any public criteria to the quality of what an individual discovered for himself or herself. It could not be said, for example, that a conclusion he or she had reached was false, or insignificant or biased. It is difficult to see how we can speak seriously at all of the education of human beings, if they are interpreted as asocial and ahistorical atoms" (p. 115).

A variant of this "nativistic" model is the view that there is one autonomy of childhood based on impulse, and another of adulthood based on reason, and that over time there is a progressive shift in emphasis from one to the other. Some see this transition as a purely developmental process that might potentially be deflected or otherwise adversely affected by education, which, in this view, is seen as a socializing agency, capable of extinguishing the tender shoots of moral autonomy and of perverting the natural development of intellectual autonomy. Others, such as Dewey ([1938] 1963), clearly see a mandate for education: "The crucial educational problem is that of procuring the postponement of immediate action upon desire until observation and judgment have intervened. Overemphasis upon activity as an end, instead of upon intelligent activity, leads to identification of freedom [autonomy] with immediate execution of impulses and desires" (p. 69).

In this view, autonomy does not consist of following one's whims, but rather in the selective application of "observation and judgment," both of which can be sharpened through education. One criticism that might be leveled against some educators, including certain adult educators, is that they have implicitly put more emphasis on "the immediate execution of impulses and desires," confusing this with the pursuit of autonomous learning.

Autonomy as an Acquired Quality. Although it may be plausible to attribute some dimensions of autonomy to childhood, few would seriously maintain that children are capable of the mature rational reflection, objectivity, or emotional self-discipline that is implied by the term *autonomy* in the present context. As people develop and "become fully human" (Strike, 1982, p. 153), they "internalize available social and cultural resources." Earlier in this chapter, it was argued that autonomous adults will not simply accept what is thrust on them. However, "children are in no position to judge the value of these cultural and social resources" (p. 153), and thus "all of us, in the first stage of our education, are Persons Lacking in Autonomy" (Phillips, 1975, p. 9). The implication of this is that the development of full adult autonomy occurs over time, as a result of certain experiences and socializing influences.

As early as 1932, Piaget discussed the socialization process of the child, describing the evolution of sequential stages that he identified as moving from "heteronomy" to "autonomy." The following list provides a summary of behavioral and attitudinal characteristics of heteronomy and autonomy:

Heteronomy	Autonomy
Egocentrism	Cooperation
Unilateral respect	Mutual respect
Conformity	Individual creativity
Rigidity	Flexibility
Blind faith in authority	Rational criticism
Other directed	Inner directed
Dependence	Independence

According to Piaget, the normal process of development in the healthy person involves progressing from heteronomy in the direction of autonomy. Another way of expressing this development is to talk of "maturity." As people grow older they mature, and it is this which distinguishes children from adults; "most human beings acquire [maturity] gradually and informally over a period of years" (Strike, 1982, p. 129). Although there is no criticism implied in saying that a child is immature, such a comment has quite a different connotation when applied to adults, because, "with the exception of the mentally ill or senile, all adults are in the maturity of their faculties" (p. 130).

Maturity, in turn, is linked to autonomy, in that "passive and uncritical acceptance of one's situation is characteristic of an essentially immature mind" (Overstreet, 1950, p. 250). As early as 1941, for instance, Angyal, in a foundational study on personality, argued that increasing maturity in the healthy adult is accompanied by an increase in independence. "According to Angyal, the psychological aspects of the individual . . . move toward greater autonomy, becoming less and less bound by the immediate situation, and the individual is more and more able to weigh possible outcomes and select that which is most advantageous, advantageous meaning that which leads to increased autonomy" (Birren and Hedlund, 1984, p. 63).

If the linkages between age, maturity, and autonomy were invariant, of course, all older people could be expected to exhibit the hallmarks of autonomy. However, as has already been mentioned, it is evident that, in any given context, some people will behave more autonomously than others; that is, they will generate alternative goals, select decisively from among them, persevere with their intentions, exert disciplined self-control, and so on. Peters (1973) notes that, "since people are not autonomous when they are born, and since many people reach old age without attaining very high levels of autonomy, some learning process which is not purely maturational is involved in becoming autonomous" (p. 176). To the extent that characteristics of autonomy may be demonstrated by people who have had limited exposure to formal education, one can dismiss the claim that education is the sole (or for that matter, even the main) contributor to the development of autonomy. However, this does not preclude the possibility that education, including adult education, can contribute to the enhancement of autonomy. The question which arises is, What is the place of education in this "learning process which is not purely maturational"?

Autonomy as a Learned Characteristic. The development of personal autonomy is almost universally proclaimed as a goal of education. Even political regimes that are not normally associated with individualism, such as that of the Soviet Union, extoll the value of personal autonomy as an educational goal (Vladislavlev, 1979, p. 17), though one suspects that they may have in mind a rather different definition of autonomy from that encountered in Western democratic countries. However, if one refers to the definition of personal autonomy proposed earlier, it is apparent that some aspects are more amenable to educational intervention than others. For instance, some qualities or characteristics, such as those of emotional autonomy or perseverance, are partly innate or, in any case, are rooted deeply in people's very earliest experiences at home and school. Other components of autonomy (for instance, the ability to rationally reflect) may be taught, at least in part, as curricular content (Telfer, 1975, p. 28; Wang, 1983). Assertiveness training, life-planning skills, values clarification, synectics and creativity training, learning-to-learn, moral philosophy, and critical thinking have all been advocated as content areas because of their alleged contribution to the development of personal autonomy.

Other dimensions (such as a self-concept of being autonomous) are not only more difficult to operationalize, but are best enhanced ancillary to, or concomitant with, some other content-oriented instruction. Thus, certain techniques of instruction, or ways of conducting teaching, have been linked with autonomy. These include collaborative learning, guided learning, discovery learning, contract-based learning, individualized instruction, learner-controlled instruction, open learning, problem-based learning, and independent study (or self-directed learning). This notion is hardly new; it is enshrined in Snyder's (1971) formulation of the "hidden curriculum" and in McLuhan's oft-quoted dictum that "the medium is the message." One thing is certain: If educators wish to build personal autonomy into the goals of their courses and activities, they must give conscious attention to the context as well as the content of their instruction. This is because so much is learned through the opportunities (or lack of opportunities) for exercising control and hence for developing a robust self-concept as a learner.

Experience clearly shows, however, that even when people are exposed to such educational approaches, not all become more autonomous. In fact, none of these interventions — content or process — leads invariably to increased personal autonomy, and none has a monopoly on the development of personal autonomy because of the multidimensional nature of the latter (Dittman, 1976, p. 467). Moreover, there is a high degree of interdependence among the various components of autonomy. Any attempt to develop one or two parts in isolation is likely to fail in the end. Similarly, if a particular strategy (such as a program of learning-to-learn) is successful, it will predictably lead to increased critical awareness, and to demands for more freedom of choice and other manifestations of autonomy. The whole question of the extent to which personal autonomy may be enhanced through instruction is dealt with in Part Four, as part of a consideration of increasing people's autonomy as learners.

Personal Autonomy and Adult Education

Before leaving the question of educational interventions, it is important to discuss, with respect to the development of autonomy, the proper and legitimate role of adult education. Six points will be made.

The first is that all forms of education should have aims that "cohere with the aims we set for life itself. Our philosophy of education must connect with, and in the end be justified by, our ethical, political and even our religious beliefs" (Hostler, 1981, p. 14). Adult education, too, derives its mandate from the society in which it occurs. This point is made by Botkin, Elmandjra, and Malitza (1979). In *No Limits to Learning,* their report to the prestigious informal think tank, the Club of Rome, they wrote: "There is a near-universal demand for increased participation at all levels. More people are aware of, and are using, their capacity to obstruct rather than to support decisions reached without their concurrence, regardless of the merits of such decisions. . . . The term participation is not new. Few words convey so powerfully the idea of the individual's aspiration to be a partner in decision-making, of the unwillingness to accept unduly limited roles, and of the desire to live life more fully. Few terms suggest so forcefully people's claim to influence both local and global decisions that shape their environment and lives, coupled with people's aspirations for equality as well as their refusal to accept marginal positions or subordinated status"(pp. 29–30).

This trend toward participatory democracy is clearly one of the "wider social changes" (Dearden, 1972, p. 449) discussed in Chapter Two contributing to increased interest in autonomy. It affects education in two related ways. The first is that for people to be able to participate fully, they need to be capable of autonomous thought and action; "since [personal autonomy] is a fundamental value of our society, a responsibility is obviously placed on education to enable such autonomy" (Strong, 1977, p. i). The second is through the inevitable demands for increased participation within education itself; as people become more accustomed to, and skilled at, informed participation and "choosing" in other aspects of their lives, they are likely to make increasing demands for similar power sharing in relation to their education. Thus, to the extent that personal autonomy is valued as a societal goal, it is reasonable to expect to find forms of adult education that attempt to foster personal autonomy.

It is, however, improper to speak of adult education as if it were a single, unified system — either conceptually or administratively. Adult education encompasses a greater diversity of locations, goals, clients, techniques, and contents than other sectors of education: "It comprises a host of courses, usually part-time and mostly conducted in the evening. . . . [It has] a multitude of different goals, some of which are broad and long term, while others are immediate and more restricted, which overlap, diverge and even conflict in subtle and complicated ways" (Hostler, 1981, p. 1). Thus, it is not reasonable to expect that all forms of adult education will have, either implicitly or explicitly, the goal of promoting personal autonomy.

The second point relates to the first. It is not uncommon to find, in the literature of adult education, the assumption that all adults are autonomous or "self-directing" and that instruction should therefore be conducted in ways that acknowledge autonomy. On the other hand, as Brookfield points out, adult educators constantly claim that the development of autonomy is a major goal of adult education. Thus, adult educators are confronted with a paradox: How can they assume the existence of certain circumstances at the outset, and at the same time hold those circumstances to be the desired goal or outcome of their activities (unless they are implicitly acknowledging that adult education has no appreciable effect)? So long as the same term — *self-direction* — is made to serve for both purposes, this apparent contradiction will continue. But the analysis in this chapter helps to show that in one context, the term *self-direction* (or autonomy) refers to certain philosophical assumptions about human nature, while in the other context, *self-direction* refers to a specific psychological orientation in the learning situation. This is discussed in the next chapter.

The third point, related to the overall theme of this book, is that for the most part, adults are not passive or inert, nor are they sitting around waiting to be "made more autonomous" by the actions of adult educators. If people are to be regarded as "self-determining" in the broadest sense, it means that they should be treated with respect by educators; to use Schön's memorable phrase, they must be "given reason." They must also, as Strike (1982) points out, be "given reasons." The fact that they are self-determining, however, does not preclude the possibility of increasing their personal autonomy in learning, but it emphatically does preclude the possibility of "making" them autonomous. There is, as Torbert states, a paradox inherent in "forcing people to be free" and, accordingly, educational structures that attempt such a task must be managed with "deliberate irony." This is a theme which will be resumed in Chapter Thirteen.

A fourth point concerning the linkages between adult education and personal autonomy rests on the confusion in the literature between autonomy as a means and as an end of education. Frequently, adult educators fall into the trap of assuming that there is a direct causal link between so-called autonomous modes of learning and the development of personal autonomy. In Chapter One, Mezirow (1981) was quoted as saying that "central to the adult educator's function is a goal and method of self-directed learning" (p. 21), and it was argued that this seemed to imply a confounding of means and ends. Does the use of methods that encourage learner-control lead to more global qualities such as critical judgment, autonomous action, and self-initiated inquiry? As discussed in Chapter Three, the answer would appear to be "no." A person may be exposed to so-called autonomous modes of learning without internalizing the values of autonomy or being enabled to think and act autonomously; conversely, it may be possible, as Dearden (1972) points out, to develop autonomy without recourse to autonomous methods.

Fifth, it is important to note that autonomy does not imply antisocial solitude or indifference to the attitudes, opinions, preferences, or well-being of others. To the contrary, autonomy (as discussed earlier in this chapter) involves cooperation, flexibility, and mutual respect. Adult education is distinguished by its emphasis on socially relevant learning within contexts of mutual interdependence (committees, congregations, families, teams, work units, clubs, and other groups), and the truly autonomous person is one who has a positive and realistic self-concept, while acknowledging the dignity and worth of others and their beliefs.

Sixth and finally, adult education does not have a monopoly on the development of autonomy as an aim. Since pre-Socratic times, philosophers have argued that education can, and indeed should, develop in people the capacities and predispositions to allow them to function autonomously. Accordingly, it has been claimed variously as the true purpose of elementary, secondary, and higher education, as well as adult education. However, with rare exceptions, education — some would maintain, even higher education (Entwistle and Percy, 1974) — has failed in this. As discussed elsewhere in this book, since autonomy is a process, rather than a product, and is continually renewed and constantly reasserted, it is an ideal candidate to be considered as the prime purpose, and organizing principle, for lifelong education, rather than as the exclusive preserve of adult education.

There is much that adult educators can do to enhance the personal autonomy of their learners, and conversely much that they might do that inhibits or denies such autonomy. For a start, educators can build the development of autonomy explicitly into their program goals, recognizing that it has three principal elements: intellectual, emotional, and moral. Second, they can engage in forms of teaching that encourage learners to define their own goals, to explore and evaluate alternative points of view, to defend their perspective in rational debate and argument, to demonstrate the courage of their convictions, and to back up or ramify their assertions with intellectually defensible rather than simply emotionally appealing arguments. They can recognize that autonomy takes a long time to develop, and that a person may exhibit differing levels of autonomy in different aspects of his or her life. And finally they can acknowledge that simply removing the barriers to a person's ability to think and behave in certain ways may not allow him or her to break away from old habits or old ways of thinking, and that deliberate interventions may be called for, though only with the full agreement and acceptance of the learner himself or herself.

Summary

It has been the purpose of this chapter to review literature pertaining to personal autonomy: how it might usefully be defined, how it may be recognized, and how it is developed.

It has been shown that, by definition, in order to be regarded as autonomous, a person needs both to be free of internal and external constraints, and to have a coherent and robust set of personal values and beliefs that give consistency to his or her life. After reviewing literature on personal autonomy, much of it derived from the philosophy of education, a composite definition was arrived at. A person may be regarded as autonomous to the extent that he or she:

- Conceives of goals and plans
- Exercises freedom of choice
- Uses the capacity for rational reflection
- Has will power to follow through
- Exercises self-restraint and self-discipline
- Views himself or herself as autonomous

Hence a person would be judged to be autonomous on the basis of his or her actions and ability to explain and justify those actions by invoking a coherent set of beliefs or criteria. It was also argued, however, that it is difficult, if not impossible, for a person to escape entirely the effects of socializing influences in determining his or her attitudes, habits, values, and beliefs. Accordingly, despite the example of Descartes, it is probably impossible for the majority of individuals to attain autonomy in the ideal or strongest sense.

Within the conception of a socialized individual, however, some people are more apparently autonomous than others. It was argued that it is impossible to judge the extent of a person's autonomy without reference to his or her personal understandings and intentions, and also that the same person may be more or less autonomous in different circumstances. Autonomy is a situation-dependent, rather than a context-free disposition, being determined partly by the situation and partly by the individual's understanding of the situation. This is a major point that will be discussed in Chapter Ten.

In discussing the achievement or acquisition of autonomy, it has been argued that personal autonomy, as a general rule, increases with age, but that it is amenable to educational intervention—both in the form of direct curricular content and in the way in which education is conducted. Moreover, it was asserted that these dimensions are not, and cannot be, independent of one another, and that the continuing development and exercise of personal autonomy is a lifelong pursuit, involving all aspects of the education system—formal as well as nonformal—and all aspects of the individual person.

With respect to the relationship between adult education and personal autonomy, six points were raised: (1) The development of personal autonomy is sanctioned by sections of society as an educational goal, but not all parts of adult education will have this as a primary goal or aim. (2) Adults are presumed to be largely "self-determining," but they are not always capable of exercising control over their own learning and this capability may be learned. (3) Since adults are seen as "self-determining," it is not congruent to force them to act autonomously against their will. (4) The presumed link between so-called autonomous methods of learning and the development or enhancement of personal autonomy is more complex than many adult educators recognize. (5) Autonomy is not incompatible with interdependence, and an advocacy of personal autonomy need not be associated with excessive individualism. (6) Adult education is not alone in its espousal of personal autonomy as a desirable goal of education and, considering the long-term and multidimensional nature of personal autonomy, it should serve as an organizing principle for lifelong education.

Earlier in the chapter, it was argued that autonomy (or "self-direction") cannot be judged in the absence of some context or environment. In the case of education, that context is learning. Attention will now be turned to the more specific issue of "self-direction" in learning. However, because there are at least two distinct meanings to the term *self-direction* within learning—one referring to the independent pursuit of learning goals outside institutional structures, and the other to the exercise of learner-control within formal instructional settings—these two will be dealt with separately.

Five

Self-Management
in Learning

In 1964, one of the doyens of adult education and its foundation professor at the University of British Columbia, Coolie Verner, wrote, "For all practical purposes, self-education is beyond the range of responsibility of adult education, since it is an individual activity and affords no opportunity for an adult educator to exert influence on the learning process" (p. 31). This assertion, however, has not deterred an increasing number of adult educators over the years either from attempting to "exert an influence" over the self-educational efforts of adults, or from undertaking wide-ranging research into various aspects of self-direction in learning.

Although most of this activity—both teaching and research—is subsumed under the general rubric of "self-directed learning," closer examination reveals that there is not one, but two distinct traditions. On the one hand, there are those who are concerned with the devolution by educators, and acceptance by learners, of responsibility for valued instructional functions within recognizable teaching/learning situations. In this book, I refer to this as *learner-control,* and an overview and commentary on this domain is provided in Chapter Seven. On the other hand, there are those who, influenced largely by the tradition of research into aspects of participation and nonparticipation in adult education, have concentrated instead on learning projects that people undertake on their own initiative, without any formal institutional structures or support: investigating the number and type of such projects undertaken, the sources of help sought, resources utilized, and the steps commonly involved. This, which I refer to in this book as *autodidaxy,* is dealt with in Chapter Six.

Spanning these two fields of research and practice is a concern with the learners themselves: the skills and competencies that have been identified with this activity, attempts that have been made to measure or assess people's predisposition toward self-directed learning, and practices (particularly educational) that have been linked with its attainment. It is the purpose of this chapter to review literature pertaining to the self-directed learner, and to attempt to distill out of it a useful profile of the self-directed learner as well as some insights into whether, and if so how, such abilities and orientations might be developed or enhanced through educational interventions.

Skills and Competencies of the Self-Directed Learner

It is widely — almost universally — assumed that in our society adults are involved in some sort of quest for self-improvement, and perhaps even for self-actualization. In the pursuit of this goal, adults involve themselves in various forms of deliberate, as well as incidental, learning endeavors. Although only a relatively small proportion of adults choose to participate in formally constituted educational programs, evidence suggests that all adults — even those traditionally classified as "hard-to-reach" (unemployed, rural, elderly, ethnic minorities, and those of low formal educational attainment) — engage in some sort of self-directed learning activities throughout their lives.

Since the phenomenon of self-directed learning is as widespread as it apparently is, one would expect to find an enormous diversity among self-directed learners, in fact as wide a diversity as among the adult population as a whole. However, although such learning may be a characteristic of adulthood, it is also manifestly clear that certain people are more competent, more dedicated, more experienced, and indeed more successful at this pursuit than others. Accordingly, a number of researchers have chosen to concentrate on studying those who learn things for themselves, and to identify the qualities or characteristics that seem to distinguish the more successful from the less successful learners. Some of these researchers seek simply to describe and catalogue the self-educational efforts of various groups of adults, in the time-honored tradition of participation research in adult education. Others appear to be motivated by a desire to use the findings in order to make changes in adult education provision or delivery: Either they are searching for clues as to how instruction might be better or more successfully organized, or else they are motivated by a desire to improve the competence of learners. A classic dichotomy: those interested in improving teaching and those concerned with improving learning.

This distinction is echoed in the ways self-direction in learning has itself been conceptualized: Some researchers have identified self-direction as primarily a matter of learning, and have made their studies and recommendations on the basis of the skills and competencies required of a learner; others have emphasized the teaching dimension of self-directed learning, and have accordingly included competencies associated with program planning or instruction (Svensson, 1989). What does seem clear is that it is neither wholly one thing nor the other, and that successful self-directed learners will probably exhibit a combination of skills, as well as some that are unique.

Not unexpectedly, approaches to developing a profile of the self-directed learner have varied enormously. First of all, there are those whose lists of competencies are based on theoretical speculation, without any empirical component. Next, there are those researchers who restrict themselves to simply collecting certain biographical and demographic data about respondents. Others go beyond this, with the collection and analysis of data concerning variables such as learning style, locus of control, psychological well-being, and life satisfaction. Still others have attempted, through a variety of techniques — including interview, analysis of learning diaries, consultations with panels of experts, interpretation of biographies, or critical incident techniques — to identify a common core of skills and competencies appropriate to the practice of self-directed learning.

Despite the enormous diversity of ways and contexts in which people have gone about developing their lists of skills and competencies, however, there is a remarkable degree of congruence in the qualities and characteristics that have been mentioned. A review of the work of twenty different sets of authors resulted in an inductively derived list of attributes and competencies that are either possessed by or desirable in independent learners. The following are the authors whose work was surveyed: Caffarella (1983), Chickering (1964), Della-Dora and Blanchard (1979), Flanagan (1970), Ford (1971), Gibbons and Phillips (1979), Guglielmino (1977), Jankovic and others (1979), Kasworm (1983b), Knowles (1984), Maras (1978), Margarones (1965), Mezirow (1981), Miller (1964), Moore (1980), Strong (1977), Torrance and Mourad (1978), Tough (1979d), Tremblay and Danis (1984), and Wedemeyer (1973). According to these various studies (see the Resource at the end of the book), the person capable of exercising control over the tasks to be mastered, and of working independently, would ideally:

- Be methodical and disciplined
- Be logical and analytical
- Be reflective and self-aware
- Demonstrate curiosity, openness, and motivation
- Be flexible
- Be interdependent and interpersonally competent
- Be persistent and responsible
- Be venturesome and creative
- Show confidence and have a positive self-concept
- Be independent and self-sufficient
- Have developed information-seeking and retrieval skills
- Have knowledge about, and skill at, learning generally
- Develop and use defensible criteria for evaluating learning

That such similar profiles of the autonomous learner abound is evidence of a definite cluster of competencies by which such people might be recognized. But the mere fact that researchers have been able to identify the prototypic self-directed learner does not prevent a number of criticisms from being leveled at it.

Criticisms of This Approach

Perhaps the most striking aspect of this list is its utopian quality; however, it is a characteristic of ideals that they tend to be idealistic, and this could therefore hardly be taken as a serious criticism of the profile if in fact it managed to serve the purposes of improving the quality and amount of self-directed learning that people undertake. But there are certain other telling criticisms that cannot lightly be dismissed. These include class and gender bias, the misleading nature of such a composite profile, failure to deal adequately with what it means to be autonomous with respect to learning, ignoring or undervaluing the place of self-confidence in undertaking autonomous learning, and perhaps most significantly, the tendency to treat self-direction as a personal quality or attribute, without regard to its situational variability.

Class and Gender Bias. A first observation concerns the class and gender bias inherent in many conceptualizations of independent learning. The concept of self-directedness in learning tends to be dominated by upper-middle-class, white male stereotypes:

> Knowles's (1975) definitive book *Self-Directed Learning: A Guide for Learners and Teachers* contains a section on the characteristics of the self-directed learner, which is actually a collection of passages on the "ideal man" [sic], written by a number of humanistic and existentialist philosophers. All the authors are male, and each of their descriptions reads like a stereotype of an ideal member of the upper-middle class. The same kind of criticism has been made of Maslow, whose "hierarchy of needs" and assumptions concerning the motivation to achieve "self-actualisation" are influential in adult education and self-directed learning circles. Maslow posits two types of people, the "growth motivated" and the "deficiency motivated." Membership in either group is a matter of personal good or ill fortune. A reading of his descriptions of both, however, reveals the "growth motivated' person to be the prototype rational, instrumental, independent, executive, middle-class male, and the "deficiency motivated" to be practically anyone else, particularly anyone who must depend on a relationship with others for their well-being and survival. Class, race and sex are not considered to be variables affecting that good or ill fortune which determines human motivation [Walker, 1984, pp. 14–15].

Research into the skills of self-directed learners needs to avoid bias in favor of either gender or any cultural or class grouping. This is particularly so when lists such as the one just presented form the basis of programs designed to develop specific clusters of competencies. It is necessary to avoid endorsing any single "ideal" of the competent autonomous learner, and it is especially important not to fall into the trap of equating "self-directed" with "independent" in the sense of socially isolated.

Misleading Composite Profiles. A second observation is that a composite list such as the preceding one can be misleading because it obscures and submerges vital differences among theorists. Take, for instance, Flanagan's 1970 presidential address to the Division of Educational Psychology of the American Psychological Association, in which he argued that the self-directed individual should have "a reasonable degree of skill and decision-making in planning. This should include skills in analyzing and defining problems, and in using various types of evaluation procedures. . . . It also includes the ability to prepare a sequential plan using a clear statement of desired outcomes and working back to obtain a definite schedule and a set of procedures for determining the required progress at each point if the plan is to be realized . . . " (cited in Geis, 1976, p. 269).

Such a vision, which places much emphasis on mechanical, linear, and analytic modes of thought, can be contrasted with Mezirow's (1981) specification: "A self-directed learner must be understood as one who is aware of the constraints on his efforts to learn, including the psycho-cultural assumptions involving reified power relationships embedded in institutionalized ideologies which influence one's habits of perception, thought and behavior as one attempts to learn. A self-directed learner has access to alternative perspectives for understanding his or her situation and for giving meaning and direction to his or her life, has acquired sensitivity and competence in social interaction and has the skills and competencies required to master the productive tasks associated with controlling and manipulating the environment" (p. 21).

Some of the differences between these two quotations are a matter of level of abstraction, and some relate to the use of language. But in themselves these are likely to be symptomatic of some other, farther reaching difference between these two perspectives. The point is that the concept of self-direction has been claimed by representatives of different basic orientations with respect both to learning and the nature of the subject matter to be learned. It is a recurring theme throughout this book that self-direction in learning, and the desirability of autonomy more generally, is claimed as a rallying point by representatives of radically different philosophical and ideological perspectives. In reviewing a range of psychological positions relevant to the development of self-direction, Skager (1979) notes that, despite differences, "the perspectives overlap to some extent. However, they differ sharply in their conceptions of the motivational basis of human learning as well as in their assumptions about the degree to which the behaviour of learners should be shaped by a controlled environment as compared to an environment which encourages spontaneous, individualised personal growth" (p. 520).

This implies that the use of the same terminology can mask profound and ultimately irreconcilable differences in the intentions of authors, and in their views of the purposes, limits, and defining characteristics of self-direction.

Inadequate Treatment of Autonomy in Learning. A third criticism that can be leveled at many of the conventional profiles of the autonomous learner is that they emphasize "situational independence" (especially from teachers and institutional constraints) but ignore other aspects of intellectual, emotional, and moral autonomy. One question that writers on self-directed learning rarely address adequately is, What does it really mean to be an autonomous learner in the full sense of the word?

There are two approaches to this question. The first (and most common) is to start with a profile of a learner, and then to ask what an autonomous one might be like. It appears that this approach has predominated in adult education, and may help to explain why the idealized vision of the self-directed learner looks so much like an idealized vision of adult learners in general: They are derived from a common conceptual framework. The alternative approach is to start with a profile of someone who is autonomous, and to ask what such a person might be like as a learner. This latter approach yields new insights into the distinction between an autonomous and a nonautonomous learner. Based on the definition given in the last chapter, one might indicate one's status as an autonomous learner by:

- Taking the initiative, with or without the help of others, in diagnosing or assessing one's own learning needs.
- Selecting appropriate sources of help with learning and, where necessary, temporarily surrendering some measure of independence for the sake of expediency in learning.
- Developing, through a process of inquiry and reflection, an appreciation for the criteria by which to evaluate the particular domain of learning being undertaken.
- Asking what is the justification for rules, procedures, principles, and assumptions that it might otherwise be natural to take for granted.
- Refusing agreement or compliance with what others (such as a teacher or trainer) state or demand where this seems critically unacceptable.
- Being aware of alternative choices, both as to learning strategies and to interpretations or value positions being expressed, and making reasoned choices about the route to follow in accordance with personally significant ideas and purposes.
- Continually reviewing the process of learning (as both a cognitive and a social phenomenon), and making strategic and tactical adjustments to one's approach in order to optimize learning potential.
- Conceiving of goals, policies, and plans independently of pressures from others to do so, or not to do so.
- Developing an understanding of phenomena in such a way, and to such an extent, as to be able to explain the phenomena to others in words and under circumstances substantially unlike those in which they were first encountered.
- Independently forming opinions and clarifying beliefs, yet being willing to relinquish such beliefs or to alter opinions when relevant contrary evidence is presented, and to do so irrespective of the presence or absence of extraneous rewards or pressures.

- Being able to pursue a learning goal with equal vigor and determination without being adversely affected by external factors, including the increase or decrease of rewards for pursuing or attaining the goal.
- Determining what is really of personal value or in one's interests, as distinct from what may be expedient, or what may be conveniently so regarded.
- Being willing and able to accept alternative points of view as legitimate and being able to deal with objections, obstacles, and criticisms of one's goals without becoming incapacitated, threatened, or angry.
- Demonstrating a sober and realistic appraisal of one's shortcomings and limitations, tempered by a cautious but positive awareness, based on past experience, of one's strengths, abilities, and motivations as a learner. (This list draws on the work of several authors, including Dearden, 1975; Krimerman, 1972; and Knowles, 1975.)

This last point is one of the most neglected qualities of the effective self-directed learner, being mentioned in passing by only three of the twenty writers whose work was surveyed earlier in this chapter. However, it will be recalled from Chapter Four that Dearden (1972) claims that "a person could not be to any marked degree autonomous, without this being an important part of his self-concept" (p.460), and Skager (1979) also includes as one of his seven attributes of the self-directed learner "self-acceptance or positive views about the self as a learner" (p. 519). Just how central is a self-concept of autonomy to the practice of self-directed learning?

Self-Confidence Versus Learned Helplessness. In her study of the relationship between librarians and self-directed learners, J. C. Smith (1986) asked public librarians about their perceptions of such learners and how to assist them: "There was an apparent reluctance on the part of librarians to describe a 'typical' or 'composite' learner, [but] despite this reluctance, a classification did emerge . . . which reflected two perceived categories of learners. One category might be called the 'confident learners.' . . . The other category that emerged from the words of the librarians might be called 'timid learners'" (p. 251).

The confident learners seemed to "have had some success in school." They were described as "eating up" their learning, "soaking it up," being people who could "really deal with this material." They were also seen as "very, very skilled," "capable," "competent," with a "strong sense of purpose." As Smith (1986) observes, "many of these adjectives are reminiscent of the characteristics that emerged from the biographies and autobiographies of self-taught individuals studied by Gibbons and others (1980)" (p. 251). The timid learners, on the other hand, were described as "fragile," "fearful," "weak," "a little lost," "reluctant to ask," "inarticulate," and "wandering" (p. 251). Smith goes on to add: "Despite the perceived differences, one librarian proposed an overriding characteristic of both confident and timid learners: 'They have in common their willingness to ask. Sure, there are a lot of people who want to learn things, [but] who just cannot take that first step. I guess that's basically it: that they're willing to take a chance to get our attention, and ask for help'" (p. 251).

The way people appear to librarians or to other agents who might assist them is not an infallible guide to their self-confidence, but it does seem reasonable to assume that there are differing levels of confidence within the overall notion of an autonomous learner. At one end of the continuum, there are those who, although they may want to learn, "just cannot take that first step" (Smith, 1986, p. 251). This phenomenon is often blamed on "learned helplessness," which is frequently invoked to explain why adults might prefer to be "taught" rather than to take responsibility for their own learning. The argument is that the more people have things done for them, the more "institutionalized" they become, and the more institutionalized they are (in both a figurative and a literal sense), the more dependent, helpless, and passive they are. It is argued that years of passivity in educational settings deprive many people of the confidence to take charge of their own learning

There is however another, potentially more useful, way of thinking about apparent lack of confidence than "learned helplessness." If the learner is considered to have developed a belief about himself or herself (or about learning, or about the subject to be learned), it is likely that such an attitude represents a reasoned response to previous experience. People who refrain entirely from self-directed learning activities or seem "timid" and apprehensive with respect to a particular learning task should be interviewed to ascertain what beliefs they hold that may inhibit their learning. Instead of thinking in terms of learned helplessness, and of the need to break the "passive set" for learning (Campbell, 1964, p. 357), it is suggested that adult educators should conceive of learners as active construers of their circumstances, making choices on the bases of their constructions. This theme will be elaborated in Part Three and in Chapter Fifteen.

Ignoring Situational Differences. Of all the definitions in the literature on self-direction in learning, that proposed by Skager (1979) probably comes closest to embodying all the elements of autonomy. After an extensive review of pertinent literature, Skager proposed seven types of personal attributes possessed by the "self-directed learner." These are (1) self acceptance or positive views about the self as learner, based on prior experience; (2) planfulness, which comprises the capacity to (a) diagnose one's own learning needs, (b) set appropriate goals, and (c) select or devise effective learning strategies; (3) intrinsic motivation or willingness to persist in learning in the absence of immediate external rewards or punishments; (4) internalized evaluation or the ability to apply evidence to the qualitative regulation of one's own learning activity; (5) openness to experience and a willingness to engage in new activities because of curiosity or similar motives; (6) flexibility or willingness to explore new avenues of learning; and (7) autonomy, or the ability to choose learning goals and means that may seem unimportant or even undesirable in the immediate social context (p. 519).

Although this is a particularly comprehensive and concise portrait of the self-directed learner, it still seems as if self-directedness is viewed as an intrinsic quality of the person rather than a property of the person in the situation. This gives rise to the fifth, and arguably the most compelling, criticism of composite profiles of the autonomous learner, which is their failure to account for situational differences in autonomy.

Profiles of the "typical" autonomous learner have a tendency to portray autonomy as a context-free disposition, rather than a context-bound one. This means that it is commonly assumed that once a person attains autonomy as a learner in one domain, such as English or ornamental horticulture, he or she will automatically be able to learn autonomously in other unrelated fields, such as mechanical engineering or child psychology. An extension of this line of reasoning is to assume that a person who is able to exert control within a formal instructional setting will also be able and willing to undertake self-directed learning in all sorts of everyday settings, and vice versa: Many profiles of the autonomous learner (such as those on which the composite list in this chapter is based) are grounded neither in autodidaxy alone, nor in independent study within formal instructional settings, but in an amalgam of the two.

The proposition that learner-control and autodidaxy are linked, indeed interchangeable, is widespread. For instance, Victor Marbeau (1976), a former Inspector-General of Public Instruction for France, and member of the prestigious Council of Europe Committee for General and Technical Education, writes, "The pupil's potential aptitude for successful self-education [as an adult] will depend upon the extent to which he or she has been exposed to situations of responsibility and autonomy in his or her school years" (p. 15). As Skager (1979) comments, "This is a plausible assertion, but little more than that. No evidence links the kind of school learning conditions referred to by Marbeau with participation in education later in life" (p. 520).

Many of the competencies mentioned in the list do not apply exclusively to the self-directed learner, but have been found to relate to successful learning generally (Smith, 1984; Della-Dora and Blanchard, 1979, p. 4). In fact, this is the position explicitly adopted by Oddi (1985), when she "focused on the personality characteristics of individuals whose learning behaviour is characterized by initiative and persistence in learning *through a variety of modes* . . . " (p. 230; emphasis added).

Intuitively, it seems likely that autonomy would manifest itself across a range of learning situations. However, although a person may have an overall predisposition toward acting autonomously (that is, being self-determining), it is clear that, with respect to any given domain of learning, he or she may not have mastered "the logic with which bodies of beliefs are criticized and developed; and the methodology which specifies the degree of support given to theory by observation" (Quinton, 1971, p. 208). In other words, he or she may not be autonomous with respect to the subject being learned.

Certainly, there are some people who seem able to apply themselves autonomously across a range of disparate content areas. However, a person can vary markedly in the degree of independence he or she exhibits from one situation to another. In this book it is suggested that there exists, with respect to autonomy, a generic or trans-situational component, as well as a situation-specific dimension. This latter would help to explain why some learners may be judged or thought of as "independent" or autonomous by their peers or instructors in one domain, yet still lack autonomy with respect to some other aspect or area of study.

There are several practical implications of this recognition. The first is that adult educators need to consider whether all aspects of their subject area are equally amenable to independent learning. Some, because of their complexity or technical nature, may be simply inaccessible to a novice working alone. Second, the educator should consider what aspects of each learner's previous education or experience could permit the exercise of autonomy, and encourage learners to make such connections for themselves by asking questions such as "how does this relate to what you already know?" or "have you ever been in a similar learning situation before?" Third, educators should avoid embarrassing learners by placing them into direct comparison with others, if such competition is likely to lead to diminished self-confidence as a learner. And finally, the facilitator must acknowledge that the ability and willingness to behave autonomously in not just an intellectual but an emotional issue, and demonstrated capability in one area may actually inhibit a learner's preparedness to risk himself or herself in another domain. Over-all, the notion that self-direction is a content-free attainment is mischievous and misleading, and has done much to retard both research into self-direction in learning and educational prac-tices designed to enhance the capability for it.

Self-Directed Learners: Born or Made?

While many, and perhaps most, adult educators can en-visage people who are more or less skilled as self-directed learn-ers, with the exception of Eisenman (1989), relatively little re-search has been carried out concerning the developmental nature of competence as a self-directed learner, or the stages through which a person might pass — even in relation to a particular sub-ject area — in attaining such competence. In the last chapter, the question of whether personal autonomy is innate or acquired was discussed; in this section, an attempt will be made to review literature about the development of self-directed learning com-petence, and to establish whether educational interventions have any noticeable impact on people's propensity or ability to en-gage in self-directed learning.

The first point to make is that it is clearly possible for people to attain competence as self-directed learners without in-struction of any kind. The work of Brookfield (1982a), Craik (1866), Gibbons and others (1980), Houle (1961, 1984), McClin-tock (1982), and Newman (1852) amply attests to the fact that many adults become competent self-directed learners without ever being taught "how to learn" (R. M. Smith, 1976, 1982, 1987).

It seems appropriate, therefore, to begin by questioning whether the capacity to undertake self-directed learning is, even in theory, capable of development through educational inter-ventions. If the acquisition of competence as a self-directed learner were simply a developmental process, then the most that educational interventions could hope to achieve would be to "speed up" movement through an invariant sequence, a preoc-cupation that Piaget has referred to derisively as "the Ameri-can question"! One author who has attempted to identify a developmental sequence in the acquisition of competence as a self-directed learner is Kasworm. After discussing briefly two alternative approaches to understanding how people come to be "self-directed," she turns her attention to a developmental perspective. Kasworm (1983b, p. 33) begins by stating that competence as a self-directed learner has three components:

1. Level of skill/behavior for engagement in learning enquiry
2. Cognitive capacities and competencies
3. Affective and value orientations focused upon both the nature of the learning inquiry and perceptual meaning of knowledge

She posits that these three dimensions are like three sides of a triangle and asks the reader to envisage a sort of three-sided pyramid made up of "slices," each slice representing a higher level of development in each of the three domains. "The progression of development from one level to the next must incorporate qualitative differences of all three elements of a level for a fundamental movement to the next more complex level" (Kasworm, 1983b, p. 33). She does not explain exactly what triggers the movement from one level to the next, although she invokes Kuhn's (1970) notion of paradigm shift, without specifying what sort of "accumulation of anomalies" might precipitate each paradigm shift. However, in discussing the "formative evolution of self-directed learning from one stage to the next" (p. 33), she identifies six conditions that "profoundly influence" the transition:

1. Learner awareness of self and values
2. Competence in language and numerical symbol knowledge and skill application
3. Problem definition, clarification and resolution perspectives and skills
4. Initial and subsequent development of cognitive information processing patterns
5. Historical and cultural context of individual in defining utilitarian value and use of knowledge in relation to self-mastery
6. *Systematically designed learning experiences to explore and facilitate learner developed self-directed learning capacity* [p. 34; emphasis added]

This last is particularly revealing, because it implies that competence as a self-directed learner is susceptible to educational interventions. The balance of her paper is devoted to explicating and attempting to intermesh Perry's (1970, 1988) scheme of intellectual development and Mezirow's (1981) formulation of perspective transformation with her own ideas about the development of capability as a self-directed learner. The author finishes by challenging what she terms the "linear set of assumed single-unit actions" that underlie and animate most models of the development of such learning competence, and by drawing attention to self-direction as "an evolutionary series of developmental actions that incorporates qualitative and quantitative differences in knowledge, value, skill and belief" (p. 45).

What sort of "systematically designed learning experience" might lead to the enhancement of self-directed learning activities? In view of the conceptual scheme advanced in this book, this really resolves itself into two questions: What sort of educational interventions enhance capability for learner-control, and what sort of approaches to education enhance autodidactic learning in everyday or natural societal settings? Since Part Four of this book is dedicated to an exploration of the first of these questions, I will confine myself here to a consideration of the second.

Schools and other agencies of formal education have been widely criticized for emphasizing external rather than internal motivation, for encouraging memorization and rote learning in preference to meaningful learning, for substituting external for internal evaluation, and for imposing rigid curricula rather than encouraging voluntary pursuit of interests (Hargreaves, 1974). The net result of these practices has been, not unexpectedly, to develop passive, incurious, syllabus-bound rote learners—hardly an auspicious foundation on which to build a capability for autonomous learning! However, the argument proceeds, if schools are as potent an influence on learners as their critics claim, could they not, if appropriately organized, also help to develop in people both the ability and the willingness to guide their own learning processes?

The literature suggests that there are two broad approaches to attempts to develop such abilities and competencies.

The first might be referred to as "direct instructional intervention" (Wang, 1983, p. 218), which involves teaching such things as data gathering, critical thinking, organizing information, systematic goal setting, and self-management. These components are taught as direct curricular content, and the exercise of such skills is reinforced and enhanced through planned practical exercises. The second approach to the development of these competencies is ancillary or concomitant: "Autonomous behaviour is not taught or learned as ordinary content in the curriculum. One can teach about autonomy, independence and responsibility, but this is not becoming autonomous in one's thoughts and actions. One learns responsibility and self-direction through experiences in which one is given the opportunity to be self-directed and responsible for one's actions. . . . Autonomy thus evolves indirectly as a concomitant to a student's total school experience" (Dittman, 1976, p. 467).

This latter perspective has manifested itself in a variety of educational approaches and interventions, ranging from collaborative planning and contract learning through to various forms of independent study and "self-directed" learning assignments. It should be noted that this is precisely the argument that links learner-control with autodidaxy, yet the bridge between the two has yet to be verified through empirical research.

Direct Development of Autodidactic Competence. Despite extensive literature on the direct development of learning competence, no research has been found that explicitly deals with programs designed to increase autodidactic activity. Although most programs that purport to increase people's skills as learners implicitly endorse the notion of autodidaxy as an ultimate goal, none has been found that reports directly on increased confidence or ability to learn independently (Wang, 1983, p. 218).

Perhaps one explanation for this may be that there are major differences between the skills required for successful learning performance in schools and formal instructional settings and those demanded in other learning contexts. Recent research has noted four such major discontinuities: individual cognition in school versus shared cognition outside, pure mentation in school versus tool manipulation outside, symbol manipulation in school versus contextualized reasoning outside, and generalized learning in school versus situation-specific competencies outside (Resnick, 1987b, pp. 13–15). There is, therefore, something incongruous about attempts to enhance the ability of learners to function outside the structures of formal institutions from within the institutions themselves. As Resnick (1987b) puts it, "The evidence developed . . . on the discontinuity between school and work [as learning environments] should make us suspicious of attempts to apply directly what we know about skills for learning in school to the problems of fostering capabilities for learning outside school" (p. 18). If educators seek to help learners to be able to learn outside of formal settings, part of the answer is probably to make the formal setting as much like the natural one as possible. This does not mean simply the physical appearance or social formality of the educational context, but trying to make the act of learning itself comparable to the learning undertaken in everyday settings. This is dealt with in more detail in Chapter Eleven.

    Concomitant Development of Autodidactic Competence. Turning now to the concomitant development of interest in and competence at autodidaxy, again there is little research evidence explicitly on this point, and as Skager (1979) notes, what is required are "long term studies of learners of different types who have been exposed to various school environments. This kind of longitudinal research . . . may be the only way to establish a firm link between schooling and self-directed learning in adult life" (p. 539). Because of this lacuna, it is necessary to rely on inference, and two types of studies are reviewed: those that posit a link between participation in formal adult education and autodidactic activity, and those that seek to link particular forms of educational provision with involvement in self-directed learning in everyday settings.

    Within the field of adult education, there is a large and well-established tradition of research into participation patterns of various groups or classes of adults in formally constituted educational activities. From this, it is apparent that only a minority of people (generally estimated at between 10 and 20 percent of the adult population) choose to engage in formal educational activities. By contrast, the overwhelming majority of adults (estimates vary from 80 to 100 percent) undertake sustained self-directed learning activities each year. Clearly, therefore, participation in adult education programs is not a gateway for access to autodidaxy; if anything, it is the other way round. However, what cannot be deduced from such statistics is whether there is any difference in the nature, quality, or amount of autodidactic learning undertaken by those who have engaged in formal courses.

Several researchers have been interested in examining the broad question of whether participation in structured adult education activities either increases the likelihood of people engaging in autodidactic activities or alters the quality of their self-directed learning experiences. One longitudinal study undertaken in Sweden (Borgström and Olofsson, 1983) concerned the extent to which participation in one form of adult education (study circles) helped individuals to develop "personal resources," where resources are defined as "money, possessions, knowledge, skills, physical and psychological energy, social relations, confidence etc., with the help of which, the individual can control and consciously command his life situation" (Johansson, 1970, p. 25).

Essentially, the research consisted of examining data from 3,300 adults who had been questioned about their adult education activities in each of the years 1968, 1974, and 1981, and comparing what they said about participation in formal adult education with what they said about the extent of their social, political, and cultural activities. The results "show that the groups beginning to take part in study circle activities consistently strengthen their resources more than those who do not take part" (Borgström and Olofsson, 1983, p. 6). Unfortunately, this particular research project did not collect data about autodidactic activities as such, although a subsequent study by one of the authors (Borgström, 1985) lends considerable support to the notion that a strengthening of political, social, and cultural resources would probably also imply a strengthening of participation in autodidaxy.

These results are highly suggestive. However, they do not indicate in what ways participation in study circles might have equipped people to undertake autodidactic activities, and indeed, as the investigators themselves are quick to question, "Can we be sure that it is participation in study circle activities that leads to a change in the resources of the individual, or is there some underlying variable which may account for both participation and the change in resources?" (Borgström and Olofsson, 1983, p. 15).

Following on earlier work by Dickinson and Clark (1975), a study by Pipke (1983) set out to establish if there is any relationship between people's motives for participation in "formal" adult education and their involvement in autodidactic activities. She reasoned that the choice to participate in autodidactic activities (which she subdivided into "self-planned" and "self-taught") was always at the expense of other pursuits in which people might engage for entertainment, relaxation, or to pass time. Consequently, her Activities Preference Inventory consisted of a series of forced-choice items, where respondents were instructed to select from between competing alternative activities. An original item bank of 144 pairs was reduced to 47 final items, made up of some active and some passive distractor activities, and some self-taught and some self-planned autodidactic activities. Respondents were also requested to complete Boshier's (1982) Education Participation Scale, which measures six motivational orientations underlying participation in adult education activities, and Wilson's (1973) Conservatism Scale.

The results were somewhat equivocal, but they suggest that autodidacts are not significantly different psychologically from other adults participating in formal instructional settings, and that if anything "persons with the highest A.P.I. scores were older, more conservative, and more likely to be enrolled in formal instructional settings for Community Service reasons than those with a lesser penchant for self-directed learning" (Pipke, 1983, p. 186). It is appropriate to echo Borgström and Olofsson's caveat that there is no definitive way of knowing whether participation in formal adult education leads to increased autodidactic activity, or if the tendency to be involved in both is indicative of some other factor.

While the preceding studies focus on the linkages, if any, between participation in formally constituted adult education activities and in autodidaxy, other researchers have studied whether certain approaches to teaching develop an orientation favorable to autodidaxy. As early as the 1960s, there was some experimental work carried out in the United States that lends support to the notion that adult education interventions might lead to increased autodidactic behavior. In 1963, for instance, Hovey, Gruber, and Terrell reported on an experimental class in which self-directed students were compared with teacher-directed students in an educational psychology course at the University of Colorado. Findings were "that self-directed study produced a small but persistent superiority in question-raising behavior and in other indices of curiosity" (p. 351). The authors comment that "curiosity may be said to have a 'gatekeeper' function in the educational system . . . and may set off a process which is self-sustaining and which may, in large part, determine the whole character and direction of the individual's future life." They venture the tentative conclusion that "the technique of placing a major responsibility on the student for his own education suggests interesting possibilities for developing attitudes towards learning which will result in the student's continuing a search for knowledge after the formal classroom experience is over" (p. 351).

Another early piece of research was reported by Campbell and Chapman in 1967. Using fourth- and fifth-grade students in what they called "learner-controlled" and "program-controlled" situations, they concluded that "giving learners more control gave them a taste for more control, as well as greater interest in the topic," and hence "that learner-control might in the long-run enhance learning by better maintaining motivation to learn." However, they caution, "Projecting into the future the gradual gain in test performance of the learner-control group relative to the program-control group, it would be years before there was an important difference, [and] perhaps it requires a more variable set of learning resources and conditions such as might be provided by learner-control of the whole curriculum for many years rather than by a single course . . ." (p. 130).

This point has particular relevance to adult education. Adults who engage in adult education activities have typically already had many years of exposure to forms of teaching that encourage their passivity, quiescence, and dependence. It is not easy to break this "passive set." Moreover, most adult education activities are short and discontinuous, lacking the protracted exposure to learner-control that would seem to be necessary to the development of competence and orientation toward autodidaxy. Finally, as already mentioned, there are few reliable guides as to the sort of skill, attitudes, knowledge, and competence that go to make up autodidaxy, and thus there is no guarantee that simply being exposed to increased opportunities for learner-control will necessarily lead to more or better self-initiated and self-managed adult learning efforts.

Recently, Caffarella (1983, 1984) reported two studies, the object of which was to investigate whether increasing learner-control through the use of learning contracts in programs of higher education increases competence in autodidaxy. In the 1984 study, she reports that "a large number of these students are presently using the competencies they learned through using the Learning Contract Format in their . . . personal learning experiences both at work and at home. . . . The competencies most noted by students . . . are related to goal and objective setting, using a variety of methods for learning, and having a better perspective on time management of learning" (p. 36).

These results are modest and have to be treated with circumspection because they are based solely on self-report data. They do, however, tend to support the ideas that "certain competencies for self-directedness in learning . . . can be fostered in part of a formal learning situation" (Caffarella and Caffarella, 1984, p. 36). However, caution is required, because "other [competencies] . . . may be blocked by the same situation" (p. 36).

In his review of "Self-Directed Learning and Schooling," Skager (1979) considers four "modes of learning or ways of structuring educational environments" that "appear to have desirable potential" because "they have been explicitly linked with self-direction." These four modes are experiential learning, discovery learning, open education, and structured individualization. As Skager himself observes, it is plausible to expect such approaches to contribute to the development of autodidactic competence, but the links have yet to be reliably established through research.

Overall, despite the assertion that the development of learners capable of pursuing their own education is a major function of adult education, evidence that it has done so is remarkably meager. This is at least in part because autonomy in learning has two dimensions — a generic or trans-situational component and a situation-specific or context-bound one. Most research into the topic, and most programs for the development of autonomy in learning, have focused on the former component and ignored the latter. Clearly there are methods of conducting education that make use of, and can potentially enhance, people's ability to be self-directing. To the extent that they succeed, their success tends to be localized to the domain or area of instruction concerned, and not to extend automatically to all learning situations. Practitioners who value this attribute in learners have to recognize that there is not necessarily any transfer, in terms of the learner's ability, knowledge, or confidence, to be self-directing in another situation.

Scales Purporting to Assess "Self-Directedness"

Before leaving the issue of profiles and competencies of self-directed learners, it is necessary to focus on an area of research and practice that has gained considerable momentum recently — that is, attempts to measure or assess people's propensity for, or ability at, self-directed learning.

Despite Cameron's (1963) dictum that "not everything that counts can be counted and not everything that can be counted counts" (p. 13, cited by Brookfield, 1983, p. 134), adult education researchers have been seized by a passionate desire to prove themselves "scientific" through the application of certain principles of scientific inquiry. This includes, among other things, attempts to categorize, enumerate, and quantify events and phenomena, many of which do not lend themselves to such quantitative approaches. Research into self-direction has not escaped this preoccupation and, as a result, various theorists have sought to develop tests, instruments, and questionnaires that purport to measure aspects of learner autonomy. Two of the best known are Guglielmino's Self-Directed Learning Readiness Scale (SDLRS) (1977) and Oddi's Continuing Learning Inventory (OCLI) (1984).

The SDLRS consists of a fifty-eight-item Likert scale, designed to assess the degree to which individuals perceive themselves as possessing the skills and attitudes conventionally associated with "self-directed learning." The original instrument was developed and refined through a three-round Delphi survey of fourteen persons considered to be experts in the area of "self-directed learning" (Herbert A. Alf, B. Frank Brown, Edward G. Buffie, Arthur W. Chickering, Patricia M. Coolican, Gerald T. Gleason, Winslow R. Hatch, Cyril O. Houle (first two rounds only), Malcolm S. Knowles, Wilbert J. McKeachie, Barry R. Morstain, Mary M. Thompson, Allen M. Tough, and Morris Weitman). When the instrument was pilot tested, the results obtained were factor analyzed, and this allegedly disclosed the presence of eight factors that Guglielmino labeled as follows: openness to learning opportunities, self-concept as an effective learner, initiative and independence in learning, informed acceptance of responsibility for one's own learning, love of learning, creativity, future orientation, and ability to use basic study and problem-solving skills.

Partly because of the preoccupation with attempts to quantify the elusive and multifaceted concept of self-direction, and partly because adult education, as a field of study, has relatively few "home-grown" research instruments, since its first appearance the SDLRS has rapidly become prominent in the field, and has formed the basis of a number of research studies (Bayha, 1983; Bejot, 1981; Box, 1982; Brockett, 1983c; Caffarella and Caffarella, 1984; Carney, 1986; Curry, 1983; Eisenman, 1989; Hassan, 1981; Leean and Sisco, 1981a; Leeb, 1983; Ravid, 1987; Sabbaghian, 1979; Savoie, 1979; Skaggs, 1981; Tzuk, 1985a, 1985b; Wiley, 1981, 1982; Young, 1985). It has also attracted a good deal of scholarly attention (Brockett, 1985a, 1985b; Field, 1989; Kasworm, 1982; Long, 1987; Long and Agyekum, 1983, 1984; McCune, Guglielmino, and Garcia, 1989; Torrance and Mourad, 1978; West and Bentley, 1989).

Clearly the SDLRS has attracted a strong following and has given rise to a rapidly expanding body of knowledge about self-direction in learning. However, despite its widespread acceptance and use, Guglielmino's scale has not escaped criticism. For instance, Long and Agyekum (1983, 1984) point to the fact that they found no significant relationship between SDLRS scores and a rating by faculty members as to each respondent's "self-directedness." Although they demonstrated some ingenuity in developing alternative explanations for this, Long and Agyekum (1983) do admit the possibility "that the SDLRS does not measure self-direction in learning" or that "SDLRS is inadequate for one group [that is, the less well educated]" (p. 85).

Brockett (1985a), in an analysis of both methodological and substantive issues in the measurement of self-directed learning readiness, identifies "problems related to the construction and layout of the instrument and, perhaps more important, the assumptions underlying the way in which the instrument defines self-directed readiness . . . from a highly school- and book-oriented perspective . . . , thus [it] may not be appropriate for adults with relatively few years of formal schooling" (p. 22).

The most wide-ranging and compelling criticisms, however, come from Field (1989), who noticed that successive users of the scale had taken it for granted that its validity and reliability had been adequately demonstrated, whereas in fact "claims about the validity and reliability rely on other claims which, when one traces them back through the literature, rest primarily on Guglielmino's original development work" (p. 128). This line of reasoning forced him to examine carefully her original work, which he argued was flawed in a number of major respects.

Field began by observing that "neither readiness nor self-directed learner are [sic] defined in the study" (1989, p. 129). Guglielmino defends this "since one of the goals of the study was to arrive at a tentative definition . . . based on the survey of authorities on self-directed learning" (1977, p. 30). Notwithstanding this explanation, Field is unconvinced and claims that "this failure to define or clarify the meaning of key terms results in a conceptual framework . . . which, in this researcher's view, is not very sound" (1989, p. 129).

Against this background, Field critiques the use of the Delphi technique: "Given the conceptual confusion surrounding the term 'self-directed learning,' Guglielmino's use of the Delphi technique to generate items may do no more than merely transfer this confusion into a set of items" (Field, 1989, p. 129). The successive rounds of the Delphi questionnaire did not challenge participants' conceptual and terminological confusions, he argued, but instead provided a means of reifying them. A similar criticism might well be leveled at the composite profile of the self-directed learner presented at the start of this chapter.

Field then turned his attention to the development of the instrument itself. Questioning the composition of the inventory, he went on to point out that many of the items were ambiguous, poorly phrased, or did not make sense when paired with the various response options; that negatively phrased items had a demonstrable and disproportionate influence on the total score; that in analyzing the data, Guglielmino used principal components analysis when she should have used common factor analysis; that, contrary to Guglielmino's assertion, there was no evidence of a multifactorial structure to the scale; and, perhaps most seriously of all, that what the scale measures "is not readiness for self-directed learning, but does appear to be related to love of and enthusiasm for learning" (Field, 1989, p. 138).

These criticisms by Field sparked a lively controversy in the pages of the *Adult Education Quarterly*. In the issue following his critique, no fewer than three sets of authors leapt to the defense of the SDLRS, with detailed counterclaims to each of the points he raised. Overall, it was argued that "Field's criticism is not constructive" (Guglielmino, 1989, p. 239), that "his findings and conclusions should be dismissed as unreliable and invalid" (McCune and Austin, 1989, p. 243), and that "Field's study has made a very limited contribution to knowledge concerning SDLRS validity and reliability" (Long, 1989, p. 242).

Whatever the outcome of this debate, it seems probable that the concern expressed in one of the articles — that "Field's research will discourage other researchers from using the SDLRS" (McCune and Austin, 1989, p. 245) — will prove to be without foundation. Indeed, if anything, spirited debate about the notion of self-directedness should be welcomed rather than deplored.

Moreover, it seems that while argument has been raging over the methodological superstructure, the conceptual hull of the good ship SDLRS may prove to be dangerously leaky. In view of the absence of a clear definition of major terms, there appears to be some confusion as to precisely what is being measured. The attribute being assessed is variously referred to, within the instrument itself, as an "attitude," a "preference," a "learning style," "readiness," "skills," "abilities," and "characteristics." This flexibility seems to have influenced users as well, because although the scale is supposed to "identify individuals *within organizations* who are high, average or low in readiness for independent learning" (Guglielmino and Associates, undated descriptive leaflet), it has been used in studies of graduate students (Caffarella and Caffarella, 1986; Tzuk, 1985a), undergraduate students (Savoie, 1979; Sabbaghian, 1979); Tzuk, 1985a; Wiley, 1981, 1982), undereducated adults (Leean and Sisco, 1981b), randomly selected members of the adult population (Hassan, 1981), and even gifted children (Carney, 1986).

The reason I have raised this issue is because this is probably indicative of the widespread, but I believe incorrect, view that "self-directed learning readiness" is context free. It is argued in this book that autodidaxy is not the same thing as independent study within formal settings, and while it may be true that there are some generic or transferable components of "self-directed learning readiness," it also seems probable that there is a substantial "subject-specific" component. People who may be perfectly capable of self-managed learning in one domain might be paralyzed when confronted with another area to master. The research of the Göteborg Group in Sweden and of the Institute for Research in Post Compulsory Education at Lancaster University in England (see Entwistle and Hounsell, 1979; Marton, Hounsell, and Entwistle, 1984), for instance, confirms the situation-specific or context-bound nature of learning competence, and it seems likely that this extends to autodidactic learning as well.

The second instrument, the Oddi Continuing Learning Inventory or OCLI, attempts to identify clusters of personality characteristics found to relate to "initiative and persistence in learning over time through a variety of learning modes" (Oddi,

1985, p. 230). Through a process of refinement, an original bank of 100 items was reduced to a final instrument containing 24 items, with a reported internal validity of .87 and a test/retest reliability of .89. According to the author, factor analysis of the results yielded three factors accounting for 45.7 percent of the total variance, of which the first factor alone, comprising 15 salient items, accounted for 30.9 percent of the variance. This general factor contains "elements of self-confidence, ability to work independently, and learning through involvement with others. Two subsidiary factors, Reading Avidity and Ability to be Self-Regulating, also emerged" (p. 229). It should be noted that, even given the author's own figures, these three major factors accounted for only 45 percent, or less than half, of the total variance in the scores.

Although this study appears to have been well controlled, and the resulting instrument is both parsimonious and elegant, there are still certain unanswered questions and issues. Like the SDLRS, the OCLI assumes generalizability of competence as an autonomous learner and, like the SDLRS, it appears to mix together "independent" continuing professional education within institutional settings (such as graduate schools) with "self-directed" or autodidactic continuing education outside formal contexts. While there may well be personality characteristics that apply in both situations, it seems that this is an untested assumption. As with the SDLRS, the Continuing Learning Inventory will require further refinement and testing, but it appears, on the face of it, to be more appropriate to the domain of independent study than to autodidaxy, and perhaps more relevant to instrumental types of learning than expressive and esthetic projects (Havighurst, 1964, pp. 17–18).

In either case, the primary purpose of these instruments is diagnosis and remediation. According to Guglielmino and Guglielmino (1982), "Major uses of the SDLRS . . . are in the areas of prediction and diagnosis. For example, it can be used as a screening tool for programs involving self-directed study, such as correspondence courses, programs for the gifted, and independent study" (p. 11), and Oddi (1986) writes that "the development of a valid and reliable tool to identify self-directed continuing learners has implications for practice . . . such as a screening tool to aid in the selection of various academic and continuing education programs" (p. 105). Both of these points of view are predicated on the dubious assumption that "self-directed learning readiness" is a context-free personal attribute, instead of being subject and context specific, as argued here, and on the equally questionable medical metaphor that "deficiencies" in readiness can be "remedied."

In this book, it is contended that people's willingness to participate in self-directed learning activities is shaped not by some abstract attribute such as "self-directed learning readiness" but by their construction of the particular situation and circumstances. Since this orientation is highly personal and idiosyncratic (as discussed in Part Three), there is little that the adult educator can do to empower the learner to feel confident and capable of exercising such control. As I will discuss in Chapter Seven, there are certain steps that the educator can take, and certain attitudes that he or she can exhibit, that will increase the likelihood of learners' accepting control in the instructional situation. But one of the most vital yet elusive qualities, as mentioned in the previous chapter, is having a self-concept of autonomy, and this is largely beyond the ability of the educator to influence — especially outside the instructional setting.

Summary

This chapter began by reviewing literature on the skills and competencies that various researchers have linked with self-directed learning. There are many profiles of the self-directed learner, but most of them exhibit some, or all, of the following defects: (1) class and gender bias, usually in favor of white, middle-class males; (2) a tacit bias toward a particular ideological position that is often masked by use of "humanistic" language; (3) failure to ground descriptions in comprehensive and internally consistent definitions of autonomy; (4) a tendency to ignore or play down the importance of self-confidence as a vital prerequisite for effective self-directed learning; and (5) an implicit assumption that competence as a self-directed learner is transposable from one learning situation to another.

The development of competence as a self-directed learner was discussed. Clearly many people have achieved a high level of skill as learners without the need of formal instruction. Nonetheless, many theorists believe education can play a part in this otherwise naturally occurring process. A number of educational interventions have been linked with self-directed learning competence. Some of these take the form of direct instruction; others involve concomitant learning through various educational strategies or approaches such as learning contracts, experiential learning, discovery learning, open education, and structured individualization. Whether direct or concomitant, the focus is usually on the generic or context-free domain of learning autonomy. However, in both cases, there is relatively little empirical evidence of a direct link between education and the pursuit of autodidactic activity, and further research on such links, if any, seems called for.

Finally, attention was focused on attempts to measure or assess learners' self-directedness. It was shown that, in addition to significant conceptual and operational flaws, such instruments are predicated on the questionable assumption that "self-directedness" is a generic, rather than a situation-specific or context-bound, accomplishment or attribute. The next chapter contains a review of research findings on autodidaxy and an indication of some of the shortcomings of the existing research tradition.

Six

The Independent Pursuit of Learning

Leakey and Lewin (1977, p. 8) give a particularly striking example of independent learning: "Close to three million years ago on a campsite near the east shore of Kenya's spectacular Lake Turkana, a primitive human picked up a water-smoothed stone, and with a few skilful strikes transformed it into an implement. What was once an accident of nature was now a piece of deliberate technology, to be used to fashion a stick for digging up roots, or to slice the flesh off a dead animal. Soon discarded by its maker, the stone tool still exists."

In addition to the spine-tingling realization that this simple artifact represents a tangible link with our most distant ancestors, it is also tantalizing to recognize that no instructor taught that proto-human how to shape a stone implement; it was entirely the product of her (or his) own imagination and experimentation. The same may be said of humankind's use of fire, the construction of the first rough shelters other than caves, and that emblematic technological advance: the invention of the wheel. In all these cases — and an infinite number of others as well — learning occurred without the aid of any teacher.

In fact, the whole of human history floats in a veritable sea of such learning; the individual and collective accretion of insight, knowledge, competence, and wisdom that results from humans' attempts "to secure more favorable treatment for themselves by appealing . . . to the greater natural forces that rule the world" (Leakey and Lewin, 1977, p. 10). That relatively simple act of creating a rudimentary tool embodied several aspects

157

of learning: observation, reflection, conceiving of an idea, and manipulation and transformation of an object to achieve some novel purpose. It also involved another aspect, one that is not characteristic of all human learning—that is, intentionality.

Although the study of learning in its "natural habitat" has intrigued and challenged anthropologists, psychologists, philosophers, and educators for generations, the systematic study of *intentional* "self-education" (which I refer to as autodidaxy) is a somewhat more recent phenomenon. As mentioned in Chapter Two, the current eruption of interest in the topic, at least in adult education, can be traced back more or less directly to Houle's study of twenty-two continuing learners, published in 1961 under the title *The Inquiring Mind*. It is for others to speculate on why it took so long for the domain of autodidaxy to become the object of sustained scholarly inquiry. However, since these first, tentative beginnings, research on autodidaxy has gathered momentum, and now, as Brookfield (1984a, p. 59) observes, "by almost any measure conceivable," it is one of the chief growth areas in adult education research.

It is the intention of this chapter to review and critically analyze the literature on autodidaxy generally: its nature and extent; the "process" itself; the help sought and obtained by learners; and theoretical, conceptual, and background studies. An attempt is made to identify key authors and landmark studies, to highlight areas that seem to offer promising new directions for research, and to suggest ways in which adult educators and others might be able to assist those seeking to learn things for themselves.

Descriptive and Verification Studies

Despite the fact that people have been aware of the existence of autodidactic activity for centuries, Tough was the first to operationalize the concept in such a way that it could be studied systematically. The basic building block of Tough's study was the "learning project," which he defined as "a major, highly deliberate effort to gain certain knowledge or skill (or to change in some other way)" (1979a, p. 1). This definition implies intentionality, and hence excludes serendipitous, incidental, or adventitious learning. Tough specified that, to be included, a learning project would need to involve a series of related "learning episodes" adding up to at least seven hours. In his 1978 review of the literature, he wrote that "the typical learner conducts five quite distinct learning projects in one year. He or she learns five distinct areas of knowledge and skill. The person spends an average of 100 hours per learning effort — a total of 500 hours per year" (p. 252).

Mocker and Spear (1982, p. 12) write that "within five years of the release of his book [in 1971], Tough's work had sparked not less than 25 dissertations, theses, and independent research studies. These, and numerous subsequent studies, used Tough's interview approach and modifications of his interview schedule to broaden the description of the self-directed learner and the learning process, while confirming and refining the findings of Tough's original work."

Although Tough's first study concentrated on "The Teaching Tasks Performed by Adult Self-Teachers" (1966b), he and those who have followed him have identified a range of learning contents of breathtaking diversity. It appears that adults learn how to build, how to buy, and how to borrow; they learn about languages and lampshades; about cooking and camping; about raising children and reasoning; about management and making wine; about music, art, literature, history, science, and psychology. In short, no domain of human existence or inquiry is exempt from the self-educational efforts of these avid amateurs, whose serious self-set study often eclipses both the breadth and intensity of even the best-informed practitioners and scholars.

Acknowledging the panoramic scope of subjects surveyed, various researchers have raised the question, How widespread is the practice of autodidaxy? Is it, for instance, limited to those who have already proved themselves through advanced secondary or perhaps even higher education? According to various estimates, the incidence of autodidactic learning may be as high as 80 to 100 percent of the adult population. It is not confined to any particular social, educational, occupational, or ethnic categories, but is widespread — almost universal — among adults. Researchers have established that learning projects are carried out:

In the general population (Tough, 1966b, 1967, 1978, 1979d; Penland, 1977, 1979)

By subgroups of the general population:
Women (Moorcraft, 1975)
African-American adults (Shackelford, 1983)
Prospective parents (Cobb, 1978)
Older adults (Hiemstra, 1975, 1976)
Older women (Grenier, 1980)
Single and divorced mothers (Bonneau, 1984)
Mothers of young children (Bogenschneider, 1977; Coolican, 1973)
Rural adults (Lensch, 1980; Peters and Gordon, 1974)
Parents of teenagers (Clarkson, 1975; Orlando, 1977)
Those undergoing spiritual growth (Wickett, 1978a, 1978b)
People undertaking purposeful change (Brillinger, 1983; Neehall, 1983)

By those traditionally classed as "hard-to-reach":
Low-income urban adults (Booth, 1979a, 1979b; Umoren, 1977)
Undereducated rural adults (Leean, 1981)
Adults of low educational attainment (Armstrong, 1971; Brookfield, 1982b)
Disadvantaged adults in urban Montreal (Serré, 1977)
Unemployed adults (Johnson, Levine, and Rosenthal, 1977)

By various occupational categories:
Gerontological practitioners (Zabari, 1985)
Farmers (Bayha, 1983)
Professionals (McCatty, 1973, 1975; Sexton-Hesse, 1984)
Nurses (Kathrein, 1981; Skaggs, 1981)
Teachers (Fair, 1973; Kelley, 1976; McCatty, 1976; Miller, 1977; Strong, 1977)
Engineers (Rymell, 1981)
Extension agents (Miller and Botsman, 1975)
University and college administrators (Benson, 1974)

Members of the clergy (Allerton, 1974; Morris, 1977)
Pharmacists (Johns, 1973; Levchuk, 1977)
Adult and continuing educators (Addleton, 1984; Zangari, 1977)
Civilians employed in the U.S. Air Force (Hood, 1975)
Family physicians (Means, 1979)

By adults living outside North America:
Jamaican adults of low literacy (Field, 1977)
Adults in Haifa, Israel (Hirschfeld, 1981)
Rural women in Cameroon (Bravay, 1983)
Professionals in Accra, Ghana (Denys, 1973)
Agricultural extension officers in Victoria, Australia (Underwood, 1980)
Teachers in England (Strong, 1977)
Adults of low educational attainment in the English Midlands (Brookfield, 1982b)
Cross section of adults in Sweden (Borgström, 1985)
Adults in Eastern Europe (Savićević, 1985)

Within groups formed around shared interests:
Women (Knoepfli, 1971)
Labor unions (Brown, 1972)
Self-help stroke recovery clubs (Banks, 1985)
Self-help groups (Farquharson, 1975)
Learning networks (G. R. Lewis, 1978; Luikart, 1976)
Political lobby groups (McCreary, 1984)

By students:
Adults matriculating into community colleges (Geïsler, 1984)
Adults enrolled in community college courses (Sheckley, 1988)
Adults participating in cooperative extension programs (Bejot, 1981)
Adult basic education students (Baghi, 1979; Kratz, 1978)
Adult high school graduates (E. A. Johnson, 1973)
In public management master's programs (Zottoli, 1984)

Criticisms of These Descriptive and Verification Studies.
Despite the number and diversity of such studies, in recent years
there have been few significant advances in this particular line
of research. Caffarella and O'Donnell (1985, p. 3) maintain that
research in this area has "reached the point of dullness," and
one is inclined to agree with their judgment that, at least with
respect to verification studies, "enough is enough"!

As Brookfield (1984a, p. 60) has observed, "It is . . . easy
for unsympathetic outsiders to critique a body of research for
its apparent methodological naivete or conceptual confusion,"
and the following comments are not intended to denigrate or
belittle the contribution that these various researchers have made
to adult education's body of knowledge. Nonetheless, a number of significant and legitimate criticisms have been aimed at
these verification studies.

The first is that the population samples are biased in favor
of urban, middle-class, English-speaking North Americans. In
his 1984 review of the literature, Brookfield describes as "highly
questionable" the assumption that "the behaviors exhibited by
this educationally advantaged collection of adults will be displayed by adults from a range of different class and ethnic backgrounds" (1984a, p. 62). The sheer volume of research on the
learning activities of such people inevitably means that more is
known about them than about other groups. Indeed, the propensity of researchers (particularly those pursuing graduate studies)
to use samples of convenience means that teachers and students
in colleges and universities, as well as other professionals, are
likely to be overrepresented in the research literature. A somewhat ritualized and inconclusive debate between Brockett (1985a)
and Brookfield (1985b) on this point did little more than to emphasize the well-attested fact that generalizations about the population at large may be invalid, given the patchy and uneven nature of research in the social and behavioral sciences.

In view of the diversity of different groups who have now
been researched, it is necessary to treat Brookfield's criticism
with some circumspection. For instance, it is interesting to note
that Brookfield himself, although denouncing the preoccupation
of researchers with samples of middle-class Americans as "a dan-

gerous act of intellectual ethnocentrism," does not refer to studies conducted in Africa (Bravay, 1983; Denys, 1973; Kondani, 1982), Sweden (Borgström, 1985), France (Cacères, 1967), Eastern Europe (Savićević, 1985), or French-speaking Canada (Pineau, 1978; Serré, 1977). One of these latter studies, published in English as well as French (Serré, 1978, p. 19) concluded that "French speaking adults in disadvantaged and less well-educated groups show a keen interest in learning. Their performance compares well with that of other groups in the number of projects engaged in and the quality of learning involved."

A second criticism is methodological. It concerns the "probing and prompting" that is called for by Tough's interview schedule. Indeed, Tough himself (1978, p. 252) writes that "in general, the less training the interviewers have in understanding the concept of the learning project and in probing successfully for additional projects, the fewer learning projects they uncover. Even interviewers trained in depth, however, state that they are probably missing some projects because people cannot recall them after several months. . . . " This admission has prompted the observation by Pedler (1972, p. 89) that the projects identified may be artifacts of the methodology; "from the account of the interviews, it appears that a lot of probing occurred so that gratuitous responses may have been recorded and the case overstated."

Certainly, the Sexton-Hesse study (1984), which used a different research approach from Tough's, found a number of respondents with no learning projects at all. Furthermore, Borgström's large-scale study in Sweden, which used a "lower limit of twenty hours" (1985, p. 5) instead of seven, found that only "14 percent had participated in self-directed learning." This is substantially lower than Tough's figure of 73 percent (1978, p. 253) and, unless the Swedish population is significantly different from the Canadian one on which Tough's findings are based, this suggests that a very large proportion of the learning projects reported by Tough were of between seven and twenty hours' duration. In his 1983 critique of this research, Boshier observed that the limit of seven hours was arbitrary, poorly operationalized (for example, did it include or exclude traveling time?), and seemed low for a learning endeavor of any consequence.

Because of the alleged unreliability of self-report data, especially that involving recall, Boshier (1983) has suggested an "alternative technique, that of study participants using diaries to record present learning activities, and thus reduce the prompting necessary for recalling past activities" (Caffarella and O'Donnell, 1985, p. 3). Tough (1978, p. 252) comments that "one experiment with daily learning diaries yielded higher figures than the interview . . . [as did] rambling two and a half hour follow-up conversations with interviewees."

Another criticism concerns the alleged inappropriateness of interview schedules, especially with less well-educated respondents. Brookfield (1984a), for instance, has criticized an over-reliance on "measurement scales, structured interview schedules, questionnaires and prompt sheets" (p. 63). He goes on to say that "it is apparent that researchers adopting formalised measures of self-directed learning . . . , administering an interview schedule in a standardised fashion, or presenting a self-completion questionnaire to subjects, are likely to be regarded with suspicion by working-class adults with poor educational attainments and distressing memories of their school experience" (p. 64).

None of these criticisms implies that autodidaxy is not worth studying, but rather that the interview method may have had the effect of overstating some aspects of autodidactic learning, while ignoring or underrepresenting others. In fact, this is indicative of an observation about educational research generally, namely, that no one methodology has a monopoly or is uniquely well suited to every research question in a particular domain. Eisner's (1981, p. 9) dictum seems appropriate: "Each approach to the study of educational situations has its own unique perspective to provide. Each sheds its own unique light on the situations that humans seek to understand. The field of education in particular needs to avoid methodological monism: our problems need to be addressed in as many ways as will bear fruit."

Accordingly, some researchers are now advocating and employing a range of different approaches to examine a particular issue from various perspectives (Peters, 1988; Spear, 1988).

This process, known as *methodological triangulation,* "involves a complex process of playing each method off against the other so as to maximise the validity of field efforts" (Denzin, 1978, p. 304). With respect to research on autodidaxy, the issue of methodological ingenuity is dealt with later in this chapter, but it is contended here that the perspective of the learner has been largely neglected in this research, and that valuable insights have been sacrificed as a result.

Overall, the existence of autodidactic learning projects has now been established beyond question. Despite some of the methodological criticisms discussed here, there seems little doubt that it constitutes an important domain in the education of adults, and researchers are now turning their attention from these descriptive and verification studies to other, more sophisticated questions, such as, "What is the actual process of learning on one's own?" "What is the significance of this practice, both to the learners themselves, and to society at large?" and "What sort of relationships do autodidacts enjoy with those who assist them?" The answers to these questions, particularly the last, have significant ramifications for the practice of adult education. Implications for practitioners are spelled out in this chapter, especially under the heading "Assistance with Learning Projects."

The Autodidactic Process

Autodidaxy is an extremely widespread activity that occurs in diverse settings and concerns a varied, possibly limitless, range of subjects. By reviewing the literature, this section tries to discover if there is a distinctive pattern of learner inquiry that might be termed *the autodidactic process.* In particular, the following questions will be considered: Do autodidacts pass through transitional stages in their learning? If so, are they consciously aware of doing so? And can they reliably reconstruct their experience as a self-teacher?

As I mentioned in Chapter Five, autodidaxy poses researchers with conceptual and practical problems because, in the autodidact, the tasks of competent instructor and proficient learner (Clark, 1973, p. 13) are fused—in the argot of organizational theory, *simultaneous role occupancy*. The problem which this raises is this: Should autodidaxy be treated as a model of teaching and researched alongside other such models (Joyce and Weil, 1980), should it be viewed as a learning situation and thus be researched from a learning point of view, or is it a phenomenon unique in education that should be studied on its own terms, without reference to (or at least without reliance on) other aspects of education? Implicitly or explicitly, different researchers have come to different conclusions, and thus the research findings seem at times confusing and incommensurable.

Some researchers have treated autodidaxy as a pattern of organizing instruction. For instance, according to Tough (1979a, pp. 116–117), there are thirteen preparatory steps that need to be performed by the autodidact:

- Deciding detailed knowledge and skills
- Deciding activities, materials, resources, and equipment for learning
- Deciding where to learn
- Setting specific deadlines or intermediate goals
- Deciding when to learn
- Deciding the pace
- Estimating level or progress
- Detecting blocks and inefficiencies
- Obtaining readings, resources, or equipment
- Preparing a room or other physical conditions
- Obtaining money
- Finding time for the learning
- Increasing motivation or dealing with motivational blocks

In his *Self-Directed Learning: A Guide for Learners and Teachers*, Knowles (1975) lists the following general stages:

- Establishing learning climate
- Diagnosing needs
- Formulating goals
- Choosing and implementing appropriate learning strategies
- Evaluating learning outcomes

Despite the allegedly "learner-centered" nature of autodidaxy, lists such as these seem suspiciously like the sort of formulas that might be offered in schools of teacher education. It is almost as if someone steeped in the realm of education, and more particularly in the profession of teaching, had superimposed a template — and a normative one, at that — over the much more fluid, organic, and unpredictable process of self-teaching.

Autodidaxy certainly involves aspects found in teaching: some sort of goal setting, finding and utilizing appropriate resources, attempting different ways of attacking the subject matter, responding to feedback, and evaluating and moving on. Such functions definitely need to be performed, but they are identified in retrospect, and the fragmentation of such a holistic process as self-teaching is like that of "vivisecting the nightingale to prove the secret of its note" (Laidlaw, quoted in Welton, 1987). Moreover, it is not a teaching method that is at the disposal of the program planner, nor a teaching technique to be used by an educational agent, because the entire initiative rests with the autodidact. The tendency of some authors to treat autodidaxy as either a method for organizing education or as "just another technique of instruction" has led to difficulties in researching this domain.

Clearly autodidacts are learners. It has often been observed that learning is an internal and invisible process, not susceptible to direct observation, and a researcher is accordingly obliged to rely either on behavioral manifestations of learning or else on the practice of asking learners to examine and report on their own internal states. In either case, there are difficulties in researching autodidacts who, because of the noninstitutional nature of their learning endeavors, are not readily identifiable or easily contacted. However, autodidacts confront difficulties and enjoy opportunities that are not commonly encountered by learners in more formal settings, and it may be that research on autodidaxy could, because of its unique nature, contribute to our understandings of the processes of teaching and learning.

Accordingly, it is argued here that autodidaxy is best understood neither a model of teaching nor of learning, but that it needs to be studied "on its own terms." This immediately raises a difficulty because, as already mentioned, one of the problems with studying autodidaxy is that, by its nature, it is entirely in the hands of the learner. Moreover, as Thomas (1967) has noted, such people are frequently pursuing knowledge or skills in order to use them, and are not conscious of themselves as learners at all, certainly not at the outset. This is not to say that they do not become aware of themselves as learners; available research evidence tends to point to the fact that they do. Indeed, it may be that acquiring the sort of critical reflectivity and self-awareness espoused by Mezirow (1985) and Brookfield (1985c) is a developmental stage through which autodidacts pass. Overall, however, this means that it is difficult to identify autodidacts, and it is also difficult to capture the early and perhaps decisive stages in their autodidactic projects (Svensson, 1989, p. 8).

Despite these difficulties, researchers have utilized a number of techniques for "capturing" information about the autodidactic process. Probably the most conventional of these involves presenting respondents with prepared lists of the functions they may be expected to perform, such as those proposed by Knowles and Tough. Not unexpectedly, their responses indicate that they do, indeed, undertake those tasks. There are at least three reasons for this. First, research subjects are legendary for their desire and willingness to please the researcher, and will therefore commonly agree to propositions that they think the interviewer wants to hear. Second, there is often a difference between the actual way in which things are accomplished and the "approved" or socially sanctioned way in which they should be accomplished, and respondents prefer to side with the "right" answer. Third, it is often the case that people have given little conscious thought to the steps involved in certain activities, and they simply respond to what appears to be a plausible sequence, since they are in no position to come up with anything better on the spot.

Although there are certain regularities in the ways in which autodidactic projects are conducted, the search for generalized lawlike relationships has tended to obscure and submerge important individual differences among autodidacts and their learning endeavors. Accordingly, researchers have employed a variety of other approaches to deal more adequately with the complex, unpredictable, and multifaceted nature of self-directed learning outside institutional settings. Those considered here are (1) reconstruction through interview, (2) written sources such as biographies and reflective essays, (3) learning journals and diaries, and (4) recurrent interviews throughout the duration of a learning endeavor.

Reconstruction Through Interview. Clearly, one potential research strategy is a reconstructive one, in which people are asked to recall and reconstruct their experience of learning something for themselves. There are many drawbacks to such an approach, not the least of which is people's frequent inability to recall the details of what might have been, at the time, crucial events in the learning process. The research work of Tough and others has been questioned because of the fallibility of memory with respect to what people learned; how reliable are retrospective re-creations of the process itself? Despite this reservation, available research findings based on recollections of learning events are rich and stimulating. Several research groups that have explored autodidaxy in this way have come up with different views of the autodidactic process.

Peters, Johnson, and Lazzara (1981), for instance, began their research on the learning projects of both literate and illiterate adults in Tennessee with the assumption that most learning projects are actually efforts to solve a problem. They devised a "hermeneutic and interpretive" research methodology involving a four-stage textual analysis, and they note in their interim report that the process of autodidactic learning is idiosyncratic in that it represents "the person's reasoning pattern applied to a specific problem situation" (Mocker and Spear, 1982, p. 20).

Leean and Sisco (1981a) followed up a Tough-like survey of undereducated adults in rural Vermont with intensive interviews with a subsample. Like those of Peters, Johnson, and Lazzara, the findings also stressed the environmental and contextual elements in autodidactic learning and, as Mocker and Spear (1982, p. 19) state, "The importance of past experiences and family background was found to be significant in the content and motivation for learning, as well as in approaches to learning and problem solving." Although acknowledging that self-directed learning may be guided by a rational problem-solving model, Leean noticed that most of the subjects were aware of times when problems were actually solved through non-rational processes or an "altered state-of-consciousness."

In their own research, Spear and Mocker (1981, 1984) found that, contrary to expectations, only rarely did adult learners preplan their learning. Instead, they discovered that autodidactic activity more often than not arose out of some "triggering event" (referred to by Mezirow as a "disorienting dilemma") or change in life circumstances, and that the structure, method, resources, and conditions for learning are all directed by circumstances over which the learner often has no direct control. To describe this, they coined the term *the organizing circumstance,* whereby the learning progresses as the circumstances created in one episode become the circumstances for the next logical step. In discussing this, Caffarella and O'Donnell (1985, p. 5) comment, "Needless to say, the organizing circumstance is an exciting new aspect of self-directed learning, and an area which calls for further research."

Other researchers who have been prepared to defy the orthodox in examining autodidaxy are Danis and Tremblay at the University of Montreal. Taking as a starting point the work of Flavell (1979) on metacognition and Maudsley (1979) on metalearning, they have found intriguing indications of the ways in which autodidacts become aware, and take conscious control, of their habitual patterns of perceiving, of searching, of learning, and of developing (Danis and Tremblay, 1987). They made a detailed content analysis of the learning experiences of ten autodidacts and conclude that the experience does not conform to either a linear or a cyclical sequence, but rather that "the self-taught adults proceed in a heuristic manner within a learning approach which they organize around intentions, redefine and specify without following any predetermined patterns" (Danis and Tremblay, 1985a, p. 139). Like Spear and Mocker, they note the impact of unpredictable events on the learning process, and conclude that "self-taught adults take advantage of any opportunity that random events may offer them in order to learn."

This is not to say that autodidacts are directionless victims of circumstance, lacking in any clear goals or intentions. On the contrary, they tend to be more purposeful, tenacious, and disciplined than other learners, and are constantly alert to the possibility of learning in all sorts of situations. There appears to be the sort of fusion of intention and response, of action and reflection, captured by Freire (1972) in the term *praxis,* and this in turn seems to be mediated by some higher-order process such as metalearning or metacognition (Tremblay and Danis, 1984). I will return to this theme in Part Four of the book, in considering strategies for developing the competence of self-directed learners.

Written Sources, Including Biographies and Reflective Essays. A second potential approach to understanding the autodidactic process is the study of those written records that autodidacts have prepared, often for themselves, though sometimes for a wider public. Many eminent (and some not-so-eminent) people have left behind biographies or autobiographies. While these are frequently an intriguing source of information about the life events that shaped their personal development and learning, or even their self-education (see for example Adams, 1931), they rarely disclose much about the learning process itself (Jackson, 1979).

"In search of commonalities that might suggest ways people become effectively self-directing in learning and accomplishment," Gibbons and his associates (1980, p. 41) write that they content-analyzed the "biographies of twenty acknowledged experts without formal training beyond high school." Although their paper makes fascinating reading, they tend to emphasize personality and situational characteristics that encourage autodidaxy, rather than exploring the internal dynamics of the process itself. They do, however, confirm the role of serendipity in many learning endeavors: "Accidents or coincidence seem to play an important part. Chance occurrences often led to a new perspective that enabled [the subjects of the study] to solve problems and make breakthroughs in understanding" (p. 48).

Perhaps the most elaborate self-analysis of the autodidactic process of learning is in a paper by Griffin (1981), in which she imaginatively reconstructs a learning project carried out in, and in relation to, her own home. Griffin identifies five dimensions that were engaged—sometimes together and sometimes individually—in pursuing her learning project: the rational, the physical (or physiological), the emotional, the relational, and the metaphorical or intuitive dimensions. She traces the constant shifting between, and interaction among, these various facets of her valuing and judging systems, but does not introduce the notion of metacognition or any higher-order process mediating the transitions.

What emerges is a picture of the enormous complexity and unpredictability of a learning effort: Critical insights were gained at various junctures, and she comments that if events had taken a slightly different turn at any point, "the results for my learning and for the project would have been quite different" (p. 6). Griffin's testimony lends weight to the findings of Mocker and Spear (1982) concerning the nonlinear nature of many such learning efforts: "There was no predictable, orderly sequence of use of the various [aspects]. Their occurrence seems almost random. [Based on my experience] I have no reason to expect that other learning experiences would follow any predictable sequence" (p. 6).

Like many other writers on autodidaxy, Griffin stresses the interdependent nature of much learning in this mode; simply because a learning project is self-directed, this does not mean that it is accomplished independently, without any outside assistance. The autodidact, as Moore (1973b, p. 669) suggests, is "not to be thought of as an intellectual Robinson Crusoe, castaway and shut-off in self-sufficiency." This point is discussed in greater detail later in this chapter.

Learning Journals and Diaries. Another methodology that has been successfully used to discover more about the nature of the learning process itself is the diary or working journal (R. M. Smith, 1986). One of the difficulties of using such an approach with autodidacts has already been alluded to; by definition such people are undertaking learning projects on their own initiative without formal institutional affiliation, and there is no simple mechanism for capturing especially the early phases of a project. Moreover, a high degree of self-discipline, not to mention critical reflectivity, is required to report on one's own learning as it unfolds. However, judging from the valuable insights that researchers in other fields have gained from the use of journals or diaries (Christensen, 1981; French, 1976; Hettich, 1976; L. C. Ingram, 1979; Merriam, 1983; Parer, 1988; Powell, 1985), it would seem a most productive line of inquiry in trying to understand the stages or phases of the autodidactic process.

Although journals and diaries suffer from the same shortcomings as other self-report instruments, they can at least reflect the ups and downs of a learning project and can, if faithfully maintained, track the learner's thoughts and emotions more closely than any reconstruction after the event. Furthermore, a diary or journal "offers an interpretive framework through which the meaning of human experience is revealed in personal accounts, in a way that gives priority to individual explanations of actions rather than to methods that filter and sort responses into predetermined conceptual categories" (Jones, 1983, p. 147).

The point has already been made that much research on autodidaxy has tended to compartmentalize existing and new understandings, to uncouple learners' intentions from their approaches, and to submerge or ignore how people construct meaning in their lives and interpret and define their actions. Learning journals are one way in which researchers may be able to gain an integrated understanding of how learners think and feel.

For instance, in his research work in a distance education setting, Parer (1988) wanted to explore how students experience correspondence study and to answer questions such as "What do they hope to gain from external study . . . ? How do [they] handle particular study guides and assignment materials? What is the nature of the social context in which external study occurs? . . . [in short] what is it 'really like' to undertake external study?" (p. 1). To answer these and related questions, he simply provided a group of volunteer subjects with small desk diaries in which they were asked to record both what they were doing when studying and how they felt about it.

Although this approach yielded many insights of value to the researcher, according to Parer, "The open-ended diaries . . .

do not seem to have encouraged students to be reflective about their studies" (p. 6). Greater guidance to the diarists about what to record is called for. Cell (1984) asked learners to keep a learning journal in which they documented their activities, their emotions during different phases of these activities, and any patterns and interrelationships they were able to discern. Similarly, Feldman (1980) asked learners to maintain a diary or journal while at the same time attempting to learn something entirely new to them. As discussed in Chapter Twelve, Feldman was interested in identifying the actual stages through which an independent learner passed in mastering a subject. He found that diary writing was in itself valuable in helping learners to conceptualize their learning in fresh, new ways.

Lukinsky (1990) goes even further. He argues that keeping a journal can be beneficial at all stages in a learning event. According to him, a person who habitually maintains a diary can often detect the intention and the need to learn something new in a "fragile, emerging sense of the problem" (p. 218) and that he or she is able to capture these "embryonic insights" that would otherwise be lost entirely or perhaps "squashed by the flow of others' ideas" (p. 218). During the actual learning process, writing a journal or diary provides "a pause in the learning activity [that] allows the individual or group to reflect upon what is now being learned" (p. 218). Finally, if a learner has maintained a journal during a period of active learning, he or she has an intimate record on which to reflect — about not only what has been learned but also how. Thus a learning journal is not just a valuable resource for researchers but also a source of insight and self-awareness for learners, assisting them to recreate the origins of their learning and to identify critical turning points in their learning projects.

Recurrent Interviews During the Learning Project. Whereas Feldman asked learners to maintain a diary or journal during their "metahobby" projects, Taylor (1979, 1980, 1986, 1987) attempted to capture the process of learning on one's own by interviewing eight respondents (six women and two men) each week for thirteen weeks as they worked through personally selected learning projects. They were also interviewed again several months later. Based on a content analysis of the interview transcripts, she hypothesized the existence of four phases or "seasons," which she labeled *detachment, divergence, engagement, and convergence.* According to Taylor (1980), these four occur in an invariant sequence though, as she mentions, "It is only near the end of a long process that we become conscious, able to name the direction of our learning" (p. 197).

In a subsequent reanalysis of the same interview data, Taylor (1986, 1987) renamed the four phases and identified four transitions that she claims "occur in a consistent order around a particular learning theme or problem being worked on" (1987, p. 183). These four phases and associated transition points are summarized briefly as follows:

- *Disconfirmation* (phase transition) — a major discrepancy between expectations and experience
- *Disorientation* — a period of intensive disorientation and confusion accompanied by a crisis of confidence and withdrawal from other people who are associated with the source of confusion
- *Naming the Problem* (phase transition) — naming the problem without blaming self and others
- *Exploration* — beginning with relaxation with an unresolved issue, an intuitively guided, collaborative, and open-ended exploration with a gathering of insights, confidence and satisfaction
- *Reflection* (phase transition) — a private reflective review
- *Reorientation* — a major insight or synthesis experience simultaneous with a new approach to the learning (or teaching) task
- *Sharing the Discovery* (phase transition) — testing out the new understanding with others
- *Equilibrium* — a period of equilibrium in which the new perspective and approach is elaborated, refined and applied [1987, p. 183; emphasis added]

Taylor (1986, p. 86) portrays these phases as a spiral or helix, arguing that "the disorientation phase arises out of an experience of equilibrium similar to the final phase described here." Taylor (1987, pp. 190–191) shows that over the period of thirteen weeks during which they were interviewed, some learners managed to complete a full cycle and even to begin a second one, while others only engaged in two of a possible four phases:

"Learners in this study proceeded at different paces in this cycle, though the sequence of experience was common."

Taylor's work is particularly interesting for the way it integrates with several other researchers' work. Like Mezirow (1981), she posits disorientation or "the collapse of the learner's frame of reference or 'assumptive world' " as the starting point for the learning process (1987, p. 184). In common with Feldman (1980), she suggests an invariant sequence to the learning cycle, but with a varied pace, and like Spear and Mocker (1981, 1984), she advances something very like the concept of the "organizing circumstance" to capture the idea that the outcome of one phase becomes the starting point for the next. She shares with Peters, Johnson, and Lazzara (1981) a view that much self-directed learning is an attempt to solve a problem, and with Frewin (1976, 1977) the need to accept ambiguity, especially during the exploratory phases of the learning project. Perhaps most significantly, however, she shares with a growing number of researchers a distinct concern with research that is too often conducted from the educator's point of view, rather than "from the learners' perspective" (Boud and Griffin, 1987).

The Heuristic Nature of Autodidactic Learning. Despite the range of research approaches that have been utilized in studying autodidaxy, the heuristic and somewhat unpredictable nature of the process has become abundantly clear. Various researchers have noted the impact of random events on the progress of a learning endeavor and the constant reorganization of intentions and plans as the project unfolds. Taylor (1980), for instance, found that learners were not able to state with precision what they expected or even hoped to learn. In fact, they only engaged fully and actively in learning once they were "able to relax without certainty as to an end state." She goes on, "By attempting to plan programs on the basis of asking learners to specify objectives at the outset, we are likely limiting the usefulness of such opportunities to that of consolidating old understandings, not coming to new ones" (p. 197). The same point is made by Frewin (1976, 1977) in his study of goal-setting behavior in autodidaxy, and by Burstow (1984, p. 200), who comments: "If I am authentically learning, if I am truly spiralling, I will not be able to predict where I will go with accuracy. If I can predict with accuracy, there is a sense in which I already know what I am purporting to learn; there is a way in which I have already arrived at where I have decided to go. At the very least, I am not giving myself fully to the process as indeed I must if authentic learning is to occur. The goal specified in the learning contract — do not forget — is not the true goal. The true goal, as Sartre had indicated, is what we desire at the end, not what we desire at the beginning."

These findings confront the researcher with something of a challenge. Clearly, autodidacts, in common with other learners, do not enter into a learning engagement without some goal or purpose in mind. Equally clearly, the autodidactic process is a complex and unpredictable one, which unfolds as it goes along. Although some autodidacts are no doubt more methodical and systematic than others, the nature of learning something entirely new (or solving a problem) precludes the setting of objectives at the outset. A complicating factor is that autodidactic learning occurs in "natural societal settings" (Jensen, 1960) or everyday learning contexts, rather than in laboratories or classrooms.

In studying such a phenomenon, therefore, what is called for are research methods that are sufficiently flexible to adapt to the constantly shifting perspective from which learners define and redefine their purposes (Thomas and Harri-Augstein, 1985, p. 310). Those studies that have employed naturalistic techniques (Hiemstra and others, 1981; Merriam and others, 1983; Lincoln and Guba, 1985) in order to portray learning in its "natural habitat" (Häyrynen and Häyrynen, 1980; Larsson and Helmstad, 1985; Marton and Säljö, 1976a, 1976b; Svensson, 1989; Thomas and Harri-Augstein, 1985) have revealed how rich and informative such an approach can be. With rare exceptions, such as Danis and Tremblay (1985a, 1985b) and Taylor (1979, 1980, 1986, 1987), this perspective has not been applied to the study of autodidaxy, and evidence is presented here from other bodies of research to support the claim that it is an appropriate approach to the study of self-directed learning.

Sources of Information

Most autodidactic learning projects are concerned with some substantive content or other, and this necessitates the learner's making use of various sources of information. Many researchers who have established the existence, direction, or duration of autodidactic projects have also inquired as to the sources of information that autodidacts use.

When someone sets out to learn something entirely new to them, it seems clear that they will make use of a variety of resources and, at the beginning at least, this is more likely to be on the basis of ready availability than any "objective" measure of their appropriateness. Since the range of resources used is limited only by the imagination or ingenuity of the learner, it is, for all practical purposes, limitless. Moreover, it is difficult to collect reliable information because of questions of definition. In her research, McCreary (1984) found that it was often difficult to distinguish "sources" of information from "channels" used. One person using a library might claim to have used a human planner (the reference librarian) while another classifies this as a nonhuman planner, because he or she has in mind a book or even the library as an institution. For these reasons, aggregate lists of sources consulted, which abound in the literature, are of only passing interest.

Not unexpectedly, most autodidacts in this society make extensive use of printed material, and accordingly "reading . . . is an especially important learning activity in many self-planned learning projects" (Tough, 1979a, p. 119). This fact has provided the basis for considerable research on "adult independent study" by librarians. It has also attracted the attention of publishers—both academic and popular (Rogers, 1979)—and of researchers such as Rothkopf (1976) with a special interest in learning from the printed word. The fact that so much emphasis is placed on the written word clearly has important implications for those with limited literacy skills, and this may in turn influence the nature of the learning projects undertaken by poorly educated adults.

Although functional illiteracy may act as a barrier to some adults' undertaking learning projects, the increasing availability of various forms of advanced technology—especially radio and television—has heralded a new era in both intentional and incidental learning. We are constantly bombarded with information by the electronic media, to the extent that, as Brookfield (1986, p. 25) observes, it "is not a river of messages, symbols and images into which we occasionally dip, but rather an ocean in which we perpetually swim." This superabundance of potential information has brought in its wake new problems, not the least of which is the need for adults to become "media literate" (Brookfield, 1986).

In part, this necessitates the development of an informed skepticism about the messages and values portrayed in the media, including a deliberate demystification of the ways in which the media might be used to manipulate people's thoughts and feelings. In part, too, it involves forms of media that are more interactive and therefore more subject to the control of the learner. A television broadcast, for instance, occurs at a predetermined time and pace, and the autodidact has relatively little opportunity to stop it, to analyze, to reflect, or to disagree, because it is basically "one-way." A videotape of the same information, however, although it is still "one-way," can at least be played at the convenience of the learner, interrupted, replayed, and discussed with others. Thus the learner has enhanced control over the medium and more time for considered reaction and response.

In considering the subject of interactive electronic sources of information, it is necessary to discuss what is arguably the most potent of all, namely microcomputers (Tough, 1979a, p. 124). In his exciting and provocative book about the future of education, Gooler (1986, pp. 178–179) envisages a time when the "Education Utility" might parallel other familiar utilities such as electricity, telephone, gas, and water services, by channeling learning resources, via computers, direct into schools, libraries, offices, factories, and even homes: "The potential of the Utility as a cornerstone of the lifelong learning society is awesome. One can envision a society in which adults freely and regularly explore new worlds of knowledge and information, even more so than today. Available statistics indicate that large numbers of adults pursue various kinds of learning projects. Given widespread availability of the Utility, I predict even more in the future will pursue their own learning activities. . . . Furthermore, I expect the Utility will encourage more networking among adult learners. . . . The Utility may, in fact, create a kind of seamless education system, blurring some of the current very sharp demarcations between elementary/secondary, higher and adult education activities. Learning may become genuinely 'lifelong.' "

Turning from the future to the present, it is interesting and potentially useful to discover, for instance, that farmers use commercial radio and university field days as important learning resources (Bayha, 1983), that adult education directors find interpersonal learning cliques a useful source of professional knowledge (Beder, Darkenwald, and Valentine, 1983), and that self-taught experts and avid hobbyists use other enthusiasts as resources and supports for their learning (Brookfield, 1981b). According to Shackelford (1983), African-American adults use acquaintances as their most frequent resource, a finding also reported by Booth (1979a, 1976b) with low-income adults. Librarians would certainly be interested, and perhaps somewhat troubled, by Shirk's (1983) finding that libraries and librarians were ranked low by adults as learning resources.

Up to now, the dominant approach to research on sources of information has been to consider the inherent qualities or characteristics of the source itself. However, what is of equal and perhaps even greater interest and importance is the learner's judgment about the resource. What value or potential is it seen as having from the point of view of the individual, and how confident does he or she feel about using it? Suggestions for such research are given in Chapter Fifteen.

Assistance with Learning Projects

Perhaps of greatest interest to the practicing adult educator is research on the assistance required by autodidacts. As early as 1964, Miller pointed out that "if we are to become serious about developing the autonomous learner, the nature of the helping relationship is an extremely important matter to investigate, and should constitute a research objective of high priority in adult education" (p. 225). In the same year, Solomon (1964, pp. v–vi), in his introduction to a book about continuing learners, declared that "it is important . . . to know of the kinds of behaviors and roles taken by [self-teachers] in relation to family, friends, associates, and the larger society."

It was from these early cues that Tough took the direction for his research. In his earliest published monograph, entitled appropriately *Learning Without a Teacher: A Study of Tasks and Assistance During Adult Self-Teaching Projects,* Tough (1967, p. 29) wrote: "When one first thinks about self-teaching, it seems reasonable to assume that the self-teacher learns without much assistance from any other person. . . . [But] after conducting several exploratory interviews and analyzing his own self-teaching, it became evident to the writer that some self-teachers obtained assistance with several major tasks from a fairly large number of persons and that some of this assistance clearly influenced the self-teacher's progress. Each assistant provided advice and information, renewed the learner's confidence and enthusiasm, or assisted in some other important way. Selecting and reaching an appropriate assistant was sometimes very difficult or time-consuming for the self-teacher, but failure to obtain the assistance could hinder or even halt his progress."

Tough (1967, pp. 29–30) suggested four major reasons why an autodidact might seek assistance with his or her learning: first, unfamiliarity with the field or its terms and concepts and therefore not knowing where to begin; second, lack of knowledge about the steps required to master the subject or skill being learned; third, the need for emotional support and encouragement; and finally, help with specific problems or items of information as the learning proceeds. He also developed a typology for categorizing types of assistants: "In the present study, friends, neighbors and relatives were divided into those who were especially close (intimates) and those who were not (acquaintances). Subject matter experts were divided into those who were approached primarily because of a personal relationship and those who were not. Two other categories, librarians and fellow learners, were added" (1967, p. 31).

Several investigators have since noted the type or amount of assistance sought and obtained by autodidacts, frequently using Tough's classificatory scheme to report their findings (for instance, Robinson, 1983). Others, however, have attempted to classify the type of assistance sought, rather than the type of assistant.

One investigator who has studied in detail the help sought by autodidacts is Tremblay (1981, 1983). Based on semistructured interviews with twenty experienced autodidacts, she obtained some 2,000 statements concerning various forms of help that self-directed learners sought. These were then content-analyzed to generate a classification scheme concerning needs for help, difficulties encountered, criteria for selecting a resource, and finally the competencies and qualities of a helper. Under this last heading, Tremblay identifies four themes: management of the learning project, content expertise, communication skills, and interpersonal relationships. Not unexpectedly, respondents noted the need for help with planning, organizing, and evaluating their learning projects, and they therefore commonly sought out people who were experts and able to suggest further resources to assist with their learning projects.

According to Tremblay (1983, p. 235), an ideal helper needs to be a good listener in order to grasp what an autodidact needs as well as an effective communicator to explain and clarify points of difficulty or confusion. He or she needs to be flexible, to adjust to the needs of the learner, and above all, as discussed in Chapter One, neither to deprive the learner of "ownership" of the situation nor to force his or her point of view onto the learner.

The helper also requires certain interpersonal skills. Respondents in Tremblay's study commonly mentioned warmth; inspiring confidence in themselves and encouraging self-confidence in the learner; showing respect for, and interest in, the learner; and providing encouragement as often as needed. Both Tremblay and Burstow stress the authentic responsive nature of the relationship between an autodidact and the people selected as assistants. Burstow (1984, p. 199) writes that "meaningful learning, meaningful change, according to a Sartrean paradigm, is not facilitated by detachment or technical know-how. It is not facilitated either by creating a vacuum or bombarding the learner with highly adroit flipchart diagrams or multimedia presentations. It is facilitated by intimate understanding, by concern, by involvement. . . . What follows from this is the notion that self-directed learning itself needs to be modified to make more room for the 'other.' "

Tremblay (1981, p. 70) emphasizes that the relationship between an autodidact and his or her assistants cannot be reduced to a formula: "De plus, il souligne que l'aidant ne devrait pas être prisonnier, d'une seule approche ou d'un choix déterminé de techniques. . . ."

From the foregoing, it can be seen that assisted autodidaxy requires the helper to have some subject matter expertise but perhaps more important to have a genuine responsiveness to the needs of the learner. Moreover, the ideal relationship is not, as some have depicted it, a technical one — with the helper acting merely as a resource person — but includes a substantial component of warmth, empathy, authenticity, and interpersonal contact. As Garrison (1987, p. 312) points out, this is also the aim of those working to support self-directed learners through distance education. Such people have sought to develop appropriate and supportive access to learning opportunities "in the convenience of the home, workplace or community . . . through their pioneering and creative application of new communications technology." There are no simple guidelines for an educator to follow; such relationships take time to establish and depend on mutual respect and candor. The person offering assistance to the learner must first and foremost have an interest in the learner's welfare as a person, and this is something that cannot be feigned, just as a lack of interest cannot be disguised.

Considering the apparent importance to successful learning of the relationship that exists, or might exist, between an autodidact and his or her assistants, it is surprising how relatively little research has been undertaken on it. There are, however, four similar relationships about which a reasonable amount is known, and these may be taken as partial analogies from which to draw parallels. They are the relationship between a mentor and protégé, between an adviser and a graduate student, between a counselor and a client, and finally between a librarian and a library user. Each of these four will be considered in order to assess the insights they offer into the role of the assistant or helper in autodidactic learning situations.

The Mentoring Relationship. The first of the relationships that resembles, and arguably embodies elements of, assisted autodidaxy is the mentoring relationship, which has been extensively researched in both corporate (Bolton, 1980; Clawson, 1979, 1980; Missirian, 1980; Phillips-Jones, 1982; Woodlands Group, 1980) and educational contexts (Bova and Phillips, 1984; DeCoster and Brown, 1982; Lester and Johnson, 1981).

The prototype was Mentor in Homer's *Odyssey,* the tutor to whom Odysseus entrusted his son Telemachus when he set off to fight in the Trojan wars. Mentor played a number of roles, including "that of teacher, father figure, trusted adviser and protector to an inexperienced young man" (Daloz, 1983, p. 24). In the organizational context, mentors are often seen as sponsors or patrons "who can offer the wisdom of years of experience from which to counsel the younger individual as they move ahead in their careers" (Klauss, 1981, p. 489).

In the educational setting, a mentor closely resembles a Rogerian facilitator; the mentor does not assume a traditional authority role, but instead "provides a learning environment . . . and relationship for the protégé to expand his or her learning potentials and goals for himself or herself" (Ruth and Frey, 1983, p. 5). Central to this supportive learning environment is the highly personal nature of the relationship between a learner and a mentor, for "if there is disharmony between the mentor and protégé, such as tension arising when the protégé becomes overly dependent or condescending towards the mentor, then learning will not be achieved" (Klauss, 1981, p. 491).

In the same way that a nondirective teacher does not impose learning goals on a learner, the mentor helps the protégé to focus on goal setting, particularly in the areas of personal development and learning experiences, without determining how the protégé should think or behave. As Daloz (1983, p. 27) expresses it, "The trick for the teacher or, in this case, the mentor is to recognize the agenda or goal on which the learner is already embarked, and which the teacher can only facilitate or thwart, but not himself invent."

According to Levinson and others (1978, p. 98), mentoring is "defined not in terms of the formal role, but in terms of the character of the relationships and the function it serves: a mentor's primary function is to be a transitional figure. . . ." The mentors gradually withdraw as the learners or protégés "grow in their own sense of intellectual competence, as well as in their sense of purpose, their feelings of autonomy, and their personal integrity" (Bova and Phillips, 1984, p. 16). Because the mentoring relationship is a transitional one, its character is likely to change over time, and Bova and Phillips (1984) cite a six-stage developmental model of mentoring (see Table 6.1).

Table 6.1. Developmental Model of the Mentoring Relationship.

1	2	3	4	5	6
Entry	Mutual trust building	Risk taking	Teaching of skills	Professional standards	Dissolution

Source: Bova and Phillips, 1984, p. 8. Reprinted with permission.

To the extent that the relationship between a mentor and protégé is analogous to that between an autodidact and his or her assistant(s), the model in Table 6.1 may be a useful way of visualizing the stages or phases through which an autodidact passes in achieving autonomy. This point will be discussed again in Chapters Nine and Ten.

The Supervisory Relationship. The second situation that is seen to be analogous to that of assisted autodidaxy is the relationship that exists between a graduate student and his or her research supervisor. At first sight, these two situations may appear to have little in common: One occurs in a formal educational setting, the other is typically very informal; one concerns the mastery of a body of knowledge to be assessed by outside experts, the other involves solving a particular problem to the satisfaction of the learner; one commonly involves a disparity in age, experience, and status between the two parties, the other is more egalitarian.

Although these are important differences, there are also striking similarities. These revolve around the fact that energy and initiative for learning in both cases reside with the learner; that both situations necessitate a high degree of commitment and independent work by the learner; and that, in the final analysis, the relationship between the parties is still a human relationship rather than a strictly technical or functional one (Bargar and Mayo-Chamberlain, 1983; Sorenson and Kagan, 1967).

In an early study of doctoral students and their supervisors, Sorenson and Kagan (1967) examined the elements of successful supervision. They concluded that far from being a simple matter of selecting students solely on the basis of academic attainment, or even certain personal characteristics, "what is needed instead is a system of selection and guidance that takes into account the abilities, personality traits and expectations of faculty members and students and matches each student to a sponsor with whom he or she will be compatible" (p. 24). Compatibility should, they claim, be based on at least three dimensions: dependence versus independence; nurturance versus distance; and "epistemological preference," which they define as having to do "with beliefs about the nature of truth and knowledge and how they are derived" (p. 24).

A more extended discussion of the components of the supervisory relationship was provided by Rugg and Norris (1975), who used a fifty-one-item questionnaire with graduate psychology students to identify ten first-order factors that affect learner satisfaction with supervision. In descending order, the factors identified were Respect for Students, Structure and Guidance, Research Productivity, Research Methods Expertise, Interpersonal Rapport, Stimulating Teaching, Supervisor Accessibility, Subject Matter Expertise, Faculty Maturity, and Communications Training.

Clearly, several of these dimensions are relevant only to the formal educational context, and have no direct parallel in the situation of autodidaxy. However, it is interesting to note Rugg and Norris's (1975, pp. 51–52) observation that "the importance of factors such as supervisor expertise, accessibility, and rapport along with the predictive strength of the Structure and Guidance dimension suggests that it may be a misconception for faculty to view their role in individualized, non-classroom learning situations as requiring little of their time, effort, or personal guidance. On the contrary, the student views reflected here showed that high ratings of the supervisor and the experience [of learning] tended to be associated with high supervisor involvement." The issue of the need for direct assistance is considered again in discussing the counselor-client relationship later in this section.

In recent years, the personal and interpersonal dimensions of supervision have received even more attention. For instance, in an article on "Cultivating Creative Endeavor in Doctoral Research," Bargar and Duncan (1982, p. 24) state that in the ideal situation, the adviser should "(1) establish an empathic relationship with the student that will enable her to understand, at some optimal level, the cognitive and affective dimensions of the student's research endeavors; (2) help assure that the problem is consonant with the student's own developmental endeavors and her own creative capacities; (3) ensure that the student retains major control of the research problem in all its complexity; and (4) avoid invoking arbitrary time constraints yet openly maintain normative expectations for progress. . . . "

One of the recurring problems in graduate research, and a potential problem for the autodidact seeking help as well, is the issue of "ownership." The intention is "to maximise the student's personal and professional investment in the research problem, thus helping assure the highest level of the student's independence in the scholarly activity" (Bargar and Duncan, 1982, p. 22). In practice, however, ownership of the research often appears to be shared ("Whose scholarly reputation is on the line during the final, oral defense?" [p. 22]). According to Bargar and Duncan (1982, p. 22), there are several indicators that might show when an adviser is taking over a problem from the student: "The most obvious of these appears when the advisor discovers his own solution to some aspect . . . and feels that this is *the correct* solution. There seems to be little harm in the advisor discovering potential solutions to troublesome aspects of the problem . . . [but] the harm seems to grow with the degree of pressure the advisor puts on the student to accept such solutions. . . . "

To avoid the likelihood of ownership subtly being wrested from the grasp of the learner, Bargar and Duncan (1982) suggest the following five ways in which helpers can actually help:

1. Identify potential resources of which the learner may be unaware.
2. Help the learner to refine his or her present understanding.
3. Assist the learner with analyzing the problem, and help to overcome blocks, including emotional blocks. (Heisenberg [1971, p. 210], the physicist, has defined an expert as "someone who knows some of the worst mistakes that can be made in his subject, and how to avoid them." Helpers can intervene at times when "worst mistakes" are most probable.)
4. Encourage the learner to synthesize the most novel, exciting, or important discoveries, without "supplying the learner with his own ready-made insights" (Bargar and Duncan, 1982, p. 27).
5. Provide informed, balanced, and helpful feedback when this seems called for.

This last point is taken up by Phillips (1981) in her research on the experience of British students undertaking doctoral studies. She writes that, over time, "the students gradually imposed their own boundaries of action and time as they learned how to evaluate their work by interpreting the feedback for themselves, instead of relying on their supervisors to do this for them." She goes on,

> At first, the postgraduates had been unable to do this, but most of them gradually acquired the ability to perceive, interpret and act upon the information contained in the feedback . . . [and] to reflect on their own performance and evaluate it.
> This resulted in a gradual increase in autonomy so that their perception of the supervisory role changed. Instead of seeing it as one of tutor, primarily concerned with generating external approval and information, the supervisory role was perceived as one of colleague [p. 12].

Three important points for the study and practice of autodidaxy emerge from this analysis. The first is that, once again, the personal dimension in the supervisory role is emphasized. The supervisor is no more a "mere resource" to the student than the mentor is to the protégé; in both cases, the relationship bears a marked similarity to the situation of an autodidact seeking help with a learning project. The second is the issue of "ownership." Has the helper actually relinquished control or is she or he exerting subtle pressure on the learner to "do things my way"? It will be recalled from Chapter One that the sense of ownership is one feature that distinguishes autodidaxy from learner-control. The third point is whether or not learners have the sense of being "in command" of the learning situation: Have they accepted responsibility for such functions as imposing their own boundaries on time and action and evaluating their own work, or are they still "relying on their supervisors to do this for them" (Phillips, 1981, p. 12)?

The Counseling Relationship. As with the situation of the graduate student, most writers on counseling stress the need for the client (or learner) to maintain "ownership" of the situation. If the counselor takes over by telling the client what to think or how to behave, the client can become dependent rather than independent. The relationship between counseling (in the form of therapy) and education is widely accepted. Educators frequently talk in terms of diagnosis, of prescription, of analysis and remediation; indeed the language of counseling has infiltrated much of the discourse of adult education (Candy, 1986; Harris, Legge, and Merriam, 1981).

Many adult educators are familiar with the work of Carl Rogers and his notion of student-centered teaching, but as he makes perfectly plain, student-centered teaching is simply the educational analogue of client-centered therapy, and this connection is a recurring theme in his book *Freedom to Learn*. In that book, Rogers (1969, pp. 164–166) outlines a number of roles for the facilitator of learning, which are highly relevant for the person seeking to help the autodidact:

1. Setting a supportive climate of inquiry
2. Helping to elicit and clarify the purposes of the learner
3. Relying on the learner to implement those purposes that have meaning for him/her as the motivational force behind significant learning
4. Organizing, and making available, a wide range of resources
5. Regarding him- or herself as a flexible resource
6. Accepting both intellectual and emotional expressions from the learner
7. Collaborating as a co-learner and equal partner
8. Being authentic in sharing both thoughts and feelings with the learner
9. Being alert to the expression of strong feelings (such as anger, pain, or conflict) by the learner, and being empathic rather than judgmental
10. Recognizing his or her own limitations, and acknowledging the difficulties of establishing really deep, meaningful interpersonal relationships with the learner

In order for a teacher or trainer to be able to respond appropriately to the learner's (or client's) needs in such a nonjudgmental, noninterventionist, and supportive way, personal qualities such as empathy, respect, authenticity, and warmth are frequently cited as desirable. But in the same way that nondirective counseling is not always appropriate in the health care situation, nondirective teaching is not always appropriate in the learning situation. The counselor is not simply a mechanic of the emotions, but also needs to have excellent skills of communication and analysis; so too the person assisting a learner needs a combination of skills. In fact, it is perhaps this perspective that encouraged Curran (1972) to claim that the distinction between counseling and education is a false one, in his formulation of *Counseling-Learning: A Whole Person Model for Education*.

He notes that counseling is, for many people, associated exclusively with the emotions, whereas education is concerned solely with the intellect. However, people are not compartmentalized in this way. Hostler (1981, p. 33) expresses it thus: "A person is far more than an embodied intellect: he or she has also a moral conscience, an aesthetic sense, a wide range of emotions and a spiritual sensibility, besides many idiosyncrasies of taste and temperament, which we significantly call 'personality.' Criticism has grown in recent years of the way adult educators have tended to ignore all these other facets of the self (Alexander, 1975, p. 23) and their current concern is to promote a more rounded and comprehensive kind of growth."

It seems, then, that despite the widespread and somewhat uncritical acceptance of Rogers's ideas in adult education, the nondirective approach is not universally welcome, nor is it always appropriate, even when dealing with self-directed learners. The nondirective approach has come under challenge in the health sciences, where it has been shown to be inappropriate and unacceptable for some clients, especially when they are seeking direct guidance. In the same way, as already mentioned in this chapter, autodidacts seek both emotional support and direct assistance with content, and, in the latter case, a nondirective approach and a failure to answer specific questions could increase learner frustration and perhaps even extinguish the first tentative sparks of interest in a learning project.

The process of helping an independent learner is every bit as complex and demanding as that of counseling a client. In the same way that there are times for direct confrontation and correction in a counseling relationship, there are also times for clear responses and unequivocal answers (where they exist) in helping someone to learn.

The Librarian-Client Relationship. A fourth analogy for assisted autodidaxy is the relationship that does, or at least can, exist between a librarian and a client. Perhaps surprisingly, some of the best research on autodidaxy (referred to as *adult independent study* in the library literature) has been by librarians and information scientists, and some of the most far-reaching and innovative proposals for the provision of support come from the same source.

Libraries have a long connection with self-managed adult learning (Birge, 1979; Burge, 1983; T. Kelly, 1970; Lee, 1966).

As mentioned in Chapter Two, throughout the nineteenth century, particularly in countries such as Australia, Canada, New Zealand, and the United States, the spread of literacy and the establishment of reading rooms accompanied the explosion of interest in many early forms of adult education — mechanics' institutes, literary and scientific societies, adult Sunday schools, and so on. Frontier College, for instance — one of Canada's most spectacular indigenous adult education innovations — grew directly out of the Reading Camp Association (Bradwin, 1928; Fitzpatrick, 1920).

In more recent times, the public library has become the focal point of initiatives to provide educational and self-educational opportunities to a wide range of the adult population (Gould, 1976; Mavor, Toro, and DeProspo, 1976) within a lifelong learning perspective (Conroy, 1980). Although many recent studies have been concerned with questions of organizational policy and institutional access, there has also been a reappraisal of the work of the librarian, changing from a custodial to a more consultative and advisory role (Carr, 1979; Dadswell, 1978; Dale, 1979, 1981; Reilly, 1978, 1981; J. C. Smith, 1986): "The agent and the learner create complex relationships over time, entailing far more than the provision of useful resources and appropriate referrals. . . . Collaboration, reciprocity, and trust lead to empathy, confidence and candor in effective unity and integrity in the learning alliance, and exist beyond the content of the learning" (Carr, 1979, p. ii).

This level of support and interpersonal rapport is far removed from the everyday stereotype of the librarian as a stern guardian of books and of the knowledge they contain. In fact, it raises the question of how librarians *feel* about being approached for help. In a 1986 study, Smith asked a number of public librarians about their perceptions of autodidacts and how best to assist them. As discussed in Chapter Five, despite their reluctance to categorize people, Smith was able to discern two basic types of autodidacts, which she labels *confident learners* and *timid learners*. One librarian indicated how her approach might differ according to how she viewed the learner: "I'd probably be more motherly to the sort of person who looks, you know, weak and in need of lots of support. I'd be more 'jokey' and relaxed with a person who is very confident" (J. C. Smith, 1986, p. 251).

Many of the librarians had a few maxims or rules of thumb for dealing with autodidacts: the importance of *all* questions, the proactive approach, and respecting the user's privacy:

1. The importance of *all* questions
   - "That's it, more than anything: Just being considerate and treating every question like it's important."
   - "We never, *never* give the impression that 'Golly, how can you be so stupid as to ask for that?'"

2. The proactive approach
   - "You don't sit around waiting for the people to come to you, you go out and approach them."
   - "So we definitely don't say, 'The books are over there.' We try to question them and see if the initial question really reflects what they want to know; or if that is just their way of getting into the subject."

3. Respecting the user's privacy
   - "I have to know when to stop and realize there is a limit with some people that I can go."
   - "I think you just have to know at what point you have to stop" [J. C. Smith, 1986, pp. 251–252].

There are several points here that might profitably influence the practice of assisted autodidaxy. The first is the reiteration of the interpersonal nature of the relationships between the learner and the librarian "entailing far more than the provision of useful resources and appropriate referrals" (Carr, 1979, p. ii). The second is the notion of confident and timid learners, and how both self-perceptions and the perceptions of the helper affect the quality of the relationship and the nature of the help given. The third point is that librarians, like qualitative researchers, have to look beyond "the words as they come at you," and find the meaning behind the words. When this meaning is discovered, and the librarian has a better sense of what the learner really wants, "it is possible that the librarian and the learner mutually arrive at a point where truly facilitative interaction takes place" (J. C. Smith, 1986, p. 252).

Self-Direction Versus Other-Direction

If humans were completely autonomous and asocial beings, the concept of self-direction in learning would be unambiguous and relatively easy to identify. However, it is in our nature to be influenced by those around us, especially by significant others in our lives. Accordingly, many of our learning needs derive from membership in various social groupings (classes, families, churches, clubs and societies, occupations, sporting teams, and so on), and much of our learning likewise takes place in the context of such social settings.

Even considering completely individual learning efforts, there are very few that are conceived, planned, and conducted by the autodidact without any outside assistance. In some cases, the self-directed learner will utilize nonhuman planning aids, such as television programs, programmed instructional materials, or workbooks. At other times, he or she will turn for assistance either to individuals (who may be classified as "professional" or "amateur") or to groups (such as workshops or classes). These distinctions are noted by both Tough (1978) and Penland (1979); however, they differ sharply in their findings as to the relative importance of each type of planner.

Whereas Tough (1978) claims that only 3 percent of learning efforts have a nonhuman planner, Penland (1979) claims 22.7 percent, and while Tough shows 73 percent of learning projects to be self-planned, Penland's research reveals that only 25.3 percent are planned by the learner. These differences are clearly significant in the overall pattern of research, although they are almost certainly artifacts of the respective research designs (Penland, 1979, p. 171). Disregarding these differences in percentages, the problem is how to distinguish self-planned from other-planned learning endeavors. Tough himself consistently refers to the "other" or the "hidden" 80 percent of adult learning, and invokes the image of an iceberg (1978, p. 253; see also Brookfield, 1981a) to make the point: "Imagine that the entire range of the adult's learning effort is represented by an iceberg. For many years, adult educators paid attention to the highly visible portion of the iceberg showing above the surface of the water. Attention was focused on professionally guided learning — the providing of courses, classes, workshops, and other learning groups, plus apprenticeship, tutorials, correspondence study, educational television, programmed instruction, and so on. Virtually everyone still agrees that all of this professionally guided learning is an extremely important phenomenon in the world today. At the same time, though, it turns out to be only 20 percent of the total picture, only the visible part of the iceberg. The massive bulk that is hidden below the surface turns out to be 80 percent of the adult's learning efforts. . . . "

There are two drawbacks to this analogy. The first is that it is unclear whether the percentages relate to adult education in total or to the activities of an individual learner. Does it mean that 20 percent of adult learners account for 100 percent of professionally guided adult learning, or that 20 percent of any given adult's learning will be professionally guided? This slippage is evident in the literature.

The second, and more significant, drawback is that it implies a clear, easily identifiable break between the other-planned (above the waterline) and self-planned (submerged) forms of adult learning. But it is not so easy in the real world of learning research to identify whether the learner is "self-directed" or "other-directed." On the one hand, there are instructional situations that are so loose, so informal, so democratic, and so learner-centered that an outside observer would be hard-pressed to say whether the learning was self-planned or not. On the other hand, there are autodidacts who go to experts for help, enroll in courses or workshops, or attend seminars. If the overall goals, the criteria for judging success, and the prerogative to accept or reject the information presented all still rest with the learner, has such a person surrendered the claim to being self-directing? Consider the following scenario:

> In Singleton, in the Hunter Valley, a family comes together for an evening. The talk is about people everyone knows. Then it turns to the crisis in the coal mines. Management, anxious to severely reduce the cost of labour so Australian mines can compete with South African, Brazilian and Chinese mines, is sacking workers and attacking work practices. A miner starts talking

about the inefficiency and rorts [impropriety] of management, which, if eliminated, would help make mines more competitive. Before we know it, we've got a list of management malpractices, from the unnecessary sub-contracting of transport to catered lunches, a list that will never appear in the *Sydney Morning Herald* or on the Channel 10 News. A little later on in the evening, one woman says to another, "You said you wanted to learn how to make rock cakes. Come on, I'll show you." And they bake the cakes and we eat them. A few weeks later, we're up in Singleton again after another family gathering. We're saying goodnight and people are getting into their cars, next to a rose bed. It's a lovely spring night and no-one is in a hurry. We're looking at the roses, which are 25 years old and shooting new growth. In two minutes, I'm taught how to prune roses, where to cut them to make new branches go where you want them to [Foley, 1987, p. 41].

According to Foley, "Education like this goes on all the time, without fuss, without system, without planning and most of all without *self*-direction. People with expertise pass their knowledge and skills on to others in a relaxed and natural way." Of course, the examples given here would probably not pass muster as self-directed learning projects, because they lack both the intentionality and intensity usually associated with such projects. Nevertheless, the issue raised is still valid; how much help or assistance can a learner receive with his or her learning and still claim to be self-directed? To build on Tough's metaphor, it is that part of the iceberg that is sometimes above the surface, sometimes below, glimpsed for an instant, then submerged again beneath the stormy seas of research where there is great potential for confusion, and accordingly this distinction has created both conceptual and practical difficulties for researchers.

As discussed in Chapter One, there are many instances where an autodidact might call on another person for help while retaining the initiative and control over the learning event. An example might involve a learner telephoning an acknowledged expert in his or her field for an answer to a specific inquiry. In this instance, the learner would clearly reserve the right to take or leave the advice, and the person telephoned would in truth be a "resource person." Not all situations are as clearcut as this, however, and there are real difficulties in ascertaining whether or not a learner is still in control of a particular learning endeavor. As discussed in Chapters Four and Five, "self-direction" depends, at least in part, on the learner's own view of the situation. Accordingly, the use of naturalistic and interpretive modes of inquiry is called for in this particular domain of research on autodidaxy.

Self-Directed Learning in the Context of a Group. Before leaving the subject of assistance with autodidactic projects, it is necessary to recognize that not all "self-directed learning" is a solitary activity, and at least some autodidactic projects arise from, and occur within the context of, membership in a group. There is an embryonic research tradition on this particular aspect of autodidaxy, with contributions by Banks (1985), Beder, Darkenwald, and Valentine (1983), Brookfield (1983), Elsey (1974), Luikart (1976, 1977), McCreary (1984), Percy (1981), Ross (1984), and Spath (1982).

As early as 1967, Thomas compared and contrasted the role of "student" with that of "member" in the learning situation. The student role is familiar in schools, colleges and universities, and most mediated adult education. It is typified by external direction of the learning process and by clear role definitions, including a consciousness on the part of the learner of his or her role as a student. The member, on the other hand, "is neither dependent upon institutional authority nor particularly self-conscious about the engagement in learning. It is the collective goal that is important, not individual enhancement, and thus the learning is merely a means to a collective end. The member did not, for the most part, become a member to learn something of advantage to himself, but to do something . . ." (p. 71).

Having established this basic assumption, Thomas (1967, p. 71) goes on to discuss the role of a "teacher" in such a situation:

> The goal is both determined and, to a degree, described in detail by the group, and the teacher is hired to provide help towards that goal. If the teacher deviates too far from the member's perception of the means to that goal, either the group dismisses the teacher, or members begin to drift away from the group. The

teacher carries with him the presumed authority of relevant knowledge and to a certain degree the authority of the institution from
which he comes, but it is a fragile authority which must be proved
and won repeatedly in intercourse with the group. . . .

   The physical venue of this experience is almost always
the learner's familiar action-bound setting—the union hall, the
conference room, the community centre—and the teacher comes
to him rather than he to the teacher.

At least two important implications for research are raised
by this notion of studentship versus membership. First, there
is reason to believe the learning outcomes obtained in situations
of studentship and membership will differ sharply. This is dealt
with in Chapter Ten, in discussing the work of Säljö and others
of the Göteborg group in Sweden. Thus, it would be desirable
for researchers to be able to distinguish these situations from
one another. However, there may be no external differences on
which to base such a distinction. For instance, although it is
most likely that learners in a conventional "school" or training
situation would think of themselves as students, the mere fact
that an activity takes place in the "learner's familiar action-bound
setting" is no guarantee that they would view themselves as members. The distinction is an internal one, made by the learners
themselves, and it would therefore be necessary to refer to the
internal processes, intentions, and understandings of the participants. This perspective is rarely encountered in the literature on autodidaxy.

Second, the "teacher" has only a "fragile authority which
must be proved and won repeatedly." Unlike many learners,
autodidacts have the power to "hire and fire" their helpers, and
thus research on the bases of the assistant's authority and ac-
ceptability in the eyes of the learner would seem to be a profita-
ble direction for research. Both of these possibilities are discussed
in Chapter Fifteen.

Summary

For a long time, the independent learning efforts of adults
were not studied in any systematic way. It was commonly assumed that what adult learners wanted to learn, and the ways

in which they went about undertaking such learning, was their own business and in any case could not be influenced by those working as professional adult educators. Since the early 1960s, however, adult self-directed learning has been exhaustively studied, and a number of people have made suggestions about how adult educators (and others in the community) can best contribute to this aspect of developing a "learning society" (Kidd, 1983, pp. 529–531).

In studying the phenomenon of adult self-directed learning in natural societal settings, the following generalizations seem to be supported. First, very few learning endeavors are entirely self-directed, but depend instead on individual motives and interests shaped and modified through interaction with other people. Thus, self-directed learning rarely exists in its "pure" form and, like personal autonomy, is nearly always a "matter of degree."

Second, accident or serendipity plays an important role in determining the direction that many learning projects take. Chance meetings, offhand comments, resources accidentally discovered or mentioned in conversation, and changing life circumstances all contribute to the form and extent of individual learning projects, and few if any of these features could be anticipated or predicted at the beginning. Linked to this is the nonlinear nature of such learning efforts, which often zigzag from one "organizing circumstance" to the next in an apparently random way.

Third, many autodidactic projects arise from, and seek to resolve, some problem situation. As the nature of the problem either becomes clear, or changes, so the learner is able to focus on different aspects, and this contributes in part to its apparently haphazard progress.

Fourth, most autodidacts are not aware of themselves in the role of learner. This means that approaching them in the role of, and from the perspective of, a teacher or educator may well not meet their perceived needs at that particular time.

Fifth and finally, self-directed learning is rarely completely solitary. It often occurs in the context of a social grouping (a family, work team, club, or community group), and this introduces complexities into the degree of interdependence exhibited by apparently individual learners. The social nature of learning is important for researchers and those who want to help self-directed learners.

Implications for Practice

Much of this book is aimed at structuring education in such a way that adults can be encouraged and empowered to learn things for themselves. Once they accept this challenge, however, they almost invariably turn to others, including sometimes adult educators, for various forms of help. The research reviewed in this chapter suggests that those helping self-directed learners need to recognize the following features:

- The success of a self-directed learning project depends largely on the extent and type of assistance obtained by individual learners, and on the quality of the personal relationships established between the learner and his or her helper(s).
- The quality of the relationship is a function of the perceptions and expectations of both partners, within a context of shared interests and mutual liking and respect.
- The learner is likely to pass through certain stages or phases in the learning endeavor, and the need for assistance will vary accordingly. In particular, there are times when direct input and subject matter expertise are called for, and other times when the main requirement is for emotional support and encouragement.
- The relationship needs to be viewed as a transitional one that is likely to have a definite end point once the learning project is complete, or when the learner has attained a degree of autonomy with respect to the subject matter being learned.
- The assistant should ideally be a good listener and an effective communicator, capable of helping the learner to clarify and articulate his or her needs and purposes and able to respond to the changing needs of the learner as the learning progresses.
- The assistant needs to avoid interfering with the learner's sense of "ownership" of the learning project, or forcing his

or her own point of view onto the learner. However, the assistant might on occasion have to take the initiative by reaching out to the learner if he or she senses that the learner is confused or uncertain about the next step.

- The assistant should help the learner to identify and overcome potential blocks to learning, and in particular, based on his or her past experience, to point out areas that are likely to prove difficult or demanding.

- The assistant should provide informed, balanced, and helpful feedback when requested to do so by the learner, while at the same time helping the learner to become "self-correcting" and to internalize the evaluative criteria that distinguish an expert from a novice in the domain of learning.

Above all, assistance must be viewed not as a purely technical or functional relationship, but as an act of sharing, marked by warmth, empathy, and authenticity. If the massive structure of human civilization has been built through many individual acts of learning such as that in which our earliest progenitor shaped a stone tool, the mortar that holds it together is cooperation: "Humans could not have evolved in the remarkable way in which we undoubtably have unless our ancestors were strongly co-operative creatures. The key to the transformation of a social ape-like creature into a cultural animal living in a highly structured and organized society is sharing . . ." (Leakey and Lewin, 1977, pp. 10–11).

At the dawn of civilization, this cooperation was limited to sharing jobs and food; in our present age, we share more intangible things such as knowledge, skill, and wisdom. In the chapter that follows, self-directed learning within instructional settings will be considered, but always against a backdrop of the essentially social nature of human teaching and learning.

Seven

Learner Control
of Instruction

It is impossible to say with certainty when teaching first occurred, but common sense would suggest that the very earliest forms of instruction were relatively informal and consisted of parents teaching their children or of people sharing with others in their family or tribal group insights about survival in their harsh primitive environment.

However, as the social complexity of human existence increased, so too did the need to store information, and to communicate it both horizontally, between groups, and vertically, between generations. This then gave rise to more formal types of instruction. Aside from the teaching and learning that inevitably took place within families and other small social groupings, at various times and in various cultures it has been the practice to take some people aside to instruct them specifically in tasks and areas of knowledge considered vital to the continuation of the culture.

In preliterate societies, these chosen individuals were singled out to become repositories of the collective knowledge and wisdom of the entire group: living libraries, in a sense. They were accorded a special status by the community, and were deliberately taught, usually by elders who themselves had earlier been marked to bear the responsibility of cultural preservation. The methods of instruction varied from situation to situation, but conventionally the transmission of knowledge was oral, often supported by an elaborate system of images, symbols, and rituals to help to fix the meaning in the learners' minds.

Learning in situations like this was governed by three factors that distinguish it from much — though not all — of the learning that takes place in contemporary Western cultures. First, the learner was not acting on his or her own behalf, but rather in the interests of the larger community. Thus the learner subjugated personal ambition to the common good. Second, the body of knowledge to be mastered was finite and either static or at most only slowly changing. Third, there was the belief, agreed and assented to by both parties, that the teacher or elder knew more than the learner. This acknowledged difference in status implied that the teacher should be the architect of the learning experience, and the learner or novice should submit to the teacher's sovereignty.

About 5,000 years ago, in civilizations that we recognize as precursors of our own — in Egypt and Babylonia, Judea, Greece and Rome — teachers began to emerge in a variety of guises: priests, prophets, poets, philosophers, and pedagogues. As with preliterate societies, such people were usually accorded a special status because the ability to read and write gave them access to temple, commercial, and court records, as well as to the accumulated wisdom of earlier ages. Although mastering the intricacies of reading and writing involved an arduous apprenticeship, students willingly submitted themselves to the discipline of instruction. Again, this was partly out of a sense of duty or responsibility, but personal ambition also figured in their motivation; once they had acquired the esoteric mysteries to which an education introduced them, they could then take their places alongside the teachers as custodians of culture.

However, if the advent of writing assured teachers of a certain elite status in the ancient world (Castle, 1970, p. 3), it was the invention of printing and the subsequent spread of literacy that, perhaps more than anything else, signaled an end to their intellectual monopoly: "The advent of the printed word created an intellectual emancipation for millions, resulting in a degree of freedom from interpreters of the learning environment — priest, pedagogue or prophet — never known before" (Br bner, 1973, p. 2). This dramatic change was felt most immediately and most intensely in the church, where the infallibility of the priestly class was called into question once adherents were in a position to read scriptures for themselves. But it was only a matter of time before secular education was also transformed, when the opinions of various authors could be analyzed and compared and the utterances of teachers could be challenged.

This is not to say that critical analysis and discussion were unknown before printing; there is a long and well-established tradition of discussion, disputation, and debate about the meaning of ancient authorities and prophetic precedents. However, this was usually confined to "experts"—scholars, scribes, and statesmen—and did not conventionally extend to the learners themselves. It is the democratization of learning and willingness to allow learners to control parts of the instructional process that distinguishes present-day education both from its ancient counterpart and from educational approaches that still prevail in many traditional and preliterate societies.

In this chapter, I will examine briefly what is meant by learner-control and the various domains over which it is logically and practically possible to give learners control. I will consider the arguments that have been advanced in its favor, especially in adult education, and examine evidence both for and against the devolution of responsibility to learners for various instructional functions. It will be argued that, despite its alleged learner-centeredness, much of the research and writing on this subject is from a teacher-dominant perspective, and that comparatively little research has been conducted on the issue of learner-control from the perspective of learners themselves. This then leads to a discussion of the implications of increasing learner-control within formal instructional settings, and in particular of the difficulties experienced by many teachers in making the transition. The chapter concludes with an analysis of the view of learners and learning that are implicit in most current conceptualizations of learner-control in adult education.

Learner-Control Versus Teacher-Control

Until recently, in schools, in colleges and universities, and indeed in adult education itself, the most common model of education has been teacher-directed. To a greater or lesser extent, the objectives, content, pacing, sequence, methodology, and evaluation were all in the hands of the teacher, to whom learners had to submit themselves in order to be "taught." However, "it is becoming increasingly evident to observers of educational trends that the traditional role of the instructor is now changing more rapidly and profoundly than at any time in history" (Brabner, 1973, p. 1). Many educationists have begun to recognize that teacher-controlled instruction is unwieldy, undemocratic, and unsound as a way of conducting education, and that (especially with respect to the education of adults) it ought to be abandoned in favor of a greater degree of learner-control (Schuttenberg and Tracy, 1987; Toppins, 1987).

Differing Levels of Learner-Control. As discussed in Chapter One, it is possible for learners to exert a greater or smaller degree of control over certain aspects of the instructional situation. Accordingly, learner-control is not a single, unitary concept, but rather a continuum along which various instructional situations may be placed. Similarly, because it is possible to have differing levels of learner-control, it is also possible for people to demonstrate differing levels of commitment to the construct of learner-control. For some people, it implies a significant and profound shift in the locus of responsibility for critical and valued instructional functions. For others, however, increased learner-control is achieved through various forms of individualized instruction.

Some two decades ago, Clark (1973, pp. 10–11) wrote: "For some time, educational literature has reflected an increasing interest in individualizing the processes of instruction. Consequently, frequent reference is made to individual study, independent study, and self-directed learning. While most of the learning occurring under these various terms does accommodate individual needs and self-pacing, they are still very much under the direction and supervision of an instructor or educational agent."

In terms of the conceptual scheme developed in this book, simply individualizing, or for that matter even personalizing, a program of instruction is not synonymous with learner-control, although it may represent a first step toward that goal. In this book, it is argued that creating individual programs does not necessarily increase the learner's control over the instructional situation; indeed, ironically, it may do the reverse. If learners are "locked into" a predetermined program of instruction, even though it has been specifically designed to meet their apparent needs, there may be relatively little room for them to follow up interests as they change and develop. In the United Kingdom, during the 1970s for instance, there were many experiments in higher education designed to increase the independence of students. But, as Percy and Ramsden (1980, p. 5) state, "The 'independence' involved was [often] conceived as a means of promoting student motivation, of adjusting the pace of academic work to take account of student differences and of developing better specific problem-solving techniques. In real senses the students were not independent of their teachers at all. A teacher does not have to be physically present for learning to be teacher-dependent. Project work, distance learning, resource-based learning, Keller Plan, programmed learning, essay writing, seminar preparation, background reading: all of these may or may not incorporate elements of student control over learning, but by no means do they imply independence."

This book is not concerned with those educational approaches that simply grant some degree of flexibility in pacing, sequencing, or even methodology, while still retaining for the instructor the major prerogatives of determining objectives and assessing learning outcomes. Although such approaches may indeed make for more flexible and responsive educational programs, they do not in any significant way shift the locus of control from the teacher to the learner, and bear only a superficial resemblance to the situation of autodidaxy discussed in Chapters One and Six. There are, however, many initiatives and educational innovations that do seek to devolve to learners decisive control over significant elements in the instructional situation.

In Chapter One, I used a sliding scale or continuum to express this changing balance of authority on the part of the teacher and responsibility on the part of the learner. Such a diagram has several useful purposes: (1) it makes it possible to visualize an otherwise abstract relationship; (2) it expresses the notion of reciprocity and equilibrium in the teaching/learning situation; (3) it implies the idea of gradual or progressive change from one model (teacher-controlled) to another (learner-controlled); (4) it suggests that the movement from dependence on the instructor to independence from the instructor may be a developmental sequence; (5) it shows that even in highly teacher-controlled situations there is still some residue of learner-control; and (6) perhaps most important, it implies the reverse, namely that even in the most liberal of learner-controlled situations, the teacher may still, in the eyes of the learner, have some residual authority to make decisions binding on the learner (Chené, 1983, p. 44). This last point is particularly important for those who believe that it is possible for a trainer or instructor ultimately to become both invisible and redundant. This matter will be discussed again in Part Four.

Despite all these advantages, it must be remembered that the diagram is a greatly oversimplified representation of reality. Perhaps its greatest drawback is that it implies control is a unidimensional construct. However, if one attempts to answer the question "Learner-control of what?" it soon becomes apparent that learner-control is a multidimensional entity. Many authors have attempted to specify what these various dimensions are.

Dimensions of Learner-Control. In their 1979 study *Moving Toward Self-Directed Learning,* Della-Dora and Blanchard write that "there are differing degrees of teacher directedness as there are of self-directedness and so a range of possibilities is described to illustrate the two modes as points between them . . . in areas of: (1) deciding what is to be learned, (2) selecting methods and materials for learning, (3) communicating with others about what is being learned, and (4) evaluating achievement of goals" (p. 5).

A European meeting of experts on various forms of autonomy in learning, held in 1979 under the auspices of Unesco, identified five components along which learners could vary from one another: setting objectives, duration and pacing of learning, pedagogical methods, selecting learning aids and media to be used, and evaluation of learning outcomes (Jankovic and others, 1979, pp. 12–14). Another way of considering autonomy in learning was offered by Boud and Bridge (1974), who identified four linked dimensions to learner-control. These are: PACE (that is, times and places at which the learner finds it most convenient and appropriate to learn), CHOICE (by which they mean the overall choice of which course, or part of a course, to study, including the selection of minor and major options), METHOD (selecting between modes — individualized study packages, lectures, and traditionally organized courses — selection of texts, and so on), and CONTENT (choosing precisely what to learn according to one's personal goals and interests).

Probably the most comprehensive analysis of the components of learner-control is that offered by Cottingham (1977), who proposed a six-part "classification system for independent learning." According to Cottingham (1977, p. ii), "An independent learner is one who comes to control his or her own learning through the acquisition and mastery of instructional principles, techniques, and methodologies enabling the student to plan and arrange conditions for successful learning." The following list constitutes the classes and subclasses of the classification system for independent learning as identified in that research:

1. Learner-control of the instructional event
   - Maintaining contact with the instructional event
   - Using indirect learning guidance
   - Using direct learning guidance
   - Responding to the instructional event
   - Controlling feedback

2. Learner-control of evaluation
   - Evaluating achievement
   - Evaluating progress

3. Learner clarification of goals
   - Specifying behaviors
   - Developing standards of performance

4. Learner-control of diagnosis
   - Diagnosing performance levels
   - Diagnosing performance problems

5. Learner-control of prescriptive decisions
   - Managing instruction
   - Selecting and developing instructional events

6. Learner-control of motivation
   - Clarifying consequences
   - Controlling the contingencies of reinforcement [Cottingham, 1977, p. ii]

Theoretically at least it would be possible for a learner to be at different levels of autonomy on each of these six dimensions, thus giving rise to various permutations of independence in differing aspects of the learning situation. In recognition of this possibility, Moore (1973b, p. 672) proposed a series of questions to identify the relationship between learners and teachers and to ascertain where control of each instructional process lies:

> Is learning self-initiated and self-motivated?
> Who identifies goals and objectives, and selects problems for study?
> Who determines the pace, the sequence and the methods of information gathering?
> What provision is there for the development of learners' ideas and for creative solutions to problems?
> Is emphasis on gathering information external to the learner?
> How flexible is each instructional process to the requirements of the learner?
> How is the usefulness and quality of learning judged?

According to Moore, the "powers of learning" are manifested in three sets of events, which he called establishment events, executive events, and evaluative events. In his 1983 work, he renamed the components *goal setting, implementation, and evaluation* (p. 164). By asking the preceding questions of any given course or teaching/learning situation, Moore claims that it should be possible to classify any program either as autonomous or nonautonomous on each of the three heads — establishment events, executive events, and evaluative events. This procedure yields a matrix where the program is said to be autonomous (A) or nonautonomous (N) with respect to each domain (see Table 7.1).

Table 7.1. Typology of Programs
Classified by the Degree of Learner Autonomy.

	Establishment	Executive	Evaluative
1	A	A	A
2	A	A	N
3	A	N	A
4	A	N	N
5	N	A	A
6	N	N	A
7	N	A	N
8	N	N	N

Source: Moore, 1972, p. 82. Reprinted with permission.

The paradigmatic case of perfect autonomy (Krimerman, 1972, p. 336) would obtain where the learner had complete control over all three dimensions (AAA), and the extreme case of teacher-control would exist where the learner had control over none of them. However, Moore (1973b, p. 673) is careful to point out that "like AAA, NNN cannot exist in reality, since no learner is entirely free of others' influence or entirely dependent on others."

Moore's scheme raises an important question: Is it realistic to treat the three domains as independent of one another? In Chapter Four, the point was made that there is a high degree of interdependence among the various components of personal autonomy, and any attempt to develop one or two parts in isolation is unlikely to succeed. In that case, the reference was to the personal aspects of autonomy in learning, but as Boud (1981, p. 25) points out, the same is also true of the situational dimension: "The exercise of autonomy cannot be realistically limited to any one part of the learning process: for example, in course content but not assessment or in choosing one's own pace but not one's objectives. Autonomous learning, as all learning, involves the whole person, not just the intellect; what is to be learned should not be seen separately from the motives and desires of students."

The implication of this is that learner-control in the full sense of the term is not a minor adjustment to the educator's approach, nor a token gesture in consulting learners about some aspect or other of course design or teaching strategy. Skager (1979, p. 539) makes the point that "if self-direction is significantly influenced by one kind of schooling or another, the presumption is that this occurs because there is some sort of consistency . . . irrespective of content and level . . . in how learners are expected to go about the learning process." If implemented fully, learner-control represents a fundamental shift in the balance of power and locus of control and leads inevitably and inescapably toward a radically altered role for both the learner and the teacher.

Moore's scheme also raises another problem. Like Krimerman's model of personal autonomy, which was discussed in Chapter Four, it raises the question of how realistic it is to judge whether or not a program is autonomous based on externally visible criteria. In this book, it is argued that educational programs cannot be classified meaningfully according to their degree of autonomy. Clearly it would be possible for different learners to have varying perceptions as to how much independence they enjoyed in each of the three domains, and likewise there could be a significant difference between the perceptions of the teacher or trainer and those of the learners. Although it may be possible to distinguish programs according to the extent to which they permit differing levels of learner-control, learners may not feel competent to exercise such control. The major determinant of learner-control is the learner's subjective understandings and feelings of potency, not the objective, especially teacher-centered, aspects of the situation.

Learner-Control and Adult Education

Under a number of guises, including self-direction, open learning, participatory learning, and student-centered instruction, the issue of learner-control has become a major focus in the "practice and discourse" of adult education in recent years (Usher and Johnston, 1988). In part, this reflects the view that adults undertake considerable self-directed learning in their everyday lives, and that instruction should, as far as possible, take account of this predisposition. In part, however, learner-control is projected as a distinctive characteristic of adult education, which sees itself as challenging the traditional teacher-directed or "banking" approach of much formal education, and thereby "helping to correct some of its adverse effects" (Abercrombie, 1981, p. 41).

Admittedly, adult education does have a long and proud tradition of encouraging personal empowerment and social emancipation. However, it is a gross oversimplification and distortion to pretend that all forms of formal education are equally pernicious in terms of denying people control or, for that matter, that adult education is distinctively different from the rest of the educational system. As Keddie (1980, p. 45) argues, "Within a sociological frame of reference, it becomes apparent that adult education is more like the rest of the education system than unlike it, both its curriculum and its pedagogy, and I shall treat the claim to distinctiveness as an ideological claim which requires explanation." Research evidence from elementary, secondary, and higher as well as adult education shows that learner-control is by no means the exclusive prerogative of adult education.

Interest in learner-control has enjoyed fluctuating fortunes over the years. For instance, in his classic work on *The Meaning of Adult Education,* Lindeman (1926b, p. 119) viewed teachers as facilitators whose "function is not to profess, but to evoke . . . to draw out, not to pour in," and a decade later, Bryson (1936, p. 99) argued for greater learner-control when he observed that "one man cannot tell another how to think; he can simply tell the other how he thinks himself." Presumably, it was with these and other similar perspectives in mind that at the 1970 Adult Education Research Conference, Landvogt (1970, p. 4) claimed that "early literature of adult education emphasized and seemed committed to guided learning [learner-control]." However, she went on to observe, "Present literature appears to be negating learners' responsibilities in making decisions in the curriculum development process and gives little attention to procedures for securing active involvement." This comment is ironic, because it was in that same year that

Knowles's first major work—which included the now-familiar term *andragogy* in its title—appeared in print, stressing the construct of self-directedness.

The term *andragogy* readily entered the vocabulary of adult education and gained widespread popular acceptance. The early 1970s were a propitious time for the emergence of andragogy. The year 1969 had seen the appearance of Rogers's landmark work on student-centered teaching, *Freedom to Learn: A View of What Education Might Become,* and according to Jarvis (1984, p. 35), at that time "the structures of society were stretched and changed," and there was a generalized manifestation of an "expressive revolution" in the arts, youth, culture, and music. As part of this general movement, self-expression and personal development were in vogue, and thus andragogy, which Jarvis (1984) describes as "best understood in curriculum terms as an expression of the romantic curriculum" (p. 35), was launched "into a philosophy that was similar to it and, therefore, quite receptive to it. . . . Andragogy emerged at a time when the structures of society were conducive to the philosophy underlying the theory, and . . . its own structures reflected the structures of wider society" (p. 37).

However, the romantic curriculum was no invention of the 1960s or 1970s but, like an educational Halley's Comet, had made periodical reappearances in the educational galaxy. Jarvis traces Knowles's own intellectual heritage back through Lindeman to Dewey, and ultimately to Rousseau. But even Rousseau was not the first to concentrate on humankind's natural propensity for learning. McClintock (1982, pp. 57–58) argues that in classical antiquity, it had been the true purpose of all education to prepare learners for a world of self-directed inquiry or, as he terms it, *study:*

> Bluntly put, in the world of study that existed until modern times, teaching was trivial; that is teaching was trivial in the rigorous sense: it pertained primarily to the trivium, to regulating a student's elementary exercise in grammar, logic, and rhetoric.
>
> Trivial teachers had the self-effacing mission of making themselves unnecessary. The young needed help and discipline in working their way through the first steps of study, in acquiring

the basic tools without which all else would be arcane. The teacher, the master of exercises, gave indispensable aid in making that acquisition; but as soon as it was made the student would give up studying the elementary arts and go on to more important matters. Reliance on the brute discipline doled out by the master of exercises was demeaning, and numerous sources show how men believed it to be important to get done with the arts, to end dependence on magisterial instruction so that one could begin to study freely, as curiosity dictated . . .

Although such a vision of teaching has a surprisingly contemporary ring to it, at some point this ancient notion of *self-culture* with a form of "schooling that respects the autonomy of study" gave way to *instruction,* a "system of injecting knowledge into inert and empty spirits": "Schooling keyed to the self-active student" was replaced by the "delusion that the teacher, on his own initiative, can shape plastic pupils and unilaterally fill their vacant slates with the wisdom of ages" (McClintock, 1982, p. 54).

According to McClintock, the lamentable process of this transformation can be traced back to the Reformation. Prior to then teachers had been content "merely to help in the self-development of their fellows." However, from the Reformation onward, people "found it hard to maintain restraint; . . . they discovered themselves burdened, alas, with paternal responsibility for ensuring that their wards would not falter and miss the mark . . . " and it was therefore only a matter of time "before schools would be held accountable for the people they produced . . . " (p. 60). An inevitable consequence of this shift in locus of responsibility from the learner to the teacher was a concomitant shift in control of the learning situation:

> Initiative has everywhere been thoroughly shifted from the student to the teacher; a world of instruction has completely displaced the bygone world of study. Rarely does one hear that study is the raison d'etre of an educational institution; teaching and learning is now what it is all about, and with this change, has come a change in the meaning of the venerable word "learning." Once it described what a person acquired as a result of serious study, but now it signifies what one receives as a result of good teaching. The psychology of learning is an important topic in educational research, not because it will help students improve their habits of study, but because it enables instructors to devise better strategies of teaching.

> Furthermore, in the same way that the meaning of "learn-
> ing" has changed, so has that of "study." It has ceased to be a
> self-directed motivating force, which to be sure may have needed
> a master of exercise to help sustain it through the dull prelimi-
> naries. No longer the source, study itself has become a conse-
> quence of instruction . . . [McClintock, 1982, p. 62].

Thus in placing the needs and interests of the learner at the center of the educational process, adult education finds itself to be "reaffirming a great tradition": a return to the pattern of education that historically predominated. However, in advocating learner-control of instruction, many adult educators have overlooked the need for a "master of exercises" to help to sustain the learner "through the dull preliminaries," a point that was discussed in Chapter Three under the heading "The Limitations of Learner-Control."

Arguments for Increasing Learner-Control

Although the development of personal autonomy in the wider sense (see Chapter Four) is commonly cited as the reason for increasing learner-control in adult education, other rationales are also advanced. A number of these were critically reviewed in Chapter Three, where it was shown that many of the benefits alleged to result from increased learner-control were in fact ideological assertions not necessarily supported by empirical evidence. One major category of reasons for supporting learner-control, however, was not reviewed in Chapter Three. It is the belief that giving learners control over certain instructional functions leads to demonstrably superior learning outcomes. These outcomes can be expressed in terms either of better subject matter acquisition, and consequently of improved performance on measures of attainment such as tests, or of more global noncognitive gains such as "student interest and involvement, breadth of understanding, application of what is learned to the solution of real-life problems, self-confidence and self-esteem, ability to work effectively with others, understanding of goals and direction, and self-motivated continued learning" (Wight, 1970, p. 246).

Given the extravagant claims made for increased learner-control, student-directed instruction, and self-directed learning over the past thirty years, there has been a consistent and, to its advocates, frustrating failure to establish the superiority of learning outcomes in learner-controlled situations.

Some of the best experimental work dates back to the 1960s, one of the reported studies from this period being carried out by Mager and his associates in an industrial training setting. A group of newly appointed trainee engineers was given responsibility for arranging their own induction course, including orientation sessions, input on specific processes, and work placements. The trainees were provided with "24 pages of detailed course objectives which specified the desired terminal behavior. The net effect was that the students had to decide what they needed to learn, in addition to what they already knew, in order to reach the objectives" (Mager and Clark, 1963, p. 73).

According to the experimenters, the results were impressive compared with their traditional training and induction courses: Training time was reduced by 65 percent; the graduates of the program appeared better equipped than previously; less time was needed by instructors, administrators, or technical experts; both the content and sequence varied markedly from student to student, and, in the case of the sequence, the order in which learners undertook learning tasks differed sharply from that which had been previously used by the instructor.

Two points need to be made about this, however. The first is that the provision of detailed behavioral objectives probably renders the learner to some extent dependent on the person or agency that established the detailed objectives, and thus removes this approach from the realm of learner-control as defined here (Kotaska, 1973; Kotaska and Dickinson, 1975). Second, even the experimenters were conservative in appraising their success: "[These results] suggest that the success of auto instructional programs may say less about their effectiveness than about the ineffectiveness of traditional procedures" (Mager and McCann, 1961, p. 20).

Around the same time, McKeachie (1960) undertook a protracted investigation of student-centered teaching methods that included self-directed study. He was forced to conclude that such methods are "no panacea" for the problems of higher education. The same theme is echoed in his 1962 review of research on instructional techniques, where the overriding finding was that of "no significant differences" between educational methods. Similarly, after a three-year investigation of self-directed study in many different university courses, Gruber and Weitman (1963, p. 222) were forced to the rather weak conclusion that, as far as learning of conventional course content is concerned, giving students responsibility for their own learning and substantially altering the attendance requirements at formal lectures and tutorials "resulted in either small losses or small gains, the gains being somewhat more common than the losses."

In 1964, V. N. Campbell carried out a series of elegant experiments in learner-control, but the best he was able to claim was the negatively worded finding that "in no experiment did self-direction have an adverse effect on learning" (Campbell, 1964, p. 358). Dubin and Taveggia (1968) reviewed and reanalyzed the findings from ninety-one previous studies comparing the effectiveness of various college teaching techniques conducted between 1924 and 1965, and they conclude that "these data demonstrate clearly and unequivocally that there is *no measurable difference* among truly distinctive methods of college instruction when evaluated by student performance on final examinations" (p. 35; emphasis added).

More recently, Rosenblum and Darkenwald (1983) carried out a neatly conceived study to test whether adult students who participated in planning their course of studies performed better that those not consulted. Although this is not strictly learner-control in the full sense, such involvement in program planning draws its support from much the same values and beliefs about adult learners as learner-control does. Their study involved a yoked-control group. The experimental subjects participated in planning the course that both they and the control subjects subsequently took. Their findings were, if anything, contrary to expectations because the group who were not consulted actually performed marginally better than those who did participate, though the difference favoring the control group was not statistically significant (p. 151). What they had expected to find was that participation had a beneficial effect on performance. Instead, they concluded that "participation in planning results in a better designed or more relevant course" and that this, in turn, may result in "greater achievement and satisfaction" (p. 152).

Rosenblum and Darkenwald's findings seem very consistent with those reported by Fry (1972), who assigned learners to one of four conditions: student-controlled, expert (teacher-controlled), random presentation, and control (no instruction). Distinguishing learners according to their level of aptitude and their level of inquiry (or self-directedness), Fry reports that "as expected, high-aptitude–high-inquiry subjects learned significantly more under a high degree of student control, and high-aptitude–low-inquiry subjects learned significantly more under a low degree of student control. Results for low-aptitude candidates were inconclusive. *Overall, subjects learning under a high degree of student control learned the least. However, they formed the most favorable attitude towards the method of instruction*" (p. 459; emphasis added).

Within the framework of the argument advanced in this book, it seems likely that the generally inconclusive and equivocal results obtained over such a range of studies are explicable, at least in part, by the research approach conventionally adopted. Customarily, the evaluation of "learning" has focused on *quanta* of knowlege:

> Within the psychology of learning, the underlying conception of learning has in most cases been rather simple. The dominating interest has been focussed upon how many stimuli can be reproduced under various conditions. There are few studies where there have been attempts to study what is learned when people are exposed to oral or written discourse. In most learning experiments, a criterion test is used and the effect of treatments, if any, is read from the sum value that a subject or a group of subjects obtain. There is thus, basically, a definition of learning which is founded on a quantitative or atomistic conception of knowledge and learning. . . .
>
> It seems a worthwhile end in itself to study what is learned as revealed through what subjects say in a situation where they themselves have to produce answers and interpretations. Study of what is learned is one of the major features of non-verbatim, as opposed to verbatim, learning . . . [Säljö, 1975, p. 14].

If, in situations of learner-control, experimenters had studied what is learned rather than how much is learned (Säljö, 1975, p. 9), the findings may well have been somewhat different, and might have vindicated the optimism of the many psychologists and educators who "cling to the hope that a convincing demonstration of the efficacy of self-directed study is 'just around the corner'" (Gruber, 1965, p. 2).

Despite the generally lackluster and inconclusive findings concerning learning of subject matter, many adult educators persist in espousing the need for increased learner-control, sometimes even in the face of learners' reluctance to accept it. Frequently, this is a result of some ideological commitment, a factor that will be discussed later in this chapter. Frequently, too, it reflects a belief that learner-control results in other, nonquantifiable gains and "that the individual develops beneficial competencies through the exercise of autonomy and freedom" (Mocker and Spear, 1982, p. 9).

It is not exactly clear what beneficial competencies may result from increased learner-control, but at least three seem to be implied: first, an increase in reasoned decision making; second, an increased willingness to accept responsibility in future teaching/learning situations; and third, a propensity to undertake further self-directed learning outside formal instructional settings. Each of these will be discussed in turn.

All learning requires the learner to make choices. This extends from macro decisions such as selecting what to learn from among a perplexing diversity of choices to more micro decisions such as choosing between competing explanatory systems in building up a personal understanding of the object of his or her study. One of the features of teacher-directed instruction is that it limits the scope for independent decision making, and thereby reduces the likelihood of inappropriate or incorrect choices. However, the more control the learner has, the wider the range of choices to be considered and the greater the responsibility to choose wisely. Accordingly, learner-controlled methods of instruction inevitably place a great emphasis on decision making as a skill of learning.

Many educators—particularly those working with adult learners—subscribe to the view that when a person is given a choice in a learning situation, he or she will select that which is individually best. This "neo-Darwinian" position (Olson, 1945; Skruber, 1982) casts the teacher or trainer in the role of an anthropologist who stands by to observe and record the choices made by learners, or possibly a gardener who "merely co-operates with an automatic process of growth" (Hostler, 1981, p. 27).

Apart from the fact that this view of learning does not admit any positive role for the educator, it is difficult to see where a learner would obtain the criteria needed for selecting from among the various alternatives available to him or her. Geis (1976, pp. 252–253) argues that, in universities at least, the combined effect of widening choices and giving increased learner-control is "to help to develop a repertoire of choosing—[and] to develop the capacity for intelligent decision-making." He goes on to note that "it has become fashionable of late to speak of the student as a consumer of education. . . ." On the one hand, this has led to considering education as a "product," and to pressure for teacher accountability. But adopting a consumerist view of education has another side to it, namely "the education of student as consumer."

According to Geis (1976, p. 268), it is not enough simply to remove constraints and to give learners increased choices: "Freedom is not merely lack of constraints. It occurs when the individual has developed several alternate repertoires which allow him [or her] to operate successfully in a variety of environments." Thus, "educational freedom . . . becomes something more than the elimination of the boundaries and narrow pathways of traditional education. . . . The educational challenge lies not only in developing these 'consumerism skills' but also in providing the student with them early enough so that he or she can intelligently manage a system of education which itself is open and provides—requires—choices" (Geis, 1976, pp. 267–268).

The implication of this argument is that increasing learner-control, especially in areas where there is a discipline-based body of knowledge to master, does not consist solely of abdicating responsibility to the learners. Instead, it involves inducting the learners into the criteria that they need to apply in making informed choices about what to learn and possibly also about how to learn. Taking this need for instruction in intelligent choosing with Gruber's observation that although "attitudinal changes develop rather slowly, they are a necessary prerequisite to stable changes in intellectual work habits" (Gruber, 1965, p. 5), it seems that "the student may need specific training to develop new patterns of active intellectual work" (p. 6).

Gruber (1965) outlines the phases in developing self-reliance in learning, extending over the entire duration of a student's time in college, and in his paper on "Educating Toward Shared-Purpose, Self-Direction and Quality Work," Torbert (1978) deals specifically with the difficulties which both students and educators encounter in fully internalizing the radically different model of education that learner-control in the full sense entails. Torbert (1978, p. 129) notes that he himself, although intellectually committed to handing over control to learners, "required seven years of very intense and diverse existential learning experiences with remarkable teachers and colleagues, as well as . . . two terms experimenting with the particular conditions of the S.M.U. business school before I could take a role in enacting the well-defined liberating structure reported here." Clearly, the protracted nature of such programs has important implications for what may reasonably be achieved in adult education, where the contact is typically much briefer and more discontinuous.

This leads to a consideration of the second type of collateral learning that is reputed to flow from increased learner-control; namely, an increased willingness to accept control in future learning situations. As discussed in Chapter Three, as early as 1967, Campbell and Chapman suggested that "giving learners more control gave them a taste for more control, as well as greater interest in the topic" (p. 130). Two years earlier, Gruber (1965, p. 5) had reported a similar finding with respect to increased learner-control: "Perhaps the most uniform finding of research in this area is that students initially *dislike* greater responsibility but come to accept it in the course of a semester, and that their brief experience with self-directed study does produce a more favorable attitude toward independent intellectual work. . . . Of course, there is little reason to believe that a single brief experience with self-directed study in an educational atmosphere fundamentally hostile to intellectual independence (cf. Gruber and Weitman, 1962) will produce attitudinal changes of great longevity."

Gruber and Weitman (1962) also noted that there was an increase in emphasis placed on the value of doing independent intellectual work by students. They comment that this finding is all the more striking because this more favorable attitude towards academic independence occurred in a group of courses "in which the students' evaluations of the experimental courses were unfavorable, and in which their final examination performance was inferior to the control group" (p. 23–25). This is a valuable insight that relates to Wispe's (1951) study discussed earlier, which revealed that enjoyment was not necessarily synonymous with value in the students' evaluations.

With respect to the connection between learner-control and the willingness and capacity to undertake autonomous learning generally, the evidence that "certain competencies for self-directedness in learning . . . can be fostered in part of a formal learning situation" (Campbell and Chapman, 1967, p. 123) is stronger and more direct. Probably the most comprehensive empirical study of the development of competence as an autonomous learner is the work of Wang and her associates at the Learning Research and Development Center at the University of Pittsburgh. After more than a decade of carefully controlled experimental work, regarding both the direct and concomitant development of competence as an independent learner, Wang (1983, p. 221) writes: "To summarize, if students function in carefully structured learning environments where opportunities are provided for skills acquisition, and where continuous emphasis is placed on self-direction, self-initiative, and self-evaluative behaviors, it is postulated that students should gain an increased sense of self-efficacy and personal control. Furthermore, it is assumed that academic successes are more likely to increase students' perceptions of personal control if the successes are achieved without a huge degree of dependence on external agents such as teachers."

Two notions are central to this claim. The first is the idea of the students' "sense of personal control," which is dealt with in Chapter Thirteen; the second is the notion of "carefully structured learning environments." As mentioned previously, there is no evidence to suggest that disorganized or haphazard programs involving intermittent or partial learner-control will lead to the sustained development of competence to function in this mode.

Somewhat more tenuous is the linkage, if any, between learner-control and the development of an ability and willingness to undertake autonomous learning under different circumstances outside formal instructional settings (R. K. Brown, 1966; Kratz, 1978; Langford, 1974; Schleiderer, 1979). In view of the fact that since the incidence of autodidaxy already exceeds by a massive margin participation in any form of formal adult education, it would be difficult to argue convincingly that the *quantity* of autodidactic learning was linked to learner-control, although its quality may well be. Research to test any such presumed link would need to examine not the quantity, but the nature and quality of learning projects undertaken by learners with previous exposure to learner-controlled methods of instruction.

Overall, there seems to be some evidence that prolonged exposure to techniques of instruction that emphasizes high degrees of learner-control can increase people's competence at, and preference for, independent inquiry. The question to which advocates must address themselves, however, is "Why bother?" As Gruber (1965, p. 9) observes, "It is plain to see that maximal independence is only an *intermediate* goal. . . . Our aim is not independence for its own sake. For this reason, in improving our methods of developing intellectual self-reliance, we must give deeper thought to the kind of human relationships our educational methods foster." Thus, those whose advocacy of learner-control rests on the desirability of increasing people's competence as independent learners must go beyond this achievement to answer questions such as "What outcomes do we expect from such programs? What ideal person do we envision? What community? What world?" (Gibbons and Phillips, 1982, p. 84).

The Transition from Teacher-Control to Learner-Control

It is relatively easy to advocate a change from one instructional approach to another, but a different matter to see it through in practice. This is particularly so when the change involves, as the transition from teacher-control to learner-control does, a reshaping of the foundations underpinning the teacher-learner relationship. At the minimum, the change from teacher-control to learner-control has implications for teachers, students, and the organization; in the wider context, it frequently has an impact on others outside the immediate instructional setting, including other teachers or trainers, family, friends, colleagues, employers, and perhaps even society at large.

The transition toward increased learner-control is not so much "tinkering with accessories to the instructional machine" as it is "rebuilding the mechanical core" (Ainsworth, 1976, p. 276). For the teacher, trainer, coach, or facilitator, it involves a significant shift in the locus of control, and a radical change from "providing instruction to a class, to facilitating learning for individual learners" (Wedemeyer, 1981, p. 78). Even a teacher or trainer intellectually committed to such an approach might find it difficult to adapt emotionally and behaviorally (Wight, 1970, p. 252), because, as Wedemeyer (1981, p. 79) states, "The prospect of having to guide and enrich the learning of students who learn at different rates, by different styles, who may be physically distant, and who exercise a degree of autonomy over their learning, can be frightening to teachers trained in traditional classroom norms, techniques and psychology."

For learners, too, the transition can be challenging and unsettling; it is difficult to overestimate the impact of previous experience: "Persons whose entire academic experience has been organized for them or whose personal survival has required social conformity cannot be expected to begin self-direction easily. When students enter college [for instance], they are not only confronted with the freedom to choose . . . but with the institution's expectation that they will make these choices for themselves. This is a bewildering and anxiety-producing situation for students and brings into play memories of their earlier educational experiences" (Shipton and Steltenpohl, 1980, p. 15).

Some of the difficulties encountered by learners in adjusting to a learner-controlled situation are dealt with in Chapters Twelve and Thirteen.

Goodbye Teacher? As discussed in Chapter Six, there are numerous arguments in support of increasing learner-control. However, such a transition is likely to be greeted by educators with mixed enthusiasm, for, as Geis (1976, p. 266) writes, "Most innovative instructional systems produce major changes in the professor's role. The introduction of student choice, for example, is likely to require the professor to refashion himself as an instructional guide, manager, counsellor, and inventor instead of an academic know-it-all. The magnitude of the changeover should not be underestimated. The content expert who equates teaching students with telling them what he knows is not likely to have the skills of counsellor, guide, and evaluator. Depriving him of his traditional role and simultaneously requiring him to acquire sophisticated new roles will produce trauma."

Although this quotation refers to higher education, many of those involved in adult education as instructors confront the same redefinition of roles. In 1968, in the heyday of euphoria over individualized instruction, Keller wrote an article entitled "Goodbye Teacher. . . ." As it turns out, he was merely signaling the passing of the teacher as "classroom entertainer, expositor, critic and debater" (p. 88). However, from time to time, educational innovations such as programmed learning, computer-manager instruction, and teaching machines have been hailed as marking the demise of teaching. Given this background, it is hardly surprising to find that at least some teachers feel threatened by learner-control and the consequent redefinition of their role as a "facilitator of learning." Like learners, "teachers have self-concepts too, and they will tend to reject a role which seems to violate the concept of self-as-teacher built up over many years of preparation, modeling and experience . . ." (Wedemeyer, 1981, p. 78).

What, then, is the role of the adult educator in situations of increasing learner-control? Many theorists and writers have attempted a specification. Tough (1979a), for instance, emphasizes the transition from the role of "director" to that of "resource" or "helper." The function of the teacher in this relationship is "providing information, advice (or suggestions and recommendations), and reasons that help the *learner* make the decision and understand the reasons for it. The helper provides detailed information about the various possibilities that are open, but lets the learner himself make the decisions" (p. 177).

Gibbons and Phillips (1978, p. 299) have portrayed the sort of roles that a teacher might be expected to fulfill in a learner-control regime in the following terms:

> Teachers become involved much more often in small-group and one-to-one interaction with students. In these closer encounters, they find themselves more often dealing with process than content. Rather than teaching specific subject matter and skills, they will more commonly find themselves diagnosing students' abilities, advising them on programs for further development, negotiating individual contracts, arranging contacts in the community, and helping students solve personal and motivational problems related to their self-directed studies. When they are teaching in the traditional sense, the content tends to be such process skills as personal planning, organizing necessary resources and managing time. And when teachers go into the community to find experts who will teach and to negotiate new locations where students can study and work, it means they must learn entrepreneurial skills seldom required of educators in teacher-directed programs.

Wedemeyer (1981, p. 80) writes that, with respect to what he terms *open learning,* "New faculty roles, in which there is less teaching of the lecturing style and more individual counselling, are implied. Faculty may find themselves nudged towards the Platonic model, with teacher as mentor, guide, developer of learners, and problem solver, rather than information and law-giver." Farnes (1975, p. 5) adds that, in situations of learner-control, "The responsibility of the tutors would need to be extended; they would help the students define their learning objectives and area of study; encourage students with similar or complementary interests to co-operate in self-help groups; make recommendations about suitable materials that could be obtained locally [or] nationally . . . ," and Wight (1970, p. 250) likens the role of the educator in this new paradigm to that of a coach: "In the beginning, he provides the rules and structure, he helps each person develop the skills and understanding to play the game or to perform effectively, and he works with each individual to help him continuously improve his performance. . . . But it is the player, not the coach, who plays the game, and in Participative Education, the game is learning."

In his thoughtful analysis of the relationship between a self-directed learner and an instructor, Pratt (1988) advocates a sort of "staged withdrawal" in terms of both support and direction as the learner becomes more accomplished in the domain *and* more confident of his or her own abilities.

Collectively, these descriptions closely resemble the prototypic "helper" in the situation of guided or assisted autodidaxy discussed in Chapter Six. However, it is argued here that until the learner senses that total control of the situation has passed from the teacher and, moreover, feels competent to exercise the control, the situation is still one of independent study, rather than autodidaxy, with "ownership" still vested in the teacher.

Difficulties in the Transition. Because these roles differ so sharply from those to which many adult educators are accustomed, it is hardly surprising to find that attempts to increase learner-control often encounter difficulties. Harrison (1978, p. 166), for instance, comments that teachers or trainers often prove more intractable than learners, and that "our experience is that participants are far more ready for responsibility than educators are to give it to them." He goes on to observe: "Self-directed learning requires a fundamental shift in the locus of control in the classroom, and this shift is difficult for many educators to make. Once participants have gone beyond the diagnostic phase and the self-directed activity is well launched, there is often little for the educator to do. The needs of most educators for authority, visibility, and a sense of personal significance are not very well met by the self-directed format" (p. 166).

In Britain, in the mid 1970s, the Nuffield Foundation sponsored an extensive research project concerning independence in learning within higher education, and the report of the research group includes the following warning: "All new schemes run the risk of being regarded with a mixture of suspicion and anxiety by some . . . teachers not immediately involved. There may be ignorance on the part of others about what is happening; uneasiness that they should be doing something similar; concern that their students who are also involved in the new course may develop a more critical attitude; or suspicion that in some way academic standards may be threatened. This last anxiety is particularly strong where students are involved in decisions about the curriculum and assessment procedures . . . " (Nuffield Foundation, 1975, n.p.).

Difficulties are also experienced by individuals who, "even if they can accept the approach and their new role intellectually," often find it hard "to adapt emotionally and behaviorally." Frequently, they have no stable role model, nor any clear concept of what their alternative job description might look like: "Over a period of many years as students and instructors in the traditional educational system, they have developed a pattern of conditioned responses to the stimuli of the classroom. This pattern is very difficult to change, particularly when many of the students will resist the change and try to force the instructor back into the familiar, traditional role" (Wight, 1970, p. 252).

Concern over changes in teaching take two forms. On the one hand, many teachers feel that they personally might become redundant and, as Jankovic and others (1979, p. 31) point out, "There will be no evolution in the attitude of the teacher unless he is assured that [learner-control] is not seen as a rejection of his contribution, a negation of his specific role of teacher. . . ." The other concern is more general, the belief that somehow learner-control will ultimately result in the disappearance of teaching itself. In addition to these general concerns, there are many other potential stumbling blocks to increasing learner-control. Literature reveals that educators commonly report

- A sense of inadequacy and lack of preparation to act as a mentor, guide, counsellor, and problem solver, rather than "information and law-giver" (Wedemeyer, 1975, p. 60).
- A feeling of frustration and helplessness in watching students struggle with problems which the trainer knows could easily be solved or avoided (Gibbons and Phillips, 1978, p. 299).
- Inadequacy and unpreparedness to deal with the increasingly divergent demands made by adult learners as they pursue individual learning programs.
- Being daunted by the task of preparing independent study materials and programs of learning (Ainsworth, 1976, p. 282). "The amount of detailed design and preparation of learning

materials required for self-directed learning goes far beyond that involved in putting together a syllabus and organizing some lecture notes. Many educators do not possess the design expertise required" (Harrison, 1978, p. 166).

- Increased rather than lessened demands on their time. "Contrary to popular belief, a self-instructional course is not self-running, and it is completely false to suggest that it saves the instructor's time. There is nothing more effective in the use of the instructor's time than classroom-based instruction, where everything — information-dissemination, test-taking, failure-diagnosis — is done according to a schedule, in a group mode, with one explanation serving a large number of students, and where individual assistance is reserved for exceptional cases. Certainly, self-instruction relieves the instructor of the burden of disseminating information, but this is more than offset by the demands of increased individual counselling, and the increased testing, scoring, and diagnosis which commonly accompanies self-instruction" (Ainsworth, 1976, p. 279).

- Removal of the usual on-the-job reward system of taking credit for student learning (Gibbons and Phillips, 1978, p. 299).

- A deep-rooted feeling of inadequacy and lack of autonomy, and a consequent unwillingness or inability to develop this capacity in others (Della-Dora and Blanchard, 1979, p. 9).

- Lingering doubts about the efficacy of such an approach compared with more traditional methods. As Boud and Prosser (1980, p. 27) comment, "A tutor in a course based on these principles must believe that students will be able to define their own goals, design their own programme, and assess their own achievement. And this he must believe without reservation for, if not, the limiting dependency relationship of students on staff will inhibit the growth of these attributes.

- A concern about being idle or "unprofessional" (Harrison, 1978, p. 166). In one experimental program in England, the senior tutor was explicit: "Every so often I get in a real neurotic state because I keep thinking this is just too loose for words. I feel as though I'm shirking my responsibility as a teacher, I should add more to these blank programme sheets, put a lot of things in those empty boxes" (Abercrombie and Terry, 1978, p. 92).

- A fear of becoming redundant, of being successful within the terms of a learner-controlled curriculum. As one faculty member expressed it, "Is participant tutorage going to reach the goal I want at the end — that I shall not be of use any more, that I've passed on all my experience, my experience has developed the students so they can operate by themselves to be self-learning people?" (Abercrombie and Terry, 1978, p. 92).

- Viewing learner-control as "yet another well-intentioned but impractical fad [which] will go away if ignored" (Ainsworth, 1976, p. 276). And, perhaps most telling of all,

- The fear of being pushed into the background; that the trainer's traditional authority and status will be undermined as the learners become more self-directing and more independent (Jankovic and others, 1979, p. 31).

Overall, it is clear that the shift to learner-control is not merely an administrative change, but a significant attitudinal one as well: "Changes in teaching methods cannot . . . be fully effective without changes in attitude. The student's ability to adopt responsibility for his learning, and the teacher's ability to foster this process, require profound changes in their basic assumptions about the relationships between student and teacher. The authority-dependency relationship . . . cannot be changed without affecting, and being affected by, its old and deeply-rooted foundations in the rest of our social system. Confusions of feeling, as well as of thought, are muddled up with the issue to a greater extent than current educational practice seems to take into account" (Abercrombie and Terry, 1978, p. 82).

Because of the magnitude of the change involved, it is difficult to overstate the strength of feelings that such an approach can engender in teachers and trainers familiar with and committed to a more traditional model. Wight (1970, p. 274) deals at length with these difficulties, citing one traditional educator who described giving learners responsibility for their own learning as "just damned rhetoric that can lead to nothing but mischief." He continued on to say that "one does not put lunatics in charge of the asylum" and called this "the fool for a master school of education. Everyman his own professor. As a teacher, I cannot communicate to you the seriousness of a situation wherein students — however intelligent, sincere, and goodhearted — are encouraged to learn on their own hook. They simply do not have the discrimination to make their way through the maze of erroneous books, for one thing." Wight (1970, p. 275) comments on these reactions by observing that "any change or attempted change in educational methodology in our schools and colleges will have to take into consideration the attitudes and assumptions of the teachers and instructors. We can expect that it will be quite difficult to establish meaningful dialogue with some. Their reactions to a suggested change as drastic as Participative Education [learner-control] will quite likely be more emotional than rational. . . ."

Teacher Beliefs and the Promotion of Learner-Control

Whenever people react emotionally to an issue, either for or against, it almost certainly indicates that deeply held beliefs are involved. There seems little doubt that encouraging learner-control represents a dramatically different educational mode from the familiar teacher-controlled model, and perhaps not all trainers or instructors would be able to make the transition. Clearly, "teachers . . . tend to specialize in the mode in which they are most skilled and with which they feel most comfortable. Each mode does seem to require basically different orientations to curriculum and instructional processes" (Blaney, 1974, p. 23). In view of the obvious importance of attitudes and values in the implementation of learner-control, it is worth inquiring as to what exactly is required of trainers and instructors in order to make the transition successful. In his essay on "Fostering Self-Direction," Combs (1972, pp. 59–63) identifies four variables:

> *We Need to Believe This Is Important.* It seems self-evident that independence and self-direction are necessary for our kind of world. . . . Unfortunately, because a matter is self-evident is no guarantee that people will really put it into practice. . . . To be effective as an objective, each of us must hold the goal of self-

direction clear in our thinking and high in our values whenever we are engaged in planning or teaching of any kind. . . . To begin doing something about self-direction we must, therefore, begin by declaring its importance; not as a lofty sentiment, but as an absolute essential. It must be given a place of greater concern than subject matter itself, for a very simple reason: It is far more important than subject matter. . . .

Trust in the Human Organism. Responsibility and self-direction are learned. They must be acquired from experiences, from being given opportunities to be self-directing and responsible. You cannot learn to be self-directing if no-one permits you to try. Human capacities are strengthened by use, but atrophy with disuse. . . . If we are to produce independent, self-starting people, we must do a great deal more to produce the kinds of experiences which will lead to these ends.

The Experimental Attitude. If we are going to provide . . . people with increased opportunity for self-direction, we must do it with our eyes open expecting them to make mistakes. This is not easy, for the importance of "being right" is in our blood. Education is built on right answers. Wrong ones are regarded as failures. . . . To be so afraid of mistakes that we kill the desire to try is a tragedy. Autonomy, independence and creativity are the products of being eager to look and willing to try. . . . In the world we live in, victory is reserved only for the courageous and inventive. . . .

The Provision of Opportunity. . . . If we are to achieve the objective of greater self-direction, I see no alternative to the fuller acceptance of students into partnership in the educative endeavor. Our modern goal for education, "the optimal development of the individual," cannot be achieved without this. . . . Few of us are deeply committed to tasks imposed on us; and students are not much different. Self-direction is learned from experience. What better, more meaningful experience could be provided than participation in the decisions about one's own life and learning?

To these four variables, it is necessary to add a fifth. In order for someone to advocate and actively to encourage an inquiry approach in others, many authors stress that "teachers . . . and other educators must be moving toward becoming self-directed learners themselves if they hope to succeed in helping students move in this direction" (Della-Dora and Blanchard, 1979, p. 9). As early as 1960, Chamberlain pointed out that twelve out of twelve adult education professors at American universities rated highest, of qualities for graduate adult education teachers, the ability to "carry on self-directed study," and

Strong (1977, p. 15) cites this in support of her contention "that the ability to learn autonomously oneself relates to being able to guide autonomous learning." The point is perhaps made most eloquently by Torbert (1978, p. 122). When teachers stop doing things "to" students, or even "for" students, and instead to do things "with" them, they are involved "in creating a special kind of social arena—a kind of social theater in which everyone is both participant and observer—and this arena, in turn, requires of the leadership the most profoundly spontaneous inquiring behavior. Only authentically inquiring behavior succeeds in 'converting' others to the practice of inquiry."

It is interesting to note, in passing, how comparatively recent is the widespread acceptance of such collaboration as a cornerstone of adult education. Freire's problem-posing education, for instance, "relies on dialogue between the teachers and learners to stimulate critical thinking, creativity, and reflection upon reality. In problem-posing education, the teachers work 'with, not for' the learners" (Conti, 1978a, p. 22). Although most adult educators would readily assent to this proposition, it first appeared a scant seven years after Coolie Verner, one of the patriarchs of the field, had pronounced that "adult education is a relationship between an educational agent and a learner *in which the agent selects, arranges, and continuously directs a sequence of progressive tasks* that provide systematic experiences to achieve learning, for those whose participation in such activities is subsidiary and supplemental to a primary productive role in society" (Verner, 1964, p. 32; emphasis added).

Teacher's Beliefs About Autonomy. What, then, is the origin of the attitudes and personal predispositions that lead to the implementation, by educators, of programs stressing learner-control? Some have suggested that such "self-directing behavior" is the result of various personality attributes. In particular, Huggins's research (1975) showed evidence to support the contention that higher self-concept is related to the promotion of autonomy in learners, but also expressed caution concerning the complexity of the variables involved. M. L. H. Smith (1968) examined the relationships among self-actualization, dogmatism, and the teachers' self-reported facilitation of student self-directed learning. The results confirmed her hypothesis that more open-minded and more highly self-actualized teachers did report behaviors likely to facilitate the development of self-direction in learners, and accordingly she recommended "a need for greater emphasis on self-actualization and open-mindedness in preservice and inservice teacher education programs" (p. ii).

Another suggestion is that the form of teacher education or previous learning experiences to which educators had been subjected might explain their predilection for learner-control. This notion was the focus of A. A. Johnson's 1973 study; the findings, however, were that there was no clear relationship between teachers' experience of an individualized mode of teacher education and their self-reported propensity to facilitate learner-control in others. A supplementary finding was that predisposition toward learner-control as a goal was not linked significantly to the teachers' success in that mode of instruction.

Although simple explanations for the origins of teachers' beliefs have failed, nonetheless it seems true that some teachers favor the notion of learner-control. Such a preference has been called a pedagogical orientation and, over the years, there have been numerous attempts to develop reliable and valid measures of teachers' pedagogical preferences. One of the earliest was Kerlinger and Kaya's *Attitude Toward Education Scale* (1959). However, researchers have been relatively slow to develop instruments specifically relevant to the adult education context.

In 1969, Landvogt put forward "a framework for exploring the adult educator's commitment toward the construct of 'guided learning.' " Six years later, in 1975, Hadley offered an instrument designed "to determine adult educators' orientation: andragogical or pedagogical," and three years later again, Conti (1978b) tested his *Principles of Adult Learning Scale,* which is not, however, designed to measure espoused philosophies so much as "teacher behavior related to the collaborative teacher-learning mode." More recently, Zinn (1983) developed and has field tested another instrument — the *Philosophy of Adult Education Inventory* — intended to evaluate "an individual's personal philosophy of adult education with respect to five prevailing adult education philosophies: Liberal, Behaviorist, Progressive, Humanist, and Radical" (Zinn, 1983, abstract).

With notable exceptions, such as the work of O'Gorman (1981) and Holmes (1980), there has been remarkably little research to establish the reliability or the validity of these various instruments, or the links between espoused philosophies and professional practice. In part, this may represent the recognition that action is not linked to theory (at least to personal theory) through a simple causal connection; that practitioners do not have a rationally developed, internally consistent perspective or worldview that invariably and inevitably manifests itself in consistent professional practices.

In recent years, there has been some attempt to examine whether teachers' beliefs are indeed congruent with their practice (for example, Borko, 1978; Cone, 1978; Russo, 1978). The results have been mixed, and several scholars have attributed the failure to find clear linkages to the fact that action itself embodies thinking, and thinking cannot be separated from action. This view is fundamental to the process of action research (Kemmis, 1982), which, in recent years, has given rise to a new generation of studies on teacher thinking (Elbaz, 1983; Elliot, 1976–77; Floden and Klinzing, 1990; Halkes and Olson, 1984; Oberg, 1983; Sanders and McCutcheon, 1984).

The factor that, above all else, gives coherence to how teachers behave is the desire "to be good teachers — to act effectively, to accomplish our purposes. We seek to be competent, not to fail, so our theories also account for what it takes to be effective" (Sanders and McCutcheon, 1984, p. 6). This clearly raises the question of what teachers mean when they think about effective teaching: "For example, a teacher might value teaching that enhances students' taking responsibility for their own learning, for growing in their ability to be in charge of what they do in order to learn . . ." (Sanders and McCutcheon, 1984, p. 7). Sanders and McCutcheon go on to point out that a person who felt this way "would use that value-rooted expectation in judging his/her own teaching as well as that of another" (p. 7). However, one of the greatest difficulties for teachers in assessing the effectiveness of their instructional behavior is that the consequences of teachers' actions depend on how *learners* perceive and construe them: "While a teacher may be acting in ways intended to encourage a student to enjoy and be successful in a lesson, some students may perceive that action as punitive or oppressive. Others may find it boring. In such cases, the consequences will very likely differ from those intended by the teacher" (Sanders and McCutcheon, 1984, p. 3).

This point is often overlooked by writers on learner-control, who seem to assume that "learner-control" is a commodity that can be given to learners. In fact, it is a subjective feeling that lies almost entirely outside the competence of the teacher or trainer. Whether or not learners feel that they can exercise control is discussed in Chapter Thirteen.

This gives rise to a final point. Because adult educators have different criteria for success and for judging their effectiveness, they will advocate and use learner-control methodologies for a variety of reasons. Boot and Reynolds (1983, p. 13) state that

> . . . the same techniques may be advocated by different practitioners for quite different reasons. Broadly speaking, advocacy seems to be based on one of three rationales, which we might describe as instrumental, theoretical and ideological. The first represents a search for methods which are stimulating and motivating because they make for more interested and enthusiastic learners. The second is a concern for practice which reflects the theory of learning that sees experience as the raw material from which knowledge is constructed. The third is a belief that educational practice must be founded on the same principles of democracy and freedom desired in society as a whole.
>
> Obviously this is an oversimplification, but the point we would like to make is that because their guiding rationales may be different, teachers are likely to find themselves adopting quite different strategies for resolving the issues that arise in practice.

It has been noted elsewhere in this book that learner-control (and autonomous learning generally) is favored by educators whose philosophical and ideological perspectives differ sharply from one another. Very often the differences are not immediately apparent, and researchers are obliged to probe beyond the superficial justifications offered by educators to fully understand the dynamics of any particular situation.

Capitulating to Pressure: Pseudoautonomy

Before leaving this consideration of teachers' motivations, it is necessary to consider some of the external pressures that might force a teacher to grant more learner-control. In Chapter One and earlier in this chapter, the point has been made that learner-control is a multifaceted or multidimensional entity. However, these dimensions are intimately intertwined, and it is not possible to give learners control over one or two aspects while retaining other prerogatives for the educator. Despite the interdependence of these dimensions, there are many situations in which adult educators have tried to limit learner-control to certain aspects of the situation, while maintaining control over other parts (such as the evaluation of learning outcomes) for themselves. Frequently, this is because they find themselves trapped in a conflict of values when it comes to increasing learner-control (Geis, 1976, p. 263).

On the one hand, there are strong pressures for them to professionalize: to gain qualifications in order to teach; to join professional associations; to be expert at program planning, discussion leading, demonstrating, evaluating; and generally to be accountable for the effectiveness of their instruction. In many cases, the tradition of the "gifted amateur" and the volunteer lecturer, which animated and characterized the work of early adult education enterprises such as the Workers Educational Association, mechanics' institutes, Chautauqua, and Frontier College, has given way to an overcredentialed replication of the formal education system.

On the other hand, adult educators are called on to hand over more and more control to learners, yet little in their training or in their experience as learners prepares them adequately for such a role. For many, "facilitation" is still a vague and barely understood concept, regarded with a mixture of suspicion and anxiety. Besides, it is difficult for an instructor to feel committed to a situation in which the prerogatives for objective setting; selecting content, pacing, and sequence; and carrying out evaluation have all been ceded to learners. One corollary of this dilemma is that some practitioners "go through the motions" of devolving responsibility onto learners, yet without commitment or conviction.

To describe this phenomenon of compliance, the term *pseudoautonomy* has been coined, borrowing from Kremer's (1978) formulation of *pseudoprogressivism*. In her study of classroom teachers and the relationship between their espoused beliefs and actual teaching practices, she found two things: "First, teachers profess favorable attitudes towards progressive educational goals, but have a relatively low perception of the knowledge conducive to goal attainment and low expectations of achieving them. Second, the consistency between attitudes and classroom behavior is indeed contingent on the congruence between attitudes and personality traits" (p. 996).

Without denying at all the sincerity of many adult educators' commitment to learner autonomy, it is possible that peer pressure and perceived social desirability might push some practitioners into espousing beliefs that do not reflect their true inner personal convictions:

> In my experience as both an adult learner and teacher of adults, I have realized some significant incongruities in my espoused theory and theory-in-use (Argyris and Schön, 1974) concerning the idea of andragogy and self-directed learning. As an adult learner, . . . I criticized others who engaged in primarily pedagogic approaches to learning. I was particularly critical of those adult educators who themselves espoused theories compatible with self-directed learning, but whose theories-in-use were substantially teacher-directed activities.
>
> [However,] in the course of being a teacher of adults, I rationalized my own failure to incorporate self-directed learning concepts with a variety of excuses: students didn't want to be self-directed, but would rather depend on me as the teacher; the institution did not sanction or encourage non-traditional learning practices such a self-directed learning; course content did not lend itself to such non-traditional practices; and the most deceptive of all, I was practicing good adult education practices when in fact I was only at best practicing benevolent pedagogy [Skruber, 1982, pp. 6–7].

An interesting example of this sort of "pseudoautonomy" or "benevolent pedagogy" is apparent in an interview between Boucouvalas and Pearse, a prison educator, reported in the *Journal of Correctional Education* under the title, "Self-Directed Learning in an Other-Directed Environment" (1982). Pearse begins by describing his progressive disillusionment with the traditional, teacher-directed mode of instruction, and he then goes on:

> After I had engaged in this type of pure teacher-directed instruction for about eight years, I began to realize that the learner was doing twenty percent of the work, and I was doing eighty percent. Of course, I used to walk around the school area and tell everyone what fantastic classes I was having. I had complete control over my classroom — no discipline problems, no rowdiness — and people were even learning! Of course, it was based on what I expected. Despite individualization, the learning was still under my control and direction. It wasn't the learner's plan — it was mine with which the "successful" ones were complying. . . .
>
> Then it slowly became clear that this approach which we're calling "self-directed" was the best thing that could happen to a maximum security institution since it tended to foster a different kind of control — an internal kind on the part of the inmate . . . adult learner. No longer is the learner just a passive participant. He becomes involved in the prescription process [note medical metaphor] where he agrees to assume individual responsibility for his own informal learning contract . . . " [Boucouvalas and Pearse, 1982, pp. 31–32].

However, Pearse's reluctance to "let go" of certain prerogatives is disclosed when he goes on to elaborate the advantages of increased learner-control: "In retrospect, the self-directed approach provides consistent motivation and performance on the part of the learner *and a precise monitoring system for the facilitator*" (Boucouvalas and Pearse, 1982, pp. 31–32, emphasis added).

Clearly, the teacher who needs a "precise monitoring system" is worlds apart from the facilitator of learning who believes implicitly and without reservation "that students will be able to define their own goals, design their own programme, and assess their own achievement" (Boud and Prosser, 1980, p. 27). Hamm, in his "Critique of Self-Education" (1982, p. 102) is even more forthright about such benevolent pedagogy masquerading as learner-control: "Is there not a deception in the suggestion that teachers 'set expectations,' 'help students to explore alternative activities,' 'provide a general program structure,' 'set realistic goals and deadlines' (Gibbons and Phillips, 1978, p. 298) and so on, while letting students think they are making the important decisions? Is this more than merely an aura of freedom?

If one is not by those techniques attempting to convey the sense of freedom without actually granting the freedom, there is little difference between it and conventional teaching."

Over what, then, must learners have control if the situation is to be described as autonomous? Geis (1976, p. 272) cites Holland (1969) when he points out that "providing choice for certain dimensions of learning (for example, mode, pacing) is something of a sham if the objectives are not manipulable by the students," and Heron (1981, p. 63) claims that control over evaluation of learning is the key issue: "Assessment is the . . . area where issues of power are most at stake. If there is no staff-student collaboration on assessment, then staff exert a stranglehold that inhibits the development of collaborations with respect to all other processes." Interestingly, Denton (1986, p. 15) takes up almost exactly the opposite point of view, arguing that "grades [do not] sabotage self-direction in adult learning." At first sight, this finding seems to run counter to much of the conventional wisdom in adult education. However, it appears that Denton is using the term *self-direction* to refer to the broader concept of self-determination or personal autonomy whereby, as argued here, a learner may choose to make a strategic suspension of his of her self-management of learning in order to be taught something.

Focusing instead on self-direction in the sense of self-management of learning, if Heron is right in his diagnosis, it casts doubt on the degree of control exercised by learners in the program described by Felder (1964, p. 338), who argues that "it might be hoped that others could be brought into the final evaluation of a student's independent study. If increased freedom is to be matched by increased responsibility, a partial motivation for carrying out this responsibility could well come from the knowledge that independent study will be critically evaluated by someone other than the faculty member directly involved with the student"!

Clearly, this is not consistent with the spirit of devolving responsibility to learners as discussed earlier, and this raises the following questions: How is it possible to practice this sort of deception? Are adult educators knowingly involved in such duplicity? Surely a teacher or trainer is either for or against learner-control, and if in favor, then wholly so? The first response is that, as Landvogt (1970, p. 6) pointed out in "A Framework for Exploring the Adult Educators' Commitment Toward the Construct of 'Guided Learning,'" "It was apparent that commitment to various ideas which are part of guided learning probably was not an 'either/or' proposition, but a matter of degree. An adult educator may be more or less committed to guided learning than he is to other teaching styles. . . . " As previously mentioned, such a view is not tenable when learner-control is taken to its logical conclusion, because having embarked on that course, the educator must be willing, at some time in the future, to surrender control entirely to the learner.

Second, it is not that adult educators are guilty of deliberately misleading learners about their intentions, but rather that they are often unaware themselves of the disjunctions between their espoused theory and their theory-in-use (Argyris and Schön, 1974). Thus, they might support the notion of learner-control at an intellectual level, without being aware of the long-term ramifications for students, or indeed for themselves, in advocating such a view. Related to this is the fact that educators frequently fail to recognize the holistic nature of the teaching/learning situation, and believe that it is possible to compartmentalize the program, handing over control of some aspects to the learners, while at the same time retaining certain prerogatives for themselves.

If the ultimate intention of increasing learner-control is to have learners accept increased responsibility for valued instructional functions, it may seem strange to consider the perspective of the educator at all. However, one of the distinguishing characteristics of the learner-control continuum is that at every point, from the extreme case of total teacher-control to the opposite extreme of learner-control, both parties to the instructional transaction have a perspective that guides their response to the situation. Moreover, as will be discussed in Chapter Fourteen, many difficulties in the instructional situation arise from a mismatch in the perceptions or intentions of the parties involved.

Summary

It has been the purpose of this chapter to review literature on learner-control in adult education, to analyze critically the transition from situations of teacher-control to learnercontrol, and, in particular, to identify difficulties in this transition from the perspective of the teacher or trainer.

The chapter began by contrasting learner-control with teacher-control. It was argued that learner-control is not, as commonly perceived, a single dimension, but rather a complex entity involving control over multiple aspects such as objective setting, content, method, sequence, pace, and evaluation of learning outcomes. Having distinguished these components, however, it was stated that it is impractical to restrict control to several of these facets and that accordingly it is useful to think of a continuum where all of these various components interact and mutually modify one another.

As many of the arguments both for and against learnercontrol have already been discussed in Chapter Three, these were not repeated here. However, a major claim, namely that learner-control leads to enhanced learning outcomes, was reviewed. It was found that when learning is defined in conventional terms as the acquisition of a certain *amount* of information, there is very little evidence to support its superiority. However, there are definitely advantages to giving learners increased control: First, prolonged and consistent exposure to learner-control seems to lead to collateral gains in curiosity and critical thinking; second, the quality and retention of understandings seem to be enhanced when learners have to "sort out" essential from inessential information; and third, learning outcomes are probably better if learning is measured qualitatively instead of quantitatively.

Attention was then turned to the implications of the restructuring of basic power relationships that is implicit in the full implementation of learner-control. It was shown that the dramatic and far-reaching nature of such proposed changes affects both teachers and learners, and that its successful implementation requires both teachers and learners to adjust their attitudes toward and expectations of each other. It was shown that teachers cannot unilaterally "give" control to learners unwilling to accept it, and that increasing learner-control demands a negotiated consensus between the parties involved.

Clearly, the perspectives of both teachers and learners are vital in this area, but since the learner's point of view is dealt with in considerable detail in Chapter Thirteen, the teacher's side of the matter was considered here. In discussing the difficulties confronted by teachers, it was shown how situations of learner-control potentially threaten the notion of teaching as conventionally defined. The construct of facilitation of learning is regarded with some circumspection by many teachers, even those intellectually committed to attempts to shift the locus of control to learners. It was argued that, whether in favor of learner-control or not, teachers' actions tend to be guided by higher-order beliefs about the nature and purpose of education, and these manifest themselves in their responses to particular situations.

The construct of "pseudoautonomy" was introduced to describe the situation in which adult educators attempt to devolve some responsibilities onto learners but without either genuine commitment or a clearly articulated view of the long-term implications of their actions. Trainers who "go through the motions" in this way are frequently unaware of the dissonance between their overt actions on the one hand and the beliefs and understandings that they hold to be true on the other. Finally, it was argued that researchers should attempt to understand the issues surrounding devolution of control from the point of view of the teacher, by attempting to adopt a "teacher's-eye view." However, this is only one perspective, and any given situation can also be understood from the perspective of the learner.

Overall, three findings emerge from this chapter. The first is that teachers and learners alike are engaged in attempts to maintain personal equilibrium. The shift to genuine learner-control, however, represents a significant challenge to established practices and beliefs, and there is therefore evidence to suggest that teachers and learners alike may encounter difficulty in making the transition.

A second finding is that adult learners judge and evaluate the demands of learning situations and that, like students in more formal settings, they adjust their learning strategies to what they perceive to be the demands of the task. Adult educators, like other teachers, have expectations of learners that they subtly transmit to the learners who respond accordingly. Neither adult educators nor learners make the transition to learner-control without some residual interference from their preadult education experiences: "One has only to see a group of foundry foremen, helicopter pilots or nursery school teachers taking their seats for, say, a 'safety' lecture in a space laid out like a traditional classroom to realise how quickly all the old associations come crowding back" (Thomas and Harri-Augstein, 1985, p. 10).

The third point is that a rather different picture of learner-control might emerge if researchers were to adopt the perspective of the participants, and to explain the dynamic nature of choices made in the instructional situation from the vantage point of the teachers and learners themselves. The theoretical underpinnings for this approach are dealt with in the next chapters.

Part 3

New Theoretical Insights on Self-Directed Learning

> Developments in cognitive psychology and in the study of language and thought over the last twenty-five years have resulted not so much in a different theory of learning as in a redefinition of knowledge. There is a heightened awareness of knowledge as a human creation, and this is linked with the realization that each learner has to construct or reconstruct it for himself or herself. If knowledge in one sense is food, the learner has first to take it apart (digest it) and then to build it into his or her existing structures of understanding. It only becomes meaningful once it is integrated with what he or she already knows.
>
> *—Sutton, 1981, p. 4*

Part Three, comprising Chapters Eight through Ten, acts as a bridge between the largely historical review and analysis in the first half of the book and the more anticipatory and future-oriented focus of the latter half. Parts One and Two examined the emergence and development of self-direction as a vital area of theory and practice in adult education, and reviewed the major themes or trends that have predominated in thinking and writing about it. Parts Four and Five, on the other hand, concern strategies for developing self-directed learning competence, issues for research in the future, and new ways of conceptualizing self-direction within the context of lifelong learning and

245

societal transformation. There are, however, some major discontinuities between traditional and emerging views of self-direction. In the past, self-direction was seen essentially as a personal quality or attribute; knowledge as a fixed and enduring set of "facts" to be mastered; learning as a process of acquiring attitudes, skills, and knowledge from outside the self; and individuals as substantially asocial atoms, independent of their social and cultural environments. In the new view, though, self-direction is acknowledged as a product of the interaction between the person and the environment; knowledge is recognized as tentative, evanescent, and socially constructed; learning is defined as a qualitative shift in how phenomena are viewed; and individuals are seen in a complex and mutually interdependent relationship with their environments.

It is the purpose of Part Three to reformulate and refract the ideas and concepts traditionally associated with self-direction so that the proposals and recommendations made later can be seen as a coherent new way of thinking about and promoting the development of self-direction in learning. Accordingly, rather than a bridge, this section might better be described as an "air lock" or "intellectual decompression chamber" in which conventional thinking might be progressively revised as a result of being challenged by new ideas about self-direction in learning.

Chapter Eight adopts a theoretical position of constructivism. It is argued that learning consists of subsuming new ideas, experiences, and skills within existing cognitive frameworks. Since such frames of reference are inherently individualistic and idiosyncratic, all learning, both as a product and a process, is in a sense self-directed. This approach to thinking about learning, however, necessarily involves a new way of considering knowledge; it has inescapable implications for whether—and if so how—people's skills as self-directed learners can be enhanced, and it also sanctions more naturalistic approaches to research.

Chapter Nine takes the constructivist approach further. Essential decisions such as what to learn, how, and in what order to approach learning tasks, how to make sense of new ideas or information, and how deeply to delve into the subject being studied must all be confronted by the self-directed learner. This chapter examines, from the learner's point of view, how these decisions are arrived at and again emphasizes that learning involves a qualitative shift in conceptions rather than a quantitative addition to a stable store of knowledge.

Chapter Ten adds to this picture by stressing that self-direction is not a quality that exists in the person or the situation independently but rather is a result of the interaction between a person and a situation. It is pointed out that a person's ability to be fully self-directing is constrained by the nature of the learning situation, by the nature of knowledge, by the learner's social context, and by his or her own view of the situation. While these features can, at least to an extent, be transcended, they cannot be ignored by those who seek either to study or to enhance the capabilities for self-direction in learning.

Eight

Understanding the Individual Nature of Learning

Despite the thousands — probably millions — of words that have been expended on the subject of self-direction in learning, very few authors ever make explicit what they mean by the term *learning*. This is hardly surprising, since there is widespread consensus about the "commonsense" understanding of what is involved when someone learns and the term is so widely used that it would probably be considered pedantic to devote attention to discussing what is or might be meant by the word. However, recent research — especially by scholars in England and Sweden and to a lesser extent in Australia — has provided some provocative insights, and in doing so has shed new light on what is meant by, and involved in, self-directed learning.

With some notable exceptions (Bantock, 1961; Becker, Geer, and Hughes, 1968; Boud and Griffin, 1987; Parlett and Hamilton, 1977; Perry, 1970; Thomas and Harri-Augstein, 1985), much modern research on learning has until recently been dominated by four factors: an atomistic or quantitative view of knowledge, a behavioristic or neobehavioristic view of people, a preference for the perspective of the researcher over that of the learner, and a tendency to conduct research in laboratories or other artificial settings. Recent research, however, differs on each of these counts; first, it views learning as a qualitative transformation of understandings rather than a quantitative accretion; second, it sees learners as active construers and "makers

249

of meaning"; third, it concentrates on portraying the experience of learning from the learner's perspective; and fourth, it seeks to examine the phenomenon of learning in all its complexity, as it occurs in "natural" or "real-life" settings.

The Meaning of Learning

One of the most original contributions to a changed understanding of "learning" is attributable to the work of Säljö, a researcher from Sweden. In 1978, he took a group of Swedish university students and asked them the simple question: "What do you actually mean by learning?" By analyzing their various responses, Säljö was able to identify five rather different underlying conceptions:

1. *Learning as the Increase of Knowledge.* Answers in this category tended to be vague, describing learning in terms of its outcome, rather than its essence, and moreover based on a view of knowledge as a "quantum" that can be accumulated.
2. *Learning as Memorizing.* Although responses in this category reveal something about the cognitive processes of learning, they rest on the assumption that learning involves transferring units of information or pieces of knowledge from a source outside the learner—a teacher or a book or an experiment—into the learner's head.
3. *Learning as the Acquisition of Facts, Procedures, and so on That Can Be Retained and/or Utilized in Practice.* The main difference between this conception of learning and the one before it is the notion of application. This has the implication that items of information or experiences might be scanned for their practical utility or applicability and hence that some sort of valuing or judging rather than simple memorizing is also involved in learning. This implies the existence of some sort of cognitive mechanism whereby new information is compared with what is already known, and is stored according to its similarity to other items of knowledge already held.

4. *Learning as the Abstraction of Meaning.* This conception moves away from viewing learning as primarily a matter of reproducing aspects of an outside reality, to one of abstracting meaning from what is seen and heard. The reproductive conception is replaced with a reconstructive one, and learning events and materials are seen not as ready-made knowledge, but as the raw material from which learning can be extracted.

5. *Learning as an Interpretive Process Aimed at Understanding Reality.* This is by far the most sophisticated conception of learning, because it emphasizes the interpretive nature of learning and the relationship between the learner's valuational system and the outside world.

In discussing these five conceptions of learning, Säljö, (1979, p. 19) goes on to comment: "A prominent feature of especially the second conception described above is the idea that knowledge is external to students and the process of learning essentially means a more or less verbatim item-by-item transfer of knowledge from an external source into the heads of the learners where it is filed. In contrast, the essence of conceptions 4 and 5 seems to lie very much in an emphasis on the assumption that knowledge is construed by individuals as a result of an active effort on the part of the learner to abstract meaning from a discourse and also to relate this meaning to an outside reality."

This shift in perspective, from viewing knowledge as something external to be "mastered" to an internal construction or an attempt to impose meaning and significance on events and ideas lies at the heart of what has become called the *constructivist paradigm.* In this view, learners are not passive beings who respond to "stimuli," and learning is not merely the appropriation of previously devised labels and categories. Instead learning is an active process of constructing meaning and transforming understandings. One corollary of this is that because no two people have had identical experiences, each person constructs a more-or-less idiosyncratic explanatory system: a unique map of the topography that we call reality. This has inescapable ramifications for evaluating *what* people have learned, and it also calls for approaches to research that recognize the highly individualistic nature of *how* people undertake learning endeavors.

It is the purpose of this chapter to present, in a condensed form, the major features of this constructivist view of learning, and to indicate what significance such a shift in perspective might have for thinking about, studying, and promoting self-directed learning.

An Overview of Constructivism

Constructivism is a broad and somewhat elusive concept. According to Gergen (1985), the term has been used in reference to Piagetian theory, to a form of perceptual theory, and to a movement in twentieth-century Russian art and architecture. However, more important for the present purpose, it has also been applied to an approach to understanding thinking processes, based on the notion that discourse about the world is not a reflection of the world but is a social artifact. In this sense, constructivism has its origins in, and is linked to, areas of study as diverse as philosophy of science, ethnomethodology, history and sociology of knowledge, literary theory, symbolic anthropology, deconstruction of meaning, dramaturgical analysis, and recent advances in historiography. An impressive pedigree!

Like positivism, constructivism (or constructionism, as some prefer to call it [Gergen, 1985]) is not a single monolithic theory, but rather a cluster of perspectives united by underlying similarities in worldview. Although some theorists have linked constructivism to the pioneering work of Lewin in the 1930s and 1940s (Sarbin, 1977), its intellectual origins can be traced back to philosophers such as Spinoza, Kant, and Nietzsche and ultimately to Plato (Gergen, 1985, p. 269).

Until recently, the principles of constructivism were not widely known or accepted, although the notion espoused by constructivists — that knowledge cannot be taught but must be constructed by the learner — is not new. Von Glasersfeld and

Smock (1974, p. xi) trace the origins of constructivism back as far as "a fragment of the pre-Socratic *Parmenides* in the 5th century BC," and what they refer to as "the suspicion . . . that knowledge and explanation might have more to do with the knower and the explainer, than with what was being known or explained" (p. xii) appeared as early as the eighteenth century in the work of George Berkeley (1710) and Giambattista Vico ([1710] 1858).

Paradoxically, it is the field of science, so frequently assumed to deal with "hard" facts and "real" data, that has done most to bring constructivism to the fore as an alternative way of viewing knowledge. A century ago, in 1886, Mack recognized the tenuous base of positivism in science when he wrote: "We are accustomed to regarding the object as existing unconditionally, although there is *no such thing as* unconditional existence" (cited in Toulmin, 1970, p. 30). Einstein and Infeld (1952, p. 310) also recognized a form of constructivism in their discussion of the nature of science itself: "Science is not just a collection of laws, a catalogue of unrelated facts. It is a creation of the human mind, with its *freely invented* ideas and concepts. . . . The only justification for our mental structures is whether and in what way our theories form as a link with the world of sense impression."

It seems ironic that, just at the time that research in education has been striving to render itself more "scientific" (meaning more concerned with invariant laws and objective data), research in science has become more concerned with the relativity of knowledge (Feyerabend, 1975; Kuhn, 1970; Lakatos, 1970; Manicas and Secord, 1983; Pope, 1982, 1983, 1985; Popper, 1963).

Although the philosophy of science has led the way, there have also been dramatic shifts in this direction in other domains, too. For instance, Geertz (1973) and Lévi-Strauss (1962) in anthropology, Schutz (1967) and Berger and Luckmann (1967) in sociology, and Heider (1958) and Kelly (1955) in psychology, among others, have all emphasized how people invent, organize, and impose structures on their experiences, and have argued that knowledge is thus essentially a social artifact. However, as Magoon (1977) observes, these changes in the parent disciplines are not well understood by many educational researchers.

One of the central tenets of constructivism is that individuals try to give meaning to, or construe, the perplexing maelstrom of events and ideas in which they find themselves caught up. This extends to attempts to construe constructivism itself. It is intriguing to see how people commonly try to subsume constructivist ideas under some more familiar, and therefore more comfortable, category or label. Writing of his own work, G. A. Kelly (1970, p. 10) notes with wry amusement: "Personal construct theory has been . . . categorised by responsible scholars as an educational theory, a learning theory, a psycho-analytic theory (Freudian, Adlerian and Jungian — all three), a typically American theory, a Marxist theory, a humanistic theory, a logical positivistic theory, Zen Buddhistic theory, a Thomistic theory, a behaviorist theory, an Apollonian theory, a pragmatic theory, a reflective theory, and no theory at all!"

There are at least two problems with these sorts of categorizations. The first is that constructivism is not a single theory, but a cluster of related perspectives that are united in their underlying view of the world. There is thus a good deal of variability *within* constructivism. Second, "constructivism in its pure, radical sense is incompatible with traditional thinking" (Watzlawick, 1984, p. 15), and therefore it cannot be incorporated into traditional categories. As von Glasersfeld and Smock (1974, p. xi) observe, constructivism offers, among other things, "an alternative way of looking at knowledge, knowledge acquisition, and the process of cognition. The approach is neither easy nor comfortable."

For both these reasons, constructivism defies ready classification within existing theoretical frameworks. Even for those who have found themselves questioning established views about the production and transmission of knowledge, constructivism demands a substantial revision of ideas and perspectives; in fact, as von Glasersfeld (1974, p. 2) observes:

> Revision may be too gentle a word for the kind of reorganisation of ideas which . . . is indispensable for an understanding of the theory of knowledge which . . . constructivist formulations entail. It is not a question of merely adjusting a definition here and there, or rearranging familiar concepts in a somewhat novel fashion. The change that is required is of a far more drastic nature. It involves demolition of our everyday conception of reality and, thus of everything that is explicitly or implicitly based on naive realism; it shakes the very foundations on which nineteenth century science and most of twentieth century psychology has been built, and it is, therefore, not at all unlike the change that was wrought in physics by the joint impact of relativity and quantum mechanics.

What, then, is the essence of this way of looking at educational issues? The basic concern of constructivism is with how people make sense of the perplexing variety and constantly changing texture of their experience. Unlike positivism, which tends to view knowledge as deriving from a more or less competent mapping of an external reality, constructivism "asks one to suspend belief that commonly accepted categories or understandings receive their warrant through observation" (Gergen 1985, p. 267). Constructivism is presented by its proponents as infinitely richer and more complex than most empiricist/positivist approaches to understanding social phenomena. Its detractors and critics, like those who criticize interpretive approaches generally, point to its excessive emphasis on the individual, although recent work in social psychology has been attentive to the social and historical context of individual meaning-making (Buss, 1979; Gergen, 1985; Sullivan, 1984; Watzlawick, 1984; Wexler, 1983).

According to Sarbin (1977), constructivism is subsumed under the root metaphor of contextualism (Pepper, 1942), which emphasizes constant change and novelty. Events are in constant flux, and the conditions of one event alter the context of a future event. In view of the way self-directed learning activities often unfold (Spear and Mocker, 1981, 1984), an approach that emphasizes and allows for the ebb and flow of circumstances would seem to be preferable to one that presumes a simple linearity. Because constructivism is more like a "shared consciousness" (Gergen, 1985) than a cohesive movement, there are many formulations of what it entails. However, at what might be called a metatheoretical level, constructivist thought usually manifests some combination of the following assumptions:

1. People participate in the construction of reality.
2. Construction occurs within a context that influences people.
3. Construction is a constant activity that focuses on change and novelty rather than fixed conditions.
4. Commonly accepted categories or understandings are so-cially constructed, not derived from observation.
5. Given forms of understanding depend on the vicissitudes of social processes, not on the empirical validity of the per-spective.
6. Forms of negotiated understanding are integrally connected with other human activities.
7. The "subjects" of research should be considered as "know-ing" beings.
8. Locus of control resides within the subjects themselves, and complex behavior is constructed purposely.
9. Human beings can attend to complex communications and organize complexity rapidly.
10. Human interactions are based on intricate social roles, the rules governing which are often implicit rather than overt.

To attempt to deal adequately with constructivism in its fullest sense lies well beyond the scope of this book. Instead, it has been decided to concentrate selectively on three dimensions that are of greatest relevance to educational research and prac-tice: assumptions about human nature, the nature of knowledge, and the meaning of learning. These three domains are bound up with one another; collectively they may be said to constitute a paradigm or worldview. Thus, if one has a particular view of knowledge it tends to affect one's ideas of how learning should (or at least might) take place, and this in turn implies a particu-lar view of people generally (Lawson, 1982, p. 41). Alternatively, seeing people in a particular way is likely to affect one's view of people as learners, which consequently implies a certain under-standing of the nature of knowledge. For instance, a researcher who sees learning as essentially a matter of mastering a stable body of "facts" is likely to adopt a substantially different approach to research from the one who sees learning as a dynamic interaction between a learner and a constantly changing world: As Kessen (1966, pp. 58–59), observes, "The [learner] who is confronted by a stable reality that can be described adequately in the language of contemporary physics is a [learner] very different from the one who is seen facing phenomenal disorder from which he [or she] must construct a coherent view of society."

The discussion that follows concentrates on the three basic domains just mentioned: a constructivist view of people, a constructivist view of knowledge, and constructivism in teaching and learning. For convenience in exposition, these three domains are treated separately, but in practice they are highly interdependent, and any attempt to subdivide them like this is inevitably artificial. In discussing constructivism, von Glasersfeld (1984, p. 37) makes the same point: "Language inexorably forces us to present everything as a sequence. The three sections of this essay, thus, will have to be read one after the other, but this inevitable succession should not be understood as a logically necessary order. What is contained in each of these sections could be outlined only very approximately as independent themes, because, in constructivist thought, each is so closely interwoven with the other principal themes that, presented separately, each would seem to be little more than a finger exercise. Singly, the arguments . . . presented here certainly cannot create a new way of thinking about the world; if they can do that at all, it will be through the fabric of their interrelations."

Thus, accepting constructivism involves suspending some commonly held beliefs and embracing instead a different view of how people make sense of their realities. Since this is central to understanding learning, it is also a vital starting point in considering the nature of self-directed learning.

A Constructivist View of People

One of the core components of constructivism is the belief that people, particularly adults, are not shaped by circumstances beyond their control. Many contemporary theorists have sought to explain human behavior either through the "push" of stimuli located in the environment or the "pull" of needs located within the person (Simons, 1986). In either case, it has been common to portray people as more-or-less passive and inert beings, jerked this way and that by forces over which they have no control. Constructivists, on the other hand, maintain that people are embarked, from the time of their birth, on a continuing voyage of inquiry and exploration, and that "instead of buying the prior assumption of [the human being as] an inert object, either on an implicit or explicit basis, we propose to postulate a *process* as the point of departure for the formulation of a psychological theory. Thus the whole controversy as to what prods an inert organism into action becomes a dead issue. Instead, the organism is delivered fresh into the psychological world, alive and struggling" (Kelly, 1966, p. 37).

It is assumed by constructivists that people "have two basic attributes, an innate and powerful drive to relate to others, and a continuing attempt to make sense of their experiences" (Ryle, 1975, p. 1), and that they pursue these goals by selectively interacting with others and, at the same time, adapting or creating for themselves representational models of reality that become guides to their actions. Central to this view of people is the notion of choice. Certainly, people have both a genetic and a cultural inheritance, but as Mair (1977, p. 267) points out, "We are not bound by our conditioning or our family dynamics, or delineated completely by our heredity, unless we choose so to be. . . . We can be different if we go out and do differently, we can become different by acting differently."

Constructivists maintain that the individual can, in principle at least, always find an alternative way of looking at a situation, that "events are subject to as geat a variety of constructions as our wits would enable us to contrive" (Pope, 1985, p. 10). As Kelly (1955, p. 15) puts it, "No one needs to paint himself into a corner; no one needs to be completely hemmed in by circumstances; no one needs to be a victim of his [or her] biography." People are viewed as "self-constructing" (Birren and

Hedlund, 1984) because what they "become" (Allport, 1955) is the product largely of their own activity.

The self-constructing person is a familiar prototype in the literature of philosophy, of psychology, and of education, being referred to variously as "an adequate personality," "mature," "self-actualizing," "fully functioning," "authentically emerging," or simply "becoming" (Robbins, 1988, p. 26). As discussed in Chapter Two, the "self-forming power" of the human soul "is a fearful as well as glorious endowment. . . . Possessing this, it little matters what or where we are now, for we can conquer a better lot, and even be happier for starting from the lowest point. Of all the discoveries which people need to make, the most important, at the present moment, is that of the self-forming power treasured up in themselves" (Channing, 1883, pp. 14–15).

The adoption of a constructivist view of people has important implications both for the study and for the enhancement of autonomy (Kenny, 1988) and self-direction in learning. The first is that the self-constructing person would, by nature and by definition, have a tendency toward being autonomous (see Chapter Four). He or she would be presumed to have both the ability and the willingness to be introspective and self-aware, as well as having an inclination towards self-improvement. This does not imply that adult learners would always be able to manifest such autonomy in every learning situation, but it does mean that educators need to make allowances for this tendency, and to create situations in which such learners could develop and exert their innate drive towards acting independently.

Second, the use of the term *self-constructing,* rather than *self-constructed,* implies a continuing process rather than a finished state. Because it connotes action, autonomy is seen as a continually renewed and renewable condition — what Overstreet (1950, p. 284) refers to as the "peculiar new dignity of a maturing adulthood" rather than a static accomplishment. It is perhaps useful to think of people, in whatever they are doing, as being in a state of dynamic equilibrium whereby they respond to any disruption or perturbation of this equilibrium by seeking to restore the balance. Several authors have argued that people consciously seek to be autonomous, and events that suppress or deny their autonomy will be resisted. This is consistent with the long-established principle in adult education that adult learners must be listened to, and respected as people, or else they will "vote with their feet."

A third implication of adopting such a perspective is that autonomy is not something that happens to people, or something that can be given to them: While an adult educator may be able to give learners the chance to exercise freedom, it is not possible to give them autonomy.

Fourth, if people are seen as "self-constructing," there must be some inner life, some central tendency or coherent belief system around which their self-constructions are organized. This means that behavior (for instance, choosing to undertake a learning project or declining to accept control of a learning situation) must be seen as intentional and logical, within the learner's own frame of reference (Magoon, 1977, p. 652).

Fifth and finally, because people are seen as active construers, constructivism requires that educators seek to understand and, as far as possible, to enter into the perspective of learners. This goes far beyond simply "starting where the learner is," and extends to attempts to see instructional events themselves from the point of view of the learner. Constructivism also sanctions both action research and other naturalistic inquiry methodologies. This is dealt with at greater length in Chapter Fifteen, but one corollary of adopting a constructivist view of people in considering self-directed learning is that particular weight needs to be given to their view of the situation. Researchers should, as far as possible, seek to elicit from respondents, and to represent as faithfully as possible, the views of self-directed learners themselves about their interests, attitudes, intentions, and understandings.

It must be noted, however, that the constructivist view presented here, which itself emerged largely in response to the dominant positivistic paradigm, has been criticized, both by positivists and by those opposed to positivism. Not unexpectedly, those imbued with a positivistic outlook have criticized interpretive approaches as representing a return to mentalism and highly subjective and "prescientific" accounts of phenomena. They also object to "the inability of the interpretive approach to produce valid knowledge in the form of wide-ranging generalisations, or to provide 'objective' standards of verifying or refuting theoretical accounts" (Carr and Kemmis, 1983, p. 94).

Perhaps more seriously, constructivist approaches have been criticized "from within," by those advocating a "critical perspective." It has been pointed out that merely describing a situation from the perspective of the participants, no matter how skilfully and systematically, ignores the fact that there are external features of social reality that are very influential in shaping that reality. Individuals are often caught up in "crucial problems of social conflict and social change" (Carr and Kemmis, 1983, p. 94) of which they may be unaware. One of the roles of the adult educator, therefore, may be to help learners to recognize and thus to emancipate themselves from various cultural, historical, and social forces that influence their lives and inhibit their ability to behave autonomously (Mezirow and Associates, 1990).

This is not to say that those who favor a critical approach to social inquiry reject the importance of the actor's point of view. As Sullivan (1984, p. 123) points out, "Critical interpretation does not relinquish the conscious intentions of actors. In fact, a critical interpretation of the personal world is grounded, at the outset, in the 'intentional project' of the actors or agents." However, as Sullivan goes on to say, "If we stopped here, we would be guilty of a crass form of idealism. The full scope of institutional living cannot be reduced to conscious intentions of agents. . . . Notwithstanding intentional action, human action must also be understood as being caused by social conditions over which the agent exerts no conscious or intentional control" (p. 124).

This constitutes one of the major limitations of constructivism — that simply exploring with learners their personal constructions of autonomy does not address the factors that may inhibit, constrain, or determine either their constructs or their ability to act freely. The question of constraints on people's activities, including self-directed learning, is an important consideration in this and following chapters.

The Constructivist View of Knowledge

The study of the origin, nature, methods, and limits of human knowledge (epistemology) is a complex branch of philosophy, and clearly it is beyond the scope of this chapter to deal adequately with such a broad subject. However, it is not possible to talk of any kind of learning, including autodidactic learning, without adopting some view of the nature of knowledge. Accordingly, this is a recurring theme in this book, and is also dealt with in detail in Chapter Twelve.

When authors advocate a particular approach to teaching (or learning), only rarely do they make explicit their view of what constitutes valid knowledge, of how it is created, shared, or reproduced. Thus, it is necessary to infer the theory of knowledge on which various formulations about learning (and, in particular, autodidactic or independent learning) are based. As mentioned previously, until comparatively recently, the dominant view of knowledge — at least in the behavioral sciences — was derived from a positivistic perspective. In this so-called received view, knowledge was thought of as an accumulated body of empirically verified "facts," derived directly from observation and experimentation: "'Knowledge,' not only in common usage, but also in most of the current psychological and philosophical literature, is always tacitly assumed to be knowledge of an existing world. That is to say, what we know is assumed to be an aspect of an independent reality, a reality that exists by itself and in itself" (von Glasersfeld and Smock, 1974, p. xiv).

This objectivist or naive realist view has been very influential in shaping conceptions of teaching, because it implies that there is an objective reality, to which learners should be introduced. It has also influenced many approaches to research, where it is considered to be the purpose of the researcher to discover and represent this objective reality as faithfully as possible (Koetting, 1984; Merriam and Simpson, 1984; Soltis, 1984).

The constructivist perspective differs significantly from

the view of knowledge as deriving from a process of copying or replicating (von Glasersfeld, 1974, p. 7). While not denying the existence of an outside reality, "It is fundamental to the constructivists' view that the environment can never be directly known, but that conception determines perception. We know reality only by acting on it. This means that knowledge is neither a copy nor a mirror of reality, but the forms and content of knowledge are constructed by the one who experiences it. The active interaction between the individual and the environment is mediated by the cognitive structures of the individual. What we learn in interaction with the environment is dependent upon our own structuring of those experiences. Thus, according to this view, people do not merely respond to the environment, they construe it" (Nystedt and Magnusson, 1982, p. 34).

It is important to emphasize that constructivists acknowledge the existence of a "real" reality beyond the individual knower. One of the charges sometimes leveled against constructivism is that it adheres to the metaphysical position of solipsism, or the claim that there is no reality outside the self, and that all human perception and experience exists only in the mind. A detailed refutation of this claim lies outside the scope of this chapter (see for example von Foerster, 1984), but Kelly (1955, p. 6), in the original assumptions underlying personal construct theory, states that "we presume that the world is really existing, and that man is gradually coming to understand it." And in 1969, he indicated that a person's constructions of reality may not even be congruent with reality as experienced by others: "The fact that my only approach to reality is through offering some responsible construction of it does not discourage me from postulating that it is there. The open question is not whether reality exists or not, but what we can make of it" (p. 25).

The proposition that different people construe the same reality in different ways sometimes proves to be a stumbling block, even to those who are able to accept the notion of people as active construers. The point might best be grasped by referring to an example. Imagine a situation in which an instructor is talking about the difficulties faced by students from lower socioeconomic groups. One student—a man dressed in dirty overalls — suddenly picks up his papers and abruptly leaves the class, nodding curtly to the instructor as he goes. When asked to recount this incident, one observer claimed that the man who left seemed agitated and angry and was obviously upset by the lesson. Another person reported that the man who left was clearly upset that he had to leave at that particular point, because he was very interested and involved in the topic.

While the same behavioral information was available to both observers, they had clearly drawn quite different inferences based on what they had seen. Both people made a connection between how the man was dressed and his probable socioeconomic status. Both also made an inference based on the agitated state in which the man left the class. In one case, it was assumed that the man was offended — and left because of that; in the other case, the man's restlessness was attributed to the fact that he had to leave, not the other way around.

It is a common experience for people to misconstrue others' motivations. Such misunderstandings might be based on past experience, on information provided by a third person, on some small gesture (real or imagined), or on a number of other fragments of evidence. Even an explanation by the persons concerned about their motivations is frequently not enough to dispel a particular impression once it has been formed.

As people interact, they are constantly judging one another and often searching for evidence that supports their own interpretation of the situation. To one observer, the man's agitation meant that he was offended, to another that he was torn between wanting to stay and needing to leave. Such "evidence" need not be objectively "true" for it to function as a powerful guide to their actions. All the time, people are testing out whether their construing of a situation adequately accounts for what they see, hear, and experience. However, central to constructivism is the perhaps radical proposition that all we can ever know for certain about the real world is what it is not. Watzlawick (1984, pp. 14–15) illustrates this provocative thesis by means of an analogy:

> A captain who on a dark, stormy night has to sail through an uncharted channel, devoid of beacons and other navigational aids,

will either wreck his ship on the cliffs, or regain the safe, open
sea beyond the strait. If he loses ship and life, his failure proves
that the course he steered was not the right one. One may say
that he discovered what the passage was *not*. If, on the other hand,
he clears the strait, this success merely proves that he literally
did not at any point come into collision with the (otherwise unknown) shape and nature of the waterway; it tells him nothing
about how safe or how close to disaster he was at any given moment. He passed the strait like a blind man. His course *fit* the
unknown topography, but this does not mean that it *matched* . . . the
real configuration of the channel. It would not be too difficult to
imagine that the *actual* geographical shape of the strait might offer
a number of safer and shorter passages.

It would not be difficult to imagine either that another person
could, under similar circumstances, sail a different course that
also *fitted,* without necessarily *matching,* the contours of the channel. Kelly (1955, pp. 8–9) uses much the same imagery to explain his notion of personal constructs: "People look at their world
through transparent patterns or templets which they create and
then attempt to fit over the realities of which the world is com-
posed. The fit is not always very good. Yet without such patterns, the world appears to be such an undifferentiated homo-
geneity that people are unable to make any sense out of it. Even
a poor fit is more helpful than nothing at all."

Systems of personal constructs (which are also referred
to, among other things, as cognitive structures or schemata) may
be likened to the above-mentioned courses in that they *fit* the
features of people's worlds, without necessarily *matching* each
other or the contours of the "real" world as experienced by someone else, such as a researcher. To the constructivist, knowledge
does not necessarily reflect or map exactly the external reality,
but consists of a set of workable hypotheses, or "templates," constantly being put to the test in interactions with other people's
constructions of the "same" situation. Not only are such construct systems complex and intricate, but it seems certain that
no two people would ever have exactly the same cognitive structures.

Earlier in this chapter, it was asserted that people "adapt
or create for themselves representational models of reality that
become guides to their actions." Now it is possible to restate
this assumption in the form that people "adapt or create for them-

selves representational models that become their reality, and that thus act as guides to their actions."

For many, it is unacceptable to suggest that learners *construct* their own realities, and even more heretical to maintain that they then experience this reality "as though" (Rix, 1983, p. 9) it were external to themselves. As von Glasersfeld (1974, pp. 3–4) says, "Such a statement would be rather shocking. We would all like to be hard scientists, and such an 'as though' threatens to pull the rug out from under our feet. It smells of solipsism, and that is something to which, by and large, we have developed an intellectual allergy; it makes us extremely uncomfortable, to say the least."

In fact, the notion of "as though" is a powerful one in education. Some extol its use in educational situations where they are seeking attitude and behavioral change, and where they call on learners to experiment with new behaviors "as though" they had in fact changed. However, it is argued here that whatever the "objective" reality, learners respond to events "as though" they were true. This means that learning often proceeds from a series of personal propositions that, if not disproved, are assimilated into explanatory schemas "as though" they were demonstrably true. After a while, they become so thoroughly internalized that, to all intents and purposes, they are true for the individual. Clearly it is one of the educator's roles to help learners to recognize incorrect, biased, or dysfunctional personal beliefs, so that the learner has the chance to change. This is a subtle and intricate process, however, which is not accomplished simply by confronting the learner, but it involves careful exploration in a nonthreatening environment (see Chapter Eleven).

The acceptance of a constructivist perspective poses the researcher and the instructor alike with the problem of how to gain access to each individual's personal worldview. Observation can do little more than to provide data about behavior rather than about intentions (and even then, it is distorted through the construct system of the observer). Asking questions presupposes first that the respondent is able to articulate his or her understandings and intentions, and second that he or she uses words to mean the same as the researcher does—a particular problem in the case of autodidacts. Moreover, there is always the likelihood of obtaining the respondent's "espoused theory" rather than his or her "theory-in-use": the attitudes, values, beliefs, and intentions that actually lie behind action.

To overcome these problems, researchers have developed a range of strategies, including participant observation, case study, critical incident technique, *Q* sort, stimulated recall, repertory grid, open-ended interview, and so on. In doing so, although they have strived for unobtrusiveness and naturalistic research techniques, they have often lost sight of the "realization that their 'subjects,' even when out of direct contact with the investigator (as in a questionnaire situation), nevertheless react differentially to the research stimulus" (Lincoln and Guba, 1985, p. 94). This phenomenon is referred to as *reactivity,* and it seems particularly ironic that constructivist researchers might lose sight of the very essence of constructivism, namely the construing respondent, and assume that their research methods are somehow immune to these reactive processes. In his review of methodological problems confronting personal construct psychology, Neimeyer (1985, p. 118) points to the fact that in truly constructivist research, "the constructs a subject records . . . are not *elicited* from some pre-existing repertoire, but are *created* in response to experimental demands." To assume otherwise is tacitly to sanction a positivistic understanding of personal knowledge.

If problems associated with gaining access to people's worldview are a major stumbling block for constructivism, another compelling criticism is its apparent overemphasis on individualism. According to Quinton (1971, p. 201): "Ever since Descartes brought it into the centre of philosophical attention, epistemology has been a thoroughly individualistic discipline or, as it is usually put, a thoroughly subjectivist one. The individual knower or subject is represented as setting out on his cognitive career with nothing more than the senses and reason that he stands up in. He gets to work on the virgin territory of the unknown with this rudimentary survival kit and in due time, through his industrious activities of construction and inference, he accumulates a substantial body of general theory and a some-what less stable stock of singular beliefs."

When this idiosyncratic view of knowledge is taken to ex-tremes, it appears that each person's worldview and explana-tory system is entirely unique, a position referred to as *radical subjectivism*. Such a position would render all forms of commu-nication, including direct teaching, and vicarious experience, virtually impossible, and, as Crittenden (1978) points out, "There are probably very few serious defenders of the complete sub-jectivism that intellectual autonomy in the strict sense entails" (p. 108). Quinton (1971, p. 203) goes on to observe that "this Crusonian story of initially solitary knowers building up their private stores of knowledge and only then entering into exchange relationships is plainly unacceptable. It utterly fails to recog-nise the extent to which we are cognitively members of one another. As Popper says: 'quantitatively and qualitatively by far the most important source of our knowledge is tradition' (1963, p. 27). My private or personal knowledge, what I have discov-ered by my own observations and stored in my memory, together with what I have inferred from this, constitutes minute frag-ment of what I claim to know. And if quality is a matter of scope and importance rather than of certainty, all but a vanishingly small proportion of my general, theoretical knowledge is derived from others."

As mentioned earlier in this chapter, research and teach-ing within a constructivist framework may well give due atten-tion to the personal understandings and attitudes of individual people. However, researchers and educators must not lose sight of the wider social and cultural issues that influence, and in many cases determine, how particular individuals see their personal worlds. Crittenden (1978, pp. 113–114) makes a similar point when he criticizes the "simplistic image of learning; each hu-man organism independently interacting with its environment and deriving its own concepts out of this experience. . . . As hu-man beings, we are not isolated individuals constructing our private realm of concepts out of the data of our raw experiences. We acquire concepts, and learn to apply them in interpret-

ing and understanding our experience through the social processes . . . of various human practices." This is an extremely valuable point in considering the limits to self-direction in learning.

At the beginning of this chapter, it was stated that, until
recently, constructivism had played a relatively minor role in
epistemology. However, this is not to say that all educators have
failed to emphasize a constructivist perspective in their work or
in their writings. For instance, in *Democracy and Education,* Dewey
(1916, p. 89) wrote that "education is a constant reorganizing or
reconstructing of experience. What is really *learned* at any and
every stage of experience constitutes the value of that experience."
Piaget, whose contribution to developmental psychology has influenced generations of educators and educational researchers,
is also well known for his articulation of a genetic (or constructivist) epistemology (Sigel and others, 1981; von Glasersfeld, 1974).

In their book *Teaching as a Subversive Activity,* Postman and
Weingartner (1971) discussed the relative nature of knowledge
and recognized the subversive implications of such a view for
conventional education. They argued that the issue was a direct
challenge — possibly even a threat — to teachers who saw their
role as passing on established truths. This is because, if knowledge is seen to be relative, the student is free to question the
utterances of the teacher. The role of the latter was conceived
as helping to release and develop the capacity of learners to inquire for themselves.

In the same year, Young edited a book entitled *Knowledge and Control* in which Esland (1971, p. 96) wrote of the fluid,
negotiable (in the navigator's sense of searching for a safe or
workable passage), and tentative nature of knowledge, especially
once disciplinary boundaries are dismantled: "If knowledge is
de-reified, it is, then, a much more negotiable commodity between teacher and pupil . . . there is no reason to suppose that
these will remain within the boundaries of what are now heuristi-
cally labelled as 'subjects.' New configurations of knowledge are
likely to emerge from the combinations of questions which arise
in the learning situation . . . the boundaries are only human constructs and can, therefore, be broken."

The acceptance of a constructivist approach to knowledge has significant implications for researchers and teachers. In science education, for instance, it has resulted in a virtual paradigm shift away from positivism and naive realism (Pope, 1982, p. 4) and, among other things, to the formation of a Special Interest Group of the American Education Research Association on Subject Matter Knowledge and Conceptual Change.

In the domain of "self-directed learning" it seems that individual learners place their personal constructions on learning situations as well as on the content they are learning, and, as discussed in Chapter Fifteen, this calls for research methods that emphasize the unique and idiosyncratic nature of each individual's system or structure of meanings, while recognizing the shared nature of much human understanding.

Constructivism, Learners, and Learning

If knowledge is viewed the preceding way, as tentative and socially constructed, it is clear that "a constructivist's epistemology has implications for both the scientist and the teacher because it leads directly to the specific proposition that knowledge cannot be taught but only learned (that is, constructed). Cognitive structures are never passed ready made from a 'teacher to a pupil' . . . because cognitive structures (that is, knowledge) must under all circumstances be built up by the learner" (von Glasersfeld and Smock, 1974, p. xvi).

Such a perspective runs counter to much conventional wisdom and established adult educational practice. Even in individualized instruction, where the ostensible focus is on individual differences, it is still commonly assumed that knowledge can be broken down into "natural" constituent elements and that it can be transmitted virtually intact from teachers to learners, although it may be reassembled by learners in idiosyncratic ways. However, the constructivist view of learning, based as it is on the individual construction of reality, is particularly congruent with the notion of self-direction. Writing of open education from a constructivist perspective, Rathbone (1971, pp. 100, 104) states that the learner is regarded:

> . . . as a self-activated maker of meaning, an active agent in his own learning process. He is not one to whom things merely happen; he is the one who, by his own volition, causes things to happen. Learning is seen as the result of his own self-initiated interaction with the world: the [learner's] understanding grows during a constant interplay between something outside himself — the general environment, a pendulum, a person — and something inside himself, his concept-forming mechanism, his mind. . . .

> In a very fundamental way, each [learner] is his own agent — a self-reliant, independent, self-actualising individual who is capable on his own of forming concepts and of learning.

Within such a conception, learning cannot be simply a matter of memorizing or "acquiring" knowledge. Instead, it is a constructive process that involves actively seeking meaning from (or even imposing meaning on) events. In a review of literature concerning academic tasks, Doyle (1983, pp. 166–172) summarizes an emerging constructivist theme in education with the following characteristics:

> Comprehension of texts is an active constructive process, not merely reception or rehearsal of information. Personal knowledge of the world is organised into associational networks or schemata.

> Prior knowledge plays a significant role in this process of construction, in problem solving, and in learning. One of the major findings of research in this area is that domain-specific knowledge plays a central role in problem-solving and learning within a content area.

> Solution strategies are learned "naturally" through experience; from these natural strategies, learners invent procedures for solving routine problems. Sometimes these problem-solving strategies are systematic, but wrong.

> Academic work requires both domain-specific knowledge and complex solution strategies.

> Age and ability of the learner influence subjective complexity of academic tasks. Mature learners are selective and efficient in extracting information relevant to a task, less mature learners attend to a broader range of stimuli and are less likely to select and process information to fit the demands of a particular task.

Central to these characteristics of academic work, and indeed to constructivism in education generally, is the notion of some representational model — a system of personal constructs, associational networks, or schemas — built up and modified on the basis of experience. This system of personal constructs provides the "anticipatory scheme" (see Chapter Twelve) that the learner uses to make sense of any given situation. According to von Glasersfeld (1984), the mental activity of bringing two or more of these schemas into relation with one another for the purpose of searching for similarities and differences (Kelly, 1955; Erickson, 1987) lies at the very heart of constructivist accounts of learning. Thus, the development and refinement of the learner's cognitive map occurs through a constant process of interaction between hierarchic integration (Crockett, 1965) or subsumption (Ausubel, 1968) on the one hand and cognitive differentiation (Crockett, 1965) or discrimination (Ausubel, 1968) on the other. As Crockett observes, "This increase in differentiation and hierarchic integration is found not only in development from childhood to adulthood, but also in the development of new knowledge in a mature individual; *thus, an adult being exposed to a content area that was initially foreign to him would proceed through the same stages in development as the maturing child,* though the process would probably be completed more rapidly than in the child" (pp. 49–50; emphasis added).

Thus, constructivism in education is concerned with two things: how learners *construe* (or interpret) events and ideas, and how they *construct* (build or assemble) structures of meaning. The constant dialectical interplay between construing and constructing is at the heart of a constructivist approach to education, whether it be listening to a lecture, undertaking a laboratory session, attending a workshop, reading a text, or engaging in any other learning activity.

This brings to light a crucial point. Many educational innovations such as open learning, activity-based learning, and discovery learning place great emphasis on the active participation of the learners, apparently under the impression that activity per se is the key to enhanced understanding and retention. However, as Kuhn's (1981) ingenious experiment showed, it is not simply active engagement that seems to influence learning outcomes, but the process of developing anticipatory schemes (see Chapter Twelve). Many educational innovations tend to confuse physical activity and situational independence with intellectual activity and epistemological independence. Even mathematics, which one might think of as objective and rule governed, is a subject where understanding is constructed, rather than discovered, by the learner: "The mathematician's enterprise . . . is after all a human activity and, as such, it is dependent on human cognition. If cognitive processes are, indeed, processes of construction rather than replicating or depicting an *a priori* existing reality, then the focus of any explanatory effort must shift from what there *is* or *may be* to *how we arrive at* the conceptual constructs we actually have. Richards' (1974) discussion, consequently, develops the dichotomy of a 'logic of discovery' and a 'logic of reconstruction' " (von Glasersfeld and Smock, 1974, p. xix).

Von Glasersfeld and Smock (1974, p. xx) then go on to explain the implications of this difference for teaching: "The method of mathematical instruction cannot be the imparting of mathematical 'truths,' but must, instead, be the setting up of circumstances which will induce the learner to achieve in his own mind—that is, to reconstruct—the conceptual entities and relational functions the mathematicians have 'discovered.' The logic of *reconstruction,* thus, becomes crucial to the didactic endeavor and Richards' analysis suggests that to ensure the learner's reconstruction, a good deal more is needed than the mere description of the mathematical constructs he is to acquire."

The task for the trainer clearly shifts from "mere description" of the constructs the learner is to acquire to attempting to understand the existing understandings and meaning systems of the learner through the use of repertory grids, concept maps, Q sorts, learning journals, and other techniques that provide a window into these understandings. This is not to say, however, that there are no standards against which a learner's constructs might be assessed, although one might be forgiven for thinking this on the basis of comments such as the following: "Individualization in learning goes well beyond any single no-

tion of 'each according to his own speed.' Open education sees
a fundamental independence of each learner from all others,
from all would-be assistants such as teachers . . . and from all
codified knowledge as it exists in universities or texts. It holds
the individual [learner] capable of interacting with and learning something from nearly any responsive elements in his environment" (Rathbone, 1971, p. 103).

Constructivism is sometimes criticized for its apparent
willingness to accept each person's interpretation of events as
being as valid as every other person's, as if there were no criteria
for judging among them. However, not all constructions are
equally useful or valid, and one purpose of education may be
to allow people to "reconstrue" events and ideas in ways that
lead to more functional outcomes for them (Freire, 1972), for
instance by thinking through the implications of their positions
or imagining the logical consequences of following a particular
line of argument. It is often difficult to do this in isolation, or
at least in the absence of guidance, and this may constitute one
of the major arguments in favor of guided instruction; otherwise learners are "trapped" by their own constructions, without
having access to alternative ways of viewing events and ideas.

As discussed in the previous part of this chapter, the
willingness to accept uncritically each respondent's interpretation is one of the criticisms aimed at constructivism by advocates of a critical science approach: "If psychological interpretation . . . simply reiterated and repeated the life world of some
particular cultural form, it would be redundant. One could call
such interpreters 'scribes' rather than interpreters, since nothing new would be added to the situation" (Sullivan, 1984, p. 118).
This is a timely observation in the present context. If research
into self-direction does no more than "simply catalogue" learners' understanding, it is unlikely to result in a useful reinterpreta-
tion of the dynamics of "self-directed learning." By the same
token, accepting the premises of constructivism, "it would be
foolish to venture that there must be one correct interpretation. . . . The whole process of interpretation must be carried
out with a considerable degree of humility and openness [which]
is characterised as a dialogue between the interpreter and the
interpreted" (Sullivan, 1984, p. 119).

Public and Private Forms of Knowledge. Despite its central importance, the subject of epistemology is frequently ignored in programs of educational research. This means that people's views of what constitutes knowledge are rarely challenged, and so rarely thought through explicitly. One particularly useful way of looking at knowledge is the scheme proposed by Habermas, and elaborated with respect to adult education by Mezirow (1981, 1985). Habermas proposed that there are three distinct domains of knowledge. Two of the domains concern "public" and one concerns "private" forms of knowledge (Polanyi, 1967; Thomas and Harri-Augstein, 1985).

The first part of the public domain concerns knowledge about the environment, and how to manipulate, control, and work within the environment. Instrumental action is governed by technical rules, and involves predictions about observable events — physical and social — that can prove correct or incorrect (Mezirow, 1981, p. 4).

A second form of public knowledge, which Habermas (1970) typifies as "practical" or "communicative" knowledge, "is governed by binding consensual norms which define reciprocal expectations about behavior and which must be understood and recognised by at least two acting subjects. Social norms are enforced through sanctions [and] . . . while the validity of technical rules and strategies depends on that of empirically true or analytically correct propositions, the validity of social norms is grounded only in the intersubjectivity of the mutual understanding of intentions and secured by the general recognition of obligations" (Habermas, 1970, p. 92).

In this view, the creation, distribution and interpretation of knowledge are social processes involving everyone (Lawson, 1982, p. 36). Becoming knowledgeable involves acquiring the symbolic meaning structures appropriate to one's society, and, since knowledge is socially constructed, individual members of society may be able to add to or change the general pool of knowledge. Teaching and learning, especially for adults, is a process of negotiation, involving the construction and exchange of personally relevant and viable meanings (Pope and Shaw, 1979; Thomas and Harri-Augstein, 1982, p. 2). This trend is "reacting to the excesses of the mechanistic, positivist account of knowledge" (Crittenden, 1978, p. 108), and is in turn part of a larger backlash against positivism generally (Carr and Kemmis, 1983; Manicas and Secord, 1983; Phillips, 1983).

The third area of cognitive interest, or domain of knowledge, is private, and Habermas characterizes it as "emancipatory." This domain is not concerned with the external world as much as it is with the learner's own self-awareness. According to Mezirow (1981, p. 5), "This involves an interest in the way one's history and biography has expressed itself in the way one sees oneself, one's roles and social expectations. Emancipation is from libidinal, institutional, or environmental forces which limit our options and rational control over our lives, but have been taken for granted as beyond human control."

It sees knowledge is idiosyncratic and personalistic: Each person has a unique worldview, based on his or her unique, cumulative life experience. There is no order to knowledge but that which the learner sees in it, and thus curriculum in the sense of a stable, ordered, logical exposition of subject matter is impossible. Teaching, therefore, can be no more than facilitating learning, which, by definition, is "coterminus with life" (Lindeman, 1925, p. 3). Mezirow (1981, p. 6) claims that this is the most distinctively adult form of learning because it refers to the learning that occurs as people move through "the existential challenges of adulthood, . . . negotiating an irregular succession of transformations in meaning perspective."

For many, it is this third domain that is the natural "home" of self-direction, and those who advocate increased self-direction in learning frequently do so from a perspective of personal emancipation (Mezirow, 1990). It is, however, possible for people to undertake self-directed inquiries in the other two "knowledge-constitutive domains" as well, although the public and socially validated nature of such knowledge clearly acts as a limit or constraint on how much self-direction is possible.

The constructivist approach discussed in this chapter, which deals with attempts to understand the meaning of intentional actions, fits within the second of Habermas's knowledge-constitutive domains, and as such may suffer from the criticism leveled at the hermeneutical sciences generally, namely that they "tend to ignore the role of authority and power in meaning constitution" (Sullivan, 1984, p. 124).

Summary

The purpose of this chapter has been to introduce the major tenets of constructivism and to consider some of its implications for understanding of self-direction, including self-directed learning. This is based on the notion that constructivism, although it is a complex and somewhat controversial philosophical and epistemological position, provides a better "fit" with the phenomenon of self-direction than does the more conventional positivist view.

The chapter began by contrasting the assumptions underlying constructivism with the more familiar positivistic position that "the activity of 'knowing' or 'cognizing' [is] viewed as a kind of copying or replicating. The copying subject was thought to acquire or build-up inside himself a replica or image-like representation of the outside things, i.e. the *real* object which he is getting to know" (von Glasersfeld, 1974, p. 7). Central to constructivism is the idea that people are "self-constructing," and that they can reconstrue their circumstances through the application of their personal worldview. The behavior of people is seen as purposive and intentional, and thus researchers and those seeking to help learners need to attempt to enter into the understandings that people have of their own situations. Five major corollaries of this assumption were mentioned: (1) the striving for personal autonomy is a natural state of affairs, though it may be retarded or constrained by social circumstances; (2) personal autonomy is a process rather than product; it is continually renewed, rather than being a static accomplishment; (3) autonomy is determined partially by personal characteristics, and partially by environmental circumstances — people can be given freedom, but they cannot be given autonomy; (4) people's search for a dynamic equilibrium is mediated by, and accomplished through, a complex belief system or set of personal constructs having both cognitive and affective dimensions; and (5) constructivism sanctions both action research and naturalistic inquiry methodologies.

It was argued that, as people develop and mature, they acquire a set of personal constructs (also called associational networks or schemata) that act as the perceptual filter through which they observe, experience, and evaluate events. These personal constructs are not immutable — they can be changed — but they provide the framework through which, and into which, all new learning is appropriated.

Although there is presumed to be an external reality, knowledge is not derived from mapping or reflecting the externalities of the real world, but is constructed by developing representations that *fit* rather than *match* this external world. Since each person experiences reality slightly differently, knowledge is always somewhat idiosyncratic. However, it is easy to lose sight of the fact that many aspects of a person's knowledge are actually shared with others, being influenced by factors such as age, gender, class, and cultural background, and that much knowledge is accordingly intersubjectively grounded and consensually validated, rather than being completely individualistic.

Teaching is not a process of transmitting knowledge intact to learners, but a matter of negotiating meanings. Learning was asserted to be an active process of *constructing* a system of meanings and then using these to *construe* or interpret events, ideas, or circumstances. As such, the constructivist view of learning is particularly compatible with the notion of self-direction, since it emphasizes the combined characteristics of active inquiry, independence, and individuality in a learning task.

The purpose of the next chapter is to explore, from this constructivist point of view, how learners make sense of new information, and in particular how they orient themselves to novel learning situations. With an improved understanding of the dynamics of the learning encounter, adult educators will be in a better position to assist and guide self-directed learning efforts.

Nine

How Learners
Approach Learning
Situations

There is a sense in which all of life's experiences are potentially educative; in fact human existence is marked by its chaotic nature and the consequent need for continual adaptation and renewal through informal and incidental learning. Within this virtually limitless domain of ubiquitous unanticipated and random learning, however, there is a pattern of consciously planned, intentional, deliberate, and often systematic efforts to learn. Such endeavors cover an extremely diverse spectrum, some being organized and mediated by external agencies—such as schools, colleges, and training departments—and some being planned by learners themselves.

While in no way denigrating the value of incidental learning, the concern of this book, and of this chapter in particular, is with how learners approach situations that are explicitly educational in intent. In those situations that are wholly planned by an outside agent, at least some of the decisions are made for the learner—notably the order in which ideas are encountered, the general boundaries or parameters of the field, and some aspects of how to understand and interpret the material. Even here, however, the learner has a considerable degree of freedom in how he or she conceives of the subject, what connections and relationships are perceived, and what underlying principles or themes are discerned.

As the learner accepts more and more responsibility for various instructional factors, these aspects of learning are still his or her own prerogative. However, added to them are concerns about the optimal order in which to deal with the material, how to understand the concepts and issues involved, how deeply to penetrate the "signs" to the things signified, and how to delineate or identify the boundaries of the area being studied. In this chapter, I will consider the following issues that — explicitly or implicitly — must be confronted by all learners, but particularly self-directed learners: what to learn, how to approach learning tasks, in what order to tackle learning, how to understand or interpret new ideas, and how deeply to enter into a subject. Each of these considerations will be discussed in turn.

What to Learn

Although it is anathema to many educators, especially those that favor the use of preplanned behavioral objectives, most self-directed learners embark on their learning projects with only a shadowy intimation of where their inquiries may lead. This is not universally true, of course; certainly some self-directed learners know in advance precisely what they want to achieve and how they will evaluate their attainment. Thus a person who wants to build a patio onto the house, to reupholster a leather armchair, to research the history of the family, or to learn enough Spanish to have a holiday in Mexico will often have a very specific goal in mind and will decide alone when the objective has been satisfactorily attained. Many self-directed learning projects, however, have a more nebulous beginning, and they develop to an extent and in directions that could scarcely have been anticipated at the outset.

Thus the decision about what to learn, or indeed about whether to learn at all, is often less clear for a self-directed learner than for a person enrolling in a course or program. Sometimes unexpected circumstances such as the birth of an exceptional child, an unanticipated job opportunity, joining a club or organization, or a chance meeting will create an interest or a need to learn, and it is from such humble beginnings that a lifelong pursuit may eventually evolve. The serendipitous and heuristic nature of much self-directed learning has already been discussed in Chapter Six. The point is that even something as basic as "what to learn" is not always clear at the start, and there may be a progressive refinement, or even wholesale reformulation of learning goals as a project unfolds and develops (Spear, 1988).

How to Approach Learning Tasks

To some extent, the approach adopted by a learner is a function of his or her preferred learning style, to some extent it is influenced by the nature of the subject matter itself, and significantly it is affected by the learner's perception of the demands of the situation (Svensson, 1989).

In formal educational settings, aspects of the approach to learning are implicit in the instructional situation. Thus the use of lectures, readings, seminar groups, or individual project work will call forth particular learning strategies that may or may not represent the learners' natural preferences or even the optimal strategy for mastering a particular domain. In the case of self-directed learning, however, where fewer such constraints apply, the learner is free to choose how to tackle some learning project, and accordingly the approach taken might be considered to be indicative of his or her "natural" or preferred learning style.

This is not to say, however, that the choice is always optimal. Many learners may have a restricted repertoire of learning skills, or alternatively they may have available a range of strategies but lack the competence needed to decide which approach is preferable in any given situation. Accordingly, as discussed in Chapter Eleven, any intervention to enhance self-directed learning competence needs, among other things, both to expose learners to a diverse range of strategies and to equip them with the necessary metalearning skills so that they recognize which approach is best in any given situation (Kirschenbaum and Perri, 1982, p. 91).

The relationship between the *content* and the *process* of learning (the "how" and the "what") has been shown to be quite intimate, so that any attempt to enhance learning competence needs of necessity to be grounded in some particular subject matter (Ramsden, 1988). Years ago, Bruner in his book *Toward a Theory of Instruction* (1966, p.72) made this important point with respect to the teaching of mathematics: "A body of knowledge, enshrined in a university faculty and embodied in a series of authoritative volumes, is the result of much prior intellectual activity. To instruct someone in these disciplines is not a matter of getting the learner to commit results to mind. Rather, it is to teach him or her to participate in the process that makes possible the establishment of knowledge. We teach a subject not to produce little living libraries on that subject, but rather to get a student to think mathematically for himself or herself, to consider matters as an historian does, to take part in the process of knowledge-getting. Knowing is a process, not a product."

This principle extends well beyond mathematics education: "Knowing is a process, not a product," and the aim of education at least in formal disciplinary areas is to teach learners to think as a linguist, a mathematician, a historian, a physicist, or an engineer (Brown, Collins, and Duguid, 1989).

Self-directed learning, if it is to be effective, necessarily requires the element of "cognitive apprenticeship" (Brown, Collins, and Duguid, 1989, p. 37) to be present. In other words, it involves "enculturation into authentic practices through activity and social interaction in a way similar to that evident . . . in craft apprenticeship" (p. 37). For the educator, this may involve a lengthy process of modeling his or her skills and knowledge, allowing the learner to gain insights by example and to see how an accomplished practitioner thinks and performs in action.

There are two important corollaries of this. The first is that, as discussed elsewhere in this book, the development of learning competence cannot be successfully achieved in a content-free way: How to approach learning needs to be considered in the context of learning a particular content for a particular reason.

Second, there are limits as to how much self-directed learning can occur in isolation. Except for those forms of learning that concern private knowledge not subject to public validation—the self-reflective or emancipatory learning discussed by Mezirow (1981, 1985, 1990)—most learning requires the acquisition of a way of thinking about a subject — a process rather than a product — and accordingly, interaction with other knowledge users is necessary.

In What Order to Tackle Learning

Almost as a subset of the question of how to approach a learning task, the learner must decide in what order to deal with issues, ideas, concepts, skills, and examples relevant to his or her area of inquiry. In a teacher-directed course, this is most often taken care of by the curriculum, and is based on some combination of the inherent logic of the subject and the learner's readiness to progress to the next theme or topic to be covered. In the case of self-directed learning, however, "the studies are not usually preplanned as in organized education, but developed on the basis of what opportunities have been natural to take advantage of, what seems to be the most complementary opportunity to utilize next" (Svensson, 1989, p. 9).

Moreover, in making these choices, the self-directed learner is usually ignorant of certain features that a teacher or trainer might take for granted: the rules of discourse governing the subject, the lines of inquiry that may have been discredited or discontinued, and the relative complexity of various ideas or aspects. This lack of knowledge confronts the learner with the problem of how to find a way into and through a body of knowledge that is unknown at the outset. Without the benefit of any explicit guidance, a self-directed learner is obliged to map out a course of inquiry that seems appropriate, but that may involve a certain amount of difficulty and disappointment that could have been averted. To avoid such detours and deadends, many self-directed learners rely on the advice of others who may be expected to be more knowledgeable about the domain being studied. The challenge for the educator is to provide guidance without providing too much direction, to help the learners in identifying areas of difficulty without detracting from their sense of "ownership" of the learning project.

As mentioned earlier, the optimal route through a learning sequence is not determined solely by the apparent structure of the subject matter itself, nor by the pattern that proved appropriate for someone else. Instead, the order in which an individual learner may best cope with a new set of skills or realm of ideas is strongly influenced by the demands of the situation for which the learning is being undertaken, the needs and interests of the learner, and the pattern of his or her past experiences and understandings of the domain. This difference may be expressed in two different views of learning. In the first,

> learning a subject is akin to building a house; first we have the foundations (prescribed basic knowledge) and then we can build on this brick by brick (*quanta* of knowledge), each neatly fitting within the existing structure. Clearly, with such a model of learning, it is nonsense to attempt to build the second floor until the foundations and first floor are complete; that is, to expect students to fit in blocks of advanced knowledge before they have consolidated the lower levels. . . .
>
> An alternative, and more appropriate metaphor for learning if we are to remain in the field of construction, is that of building a steel-framed structure in outer space — an interconnected network of potentially infinite extent, to which it is possible to add pieces in almost any order as long as they interconnect in some way, and form a pattern which makes sense to the builder. In this model there is nothing to prevent us completing the whole structure in outline before filling in the finer detail, or indeed starting at one place rather than another [Cornwall, 1981, p. 201].

Recent research into cognitive psychology has shown that in fact learning is more often like the second than the first model; that is, the learner develops certain broad outlines of his or her understanding, and then gradually fills in the details, paying selective attention to those features that "fit" into his or her personal schema. Thus in endorsing a self-directed approach to learning, advocates are also implicitly supporting a particular view of knowledge and of learning generally. In those situations where quality, safety, or meaningfulness of learning would be severely hampered by learners pursuing issues without guidance, one would need to reconsider the wisdom of advocating self-directed rather than teacher-directed learning.

How to Understand or Interpret New Ideas

When a person confronts an entirely new topic for the first time — an event, idea, or experience for which she or he has no personal precedents — the automatic response is to try to make sense of it by searching for similarities with things that are familiar. The Rorschach ink blot test is a good example of this: The respondent is presented with some shapes on paper that really have no meaning in themselves, but that are capable of being viewed as a butterfly, a pair of lips, or a mountain in the mist.

The tendency to impute meaning to events or objects is certainly not limited to ink blots; psychologists and educators have increasingly recognized that the frames of reference that we bring to situations significantly shape how we view and react to them. In 1968, Ausubel made his often-quoted statement: "*Existing cognitive structure* . . . is the principal factor influencing meaningful learning and retention. Since logically meaningful material is always, and can only be, learned in relation to a previously learned background of relevant concepts, principles, and information . . . it is evident that the substantive and organizational properties of this background crucially affect both the accuracy and the clarity of these emerging new meanings and their immediate and long-term retrievability" (pp. 127–128).

Based on these convictions, Ausubel made his even more famous recommendation on the need for teachers to provide learners with "advance organizers," which he described as "introductory materials at a high level of generality and inclusiveness presented in advance of the learning material" (p. 131). Although Ausubel's work has not escaped criticism, the notion that teachers should attempt to bridge from the known to the unknown, by making use of whatever relevant knowledge exists in the learner's cognitive structure, is widely accepted.

Special problems present themselves, however, in the case of those who are attempting to learn something without the assistance of a teacher or trainer. In such cases, the learner still strives to make sense of the new idea or experience, but with-

out the benefit of any help by an external agent to render the
new learning compatible with the learner's existing understandings. In any given learning situation, it is possible that a person could apply any one of several "frames of reference" in attempting to understand something new. In an unpublished paper
on "School Science: Falling on Stony Ground or Choked by
Thorns," Claxton (1982) explains very simply and lucidly how,
based on past experiences, a learner could attempt to understand and explain the scientific concept of flotation or what happens if a solid object is placed into or onto a "squishy" medium.
He calls the alternative frames of reference *minitheories* and goes
on to explain four plausible scenarios (see figure, p. 287):

> Suppose the learner does not yet possess a trans-situational mini-
> *theory* about water, but does possess mini-theories about *drinks,*
> *baths, boats* and *beds,* all of which surround the gap in which the
> target phenomenon is located. The learner can extend any one
> of these theories into the gap in order to generate a prediction,
> because each of them has something to say about the situation
> of lowering a solid object onto or into a "squishy" medium. If the
> learner chooses *drinks,* he [or she] may say that the water level will
> remain unchanged — because when a spoonful of sugar is put into
> a cup of tea, no change in the overall volume is noticed. If he
> [or she] extends *boats,* the same answer will be arrived at, because
> neither the sea nor the local pond visibly rises or falls when a real
> or a toy boat is launched. If the *beds* mini-theory is used, how-
> ever, the learner may predict that the water level will go down —
> because the bed goes down when he or she lies on it. And, finally,
> if the choice is made to base a prediction on *baths,* then he [or
> she] will say that the level will go up, because that is what hap-
> pens when he [or she] gets into the bath. . . . Note that only *baths*
> generates the correct prediction, and also something like the sym-
> bolic science explanation. Note also that every other answer is
> a perfectly rational deduction from an inappropriately applied
> theory. And note too that there is no way that the learner can
> know which will turn out to be "correct" ahead of time: he or she
> has no alternative but to gamble on the basis of existing knowl-
> edge [Claxton, 1982, p. 5; corresponding figure on p. 287 used
> by permission].

This is precisely the situation confronted by the autonomous learner. New information, experiences, or ideas have
somehow to be accommodated within the learner's existing cognitive framework. In any given situation, it is likely that the
learner could bring to bear one of several different ways of think-

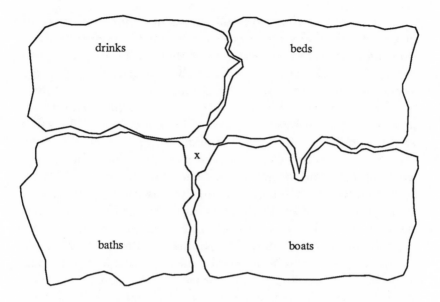

ing about and viewing the phenomenon of interest, but in the absence of any outside guidance, there is no definitive indication as to which point of view should be adopted.

This dilemma has occasionally been raised as an objection to self-directed learning. It has been argued that learners lacking explicit guidance may invest their energies in exploring and attempting to understand some phenomenon of interest for which they lack the necessary vocabulary or conceptual framework. Self-directed learners, therefore, run the risk of misunderstanding the subject of their study and hence of being miseducated.

Clearly there is an element of truth in this concern, and educators can do much to avoid the need for learners to "rediscover the wheel" in their attempts to comprehend some body of knowledge. Likewise, they can help to avert frustrations and deadends that might otherwise bedevil the independent learner. However, implicit in this argument is the tacit belief that there is a "right" or "correct" way of viewing particular issues in education and moreover that educators can direct learners into such approved channels of thought.

Recent research, especially in science education, has emphasized that in any given group of learners—even those confronting a subject for the first time—there will be a finite number of alternative ways of thinking about and understanding a phenomenon of interest. In addition, there is also usually a "preferred" or "correct" way of thinking about the phenomenon that is sanctioned by the canons of formal science. The same research, however, has revealed that "telling students the 'right' conception cannot work, because change involves an active working upon and interaction between the old way of thinking and the new. . . . Changes in conceptions require teachers to arrange situations where students must confront the discrepancies between their present way of thinking about the subject matter and the new way desired" (Ramsden, 1988, pp. 21–22).

In the case of self-directed learners, there may be no built-in or inherent mechanism to ensure that a learner does confront discrepancies between his or her present way of thinking and that which is sanctioned by the discipline or body of knowledge involved. It is as if a person learned to speak a foreign language entirely from books, without ever hearing the language spoken. He or she would need to actually speak with other language users before being able to claim to have learned the other language correctly.

It is one of the teacher's or instructor's responsibilities in formal learning contexts to give serious attention to the learner's preexisting and emergent conceptions about the subject matter being taught and learned. Furthermore, he or she needs to provide a supportive environment in which the learner is encouraged to confront and work through the implications of discrepancies between the present and desired way of viewing the subject. In the case of a self-directed learner, however, no such control or checking mechanism is operating unless the learner imposes it for himself or herself. The nearest approximation to building in some sort of comprehension check on the learner's conceptions is to ensure that she or he attempts at least to understand fully the basic principles involved and not simply the specific examples given. This, in turn, raises the issue of how deeply a learner tries to enter into a subject he or she is learning.

How Deeply to Enter into a Subject

One decision which any learner — self-directed or taught — must make is how deeply to delve into the subject matter being studied; that is, whether to aim for deep-level or surface-level learning outcomes (Häyrynen and Häyrynen, 1980, p. 10). Clearly this decision is not made independent of the other aspects of the learner's approach; indeed whether or not the learner seeks to adopt a critical, questioning stance or simply to repeat or memorize the material is a central aspect of the learner's orientation, and a reflection of how significant the learning is to the learner. It is reasonable to expect that a project that has pervasive and far-reaching implications for a learner's life would be regarded and approached differently from one with a lower level of personal significance. In his critical analysis of research into autodidaxy, Brookfield (1984a, p. 66) questions the tendency "to treat all learning projects as possessing equal significance to the learner." He goes on to add: "To compare dealing with bereavement or divorce with learning how to repair a car or wire a basement is methodologically unsound. Similarly, organizing an anti-nuclear advocacy group is an activity of a very different order from becoming expert in Armenian cuisine. The danger of emphasizing mechanical aspects of learning projects such as the number of hours spent in learning, the number of assistants used, or the non-human resources most frequently adopted, is that of coming to regard all self-directed learning as exhibiting some kind of conceptual or substantive unity" (pp. 66–67).

It is important to avoid simplistically equating the level of learning with its emotional impact or significance for a learner, but Brookfield is hinting at the need to discover the affective connotations a learning effort has for the learner — a perspective not commonly encountered in the literature on autodidaxy. One useful way of looking at this question might be to ascertain the purpose to which a new piece of learning is to be put.

As early as 1964, Havighurst distinguished between instrumental and expressive education, which he described as follows:

> Instrumental education means education for a goal which lies out-
> side and beyond the act of education. In this form, education is
> an instrument for changing the learner's situation. For example,
> the learner studies arithmetic so as to be able to exchange money
> and buy and sell things and to become a competent scientist or
> teacher. Or the learner . . . studies in his vocational field so as
> to get a promotion, or studies cooking so as to become a better
> housewife. Instrumental education is thus a kind of investment
> of time and energy in the expectation of future gain.
>
> Expressive education means education for a goal which
> lies within the act of learning, or is so closely related to it that
> the act of learning appears to be the goal. For example, the learner
> studies arithmetic for the pleasure of learning about numbers and
> quantities. The learning of arithmetic is its own reward. Or the
> learner . . . studies the latest dance "for fun," and not to become
> a teacher of dancing or even to make new friends. Expressive edu-
> cation is a kind of consumption of time and energy for present
> gain [Havighurst, 1964, pp. 17-18].

As Havighurst (1964) goes on to note, the difference between instrumental and expressive aspects of education should
not be overemphasized, because "there is some intrinsic enjoyment in almost every instrumental form of education, at least
if the learner is reasonably successful; and there is some instrumental or extrinsic outcome from almost every expressive
form of education" (Havighurst, 1964, p. 18n). However, despite
this reservation, the distinction has proved useful, particularly
in studies of participation and nonparticipation in various forms
of adult education (Aaltonen, 1979; Ordos, 1980), but no published reference has been found to its application in studies of
autodidaxy. Still, it seems that, according to the purposes described by learners themselves, many projects could be described
as instrumental while others are more esthetic and expressive.
This differentiation is important because it affects the strategy
employed by the learner, which in turn has been shown to influence the learning outcome.

One potentially fruitful avenue of inquiry in attempting
to gain a better understanding of this phenomenon of learning
something completely new may be found in the work of Häyrynen and Häyrynen in Finland. For the past decade or longer,
they have been engaged in an attempt to understand the mechanisms by which adults learn things from their environment.

According to Häyrynen and Häyrynen (1980, p. 8), "In the first stages of learning and thinking, a person orients himself to a new task. Actually, the first stage includes the perception of a new task, and its formulation as a problem. In new situations, a person makes a preliminary synthesis, that is, recollects all his knowledge, analysing the task on that basis. At the same time, he has to decide whether the task involves development of a new idea, a tool or maybe a new emotion."

Clearly this preliminary orientation involves an attempt to construe, or make sense of, a skill or task on the basis of past experience, and as Häyrynen and Häyrynen (1980, p. 8) state, "Thinking does not actually start until previous abilities prove insufficient. Thinking, thus, is a total process in which a person formulates his situation and creates conditions for oriented learning." Häyrynen and Häyrynen based their ideas on the work of the Göteborg Group in Sweden (Gibbs, Morgan, and Taylor, 1982; Marton, 1975, 1981; Marton and Säljö, 1976a, 1976b; Säljö, 1975, 1979a), which distinguishes between a surface level and a deep or transformational approach to learning tasks.

Deep-level learning involves an attempt to delve beneath the words or symbols to the underlying ideas or "the things signified." It requires a critical and analytical disposition, a deliberate search for the meaning of the subject, and an attempt to identify the relationships between ideas already held and those newly encountered. It contrasts sharply with *surface-level learning,* which concentrates on the externalities of subjects and is characterized by the rote memorization of (apparently) unrelated items of information. (In the context of formal educational settings — schools, colleges, universities, and training courses with assessments — there is a third kind of learning orientation — *achievement oriented* — which has to do with using deep-level strategies simply to attain high grades or to please the teacher or trainer, rather than because of any genuine interest in the subject itself. However, such an approach is relatively uncommon in situations of authentic self-directed learning, where the initiative for, and criteria concerning, the project reside with the learner rather than an outside agent, and consequently it is not dealt with in detail here).

Recent research has established a connection between the depth of learning outcome and the strategy employed. Thus, those who achieve deep-level or transformational learning do so because they use deep-level strategies. Similarly, those whose learning is surface level can attribute such outcomes to using surface-level approaches. Although there is not complete equivalence between approach and outcome, it is evident that deep-level learning — the kind most likely to result in a serious questioning of the issues and concepts embodied in an area of study — is unlikely to eventuate if a learner restricts his or her approach to rote memorizing of isolated facts or formulas.

According to Biggs (1987), each approach to learning (surface, deep, or achieving) is itself the product of two components: a motive and a strategy. The *motive* is the learner's intentions and purposes in undertaking a learning task: "If, in an educational situation, one decides that a pass is sufficient, then it seems to make best sense to rote learn only those facts and details which are judged (or guessed) as most likely to be tested. If one is interested in a particular subject, then it makes best sense to find out as much as possible about it, and work out what it all means. . . . It must be emphasized that it is the *learner's* psycho-logic that is at issue here, not the teacher's or the researcher's" (Biggs, 1987, p. 11).

The *strategy* is the way the learner goes about the learning task. In the case of surface approaches, the strategy is to memorize isolated items of information and, as Newman (1852, p. 238) puts it, "to load the mind with a score of subjects against an examination, . . . [to] devour premiss and conclusion together with indiscriminate greediness, . . . [to] hold whole sciences on faith and [to] commit demonstrations to memory."

In the case of deep-level learning, those "wanting to understand a topic would be unlikely, unless singularly lacking in metalearning ability, to choose a strategy based on rote learning" (Biggs, 1986, p. 133). Instead, they would need to develop an orientation towards learning in which they

- Are interested in the learning task and derive enjoyment from carrying it out

- Search for the meaning inherent in the task (such as the author's intention or purpose)
- Personalize the task, making it meaningful to their own experience and to the real world
- Integrate aspects or parts of a learning endeavor into a whole (for instance relating evidence cited to conclusions drawn)
- See relationships between this domain and their previous knowledge
- Try to theorize about the task or, in Bruner's phrase, go "beyond the information given" [Biggs, 1987, p. 15]

It is possible for motives and strategies to be dissonant. A person who, for instance, simply wants to obtain an overview of some author's ideas, instead of adopting the obvious course of skim reading, might laboriously read the entire work from cover to cover, underlining, highlighting, and taking copious notes: a strategy much more likely to be found in deep-level learning. Conversely, a person who seeks a deep level of understanding of some topic, but who lacks the necessary analytical skills, may find that his or her attempts to memorize apparently relevant information are inadequate to gaining that understanding. For the most part, however, learners demonstrate motive-strategy congruence, and the glue that holds these dimensions together is "metacognition," or more specifically "metalearning," which, as Biggs (1987, p. 75) comments, consists of two phases: "being aware of the available options and exerting control over those options."

Unfortunately, evidence suggests that much formal education encourages surface-level learning, and many commonly used processes of evaluation likewise encourage rote memorization. Even adult education (at least that part that is concerned with public knowledge) can sometimes be guilty of emphasizing the "rote" or "reproductive" learning of material, rather than encouraging learners to enter deeply into the subjects they are studying. Educators, therefore, have a substantial challenge if they propose to create learning environments that genuinely promote metacognitive outcomes (Baird and Mitchell, 1986). As Biggs (1986, p. 140) puts it, the counterpart of metalearning is metateaching, "procedures that . . . work simultaneously towards ameliorating factors that encourage surface learning, and emphasizing factors that encourage deep learning." The attempt to encourage metalearning abilities as part of the process of enhancing self-direction is discussed in Chapter Eleven.

Toward a New Understanding of Learning

Much of the foregoing has concerned the learning of propositional bodies of public knowledge. However, as discussed previously, a great deal of learning — especially self-directed learning — is emancipatory, concerning personal insights that are not codified and not necessarily shared by others. In either case, whether the knowledge to be learned is "public" or "private," the pervasive issue of how learners strive to make sense of their realities, and how they impose meaning on the events and circumstances they encounter, is still central to an understanding of how learners approach learning situations.

The approach that learners (and for that matter teachers) take to learning tasks is a reflection of how they view learning. If, for instance, learning is viewed as simply a matter of acquiring, mastering, or subsuming some set of concepts that have an independent existence outside the learner, then it makes sense to talk in terms of how much a person has learned. It is also sensible to consider learning-to-learn as the acquisition of a set of context-free skills that may be applied to any given learning situation.

In this chapter, however, and indeed throughout this book, learning is thought of as a qualitative shift in how a learner views or thinks about a person, situation, idea, experience, event, or other phenomenon of interest. Since learning is defined qualitatively, it implies that the evaluation or measurement of learning must also be qualitative, and must address the question *what is learned* rather than *how much* is learned. It also implies that learning is a relational construct; a person will approach learning in a particular way as a result of how he or she views the subject and the demands of the learning situation. A learner's preexisting conceptions, however, are not simply superimposed on a new subject or experience, but are certainly used to make sense of such subjects or experiences, and once learning has taken place, the learner can never view the phenomenon in exactly the same way again. Learning therefore entails an interactive relationship between new ideas, experiences, and insights and existing frames of reference, where each interacts with and mutually modifies the other (Ramsden, 1987). In practical terms, this means that educators need to allow learners the opportunity to experiment with new ideas and new behaviors; new ways of thinking about subjects or of acting cannot be taught without the opportunity for the learner to integrate them into his or her existing worldview.

There is a very strong relationship between what is learned (the referential aspect of learning) and how it is learned (the structural aspect of learning). Take, for instance, a person who is striving to learn about gardening. If he or she adopted a surface approach, this would imply an attempt to remember huge amounts of detail concerning the size, appearance, habit, nutritional demands, and other aspects of how, when, and where to plant particular types of seedlings which, as Eizenberg (1988, p. 180) notes, "becomes increasingly more arduous and tedious as the volume of material to be digested increases." If the learner chose a deep-level approach, on the other hand, he or she would try to understand the basic principles rather than specific instances which, again as Eizenberg (1988, p. 180) states, "is more efficient and effective in the long term as a way of remembering facts and is, of course, a more satisfying way to learn."

In order to adopt a surface-level approach to learning, it would be necessary to think of knowledge as essentially atomistic, individual fragments of information that are only connected sequentially and not in any profound way. Deep-level learning, on the other hand, rests on the assumption that knowledge is hierarchical; that is, some concepts are broader or more inclusive than others and there is a difference between principles and instances, and knowledge can be understood holistically (Svensson, 1984).

It is important to recognize that the "how" and the "what" of learning are intimately interwoven: The learner who seeks underlying principles will find them; the learner who strives just for rote memorization is unlikely to recognize any such inherent logic or structure in the subject. Thus the overall approach a learner adopts will significantly influence the shape of his or her learning outcomes. Not only must educators recognize the relationship, but they can assist learners to become more self-aware by asking them to reflect on how they approached particular learning tasks or activities, and how they preferred to learn certain content.

To relate this to self-directed learning, it is evident that learners are not always best served simply by removing obstacles to their autonomy. A learner whose view of knowledge is restricted to the more basic and absolutistic end of Perry's (1970, 1988) continuum — discussed in Chapter Twelve — is likely to adopt more atomistic/surface approaches to learning and accordingly to obtain only surface-level learning outcomes. Conversely, a learner who understands knowledge as relativistic, contextual, and tentative will probably adopt a more holistic/deep-level approach and will accordingly attain a more profound level of meaningful learning. Educators can help learners to come to this understanding by talking about and demonstrating the way knowledge is created in the domain, by showing how concepts have evolved historically, and by emphasizing the sorts of questions and issues that are being studied or debated at the "leading edge" of the field of study.

The problem, already alluded to in this chapter, is that learners cannot simply be told that knowledge is more complex than they might otherwise believe, but must be given the opportunity to confront the inadequacies and shortcomings in their present conceptions (in this case, conceptions of knowledge). As Biggs (1986, p. 142) notes, this requires the opportunity "to talk about their learning processes in a language distinct from that used to talk about the content of their learning." Providing learning situations in which this may happen is one of the challenges confronting those educators who wish to enhance the capacity for informed self-direction in learning. It is necessary to engage learners in thinking about and discussing their own approach to learning, and consciously exploring alternatives. This seems to be an essential component in developing an awareness of one's own learning process and preferences; yet, as Baird and Mitchell (1986) point out, many learners resent and resist this sort of activity as "a waste of time," "the instructor avoiding his or her responsibilities," or "not what we have come here to learn." To the extent that the learners are viewed as autonomous adults, such objections must be treated seriously, and the reasons for concentrating on such metalearning outcomes must be discussed.

Summary

Putting aside the question of serendipitous learning in everyday situations, any person who more or less deliberately sets out to learn something has to answer a series of questions that Biggs (1986, p. 143) summarizes as follows:

Motives	"What do I want?"
Goals	"What will it look like when I've got there?"
Task demands	"What do I need to get there?"
Context	"What resources have I got to use?"
	"What constraints must I contend with?"
Abilities	"What am I capable of doing?"
Strategies	"Well, then. How do I go about it?"

Although it is not suggested that the questions will be framed as baldly as this, or in this particular order, successful learning involves some awareness of the first five issues, and control over the sixth. Whether in formal learning situations, or in natural societal settings, the learner needs to confront these questions and, since they are about *process* rather than the *content*, all learning involves some metacognitive functioning: "High quality human performance inevitably requires metacognitive as well as cognitive components. To perform well, one needs to be aware not only of the knowledge and algorithms required by the task, but of one's own motives and resources, the contextual constraints, and to plan strategically on that knowledge. . . . Learning is no exception" (Biggs, 1986, p. 143).

In short, there are qualitative differences in the way learners approach learning tasks. These depend on the learner's intentions, understanding of the subject matter, interpretation of the demands of the learning situation, his or her repertoire of learning strategies, and ability to exercise control in the selection of different approaches to learning. All of these dimensions involve some higher-order metacognitive awareness.

Self-directed learning is no exception. If the quality of learning is to be maximized, educators must create situations in which learners can develop their range of learning skills, their understanding of knowledge, and their awareness of themselves as learners. These themes are dealt with in Chapters Eleven, Twelve, and Thirteen, respectively. This is a complex and demanding process that transcends the imparting of content, that affects all subjects or areas of study, and that applies to all phases of the educational spectrum. In the final analysis, teaching for self-direction demands nothing less than a radical rethinking of the paradigm that underlies most formal education — teaching, curriculum, and assessment — and brings into question many of our fundamental assumptions about what it means to learn. This theme is dealt with at length in Chapter Eleven. First, however, Chapter Ten further explores constructivism in education, and places particular emphasis on the way the situation or context influences people's ability to think of themselves as self-directed and to act accordingly.

Ten

Factors
That Influence
the Capacity for
Self-Direction

Whether people believe that autonomy is attained as a result of a normal process of maturation and development, or through deliberate exposure to certain educational and social experience, there is nonetheless a widespread acceptance of the idea that it is possible for a person to *become* autonomous, and that such an attainment is a central part of being an adult. It seems to me that there are at least two main problems with this line of reasoning. The first is that adulthood and autonomy are defined in terms of each other, so that adults are assumed to be autonomous and autonomous people are defined as adult.

The second, and perhaps more important problem, however, is that autonomy is assumed to be a unidimensional and once-and-for-all attainment; having reached adulthood, a person would exhibit autonomy uniformly in all aspects of his or her life. This, however, is not borne out in practice; often a person will exhibit qualities of intellectual but not moral or emotional autonomy (or vice versa). Furthermore, it is not uncommon to find a person who behaves very autonomously in some aspect of his or her life (for instance at work, or in the home) but seems very dependent when it comes to other aspects (for instance in their religious beliefs or in a learning situation).

As discussed in Chapter Four, it is clear that personal autonomy is not a single unidimensional construct, but one that has several distinct aspects or facets to it. Neither is it a single once-and-for-all attainment, but rather a constantly renewed and situationally variable attribute. In a sense, this means that no one ever *becomes* fully self-directed in any final sense, but in certain circumstances, or at certain times, people may behave more autonomously than at others. Such variability should not necessarily be construed as an undesirable or pathological situation, but rather as a recognition that individuals respond differently in different situations. In certain circumstances, a person might feel unable or unwilling to question the pronouncements of experts, to take the initiative in a new or unfamiliar situation, to determine what he or she believes in the absence of support or guidance from others, or to manifest personal autonomy in the broadest sense.

Limits to Self-Direction in Learning Situations

As with autonomy generally, many people commonly believe that there is such a thing as context-free autonomy as a learner. As discussed in Chapter Five, researchers have expended a great deal of effort on identifying the characteristics, qualities, skills, and attributes of successful self-directed learners and in devising educational approaches designed to help people in developing the desired profile as competent self-directed learners. Although there are certainly educational strategies that can potentially enhance learner self-directedness, it is "a developmental process with no finite end-states" (Gerstner, 1987, p. 172), and hence the search for the definitive qualities of *the* self-directed learner is doomed to fail. It is quite possible to find adult learners who can function perfectly competently in one area or domain, but who seek out help and guidance in another field. Indeed the myth of universal competence as a learner is not only misleading, but is potentially disabling, both for learners and for teachers, since it may engender feelings of inadequacy or guilt in someone who fails to deal equally well with all domains of learning.

At least four different strands of research converge to support the notion of situational variability in learner self-directedness: the context-dependent nature of adult learning generally; the socially constructed and consensually validated nature of knowledge; recent work on the situated nature of cognition and of learning; and the influence of a learner's perceptions of the demands of a learning situation, along with his or her "sense of personal competence." In addition to this, the sociologist's notion of the individual-in-social-context also illustrates the situational constraints on self-direction in learning. Each of these aspects will be considered in turn, before I offer some tentative observations and recommendations on its implications for educators.

The Context-Dependent Nature of Adult Learning. One of the by-products of the continuing emphasis on self-direction in learning is the often tacit belief that learning is a solitary matter, in which a learner interacts only with a body of knowledge that he or she is striving to acquire. Despite the attention paid to the assistance that is demanded and received by independent learners, much of the literature stresses the individuality of adult learning efforts.

In fact, however, by far the majority of adult learning occurs in social contexts and derives from social pressures of various types. The literature of adult education has consistently emphasized the collaborative, interdependent, and basically social nature of learning, but the constant stress on *self*-direction often obscures the facts that (1) most learning needs derive from membership of social groups (such as families, clubs and organizations, and work settings); (2) most learning takes place in group settings rather than in complete isolation; (3) even those who begin their learning alone commonly seek out other learners against whom to measure their progress and with whom to share the experience; and (4) in order for learning to be recognized as such, it usually necessitates submitting what has been learned to be validated by others. In addition to all this, the actual *content* of most adult learning is social in nature, concerned either with aspects of social behavior or with the interrelationship of the learner with other people.

Accordingly, much adult learning is not as self-directed as it appears to be. It occurs because of the learner's membership in a social group, and what is deemed to be worth knowing is likewise based on the opinions and expectations of others. This constitutes a major limitation to the learner's apparent self-directedness. I will return to this theme later in the chapter.

The Socially Constructed Nature of Knowledge. Closely linked to the social context of learning is the socially constructed nature of knowledge. Admittedly, as discussed in Chapter Eight, there is a domain of learning in which self-directed learners engage — learning about themselves — that gives rise to personal and private meanings that are not subject to verification or approval by others. Sometimes this is the ostensible purpose of their project. They read philosophy, join an encounter group, attend church, or keep a diary, with the intention of learning more about themselves. At other times, this learning is incidental, and occurs more or less fortuitously alongside their pursuit of some other content. Often, this incidental learning concerns insights into themselves as learners: how they prefer to learn new material, their motives, their level of tolerance for ambiguity, or how they interact with other people. In either case, the knowledge they acquire is self-knowledge, and it is typically less orderly than conventional discipline-based knowledge.

However, a large proportion of adult learning is concerned with attempts to appropriate and use bodies of knowledge for which there are public criteria in existence, and where learning, at least at the outset, necessarily involves accepting the rules that govern the subject area or domain. What this means is that in order both to learn something and to verify that it has been learned, the learner must engage in dialogue and interaction with others in the community of knowledge users.

Perhaps more important for the present purpose, this socially constructed aspect of knowledge also means that each subject, discipline, or field of study has its own particular and unique concepts, rules, and examples that distinguish it from other areas of study. Accordingly (as discussed in Chapter Twelve), the learner wanting to master some particular body of knowledge has to acquire the "domain-specific" aspects that allow him or her to learn the chosen subject. The question is How vital are these domain-specific aspects of learning? Are there general abilities or context-free skills that would allow the self-directed learner to acquire any subject matter desired? Recent research in cognitive psychology has done much to clarify the distinction between "general" and "content-specific" learning competence.

Language provides a readily available illustration. In order to learn about any body of propositional or discipline-based knowledge in our society, it is necessary to have reasonable facility in spoken or written language. But this in itself is not enough, because most fields of study have a specialized vocabulary that must also be acquired in order to gain access to the body of knowledge. What is more, many fields of study and practice use "everyday" words and phrases, but in a special way. People often resent the use of technical terminology—and especially of everyday words in a specialized way—claiming that it is simply jargon designed to exclude some people and make them feel inferior. Of course technical knowledge can be misused in this way, but "specialized knowledge is not just a set of technical terms. The terms imply taxonomies which organize reality differently from commonsense. Understanding technical discourse means being familiar with these specialized taxonomies and the principles which led to their construction" (Martin, 1989, p. 37).

How, then, can a learner—particularly a self-directed learner—who is unfamiliar with a certain body of knowledge even begin to understand it? If specialist knowledge is required to understand a given field, and if it forms part of that field, how can a novice break the vicious cycle of "not knowing"? The answer seems to be that there are certain forms of higher-order or strategic knowledge that allow a learner to orient himself or herself to a new learning task. However, as discussed in Chapter Twelve, a learner must enter at least a certain way into the subject he or she is trying to learn, and accordingly, "a foundation of domain-specific knowledge seems requisite to the efficient and effective utilization of strategic knowledge" (Alexander and Judy, 1988, p. 384).

In fact, the division of strategies into general and domain-specific is not quite as dichotomized as may at first appear: "There *are* general cognitive skills; but they always function in contextualized ways" (Perkins and Salomon, 1989, p. 19). Perkins and Saloman (1989, p. 23) go on to note that "general cognitive skills do not function by somehow taking the place of domain-specific knowledge, nor by operating exactly the same way from domain to domain. Rather, cognitive skills are general tools in much the way that the human hand is. Your hands alone are not enough; you need objects to grasp. Moreover, as you reach for an object, whether a pen or a ball, you shape your hand to assure a good grip. . . . Likewise, general cognitive skills can be thought of as general gripping devices for retrieving and wielding domain-specific knowledge. . . ."

This means that no self-directed learner can be equally competent across the range of all potential learning situations. While he or she may possess an extensive repertoire of strategic or general learning skills, each new domain will have its own domain-specific vocabulary of concepts that must be mastered before more advanced ideas can be tackled. Alexander and Judy (1988, p. 376) distinguish three levels of knowledge: declarative, procedural, and conditional. "Declarative knowledge refers to factual information (knowing what), whereas procedural knowledge is the compilation of declarative knowledge into functional units that incorporate domain-specific strategies (knowing how). Conditional knowledge entails the understanding of when and where to access certain facts or employ particular procedures."

Since these three aspects are cumulative, it can be seen that learning of at least some domains of public knowledge involves acquisition first of declarative and procedural aspects before progressing to conditional components. Since this is so, learning involves some sort of "cognitive apprenticeship" (Brown, Collins, and Duguid, 1989, p. 37), whereby the learner is progressively introduced to how words, concepts, and tools are used by practitioners in practice.

Again, the example of language might help. It is possible for a person to learn individual words and phrases within a language from a dictionary or phrase book, but vocabulary acquired in this way is often stilted and may be used quite erroneously, as in "I was meticulous about falling off a cliff" or "Mrs. Morrow stimulated the soup" (Brown, Collins, and Duguid, 1989, p. 32). Such mistaken usage occurs if words are treated as self-contained pieces of knowledge (meticulous = very careful; stimulated = stirred up), whereas in fact "words and sentences are not islands, entire unto themselves." Individual words, phrases, and sentences draw at least part of their meaning from their context, and the same is true of other aspects of knowledge. As Brown, Collins, and Duguid (1989, p. 33) express it, "All knowledge is, we believe, like language. Its constituent parts index the world and so are inextricably a product of the activity and situations in which they are produced. . . . Even well-defined, abstract technical concepts are not wholly definable and defy categorical description; part of their meaning is always inherited from the context of use."

In short, this means that public knowledge is both socially constructed and situationally variable and that any learner, including a self-directed learner, has to acquire the special domain-specific aspects of his or her chosen subject. Of course there is some transferability of learning skill, and of subject content, from situation to situation. However, the extent to which skills and insights gained in one context can be transferred to another is somewhat restricted, and any talk of universal competence as a self-directed learner must therefore be treated with caution.

The Situated Nature of Cognition and Learning. Knowledge is not only socially constructed and situationally variable, but much of it is also distributed among the community of knowledge users. In her presidential address to the American Educational Research Association, Resnick (1987b, p. 13) gives the following very elegant example, drawn from "the highly technological work environment of US Navy ships":

> The activity of interest occurs on a ship being piloted into and out of San Diego harbor and involves six people with three different job descriptions. On the deck two people take visual sightings on predetermined landmarks, using special telescopic devices

mounted on gyrocompasses that yield exact readings of direction. They call out their readings to two other individuals, who relay them by telephone to a specialist on the bridge. This individual records the bearings in a book and repeats them aloud for confirmation. Next to the recorder, another individual uses specialized tools to plot the ship's position on a navigational chart and to project where the ship will be at the next fix and beyond. These projections of position are used to decide what landmarks should be sighted next by those on deck and when a course correction will be required. The entire cycle is repeated every one to three minutes.

No individual in the system can pilot the ship alone. The knowledge necessary for successful piloting is distributed throughout the whole system. Furthermore, important aspects of that knowledge are built into tools. These aspects of knowledge, although not needed by the people who actually pilot the ship, are needed by cartographers and gyrocompass builders. Thus, there is a further sharing of knowledge—with tools, and with the builders of tools, who are not present during piloting, but who are part of the total knowledge system required for successful piloting.

A person wishing to "learn" about navigation would discover that no single person had all the knowledge or skill necessary to the entire process, and that although navigation of this particular vessel embodied some commonalities with other ships, there were also some unique qualities or characteristics as well.

Most adult learning is like this example, if not in detail then at least in principle. When a self-directed learner begins to acquire an understanding of some domain—whether it be religious experience, ornamental horticulture, child rearing, or management theory—he or she is necessarily limited to the perceptions of individual practitioners who, in all likelihood, have derived their understandings from a unique set of personal experiences. If the learner goes to the opposite extreme, and tries to learn about the field from abstract, metatheoretical studies, he or she is likely to be defeated either by the specialized vocabulary used (Martin, 1989) or by the absence of linkages with his or her own concrete experience base. In either case, the self-directed learner is bound by the nature of knowledge in the field and by the fact that at least some parts of the required knowledge are embedded in the detail of "authentic practice" (Brown, Collins, and Duguid, 1989).

The self-directed learner in all but the most intimate of personal learning has to rely on and collaborate with those who are practitioners in the field or area of his or her learning. Those who assist the self-directed learner "begin by providing modelling in situ and scaffolding for learners to get started in an authentic activity. As the learners gain more self-confidence and control, they move into a more autonomous phase of collaborative learning, where they begin to participate consciously in the culture. The social network within the culture helps them develop its language and belief systems and promotes the process of enculturation" (Brown, Collins, and Duguid, 1989, p. 39).

In short, the situated nature of learning ensures that almost all self-directed learning has a social as well as a cognitive component, and furthermore that there is limited transferability of competence from one learning situation to another.

The Demands of the Learning Situation. In formal instructional settings—even those which may be characterized as socially informal—there are contextual factors that limit or inhibit a learner's self-directedness. Clearly the approach taken by the teacher or trainer, including content, pacing, sequencing, and depth of coverage, will influence what a learner learns and how he or she goes about it. Any form of evaluation or assessment is particularly influential in determining what learners learn and how, and evaluation must therefore be carefully constructed to emphasize the educational outcomes—both substantive and collateral—that are particularly valued. Crooks (1988) gives detailed advice on how evaluation tasks should be constructed to maximize the sort of learning that is actually preferred: deep-level understanding and transfer of learning to novel situations and other thinking skills. "All too often," writes Crooks (1988, p. 467), ". . . evaluation places heavy emphasis on the recall or recognition of comparatively isolated pieces of information. . . . This encourages surface (memorizing) approaches to learning."

In addition to these "external" aspects of the learning situation that conspire to reduce the learner's self-directedness and ability to be autonomous, there is another important class of "internal" constraints as well. Basically, these are of two types, concerning either the learner's self-concept or his or her construction of the learning situation. As discussed earlier in this book, past learning experiences in school, college, or formal training situations frequently help to shape a person's self-concept and not infrequently to convince him or her that learning is a difficult and painful process that should be avoided where possible. However, not all personal beliefs about learning are generalized, and thus a learner's approach to self-directed inquiry might vary from situation to situation. Beliefs such as "I can't understand math," or "I'm no good at foreign languages" can operate powerfully—if selectively—to limit a learner's potential for self-directedness. It is not difficult to imagine a situation in which a person who, although having established credentials or extensive experience in some field, simply trembles at the prospect of having to learn something new in an unfamiliar field or one where previous educational experience was unfavorable.

Indeed, past educational experiences might serve to deny adults access to the deeper levels of meaning, which determine what counts as knowledge in their culture (Bernard and Papagiannis, 1983; Bernstein, 1977; Stalker-Costin, 1986). This causes Häyrynen and Häyrynen (1980, pp. 5, 8) to observe:

> We have tried to prove that the limitations in their learning abilities are mainly social by nature and often relate to social inequality. . . .
> We cannot emphasize too much the importance of a comprehensive basic education. . . . Adult education works in situations in which individuals and social classes are victims of repressive circumstances. They [the learners] have not always been able to develop language or conceptualized thinking, perhaps not even good esthetic taste, to a stage fulfilling the norms of good education.

Of perhaps equal—if not greater—importance are the learner's perceptions and expectations of particular learning situations. In the case of courses and programs conducted in schools, colleges, or other recognizable instructional settings, research shows that learners adjust and adapt themselves to what they *believe* are the instructor's expectations, and what they *anticipate* will be required in tests and assessments at the end. Such expectations are highly persuasive in determining learning strategies and depth of learning outcomes sought (see Chapter Nine). Because of this, instructional settings are inherently restrictive of learners' abilities to be fully self-directing.

However, even fully self-directed learning in everyday contexts is also influenced by learners' perceptions. In language learning situations, for instance, a learner may fear appearing foolish and therefore hold back from practicing the language with native speakers. Someone wanting to learn how to sail, or paint, or cook might because of past failure, unfavorable connotations, or the fear of "looking stupid" likewise avoid taking what they perceive as a risk by actually practicing the skill to be learned. The list of potential barriers to undertaking self-directed learning is indeed formidable, but the point is that even an experienced, competent, and motivated learner, who has successfully learned other things in the past, may still be disabled, by "societal rules and norms, distance between the learner and teacher, [or] competence of the learner to exercise choice" (Shores, 1985, p. 82), from undertaking a particular learning project.

Thus it appears that the type of learning project, the level of learning, and the learner's purposes all interact in complex ways that affect the learning outcome. It has been argued here that the ability to master the basic "codes" of a task or subject is dependent in part on the learner's existing intellectual capabilities, in part on past education, and in part on his or her intentions and purposes. Since this combination will vary from situation to situation, a learner's autonomy is also likely to vary from one context to another, and educators must avoid the automatic assumption that simply because a person has successfully learned something in the past either in an instructional setting or outside it, he or she will be able to succeed in a new area: Orientation, support, and guidance may all be required in the first stages of a learning project.

Socialization, Habitus, and Limits to Human Agency

This discussion of perceptions leads to a consideration of what is arguably the most influential determinant of the pattern of self-directed adult learning, namely, the way in which individuals have been and are socialized to think about learning and about themselves as learners. In his book *Adult Learning in the Social Context,* Jarvis (1987, p. 13) writes: "As the individual grows and matures within the context of social living, the person becomes, in part, a reflection of the sum total of experiences that the individual has in society. But that culture is not a single undifferentiated phenomenon, it varies by socioeconomic class, by ethnic community, by region and even by gender. . . . Hence every aspect of the person is social; even the language a person acquires is social."

Sociologists have coined a special term to refer to this phenomenon of the individual's internalizing aspects of his or her culture. It is referred to as *habitus* (Bourdieu, 1977; Giroux, 1983; Harker, 1984), and an individual's habitus is a vital link in mediating the impact of social structures, expectations, and external circumstances on individual action and behavior.

Earlier in this chapter, and elsewhere in this book, I have talked about how matters such as language, dress, "style," self-concept, and aspirations all tend to converge in shaping both what and how individual learners choose to learn. These features in turn are strongly influenced by external factors such as the learner's gender, ethnic background, and social class. Thus, such issues as the type of topics pursued by self-directed learners, the depth to which they choose to pursue their inquiries, the amount of learning they feel able to undertake, the barriers they perceive to their own learning endeavors, and the conceptual and cultural frameworks against which new learning is undertaken — in short every aspect of learning — is profoundly influenced by the individual's social context.

Fortunately, the habitus is not fixed and immutable; if it were, then each individual would be locked into a conveyer belt that carried him or her inevitably and unerringly from the cradle to a predetermined destination. The habitus, however, is not reproduced like a "photocopy" (Harker, 1984, p. 122) but by the dynamic interaction of school, family, workplace, and other aspects of "the material and social environment" (p. 120). This means that individuals can exercise some freedom of choice and can, within certain structural limits, reconstruct and reinvent their social circumstances, but these possibilities exist for relatively few individuals, and "certainly *not* for whole classes" (Harker, 1984, p. 122).

It appears, then, that at both the micro (classroom) and the macro (societal) level, "the study of learning is as much the prerogative of the sociologist as it is of the psychologist" (Jarvis, 1987a, p. 14), and that adult educators cannot afford to treat self-directed learners as completely independent of their social and cultural circumstances. In particular, although the processes of social reproduction are much more complex than early analysis suggested (Giroux, 1983; Harker, 1984), adults are powerfully affected by aspects of their backgrounds—including family and prior education—in ways that limit and constrain their ability to be self-directing in certain learning situations.

Summary

This discussion about the contextual limitation to self-direction in learning has several major outcomes.

First of all, it emphasizes that any plan or program to develop self-directedness—and this after all is the main purpose of Part Four of the book—can only achieve marginal improvements in general aspects of learning competence and learning confidence; the need for detailed "domain-specific" skills will persist so long as knowledge is constructed the way it is at present, and educators must accordingly be prepared to offer assistance by orienting learners to the particular problems and possibilities inherent in each individual learning situation.

Second, it has been emphasized that almost all learning is socially based and hence interdependent. The term *self-direction* has misled many into elevating the individual above the collective, whereas the nature of knowledge and the nature of learning inherently places learners into relationship with others. The myth of the solitary learner—the intellectual Robinson Crusoe— is as untenable as the notion of a world full of wild-eyed individualists owing nothing to social structures or to each other (Rosenblatt, 1984, p. 94).

Third, it is apparent that self-directedness is a person-situation variable; that is, it is not a quality that inheres in the person independent of the situation, or in the situation independent of the person. As the first of seven major assumptions in his book *The Design of Education,* Houle (1972, p. 32) wrote: "Any episode of learning occurs in a specific situation and is profoundly influenced by that fact." Boyle (1981, p. 23) in his book on *Planning Better Programs* defines the reality "in the educational sphere as being mutual; that is neither lying in the learner alone nor in the instructional environment alone." Learners find themselves in learning situations which they construe or make sense of in unique ways. No external agent can create a situation in which potential learners will view the learning possibilities identically, and, as discussed in Chapters Eight and Nine, the interpretive or constructivist understanding provides not only a model for how learning takes place, but for how learners think about, orient themselves to, and engage with learning situations.

In a characteristically elegant essay on adult learning, Kidd (1966, p. 72) highlighted the multidimensional quality of learning in the following terms: "There is a perpendicular dimension of learning continuing through the entire life-span and consonant with all of the divisions of education. There is a horizontal dimension of learning penetrating into every form of intellectual and spiritual activity known to man. . . . There is a depth dimension to learning responding to immediate and simple needs, on, up, and in the most sublime search for the truth that makes us free."

As an individual stands poised, at any given instant, on the intersection of these three axes, the choices he or she makes are the profoundest expression of self-direction. Once those choices have been made, self-direction of an entirely different order influences how the decision is implemented and put into effect. In both cases, there are important situational limits and constraints on the exercise of self-direction in learning.

Part 4

Promoting Self-Direction in Learning

> Isolated instruction in thinking skills, no matter how elegant the training provided, is unlikely to produce broadly used thinking ability. Thinking well requires more than knowing a selected set of strategies or techniques for problem solving and learning. It also requires knowing when these strategies are appropriate, and it requires the motivation to apply them. . . . This implies that higher order skills must suffuse the [educational] program from kindergarten on and in every subject matter. Training in general skills must be supplemented and supported by application throughout the curriculum. Various subject matters . . . should be taught with an eye to developing the powerful thinking methods used by experts in those disciplines. Students must come to think of themselves as able and obligated to engage in critical analysis and problem solving throughout [learning].
> — *Resnick, 1987a, p. 48*

The ability and willingness to undertake learning on one's own is not an end in itself, but is rather a means to an end. Consequently, any educational intervention that seeks to develop or enhance learners' self directedness must be predicated on some longer-term view of the sort of people — and ultimately the kind of society — it is hoped to produce. It is necessary to make this statement at the outset, in order to avoid the temptation of defining too narrowly the ultimate outcomes for which one is striving.

In Chapter Five, a fairly extensive survey was undertaken of previous attempts to identify the qualities or characteristics of the ideal self-directed learner. Too often, theorists and practitioners alike have fallen into the trap either of defining self-directedness too broadly, and ignoring the distinctive features of self-directed *learning,* or too narrowly, and accordingly of attempting to recognize, develop, or enhance only a limited range of capabilities in learners. In this book, it is argued that the ability to be fully self-directed in learning has three major components. The first is to have mastery of a range of "technical skills" that allow a person to identify learning purposes, to locate learning resources, and to manage learning endeavors. To some extent, these accomplishments are relevant across a range of potential learning situations, and it is appropriate to concentrate on educational strategies that allow for their development and practice. These capabilities include (1) the ability to plan personal and group activities, which includes definition of objectives and time management; (2) the ability to identify and obtain, and the skill to use various sources of information (from verbal and written through audiovisual to computerized information); (3) the ability to read, watch, and listen with different objectives in mind (identifying relevant facts, identifying and critically assessing the main ideas, separating the crucial from the irrelevant, speed reading and skimming, decoding visual messages, comparing information); (4) skill in note taking, recording, paraphrasing, quoting, systematizing data, writing précis, and keeping records; (5) numerical literacy, including manipulating numbers and drawing and reading visual diagrams, tables, graphic presentations, visual messages, and so on; (6) command of a foreign language (implying a certain vocabulary and simple structures to be followed); (7) the ability for self-evaluation in all stages of work and assessment of results; and (8) problem-solving ability as the combined outcome of the preceding skills and abilities (after Vukadinović, 1988, p. 34). These abilities may be thought of as building blocks that are fundamental to all learning endeavors, and they are the subject of Chapter Eleven.

It has also been argued in this book, however, that such content-free attainments can only carry a learner part of the way into a learning endeavor. Indeed, since all learning involves some substantive content, true self-direction necessitates having sufficient familiarity with the subject matter of one's learning efforts to be able to distinguish convincing from unconvincing knowledge claims. In other words, when a person is just beginning his or her study of a subject or domain, he or she does not "appreciate the inherent structure of the discipline, the interconnectedness of its elements [or] its own internal logic which determines its modes of inquiry and its canons of proof" (Auchmuty, 1980, p. 51). It is only after someone has been reading, studying, and thinking about an area of knowledge for some time that he or she is capable of true "self-directed" inquiry in that subject. Accordingly, Chapter Twelve looks at how instruction might be arranged in order to increase learners' autonomy with respect to subject matter.

The final chapter of this part concerns what is arguably the most important yet most elusive aspect, namely the development of a sense of personal control or of "learning competence" (Usher and Johnston, 1988, p. 147). In order to behave autonomously in a learning situation, a person requires not merely intellectual but also moral and emotional autonomy. This involves a robust self-concept, along with a strong sense of purpose and an emerging commitment to the value of the learning experience. It is in this domain, perhaps more than any other, that attempts to enhance self-direction in learning "spill over" into attempts to enhance self-determination more generally. This challenging aspect is discussed in Chapter Thirteen.

Eleven

Developing Skills for Self-Directed Learning

It may fairly be taken as one of the enduring and indeed universal missions of education to contribute to people's abilities to learn. This preoccupation is one of the very few that seems to be shared by all educators from preschool to postgraduate study, and in all ages from the distant past to the uncharted future: Educational programs should help learners to become better learners still.

As a result of this widespread concern with increasing learning competence, there is a vast body of literature—in preschool, elementary, secondary, higher, and adult education—that addresses the skills of learning and how they can be enhanced through various educational approaches. Sometimes these educational strategies seek to teach learning skills as direct curricular content; that is, they include lessons, workshops, and practice sessions on skills such as time management, goal setting, note taking, and even critical thinking. Increasingly, however, it is being recognized that these "skills" are not context-free attainments, but are best taught and learned in the context of real learning tasks. As a result, learning skills are often embedded within other curricular content, so that learners may develop their competence in both the content and the process areas simultaneously.

Within this overall concern to improve the learning competence of learners, there is a strand concerned with the enhancement of self-directed learning skills, and this has given rise to a range of approaches that aim to stress learners' ability to take responsibility for their own self-education. Thus, in addition to what might be thought of as general learning skills (listening, reading, note taking, questioning, information seeking, and so on), there are other skills such as time management, critical thinking, goal setting, and problem solving that are particularly central to self-directed learning efforts.

The purpose of this chapter is to examine educational interventions through which these various competencies might be developed, and in particular to consider the extent to which they might be transferable to "out-of-school" or everyday learning situations.

Developing Skills of Autonomous Learning

The belief that adult learners should, to a significant degree, be able to conduct their own education is widespread in the field of adult education. However, practitioners differ sharply as to how this capability might be enhanced, if at all. It is possible to discern a number of different groups, each based on varying perspectives about the development of learning competence through the conduct of adult education.

The first group are those who believe that the ability to be self-directed in learning is a universal characteristic of adulthood and accordingly that no special provision needs to be made to develop or enhance this capacity. People who think this way usually advocate the removal of constraints as far as possible, in the belief that adult learners' natural propensity to be self-directing will inevitably manifest itself in the learning situation. This point of view is tacitly endorsed by those who argue for a minimum of structure in the conduct of adult education activities.

Turning to those who believe that self-directedness can be deliberately enhanced, a range of possible intervention strategies may be identified. First are those who argue that skills of independent learning can be identified, and taught through direct instruction. Competencies such as note taking, listening, reading, and performing mathematical procedures, which Wang (1983) characterizes as "academic skills," can be built into the curriculum at all levels. The assumption that all adults have necessarily mastered these "basic skills" has been brought into question, however, and adult educators may well have a role to play in helping learners to master these building blocks of learning. Other "higher-order" skills, including information retrieval, time management, goal setting, problem solving, and even critical thinking, which Wang (1983) characterizes as "self-management skills," are also isolated and taught as more or less content-free accomplishments.

These approaches have been criticized from two separate directions. On the one hand there are those who argue that skills of independent learning cannot be taught and learned as regular curricular content but that they may only be developed through the opportunity to exercise such personal discretion in the learning situation. Dittman (1976, p. 467), for instance, writes that "autonomous behavior is not taught or learned as ordinary content in the curriculum. One can teach *about* autonomy, independence and responsibility, but this is not *becoming* autonomous in one's thoughts and actions. One learns responsibility and self-direction through experiences in which one is given the opportunity to be self-directed and responsible for one's actions. Therefore, if we want students who will be capable of making autonomous judgments, we must provide a learning environment in which they are encouraged to make autonomous judgments."

Based on this line of argument, their approach is to make use of "learner-controlled" methods of instruction—strategies that give learners an increasing say in the content, sequencing, pacing, location, or method of learning. Admittedly, there is evidence to suggest that increasing learner-control can increase both the ability and the willingness of learners to exert control over valued instructional functions, but the task is a complex one and merely placing learners in such situations is no guarantee that they will be equipped to handle those situations adequately—especially if previous education has diminished their capability to think and act autonomously. The limitations of relying on learner-control to develop self-direction in learning are dealt with elsewhere in this book.

On the other hand, many study-skills courses and learning-to-learn programs are criticized because they are based on an inadequate understanding of the complexity of learning: "The assumption underlying almost all attempts to improve student learning is that studying consists primarily of techniques, and that to increase skill in using specific techniques is therefore to increase learning outcomes. I believe that this assumption, and the approach to advising and training students in study skills that follows from it, is fundamentally misguided" (Gibbs, 1983, p. 84).

In a paper on "Understanding Why Students Don't Learn," Gibbs, Morgan, and Taylor (1980) explain the limitation of simply conducting learning-to-learn courses or programs that focus on doing particular things in particular ways. For instance, they cite the example of a study skills adviser who recommends that learners should sit close to the front of a class "because he has evidence that those who sit at the front do better. It is assumed that such behavior will *cause* success" (p. 2). Clearly, this is a very tenuous assertion, and although it is certainly possible to distinguish successful from unsuccessful learners, it is very difficult to attribute these differences simply to particular patterns of behavior: "It is often very unclear what students are actually *doing* when they are studying [that is, learning]. . . . It may be possible to record some aspects of the observable behavior, but this is unlikely to tell you very much about the underlying cognitive processes — the purposes, plans and thoughts which direct and make use of this behavior" (p. 3).

This then directs attention to certain higher-order aspects of learning-to-learn and, in particular, to the possibility that "purposes, plans and thoughts" might be related to the learning of specific content. Accordingly, there is yet another group that believes that learning competence can only be developed in the context of particular subject areas. In other words, the ability to learn, and indeed to learn independently, must be embedded in the context of the individual learner's previous knowledge and of his or her purposes, intentions, and understandings, because there is a complex interaction between motive and strategy (see Chapter Nine) in any given learning situation. The corollary of adopting this perspective is that the teacher/trainer tries to develop learning skills within the context of his or her particular subject area. Although such strategies are clearly more consistent with the context-dependent nature of learning competence, as argued in Chapter Ten, they may still fail to take account of learning as the construction of personal structures of meaning (see Chapter Eight).

Accordingly, the last group has a rather different view of learning from the others, and this in turn influences their approach to the development of learning competence. For a start, they define learning in terms of a qualitative change in the learner's way of "seeing, experiencing and conceiving aspects of the real world around them" (Ramsden, 1988, p. 13). Consequently, they place an emphasis on how learners construe or make sense of the subject area they are learning, and on how these cognitive structures are affected when learning takes place.

Furthermore, proponents of this point of view argue that "the *content* and the *process* of learning (the 'what' and the 'how' of learning) form part of a unified whole" (Ramsden, 1988, p. 19). They share this perspective with members of the previous group, but are more explicit as to the linkages. They hold that learners need to understand what Schwab calls the "syntactic structure" of conceptions in the field, in other words, that they need to develop a "knowledge of the *methods* that disciplines characteristically use to study the phenomena in their domains" (Ramsden, 1988, p. 22). Members of this group also stress that optimal learning occurs once "the phenomenon of learning in itself has become an object of reflection . . . something which can be explicitly talked about and discussed and can be the object of conscious planning and analysis" (Säljö, 1979a, p. 446).

On the basis of these various convictions, advocates of this last (and most sophisticated) perspective on learning competence emphasize three interrelated themes: the need for the facilitator to take account of the learner's existing cognitive structures and previous knowledge, the need for the learner to gain an understanding of the "syntactic structure" of the field that he or she is learning, and the learner's development of a metacognitive awareness or conscious control over his or her learning skills and activities. In the discussion that follows, both in this and succeeding chapters, I will focus on this particular view of learning competence and its implications for how such learning competence may be enhanced.

Approaches to Increasing Independence in Learning

There are literally hundreds of approaches to teaching that are alleged to result in enhanced capacities for learning in general and for self-directed learning in particular (Kirschenbaum and Perri, 1982). Prominent among these are strategies such as contract-based learning, experiential learning, and various other forms of learner-controlled instruction that seek to shift to learners increased responsibility for various parts of the teaching/learning process. As previously mentioned, such approaches are usually advocated in the belief that the best way to become self-directed is to behave autonomously. In Chapter Thirteen, as elsewhere in this book, it is argued that providing such opportunities is a *necessary* but not a *sufficient* condition for the development of competence as a self-directed learner. Thus in addition to giving learners control over certain relevant aspects of the instructional situation, adult educators can develop and enhance the capabilities for self-direction in other ways too. The following strategies have the potential to encourage self-direction, although they may not, at first sight, involve the learners in acting autonomously: making use of learners' existing knowledge, encouraging deep-level learning, increasing question-asking by learners, developing critical thinking, enhancing reading skills, improving comprehension monitoring, and creating a supportive climate for learning.

Making Use of Learners' Existing Knowledge Structures. To say that teaching should begin "where the learner is" is a truism. The question is, how can teachers find out what learners already know, especially in a novel or unfamiliar domain? It is widely accepted that adult learners "rarely have *no* knowledge about a topic, or *no* strategy when they tackle a problem. There is almost always some understanding, however limited" (Ramsden, 1988, p. 22). However in a new area, the learner may not have arranged his or her understandings according to the conventions of the field, and indeed may not be familiar with some of the technical terminology used in the field, although he or she might very well recognize the concepts and relationships that are relevant to a study of the domain, and will certainly try to construe the new field according to frames of reference derived from past experience (see Chapter Nine). This means that many conventional pretests, which make use of the concepts and ter-. minology common in the field, will not necessarily reveal learners' preexisting understandings. Accordingly, it is necessary to use other methods to find out what learners already know about a subject being studied.

One of the easiest and most useful ways of finding out what learners already know is the concept map. A concept map is an attempt to depict, in a diagrammatic form, ideas, examples, relationships, and implications about particular concepts as they are perceived by a learner. Usually the central or core idea is placed at the center of the page, and radiating from it are a number of spokes or lines leading to other concepts that are related to, or indicative of, the central idea. These are then linked to other notions, which in turn may be further linked both to one another and to even more "nodes" on the network in complex and multidimensional ways. There is no inherent limit to the number of concepts that may be included in a single map, although common sense dictates that it would be impractical to depict more than a fraction of the total connections that a normal adult has available in understanding any particular domain of human discourse, given the richness and complexity of our cognitive schemata.

Concept maps (by a variety of names) have proved useful in helping learners to visualize their patterns of understanding and of making explicit those assumptions and relationships that are usually implicit and unarticulated (Buzan, 1978; Hampden-Turner, 1982). An appreciation of one's own tacit network of concepts is a vital prerequisite to learning and an essential corollary of learning about one's own learning. A concept map might consist of as little as a hasty diagram scrawled on the back of an envelope, through to an elaborate and complex representation created using sophisticated computer software (Fisher and others, 1987). Its strength as a learning-to-learn device is, as Novak and Gowin (1984) point out, its remarkable flexibility and ease of use and its truly idiosyncratic and relatively unstructured form.

An alternative approach for tapping into learners' preexisting frames of reference or "personal construct systems" is the repertory grid. Repertory grids owe their existence to Kelly's *Psychology of Personal Constructs* (1955) and to considerable subsequent work that builds on Kelly's ideas (see, for example, Beail, 1985; Fransella and Bannister, 1977; Pope and Keen, 1981). Basically, repertory grids represent an attempt to selectively sample part of a person's frame of reference with respect to some domain of human existence. The technique, in its simplest form, consists of presenting the respondent with three items from an array of qualitatively similar elements ("situations from which I leave learned," "books I have read," "teaching methods I have experienced," and so on) and asking him or her to say in what way two of the items are similar and thereby different from the third.

This process, when repeated a number of times with differing combinations of trigger items (that is, different triads), produces a series of bipolar descriptors (for example, "interesting-boring," "threatening-safe," "easy to understand–difficult," "useful-irrelevant," and so forth) that can then be used by the respondent to differentiate all the items in the array — not just the three used to generate it. This process yields a two-way matrix having the "constructs" down one side and the "elements" or items along the other axis, and each element can be given a score or rating on each construct dimension. The resulting data are susceptible to various forms of statistical analysis — more or less sophisticated depending on the purpose — and the results may be given back to the respondent in a diagram or other pictorial form for reflection and personal analysis. An extension of the basic repertory grid technique is to program a computer that can interactively interrogate a respondent and provide him or her with immediate feedback on his or her view of the world, privately, and without the intervention of another person. This is a particularly powerful device for learning-to-learn. A fuller description of the use of the repertory grid may be found in Candy (1990).

Encouraging Deep-Level Learning. As discussed earlier in this chapter and in Chapters Eight and Nine, there has recently been a major shift in emphasis within educational research, from viewing knowledge essentially as an accumulation of fragmentary facts to seeing it largely as a socially constructed artifact. This shift in emphasis has also caused conceptions of learning to change — from the previous view that learning involved appropriating a given quantum of knowledge to the emergent view that learning involves a qualitative change in the learner's conception about phenomena.

In reconstruing what is meant by *learning,* researchers have begun to look much more closely at *what* is being learned, rather than *how much.* Strategies that seek to look for qualitative changes in people's understandings have resulted in the recognition that in some tasks learners seem to pay more attention to the externalities of a body of knowledge and at other times they manage to develop a much deeper level of understanding of underlying principles.

In the mid 1970s, Marton and his colleagues at the University of Göteborg in Sweden began to explore how and why some learners were only able to reproduce the contents of learning tasks, whereas others seemed able to transform material they had read or heard and to point out underlying principles and implications. In the original research, university students were asked to read lengthy passages from academic texts, and were then asked two sets of questions — about the content of what they had read, and about their approach or how they read it. Perhaps predictably, their research showed that students approach learning tasks in fundamentally different ways. Some strive to understand the basic message and work hard to achieve a really profound insight into the author's intentions; others attempt to memorize the content of the passage without seeking to understand it or its connection to what they already know. This work gave rise to the now-famous distinction between surface- and deep-level learning, which has already been discussed in Chapter Nine, and to the realization that learning outcomes are fundamentally related to the approach taken by the learner in terms of his or her intentions.

Since this original work (Marton and Säljö, 1976a, 1976b; Svensson, 1976), it has been found that the surface/deep distinction applies to all sorts of learning situations and not simply to learning from text (Biggs, 1979, 1987; Entwistle and Ramsden, 1983; Häyrynen and Häyrynen, 1980; Marton, Hounsell, and Entwistle, 1984). Given that it is usually assumed that a deep approach is preferable to a surface one, researchers and teachers have been interested in exploring how learners might be encouraged to adopt more deep-level approaches to learning tasks. Because learning approaches are a product of the interaction between the individual and the particular learning situation (that is, unlike learning styles, they are not a characteristic of a learner in every situation), the interventions themselves must be related to the specific context. In discussing attempts to have surface learners adopt a deep approach, Biggs (1987, p. 103) notes:

> The question of what to do about high surface learners highlights a dilemma familiar in the aptitude treatment interaction (ATI) literature (Cronbach and Snow, 1977): to *match* the learner with treatment (for example to teach surface-achieving students factually, with high structure) or to *mismatch* student and treatment (to teach in a way encouraging a deep approach, with high structure-fact ratio). The first accepts the learner's current way of operating and optimizes on that; the second attempts to improve the way the learner operates. The answer hinges around the extent to which the learner's approach is modifiable . . . and on the extremity of the case. Probably sound strategy would be to teach at first in a "surface discouraging" way. . . . The fallback teaching strategy would then be to provide high factual goals and teach low level survival strategies for each task. Mastery learning strategy (Block, 1971) is one example of an approach that seems well suited to the surface learner: the content and task objectives are highly structured for the student, and the high success rate is specifically aimed at improving the student's academic self-concept.

Overall, attempts to increase deep-level approaches to learning confront both practical and ethical problems. On the practical side, there is the difficulty of how to encourage learners to take an interest in a topic that they have relatively little motivation to learn. While it may be possible to help learners to develop deep-level strategies, this does not necessarily lead to deep-level motives, yet approaches are made up of a motive (what the learner intends or hopes to achieve) in combination with the strategy (the technique or combination of techniques the learner employs to achieve the learning task). On the ethical side, the attempt to have learners develop a deeper orientation is nothing less than an intervention in the learner's prerogatives as an adult and, as Godbey (1978, p. i) observes, "It is no defence to say that someone else arranged for the learning experience to be set up, decided on a curriculum, and set up the institution in which the learning situation came about. Still, the teacher must be able to look clear-eyed into the mirror and say, 'What I am attempting to do with other human beings is for their good and for the good of humanity.' . . . The person who cannot, in good conscience, make that statement should find other employment."

Increasing Question-Asking by Learners. One strategy that may be used to encourage deep-level learning is to increase questioning behavior by learners. However, as Hynes (1986, p. 33) points out, "There is a subtle difference between *telling* students to ask questions, *telling* them to think about what they did last lesson, *telling* them to find problems in the topics being studied, and *teaching* them to perform those activities or creating an atmosphere in which they can take more initiative for their own learning."

It is widely recognized that conventional teaching often provides answers to questions that learners have not even asked. In other words, instruction commonly fails to address the interests of learners, and hence reinforces the myth that effective learning consists of appropriating previously packaged clusters of ideas. One strategy that seeks to shift the onus of responsibility to learners is to provide some sort of stimulus (a reading or a lecture or a video for instance) and then have learners generate as many questions as they can about the topic presented.

Such questions usually fall into two categories: those that invite a factual answer and "thinking questions" that involve a more complex interpretive response. In discussing his use of this strategy to encourage metacognition in an Australian history class, Hynes (1986, p. 36) writes: "A fact question, like 'How many lashes did the convicts receive?' required a simple factual answer. I then went on to explain what a 'thinking question' was and, after discussion, students were able to come up with a variety of 'thinking questions,' especially if they started off with the words 'What if . . . ?', for example, 'What if a mutiny occurred on a convict ship and the convicts took over?'"

Hynes discusses how an entire teaching program, including inquiry projects, can be built around a cluster of questions generated by the learners themselves, and he observes how gratifying it can be to see students pursuing often quite difficult questions that they set for themselves and over which they accordingly feel some sense of ownership (this concept was discussed in Chapter One of this book). Basically, if there is a group of learners, they may be asked to read some introductory material and to write down questions that occur to them as they are reading. These questions are then pooled and wherever possible are expressed in the form of "thinking questions," which in turn are ranked or placed in some sort of order. The questions generated by the learners thus become the skeleton for the course or program, and may also provide the basis for collaborative study groups or even individual projects. Hynes (1986, p. 39) concludes his observations about the vital importance of learners asking questions by stating: "Taking responsibility for one's own learning involves questioning and individual research."

Developing Critical Thinking. Closely related to question-asking is the development of critical thinking. Historically, critical thinking is one of the most highly esteemed goals in education — from elementary to advanced graduate level. In Western democratic countries, the freedom to form opinions and to make informed, independent judgments on the basis of wide, critical reading is regarded as essential to full, active participation in the democratic processes of government.

As mentioned elsewhere in this book, personal autonomy is also a valued educational ideal that has likewise animated educators of all ages, and consequently these two great pillars of education — autonomy and critical thought — have frequently been cited as desired outcomes of education in various systems and for learners of all ages. The relationship does not end there, however, for whether autonomy is defined in terms of emotional freedom or of intellectual independence, there is a corresponding conception of critical thinking to match.

For instance, in his critical theory of self-directed learning, Mezirow (1985) has argued that autonomy consists of throwing off the bonds of one's previous enculturation, and of consciously and intentionally becoming critically aware of debilitating rules, norms, expectations, values, and beliefs that stand between the individual and full realization of his or her autonomous nature — as a learner and as a person. Others, however, such as Bodi (1988), who tend to define autonomy more in terms of intellectual accomplishments and the ability to evaluate ideas and arguments from an independent and objective point of view, are also able to point to the need for critical thinking as essential to *their* perspective. The results are twofold: first, there is an almost overwhelming mass of literature on both practical and theoretical aspects of the development of critical thinking, and second, the footprints left by advocates of personal autonomy and of critical thinking are commonly parallel, frequently cross one another, and often are quite indistinguishable.

Like the literature on autonomy, that on critical thinking is confused and confusing. As Furedy and Furedy (1985, p. 57) observe, "As widely as it is accepted in a general way, the meaning of critical thinking is not precisely agreed on. In the literature, the essence of critical thinking has been seen as reflective scepticism, applying standards of reason to arguments, or merely understanding what another person is thinking. A critical spirit or attitude is defined as widely as 'the habit of using critical skills' (Hitchcock, 1983, p. 2) or a set of attitudes and character traits."

Given this range of views of what critical thinking is, it comes as no surprise to find that there are many suggestions as to how it can be developed. Broadly speaking, however, these resolve themselves into psychologically and philosophically based approaches; whereas psychologists have sought to discover and then to teach the processes used by good thinkers, philosophers have chosen to use the analysis of extended discourse on complex topics as a vehicle to promote disciplined inquiry.

One of the most important debates in the field of critical thinking "exactly parallels psychologists' discussions of whether general cognitive skills or specific knowledge is most central to intellectual competence" (Resnick, 1987a, p. 31), which was discussed in Chapter Ten. On the one hand, there are authors such as McPeck (1981) who argue that no general reasoning skill is possible and that all instruction in thinking should be situated in particular disciplines. At the other extreme, there are those such as Ennis (1985) and Paul (1982) who argue for the development of general reasoning capacity that transcends specific knowledge domains. As with most such sharp dichotomies, it seems likely that some sort of compromise position is most appropriate: "There is something disturbing about casting . . . *general* and *contextualized* as though they were exclusive of one another. . . . There are general cognitive [and critical thinking] skills; but they always function in contextualized ways" (Perkins and Salomon, 1989, p. 19).

This is basically the perspective proposed by Brookfield (1987) in his book *Developing Critical Thinkers.* In what is arguably the most comprehensive treatment of critical thinking in adult education, Brookfield describes effective strategies for facilitating the development of critical thinking: creating a supportive social climate (dealt with later in this chapter); listening and watching attentively for verbal and nonverbal cues in order to pose critical questions; sensitively challenging old modes of thought and especially unqualified assertions; reflecting back to learners their attitudes, rationalizations, and habitual ways of thinking and acting so that they can see themselves from a different perspective; and providing an opportunity for reflective evaluation or "stock-taking" in the process of critical thinking.

To this list, we should add: making learners aware of the conventions and principles of the subject being learned, teaching what sorts of questions to ask and when, and showing how much and what kind of evidence is enough to determine the validity of a statement. Taken together, such instructional approaches should contribute significantly to the capacity of adult learners to function independently, not simply accepting responsibility for the external features of their own education but undertaking learning effectively in new and unfamiliar domains.

Enhancing Reading Skills. Clearly, a great deal of personally significant learning occurs through interpersonal contacts, via direct experience and from media such as radio and television. However, the fact remains that one of the most common forms of learning in our society is through reading. Attaining literacy is taken as one of the basic goals of all educational systems in the Western world, and indeed is an objective that seems to be shared by educationists worldwide. However, the goal is somewhat illusory, because literacy (like autonomy) is not a single once-and-for-all accomplishment, but one where varying levels of attainment are possible in different subject areas (Chall, 1979; Mandl, Stein, and Trabasso, 1984; Resnick and Resnick, 1977). This means that there are often both technical terms and forms of sentence construction that only make sense to a reader who already knows something about the subject; thus whatever the reading task, "we bring far more knowledge 'to' the page than we actually get 'from' it" (Morris and Stewart-Dore, 1984, p. 17). As Anderson (1977, p. 423) expresses it, "Text is gobbledygook unless the reader possesses an interpretive framework to breathe meaning into it."

To some extent, this assertion is counterintuitive — the commonsense view of reading is that the meaning is there, on the page, waiting to be extracted through reading. In fact, however, "It is our background knowledge of language structures, word meanings and sounds, together with our background knowledge of the particular topic described which helps us to make *predictions* about what we are reading. The more we are able to predict what a particular piece of text will be about, the

more we are likely to be able to read it with understanding"
(Morris and Stewart-Dore, 1984, p. 17).

Earlier in this chapter the point was made that effective
learning involves acquiring both the substantive and the syntactic structure of the subject area being learned. In part, this
insight comes from recent research into the reading processes
which also emphasizes that understanding is dependent on both
"semantic"and "syntactic" clues. It appears that beyond a certain minimal ability to recognize and to decode individual words
as they appear on the page, learning from text involves a much
more complex process of "breathing meaning" into what we read,
and the ability to do this is largely subject-specific. In discussing this, Morris and Stewart-Dore (1984, p. 21) write:

> *Content Area Reading* is the reading associated with the learning
> of a particular subject or the performance of a particular subject
> area task. Thus, if we are studying History, we read historical
> works and try to learn and understand the factual content. When
> studying Science we read scientific explanations or instructions.
> In Cooking we read to follow directions to complete a recipe.
> While in Accounting we have to cope with a large amount of
> specialized vocabulary related to commercial concepts. Each area
> of specialization, Science, Geography, Home Economics, Phys-
> ical Education, Music, Art and so on, has its own body of litera-
> ture, which presents the content of that area in a language style
> of its own. Once we recognize that different bodies of knowledge
> have their own literature and language style, we can see that the
> learning implications extend beyond the school scene to the world
> of work and everyday life. There is the reading associated with
> Electricians, Lawyers, Motor Mechanics and so on. The list is
> almost endless.

Morris and Stewart-Dore (1984, p. 30) argue that "efficient reading is necessary for independent learning," and that "if we want
to prepare enquiring and independent learners who are flexible problem solvers, able to adapt to a variety of situations, then
we do need to focus on the processes of gaining and applying
information" through reading. To achieve this goal, they propose a four-step model comprising the following stages: (1)
preparing for reading, (2) thinking through the reading, (3) extracting and organizing information, and (4) translating
information.

These four stages are related to one another, and each is supported by a substantial body of research literature. The first stage, preparing for reading, essentially involves obtaining an overview of the structure of the reading, especially major concepts, ideas, and arguments; identifying any special tables, charts, diagrams, maps, graphs, and so on; and noting any specialized vocabulary that is essential to an understanding of the whole text.

The second phase, thinking through the reading, addresses the common problem of reading without understanding. Thinking through the reading involves having learners reflect more deeply on the text and learning from each other through interactive discussions and critical analysis. It is worth distinguishing three levels of comprehension: literal comprehension, interpretive comprehension, and applied comprehension. In setting learners reading tasks, adult educators should specifically target some of the tasks towards each of these three levels of comprehension.

Extracting and organizing information represents a stage beyond simply understanding. It involves distinguishing "the forest from the trees," or, in Ramsden's (1988, p. 23) startling image, the mountains from the plain: "For [many] students, texts are a flat landscape of facts to be remembered, rather than an area dotted with salient features representing principles or arguments around which stretch plains of evidence."

Extracting information necessitates identifying major themes, assertions, and principles and distinguishing these from examples, illustrations, or supporting evidence. It is often possible to extract information in diagrammatic or point form, that is, to transform it from the linear prose in which it is presented. Organizing information entails moving around large "chunks" of ideas, and perhaps producing a skeleton outline or schematic diagram (such as a concept map) or "structure-of-meaning" diagram to show how main ideas are related to one another (Harri-Augstein, Smith, and Thomas, 1982, pp. 75–86). In this sense, reading is itself a form of self-directed learning and a microcosm of the larger process of learning for oneself.

The fourth stage is translating information from reading to writing or performance. The ultimate end product of learning from reading is the ability either to express ideas clearly and cogently in one's own words or to be able to perform some skill or procedure correctly. A variety of outcome exercises is possible, but the adult educator needs to model the expectation that learning will result in changed conceptions by having learners manifest as creatively as possible some qualitative shift in understanding, insight, or perspective as a result of reading.

Although reading is a foundational skill of learning, it is far from basic. It is, in fact, a higher-order cognitive process, and one that varies depending on the learner's purpose, familiarity with the subject matter, and the nature of the learning task (Resnick, 1987a, p. 11). Reading is a "kind of conversation between the reader and the text. The reader puts questions, as it were, to the text and gets answers. . . . In the light of these he or she puts further questions, and so on" (Harri-Augstein, Smith, and Thomas, 1982, p. 4).

The purpose of instruction in reading is to internalize this process, which Goodman (1976) has characterized as a "kind of psycholinguistic guessing game," so that learners can frame appropriate questions and recognize relevant and adequate answers — a process that calls for a high degree of inference along with some topical knowledge (Resnick, 1987a, p. 9). Literacy is taken for granted, especially by the time people reach adulthood. In fact, literacy is only partially a generic skill; it is largely subject-specific, and educators need consciously and intentionally to develop "subject literacy" so that learners can learn independently in areas of their choice.

Improving Comprehension Monitoring. Although there are many similarities between learning on one's own and being taught, there are also major differences. When an instructor is involved, his or her role includes constantly checking for any misunderstandings and arranging materials in a form and sequence that is best for the learner. When a person is teaching him- or herself, however, those vital tasks are also in the hands of the learner, and the problematic situation arises that the learner needs constantly to monitor his or her own understandings in order to see whether new learning makes sense.

As a person's level of expertise rises, so too does the ability to make effective judgment about his or her level of comprehension. Markman (1981) for instance has argued that experts are probably better able to monitor their comprehension than are novices because

1. They have a more systematic knowledge of the subject area, and this permits facts and examples to be incorporated into higher order structures.
2. More detailed and organized knowledge structures create expectations on the part of the learner, and those expectations fulfill a vital role in helping to assess whether learning is adequate.

In short, experts develop abstract knowledge structures that give them a distinct advantage in monitoring their own learning. How can a learner — especially one who is "primarily responsible for his or her own mastery of a task" — perform this vital role of monitoring learning? Weinstein and Rogers (1985) identify (in the context of reading) four different breakdowns that can affect comprehension: (1) failure to understand particular words, (2) failure to understand particular sentences, (3) failure to understand the relation between sentences, and (4) failure to understand how the text fits together as a coherent whole.

It appears that each of these comprehension failures might stem from one of three possible causes: (1) unfamiliar information, (2) internal inconsistency (within the text), or (3) external inconsistency (with the reader's previous knowledge). Whenever learners encounter one or other of these problems, they may make use of several alternative strategies, including:

1. Ignoring the problem and reading on
2. Suspending judgment
3. Forming a tentative hypothesis
4. Rereading the current passage
5. Rereading previous content
6. Seeking out expert assistance

According to Weinstein and Rogers (1985, p. 626), in teaching learners to be independent, "We explore the implications of taking these courses of action. . . . Our goal is to help make learners' tacit knowledge of monitoring strategies more explicit and thereby increase their expertise [in comprehension monitoring]." Comprehension monitoring is more than a learning strategy, it is a metacognitive procedure whereby learners reflectively monitor their own performance as learners and learn to adopt alternative strategies for themselves.

Creating a Supportive Climate for Learning. In the domain of science education, researchers have in the past few years recognized that learners frequently bring to bear quite complex personal explanatory systems that they use to understand scientific phenomena. These systems are often derived from an amalgam of past experience, popular television and reading, and half-remembered formulas and experiences from school, which Claxton (1982) labels "gut science," "lay science," and "school science," respectively. Together, they make up a personal science, but such personal scientific understandings are often at odds with the explanations and constructs sanctioned by formal science. Hence, they are frequently labeled "misconceptions" by teachers and researchers because they deviate from the formally sanctioned wisdom of established science.

An alternative perspective, however, is to think of such personal views not as "misconceptions" but as "alternate conceptions" that are valid but limited in their explanatory power or internal coherence. The importance of such "alternate conceptions" cannot be overemphasized in self-directed learning, because it is into such personal frameworks that learners seek to fit new learning. In situations of teaching, it is usually desired to have learners move in the direction of embracing, understanding, and espousing the scientifically correct or approved view, but "changing students' conceptions demands more than the transfer of concepts from teacher to student. . . . This suggests that teaching methods that enable students to work on discrepancies in a supportive environment — one that permits incorrect thoughts to be retraced and remedied — are likely to be appropriate. Simply teaching students the 'right' conception cannot work, because change involves an active working upon and interaction between the old way of thinking and the new . . . " (Ramsden, 1988, p. 21).

The need for such a "supportive environment" is by no means limited to science education; in fact, it has been recognized as a central feature of good adult education practice for decades. As Knowles points out in *The Adult Learner* (1984, p. 120), almost all learning theorists — behaviorists, cognitivists, humanists, and personality theorists — endorse the need for an "atmosphere of adultness" in which "conditions of mutuality and informality" combine to provide a supportive human and interpersonal climate.

The elements of such a climate are well known: low threat, unconditional positive regard, honest and open feedback, respect for the ideas and opinions of others, approval of self-improvement as a goal, collaboration rather than competition. These qualities must be manifest not only in the emotional, but in the intellectual climate; the teacher and the taught must be prepared to suspend critical judgment and to explore together the strengths and weaknesses of their respective viewpoints, so that the learner in particular is free to experiment with alternative conceptions and perspectives before making a commitment to a new or revised framework.

Developing Skills for Learning in Everyday Settings

The argument so far has been focused on the learning of specific subject matter usually referred to as disciplinary, propositional, or "preceptual" (Laurillard, 1988, p. 216) knowledge. However, a great deal of adult self-directed learning occurs in, and in relation to, real-life settings where knowledge may not have been codified in these ways. What different or additional learning skills are called for in learning in "everyday" settings?

It has been maintained throughout this book that there are significant differences between learning in formal instructional settings and in natural societal or everyday settings.

These differences have been maintained in the distinction between learner-control and autodidaxy: two faces of self-directed
learning.

Recent research has thrown further light on these differences and on their consequences for programs that seek to enhance learning abilities. In her 1987 presidential address to the
American Educational Research Association, Resnick (1987b,
pp. 13–15) identified four major differences between the skills
required for successful learning performance in schools and formal instructional settings, and those demanded in other learning contexts. These differences are individual cognition in school
versus shared cognition outside, pure mentation in school versus
tool manipulation outside, symbol manipulation in school versus
contextualized reasoning outside, and generalized learning in
school versus situation-specific competencies outside.

In view of these discontinuities, there may be something
incongruous about attempts to enhance the ability of learners
to function independently outside the structures of formal institutions, from within the institutions themselves. As Resnick
(1987b, p. 18) puts it, "The evidence developed . . . on the discontinuity between school and work [as learning environments]
should make us suspicious of attempts to apply directly what
we know about skills for learning in school to the problems of
fostering capabilities for learning outside school."

Adult education is distinctive because much of it occurs
in, and in relation to, work situations. It is essential, therefore,
for adult education programs that seek to develop capabilities
for self-directed learning to ensure that as far as possible attention is given to the criteria for effective functioning as a learner
in everyday settings. Frequently, it has been assumed that if
a person can perform well in structured learning settings, then
these skills will easily translate into competence in more fluid
and less structured environments — such as at work or in the
home. However, recent work on "everyday cognition" (Rogoff
and Lave, 1984), on "situated cognition" (Brown, Collins, and
Duguid, 1989), and on out-of-school learning generally has emphasized the important differences between these contexts and
the need "to redirect the focus of schooling to encompass more

of the features of successful out-of-school functioning" (Resnick, 1987b, p. 19). In part this may be achieved by locating programs wherever possible in real-life settings, in part by making use of resources (including instructors and guest speakers) from the workplace or situation involved, in part by simulating salient features of effective practice and practice-based learning in the instructional setting, and in part by encouraging thoughtful discussion about expectations concerning what it is like to be functioning in the actual out-of-school setting. The facilitative role of the educator is dealt with at length in Jenks, Murphy, and Simms, *Experience-Based Learning and the Facilitative Role of Teachers* (1978), and in Barrows and Tamblyn, *Problem-Based Learning: An Approach to Medical Education* (1980).

Summary

The conventional approach to the development of competence as a self-directed learner has been to place adults into situations where they are expected to assert control over valued instructional functions. This approach is based on the combined beliefs (1) that adults are inherently self-directing, (2) that the best way to learn autonomous behavior is to behave autonomously, and (3) that the ability to learn independently in one situation or context is generalizable to an ability to do so in a different setting.

Although there are sound reasons for these assertions, there is also support for the view that being able to learn for oneself is a developable capacity, which, however, has a subject-specific dimension to it. Accordingly, if adult educators want to enable their learners to become more competent at self-directed inquiry, they must explicitly plan to do so. In this chapter a selection of such approaches has been discussed.

The most appropriate strategy for the development of learning skill would seem to be within the teaching of specific content areas. Although there are some context-free learning skills, recent research has emphasized the role of context in learning activities and cognitive performance generally: "Concern with contextual variation in skills has been influenced by cross-cultural observations that people who have difficulty with a task embodying a particular skill in the laboratory spontaneously evidence the skills in their everyday activities. Micronesian navigators who show phenomenal skills in memory, inference and calculation when travelling from island to island perform abominably on standard tests of intellectual functioning. Subjects who perform poorly on logic or communication problems in a test situation often reason precisely and communicate persuasively in more familiar contexts" (Rogoff, 1984, p. 2).

New learning builds on and is constructed through the learner's existing "frames of reference." In all learning, but particularly adult learning, new information is understood via the learner's preexisting cognitive structures. This has three major implications. First, learning must be thought of in terms of a qualitative change in the learner's conceptions rather than a quantitative accretion in his or her store of knowledge. Second, the teacher or trainer cannot afford to ignore the range of alternative conceptions that learners bring to the instructional situation, and attempts should be made wherever possible to draw out such patterns on which to base instruction. Third, if a learner is tackling some new task — whether in learning about his or her own perspective or place in the world, or in trying to master a body of "propositional knowledge" — a constant monitoring of his or her personal understandings of that domain is essential.

Encouraging an orientation toward deep-level learning is preferable to strategies that lead to surface-level or reproductive learning. Assessment procedures and other features of the learning environment in formal instructional settings commonly have a tendency to reward learning strategies that lead to surface-level or rote learning. In adult education — particularly in self-directed adult learning — learners should be acquainted with the differences between surface-level and deep-level processing, and should be instructed deliberately in strategies that lead to deep-level learning. Among these are metacognitive awareness, self-monitoring of learning outcomes, and critical thinking about the subject being learned.

Critical thinking can be encouraged as both a skill and an attitude or predisposition, and is a significant determinant of likely success in self-directed learning. In order for adults to be able to succeed in self-directed learning endeavors, it would seem to be vital for them to have or to develop the capability to think logically, critically, and analytically about the subject they are learning. There is some evidence that critical thinking has both a generic and a subject-specific component; it is the responsibility of adult educators both to model critical thinking and to create situations in which learners are encouraged to develop, practice, and exhibit this capability — especially by the analysis of both written and spoken arguments.

Reading skills are, to an extent, content-specific, and the adult educator cannot presume that even highly educated learners will already have mastered the strategies for reading in a particular subject area. Despite the widespread conviction that literacy is a generic attainment, research shows that each subject has its own vocabulary, its distinctive forms of writing, and its accepted structures of written discourse. A learner who is unfamiliar with the conventions in the field he or she is learning is at a distinct disadvantage, and to prepare people for self-directed learning, the adult educator needs to devise strategies that introduce the potential learner to the conventions of the field and allow him or her to optimize learning outcomes from the written word.

In the absence of an instructor to check for confusion or growing misapprehensions, the self-directed learner must develop the capability to monitor his or her own progress and understanding. Since learning comprises considerably more than the rote memorization of isolated and unconnected fragments, learners must become adept at constantly reviewing their learning, checking against existing knowledge, and ensuring that new information is comprehensible, internally consistent, and leads to sustainable predictions. Adult educators should model this sort of comprehension monitoring by having learners discuss their understandings and expectations at various points in the learning process, so that this process is internalized and becomes second nature.

Central to effective adult learning is the establishment and maintenance of an appropriate learning climate, an environment of trust and collaboration in which learners feel free to risk themselves and to explore new ways of thinking, feeling, and acting without the threat of censure or ridicule.

Finally, the issue of developing skills for lifelong learning was dealt with. However informal and nonthreatening an adult education environment is, it is nevertheless an educational setting that may differ in important ways from the learning that occurs spontaneously and naturally in everyday contexts. The challenge is to assist learners to develop the skills and the confidence to be effective learners in less structured milieux.

It has been the purpose of this chapter to challenge the widely — but nonreflectively — held view that the best (or indeed the only) way to enhance people's self-direction in learning is to place them in situations of learner-control. There can be little doubt that exposure to situations that require learners to think and act autonomously is a vital aspect of developing their capacity for self-directed learning. However, self-directed learning — especially of discipline-based knowledge — calls on attitudes, skills, and knowledge that can be intentionally developed through planned educational interventions. Some of these aspects are generic, others are content-specific; some relate to learning generally, others specially to self-directed learning. In all cases, however, there is a role for the adult educator — as there is for all educators — to work for the intellectual, emotional, and personal emancipation of learners as a vital prerequisite to the development of a learning society.

The next chapter takes the issue of subject-specific autonomy a step further by examining the need for, and strategies for, introducing learners to the basic "codes" or "rules of discourse" that govern particular subject areas.

Twelve

Facilitating
Independent Mastery
of Subject Matter

When a person confronts an entirely new area of knowledge or skill, one with which she or he has no familiarity, there is the problem of where to begin in attempting to learn it. In his paper on "The Authority of Ideas and the Student's Right to Autonomy," Strike (1982, p. 41) puts it this way: "The ignorance of the person just beginning the study of a subject has a special character. It is not just that the novice is ignorant of the facts and theories of the subject matter; the student is also ignorant of the principles that govern thought about the subject matter. He [or she] does not know what the problems of the field are, . . . what approaches to take to solve a field's problems, and . . . how to identify a reasonable solution to a problem."

Gradually, however, through a process of inquiry and personal experimentation, the learner comes to recognize the boundaries of the subject or skill, and to internalize the "rules" or "codes" that inhere within it. This involves acquiring the basic "vocabulary" of concepts in the subject being learned, and, since each subject has its own rules of discourse, a person cannot properly be said to have learned a subject until he or she is familiar, at least at some minimal level, with the rules of that domain.

Frequently, autonomy in learning has been equated with situational independence—that is, the ability to operate as a learner with minimal supervision or institutional support and affiliation. Although this is clearly an important aspect of learner

343

autonomy, it is only part of the story. All learning efforts concern some substantive content or other, yet, as I have discussed in Chapter Six, many researchers have classified learning projects according to the subject matter being learned, few seem to have considered the processes whereby a learner actually becomes autonomous with respect to the material itself. Nearly always, when we speak or write about learner self-direction, a degree of expertise or subject matter competence is also implied; we do not simply want people who can find resources for themselves, manage their time appropriately, or set learning goals, but rather learners who know and understand enough to be able to distinguish plausible from implausible knowledge claims or convincing from unconvincing evidence. Thus it seems that autonomous learning has, in addition to its situational component, an epistemological or knowledge-based component as well.

In this chapter, three major notions with respect to the attainment of such subject matter autonomy will be advanced. First, the attainment of independence with respect to a particular subject is a developmental phenomenon. As people move through various phases in a learning endeavor, their ability to function independently—as Brookfield (1981a, p. 23) puts it, "to call into question the pronouncements of experts"—increases.

Second, at the heart of growing independence as a learner is the development of personal "frames of reference" or "anticipatory schemes" (Kuhn, 1981). It is asserted that each learner builds up, for himself or herself, a "mental map" of the subject matter being learned, and that one indication of autonomy is when a learner is able to offer, on the basis of such anticipatory schemes, coherent, plausible, and internally consistent explanations concerning the subject that is being learned.

Third, epistemological independence is highly content-specific. A learner who is very competent, experienced, and knowledgeable in one domain may be a complete novice in another area, and must accordingly function dependently, at least at first. Contrary to the assertions of some, the attainment of autonomy in learning is not a universal, content-free accomplishment.

The chapter concludes with some observations about how adult educators can help learners to develop their subject matter expertise, and thereby to enhance their ability to learn independently.

The Development of Subject Matter Autonomy

In Chapter Eight, I drew the distinction between "public" and "private" knowledge. Public knowledge relates to what Habermas has called the "practical" and "communicative" domains; it is socially constructed, consensually validated, and incorporates norms and criteria for evaluating or judging knowledge claims. Private (or emancipatory) knowledge on the other hand deals with the world of personal experience and judgment: the insights that people gain into themselves as learners, how they prefer to learn new material, their motives, their level of tolerance for ambiguity, and how they interact with other people. Private knowledge also includes a whole range of insights and understandings that are tacit and highly situation-specific, and that accordingly are not as accessible to public scrutiny and review as learning of conventional discipline-based or propositional knowledge (Elbaz, 1983; Erickson, 1987; Kelly, 1955; Polanyi, 1962; Schön, 1983, 1987).

In this chapter, I do not intend to deal with such private knowledge, either in the form of self-learning or of "personal practical" knowledge, because (at least in this regard) learners can already be assumed to be autonomous. Instead, I intend to examine how learners gain autonomy when dealing with propositional knowledge, which is often codified and "discipline-based," where the rules are public, and where the autodidact's learning can be publicly tested and acknowledged.

Putting aside, therefore, self-directed learning about oneself, more often than not, the autodidact must accept and acknowledge the existence of norms or standards against which to judge, and on which to base, his or her learning. Chené (1983) has observed:

> Whether the learners are currently in relation to a teacher or not, the mediation of another person is necessary for them to assert the value of what they are aware or, of what they know. . . .

> Similarly, skill performance is evaluated according to a standard which, at least at the beginning of the learning process, is outside the self. Embroidering, using a computer, meditating or jogging, to be recognized as such, have to conform to a set of criteria which have been communicated by somebody else, or taken from somebody else. . . .
> *Epistemologically, the relation to others is fundamental to knowledge and the psychological independence from the teacher conceals the problem of the norm in learning.* In fact, the teacher cannot disappear without reappearing in another form, since learners have to test their knowledge against somebody else [p. 43; emphasis added].

Thus, as Chené points out, it is not possible for a learner ever to be fully autonomous with respect to propositional knowledge. However, given this general proviso, it still makes sense to speak and write of people becoming sufficiently familiar with the subject of their study that they can judge between expert opinions and perhaps, in some situations, even contribute to boundary or standard setting for the field (Brookfield, 1981b; Gross and Gross, 1983; Kuhn, 1970). As Quinton (1971, p. 214) writes, "Cognitive autonomy is achieved when the capacity for the criticism of authorities and of personally-formed beliefs . . . has become an operative skill. . . . "

In Chapter Eleven, I argued that the development of such a critical capacity with respect to any given subject matter is a hallmark of the truly self-directed learner. Central to this task of developing a critical stance is the approach adopted by the learner. In Chapter Nine, I discussed the distinction between surface and deep-level learning; this distinction is particularly vital here because a learner could not be considered to be truly autonomous if his or her learning were restricted to surface-level approaches, but only if she or he had engaged in deep-level learning.

The ability to specify whether or not a person has achieved autonomy in some subject area presupposes the ability to identify the "level" of their learning accomplishment. This, however, is not always easy: "In some discipline-based domains such as chess or aviation, the different levels of mastery and the criteria for their attainment are clearly and explicitly established (for example, Expert or Master level play in chess). For other domains (such as medicine, carpentry or political leadership) the levels of achievement are less clearly defined" (Feldman, 1980, p. 10).

Although it might be difficult to judge the "level" of a person's learning, because of the idiosyncratic ways in which people represent their understandings, one feature does appear clear. Attaining autonomy with respect to some particular subject is not an instantaneous process, but one that involves some cumulative, or indeed developmental, aspects. Many researchers into autonomous learning have identified the phenomenon of learners' growing independence with respect to the subject of their study. For instance, Brown (1983) in her "Confessions of an Autodidact" gives a glimpse of how feelings of inadequacy, lack of confidence, or even shame can be turned into pride, enthusiasm, and determination as the autodidact encounters success in his or her project. Brookfield (1981a, p. 23) writes of the learning experience of self-taught experts who develop what he calls "critical confidence," that is, "the growing belief that one's knowledge was such that one could call into question the pronouncements of experts in the learner's field of interest." In the report of his study, Brookfield (1981a, p. 23) gives a number of illustrative quotations that reveal the feelings and attitudes of learners who know their subject:

> "The world's top ichthyologist is H. A. I don't keep his books any more, because I disagree with a lot of his theories on tropical fish keeping. I didn't at first. I don't suppose I read anything else but A., and another American W. But after a few years, you start to realise that their idea of fish-keeping clashes with your own. Anybody who's a thinking person, anyway." (Self-taught expert on tropical fish)
>
> "I think I've developed my own philosophy. I'm able to assess other people's philosophy from a definite standpoint. I've read a few people's philosophies and so assessed them." (Self-taught expert on philosophy)
>
> "I think I know enough about my subject to be able to spot a lot of mistakes in the books I read. When I buy a new book, I find I'm making alterations all the time, while I'm reading it. Things I know to be wrong are printed in there. If you look at any new books of mine, you'll find the margins are full of comments I've made about it." (Self-taught expert on railway management and modelling).

How is it that these people, who at one time knew little or nothing about the field which they now claim as their own, manage not only to acquire the subject matter, but to go beyond conventional wisdom, to achieve expertise themselves? What are the steps or stages that a learner goes through in attaining proficiency in a new subject area? One person who has addressed this issue is Feldman who, in his book *Beyond Universals in Cognitive Development* (1980), advances the notion that all learners — even prodigies — must go through certain steps or stages on their way to autonomy.

Feldman studied a number of child prodigies who demonstrated superior talent and capability, and as a result he identified what he terms "developmental levels and transitions within the variety of discipline-based domains." In order to test the generalizability of these "non-universal developmental phenomena," Feldman (1980, p. 18) asked university students "to begin a hobby that they have always wanted to learn, but had not had time to try." He goes on to describe the process and its outcome:

> Their learning assignment for the semester is to spend a reasonable amount of time learning how to do something challenging with which they have had little experience. The only constraint is that the hobby they choose has to be sufficiently difficult that they are unlikely to master it fully in a semester's time. They are instructed to reflect upon the experience in a journal and try to relate their experience to developmental theory. . . .
>
> Amazingly, almost all of the students thus far have been able to conceptualize their "metahobby" projects in terms of developmental levels and developmental transitions which seem plausible and natural. The metahobbies have ranged widely — belly-dancing, ethnic cooking, sculpture, skiing, autobody work, calligraphy, radio broadcasting, to name only a few. The range is remarkable, but the common threads are, from our point of view, even more impressive [p. 18].

Through these independent learning endeavors, Feldman attempted to study the processes whereby an independent learner masters a subject. There is reason to suppose, on the basis of these findings, that the learner's attainment of autonomy with respect to any particular subject matter or content is likely to pass through distinct stages—slower or faster for each individual. Feldman calls this a "nonuniversal" development because, although it happens in an invariant sequence and involves the hierarchical integration of ideas, it is not universal (that is, not everyone learns it) and it does not happen spontaneously.

This is a valuable insight for two reasons. First, the fact of its cumulative nature implies that instruction (or even lack of instruction) cannot materially alter the necessity to go through certain stages of understanding (or perhaps even misunderstanding). The most it can hope to achieve is to "speed up" the progression through what appears to be an invariant sequence. Second, the fact that its accomplishment is not universal, and hence requires at least some special conditions for its attainment, emphasizes the "complementarity between a field of endeavor and a set of individual predispositions or talents" (Feldman, 1980, p. 19).

A second important finding emerges from Feldman's work, for in discussing the students' responses to their learning projects, he goes on to add: "There is a real sense that the students' analyses are not simply a relabeling of experience. The notion of developmental levels and transitions within the variety of discipline-based domains selected seems to make a profound difference to these students as they reflect on their experiences . . . " (p. 18).

The notion that subject matter autonomy depends, at least in part, on reflecting on one's individual structures of meaning, as well as on the underlying structure of knowledge, is an intriguing one. It has been discussed elsewhere in relation to reflection in learning (Candy, Harri-Augstein, and Thomas, 1985), and is also foundational to aspects of deep-level learning and critical thinking discussed in Chapter Eleven.

Thus far, I have talked about the likely existence of steps or stages in the development of autonomy, but what exactly are they? Several researchers have explored adult learning of a second or subsequent language in an attempt to understand this process (Abe, Henner-Stanchina, and Smith, 1975; Curran, 1976; Henner-Stanchina, 1976; Nolan, 1981a, 1981b). Curran (1976), for instance, postulates that in all learning situations—formal and nonformal— adult learners struggle to maintain a sense of autonomy, even when the subject matter is unfamiliar or the teaching method is a dependent one. On the basis of extended observations of second-language learners in various settings, he hypothesized that learners move through a five-stage process with respect to any particular content (see Table 12.1).

Table 12.1. The Development of Autonomy
in Adult Second-Language Learning.

I	II	III	IV	V
Total dependency	Learner attempts to move ahead independently	Learner functions independently in the language	Learner becomes open to correction	Positive self-concept; fully autonomous learning
Embryonic Stage	Self-assertion Stage	Separation or Birth Stage	Reversal Stage	'Adult' Stage

Source: Adapted from Curran, 1976, p. 105. Used by permission.

Nolan (1981a, 1981b) set out to test the generalizability of Curran's scheme. Distinguishing learners in the beginning phase of their language learning project from those in an advanced stage, he asked learners to describe their perceptions and feelings about themselves as second-language learners at each phase. In the beginning "they described themselves as learners in both positive and negative terms. They described themselves as frustrated, childish, insecure, foolish, embarrassed, belittled, humiliated. They also described themselves as enthusiastic, confident, comfortable. . . . The first stage or period was described in cognitive terms as one of intense work—sheer drudgery as one subject put it—in which the learner, although highly motivated, frequently felt frustrated and foolish in the learning situation . . . (p. 144).

These learners would be described as situationally autonomous (that is, free of direction by others), but not yet as epistemologically autonomous. It is interesting that those with higher levels of formal education, far from being at an advantage, reported themselves as experiencing the most frustration and loss of self-esteem at this stage: "A subject who holds a Ph. D. degree described the early stages of his second-language learning experience as 'an assault on his self-esteem.' A Roman Catholic clergyman reported his early learning period as a torturous time when he felt like 'a child or an idiot'" (Nolan, 1981b, p. 145).

Thus, it appears that previous educational attainment may not necessarily be an advantage and may even become an impediment, in terms of emotional adjustment to the learning situation. Fortunately, however, these feelings of helplessness and despair did not persist, as Nolan (1981b) again explains: "There then seemed to occur a breakthrough period reported most often by those whose learning had occurred in an intense, monolingual setting. This breakthrough experience accompanied the adult learner's arrival at a threshold level of linguistic competency, where the learner found it relatively easy to communicate. As one ex-Peace Corps Volunteer put it, "It is the sudden realization that you are keeping up with the conversation without trying." Others described it as a liberating moment. . . . Not all subjects interviewed reported this experience. Those who did, [however], described it as a very dramatic event which they had no trouble remembering . . . " (p. 144).

This quotation serves to emphasize the fact that attainment of subject matter autonomy is, as Feldman states, "nonuniversal." At the same time, it raises the question of whether there is any generic or trans-situational component that would allow some people to develop autonomy while others do not. It may be argued that the ability to become autonomous with respect to one domain or area occurs within a broader developmental framework, and that it is only possible for learners to achieve full independence when they come to view knowledge in relative rather than absolute terms.

As early as 1970, Perry and his associates at Harvard identified a developmental continuum with respect to the relativity of knowledge along which university students were found to be arrayed. In introducing his full nine-stage model of intellectual development in the college years, he paints the following vignettes about three different types of students:

> Student A has always taken it for granted that knowledge consists of correct answers, that there is one right answer per problem, and that teachers explain these answers for students to learn. He therefore listens for the lecturer to state which theory to learn.
>
> Student B makes the same general assumptions, but with an elaboration to the effect that teachers sometimes present problems and procedures, rather than answers, "so that we can learn to find the right answer on our own." He therefore perceives the lecture as a kind of guessing game in which he is to "figure out" which theory is correct, a game that is fair enough if the lecturer does not carry it so far as to hide things too obscurely.
>
> Student C assumes that an answer can be called "right" only in the light of its context, and that contexts or "frames of reference" differ. . . . Although he feels a little uneasy in such a kaleidoscopic world, he nonetheless supposes that the lecturer may be about to present three legitimate theories which can be examined for their internal coherence, their scope, their fit with various data, their predictive power, etc. [pp. 1–2].

These three hypothetical students represent different positions in Perry's scheme of intellectual development. Clearly, if they were each engaged in autonomous learning, they would bring to bear different criteria to judge the adequacy of their own learning accomplishments. But educators commonly set learners independent tasks, with little conscious thought for the developmental stage each has reached. Even at advanced graduate level, there is no guarantee that learners will have attained the ninth and ultimate stage of commitment to a personal view, alongside a tolerance for alternative perspectives (Perry, 1970, 1981, 1988; Phillips, 1981).

Although this developmental continuum was derived from a study of "students" (and a rarefied and privileged group of students at that), Perry (1970, p. x) questions its wider applicability: "Can this scheme be considered a relatively enduring outline of major vicissitudes in human experience from adolescence into adulthood in a pluralistic culture? Does it help us to understand the way that 'modern man' [or woman] finds to address his [her] predicament in a relativistic world?"

Cameron (1983), for her part, argues that adults generally are spread out along such a developmental spectrum, and, since self-direction in learning is a widespread phenomenon, it is also reasonable to suppose that autodidacts would exhibit the same range of development with respect to their beliefs about knowledge. Thus, some self-teachers would be seeking the one "right" or "true" answer, while others would be seeking a better understanding of the issues involved, and possible alternative explanations or perspectives. Overall, it is difficult to conceive of learners becoming autonomous with respect to subject matter, if they had not progressed far along a general continuum of epistemological sophistication such as that offered by Perry. This implies that adult educators wishing to assist learners to attain independence need to focus on the tentative, fragile, and relativistic nature of knowledge.

Anticipatory Schemes and Autonomy in Learning

What exactly is developed as people move through these various stages with respect to their subject? Clearly, it is more than a collection of fragmentary "facts," such as those acquired through rote learning. Instead, it is some sort of understanding of the underlying principles, or the structure of knowledge in the domain concerned. It is this that allows people, in Bruner's (1957) evocative phrase, to "go beyond the information given" and thereby to assert their autonomy. Although there has been relatively little research into the mechanism whereby people attain autonomy with respect to learning tasks, a promising direction is suggested by several reports that, despite the fact they approach the question from different points of view, do tend to corroborate each other.

In conventional teaching/learning situations, whether face to face or at a distance, learners are customarily presented with prepackaged ideas. More often than not, the ideas are presented in a sequence that seems logical to the trainer or instructor, and the learner has to accommodate to the conventions of the field of study in order to master it. The learner usually does not have to "grapple" with the essence of the subject, and accordingly is often pushed in the direction of reproductive rather than deep-level or transformational learning (Ramsden, 1985, pp. 58–59).

However, if grappling with the complexities of a subject is an important part of deep-level or transformational learning, then it may be that one advantage which the independent has over the more dependent learner is the experience of "sorting out" relevant from extraneous concepts and ideas. Eraut, Mac-Kenzie, and Papps (1975), reporting on a course at Sussex University, comment on their initial disappointment when students failed to grasp the significance of certain basic economic concepts in a teaching package over which they had labored. They write: "Whilst students appeared to get very little out of the Demand Theory Package, the members of faculty who prepared it felt that they had learnt a lot from having to sort out their ideas: and it occurred to them that the 'sorting out' process might be more important than the subsequent learning. Perhaps the students could also be involved in formulating the problems, clarifying the assumptions about the situation to be studied, choosing the analytic techniques, and disentangling value judgments and empirical judgments" (p. 24).

Interestingly, Farnes, (1975, p. 3) makes almost the same comment about the experience of course teams at the Open University:

> In the Open University, it seems paradoxical to me that the people who experience exciting and immensely demanding learning tasks are the course teams; they are acquiring and organizing knowledge, evaluating and selecting materials, designing and presenting programs and activities. The students receive what appears to be a polished product from this process; they have to learn from material that has been agonized over by authors, course team members and many others. . . .
>
> If it is in the course teams that there are genuine learning experiences, should we not allow the students to participate in these learning experiences by delegating more of the job to them? . . . A major effort is necessary to get students to change their passive approach to learning and to encourage them to take responsibility.

From a review of the literature, it appears that only one study of autodidacts has identified this dimension as important to the attainment of autonomy. In their study of major recurrent tasks in self-teaching, Danis and Tremblay (1985b) identified twenty-six tasks that they found to be common to the experience of many adult self-teachers. These were grouped into five major dimensions:

> *Management of the learning process:* tasks related to the planning, conducting, and evaluating of the learning activities
>
> *Acquisition of knowledge or skills:* tasks related to the learning of specific contents
>
> *Acquisition of resources:* tasks related to the locating of the various human resources (peers, experts, friends, parents, etc.) and material resources (books, official documents, films, pamphlets, etc.)
>
> *Use of didactic abilities:* tasks related to self-instruction
>
> *Use of support:* tasks related to getting and maintaining a satisfying emotional support with regard to the learning behavior [p. 286].

One function within the cluster labeled "Use of didactic abilities" is "Sorting out contradictory information or differing ways of proceeding" (p. 291). This was rated, by learners, as one of the most frequently recurring as well as one of the most difficult tasks they have to perform (p. 297). What is needed to accomplish this task of "sorting out"?

Presumably, active involvement would be one component: It does not seem likely that "sorting out" would be compatible with a passive, dependent mode of learning. In addition, there would need to be the application of some generic intellectual skills such as critical thinking or assumption finding. However, for the most part, the skills of learning any particular knowledge are not independent of that knowledge and cannot be mastered in a content-free course on "study skills." Central to the process of "sorting out" must be the development of some categories or criteria with respect to that body of knowledge itself. In a paper entitled "The Role of Self-Directed Activity in Cognitive Development," Kuhn (1981, p. 354) reports on an experiment designed to focus on the role of "sorting out" in the development of reasoning strategies: "Our intent was to examine critically this alleged role by designing two identical intervention situations with the exception that in one, subjects selected the particular information-seeking activities they would engage in, while in the other, they did not. This was accomplished by pairing each experimental subject with a yoked control subject, who engaged in exactly the same activities as had been chosen by his or her experimental partner. Thus, each subject of the pair was 'active,' each carried out an identical set of activities and hence was exposed to identical information stemming from those activities, but only the experimental subject selected the activities to engage in."

Subjects were exposed to a series of problem-solving tasks of increasing complexity, and the experimenters were interested in "(1) a comparison of the highest problem in the intervention sequence mastered by subjects in the two conditions; and (2) a comparison of the post-test performance of the subjects in the two conditions, as well as the simple control condition" (p. 355).

All subjects improved their problem-solving capacities, which substantiated earlier findings that people generally make "significant progress in the construction of new thinking strategies when they are simply exposed to a rich problem-solving environment over a period of months" (p. 356). However, the experimental subjects made noticeably greater progress than their yoked controls, and Kuhn (1981, p. 357) offers the following explanation: "The experience of the experimental subjects in the present study differed from that of their yoked controls in that [they] were required to 'direct' their own activity in the sense of planning the specific activities they would carry out. Both groups were physically active (in manipulating the materials) to an equal extent, . . . [but] the critical difference, in our view, is rather that the experimental subjects were encouraged to develop an *anticipatory scheme* with respect to possible experimental outcomes, simply because of the fact that they had to design the set of experiments that would yield one of these outcomes. . . . It is our hypothesis that experimental subjects, because of these anticipatory schemes, were better able to 'make use of' in the cognitive sense — in other words assimilate into a theoretical framework — the data yielded by the experiments, and thus they gained more from the experience."

Although the term *anticipatory scheme* itself may be novel, the notion that learners develop cognitive schemas with respect to subjects they are learning is not new. Its antecedents, at least in the field of cognitive psychology, stretch back as far as Spearman's (1923) treatise on *The Nature of Intelligence and Principles of Cognition*. In more recent years, a similar notion may be found in sources as diverse as Ausubel (1968), Bruner (1957), Crockett (1965), Erickson (1987), Kelly (1955), Lindsay and Norman (1977), Piaget (1972), Quine and Ullian (1978), Rumelhart (1977), Thomas and Harri-Augstein (1985), and von Glasersfeld (1984).

In each case, it is envisaged that learners portray their understandings in the form of a mental representation (or "cognitive map") of the subject of their inquiries. It is generally held that, within the overall context of a person's cognitive map, they will have various schemas to represent various domains of knowledge. What Kuhn's concept of "anticipatory schemes" adds to this picture is the notion of anticipation. Learners are not mere passive observers in the learning situation, but active construers, and their constructions lead them to expect certain outcomes.

In elaborating the relevance and significance of Kelly's *Psychology of Personal Constructs* (1955) for learning, Beck (1979) emphasizes that people's understandings about the world (or some specific aspect of it) lead them to have certain expectations. They then "invest themselves" or commit themselves to these expectations. The way in which things actually turn out, Beck argues, may either confirm or disconfirm the expectation, but in either case, it offers the opportunity to elaborate or modify the learner's existing set of constructs about that domain.

This notion of anticipation was discussed with respect to reading in Chapter Eleven, and is vital to an understanding of what it means to be autonomous with regard to a subject. The true neophyte's anticipations will either be inaccurate or incomplete, whereas the person who has at least mastered the essence of his or her subject should be able to make more defensible and more complete predictions about it and, if events prove them wrong, to make better sense of the disconfirming evidence.

The Content-Specific Nature
of Subject Matter Autonomy

As discussed in Chapter Five, there are commonsense grounds for expecting autonomy to manifest itself across a range of learning situations. This is certainly implicit in many formulations of independent learning that assert that autonomy is a "developable capacity." However, although a person may have an overall predisposition toward acting autonomously in the sense of managing time, setting goals, finding resources, and critically evaluating ideas and events, it is clear that he or she might not know enough about the details of the subject being learned to distinguish convincing from unconvincing knowledge claims or reliable from unreliable evidence. In other words, he or she may not be autonomous with respect to the subject being learned: "*It is dangerous to assume that, because someone has exhibited an ability to learn autonomously, the same situation will apply with regard to an area completely different to all previous learning.* It was noted of several people in this study that whilst their basic ability to plan and to organise their learning was well established, having been involved in, say, pure science, that when tackling a practical 'do-it-yourself' project, there was a considerable need for assistance . . ." (Strong, 1977, p. 139; emphasis added).

This "need for assistance" does not necessarily represent some pathological inadequacy on the part of the learner. To the contrary, it may even be evidence of a higher-order form of autonomy that allows him or her "to choose between dependence and independence as he [or she] perceives the need" (Nuffield Foundation, 1975).

In addition to such conscious and deliberate surrendering of independence in pursuit of learning, there are many other factors that might conspire to limit a learner's autonomy. As discussed in Chapter Ten, these include the learner's preexisting concepts and beliefs concerning the domain being studied; past educational experiences that, as Häyrynen and Häyrynen and others have observed, might have effectively denied the learner access to deeper levels of meaning about what counts as knowledge in that culture; individual beliefs or "personal learning myths" (Thomas and Harri-Augstein, 1985) that the learner may have internalized concerning his or her ability to learn certain subjects (discussed in Chapter Thirteen); the learner's intentions and purposes in the learning situation; how the learner construes salient environmental and contextual factors that influence the decision about learning strategies; and other factors already alluded to, such as the learner's conceptions of "learning" and of "knowledge."

All of these dimensions interact with one another in complex ways, and, since this combination will vary from situation to situation, a learner's autonomy might be expected, likewise, to vary from one context to another. Combined with this is the point already made that the internal structures of various domains of knowledge differ markedly from one another. Overall, although there may well exist a generic or trans-situational sort of autonomy in learning, it seems to me that for all practical purposes, each situation should be treated on its own merits. It comes as no surprise to find that a learner may be judged or thought of as "independent" or autonomous by his or her peers or instructors in one domain, yet as lacking in autonomy with respect to some other field of study.

Helping Learners to Increase Subject Matter Autonomy

If the arguments presented so far in this chapter are accepted, the next question is, "What can the educator do to assist learners to become autonomous with respect to a particular area of study?" In the section that follows, four strategies are discussed: providing scaffolding, bibliographic instruction, the use of Gowin's "Knowledge Vee," and cognitive apprenticeship. None of these strategies on its own is likely to create a high degree of metaknowledge, but collectively they (along with other similar approaches) may help to shift the responsibility for critical evaluation of knowledge claims from the teacher or trainer to the learner.

Providing Scaffolding. In Zinacantan in Southern Mexico, the skill of weaving is passed on through informal but highly individualized instruction. Beginning weavers are assigned small and relatively simple tasks; experts are left to get on with their weaving once they have mastered the repertoire of basic skills and patterns involved. In the early stages, those providing instruction intervene and take over difficult parts of the weaving; the result is that even pieces from first-time beginners are of a high quality. As the learner progresses, however, verbal instruction replaces physical intervention, and direct commands are replaced by comments and observations. These aids to learning are referred to as scaffolds, and the type and amount of "scaffolding" needed and provided are adapted to the learner's level, decreasing as the learner's skill level increases, until "ultimately, the scaffold becomes internalized, enabling independent accomplishment of the skill by the learner" (Greenfield, 1984, p. 135).

Thus the first approach in helping learners to become indendent is to introduce them, gradually and systematically, to the subject matter in which they are interested. This may seem self-evident, but there are abundant examples of where an educator has failed to provide any such "scaffolding" within which the learner can erect his or her own pattern of understandings or skill development.

Bibliographic Instruction. At least some adult education concerns "book-based" rather than "skill-based" learning, and accordingly a second approach to developing subject matter independence is deliberately to introduce the learner to the structures of knowledge in the particular field. In a paper entitled "Teaching Information Structure: Turning Dependent Researchers into Self-Teachers," Frick (1982, p. 197) writes:

> A class or course on bibliographic structure should help students discriminate among various aspects of a discipline's literature. Exploring and evaluating the literature expands the research process, allowing students to become contributing participants in their own education. Not only then are students able to continue their own education, but they see the chosen discipline as a living entity rather than a static corpus of facts and begin to develop judgment.
>
> Discriminating between appropriate and inappropriate, scholarly and popular material is not only an important, but a mandatory talent. . . .

Earlier in this chapter, I alluded to the need for adult educators to show learners that knowledge is dynamic and tentative, not static and external. If learners are always presented with neatly packaged, carefully arranged, and sequentially organized reading matter, as is often the case in so-called self-instructional programs, they may never come to realize the careful system of checks and balances that exists in developing, refining, and reviewing a body of knowledge.

For those who hold that learners should have undifferentiated access to all sorts of ideas — established and radical, speculative and empirically verified, descriptive and normative — then the widespread use of electronic databases is a welcome development in the democratization of learning. However, unless the learner is to waste valuable time in recapitulating the entire intellectual history of his or her chosen domain, and in the process is to follow up many false trails and discredited lines of argument, the plethora of information is a curse rather than a boon. In order to liberate learners from a bondage to the superabundance of information, the educator must strive to develop in them "a basic understanding of how knowedge is created, communicated, synthesized within fields of inquiry, how knowledge differs structurally from one field to another, and how bibliographic sources reflect the various stages of the knowledge process" (Hopkins, 1981, p. 18).

In most areas of inquiry, there is a succession whereby ideas are eventually incorporated into the body of knowledge of that subject or domain. One common route is for ideas and reports of research to appear in working documents and unpublished papers. Next, they will often be presented at — and appear in the proceedings of — conferences or other gatherings of experts. They might then be submitted to a journal and, finally, find their way into book form. This progression is not identical for every field, but the notion that "books" represent the repository of the most tried and tested knowledge claims in a field, for instance, or that recent developments are most likely to be found in press releases or conference papers, gives a vital clue as to the essential structure of knowledge in an area of study.

Frick (1982) claims that there are four levels of "bibliographic awareness," which are arranged hierarchically. They are "(1) a knowledge of specific titles that are useful for specific tasks; (2) a knowledge of types of sources relevant to types of questions; (3) a knowledge that each of the specific disciplines inspires specific types of sources for reasons embedded in their research goals, assumptions, and methods; and (4) a knowledge that the structure of literature and information in a society or discipline both informs, and is informed by, that society [or discipline]" (p. 198). It often appears as if the experienced researcher or practitioner has an almost innate sense of what is new, what is worthwhile, and what is practical in his or her field of expertise. This sense, however, is not intuitive but derives from a prolonged exposure to the field and extensive contact with its core ideas and practices. It is thus vital to help a person "in learning how to learn and in learning how to become an independent learner who can continue to function in a society where the ability to focus on the most relevant information in a maelstrom of increasingly difficult and important data is necessary" (Frick, 1982, p. 206).

Gowin's "Knowledge Vee." When one looks at an archipelago, it is often easy to lose sight of the fact that the islands are not, in fact, isolated entities; rather they are a submerged mountain range where only the tallest peaks are visible above the water. The same is frequently true of knowledge in a particular domain; what appear as isolated or unrelated facts, principles, or examples are often part of a larger topography, but the connections are hidden from view and accordingly are not immediately apparent.

From the point of view of a novice in a field of study, many knowledge claims may appear as islands, having little in common with other knowledge claims in the immediate vicinity. This is a distinct problem for the self-directed learner. For the expert, or at least the more experienced student, on the other hand, individual items form part of a cohesive whole; there is an underlying structure that helps to explain how the apparently separate or disparate items are related to one another. Part of the process of achieving autonomy with respect to a body of knowledge is coming to recognize the underlying structure or "syntax" of the domain.

One way of doing this, of upgrading the knowledge in any particular field, is to apply the following five questions to any document or exposition presenting knowledge:

1. What is the "telling question"?
2. What are the key concepts?
3. What methods of inquiry are used?
4. What are the major knowledge claims?
5. What are the value claims?

Answers to these questions help to reveal the interconnections and underlying structures of various bodies of knowledge. Based on research using these five questions, Gowin developed a framework or heuristic device that can be superimposed on any domain to lay bare its structure and the linkages of its main components (see Figure 12.1). The "Knowledge Vee" is a device that has sides or arms; one concerns the methodological aspect of creating knowledge and the other the conceptual aspect. At the point of the Vee are the events and objects that are being studied or considered in a particular area of study. As one progresses up the "methodological" arm of the Vee, there are records of the events or objects, facts, transformation of facts, results, interpretations, explanations, and generalizations, leading to knowledge claims and, ultimately, value claims. On the other hand, as one progresses up the "conceptual" arm, there is another nested hierarchy comprising concepts, conceptual structures, constructs, principles, theories, philosophies, and finally worldviews.

These two aspects, however, are far from independent, and there is a constant two-way traffic between the conceptual and methodological sides of the diagram: "Concepts operate in an explicit way to select the events or objects we choose to observe and the records we choose to make. If our concepts are inadequate or faulty, our inquiry is already in difficulty. If our records are faulty, then we do not have the *facts* (valid records) to work with and no form of transformation can lead to valid claims. To Vee helps us to see that although the meaning of all knowledge eventually derives from the events or objects that teaches us what the records mean. The meaning must be constructed . . ." (Novak and Gowin, 1984, p. 56).

Figure 12.1. An Expanded Version of Gowin's "Knowledge Vee" with Descriptions and Examples of Elements.

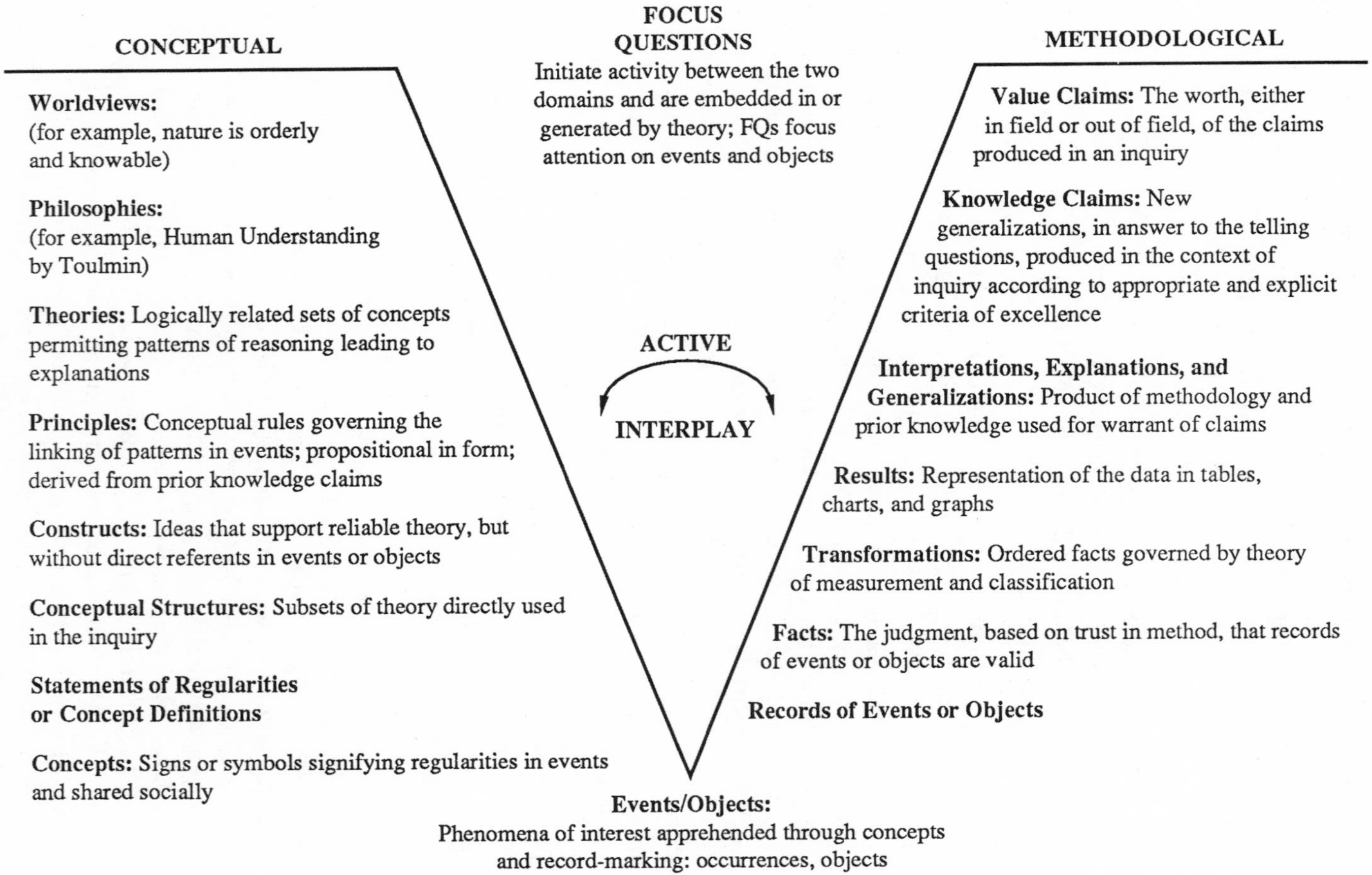

CONCEPTUAL

FOCUS QUESTIONS
Initiate activity between the two domains and are embedded in or generated by theory; FQs focus attention on events and objects

ACTIVE INTERPLAY

METHODOLOGICAL

Worldviews: (for example, nature is orderly and knowable)

Philosophies: (for example, Human Understanding by Toulmin)

Theories: Logically related sets of concepts permitting patterns of reasoning leading to explanations

Principles: Conceptual rules governing the linking of patterns in events; propositional in form; derived from prior knowledge claims

Constructs: Ideas that support reliable theory, but without direct referents in events or objects

Conceptual Structures: Subsets of theory directly used in the inquiry

Statements of Regularities or Concept Definitions

Concepts: Signs or symbols signifying regularities in events and shared socially

Value Claims: The worth, either in field or out of field, of the claims produced in an inquiry

Knowledge Claims: New generalizations, in answer to the telling questions, produced in the context of inquiry according to appropriate and explicit criteria of excellence

Interpretations, Explanations, and Generalizations: Product of methodology and prior knowledge used for warrant of claims

Results: Representation of the data in tables, charts, and graphs

Transformations: Ordered facts governed by theory of measurement and classification

Facts: The judgment, based on trust in method, that records of events or objects are valid

Records of Events or Objects

Events/Objects:
Phenomena of interest apprehended through concepts and record-marking; occurrences, objects

Source: Novak and Gowin, 1984, p. 56. Used by permission.

In their book on *Learning How to Learn,* Novak and Gowin (1984) give detailed examples, drawn from the sciences and the social sciences, of how the Vee can be used both in devising experiments and in seeking to "unpack" or understand the relationships of events and ideas in a subject being studied. They argue, for instance, that the Vee can be used in studying books, journal articles, and research reports, by "laying the Vee" on these papers and asking questions such as

1. What objects and/or events were being observed?
2. What records or record transformations were made?
3. What was/were the focus question(s)?
4. What relevant concepts or principles were cited or implied?
5. Do the records made validly record the main aspects of the events and/or objects observed?
6. Are relevant principles stated, implied, or ignored?
7. What theory was stated or implied in the research, if any?
8. Is there a conscious, deliberate effort to tie concepts and principles to the (a) events and/or objects observed, (b) records made, (c) record transformations, and (d) knowledge claims?
9. Were any value claims made, and if so, are they congruent with the knowledge claims?
10. Was there a better focus question, or do the results answer a focus question other than what was (or can be inferred to have been) stated? [p. 73]

It seems that knowledge about knowledge (metaknowledge) is one of the critical characteristics of the expert and of the successful independent learner. The Knowledge Vee, then, can be used as a technique or a device to allow people to attain greater subject matter autonomy, and hence to be more effective self-directed learners.

Cognitive Apprenticeship. The fourth strategy to be considered in increasing subject matter autonomy rests on the notion that knowledge does not exist in and of itself but that it occupies an "ecological niche," whereby it "comes coded by and connected to the activity and environment in which it is developed, is spread across its component parts, some of which are in the mind, some in the world such as the final picture on a jigsaw is spread across its component parts" (Brown, Collins, and Duguid, 1989, p. 36). The context-dependent nature of language, for instance, has already been mentioned. Mathematics, too, means something different for the physicist, the engineer, the tailor, the shopkeeper, or the carpenter, and the best way to learn the subject matter is through "learning methods that are embedded in authentic situations" (Brown, Collins, and Duguid, 1989, p. 37).

What Brown, Collins, and Duguid have in mind is *cognitive apprenticeship,* by which they mean methods of learning that seek to enculturate the learner into authentic practices through activity and social interaction. This may be seen as in some ways comparable to the "scaffolding" example with which I began this section, but the point is that learners need to see how, for example, mathematicians think and how they solve problems in real-life contexts or how economists think about and study particular industries (Williams and Delahaye, 1988). By doing this, the learners can progress

> from embedded activity to general principles of the culture. In this sequence, apprenticeship and coaching in a domain begin by providing modelling in situ and scaffolding for students to get started in an authentic activity. As the students gain more self-confidence and control, they move into a more autonomous phase of collaborative learning, where they begin to participate consciously in the culture. The social network within the culture helps them develop its language and the belief systems and promotes the process of enculturation. Collaboration also leads to articulation of strategies, which can then be discussed and reflected on. This, in turn, fosters generalizing, grounded in the students' situated understanding. From here, students can use their fledgling conceptual knowledge in activity, seeing that activity in a new light, which in turn leads to the further development of the conceptual knowledge [Brown, Collins, and Duguid, 1989, p. 39].

This approach to the development of subject matter autonomy progresses from the particular instance to general principles. It acknowledges the situational nature of much knowledge, and encourages the learner to submit to the tutelage of an expert as a necessary preliminary to his or her own autonomous endeavors as a learner.

Summary

In this chapter, I have based my argument on two basic premises. The first is that knowledge — even public, discipline-based knowledge — is socially constructed and that accordingly learning is a social process. Autonomy in the sense of totally independent thought and action is fundamentally irreconcilable with the notion of mastering a recognized body of knowledge: in a sense, autonomous learning is a contradiction in terms! Educators should not, in advocating self-direction in learning, lose sight of the fact that contact with other people is essential to most forms of learning. Self-direction does not necessarily imply solitary learning.

The second basic premise is that learners are active makers of meaning. Not simply that they are, or should be, active in the learning situation, but that learning itself is an active process of constructing and transforming personal meanings. The outcomes of any learning endeavor should be gauged in qualitative, rather than quantitative terms, and learners should, in Schön's (1983) memorable phrase, be "given reason," which means that educators should usually assume that there are good and logical reasons for what learners think and how they act, even if those reasons are not immediately apparent or not shared by others.

Following from these basic convictions, I have argued four main things. The first is that the truly autonomous learner, at least in the sense that most educators would endorse, is the one who engages in deep-level learning of a subject, seeking to go beyond the overt or surface message to the underlying meaning of the topic or domain. Not everyone will be able to function at this level, or would want to do so (Holmberg, 1984, p. 8). The achievement of subject matter autonomy is developmental and cumulative, and learners need to have the right combination of personal interests and environmental circumstances for such deep-level understandings to emerge. The educator has an important role to play in encouraging learners to enter deeply into subjects they are seeking to master.

Second, I have stressed the importance of "sorting out" as critical to the attainment of subject matter autonomy. By this,

I mean the development of "anticipatory schemes" that subsume what the learner already knows about the subject, and that allow him or her to make "intelligent guesses" about the items of information that are missing. An effective autonomous learner is one who knows enough to be able to distinguish defensible from indefensible knowledge claims in the area of his or her expertise; if educators present learners with knowledge in highly polished, prepackaged formats, they may deny the learners the opportunity of "sorting out" for themselves convincing from unconvincing evidence and may also portray knowledge as much more fixed, enduring, and settled then it actually is.

Third, I have emphasized the highly situation-specific or content-dependent nature of subject matter autonomy. The positivist fallacy, as I see it, assumes that behavior and competence can be "hacked off" from their environment, without doing violence to their integrity. I believe, on the contrary, that understandings are contextual and relative, and that the ability to function independently in one domain cannot necessarily be transplanted to another subject area. Thus educators must treat each learner and each learning situation on their individual merits, and be wary of attempts to develop autonomous learning as a generalized capability.

Fourth, and finally, I have argued that adult educators should strive to help learners to achieve a measure of subject matter autonomy: a level of expertise that allows the learner to internalize the rules or norms that are used to judge knowledge claims or performance standards in a particular domain. As Ramsden (1988, p. 23) puts it: "Teachers have a responsibility to learn about, and change, their students' perceptions of a subject's syntactic as well as substantive structure. Many problems in learning derive from sincerely held misconceptions about what subject experts (usually represented by teachers) do and how they think. An extreme version of this type of misconception is the view that a subject consists of a large amount of factual knowledge that has to be remembered, and that subject experts are experts because they know a lot of facts — a view that comes close to the absolutism of Perry's students or the naive view of learning as amassing quantities of knowledge."

I have proposed that such development should, as far as possible, be situated in real-life contexts; that it should involve the progressive induction of the learner into the "syntactic structures" of the subject; that it should encourage high-level thinking about and questioning of the nature of knowledge claims in the field; and ultimately that it should strive for metaknowledge. This involves deliberate strategies on the part of the educator to teach not simply the *content* of the subject, but the *process* by which knowledge develops and is tested in that domain.

In the next chapter, I will turn to a consideration of the social and emotional dimensions of self-directed learning, and the argument that teachers and learners (or experts and novices) "are equally moral agents, and owe one another the rights and respect due [to] moral agents" (Strike, 1982, p. 49). However, although teachers and learners may be equal *moral* agents, when it comes to learning discipline-based knowledge, "There is a significant inequality between the student (as novice) and the teacher (as expert) in terms of their current capacity to understand and assess the ideas and arguments of a field" (Strike, 1982, p. 49). This inequality between experts and novices — between those who are autonomous with respect to their subject and those who are not — has nothing to do with moral agency and everything to do with mastery of "critical standards inherent in the subject itself." As Phillips (1973, p. 139) so eloquently puts it, "Where matters of the intellect are concerned, it is fatal to confuse the statement 'I can say something' with 'I have something to say.' "

Although such an assertion may seem reactionary, until we have dismantled what Lawson (1982, p. 37) calls the "apparatus of public forms of knowledge with its associated experts in the various fields," and have created instead a world in which the production, dissemination, and evaluation of knowledge are seen as "a social process involving everyone," it seems that autonomy of the learner will always have both a different meaning and a different purpose from the autonomy of the expert. Those who seek to help others to learn must keep these different concepts of autonomy clear, and recognize that the kind of autonomy that a new learner can exercise differs in nature and extent from the self-direction of the more advanced practitioner.

Thirteen

Helping Learners
Gain a Sense
of Personal Control

In the two preceding chapters, I have focused primarily on the intellectual and cognitive aspects of self-direction in learning, mainly because these appear to be substantially neglected in much of the literature on adult self-directed learning. However, as I have been arguing throughout this book, self-direction or autonomy also has a significant emotional dimension as well, and it is to this aspect that I will now turn.

Although the development and exercise of personal autonomy as discussed in Chapter Four is valued as an ideal in our society, and despite the fact that there are logical grounds for assuming a link between the exercise of democratic freedoms inside and outside learning situations, it is not the purpose of this chapter to review the extensive literature on the general development of personal autonomy. Instead, the focus will be on the narrower domain of developing and enhancing people's ability to think and behave autonomously in learning contexts (Robertson, 1987).

As I have discussed elsewhere in this book, the literature on education (and adult education in particular) is replete with calls for educators to surrender to learners control over certain aspects of the instructional situation. Furthermore, there are many strategies and approaches that are supposed to contribute to this goal: experiential learning, free discussion, independent study and project work, contract-based learning, problem-based learning, negotiated curricula, individualized instruction, self-assessment, and so on.

It will be argued in this chapter that useful as these strategies are, they conventionally rest on two rather dubious premises. The first is the prevailing assumption that "all [learners] should want or, under certain specifiable conditions, would want more autonomy" (Dearden, 1972, p. 449). The second is that by giving people control over aspects of one teaching/learning situation, the educator is necessarily enhancing their capabilities to assert such control in other situations. These two propositions will be considered before I propose the concept of a "sense of personal control" not only as a useful analytical and explanatory device but also as a vital contruct in the development of self-directed learners.

Individual Differences
in the Acceptance of Learner-Control

Although as discussed in Chapter Three, individual differences are frequently invoked as a justification for increasing learner-control, many authors paradoxically do not allow for the existence of individual differences when it comes to people's ability or willingness to be "self-directing." This is particularly so in adult education, because of the circular way in which adulthood and autonomy are often defined in terms of each other.

However, like any other human attribute, the ability (and willingness) to exert control in the learning situation varies from person to person. As More (1974, p. 157) puts it: "To assume responsibility for one's own learning is a very difficult step to take. For some adult students, it is too difficult a step, and they are never able to take it. On the other hand, there are those students who take to it with a spirit of liberation, as if it were what they had been searching for all their lives. In the middle, there is the great mass of students who can accept this responsibility only with varying degrees of difficulty."

In the past thirty years or more, there has been a steady accumulation of research findings that demonstrate that not all learners are comfortable with, or feel they can benefit from, increased learner-control in the instructional setting (Pratt, 1988). It is the purpose of this section to examine some of the research that deals with individual differences in the acceptance of learner-control, and to explore the extent to which it is desirable (or for that matter possible) to persevere with learners beyond their initial reluctance or even hostility, to some point of acceptance of, and agreement with, learner-control.

Often, when educators have experimented with learner-control, they have encountered negative reactions (especially at first), and observed an apparent unwillingness on the part of learners to accept the increased responsibility. Dunbar and Dutton (1972, pp. 27–28), for instance, note that "from the instructor's point of view, the purpose and design of the course were clear enough and reflected their beliefs as to what was necessary for student learning to occur. . . . However, many students felt lost and confused with this unfamiliar structural design. Some responded with curiosity, exploring what could be done in the new situation. But others became passive, sullen, or even violently angry because they could not understand what was expected of them."

Gruber and Weitman (1962, p. 5 of Chapter 23), summarizing a series of research studies carried out more than twenty-five years ago, write: "A generally negative reaction to participation in the self-directed study experiments was expressed in the students' evaluations of the courses. In almost every case, students prefer the conventional method. Morale problems associated with similar experiments have been reported by Eglash (1954), Neel (1959), and Beach (1961)." Further evidence of learners' expectations was found in an experimental course for the training of adult educators at the University of Cape Town. There, Millar, Morphet, and Saddington (1986) noted a degree of impatience among learners when asked to accept an increased share of responsiblity. They note the presence of "a basic feeling underlying the questions and the silences, [that] rested on a wish 'to get down to work' or 'to get started,' 'to be practical' or 'to be plain and straightforward.' Implicit in these feelings and their expression was the assumption that the role dislocation was an interference with real purposes, an unnecessary preparation developed out of some remote theoretical interest pursued by staff and some students, and that it had nothing to do with the real tasks of teaching and learning. The concept of 'real tasks' implied here conformed closely, of course, to the patterns of traditional teaching and learning" (p. 434).

More often that not, criticisms voiced by learners who are suddenly expected to take control in the instructional setting are aimed at the teacher or instructor, who is suspected of "playing games" and accused of not fulfilling his or her normal role. Wight (1970, p. 271) states that students who have been in school "long enough to know how school is supposed to be taught" will often accuse an instructor of "not knowing his subject matter or how to teach" if he or she moves in the direction of increased learner-control, and Dunbar and Dutton (1972, p. 28) note that "when the professor enters the classroom, students are alert to, and looking for, clues as to which of the expected legitimate demands will be imposed."

Overall, research has repeatedly shown that "there seems to be a uniformly negative reaction to methods of instruction giving the student greater independence than he is accustomed to" (Gruber and Weitman, 1962, p. 5 of Chapter 23). Why is there such a negative attitude towards learner-control? There seem to be at least four plausible explanations, which might be summarized as a preference for directed instruction, learned helplessness, the development of personal learning myths, and deliberately adapting to the instructional situation. Each of these will be discussed in turn.

A Preference for Directed Instruction. One possible explanation for why learners might resist learner-controlled methods of instruction is that they simply prefer to be taught. Some people would read Dunbar and Dutton's claim that students "could not understand what was expected of them," or the reference by Millar and others to "role dislocation" from "the patterns of traditional teaching and learning," and infer from this, as Gruber and Weitman seem to, that "students prefer the conventional method" of instruction.

There is no doubt that the practice of self-directed learning is widespread in the adult population. However, there is no evidence that a preference for independent learning is universal among adults; the common assertion that "adults are self-directing" seems to be normative rather than empirical (Todd, 1981), and to embody the confusion already referred to between self-construction as a philosophical construct and self-direction as a psychological one.

If, for instance, one takes the widely researched construct of field dependence/field independence as a metaphor for dependence/independence in learning (Tzuk, 1985a, 1985b), it is apparent that not all adults are (or for that matter would wish to be) regarded as "field independent." The kinds of characteristics, preferences, and orientations distributed across the population include the predisposition to conduct one's own education, and there would seem to be legitimate and enduring differences among people with regard to their willingness and capacity to control aspects of the learning situation. Educators should respect the rights of those learners who prefer to be taught in a particular situation, because this is a legitimate choice that adults may make.

Learned Helplessness. A second way of looking at learners' apparent preference for the traditional patterns of instruction is to assume that it is itself learned. Learners have expectations both of teachers and of what constitutes legitimate teaching, in just the same way that teachers have expectations of learners (Hounsell, 1984). McKean (1977) argues that adult learners have "culturally influenced ideas" about "the kinds of activities that provide meaningful learning," and that accordingly "sometimes adult learners react negatively to attempts to involve them in self-directed learning" (McKean, 1977, p. ii). Sometimes, these "culturally influenced ideas" extend to the learner's views of themselves. Thus, it is argued, prolonged exposure to particular relationships in education often creates in learners the belief that they are incapable of independent initiative, and the only way that they can "learn" something is to be "taught."

Yet, in situations of learner-control, the learner who might be accustomed to lapsing into a passive and uncritical mode, or at least appearing to do so to win the approval of the instructor, is suddenly called on to accept responsibility for, and give direction to, a transaction that previously was the responsibility of the teacher. Gibbons and Phillips (1978) personalize and dramatize the transition, when after years of teacher-direction, the teacher suddenly adopts the role of a facilitator of learning: "'My responsibility,' she says, 'is to teach you how to design and manage your own learning, to give you every assistance I can with basic skills, and to help you make contacts with other teachers and members of the community. The responsibility for learning is strictly yours!' Suddenly, after sitting and waiting for the lesson for so long, you are . . . to write up a contract on how much you will accomplish in the rest of the semester, how you plan to go about it, and how you will demonstrate your achievement in the next meeting. Then . . . you are left alone to confront the crises: 'Can I do it on my own? Can I take the initiative? Can I overcome the obstacles? What about all the risks? Will [people] laugh at me or get angry when I call? What if I don't make it? There's no-one else to blame.' "

It is commonly assumed that those who want more direction are simply the victims of an educational system that has systematically deprived them of the opportunity to be "self-directing." Moore (1973a, p. 30) for instance, writes that " . . . it seems likely that a particular kind of person is prone to surrender his learning autonomy, and to become dependent." This choice of words is revealing, because it implies that autonomy is the natural state of affairs, which one might choose to "surrender," rather than an outcome towards which education might be structured. Ricard (1982, p. 4), too, assumes autonomy to be the normal situation; he enlists the notion of adult autodidaxy to buttress his assertion that adult learners should, as a matter of course, share control within formal educational settings.

In view of the predominant methods of instruction commonly encountered in much formal instruction, it is not surprising that, after a few years, people might come to regard themselves as "helpless," at least with respect to learning. Wight (1970, p. 252), for instance, comments: "Most students have had very little practice in school with the use of inductive, discovery, and critical-thinking modes of learning. . . . They are much more familiar and comfortable with the traditional modes — memorizing from lectures and reading assignments, completing exercises and taking tests assigned by the instructor. They need to relearn how to learn. . . ."

Students even make this observation themselves. For instance, in an early study, now over thirty years old, one student, quoted by Eglash (1954, p. 261), said: "This method won't work unless we are brought up in this system and are used to it, and unless everyone co-operates. It allows too much independent thinking." Gruber (1965, p. 3) makes a similar point about the origin and reinforcement of dependent styles of learning: "Having had years of training in certain teacher-directed patterns of education, the student is perfectly capable of privately preserving these patterns, at least in large part, unless far more drastic changes in his situation are introduced or, alternatively, unless training methods are developed to deliberately break up these patterns. Given a textbook, a course outline, and an impending final examination, there is nothing to prevent the student from recreating and maintaining the passive, cramped, teacher-directed study pattern to which he has long been accustomed. Indeed . . . if the American college student has learned little else, he has learned the strategy of passive acquiescence in uncritically assimilating the material the teacher thinks is important. There is a strategy that *works:* it has gotten him where he is. . . ."

The fact that learners might adjust their learning strategies to the demands of the situation will be dealt with in the next section, but if, indeed, the disinclination or inability to accept responsibility is actually a learned phenomenon, akin to learned helplessness, then one could argue that it would be possible, and perhaps even desirable, to jolt adult students out of their compliance and passivity. This may be achieved gradually, through the progressive devolution of control to the learners, or it may be sudden. In either case, in the ensuing conflict between teachers and taught, certainly Mezirow sees the potential for significant learning to take place — learning that is based on a realization and acknowledgment by the learner of previously tacit beliefs and assumptions. He calls this process "critical reflectivity" (1981, p. 19).

Mezirow, however, is not the first to draw attention to the potential value of confronting learners' preconceptions about teaching and learning. According to Wispe (1951, p. 161), both Cantor (1946) and Gross (1948) "attempted to study the consequences of 'skillfully opposing' and jarring loose the fixed attitudes of the students." Campbell (1964) reported a similar phenomenon. He noted that when students were simply "let loose," and told to be self-directing, they very often floundered, but if they were given "coached practice," they were much more successful: "Why did practice in self-concious appraisal by the student of his own learning activities help? Our classroom observations and early individual interviews strongly suggested the following as the primary reason: We broke their set for passive instruction, a set to do just as they are told, which is deeply ingrained after a few years of formal education. It seems to take a lot of jogging to get students out of this passive set. Verbal instructions alone seldom suffice" (p. 357).

The Development of Personal Learning Myths. One of the problems with the notion of learned helplessness is that it implies that the learner is a victim who is perhaps too helpless even to do anything about the helplessness! There is however another, potentially more useful, way of thinking about "learned helplessness." If the learner is considered to have developed a belief about himself or herself (or about learning, or about the subject to be learned), then it might be possible to change that belief: "If such human conditions are learned, they can be unlearned" (Even, 1984, p. 280). Thomas and Harri-Augstein (1983, Part l, p. 4) refer to this alternative view as a "personal learning myth," which they explain as follows: "Most people have arrived at convictions about their own learning; their models of themselves as learners. Often this has been achieved on less than adequate evidence. They have either been 'brainwashed' by someone else's assessment of them, for example parents, teachers and peers or, in having been offered less than optimal conditions to learn, they have generalised their experience as a commentary on their *own* methods. Such assumptions can very easily be self-validating. . . . "

Personal myths, like societal myths, might well be demonstrably untrue, but that does not stop them from being treated as if they were true, and such beliefs accordingly influence behavior. Thomas and Harri-Augstein (1985) give some insight into the sort of tacitly held views of "self-as-learner" that can keep people imprisoned and prevent them from achieving their potential. Sometimes, such myths concern "what students felt to be necessary physical or social conditions of learning. Many described how they must have coffee or snacks to hand all the time, but others saw even regular meals as interruptions which disturbed their efforts to learn. Some students knew that they had to set up 'properly' at a desk if they were to read something and really remember it, whilst others were generally convinced that they could only really concentrate if they were comfortably stretched out on the carpet. There were those who had to have complete silence if they were studying. Others 'knew' that they could not work without a background of radio or recorded music" (p. 11).

Even more bizarre are the beliefs that people hold about their own learning abilities. For instance: "Towards the end of the third session in a series of four interviews . . . one psychology honours student revealed the following view of his own learning. Thinking himself to be mature (26 years old) he was convinced that his memory had reached its limits. He had, therefore, to be very careful not to learn anything which was not crucially important because when he now learned anything, he inevitably forgot something else" (p. 11).

Learners also hold deep implicit views of their own innate capabilities; they have "negative myths about their bodies, their inability to think logically, the bluntness of their aesthetic sensibilities, their lack of inventiveness or their incapability to empathize with others" (Thomas and Harri-Augstein, 1985, p. 12).

It seems that personal learning myths may represent a more constructive way of understanding variability in self-directed learning activity than the idea of learned helplessness. The corollary of accepting this view, however, is that if learners are to become more self-directing, and are to question the often disabling and dysfunctional assumptions they make about themselves, they would need to be confronted with opportunities to see themselves differently. Thus the adult educator would need to create situations in which learners are forced to confront and to analyze their internalized self-concepts, or beliefs about learning generally.

Deliberately Adapting to the Instructional Situation. If it is true that prolonged exposure to "other-direction" robs people of their natural or spontaneous "self-directedness," it would be reasonable to expect that more formal education would lead to lower levels of "self-directedness" in learning, and indeed Chickering (1969, p. 285) cites several studies showing that "those who persist longest in college — compared with their peers who leave or interrupt their education — are more authoritarian, more rigid, less creative, less complex." He adds that "numerous studies of attrition show that the most creative and complex are the ones who leave."

Although this is a lamentable indictment of the formal education system, creativity and complexity are not the only hallmarks of independent learning. In her research on the relationship between field independence and self-directed learning, Tzuk (1985a, p. 139) shows that "significant differences in field dependence/field independence exist between adults studying in various educational levels . . . " and Peterson and Eden (1981, p. 60) claim that "persons with more formal education are likely to be field independent." Since field independence has been found to correlate, at least moderately with "self-directedness" in learning (Tzuk, 1985a, p. 144), the net effect of these findings is to indicate that more highly educated individuals are more likely to participate in, and be successful at, independent learning of various types.

How can this discovery be reconciled with Chickering's observation that many students, even those with advanced graduate level studies, seem unwilling to accept responsibility for independent study? The answer would seem to be that many have deliberately acquiesced and adjusted themselves to the implicit requirements for success in the formal system, and that this modus operandi carries over into their contacts with adult education.

It seems clear that there is frequently a disjunction between the apparent requirements for success in instructional settings and those that actually count. Wight (1970, p. 236) notes: "The teacher may ask for active involvement—thinking, questioning, problem solving, evaluating, creating—but his or her actions, the methods used, and the rewards of the system are for passive activities. Listening and accepting without questioning are stressed more than thinking, memorization more than problem solving, and conformity is valued over creativity."

Over the past decade or fifteen years, a number of researchers in various parts of the world have studied the influence that students say that the learning environment—and especially its assessment procedures—has on their learning (Crooks, 1988). In their various studies of the dissonance between the formal requirements of educational environments (thought, creativity, competence, independent thinking, critical thinking) and the actual requirements as perceived by students (memorization, fact gathering, conformity, rote learning), authors such as Becker, Geer, and Hughes (1968), Miller and Parlett (1974), Ramsden (1979), and Snyder (1971) have drawn attention to the strategies that learners use to master the "hidden curriculum."

For example, Becker, Geer, and Hughes (1968) apply the idea of "situational adjustment" to the experience of the college student: Students learn the requirements of social situations and what makes for success in them, so that they turn themselves into the kinds of persons that the academic context demands. Becker argues that the academic situation requires attendance and written work, but does not reward students for showing intellectual involvement, even though the institution says that it does.

Research in Britain has supported and amplified Becker's findings, although the results are based on small samples. Miller and Parlett (1974), for example, found that the academic environment defined by examinations in a Scottish university led to the employment of distinctive strategies of adaptation by different students. The authors show that one group of students (labeled "cue-seekers"), who went out of their way to make a favorable impression on faculty and who studied very selectively for examinations, obtained the best degree results. This group of students were often uncomfortably aware that these strategies were detrimental to learning.

Ramsden (1979) draws a parallel between these studies of students who "know the game" and who adjust their behavior accordingly and the work of the Göteborg Group in Sweden, who have studied the approaches to learning used by students in reading academic articles (Marton, 1975; Marton and Säljö, 1976a, 1976b). Of the Göteborg Group's studies in Sweden, Ramsden (1979, pp. 415, 426) writes: "The notion of deep level processing shows a remarkable similarity to what lecturers in many disciplines have described as a desirable goal of higher education—the development of 'critical thinking.' . . . [Yet] whether a student's approach to a learning task is to tackle it in a superficial way or to strive for meaning is very much affected by his or her perception of that task, which in turn is influenced by level of interest, personal commitment, and previous knowledge."

Thus, instead of viewing learners as hapless victims of circumstance, buffeted by approaches to teaching over which they have no control, and instead of thinking in terms of learned helplessness, and of the need to break the "passive set" for learning (Campbell, 1964, p. 357), it is possible to conceive of learners as active construers of their circumstances—making choices on the basis of their constructions, searching for cues, striving to interpret and even anticipate the demands made in various situations, and adjusting their learning behavior accordingly. It is maintained that if researchers and adult educators sought out learners' constructions of various situations, attempting to understand and portray reality as it is viewed by learners themselves, a pattern of actions would be discerned that would suggest both consistency and purposefulness on the part of the learners. This is a theme to which I will return in Chapter Fifteen.

Summary. In this section, it has been shown that learners may well vary from one to another with respect to their willingness and ability to accept and exercise control over instructional events. In particular, four alternative explanations have been offered for why learners may choose what appears to be a passive and dependent learning stance: (1) they prefer to be taught (at least with respect to this subject or in this situation); (2) they have been socialized by years of experience in formal education into a passive role, and do not associate learning with a more active posture; (3) they have developed certain "myths" either about learning in general or their own capabilities in particular; or (4) they have deliberately conformed to the tacit requirements for success in the instructional situation, and have difficulty in figuring out what the instructor "really wants" in the allegedly learner-controlled situation.

      Embedded in these explanations are different views of people as learners. The first and fourth rest on the view that people are active choosers, in the one case choosing to pursue their own preferred learning style and in the other choosing to adapt consciously to outside demands. In the second and third, however, learners are seen primarily as passive victims who have been robbed, by events over which they have no control, of any concept of themselves as decisive or independent learners. Irrespective of which point of view is accepted, however, two important observations must be made. The first is that adult learners are likely to vary in their ability to accept responsibility for valued instructional functions, and should not "be left to wallow until they find their own feet." More (1974, p. 157) goes on to expand on this point: "The adult student, like anyone else, can best learn to be maturely independent by evolving out of dependency. The wise teacher will create situations in which the student can feel safe to invest himself in a relationship with the teacher and with the other students. It is from this kind of meaningful relationship that independence will spring."

      The second point is that when someone approaches an educator for help with the content or process of their learning, they are not usually asking the helper to assist them to get more control over their learning. This is an imputed goal, not an explicit one (Cheren, 1983, p. 24). Thus the decision to develop others' capacity for self-direction — what Torbert (1978, p. 116) describes as the "paradox of forcing people to be free" — is ideologically based, just as surely as the decision to deny people

freedom is. It is based on the assumption that it is "good" for
people to exercise control over their learning, and this bias needs
to be acknowledged by those who seek to encourage progress
in people's ability to be self-directing.

Transferability of "Self-Direction" Between Situations

It has been mentioned elsewhere in this book that the development of capability as a self-directed learner is rarely regarded as an end in itself, and is usually defended on the grounds
that it leads to a broader goal, namely, that of developing autonomy generally. In the same way, when an educator seeks
to devolve to learners a greater share of responsibility for their
own learning in some particular subject, this is not usually
thought of as an end in itself either. Instead, it is assumed that
"any progress along the control continuum in the direction of
increased capacity to exercise control in any area of learning
is progress toward the overall objective of greater self-direction
in learning" (Cheren, 1983, p. 24).

Intuitively, it seems likely that autonomy would manifest
itself across a range of learning situations. In everyday life, some
people seem to exhibit an ability to behave autonomously; to
think logically and analytically, even in unfamilar subject areas;
and to be able to learn virtually anything to which they turn
their attention. Such people are in the minority, however, and
even they must start from the beginning, often accepting help
and guidance from those with greater expertise, until they have
progressed a certain way with their learning (Strong, 1977,
p. 139).

When a person does make a success of learning some
previously unknown domain of knowledge or skill, it is a fairly
safe bet that they have developed, and are using, some of the
higher-order or metacognitive capabilities that were discussed
in Chapter Eleven. It is also likely that they are drawing on
similarities with some field of study with which they are already
familiar. Hence people who speak Spanish and French may
be able to learn Italian easily, not merely because they have
a "flair for languages" but also because they understand linguis-

tics, or how languages work. Similarly, a person who plays rugby and soccer may be able to learn and enjoy football, because there are underlying similarities in the respective codes that govern the different subject matter, as discussed in Chapter Twelve.

However, it is not simply familiarity with similar fields of endeavor that allows people to take up new learning, but rather the sense of confidence that comes from already being accomplished in a comparable field: "A strong sense of the self as the causal agent in learning must inevitably be at the core of the self-concept of people who plan and direct their own learning. Internal attribution implies a feeling of personal competency" (Skager, 1984, p. 42). Accordingly, attention will now be turned to the learner's sense of confidence, or the quiet assurance of being able to learn something new, and to a consideration of the extent to which such a sense of competence may be trans-situational — or "transcontextual" (Stipek and Weisz, 1981, p. 131).

The Sense of Personal Control

It is widely recognized in education that previous success as a learner commonly has a beneficial effect on people's confidence and their willingness to undertake further education. Conversely, those whose previous education was painful or unsuccessful have a tendency to avoid further grief by steering clear of educational settings that remind them of failure and inadequacy. To describe this phenomenon, Nelson-Jones (1982) has coined the term *sense of learning competence,* which recognizes that there are significant emotional, motivational, and interest variables that affect learning. The "sense of learning competence" is a subjective and rather fragile construct, yet its lack can inhibit the attainment or fulfillment of one's *actual* potential. In discussing this notion, Woolfe, Murgatroyd, and Rhys (1987, p. 93) comment: "If they are to move forward, learners need to gain increasing trust in their own judgments and abilities and become more able to weigh up their strengths and weaknesses as dispassionately as possible. One message which can be drawn from the available evidence on how people cope intellectually and emotionally with their learning is that for an adult one important facet of the overall process may well be coming to understand how to mobilize more effectively inner resources to cope with inner constraints."

One way in which many people cope with their distrust of the formal educational system — or even of direct instruction — is by undertaking various forms of self-directed learning. It may be assumed in such cases that they have, or they develop, a sense of self-directed learning competence or, as Wang (1983) calls it, "a sense of personal control." According to Wang, the sense of personal control is defined as "students' belief that they are personally responsible for their school learning" (p. 214), and it is strongly influenced by two psychological entities: Rotter's (1966) concept of "locus of control" and Bandura's construct of "self-efficacy" (1981).

In her paper on the "Development and Consequences of Students' Sense of Personal Control," Wang (1983) summarizes several studies that reveal that internal locus of control is positively related to a number of desirable attributes, including degree of classroom participation, academic performance, scores on academic achievement tests, ability to delay gratification, reflectivity, attentiveness, and rates of knowledge acquisition. She goes on to cite a range of studies from 1969 to 1979, all of which suggest that "locus of control orientation can be modified" through various educational interventions, though principally through the transactional influence between the teacher and the learner.

Appealing as this notion is, it falls into the familiar trap of assuming that the "sense of personal control," like autonomy itself, is transsituational. Instead, however, whether a person feels able to exert control in any particular situation depends on his or her view of that particular situation. The fact that an individual exhibits skills in self-directed learning in one situation must not be taken as evidence that he or she can, or would necessarily want to, be self-directing in another: "To make an informed judgment of another person's level of self-directedness, a much deeper and more empathetic understanding of that person is required. We should also be responsive to the situational specificity of self-determination, in eschewing the temptation to generalize a perceived level of self-determination in a learner from one type of situation to another. In this regard, the individualistic nature of self-determination indicates the need for situational types and differences to be defined within the framework of the *learner's* world view" (Bagnall, 1987, p. 98).

In Chapter Four, I commented that while it may be possible to give people freedom, it is not possible to give them autonomy. The same is true in learning situations. It may be possible to create circumstances in which people can exert control, and even to provide appropriately structured and sequentially arranged learning experiences in which people may develop the capacity to be "educationally self-determining" (Bagnall, 1987, p. 98); however, it is not possible to give people a "sense of personal control."

This, then, gives rise to the question, What sort of circumstances or strategies are likely to contribute to learners' developing a sense of personal control? Clearly the answer lies somewhere in the twilight zone between education and therapy, concerning as it does, such subjective and intimate dimensions as how a person construes the opportunities to exert control, and how he or she views both internal and external constraints within the situation. There are, however, some guidelines that — although they can never guarantee success — at least offer the possibility of helping learners to develop the vital, but elusive, sense of personal control. These guidelines include providing the opportunity — in fact repeated opportunities — to exert control, encouraging appropriate attributions of success and failure, making learning an object of reflection, situating learning in real-life contexts, encouraging learners to believe in their own abilities, and creating a climate of self-direction and inquiry.

Providing the Opportunity to Exert Control. It may seem self-evident, but if people are to develop a consciousness of their ability to learn without an instructor they must be given some opportunities to do so (Combs, 1972, p. 63). This is not to be taken as support for "throwing learners in at the deep end," for clearly unsuccessful experiences could have exactly the opposite effect to that intended. What it does imply is that educators need to progressively relinquish control, while at the same time providing some form of safety net in case the learner experiences difficulty. More (1974, p. 158) expresses it this way: "Adult students need help when they take their first step of assuming the responsibility for their own learning. They need support as they recognize how heavy it is. Learners need reassurance when they falter, and praise when they succeed."

In the literature on self-direction in learning, it seems that the provision of opportunities to exert control has often been portrayed as sufficient in itself to create or enhance the ability to do so. Although it may be a *necessary* condition, it is hardly *sufficient,* and educators need not only to support learners during the transitional phase but, as discussed later, to take other positive steps to assist learners in developing the sense of personal control.

Providing Repeated Opportunities to Exert Control. The literature suggests, and common sense supports, that learners require more than spasmodic or superficial exposure to situations of learner control if they are to develop a robust concept of self-directedness: "Of course, there is little reason to believe that a single brief experience with self-directed study in an educational atmosphere fundamentally hostile to intellectual independence will produce attitudinal changes of great longevity" (Gruber, 1965, p. 5). Unfortunately, conventional adult education — unlike formal schooling — represents only a very small fragment of all the forces that are acting in an adult's life. Thus, its ability to have any lasting impact on an adult's view of his or her own self-directedness is severely constrained. There are, of course, examples of how a particular adult education experience has had an emancipatory effect in someone's life, but in the majority of instances, where the development of a sense of personal control is only ancillary or concomitant to the acquisition of some other content, its chances of succeeding are greater the longer and more extensive is the learner's exposure to situations of self-direction in learning: "If students function in carefully structured learning environments where opportunities are provided for skills acquisition and where continuous emphasis is placed on self-direction, self-initiative, and self-evaluative behaviors, it is postulated that students should gain an increased sense of self-efficacy and personal control" (Wang, 1983, p. 221). The implications of this, particularly for those educators who work within government, industrial, or commercial organizations or who have prolonged contact with a group of learners, is that programs must be structured to give repeated and consistent chances to exercise control.

Encouraging Appropriate Attributions of Success and Failure. Central to the development of a sense of personal control is the belief that one actually is in control of one's learning outcomes. However, unsuccessful learners often believe that matters are out of their hands—that when they succeed it is a matter of luck, and that when they fail, it represents a lack of competence. Such beliefs are particularly disabling because they engender the view that successful learning cannot be controlled and that failure will derive from a lack of competence, and hence people with such beliefs are likely to shy away from learning situations.

An educator can help, however, by "encouraging learners to attribute success to their own ability (hence encouraging an optimistic prognosis) but failure to *lack of effort* (which the learner can do something about)" (Biggs, 1987, p. 106). In the early 1970s, deCharmas demonstrated that children at elementary school could be given a greater sense of personal control through "personal causation training." Individuals were found to differ from one another along a continuum that he named the *Origin-Pawn Dimension,* where "origin" refers to the extent to which people initiate intentional behavior and "pawn" refers to the extent to which people experience themselves as the instrument of some outside source over which they have little if any control. The author describes a number of ways in which learners were helped (1) to determine realistic goals for themselves, (2) to know their own strengths and weaknesses, (3) to determine concrete actions to take in order to achieve these goals, and (4) to evaluate their success in reaching the goals.

Clearly it is not possible to help people to view themselves as Origins by pushing them around like Pawns and telling them to behave in a self-directed way. As deCharmas (1972, p. 97) comments, "Not to push people around is a beginning in treating people as Origins, but we soon found that letting them do anything they wanted to do was *not* treating them as Origins either. To treat people as Origins is to help them to take responsibility for their own behavior. To the extent that a student is immature and incapable of taking responsibility, it is the duty of the teacher to step in, impose some restraints, and find ways to develop in the students the capacity for taking responsibility."

It is instructive that deCharms chose to concentrate on the personal sense of control of younger children. As Biggs mentions, the real basis of a sense of personal control (or a lack of it) is often deeply rooted in early childhood or in the cumulative effects of a lifetime of educational and social experiences. Hence, although it is worth the effort, adult educators and counselors should not underestimate the difficulty of engendering a more hopeful sense of self-efficacy in adult learners.

Making Learning an Object of Reflection. One aspect of the process of increasing people's sense of personal control is raising to a level of conscious awareness the strategies and approaches that people use in tackling learning tasks. Elsewhere, I have mentioned that some less sophisticated learners often regard learning as an automatic process, something that "just happens" and that is accordingly beyond the reach of deliberate personal intervention. This was mentioned in Chapter Eleven in discussing surface-level learning, and again earlier in this chapter in considering "personal learning myths." If people are to develop a sense of personal control, they need to recognize a contingent relationship between the strategies they use and their learning outcomes, and this may well involve having learners maintain learning journals, analyzing their own approaches to learning, and discussing their beliefs about and approaches to learning in groups or with a facilitator or counselor. It seems that awareness of one's cognitive processes and motives is an essential precondition to attaining control over strategies (Biggs, 1985), and that techniques for acquiring such awareness must "be integrated into the teaching of subject matter" (Ramsden, Beswick, and Bowden, 1987, p. 169) rather than being taught as a self-contained set of learning skills.

The development of an informed awareness of one's own learning is in fact a subset of a much larger dimension of self-directed learning, namely, critical reflectivity in general. In recent years, at the confluence of streams in experiential education and humanistic psychology, the central role of reflection in learning has emerged. Boyd and Fales (1983, p. 100) define reflective learning as "the process of internally examining and exploring an issue of concern, triggered by an experience, which creates and clarifies meaning in terms of self, and which results in a changed conceptual perspective."

Brookfield, among others, has emphasized the central role that reflection plays in self-directed learning; "the most complete form of self-directed learning occurs when process and reflection are married in the adult's pursuit of learning" (1986, p. 58). In an elegant and forceful essay, Harris (1990) has pinpointed the need for adult educators to "structure activities and programs to foster self-direction and reflection in [their] clients" (p. 112) and has argued that such interventions must be adequately documented and researched not only at the individual level, but recognizing that reflection is "socially conditioned and affective in nature" (p. 113).

Situating Learning in Real-Life Contexts. Many adult education programs and activities take place in laboratories, training centers, and classrooms that are not significantly different from learning environments in school, college, and university. However, the majority of adult learning activities occur in, and in relation to, real-life contexts, where there is a social distribution of knowledge (Resnick, 1987b) and an emphasis on collaborative work modes. In order to develop a sense of personal control in learning, and "to show students the legitimacy of their implicit knowledge and its availability as scaffolding in apparently unfamiliar tasks" (Brown, Collins, and Duguid, 1989, p. 38), learning experiences should as far as possible take place in everyday situations and be embedded in familiar activities.

Encouraging Learners to Believe in Their Own Abilities. One of the more insidious side effects of much conventional education is that it systematically — albeit unintentionally — robs the learner of a sense of personal potency. Learners are given the message that they cannot learn without being taught, and that their existing understandings are inadequate or inappropriate when compared to those that are sanctioned as formal school-based knowledge. To overcome or redress this predominantly negative self-image, educators need to convey to learners a sense of confidence in the learners' abilities (Rosenthal and Jacobson, 1968). This, in turn, may be expected to result in more purposeful and confident behavior by the learner and to lead to a positive cycle of reinforcement. Thus, Wang (1983, p. 218) explains, "As a reaction to an increase in student competence, the teacher's perception of the student's ability to achieve the program's goals is likely to be modified. As the teacher's perception of each student's competence changes, the teacher's behavior toward and expectations for each student are also affected. Positive alterations in the teacher's behavior and expectations, in turn, result in changes in the student's perception of his or her competence and efficacy in acquiring academic and self-management skills. From the student's perspective, the development of competence in academic and self-management skills results in an increased sense of personal control."

Educators who hold high expectations for their students tend to convey these through complex and subtle patterns of interaction, which commonly result in the learners' living up to these expectations and, in the process, developing a more positive image of themselves.

Creating a Climate of Self-Direction and Inquiry. It is one of the important functions of adult education to provide a "springboard" or "launching pad" from which learners may be expected to "take off" in pursuit of their own independent learning endeavors. It seems that there are several qualities that would characterize both an educator and an educative environment that promoted such activity.

The first is the provision of opportunities, resources, and facilities to encourage a positive orientation toward learning.

In a monograph entitled *The Missing Link: Connecting Adult Learners to Learning Resources,* Cross (1978, p. 4) writes that "the goal of the learning society is to make adults stronger, more self-motivated and self-directed learners. One critical step in reaching this goal is to provide the services that will link learner interests to the learning resources of society." Many approaches to this ideal have been suggested, including educational brokering (Heffernan, Macy, and Vickers, 1976); educational advisory services (Moore, 1986); learning exchange networks (Perkins, 1985); shop-front education (Knowles, 1983b); the education utility (Gooler, 1986); the creation of institutions and services intended to help people teach themselves — language laboratories, technical training laboratories, information centers, data banks, and so on (Faure and others, 1972); and promoting both cultural institutions (Carr, 1985) and libraries (Burge, 1983; Reilly, 1981) as learning resources. In all cases, although the details differ, the underlying message is the same: Encourage a sense of personal control by linking learners' questions with answers, by connecting learning interests with appropriate and easily accessed resources.

The second attribute of an appropriate educative environment is that it is characterized by warm and humane interaction, preferably within a physical setting that is itself conducive to learning (Gores, 1972). In his various writings, Knowles has consistently emphasized the establishment of an appropriate learning environment as the first consideration in the conduct of adult education activities. There are many features of such a climate, including acceptance and acknowledgment of individual differences, recognition of the importance of feelings as well as ideas and skills in learning, mutual respect and risk taking, authenticity, supportive interpersonal relations, collaboration rather than competition, and informality (Knowles, 1984, pp. 119-120). Knox (1986, p. 132) also stresses the importance of climate in confidence building when he writes, "A supportive physical and interpersonal setting in which participants feel secure and welcome is especially important for adults with little formal education or without recent educational experience."

The third aspect of an appropriate learning environment is that it encourages questioning behavior. This has already been mentioned in Chapter Eleven, but a vital tool of the self-directed learner is the ability to formulate issues in the form of questions. Thus, instead of simply accepting the status quo as given, or instead of accepting the correctness of something written or said, the individual is inclined to "reflective skepticism" (McPeck, 1981, p. 7) and appropriate question-asking. Philosophers have described this predisposition as a "critical spirit" or "critical attitude," and Siegel (1980, p. 9) writes, "A possessor of the critical spirit is inclined to seek reasons and evidence; to demand justification; to query and investigate unsubstantiated claims. . . . A critical spirit habitually seeks evidence and reasons, and is predisposed to so seek." As is often the case with questions of self-direction, there is a certain circular relationship between the development of a "critical spirit" and of "a sense of personal control." However, if educators can encourage critical reflection by learners, there is reason to expect that this will have a beneficial influence on the development of a "sense of personal control" with respect to self-directed learning.

The fourth attribute of an educative environment that may lead to an enhanced sense of personal control is that educators are willing to provide a role model and to open themselves to criticism and question. As discussed in Chapter Seven, Torbert (1978, p. 122) makes the point that "only authentically inquiring behavior [by leaders] succeeds in 'converting' others to the practice of inquiry." He goes on to discuss the need for educators to be open to criticism and to "exemplify the morality they enjoin" by acting with integrity as learners themselves.

Not only must adult educators be continuing self-directed learners, they must be prepared to give up the privileged position that their role formally bestows on them. This is by no means easy, and even when they are genuinely intent on creating situations of alleged learner-control, teachers may still behave, even though they do not intend to, in classic teacherlike ways. For instance, when they make elaborate statements about the metatheoretical justification for abdicating their traditional responsibility, or use technical terms such as *experiential learning, reflection, process,* and *what really matters* in a learning situation, educators unthinkingly reinforce the belief that "authority at the deepest level still rests with staff" (Millar, Morphet, and Saddington, 1986, p. 435). It is only when staff and students are both able to address these contradictions, on a more equal basis, that learners will come to realize the fullness of what it means to have "a sense of personal control."

Summary

The notion that perceived personal control has important implications for the quality of learning derives support from various theoretical positions, including social learning theory, attribution theory, and intrinsic motivation theory. Although researchers from these various schools of thought use different methods and report their findings in slightly different terms, their evidence seems to converge on one crucial point: "Success or failure *per se* might be less important than a [learner's] perceptions of the *cause* of the success or failure" (Stipek and Weisz, 1981, p. 130).

Paradoxically, the development of a sense of personal control in learning is simultaneously central and peripheral to helping people to be better self-directed learners. It is central in the sense that this elusive and fragile feeling of personal control lies at the heart of all intentional autonomous learning. It is peripheral partly because it represents only one manifestation of a much more profound and far-reaching construct, which Thelen (1972, p. 89) has dubbed "captaincy of self," and partly because there is much more to effective learning than simply believing that one has this capacity.

If educators want people to be better at independent learning, they need to make some profound changes. As discussed in Chapter Seven, for the teacher, trainer, coach, or facilitator, it involves a significant shift in the locus of control and a radical change from providing direct instruction to facilitating learning.

Moreover, as in so many other aspects of education, actions probably speak louder than words. Boud and Prosser (1980, p. 32) point out that, of the many skills, characteristics, attributes, and areas of expertise needed by adult educators, "Their most potent influence is through their role as exemplar: their conduct should, as far as possible, model the behavior of a self-directing person and demonstrate their commitment to the peer learning community."

In the final analysis, the development of a sense of personal control is not simply a quality to be encouraged in others; it is a practice to be developed and exemplified by adult educators themselves.

Part 5

Realizing
the Potential
of Self-Direction
in Adult Learning

> The world is, above all, perplexing. At any given moment some part of my world and of yours is a source of mystery, problem, curiosity, disorder, even chaos. This is the starting point for a theory of independent learning. It is in man's restless nature to probe the mysteries and confusions of his world and to quench his insatiable thirst for understanding and for knowledge about his world.
>
> Within some part of my "life space" exists an area of confusion and as I go about bringing order to that confusion, I am engaged in the process of learning. . . . I proceed to gather information and ideas, make hypotheses and eventually, after much testing, decide that my objectives have been met. What was confused becomes clear, what was a problem has been solved . . .
>
> —*Moore, 1973a, pp. 28–29*

Although at times I have been critical of some of the research and writing that has been undertaken on self-directed learning, nevertheless I believe it to be a vital component of the educational spectrum, and the capability for self-directed learning to be well worth developing wherever possible.

In T. H. White's celebrated novel *The Sword in the Stone,* Merlyn the Magician offers some advice about learning to his young protégé Wart: "The best thing for disturbances of the

397

spirit," counsels Merlyn, "is to learn." He goes on to advocate learning and to enumerate its many advantages:

> "[Learning] is the only thing that never fails. You may grow old and trembling in your anatomies, you may lie awake at night listening to the disorder of your veins, you may miss your love and lose your moneys to a monster, you may see the world about you devastated by evil lunatics, or know your honour trampled in the sewers of baser minds. There is only one thing for it then — to learn. Learn why the world wags and what wags it. That is the only thing which the poor mind can never exhaust, never alienate, never be tortured by, never fear or distrust, and never dream of regretting. Learning is the thing for you. Look at what a lot of things there are to learn — pure science, the only purity there is. You can learn astronomy in a lifetime, natural history in three, literature in six. And then, after you have exhausted a milliard lifetimes in biology and medicine and theo-criticism and geography and history and economics, why, you can start to make a cart wheel out of the appropriate wood, or spend fifty years learning to begin to learn to beat your adversary at fencing. After that you can start again on mathematics, until it is time to learn to plough" [White, 1938, p. 254].

Based on this advice, Merlyn should perhaps be canonized as the patron saint both of self-directed learning and of curiosity-driven research. Indeed, it is fascinating to note the parallels that exist between self-directed learning and research and the qualities that are required to do either well.

In Chapter Fourteen, I attempt to review and draw together some of the many strands that run through this book. In particular, I reemphasize the situation-specific aspects of self-directed learning competence, and present a concise three-part model that identifies and specifies the dimensions involved that can constrain — or alternatively facilitate — self-direction in learning.

In the course of researching this book, and indeed in any serious study of the phenomenon of self-direction in education, it becomes apparent that the field does not suffer from a shortage of literature (Caffarella and O'Donnell, 1988). However, ironically, what does seem to be significantly neglected are studies that portray self-directed learning from the learner's perspective. Despite the heavily ideological rhetoric about self-direction as a distinguishing characteristic of adult learners, the dominant approach to research has been positivistic, in which learning endeavors are portrayed as more or less linear activities, conforming to a predictable stereotype, and attempts to enhance self-directedness have mainly been seen as manipulative strategies based on a cause-and-effect view of human affairs.

Research, itself, can profitably be viewed as an example of self-directed inquiry. But then the researcher (whose behavior can best be described as an example of "intelligent self-direction") is confronted with the question of reflexivity: "Given that I am committed to such a model to explain my own research behavior, what explanatory model is relevant to my subjects' behavior, and what method of enquiry is it appropriate to apply to it? I cannot without gross inconsistency apply to my subjects a model that is logically at odds with the one I apply to myself. I cannot responsibly argue that they are in principle to be seen as fully under the control of antecedent conditions within a scheme of absolute determinism, while it is a necessary condition of my researching them that I view myself as a self-directed intelligence within a scheme of relative determinism. I must also surely see them in principle as self-directing and intelligent agents, whose behavior is only relatively determined by antecedent conditions" (Heron, 1971, p. 4).

The inevitable corollary of this line of reasoning is to undertake investigations that give due recognition to the self-directed or autonomous nature of people as learners and that are philosophically and methodologically congruent with such beliefs. Consequently, Chapter Fifteen examines the major approaches that have been influential in the study of self-direction in learning, and concludes by proposing both some questions and some alternative research methods for the consideration of researchers and other educators concerned with portraying learning from the learner's point of view.

Fourteen

Enhancing
Self-Directed
Learning
in Adult Education

This book has involved a long and, at times, arduous journey through the treacherous territories of philosophy, epistemology, psychology, and sociology. In one way or another, it has touched on many enduring problems in educational discourse that theorists and practitioners have applied themselves to since the time of Plato and before. I have made extensive use of literature from adult as well as elementary, secondary, and higher education. It is now time to draw together the many threads running through the book, and to answer the questions, In what ways does this piece of work contribute to an understanding of "self-direction" in adult education, and how can its insights be of benefit to theorists and practitioners?

   This chapter consists of three main sections. The first is an examination of the domains of autodidaxy and learner-control, an attempt to distinguish them from one another on the basis of a constructivist perspective, and a discussion of the potential and some of the limitations of self-direction in each use. The second recapitulates the main themes throughout the book and presents a schematic representation of the variables that have been discussed that influence autonomy in learning. The chapter concludes with a three-part model for the development of self-direction in learning and some observations for both practitioners and theorists about what is involved in becoming self-directed within our societal context.

Distinguishing Autodidaxy from Learner-Control

At the start of this book I advanced—and have since maintained—the idea that learning in formal instructional settings is significantly different from learning in everyday or natural societal settings. If this distinction is indeed a valid one, then it has important implications for research, teaching, and theory building in adult education. It influences the very nature of self-directed learning activities that are, or might be, carried out in each context. This in turn affects the strategies implemented to support, encourage, or facilitate the development of learning competence. It can be seen, therefore, that the concern to distinguish these phenomena is not mere pedantry, nor is it motivated solely by an interest in the learning behavior of learners. Whether or not autodidaxy is part of the learner-control continuum has both practical and theoretical implications.

Ever since it entered the mainstream of educational inquiry in the early 1960s, autodidaxy has occupied a privileged position in the field of adult education, being hailed as a legitimate, and possibly unique, domain of adult education research. In Chapter One, I presented a diagram in which I distinguished between various levels of autodidactic learning and various degrees of learner-control, and I argued that there is a gray area in between, in which a qualitative shift occurs from one domain to the other. Accordingly, I will now return to a consideration of these two domains and the area of overlap, and their implications for both the study and practice of adult self-directed learning.

Learner-Control in Formal Education. At one extreme, there is the realm of formal education, with a substantial body of literature that concerns both how learners should and how they can be given a greater sense of personal control or self-directedness in such settings. Strangely enough, despite the existence of an enormous range of different histories, cultures, political ideologies, and structural arrangements, systems of formal education throughout the world are stunningly alike, and virtually everywhere, "[schooling] is vertical and individualistic. The unit to be schooled is the individual: he or she is the receptacle of knowledge, the unit that moves from one class or school to the other, that performs and ultimately achieves and receives a diploma and graduates. . . . If somebody wanted the schooling system to serve as a tool for placing people in niches in a society that is predominantly vertical and individualistic . . . then the system is well constructed. It can be seen as one enormous sorting device absorbing each year new millions of small children, processing hundreds of millions one more step till they either graduate at some level, with some note hung round their necks, or drop out" (Galtung, 1976, pp. 93–94).

If this portrayal of education is accepted—and some version of it is accepted by many sociologists—then two conclusions about self-directed learning are clear. First, given the ubiquity of external constraints and forces, the ability of any given individual to shape his or her educational destiny is limited. Second, any attempt to graft self-direction onto the root stock of formal education is likely to fail, since self-direction in its broadest sense is fundamentally incompatible with the role of education as a mechanism of social reproduction and cultural transmission. Thus, a great deal of the "self-directed learning" that is discussed in the context of school, college, or university settings is only tenuously linked to personal autonomy and self-determination as discussed in this book, and practitioners need to be wary of the strong social and other pressures that might force them into a position of advocating self-direction when it is neither practical nor desirable.

Many adult educators of course seek to distance themselves from the formal education system and its invidious tendency to reproduce social hierarchies and hence social inequalities. Adult education, they claim, is marked by features such as equality between teachers and learners, lateral transmission of knowledge, informality in instructional approach, and responsiveness to the needs and interests of learners. Citing adult education's long social activist tradition, they argue that self-directed approaches to education are more philosophically congruent than the directive and subject-centered methods common in institutions of formal education.

Although there is some merit in these claims, they must be treated with a certain amount of circumspection. For a start, many of the attempts to distinguish adult education from "formal education" are based on a mistaken understanding of what is meant by the term *formal*. In this context, formality has nothing to do with external features such as modes of dress, ways of speaking, layout of the classroom environment, or planning of the program. It would be quite possible for a class within a school or university (formal education) to be quite informal socially; conversely, a workshop run in industry (nonformal education) could evidence a formal approach to the proceedings, with official podiums, stilted opening speeches, and elected chairpersons. In fact, formality in this context refers to the extent to which educational activities deal with established bodies of knowledge and lead to the award of degrees, certificates, or other credentials (Coombs, Prosser, and Ahmed, 1973, pp. 10–11).

Although much adult education activity is short-term, recurrent, and non-institution-based (Simkins, 1977), the work of certain socially critical theorists in recent years (Rubenson, 1982; Hopper and Osborn, 1975; Welton, 1987) has shown that much of adult education, at least in its social consequences, is not as different from formal education as many have argued. A lot of the claims about its distinctiveness have been shown to be ideological rather than empirical (Keddie, 1980). In fact, much of the "self-direction" practiced in adult education is partial and inauthentic, deriving as much from social pressures as from any deeply held convictions about the need for individual emancipation. I have referred to this phenomenon in Chapter Seven as "pseudoautonomy."

Autodidaxy in Natural Societal Settings. What then of the opposite end of the spectrum: the self-directed learning that happens outside of educational institutions, and even without any formal institutional support or affiliation? Certainly this activity is vital to our continual growth and adaptation both as individuals and as a society. It must be acknowledged, researched, encouraged, and supported to the greatest extent possible. It is indeed a vital component in the pattern of lifelong learning and a key element in the structure of the learning society. There are, however, grounds for questioning whether autodidaxy should be considered as part of adult education at all.

More than a quarter of a century ago, Verner (1964, p. 31) commented that "self-education is beyond the range of responsibility of adult education, since it is an individual activity and affords no opportunity for the adult educator to exert influence on the learning process." In 1972, Bowers and Fisher stated that "self-directed learning [is] learning organized by the learner in which no educational agency or teacher is consciously involved. . . . *This form of learning is not regarded as education"* (p. 47; emphasis added).

Likewise, the International Standard Classification of Education (Unesco, 1976, p. 18) defined education as *"organized and sustained communication designed to bring about learning."* In discussing the meaning of *education,* the report notes: "Clearly, the term *Education* as used in ISCED includes activities that in some countries and in some languages may not usually be described as education but by such terms as training or cultural activities. On the other hand, certain forms of learning that may be quite legitimately regarded as education are excluded from the coverage of ISCED because they are not organized as here defined. *Random learning from experience, observation, and other responses to stimuli in the environment is clearly excluded.* So also is *self-directed learning,* where the learning is not consciously organized by a teacher or any providing agency, but by the learner himself, for example, through reading or self-directed training or practice" (p. 18; emphasis added).

Notwithstanding this, autodidaxy (in the form of "self-directed learning") has been embraced by adult educators as an object of study. There is no denying the importance of autodidaxy to the field of learning; what is questionable is whether it measures up to the minimum criteria of "education." Again, according to Bowers and Fisher (1972, p. 46), "Education [is] organized communication designed to bring about learning. . . .

It involves an educational providing agency that organizes the learning situation and/or teachers who direct the communication." Despite Strong's (1977) explicit support, and the clear weight of professional opinion as expressed through the research literature, it seems that autodidaxy does not exhibit the characteristics that would allow it to be treated as education.

Thomas once described adult education as floating in a sea of learning. If one could extend the metaphor, it could be argued that research into autodidaxy is rather like bailing water in, rather than out: The sheer volume of autodidactic activity is likely to swamp the adult education boat and to drown its occupants. For this reason alone, it would seem to be desirable to make a defensible distinction between autodidaxy and learner-control.

However, even disregarding self-preservation, adult educators should not be too keen to embrace autodidaxy as the dominant (or worse still, the only) mode of adult education, for there must surely be some areas of knowledge where, as Lawson (1979, p. 26) observes, "the positive conception of a teacher has to be introduced." In a way, the "positive conception of the teacher" is the feature that distinguishes autodidaxy from learner-control. It is the weakening of the notion of teaching itself and its transformation into something called "facilitation" that more than anything else, has contributed to blurring the valid and useful distinction between self-directed learning both inside and outside formal instructional settings.

Significant differences between autodidactic learning and that which happens within institutional settings do not end, however, with the existence or otherwise of a "teacher." As discussed in Chapter Eleven, recent research on everyday cognition (Rogoff and Lave, 1984), situated cognition (Brown, Collins, and Duguid, 1989), and out-of-school learning (Resnick, 1987b) shows that structures of knowledge and significant aspects of people's learning approaches are different in formal and natural societal settings. Consequently, adult educators should be wary about uncritically using strategies within educational settings (in particular, so-called self-directed methods of learning) that purport to develop competencies for learning outside them.

In addition, as I have discussed elsewhere, even when there is a genuine, thorough, and sustained attempt to develop a "liberating program structure" (Higgs, 1989) within adult education activities, its effects are likely to be limited to that situation and may not extend to other educational contexts because of three main factors: the enormous influence of past experience in determining what people regard as legitimate "education"; the relatively short-term and infrequent nature of people's involvement in adult education activities; and the situation-specific nature of learning competence, which means that people often fail to transfer skills from one situation to another or to generalize them to all learning contexts.

The "Gray Area" Between Learner-Control and Autodidaxy. Back in Chapter One, I reproduced a diagram (Figure 1.4) that suggests that there might exist a single continuum from a high degree of teacher-direction to "pure" autonomous learning or autodidaxy, with an area of overlap (the shaded area) in between. The area of overlap represents the intersection of domains where, from the point of view of an outside observer, it is impossible to discern whether the primary orientation is one of "instruction" or of "self-instruction" (autodidaxy). In adult education, a particularly good example of this is posed by mentoring. In the evocative metaphor of *learning as a journey into the unknown,* a mentor may act as a guide, "providing a map and fixing the road," or as a companion who concentrates on "helping the protégé to become a competent traveler" (Daloz, 1986, p. ix). The problem is that mentors commonly alternate between these roles, and as they do so, the situation appears to change, too: now autodidaxy, now learner-control, like the constantly shifting play of light and color in a piece of Thai silk. Because of difficulties like this, many people have assumed that self-directed learning is a single undifferentiated continuum, but it is argued here that the notion of a single continuum is misleading: Independent study and assisted autodidaxy, despite their apparent similarities, are not the same. There are subtle differences in the way both learners and teachers approach the different learning tasks, and in their respective views of assistance given and received. How then are the situations to be distinguished?

Clearly because of their apparent similarities on the outside, the question of whether any particular instance is one of autodidaxy or of learner-controlled instruction cannot be determined by objective evidence alone. It is necessary to refer to the personal meanings of the participants. What is more, contrary to conventional practice, it cannot be determined by referring solely to the perspective of the teacher/trainer or helper. This is because a learner's control over events in the teaching/ learning transaction is not objectively determinable, but depends on the learner's personal construction of the situation. Accordingly, the next part of the chapter will concentrate on the importance of the distinction from the learner's point of view.

There is reason to believe that the learning outcomes from any given learning encounter depend substantially on the learner's construction of the situation and the strategies that he or she consequently employs. In his research into commonsense understandings of learning, Säljö (1979b) asked ninety people, ranging in age from fifteen years to seventy-three years, about their conceptions of learning. He found that, even though many people had given relatively little conscious or systematic thought to learning in general, or their own learning in particular, they nevertheless commonly made three important distinctions: the importance of context, the value or quality of the learning, and the purpose to which the learning is to be put.

The first distinction concerns their increasing awareness of the influence of context on both what is learned and how it is learned. Citing Snyder (1971) and Miller and Parlett (1974), Säljö (1979a) discusses how learners become "cue conscious" or aware of the implicit rules governing learning, at least in a school context. While not all learners adjust their learning to demands such as teacher preferences and tests, nevertheless the awareness of such tacit rules is widespread (p. 448). As discussed in Chapter One, central to this aspect of learning is the concept of "ownership." In situations of true autodidaxy there can be no doubt that both the initiative and the locus of control over the events of learning reside with the learner, who accordingly feels that he or she "owns" the learning situation and its outcomes. In conditions of learner-control, however — even those with relatively limited input and direction by the teacher or trainer — there are subtle and often largely symbolic ways in which the culture of the learning situation influences the learner's choices or even the criteria she or he uses to make those choices.

The second distinction is that subjects often reported that they had started to think about the *nature* of what is learned. They distinguish between "learning" and "real learning," or between "learning" and "understanding." The main feature of real learning is that it involves going beyond the plain "facts" to some general principle. These "facts" are seen as subordinate to what should really be learned — that is, the general meaning (p. 449).

The third distinction concerns the difference between "learning for life" and "learning in school." Learning in school is typically regarded as stereotyped and routine, and not organically related to anything outside the school situation itself (pp. 448–449). Learning for life, on the other hand, is seen as relevant, meaningful, viable, and significant. This distinction, which it will be recalled exists in the minds of the learners, perhaps best captures the qualitative distinction envisaged here between learner-control and autodidaxy.

This and other research by Säljö and others of the Göteborg group in Sweden demonstrates that the way in which an individual learner construes the learning situation influences the approach taken to learning and hence the outcomes obtained. What is more, a problem can arise when there is a discrepancy or disjunction between the perspectives of the two partners involved — the learner and the instructor or other person assisting the learner. The learner might believe himself or herself to be engaged in an instructional situation, and consequently to have certain expectations of the roles of the teacher or trainer. However, the teacher or trainer may think of the learner as an autodidact. There is the potential for conflict based on these dissonant perceptions. Conversely, if the learner wants to direct his or her own learning, but the instructor is still retaining certain prerogatives, there is again the potential for a mismatch of expectations. This situation may be represented in Figure 14.1.

Figure 14.1. Comparison of Learner's and Instructor's
Perceptions of a Learning Situation.

| | | Instructor believes this to be a situation of | |
		Instruction	Autodidaxy
Learner believes this to be a situation of	Instruction	✓	x
	Autodidaxy	x	✓

These situations indicated in Figure 14.1 by an "x" represent what Millar, Morphet, and Saddington (1986) typify as
a "vacuum," that is, a disjunction in the mutual expectations
of teachers and learners. The effect of any such vacuum will
depend on the direction of the mismatch. If the learner is expecting instruction, but the teacher has in mind a situation of
guided autodidaxy, the learner will probably react to this by
demanding the structure that he or she believes to be necessary
to learning in that situation. Conversely, if the learner believes
himself or herself to be engaged in an autodidactic project, the
unwelcome imposition of restriction and structure is likely to
result in resistance. This perspective helps to explain Wispe's
(1951) early experimental results. The students' need-for-di-
rection or need-for-permissiveness is not necessarily an enduring personal characteristic, but may arise from the learner's understanding of the demands of the specific learning situation.
In the case of adult education practices, it means that educators and learners must be quite clear and explicit about their
expectations of each other and about the stage they believe their
relationship has reached at any given time. The research implications of this sort of mismatch in perceptions are dealt with
in Chapter Fifteen.

Main Themes of the Book Revisited

As mentioned in Chapter One, the construct of "self-direction" has become, for many adult educators, a guiding star. It is held up as the prime purpose, distinguishing characteristic, and predominant methodology of the field. Indeed "self-direction" is so universally acclaimed that it seems to unite, and to claim the loyalties of, educators who, in other respects, represent divergent and at times incompatible points of view. This is at once a strength and a weakness, because although self-direction has been adopted as a slogan by all manner of adult educators, its popularity has come at the price of its integrity.

Self-direction has become the unwitting accomplice of many educational schemes, some of whose intentions are the very antithesis of what might be understood as true "self-direction." Self-direction has been, and is, recruited by behaviorists and humanists, idealists and pragmatists, radicals and conservatives, positivists and constructivists. A versatile concept, it has been coopted to every purpose that adult educators espouse and pursue. The consequence of this is that the literature on self-direction is extensive, but it is also confusing. The lack of internal consistency precludes the possibility of developing a coherent theory of self-direction, or even of self-directed learning, from within the literature itself. This is the first major finding of this book.

Quite apart from these fractures, which extend deep into the substance of self-direction, it is apparent that the term itself is used in the literature to refer to four distinct concepts. These are self-direction as the independent pursuit of learning without formal institutional structures (referred to here as autodidaxy), self-direction as a way of organizing instruction (learner-control), self-direction as a personal quality or attribute (personal autonomy), and self-direction as the manifestation of a certain independence of mind and purpose in learning situations (self-management in learning). It will be noted that the first two of these relate to activities, whereas the latter two refer to personal attributes or characteristics. However, the relationships among these concepts are complex, and this complexity has led many adult educators (and others) to substitute one usage for another inadvertently. Accordingly, the second major finding of this book has two parts: first, that from a constructivist perspective, learner-control and autodidaxy are not synonymous and that autodidaxy is not part of the instructional domain at all, and second, that autonomy in learning does not necessarily give rise to personal autonomy, nor does the existence of personal autonomy always manifest itself as autonomy in any particular learning situation.

A third major theme of this book is that autonomy apparently has both a personal and a situational dimension. A good deal of research on personal autonomy has faltered because of the failure by researchers to recognize the situation-specific or context-bound nature of personal autonomy. Researchers have assumed personal autonomy to be a generalized personal attribute that manifests itself in all situations. Similarly, much research into autonomy in learning has described the features of situations, without regard to the behavior or reactions of the learners or other actors in those situations. It is not possible to look at a person and to pronounce him or her to be autonomous without reference to the context or environment (that is, at work, at home, in his or her hobbies, in learning particular things, and so on.) Conversely, it is not possible to describe a situation (such as a learning context) as autonomous without a consideration of the responses of the participants in that situation.

However, it is not simply the interaction of the person and the environment that influences the extent and nature of autonomy in learning, but rather the subjective interpretation that the actors place on the "distal situation" (Shores, 1985). It has been proposed in this book that research on self-direction (in each of the senses mentioned here) has not made significant progress in recent years because of the failure of researchers to account for the subjective meanings that the situation has for the learners and teachers involved. As discussed earlier, the strategies adopted by the learner (and accordingly the learning outcomes attained) depend on the learner's construction of the situation. Hence, a fourth major theme of this book is that viewing the situation from the perspective of the learner is vital to gaining an understanding of the strategies employed as well as the outcomes attained by learners. This applies especially to the learner's strategy for developing and maintaining a sense of personal autonomy.

A fifth major theme is that a learner's autonomy in any given learning situation has two main components. These have been referred to as "situational autonomy" and "epistemological autonomy." Each of these further subdivides. Situational autonomy comprises two dimensions: (1) the practical skills necessary to the pursuit of the learner's goals (see particularly Chapter Eleven), and (2) the learner's sense of being independent from external constraints, pressures, or direction (discussed in Chapter Thirteen). Chickering (1964) refers to the first of these domains as "instrumental autonomy" and to the second as emotional autonomy, although in the present context, personal autonomy extends beyond emotional to include intellectual and moral autonomy as well (see Chapter Four).

Epistemological autonomy, on the other hand, involves (1) the learner's ability to make informed judgments about the content to be learned, as well as (2) the ability to employ appropriate strategies of inquiry. These two components have been called "anticipatory schemes" and "learning strategies." These four features — self-management skills and the qualities of personal autonomy on the one hand, and anticipatory schemes and learning strategies on the other — are themselves influenced by further factors. The relationships are depicted diagrammatically in Figure 14.2.

It has been argued that willingness to exercise self-management skills or to exert personal autonomy are dependent on the learner's view of assistance or direction, combined with his or her self-concept as a learner in the particular situation (Goodman, 1985; Serdahely and Adams, 1979). The other two features, anticipatory schemes and learning strategies, both depend on a combination of the learner's existing frames of reference as well as his or her purposes and intentions. All of these latter dimensions are influenced, to some extent, by the learner's construction of the individual situation. The diagram in Figure 14.2 summarizes a number of the major theoretical and practical issues raised in this book.

Figure 14.2. Schematic Representation
of the Variables Influencing Autonomy in Learning.

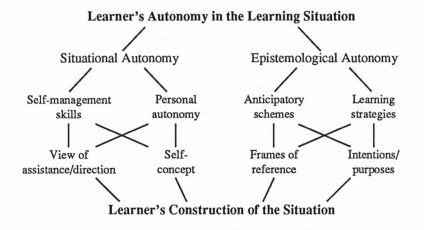

Learner's Autonomy in the Learning Situation

Situational Autonomy   Epistemological Autonomy

Self-management   Personal   Anticipatory   Learning
skills   autonomy   schemes   strategies

View of   Self-   Frames of   Intentions/
assistance/direction   concept   reference   purposes

Learner's Construction of the Situation

On the theoretical side, it is apparent that most research on autonomy in learning has tended to focus on the left-hand side of this diagram and in particular on either self-management skills or the qualities of personal autonomy. This preoccupation has effectively been at the exclusion of either the right-hand domain of epistemological autonomy or the underlying dimension of the learner's construction of the situation (see Chapter Fifteen).

On the practical side, there are a number of ways in which adult education practitioners can help learners to develop both situational and subject matter autonomy. To enhance situational autonomy, teachers and trainers can build the development of self-management and learning-to-learn skills into whatever they teach. They can encourage the emergence and exercise of personal autonomy in a variety of ways, including the appropriate use of learner-controlled methods of instruction and treating learners with respect and dignity. To enhance epistemological or subject matter autonomy, educators can provide instruction that allows for the emergence of anticipatory schemes and that builds on learners' existing subject matter knowledge, and they can help learners to develop higher-order learning strategies, including metacognitive awareness and self-monitoring. Clearly, this is a demanding mandate that goes well beyond the imparting of content and that even exceeds the facilitation of the learner's individual learning projects.

The sixth major theme of this book pertains to how learning is viewed. It has been customary to think of learning as the acquisition of quantities of information, and most research on learning has been dominated by the notion of how much is learned under differing regimes. This approach has extended to the study of learner-control and autodidaxy. However, a major element in this book has been that if learning is regarded not as the acquisition of information, but as a search for meaning and coherence in one's life and if an emphasis is placed on *what is learned and its personal significance to the learner,* rather than *how much is learned,* researchers would gain valuable new insights into both the mechanisms of learning and the relative advantages of teacher-controlled and learner-controlled modes of learning. Moreover, if constructivist assumptions are accepted, alternative research methodologies will be called for. As shown in the discussion of Gowin's Knowledge Vee, the interdependence of epistemological and methodological assumptions is a vital area of concern, and accordingly Chapter Fifteen contains a special note to researchers, although many of the issues discussed there are of direct interest to adult education practitioners as well.

A seventh theme throughout this book has been the attempt to place discussion about self-direction in education into a broader and less individualistic framework. In Chapters Eight through Ten, an attempt was made to offer a constructivist perspective on self-direction, to show that knowledge is socially constructed and that individual learners are "makers of meaning" in the sense of bringing to bear their unique and idiosyncratic frames of reference to any given learning task. This could be construed as idealizing the individual and adopting a somewhat romantic notion concerning just how much autonomy any one person actually has. What becomes apparent from a reading of the literature on critical science, however, is that interpretive approaches often exaggerate the extent to which individual intentions influence action and, conversely, that they underestimate the power of social and cultural factors to constrain personal freedom. In particular, issues of power, authority, and ideology are bound up inextricably with questions of learner-control and autodidaxy to a greater degree than is generally acknowledged in the literature on self-direction. Because self-concept, knowledge about learning, visions of the future, attitudes toward others, and convictions about education are all powerfully mediated by structures of class, gender, ethnicity, and age, adult educators who advocate and strive to develop self-directedness are inevitably involved in aspects of societal transformation.

Because of the preceding considerations, the agenda for research on self-direction that appears in the next chapter must be treated as partial. The decision to pursue an approach emphasizing individual psychology necessarily neglects sociological and anthropological perspectives. Although it is believed that the adoption of a constructivist approach may generate new and valuable lines of research within the psychological tradition, it is also hoped that this research will stimulate a more comprehensive and critical analysis of the social dimensions of autonomy in learning.

Finally, this book has outlined some directions for the development of self-directed competence. It has been suggested that any proposed program to enhance self-directed learning (as distinct from programs aimed at emancipation or liberation of the whole person) needs to go well beyond the simple recipe of placing people into situations that allow for—or even demand—a degree of self-directedness. Such programs must start with the learner's current worldview and self-concept. They should explicitly aim to develop a range of skills and attitudes, to concentrate on "higher-order" as well as foundational competencies, to acknowledge the context-dependent nature of learning competence, and to recognize the importance of the learner's own construction of events—in particular his or her "sense of learning competence" as essential to effective self-directed learning. Four important observations must, however, be made about these recommendations.

First, the development of self-directed learning capability is not the exclusive preserve of adult education; indeed the socializing influences of early educational experience are so strong that by adulthood, it may well be too late for many. Accordingly, the project of developing self-directed learning competence and confidence is a lifelong one. Second, although the "keys to promoting self-direction" discussed in Part Four look like discrete and relatively watertight compartments, in fact they are intimately interwoven, and the project of developing self-directedness cannot meaningfully be grafted onto an educational system or institution that is antipathetic to that goal. Third, as I have shown, there may be only limited transfer of self-directed learning competence from one context to the next, and the pursuit of generalized strategies is probably ill-advised and foredoomed. Fourth, approaches to the development of self-direction in learning must be congruent with the underlying assumption of self-directedness on which they are predicated. It is thus inconsistent and indefensible to implement a program — no matter how pure one's motives or how comprehensive and thorough the approach — that fails to honor the right of learners to be self-directed with respect to their own self-directedness. This need for congruence or reflexivity represents arguably the greatest challenge confronting those who seek to enhance the self-directedness of others. These considerations lead to the formulation of a model, the details of which follow.

A Model for Enhancing Self-Direction in Learning

In this book, I have argued for the implementation of approaches to education that aim — either directly or concomitantly — to enhance learners' ability and willingness to undertake self-directed learning. It is likely, though by no means certain, that such approaches to learning will "spill over" into other aspects of people's lives: their democratic participation at work and in the community; their approach to family life and social relations, and their involvement in other forms of education and training. There are also other, more immediate justifications for promoting self-direction in learning. In particular, there is evidence that self-direction can enhance learning outcomes, improve the relevance and meaningfulness of what is learned, and give people a sense of personal potency or power that is basic to the development of a learning-oriented society.

From a consideration of the themes running through this book, it is evident that the development of self-directed learning competence is a multifaceted activity and that adult educators need to give attention to at least three main dimensions along which self-direction might vary: competence, resources, and rights. I will discuss each of these in turn.

Competence. There can be little doubt that people differ from one another in their ability to be self-directed in learning. This competence has both a generic and a situation-specific aspect to it. In Part Four, especially Chapter Eleven, I delineated a set of "building blocks" that may be amenable to educational intervention. These include

- Essential skills of literacy and numeracy
- Information location and retrieval
- Goal setting
- Time management
- Question-asking behavior
- Critical thinking
- Comprehensive monitoring and self-evaluation

Some of these skills, such as goal setting and time management, appear to be relatively low level and also relatively context-free. Others however are increasingly complex, demanding both high levels of subject specific knowledge and high levels of intellectual sophistication. In view of recent research on domain specific learning strategies, it is clear that the development and enhancement of all these various competencies can be built into the way in which adult education activities are conducted. However, they require a specific metacognitive approach to teaching, and in any case few adult education activities are of sufficient duration or intensity to allow for the comprehensive buildup of such abilities and dispositions.

It is thus apparent that developing the competencies for self-directed learning is a lifelong endeavor, and that it should form part of the overall guidelines or criteria shaping the development of all educational curricula (Skager and Dave, 1977, pp. 53–60). Educators can definitely make a concrete contribution to the development of self-directed learning competence.

Resources. The second domain in which educators can seek to enhance self-directedness in learning is by providing learners with access to adequate, comprehensive, and readily available learning resources. Depending on the particular domain to be acquired, this may include intangibles such as time or money, or more tangible aspects such as newspapers and journals, libraries and resource centers, laboratories, radio and television broadcasts, computer-based instruction materials, as well as internships, practicums, and job placements. In the final analysis, the vision of the learning society implies the widespread availability of learning opportunities in a diverse range of contexts and settings.

If self-direction is narrowly defined as increasing learner-control of instruction, then it is clearly an institutional matter, and the learning materials concerned will be located within the ambit of the school, college, university, training department, or adult education agency involved. If, however, self-direction is more broadly defined as embracing the independent pursuit of learning opportunities beyond or outside formal institutional settings, then the availability of and access to the means of learning becomes a matter of social policy, which requires a political will at the very highest level. In this case, the desire to promote self-direction is not and cannot be merely a small-scale and local initiative, but must be seen in the context of regional, national, and ultimately international concerns. Because of these diverse implications, the educator needs to recognize that there are potent forces militating against the democratization of learning opportunities.

Despite the high-sounding rhetoric about the democratization of learning opportunities, education everywhere is essentially a conduit to priviledge and prestige. Those who have access to high culture, to well-paid jobs, and to social mobility do so largely as a result of education (including, in some cases, self-education). With certain notable exceptions, they are not about to relinquish their position—or, as Freire puts it, to "commit class suicide"—by making access to it any easier. Glib talk of self-direction as a universal attainment and goal of education needs to be tempered by a sober realization of the formidable ideological and practical obstacles to the attainment of such a goal.

Rights. It may be possible for a person to have the competence to learn things for himself or herself, and to have access to needed resources, and yet still to be disabled from doing so. The domain at issue here is broadly defined as personal "rights," and this is arguably the most difficult and delicate aspect in the area of self-directed learning. I am not talking here of "rights" in any narrow legal or constitutional sense, but rather in the context of enabling personal space or discretionary power to act on one's own behalf that derive from social structures. Thus "rights" in this sense has both an individual and a societal component: what is actually permitted and what the individual believes is permitted.

With respect to the individual dimension, I have discussed in Chapter Thirteen the notion of a "sense of learning competence" (Usher and Johnston, 1988), which in turn is one manifestation of a broader "sense of personal control" (Stipek and Weisz, 1981) or of personal agency (Thomas, 1980). In a way, people's ability to be self-directing, in any given context, is limited by their belief in themselves. As Harré (1983, p. 226) expresses it, "In every culture what someone does is a reflection of their beliefs as to whether they have the right to do something and/or the confidence to carry out a cognitive operation in the possible or actual presence of certain others."

I am not arguing here for the popular notion of the "power of positive thought," although that has its place in understanding the phenomenon of self-determination (Bagnall, 1987) broadly defined. What I am arguing is that people often perceive limits to their agency that are more illusory than real. In Chapter Thirteen, I discussed the idea of "personal learning myths"; here I am endorsing the view that to behave autonomously as a learner requires emancipation from such disabling self-images or stereo-types about the locus of control in learning. As discussed in Chapter Thirteen, there is much that can be done to affirm and enhance people's "sense of learning competence," although these interventions frequently border on therapy rather than educa-tion, and certainly go well beyond the widely advocated process of simply encouraging people to become autonomous by plac-ing them into situations of self-directed learning.

With regard to the societal dimensions of "rights," there are certain boundaries that limit or restrict people's absolute abil-ity to be self-directed in learning. Although invisible, these hid-den barriers work strongly to inhibit self-direction in general (Watt, 1989, chap. 8), and self-directed learning in particular. It is as if people were trapped inside a "glass tunnel," so that although they can look out on the world of learning opportuni-ties, they are unable to stray far from the routes mapped out for them. There are at least three components of this "glass tun-nel." The first is peer pressure. There are often very potent, if unspoken, restrictions imposed on self-directed learning by people's family, friends, and associates. In his classic book *The Mature Mind,* Overstreet (1950, p. 37) comments that "obsta-cles *within the culture* arise from the *unusualness* of adult study; from the fact that the enterprise of organized learning lies out-side the accustomed pattern of adult life. There is the possibil-ity of ridicule; of being made conspicuous by 'going to school' when grownups are supposed to be through with school; of lone-liness in an experience that was a companionable one during the years of childhood; of being thought inferior or stupid by seeming to need to study at an age when study is presumed to have been accomplished."

If learning is not part of the cultural norm for a particular group, then the person seeking to emancipate himself or herself through self-education has first of all to transcend the indiffer-ence or even antagonism of those with whom she or he is regu-larly in contact. An educator who is encouraging a learner to become self-directed should be aware that this may be placing that person at odds with significant others in his or her social circle.

The second aspect is the closed ranks often confronted

by the person seeking to be self-directed in learning. This may include such behaviors as letters or telephone calls going unanswered; misleading, incomplete, or unenthusiastic responses from practitioners, librarians, teachers, or other gatekeepers of the field of work and inquiry; and unduly or inappropriately harsh evaluation by those in a position to encourage or support self-directed inquiry, often based on such flimsy grounds as the aspiring learners' accent, vocabulary, dress, or other aspects of class membership.

A third dimension of the glass tunnel is even more elusive and hard to identify; it is those criteria that are used to distinguish an expert from a novice or indeed a more experienced from a less experienced learner. In almost any field of inquiry, but especially those concerning disciplinary bodies of knowledge, there is a tacit hierarchy whereby those who are familiar with the rules of discourse—the "syntax," "grammar," and "vocabulary" of the field of study—are accorded higher status than neophytes. Learners (whether self-directed or not) must submit to the rules governing the field and acquire them—often without understanding or justification in the first instance—as a prelude to truly self-directed learning (Quinton, 1971; Strike, 1982). This essential form of epistemological dependence is built in to propositional forms of knowledge. As Quinton (1971, pp. 203–204) puts it:

> My private or personal knowledge, what I have discovered by my own observations and stored in my memory, together with what I have inferred from this, constitutes a quantitatively minute fragment of the whole range of what I claim to know. And, if quality is a matter of scope and importance rather than of certainty, all but a vanishingly small proportion of my general, theoretical knowledge is derived from others.
>
> Not only is this the case now, with me or any other mature cognitive subject, but it always has been so. Indeed dependence on others is even more extreme at the beginning of one's cognitive career than it turns out to be later, when one has at least accumulated quite a substantial body of personal knowledge and has acquired the skill of critically sifting the testimony of others.

This is a theme with which I dealt at some length in Chapter Twelve.

Of course there are, and have always been, some for whom the glass tunnel is little more than a challenge to their ingenuity, persistence, and sense of purpose. People have managed to rise above disabling social or family circumstances, to transcend the limits imposed by an inadequate formative education, to manifest a lively and well-informed interest in the world around them, to develop and use a vocabulary that offers access to sometimes arcane and esoteric fields of study, and to liberate themselves from those factors that might otherwise constrain, block, inhibit, suppress, divert, or distort the capacity for human self-direction and intelligent agency in learning (Heron, 1971, p. 5). Such people, however, tend to be in the minority. The challenge for those who wish for learners to be more self-directed is to tackle the question of self-direction not simply from an individual perspective but from a social and critical point of view as well, and to recognize that increasing the rights of individual learners may entail changes in their social circumstances.

Rights, Resources, and Competence. These various aspects may be summarized in a simple, three-dimensional diagram, as shown in Figure 14.3.

With respect to any given potential learning situation, a learner may occupy a position somewhere in this imaginary cube: a position marked by his or her unique combination of competence, rights, and resources. The central message of this book may be summed up in the following way. The educator who seeks to facilitate or enhance the learner's self-directed learning has three dimensions on which to concentrate. He or she might seek to raise competence, increase rights, or provide resources. Conversely, he or she might seek to remove or reduce those features that inhibit, diminish, or restrain the learner's competence, rights, or resources. In either case, all three have an individual aspect and all three have a collective or social aspect as well. People's capacity for self-direction in learning cannot be fully realized by giving attention to any one of these elements in isolation, and moreover, individual self-directedness cannot be fully achieved without giving due consideration to the social and collective constraints that may inhibit it.

**Figure 14.3. The Three Major Domains
Involved in Self-Directed Learning.**

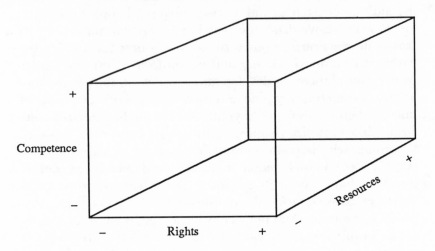

Finally, while it may be argued that seeking to move learners toward the top right corner of the diagram is a valid and defensible objective for adult education, it should not be assumed that this is exclusively the role of adult education, that the trajectory for each individual learner will necessarily be the same, or even that such a move will be acceptable to every learner or potential learner.

Summary

In self-direction many of the enduring and at times contradictory preoccupations of education converge. Self-direction is at once a social and psychological construct, a philosophical ideal, and a literal impossibility; an external manifestation and an internal tendency; both the beginning and the end of lifelong learning; the foundation stone and the keystone of the learning society; a supplement to and a substitute for the formal education system; a vehicle for the mastery of established knowledge and for the transformation of personal understandings; simultaneously a process and a product, a precondition and a purpose.

Because of this complexity, and in particular the inherently subversive nature of self-directed learning broadly defined, it is hardly surprising that writing about it is confusing and at times contradictory. In the preceding parts of this chapter, I have emphasized the individual as well as the collective or social dimensions of self-direction in learning. This brings us to Lindeman's classic dictum, written more than sixty years ago, in *The Meaning of Adult Education:* "We can progress not by giving attention to either organisms or the environment, but to both and in relation to each other . . . " (Lindeman, 1926b, p. 48). The reason that self-direction continues to attract such attention from scholars and practitioners alike is that it embodies two of education's most noble aims and most enduring mandates: individual fulfillment and societal transformation.

Fifteen

Directions
and Agendas
for Research

For reasons that I have discussed throughout this book, though principally in Chapter Two, in recent years, the notion of self-direction has become a central theme in both the theory and practice of adult education. One side effect of this pervasive movement has been a dramatic increase in the amount of literature that has appeared about the subject. However, despite or perhaps because of the volume of material appearing, recent research on "self-direction" seems to have become stalemated. This may be attributed to three main causes: The first is the absence of a consistent theoretical perspective underlying the study of self-direction; the second is the failure to create a cumulative knowledge base about the phenomenon; and the third is the indiscriminate application of the term *self-direction* to at least four distinct phenomena: personal autonomy (Chapter Four), self-management in learning (Chapter Five), autodidaxy (Chapter Six), and learner-control (Chapter Seven).

Although this chapter is directed to researchers, it should also be of interest to adult education practitioners and to other research users. It represents an attempt to review briefly the major paradigms that have influenced educational research, especially those that have been influential in the study of "self-direction." In this way, it is hoped to identify research designs and approaches that because of their compatibility with underlying assumptions concerning "self-direction," promise to offer further productive lines of inquiry.

426

Readers of this chapter will note that I am arguing in favor of the use of certain approaches within a predominantly interpretive framework, and may accordingly be inclined to accuse me of what Brookfield has dubbed "methodolatory," or a fixation on one particular approach to educational research.

Although there may be some justice in such an allegation, it is necessary to point out that advocacy of a particular approach to research does not necessarily imply rejection of alternatives, but rather a recognition that different aspects of a research problem may yield to different strategies. As I have stressed throughout the book, self-direction is a complex and multifaceted domain that is susceptible to research from a variety of perspectives. To neglect research into some of the elusive aspects of "how learners organize, do and judge their self-directed learning activities" (Caffarella, 1988, p. 6) is potentially to miss out on some of this richness.

The second reason for promoting another approach to research is precisely to avoid the bias that results from emphasis on just one main strategy. Years ago, in his insightful and widely cited work on *The Structure of Scientific Revolutions,* Kuhn, (1970, pp. 109–110) had this to say about alternative approaches to research: "To the extent . . . that two scientific schools disagree about what is a problem and what a solution, they will inevitably talk through each other when debating the relative merits of their respective paradigms. In the partially circular arguments that regularly result, each paradigm will be shown to satisfy more or less the criteria that it dictates for itself and to fall short of a few of those dictated by its opponent. . . . Since no paradigm ever solves all the problems it defines, and since no two paradigms leave all the same problems unsolved, paradigm debates always involve the question: Which problems is it more significant to have solved?"

There is no doubt that we have an extensive and valuable knowledge base about self-direction, but the adoption of an interpretive approach would have two major benefits. First, it would open up for discussion and analysis a whole new range of "problems" and areas of inquiry. Second, by researching existing domains from different theoretical points of view, the canons of methodological triangulation could be honored, and the veracity of various knowledge claims might be tested from different perspectives.

Educational Research: Alternative Paradigms

In one form or another, doing research seems to be as much a natural human function as breathing. Cohen and Manion (1985) place research along with experience and reasoning as the principal ways in which people attempt to understand their environments. In the introduction to a set of papers on qualitative research, Emery (1986, p. i) writes: "Research . . . is an ancient and ubiquitous human activity. Curiosity about others and the worlds in which they live has always been displayed through conversation, asking questions, working together to see what happens after different kinds of actions are performed, talking or gossiping about others to tease out intentions and other reasons for behavior, clarifying and understanding circumstances; all are fundamental research functions."

It is on such slender foundations that the whole massive superstructure of "research" as a formalized, specialized, and commonly as an institutionalized process is based. It is beyond the scope of this chapter to attempt to survey the vast and complex topic of social and behavioral research, or even the narrower but still overwhelming field of educational research. However, it is true that research is far from a unified and monolithic enterprise, and that there are important divisions within the research community that affect such vital areas as what is considered worth knowing, how research ought to be conducted, and what is to count as evidence in supporting knowledge claims.

Until comparatively recently, the argument about alternative approaches to educational research was commonly presented as a simple dichotomy, with pairs of terms being applied to the respective paradigms: rationalistic versus naturalistic, positivistic versus interpretive, rigorous versus intuitive, objective versus subjective, and even "hard" versus "soft." However, this rather simplistic formulation has been disturbed, first by the recognition that there are major differences within paradigms, and second by the acknowledgment of a third broad approach, namely that of critical science. An overview of these three dominant paradigms follows.

In the late nineteenth and early twentieth century, research into education began to emerge as a legitimate form of scholarly inquiry. At that time, and in fact until recently, it was commonly assumed that such research should be based on the aims and methods of established science. Educational phenomena were assumed to be governed by the same sort of regularities and lawlike relationships that characterized the "hard" or "natural" sciences.

However, many researchers, notably anthropologists and sociologists but also some psychologists and others, became increasingly disenchanted with this empirical-analytical approach, and instead sought to explain how people attribute meaning to their circumstances and how they develop and make use of rules that govern their behavior. Thus, a second major approach to the study of educational phenomena developed—the interpretive or hermeneutic (Bauman, 1978).

Although this was clearly an improvement on the positivist/empiricist approach to the study of educational issues, critics have pointed out the limitaions and weaknesses in the interpretive point of view. They argue that a knowledge of the meanings that individual actors bring to bear does not go far enough, that human beings do not live in worlds entirely of their own devising, and that people generally are subject to influences and pressures that shape their attitudes and perceptions and yet of which they are often unaware. In short, they advocate approaches to research that explore how social relations have developed historically and how individual people's interpretations may be distorted by ideological convictions (Sullivan, 1984).

It appears, then, that educational research has been influenced by several major intellectual traditions, and in the sections that follow, these will be briefly explored, before we move on to a more detailed consideration of the interpretive approach.

Positivism. Positivism is not a systematically formulated doctrine, but rather a general philosophical outlook that stresses the power of "positive" knowledge to solve major practical problems. Although its origins can be traced back to classical antiquity, it emerged in the latter half of the nineteenth century as a potent intellectual force in Western thought. The term itself is associated with the French philosopher Comte, who eschewed theological and metaphysical claims to knowledge, arguing instead that only sensorily apprehended experience could form the basis of valid knowledge and that accordingly knowledge could be advanced only by means of observation and experiment (Cohen and Manion, 1985, p. 12). When first coined, the term *positivism* itself had quite positive connotations, being associated with ideas of scientific progress and liberation from mentalism. Today, it is a derogatory epithet, used as a weapon of attack and as a term of derision. There are many versions of positivism; however most share some common features. These include (1) the belief that theory is universal and that lawlike generalizations are not bound to specific contexts or circumstances; (2) the commitment to an objective or dispassionate pursuit of "scientific truth"; (3) a belief in determinism, or the assumption that events have causes which are distinct and analytically separable from them; (4) the view that variables can be identified and defined and that knowledge can be formalized; and (5) a conviction that relationships between and among variables can be expressed in mathematically precise ways in the development and testing of theoretical propositions.

From a set of assumptions such as these flows the implementation of the "scientific method," including the specification of hypotheses at the start of research, the attempt to remain objective and detached from the area of study, the search for invariant causal relationships, and the attempt to reduce findings to quantified forms. Lying behind many of these practices is the notion that theory, conceived as a body of scientific knowledge, can be used to predict and hence to control outcomes.

There can be little doubt that, at least until recently, the assumptions of positivism, and the practices of the empirical-analytical approach, have dominated psychological research. Rist (1977, p. 42) comments that "quantitative research is the dominant methodology in educational research. It is more widely published, taught, accepted, and rewarded in educational research circles than any other approach." This same dominance seems to have extended to adult education research (Boud, 1983), where, according to Jennings (1985, p. 4), "almost all research methodology . . . has been imbued with the values associated with the empirical model. . . . The dominance that this model has assumed may reflect the concern of researchers in this relatively new field to gain 'respectability' through the empirical tradition." Despite its dominance, however, it has become increasingly apparent that "no one methodology can answer all questions and provide insights on all issues" (Rist, 1977, p. 42). This is particularly true of "self-direction" in learning, at least some features of which are simply not amenable to research in this tradition.

Interpretive Approaches. The positivist paradigm has been subjected to severe critical scrutiny and debate. In its place, many theorists have advocated a new epistemological framework, one which aims to produce "interpretive" accounts of phenomena rather than lawlike generalizations. Like the positivists, who cover a range of different positions and perspectives, opponents of positivism also subscribe to a variety of schools of thought. Nonetheless, they are united in rejecting the belief that human behavior is governed by general laws. Instead, they argue that the social world can only be understood from the standpoint of the individual actors. Carr and Kemmis (1983, p. 88) express it thus: "[Human] actions cannot be observed in the same way as natural objects. They can only be interpreted by reference to the actor's motives, intentions or purposes in performing the action. To identify these motives and intentions correctly is to grasp the 'subjective meaning' the action has to the actor."

According to interpretive theorists, human interactions are not governed by inviolable laws so much as by agreed rules which are consensually validated by people — a simple example might be the custom of shaking hands as a form of greeting. Many such rule-governed practices are symbolic, and thus interpretive approaches are sometimes referred to as "symbolic." According to Popkewitz (1984, p. 41), "At one layer, the purpose of a symbolic and an empirical-analytic (or positivistic) science is the same: to develop theories about social affairs. The notion of theory, however, shifts from a search for law-like regularities about the nature of social behavior to the identification of social rules that underlie and govern the use of social 'facts.'"

Central to the work of interpretive or symbolic theorists are the concepts of intersubjectivity, motive, and reason. Intersubjectivity refers to the consensual norms which define what is real or valid in any social situation; motives are the events or circumstances which cause other events or circumstances (that is, "because of"); reasons are the as-yet-unfulfilled expectations that influence behavior prospectively (that is, "in order to"). Positivistic research has tended to focus almost exclusively on "because of"–type motives, ignoring the intentions, values, attitudes, and beliefs that influence people to behave "in order to" achieve some desired state of affairs.

Assumptions commonly shared by interpretive theorists include (1) the belief that any event or action is explicable in terms of multiple interacting factors, events, and processes, and that "causes" and "effects" are mutually interdependent; (2) an acceptance of the extreme difficulty in attaining complete objectivity, especially in observing human subjects who construe, or make sense of, events based on their individual systems of meaning; (3) the view that the aim of inquiry is to develop an understanding of individual cases, rather than universal laws or generalizations; (4) the assumption that the world is made up of tangible and intangible multifaceted realities, and that these are best studied as a unified whole, rather than being fragmented into dependent and independent variables (in other words, context makes a difference); and (5) a recognition that inquiry is always value laden and that such values inevitably influence the framing, bounding, and focusing of research problems.

In the minds of many, the interpretive paradigm is linked with certain specific approaches to research, such as fieldwork, case-study, and participant observation. However, as Jennings (1986) points out, not only is there a good deal of looseness in the application of these terms, but in any case such methods are not necessarily tied to any one particular paradigm (p. 14);

the same method may equally be recruited by researchers operating on quite different assumptions and with different intentions.

Central to the interpretive methodologies is the need for interpretive accounts to be "coherent" (that is, to comprehend and account for insights and evidence within a consistent framework). Interpretive accounts must also make sense to the actors whose behavior is being studied; in other words, they must pass the test of participant confirmation (Carr and Kemmis, 1983, p. 91). This means that interpretive accounts in research do not seek to reinterpret the actions and experiences of the actors, but rather to give a deeper, more extensive, and more systematic representation of events from the point of view of the actors involved.

Critical Approaches. By taking account of the perspectives of the individuals who are the subjects of research, the interpretive approaches seem to be grounded in people's practical realities, and moreover they resonate with the dominant humanistic and liberal value of respect for the person (Lukes, 1973). However, despite these strengths, interpretive approaches to research have not escaped criticism, either from positivists or from opponents of positivism. Not unexpectedly, those imbued with a positivistic outlook have criticized interpretive approaches as representing a return to mentalism and highly subjective and "prescientific" accounts of phenomena. They also object to "the inability of the interpretive approach to produce valid knowledge in the form of wide-ranging generalizations or to provide 'objective' standards of verifying or refuting theoretical accounts" (Carr and Kemmis, 1983, p. 94).

Perhaps more seriously, interpretive approaches to social research have been criticized from within, because they do not go far enough. It has been pointed out that, "like the empirical sciences, the interpretive tradition seeks objectivity and value-free inquiry into the human realm of intersubjective meaning" and that in doing so, "many interpretive studies are covert forms of positivism" (Jennings, 1985, p. 5). In the view of such critics, the fear that the respondent may become "contaminated" by the subjectivity of the researcher leads to recommended methods of inquiry that threaten both to reduce the researcher to a passive role and the subject of the research to the "object" of research — ironically one of the main criticisms aimed at positivism.

A second major critique of the interpretive approach is that merely describing a situation from the perspective of the participants, no matter how skilfully and systematically, ignores the fact that there are certain external features of social reality that are very influential in shaping that reality. In particular, individuals are often caught up in "crucial problems of social conflict and social change" (Carr and Kemmis, 1983, p. 94) of which they may be unaware. In discussing the epistemology of oral history, Murphy (1986, p. 167) makes a similar point when he writes: "Just as there is a difference between using language and enquiring into its use, so the actors themselves need not have consciousness of the rules in order to follow them properly; and it is not they whom the interpreter would wish to interrogate in a search for the consistent formulation of the rules. Consequently, the ideological and cultural parameters of social action are not necessarily those which people articulate, and may lie below the surface of verbal communication."

What is required is a broader and more inclusive perspective than any one participant, or group of participants, may be able to bring to bear. As Rex (1974, p. 86) puts it: "Whilst patterns of social reactions and institutions may be the product of the actors' definitions of the situations, there is also the possibility that those actors might be falsely conscious. . . . [Researchers] have an obligation to seek an objective [sic] perspective which is not necessarily that of the participating actors at all. . . . We need not be confined purely and simply to that social reality which is made available to us by participant actors themselves."

Those who favor critical approaches argue that, by emphasizing the subjective meanings of social action, other interpretive researchers often neglect the relationships between individuals' interpretations and actions and external factors, ignoring the fact that social reality is both shaped by, and shapes, the interpretations and perceptions of individuals. Critical researchers maintain that research can legitimately look beyond the perceptions that individuals have, to the factors (often ideological) that influence such perceptions, for "the very process whereby one interprets and defines a situation is itself a product of the circumstances in which one is placed" (Cohen and Manion, 1985, p. 38).

The label "critical theory" has been applied to a range of phenomena (Carr and Kemmis, 1983, p. 129), and, like both positivism and the interpretive approaches to research, critical theory is not, and never was, a "fully articulated philosophy shared unproblematically" (Giroux, 1983, p. 7). Partly because of this, and partly because of the inherent complexity of the ideas themselves, it is difficult to find in any one place a succinct statement of the convictions underlying research with this paradigm. However, most researchers subscribing to a critical approach would assent to some or all of the following guiding assumptions: (1) much human action is outside the conscious control of personal agency, and is embedded in social conditions beyond the consciousness of the actors involved; (2) any interpretive explanation makes sense against a background of social rules, practices, and beliefs, and there is thus a "logic of the situation" that differs from the "logic of causes"; (3) unless research is restricted to merely recording actors' interpretations and understandings, it inevitably involves reformulating or "resymbolizing" events, which is an act of construction rather than of discovery; (4) researchers make use of expert knowledge that potentially sets them apart from the subjects being researched and that gives them access to a specialized language of interpretation not accessible to the people being studied; and (5) intentional agency may be frustrated by social rules, by constitutive meanings of the social order, and by "the habitual sediment of the past," and the core project of uncovering such constraints through research is one of human liberation and emancipation.

In its commitment to social change (and indeed to political reform), the critical approach abandons any pretense at neutrality, and recognizes that "questions of ethics, morality and politics are interrelated with science to orient individuals to what is right and just in a given situation" (Popkewitz, 1984, p. 46). The critical approach seeks explicitly to identify and criticize disjunctions, incongruities, and contradictions in people's life experience. Whereas interpretive approaches may be inclined towards simply revealing misconceptions and confusion while leaving situations unchanged, "the function of critical theory is to understand the relations among value, interest, and action and, to paraphrase Marx, to change the world, not to describe it" (Popkewitz, 1984, p. 45).

Research on Self-Direction

When one reviews the literature on "self-directed learning," it appears that it has been dominated by two themes: a psychological perspective and a positivistic view of knowledge. On the surface, autonomy in learning is quintessentially individualistic. The way in which individual learners approach learning tasks, their concepts of themselves, how they construe the material they encounter, and how they develop and assert their independence in learning situations are all the legitimate domain of the psychological researcher. However, it is important to recognize that many of these features are socially constructed and historically mediated, and that one could argue forcefully for a more critical and sociologically based approach to the study of autonomy in learning (Sullivan, 1984). In view of the pervasive influence of social and cultural factors, therefore, the whole phenomenon of self-direction might profitably be investigated through the use of complementary research paradigms, emphasizing sociological as well as psychological dimensions, and it may be argued that interpretive approaches suit many of the research questions surrounding this aspect of education perfectly.

Turning to the dominance of the positivistic paradigm, the search for lawlike generalizations and for mathematically precise causal relationships is perhaps most pronounced in the domain of learner-control. However, this tendency is also evident in research on autodidaxy where, as Brookfield (1984b, 1985c) points out, there has often been an overemphasis on the quantitative and quantifiable dimensions of self-guided learning endeavors, without regard to the quality of learning or of its meaning to individual learners.

That such preoccupations are manifest in the literature on self-direction seems particularly ironic, in view of the nature of the phenomenon being studied. If researchers were inquiring into the migration patterns of birds, for instance, or the behavior of large bodies of water in the open ocean, the search for lawlike generalizations might seem appropriate. But self-direction, by its very nature, is distinguished by its concern for individual cases and by its emphasis on the vagaries of human motivation and interests. It seems that the adoption of a predominantly positivistic approach to research has inhibited the emergence of valuable research findings with respect to self-direction in learning. For example, researchers have repeatedly shown that self-direction is a highly individual phenomenon, yet individual differences tend to be submerged by research methods that emphasize similarities; an individual person's ability to be self-directing may well vary from one situation to another, yet research methods often ignore such situational differences; the processes of self-directed learning (both autodidactic and learner-controlled situations) seems to zigzag and to follow unpredictable patterns, but researchers have commonly assumed a linearity in the process and have employed research methods based on such "means-end" logic; finally, learners appear to pay attention to different features of each situation in determining their level and direction of personal autonomy, but researchers have often implicitly assumed that external and publicly observable features are the criteria by which autonomy is to be judged.

In short, some of the very features that are distinctive about self-directed learning, and that accordingly appear as paradoxical or problematic, could potentially be overcome by the adoption of a research perspective that explicitly allows for such features rather than ignoring or denying them. In order to acknowledge the unique features of "self-directed learning" in its various manifestations, what seems called for is a research orientation that emphasizes individuality, that acknowledges situational variability, that takes account of the apparently random and serendipitous nature of human affairs, and that above all gives due prominence to the fact that people are active choosers and participate actively in the creation of the social world of which they are a part. The interpretive approach, it is suggested, offers such an orientation.

Central to the interpretive approaches are the personal purposes, intentions, and frames of reference that individual actors, in this case the learners themselves, bring to bear in any circumstances. In learning situations, these influence everything from the initial willingness to engage at all, to the help sought and resources used, to the outcomes arising from the learning encounter. Yet it is precisely this perspective that is almost totally absent from research and writing about self-direction. In the case of assistance sought by learners, little attention is given to the personal significance that such help might have for the learner. In the case of an autodidactic project, one rarely encounters descriptions of what the learner feels or what he or she thinks as the project takes shape. In considering the issue of learner-control, few researchers seem sensitive to the fact that the learner's perception of being in control is more vital than some arbitrary set of circumstances engineered by the instructor. It would appear that examining the attitudes and intentions of learners is essential to gaining a full understanding of their actions. However, the attitudes and understandings of self-directed learners are intensely personal and idiosyncratic, and are also deeply influenced by the concrete realities of particular situations. They are beyond the "reach" of conventional positivism, which relies so heavily on observable behavior. Moreover, as I have argued elsewhere (Candy, 1987) and in the previous chapter, there are important sociological dimensions to self-direction that have been almost entirely neglected in current research.

Toward a New Research Agenda in Self-Direction

If the preceding argument is accepted, what new directions and revised research questions might researchers pursue? The first corollary of adopting an interpretive or constructivist perspective is that the researcher becomes aware of precisely whose perspective is being presented. The issue of "self-direction" at least in formal instructional settings (and to a lesser extent in situations of autodidaxy) can be viewed from the perspective of the learner as well as that of the teacher/trainer/coach/facilitator or helper. Thus, in the discussion that follows, the domain of research interest will be subdivided according to the perspective taken—that of the learner or of the person assisting the learner.

Autonomous Learning from the Learner's Perspective

Despite protestations of learner-centeredness, it is relatively unusual to encounter studies of autonomous learning, whether in formal instructional settings or in the natural societal setting, that represent the situation in the language, and from the point of view, of the learner. However, it has been argued that the learner's subjective construing of the situation significantly influences the strategies he or she employs, which in turn is a major factor in the outcomes obtained. This subjective construing includes at least four parts: (1) the learner's view of learning in general; (2) the learner's view of this specific learning endeavor; (3) the learner's view of assistance or direction received; and (4) the learner's view of autonomous learning and the development of personal autonomy. In the remainder of this section, these four aspects will be considered; each of these, in turn, comprises a number of subsidiary elements, related to each other in complex ways.

The Learner's View of Learning in General. If one were to observe learners approaching a particular learning task, it would be possible to detect a number of different strategies. To take a simple example, confronted with the need to learn a new language, one learner may approach the task with a sort of grim determination, equipped with such paraphernalia as phrasebooks and dictionaries, tape recorders and notepads. Another may choose to live among native speakers, seeking to absorb the language in all the fullness and richness of its cultural context. Such differences in learning strategy could be ascribed to different learning styles, but on what are such differences based? To some extent, learning style preference might be related to personality, but it is also related to the way learners view learning itself, and this, in turn, depends on two things: their view of knowledge and their approach to learning tasks.

Fundamental to any study of learning—including self-directed learning—must be the learner's view of the nature of knowledge, and how this may affect his or her willingness (or ability) to be self-directed in learning (Candy, 1988). At one extreme, it is possible to discern the view that knowledge is fixed, enduring, and external and that it has to be "mastered." Such an understanding implies that learners need "study skills" in the same way that a mountaineer requires such accoutrements as crampons, ropes, and steel spikes (not to mention a head for heights!). People who view knowledge this way assume that some approaches to learning are "safer" than others, and that one must master the easier parts before launching an attack on the summit. Autodidacts seeing knowledge this way would try to familiarize themselves with the basics of their chosen field, before progressing to advanced levels, in the belief that "basic" and "advanced" are somehow properties of the subject matter rather than of the learner. It will be noted that this view does not in any way imply passivity on the part of the learner, who may well have to undertake massive exertions in order to "appropriate previously constituted knowledge" (Millar, Morphet, and Saddington, 1986, p. 440).

An alternative view of knowledge, and one that is endorsed in this book, is that it is labile, evanescent, and socially constructed. The learner is involved in actively constructing meanings and hence still requires tools, but different tools. In viewing knowledge thus, the learner becomes responsible for transforming understandings through reflection on experience (Boud, Keogh, and Walker, 1985). Learning is not, and cannot be, a matter of rote memorization, nor of simply "increasing knowledge," but is instead "an interpretive process aimed at the understanding of reality" (Gibbs, Morgan, and Taylor, 1982, p. 134).

It has already been discussed in Chapter Twelve that, as learners become more "mature," they tend to see knowledge differently. Perry's (1970) work suggests that, as students progress through the university, they frequently come to view the subject they are studying in more relativistic terms, and research with autodidacts (for example, Brookfield, 1981b; Nolan, 1981b) shows much the same phenomenon. However, attaining a level of epistemological sophistication in one topic area or domain does not necessarily influence people's view of knowledge more generally. Hence it is possible for someone to have an advanced knowledge of one subject area, yet to regard something unfamiliar as an impenetrable mystery. Not unexpectedly, such a view would dramatically alter the learning strategies employed, the kind of assistance sought, and the learning outcomes obtained.

> *Recommendation One:* Researchers should examine how learners construe differing subject areas that they are attempting to learn. By virtue of the learners' unfamiliarity with the subject matter, this may entail research techniques that stress analogy and metaphor and that call on learners to describe their learning strategies in abstract or metacognitive terms.

Acting as a sort of bridge between the learners' views of knowledge, on the one hand, and their views of a specific learning endeavor on the other, is their general understanding of what it means to learn. Säljö's (1979b) study of commonsense conceptions of learning has already been mentioned. Underlying the five main conceptions of learning that he discovered, Säljö identified an even more basic split between those who viewed knowledge as external to individuals and those who argued that knowledge is constructed by individuals as a result of an active effort on the part of the learner to abstract meaning (Säljö, 1979b, p. 14). Such a difference in the view of knowledge inevitably implies significant differences in the process of learning itself. This distinction is often referred to as the difference between rote and meaningful learning, characterized by Novak and Gowin (1984, p. 167) as follows:

Rote learning (most school learning)

Arbitrary, verbatim, non-substantive incorporation of new knowledge into cognitive structure

No effort to integrate new knowledge with existing concepts in
cognitive structure

Learning not related to experience with events or objects

No affective commitment to relate new knowledge to prior learning

Meaningful learning (creative production)

Non-arbitrary, non-verbatim, substantive incorporation of new
knowledge into cognitive structure

Deliberate effort to link new knowledge with higher-order, more
inclusive concepts in cognitive structure

Learning related to experience with events or objects

Affective commitment to relate new knowledge to prior learning

Rote and meaningful learning clearly demand that the
learner accept different levels of responsibility. In their experiment with learner-control, Millar, Morphet, and Saddington
(1986, p. 440) noted that students had two different answers
to the question, "What kind of responsibility do I have for learning?" The "old orthodoxy" is typified by the response "I am
responsible for appropriating previously constituted knowledge";
the alternative "new orthodoxy" is represented by the view that
"I am responsible for transforming my understandings through
reflection on experience."

It seems that this difference in perspective is analogous
to the distinction already discussed between surface and deep-
level approaches to learning (Biggs, 1987). However, very little research has been undertaken on the learning approaches
adopted by adults in situations either of autodidaxy or of learner-
control.

> *Recommendation Two:* Researchers should investigate
> with learners their orientation to new learning
> tasks (Häyrynen and Häyrynen, 1980); their ini-
> tial choice of a surface or deep approach and the
> criteria used in arriving at the choice; their personal
> definitions of whether learning is essentially a re-
> productive or a transformational process; and how
> their views change as they engage further in the
> learning process.

The Learner's View of this Specific Learning Endeavor. As I have discussed in Chapter Nine, when a learner is confronting a new learning task, he or she must make some preliminary judgments about how to approach the new domain. The implicit organization of the situation will undoubtedly have an influence, including such tacit dimensions as the degree of structure already present, the nature and amount of assistance available, and other demands such as those of trainers or tests likely to cause situational adjustment. Säljö's distinction between "learning-for-life" and "learning-for-school" and Havighurst's differentiation between "instrumental" and "expressive" forms of learning have already been mentioned. Although these distinctions have been shown to influence learners' approaches to learning tasks, they have been little investigated in adult education, even less in the domain of "self-direction." Thus, the approach that a learner adopts in any particular learning endeavor will be influenced by the sort of purposes the learner has in mind and by his or her level of previous knowledge of this or a similar field.

This is not to say, however, that the learner's intentions cannot change over time. Experience suggests that what starts off as an instrumental project frequently becomes expressive (and sometimes vice versa!). In discussing what they term *self-organized learning,* Harri-Augstein and Thomas (1976) argue that a learner's strategy is developed in the light of the learner's purposes, but that these purposes are not fixed. They write: "A learning event is peculiar. The learner is purposive and yet it is in the nature of learning that you often cannot know what exactly you are going to learn until you have learned it. This means that the purpose can only be specified completely when it has been achieved. . . . Effective learning almost always consists of . . . cycles in which purposes become progressively more clearly articulated, and the outcomes become more precise and determined and well mapped onto purposes" (p. 15).

In researching learning activities, it is important to avoid the assumption that purposes are fixed and external to the learning act itself. For instance, Neimeyer (1985, p. 119), in discussing both the theoretical and methodological crisis in personal construct theory (one branch of interpretivism), writes that "we've still been using, as it were, rather static, cross-section methods. We've found ways of cutting in, putting the slide under microscope. . . . But we haven't found ways of following process, seeing flow, and making sense out of it, which is very dangerous when you're dealing with something that is essentially about flow, essentially about people living over time."

Thus, to develop and refine methods of inquiry that reflect the changing nature of "self-directed" learning is a major challenge for researchers.

> *Recommendation Three:* Researchers could inquire into the changing nature of the learning tasks as learners engage more fully and enter more deeply into the material, and into the changing nature of their motivation toward learning endeavors, both in instructional and autodidactic situations. They could also explore, for individual learners, the relation between these emerging purposes and the strategies the learners employ, especially with respect to the selection and use of resources and assistance.

It is commonly supposed that when learners confront a domain for the first time, they come to it without any prior knowledge, and hence without preconceptions. Yet as I have emphasized throughout this book, this proves to be impossible, especially in adulthood. A person learning a new language must rely on his or her knowledge of other languages for parallels (whether in grammar, syntax, or vocabulary); persons learning about childrearing will conventionally refer to similar experiences, their observations of friends and relations, and perhaps most commonly, the experience of their own upbringing; one who seeks to learn physics as an adult will necessarily fall back on past experience.

In an early experiment in autonomous learning, Mager and Clark (1963, p. 72) comment, clearly with some surprise: "In addition to the results just described a rather nagging phenomenon was repeatedly observed. No matter how ignorant the learners appeared to be, no matter how slowly they appeared to learn, no matter how naive they claimed to be, male or female, subjects all entered the experiment with some relevant knowledge of electronics. Some subjects knew more than others, of course, and one or two had developed some rather interesting misinformation about the subject. Nonetheless, no subject started with zero relevant knowledge."

In recent years, educators have become more aware of the "frames of reference" that learners bring to bear in undertaking new learning tasks. There has recently begun a whole stream of research, particularly in science education, into learners' preexisting understandings of scientific concepts (sometimes referred to as naive theories, misconceptions, or alternate conceptions) and how this affects their classroom learning. In discussing the purpose and implications of this line of research, Driver and Erickson (1983, p. 39) list several underlying assumptions, including the fact that "many students have constructed, from previous physical and linguistic experience, frameworks which can be used to interpret some of the natural phenomena which they study formally in school science classes."

This assumption is neither new nor surprising; indeed it is fundamental to Ausubel's (1968, p. 127) crucial and widely cited notion that "existing cognitive structure is the principal factor influencing meaningful learning and retention." But Driver and Erickson go on to discuss a second assumption: "These student frameworks often result in conceptual confusion, as they lead to different predictions and explanations from those frameworks sanctioned by school science" (p. 39). If an individual learner seeks to subsume new material into existing frameworks, especially without content-oriented guidance from a "teacher," this may well "result in conceptual confusion," especially when his or her existing frameworks "lead to different predictions and explanations" from those common in the field at large.

Recommendation Four: Researchers should use devices such as cognitive maps (Buzan, 1978; Fisher and others, 1987; Novak and Gowin, 1984), repertory grids (Kelly, 1955; Candy, 1990; Candy, Harri-

Augstein, and Thomas, 1985; Thomas and Harri-Augstein, 1985), learning journals, and the like to find out what learners already know about existing domains of knowledge and how they attempt to reconcile new learning with existing views of knowledge.

The Learner's View of Assistance or Direction Received. Learning of any type, including autodidactic learning, is not merely a mechanical function in which a learner deals with abstract bodies of knowledge and inanimate resources. As emphasized throughout this book, it is nearly always carried out in the context of interpersonal relationships, which have a variety of emotional overtones. The relationship between an autodidact and his or her helpers is often vital to the success of a learning project, but relatively little is known about the *quality* of the relationship from the perspective of the parties involved. In part, it might be expected that a learner's views concerning both help required and obtained and direction received would relate to his or her self-concept as a learner. However, researchers have been slow to exploit this dimension of the learner's construing. Accordingly, this section deals with the somewhat neglected personal and interpersonal aspects of autonomous learning.

A beginner in any field is likely to turn for help to those from whom help is to be expected. Past experience is the best initial guide in this. If a learner has successfully used libraries before, she or he might well turn to libraries again. If friends have previously provided the needed support and guidance, then it seems likely, at least initially, that the would-be learner would seek such help again. Although this is just common sense, in the search for underlying patterns, generalizable across situations, researchers have often overlooked the simple fact that, from the point of view of an individual learner, what he or she is attempting is unique, not generalizable.

Research suggests that those autonomous learners with longer exposure to formal education tend to turn to experts, libraries, or teachers to help them when they want to learn something new. On the other hand, a disadvantaged single parent living in an impoverished inner-city area would likely look to friends and relatives for help. What might happen if the situations were reversed, if each learner were forced to rely on the sources of help selected by the other? The disadvantaged learner (who may also have left school at an early age, and mistrust books) would possibly feel confused, anxious, and timid when confronted with book knowledge. He or she would probably dismiss it as abstract, irrelevant, or theoretical. The academically competent learner may feel as out of place, albeit for a different reason, relying for help and guidance on an assortment of well-intentioned but ill-informed acquaintances. What is vital for one learner would be unacceptable to another, and vice versa. The difference resides in the connotation each learner has built up on the basis of his or her past experiences, rather than on any quality inherent in the form of help itself.

> *Recommendation Five:* Instead of striving only for general "laws" concerning assistance with learning projects, researchers could profitably direct their efforts toward exploring with learners: how they construe various forms of assistance; what criteria they use to decide between competing alternatives when the attainment of goals requires some relative loss of autonomy; what criteria they use to distinguish direction from assistance; and what renders one helper acceptable, while another is seen as threatening or inadequate.

Similar comments might be applied to the sort of information sources sought out and utilized by different learners (perhaps books, journals, documentary films, and specialized groups by the one; popular magazines, family members, or neighborhood groups by the other). Previous research has been directed toward identifying either the inherent qualities of various information sources or else the pattern of information sources utilized by particular "types" of learners.

Recommendation Six: Researchers should attempt to explore with learners how they view various learning resources, and in what way(s) some resources are seen as more helpful or more appropriate than others. They should seek to understand, from the learner's point of view, what he or she thinks is required in order to "learn."

Linked to both the assistance sought and resources utilized is the learner's concept of himself or herself as a learner. The point was made in Chapter Four, as well as in Chapter Thirteen, that a learner's self-concept affects the ability to act autonomously. Furthermore, a concept of inadequacy may either be quite generalized (for example, "I'm a failure" or "I couldn't learn if my life depended on it"), or fairly specific (for example, "I can't learn languages" or "I can't do math").

Recommendation Seven: Researchers should examine learners' concepts of themselves as learners. This would include trying to ascertain both generalized and subject-specific images of their learning competence; the origins of such notions in their past; how they change or consolidate their self-concept as a learner during the course of a learning endeavor; the particular points in learning experiences (both autodidactic and instructional) where they felt either especially blocked and incapacitated, or else especially competent and capable; and the cues embedded in the learning situation that they believe inhibit or release their potential for exercising control over the learning situation.

The Learner's View of Autonomous Learning and the Development of Autonomy. One of the most pervasive assumptions in the literature on self-direction is that there exists a connection between the conduct of education and the development and exercise of personal autonomy in some broader sense. For example, this assumption forms the basis of Sneddon's (1930) article, which includes interviews with two hypothetical adult learners whose respective taste for "self-education" had been shaped by their earlier schooling.

In the absence of empirical data, however, this is little more than a "plausible assumption." Skager (1979) calls for longitudinal studies to establish a connection between educational experiences and the "self-directed learning" activities of adults in later life. However, with the exception of two Swedish studies (Borgström, 1985; Borgström and Olofsson, 1983), there is little longitudinal data of any type concerning adults' participation in autodidactic activities, and even less regarding the relationship between educational experiences and personal autonomy in the broader sense. Moreover, in order to test assumptions about situational variability in personal autonomy, it would be necessary to work with adult learners across a range of settings, if possible, matching data about their overt behavior with their subjective evaluation of each situation (Shores, 1985).

> *Recommendation Eight:* Researchers should undertake long-term studies of individual learners with a view to discovering the components of their continuing search for personal autonomy. Researchers should explore with learners their perceptions of the meaning of autonomy, the opportunities for development of autonomy embodied in various instructional techniques, and the factors in a range of situations that learners perceive as either inhibiting or facilitating the development or exercise of autonomy. Such research should include the same learners' views of different learning situations, as well as different learners' views of the same learning experience.

Autonomous Learning from the Facilitator's Perspective

Having argued so strongly for the adoption of an interpretive paradigm, with its emphasis on the personal perspective of the actors, it might seem strange to advocate research based on the facilitator's point of view, especially since one of the major criticisms of present research on learner-control has been its over-emphasis on the teacher's perspective. While this criticism is valid, it is aimed not so much against the inclusion of the teacher's or trainer's perspective, as against the implicit assumption that it is somehow superior, in all respects, to that of the learner.

All instructional situations, including forms of assisted autodidaxy, rest largely on the quality of the relationship established between the learner and the "helper." In turn, such a relationship depends on the facilitator's genuine responsiveness to the needs of the learner. It is not, as some have depicted it, a technical relationship—with the helper acting merely as a resource person—but includes a substantial component of warmth, empathy, authenticity, and interpersonal contact.

Just as learners construe the situation in which they find themselves, and the sort of help given, so do instructors. For instance, I have already discussed J. C. Smith's (1986) study on how various learners present themselves as either "confident" or "timid" learners to librarians, and she even suggests that the librarian's appraisal will influence how he or she might deal with the learner: " 'I'd probably be more motherly to the sort of person who, you know, looks weak and in need of lots of support. I'd be more "jokey" and relaxed with a person who is very confident' " (p. 251).

The constructions that a learner places on a situation—leading him or her to appear timid or confident—influence the constructions that the helper makes, and these in turn affect the sort of help provided. Thus, research from the point of view of the instructor or the helper is not just acceptable, it is positively demanded.

> *Recommendation Nine:* Researchers should study how teachers construe learner autonomy. They should examine the extent to which individual practitioners regard it as a developable capacity, the sort of behaviors they would look for in autonomous learners, and the kinds of practices they believe lead

to an enhanced sense of personal control. Ultimately, such research could be used as a way of exploring the teacher's ideological commitments to personal autonomy as an educational goal.

Such inquiries, especially if conducted in an action reseach framework (Sanders and McCutcheon, 1984), would provide a legitimate focus for in-service professional development. They could also form the basis for meaningful negotiations between teachers and learners with respect to instructional events and strategies, so that the learner's pursuit of autonomy in learning and the teacher's search for enhanced self-knowledge could be explicitly shared goals and form subjects for discussion and analysis by those involved in the teaching/learning situation.

It is also worth considering the advantages of investigating autodidaxy, at least in part, through the eyes of those who assist autodidacts with their projects. Only one piece of research has been discovered that adopts such a perspective. Phillips (1980) pursued doctoral students through three years of their studies, interviewing them at monthly intervals. She also separately interviewed their advisers, although less frequently, and then juxtaposed the perspective of the learner alongside that of the adviser. The differences in their views of the situation were striking and serve to emphasize the need for data derived from the perspective of both parties to the teaching/learning transaction.

Recommendation Ten: Researchers should examine issues such as how the helpers view being approached for assistance, how they construe the learner's need for help, the sort of strategies they employ in trying to meet the learner's needs, and how they sense when the learner is nearing independence and no longer needs their help.

A Note on Research Methodologies

In addition to the major lines of research advocated in this chapter, it seems appropriate to comment on the question of research methodology. If ever there were a topic that lent itself to, or even demanded, an idiographic or case study approach, it must be the phenomenon of self-directed learning. The practice of individuals voluntarily undertaking self-planned and self-managed learning projects, where the initiative and responsibility for the activity rests with the learners, is surely the epitome of individualistic educational endeavor. Hudson (1966, p. 17) puts it well in *Contrary Imaginations:* "There is . . . little merit (and no point) in proposing general ideas about human beings if these are largely or completely mistaken. Nor is there any virtue in claiming that an idea is 'basically right' although obscured by the welter of people's individuality. It is the welter that we must observe and measure. . . ."

Despite this, the number of reported studies that deal adequately with the rich and varied experiences of individual self-directed learners is remarkably small. Instead, many (and perhaps most) researchers ignore or play down individual differences. The issue of research methodology is intimately intertwined with the reframing of research generally, and it is apparent that interpretivism by its nature demands a different *form of inquiry* from that which is common in adult education research generally. The interpretive approach is based on a phenomenological perspective, and, as Bogdan and Taylor (1975, p. 2) state, "The phenomenologist is concerned with *understanding* human behavior from the actor's frame of reference. . . . The phenomenologist examines how the world is experienced. For him or her, the important reality is what people imagine it to be." This perspective calls both for a shift in the sort of questions that are asked and in the perspective from which they are asked. It also demands changes in the modes of inquiry that are used. It does this in two ways.

The first is that, because interpretive research emphasizes the personal meanings of research subjects, it denies the existence of a "correct" or "true" interpretation against which research results might be measured. It admits of the existence and utilization of tacit knowledge; it allows for situational variability; it prefers to have substantive theory emerge from the data; it emphasizes the use of qualitative realities; it endorses idiographic interpretation of data; and it allows for the mutual, simultaneous shaping of entities, including the impact of the researcher on the subjects being researched. Collectively, these features form a mutually interpenetrating network of characteristics that lead to certain modes of inquiry being selected in preference to other, perhaps more familiar, approaches. The interdependence of these assumptions and characteristics means, as Lincoln and Guba (1985, p. 39) point out, that "once one is selected, the others more or less follow." It is not possible to select some of these assumptions (such as the grounded nature of theory), and apply them in a different research paradigm, just as it is inconsistent to import into a naturalistic paradigm research methodologies derived from another set of assumptions (Koetting, 1984, p. 10).

The second reason why different modes of inquiry are demanded is the reflexivity of the paradigm itself. If one makes the assumption that people impose meaning on the events they encounter, that "conception determines perception" (Nystedt and Magnusson, 1982, p. 34), or, as Lincoln and Guba (1985, p. 41) put it, that "believing is seeing," there is no reason to assume that researchers will be exempt from this human tendency. As has been repeatedly shown in the natural sciences, the position of the observer affects the thing being observed, and this is if anything more true in the social and behavioral sciences. Researchers are interpreters too (Heron, 1971), and, instead of opting for the impossible goal of "objectivity," a person espousing such an approach is obliged to adopt modes of inquiry that do not conform to the conventional criteria for trustworthiness. This is not to say that such research cannot be audited or evaluated, but rather that the conventional canons of internal and external validity, reliability, and objectivity are supplanted by substitute criteria of credibility, transferability, dependability, and confirmability (Lincoln and Guba, 1985, p. 43).

The sort of research methods sanctioned by the interpretive approach are naturalistic, which means they "attempt to present 'slice of life' episodes documented through natural language, and representing as closely as possible how people feel, what they know, how they know it, and what their concerns, perceptions and understandings are" (Wolf and Tymitz, 1976–77).

Central to naturalistic modes of inquiry is the "human instrument" (usually the researcher himself or herself), "because it would be virtually impossible to devise *a priori* a non-human instrument with sufficient adaptability to encompass and adjust to the variety of realities that will be encountered" (Lincoln and Guba, 1985, p. 39). This means that the researcher must adapt his or her line of inquiry to the responses and other evidence as they emerge, and must constantly evaluate, assess, and monitor the research process and make adjustments accordingly. As Merriam and others (1983, p. 261) observe, "While other instruments such as surveys, tests or inventories might be used for support, the human investigator possesses several characteristics that can lead to understanding behavior as it occurs in its natural setting."

This gives rise to the second general characteristic of naturalistic inquiry modes, which is that "the researcher physically goes to the site, the group of people, the institution, 'the field' to collect data" (Merriam and others, 1983, p. 261). Basic to constructivism is the context-bound nature of construing, and, so as far as possible, research methodologies based on constructivist assumptions should take place with the "entity-in-context for fullest understanding" (Lincoln and Guba, 1985, p. 39). Naturalistic inquiry rests on the dual assumptions that "human behavior is integrally related to the context in which it occurs, and that this behavior cannot be understood without knowing its meaning for the participants" (Merriam and others, 1983, p. 261). Despite its apparent appropriateness for understanding the phenomena subsumed under the rubric "self-direction," however, relatively few studies on autodidaxy or learner-control have made use of these methodologies: "In our search for generalizable knowledge, we tend to treat everyone or every situation as the same. We fail incessantly to honor uniqueness in our fervor to understand commonness" (Wolf and Tymitz, 1976–77, p. 7).

There are, however, a few studies in this domain that have made use of naturalistic inquiry modes. For autodidaxy, exemplary studies of this type include Danis and Tremblay (1985a, 1985b), Leean and Sisco (1981a), Nolan (1981a), Peters, Johnson, and Lazzara (1981), Spear and Mocker (1981, 1984),

Svensson (1989), and Taylor (1979, 1980, 1986, 1987). In the field of learner-control, excellent studies include Abercrombie and Terry (1978), Boud and Prosser (1980), Marton and Säljö (1976b), Millar, Morphet, and Saddington (1986), Ramsden (1979), Thomas and Harri-Augstein (1983), Torbert (1976, 1978), and Zubir (1983). Each of these studies has the unmistakeable imprint of real people speaking about their world — what Merriam and others (1983, p. 265) would describe as "the ring of reality which is a product of its grounded nature."

Summary and Conclusions

The chapter began with the assertion that research on personal autonomy generally, and autodidaxy and learner-control in particular, has reached something of an impasse, and it was argued that this might be attributable to "slippage" between the research paradigms employed and the nature of the phenomenon being studied. Accordingly, three dominant paradigms in educational research were reviewed — positivist, interpretive, and critical. Each paradigm was considered in turn and its major assumptions explored. It was asserted that research into "self-direction" has been dominated by the positivist paradigm, as has research in education generally. However, positivism has been shown to be inappropriate to the study of many educational phenomena, and it seems that the assumptions of positivism are, if anything, particularly antithetical to those underlying "self-direction." As a consequence, it was proposed that an interpretive approach would be more congenial to the study of "self-direction" in learning.

In the second part of the chapter an attempt was made to advocate research on self-direction within the interpretive paradigm. It was observed that research undertaken and reported from the point of view of the actors in any situation is relatively rare in adult education, and yet such an approach could revitalize research on self-direction. It was stated that, in most learning encounters, the situation may be portrayed either from the perspective of the learner or of the person assisting the learner. Accordingly, recommendations for research were divided into these two different vantage points.

With respect to research from the learner's perspective, four major themes were suggested: (1) the learner's views of learning in general, (2) his or her intentions or purposes in the situation, (3) his or her attitudes toward direction or assistance, and (4) views of autonomous learning and the development of personal autonomy. What is argued for in this chapter is neither the study of the situation per se nor of the learner, but rather of the learner in the situation. This was the focus of Shores's (1985) dissertation, but little research has been undertaken concerning the learner's "in-context" construing of autodidaxy or of the dimensions of learner-control. This chapter has identified a number of research areas that, if implemented, could lead to a new focus by researchers on the dynamics of autonomous learning.

It was also suggested that research on autonomous learning could be framed from the point of view of the person or people providing the learner with assistance. It was argued that this perspective is neither more nor less valid than that of the learner, but provides a different and complementary vantage point from which issues of autonomy and self-direction can be explored.

For the sake of exposition, the issue of teachers' and learners' conceptions was subdivided into manageable components: views of knowledge, of resources, of assistance given or received, of self-as-learner, and of the process of learning itself. But the interpretive approach, by its nature, abhors this sort of fragmentation. Instead, it endorses the notion that a person's construction of a situation comprises an integrated whole. One of the criticisms that has been made of the positivist paradigm is the tendency of the latter to alienate research subjects from their contexts, and further to compartmentalize the experiences and perspectives of subjects in artificial ways. Interpretive researchers on the other hand seek to understand how a person construes a situation in all its complexity — what is regarded as salient, what connections and relationships are perceived by the person himself or herself. One particularly challenging aspect is the need to develop research approaches that reflect the dynamic and constantly changing nature of learning endeavors (that is, that function more like a movie than a snapshot) and that ideally involve the learners themselves in exploring and challenging aspects of their taken-for-granted worldview (Dorsey, Manning, and Shindell, 1989).

Overall, this chapter suggests the acceptance of the "person-in-context" as the main unit of analysis. It calls for the attempt to understand how, in any particular situation, self-concept, overall orientation toward learning, shifting patterns of purposes, and frames of reference all interact to create the anticipatory schemes, and influence the strategies used, by either the learner or his or her assistants. If the findings derived from research of this type were integrated with the existing body of knowledge about self-direction, the result would be a comprehensive picture of self-directed learning in a variety of contexts: one panel in the rich and varied tapestry of human learning in the life span.

Resource:
A Profile of
the Autonomous Learner

Although composite profiles do not account for significant differences between situations, researchers have identified well over 100 competencies that they have linked with successful independent learning. What follows is a composite list, with the various attributes, characteristics, qualities, and competencies grouped together into "families," based on qualitative similarities. The authors are indicated to the right.

The learner capable of autonomous learning will characteristically:

Be Methodical/Disciplined

Have direction [Chickering, 1964]
Be able to focus on an area of interest [Margarones, 1965]
Exercise self-discipline [Della Dora and Blanchard, 1979]
Develop individual plans for achieving goals [Flanagan, 1970]
Be able to analyze and plan the entire learning process and to manage it dynamically [Gibbons and Phillips, 1979; Tough, 1979d]
Plan learning a long time ahead [Kasworm (after Tough), 1983b; Maras, 1978]
Plan ahead [Margarones, 1965; Wedemeyer, 1973]
Make effective use of time [Kasworm (after Tough), 1983b; Wedemeyer, 1973]

Establish personal priorities [Wedemeyer, 1973]

Have a sense of what is important [Chickering, 1964]

Translate needs into specifiable objectives [Caffarella, 1983]

Pay close attention to details of an ongoing project [Margarones, 1965]

Be able to organize [Chickering, 1964]

Be able to develop sequential plans based on clear objectives [Flanagan, 1970; Gibbons and Phillips, 1979]

Maintain detailed and accurate records of the learning project [Margarones, 1965]

Be Logical/Analytical

Be attuned to the whole [Chickering, 1964]

Be able to organize his/her thoughts [Jankovic and others, 1979]

Form generalizations, look for principles, and find basic structures of subjects [Knowles, 1984; Wedemeyer, 1973]

Enjoy questioning, testing, and analyzing [Wedemeyer, 1973]

Be able to analyze and define problems [Flanagan, 1970]

Be able to develop criteria for selecting among alternative solutions [Flanagan, 1970]

Be able to break general goals down into specific objectives and define explicit criteria for their achievement [Moore, 1980]

Engage in logical reasoning [Knowles, 1984]

Draw inferences and conclusions [Margarones, 1965]

Be able to organize data [Knowles, 1984]

Be able to analyze data and see relationships [Knowles, 1984; Margarones, 1965]

Be able to identify underlying assumptions [Margarones, 1965]

Be able to go beyond simple findings to see implications [Margarones, 1965]

Be Reflective/Self-Aware

Be able to identify needs when he or she encounters a problem to be solved, a skill to be acquired, or information to be obtained [Moore, 1980]

Decide what knowledge and skills to learn [Caffarella, 1983]

Have access to alternative perspectives for undertanding his or her situation [Mezirow, 1981]

Identify personal learning objectives [Kasworm (after Tough), 1983b]

Have an awareness of the constraints on their learning— including psychocultural assumptions (Mezirow, 1981]

Be able to diagnose current problems or needs [Tough, 1979d]

Have a self-concept as an effective learner [Guglielmino, 1977]

Clarify his or her values and establish goals consistent with those values [Della Dora and Blanchard, 1979]

Understand his or her own learning style and be willing to try others [Della Dora and Blanchard, 1979; Tough, 1979d]

Know his or her strengths and weaknesses [Chickering, 1964]

Recognize when help is needed [Chickering, 1964]

Understand his or her own values, interests, abilities, and knowledge [Flanagan, 1970]

Understand what he or she wishes to be as an adult human being [Strong, 1977]

Demonstrate Curiosity/Openness/Motivation

Be self-starting [Chickering, 1964]

Be curious, with a continual need to learn [Tremblay and Danis, 1984]

Be curious about a variety of phenomena [Knowles, 1984; Miller, 1964]

Be "cognitively open" with regard to phenomena [Miller, 1964; Wedemeyer, 1973]

Have a field of particular interest, and a desire to "own" the project [Margarones, 1965; Miller, 1964]

Have a taste for learning [Guglielmino, 1977; Jankovic and others, 1979]

Be open to new learning opportunities [Chickering, 1964; Guglielmino, 1977]

Be future oriented [Guglielmino, 1977]

Discover through investigation [Chickering, 1964]

Confront questions and problems willingly [Chickering, 1964]

Be Flexible

Be able to learn in many situations — from conversations, by reading, and by observation [Kasworm (after Tough), 1983b; Miller, 1964]

Be able to learn from listening, taking notes, reading, or memorizing [Tough, 1979d]

Stick to plans — modifying as necessary [Wedemeyer, 1973]

Be flexible in view of new evidence and changing circumstances [Chickering, 1964; Margarones, 1965]

Be able to modify his or her own behavior through an understanding of behavior modification [Flanagan, 1970]

Be able to accept or reject material [Moore, 1980]

Be able to achieve or abandon goals [Moore, 1980]

Be Interdependent/Interpersonally Competent

Be amiable and peace loving [Chickering, 1964]

Have sensitivity and competence in social interactions [Mezirow, 1981]

Have sustained relationships with faculty members [Maras, 1978]

Develop small, stable groups of friends [Maras, 1978]

Be able to work cooperatively with others, yet enjoy being on his or her own in learning [Chickering, 1964; Wedemeyer, 1973]

Be willing and able to learn from others [Della Dora and Blanchard, 1979]

Be willing and able to learn with others and to share ideas [Della Dora and Blanchard, 1979; Margarones, 1965]

Develop group plans for achieving goals [Della Dora and Blanchard, 1979]

Know how and when to ask for help or direction [Caffarella, 1983; Della Dora and Blanchard, 1979; Kasworm (after Tough), 1983b]

Analyze group dynamics and become capable of using group decision-making processes [Della Dora and Blanchard, 1979]

Diagnose learning needs with help from teachers and peers [Caffarella, 1983]

Relate to teachers as facilitators [Caffarella, 1983]

Be able to secure cooperation, support, and encouragement from advisers [Margarones, 1965]

Relate to peers collaboratively as resources [Caffarella, 1983]

Be able to relate to people of differing ages and to assume a variety of roles successfully [Gibbons and Phillips, 1979]

Be Persistent/Responsible

Be emotionally stable, objective, and impartial [Margarones, 1965]

Be serious, committed, and organized [Maras, 1978]

Be self-regulating and systematic in work [Margarones, 1965]

Be able to assume academic responsibility (that is, be syllabus free) [Maras, 1978]

Be capable of intellectual concentration [Jankovic and others, 1979]

Have an informed acceptance of the responsibility for his or her own learning [Della Dora and Blanchard, 1979; Guglielmino, 1977]

Stick to plans — modifying as a necessary [Wedemeyer, 1973]

Renew motivation for learning as required [Caffarella, 1983; Kasworm (after Tough), 1983b]

Have a tolerance for frustration [Margarones, 1965]

Be able to "stick to" a position [Chickering, 1964]

Have energy and determination at a job [Chickering, 1964]

Detect and cope with personal and situational blocks to learning [Caffarella, 1983; Kasworm (after Tough), 1983b]
Have knowledge of social barriers facing the learner [Ford, 1971]
Work to resolve problems [Moore, 1980]

Be Venturesome/Creative

Be able to develop new conceptual frameworks [Margarones, 1965]
Be capable of original thinking [Torrance and Mourad, 1978]
Be able to produce analogies [Torrance and Mourad, 1978]
Be creative [Guglielmino, 1977; Torrance and Mourad, 1978]
Construct and develop special materials and devices [Margarones, 1965]
Have a right hemisphere style of learning and thinking [Torrance and Mourad, 1978]
Be unafraid of "being different" [Wedemeyer, 1973]
Be able to discover new possibilities [Chickering, 1964]
Be able to develop alternative solutions to problems [Flanagan, 1970]
Engage in divergent thinking [Knowles, 1984]
Be intuitive [Tremblay and Danis, 1984]
Be a risk taker (but often lack confidence) [Tremblay and Danis, 1984]

Show Confidence/Have a Positive Self-Concept

Be able to disagree [Chickering, 1964]
Be unafraid of "being different" [Wedemeyer, 1973]
Be able to "stick to" a position [Chickering, 1964]
Work for his or her own satisfaction [Chickering, 1964]
Have quiet self-confidence [Chickering, 1964]
Know how to achieve his or her goals and objectives [Strong, 1977]

Pursue excellence based on personal standards [Strong, 1977]

Project to the world a clarity of purpose [Strong, 1977]

Be Independent/Self-Sufficient

Relate to others without depending on them [Chickering, 1964]

Have skills to study independently — reading, writing, listening, reflective thinking, use of time, and self-motivation [Ford, 1971]

Be able to work autonomously [Jankovic and others, 1979]

Take initiative and work independently in learning [Guglielmino, 1977]

Be able to work cooperatively with others, yet enjoy being on his or her own in learning [Wedemeyer, 1973]

Have Developed Information Seeking and Retrieval Skills

Intelligently select and use most relevant sources of information [Margarones, 1965]

Identify, and know how to use, resources appropriate to different kinds of learning objectives [Caffarella, 1983; Della Dora and Blanchard, 1979; Knowles, 1984; Moore, 1980; Tough, 1979d]

Be able to establish feedback mechanisms for day-to-day performance [Caffarella, 1983; Tough, 1979d]

Be able to choose relevant resources, on the basis of needs, potentialities, objectives, means, and limitations [Jankovic and others, 1979]

Be able to "dig up" material [Chickering, 1964]

Know of available opportunities [Ford, 1971]

Have Knowledge About, and Skill at, "Learning Processes"

Be capable of reporting what he or she has learned in a variety of ways [Della Dora and Blanchard, 1979; Margarones, 1965]

Be able to decode a message — textual, auditory, or visual [Jankovic and others, 1979]

Be able to collect information using appropriate tools and instruments [Margarones, 1965]

Have skills and competencies required to master productive tasks [Mezirow, 1981; Moore, 1980]

Be able to understand learning and behavior change [Tough, 1979d]

Be able to use basic study and problem-solving skills [Caffarella, 1983; Gibbons and Phillips, 1979; Guglielmino, 1977]

Enjoy reading, writing, listening, and discussing [Gibbons and Phillips, 1979; Wedemeyer, 1973]

Have developed skills in note taking, remembering, and relating [Wedemeyer, 1973]

Be able to gain knowledge and skills from resources [Caffarella, 1983]

Know how to use resources for learning [Chickering, 1964]

Conduct learning activities [Kasworm (after Tough), 1983b]

Develop and Use Criteria for Evaluating

Be able to select what is of value from the mass of information available [Jankovic and others, 1979]

Participate in diagnosing, prescribing, and evaluating his or her own progress [Caffarella, 1983; Della Dora and Blanchard, 1979; Jankovic and others, 1979; Kasworm (after Tough), 1983b]

Be able to evaluate the appropriateness of new skills, the adequacy of solutions, or the quality of new ideas and knowledge [Moore, 1980]

Be able to evaluate data [Knowles, 1984]

Evaluate learning activities [Kasworm (after Tough), 1983b]

References

Aaltonen, R. "The Educational and Cultural Activities of Adults in a Rural Area: The Rantasalmi Case." *Adult Education in Finland,* 1979, *16* (4), 14–21.

Abe, D., Henner-Stanchina, C., and Smith, P. "New Approaches to Autonomy: Two Experiments in Self-Directed Learning." *Mélanges Pédagogiques — 1975.* Nancy, France: Centre de Recherches et d'Applications Pédagogiques en Langues, Université de Nancy, 1975.

Abercrombie, M.L.J. "Changing Basic Assumptions About Teaching and Learning." In D. J. Boud (ed.), *Developing Student Autonomy in Learning.* London: Kogan Page, 1981.

Abercrombie, M.L.J., and Terry, P. M. "Reactions to Change in the Authority-Dependency Relationship." *British Journal of Guidance and Counselling,* 1978, *6* (1), 82-94.

Adams, H. *The Education of Henry Adams.* New York: Modern Library, 1931.

Addleton, R. L., Jr. "Self-Directed Learning Projects of Continuing Educators in Selected Alabama Four Year Colleges and Universities." Unpublished doctoral dissertation, University of Alabama, 1984. *(Dissertation Abstracts International, 44* (10A), 2988.)

Adekanmbi, G. "The Concept of Distance in Self-Directed Learning." Paper presented at third North American Symposium on Adult Self-Directed Learning, Oklahoma Research Center for Continuing Professional and Higher Education, Norman, Feb. 1989.

Ainsworth, D. "Self-Instruction Blues." *Journal of Higher Education,* 1976, *47* (3), 275–287.

Alanen, A. "Lifelong Education — Permanent Education — Recurrent Education." *Adult Education in Finland,* 1982, *19* (2) (entire issue).

Alexander, K.J.W., and others. *Adult Education: The Challenge of Change.* Report to the Scottish Education Department by a Committee of Inquiry appointed by the Secretary of State for Scotland. Edinburgh: Her Majesty's Stationery Office, 1975.

Alexander, P. A., and Judy, J. E. "The Interaction of Domain-Specific and Strategic Knowledge in Academic Performance." *Review of Educational Research,* 1988, *58* (4), 375–404.

Allerton, T. D. "Selected Characteristics of the Learning Projects Pursued by Parish Ministers in the Louisville Metropolitan Area." Unpublished doctoral dissertation, School of Education, University of Georgia, 1974. *(Dissertation Abstracts International, 35* (10A), 6422.)

Allport, G. W. *Becoming: Basic Considerations for a Psychology of Personality.* New Haven, Conn.: Yale University Press, 1955.

Anderson, J. "Informal Adult Education in the Classical World." In A. Powell (ed.), *Adult Education Papers and Abstracts.* Manchester: Department of Adult Education, University of Manchester, 1974.

Anderson, R. C. "The Notion of Schemata and the Educational Enterprise." In R. C. Anderson, R. J. Spiro, and W. E. Montague (eds.), *Schooling and the Acquisition of Knowledge.* Hillsdale, N.J.: Erlbaum, 1977.

Anderson, W. R., and Bruce, S. W. "A Plan for Matching Learning and Teaching Styles." In *Student Learning Styles: Diagnosing and Prescribing Programs.* Reston, Va.: National Association of Secondary School Principals, 1979.

Angyal, A. *Foundations for a Science of Personality.* New York: Commonwealth Fund, 1941.

Argyris, C., and Schön, D. A. *Theory in Practice: Increasing Professional Effectiveness.* San Francisco: Jossey-Bass, 1974.

Armstrong, D. P. "Adult Learners of Low Educational Attainment: The Self-Concepts, Background and Educative Behavior of Average and High-Learning Adults of Low Educational Attainment." Unpublished doctoral dissertation, University of Toronto, 1971. *(Dissertation Abstracts International, 33* (03A), 944.)

Aroskar, M. A. "Attaining Autonomy Through Curriculum Planning in Nursing." Unpublished doctoral dissertation, State University of New York–Buffalo, 1976. *(Dissertation Abstracts International, 37* (01A), 106.)

Auchmuty, J. J., and others. *Report of the National Inquiry into Teacher Education.* Canberra: Australian Government Publishing Service, 1980.

Ausubel, D. P. *Educational Psychology: A Cognitive View.* New York: Holt, Rinehart & Winston, 1968.

Baghi, H. "The Major Learning Efforts of Participants in Adult Basic Education Classes and Learning Centers." Unpublished doctoral dissertation, Iowa State University, 1979. *(Dissertation Abstracts International, 40* (05A), 2410.)

Bagnall, R. G. "Enhancing Self-Direction in Adult Education: A Possible Trap for Enthusiasts." *Discourse: The Australian Journal of Educational Studies,* 1987, *8* (1), 90–100.

Bagnall, R. G. "Educational Distance from the Perspective of Self-Direction: An Analysis." *Open Learning,* 1989, *4* (1), 21–26.

Baird, J. R., and Mitchell, I. J. *Improving the Quality of Teaching and Learning: An Australian Case Study — The PEEL Project.* Melbourne, Australia: PEEL Group, Monash University, 1986.

Bandura, A. "Self-Referent Thought: A Developmental Analysis of Self-Efficacy." In J. H. Flavell and L. R. Ross (eds.), *Cognitive Social Development: Frontiers and Possible Futures.* New York: Cambridge University Press, 1981.

Banks, S. "Informal Learning in Self-Help Groups: A Qualitative Research Study of the Remobilization and Development of Coping Competencies in Two Stroke Clubs." Unpublished master's thesis, Dalhousie University, 1985.

Bantock, G. H. "Educational Research: A Criticism." *Harvard Educational Review,* 1961, *31* (3) 264–280.

Bargar, R. R., and Duncan, J. K. "Cultivating Creative Endeavor in Doctoral Research." *Journal of Higher Education,* 1982, *53* (1), 1–31.

Bargar, R. R., and Mayo-Chamberlain, J. "Advisor and Advisee Issues in Doctoral Education." *Journal of Higher Education,* 1983, *54* (4), 407–432.

Barrows, H. S., and Tamblyn, R. M. *Problem-Based Learning: An Approach to Medical Education.* New York: Springer, 1980.

Barshinger, C. E. "Existential Psychology and Christian Faith." In J. W. Montgomery (ed.), *Christianity for the Tough-Minded: Essays in Support of an Intellectually Defensible Religious Commitment.* Minneapolis, Minn.: Bethany Fellowship, 1973.

Barth, R. S. *Open Education.* New York: Agathon Press, 1972.

Bauman, Z. *Hermeneutics and Social Science: Approaches to Understanding.* London: Hutchinson University Library, 1978.

Bayha, R. A. "Self-Directed Learning Readiness of Northwest Missouri Farmers as Related to Learning Resource Choice and Valuing." Unpublished doctoral dissertation, Kansas State University, 1983. *(Dissertation Abstracts International, 45* (01A), 50.)

Beach, L. R. "The Use of Instructorless Small Groups in a Social Psychology Course. Paper presented at 41st annual meeting of the Western Psychology Association, Seattle, Wash., June 1961.

Beach, L. R. "Self-Directed Student Groups and College Learning." In W. R. Hatch and A. L. Richards (eds.), *Approach to Independent Study.* New Dimensions in Higher Education, no. 13. Washington, D.C.: U.S. Department of Health, Education, and Welfare, 1965.

Beail, N. (ed.). *Repertory Grid Technique and Personal Constructs: Applications in Clinical and Educational Settings.* London: Croom Helm, 1985.

Beck, J. E. "Changing Construing by Experiential Learning Methods: A Framework for Research." Paper presented at third international congress on Personal Construct Psychology, Breukelen, The Netherlands, July, 1979.

Becker, H., Geer, B., and Hughes, F. *Making the Grade: The Academic Side of College Life.* New York: Wiley, 1968.

Beder, H. W., Darkenwald, G., and Valentine, T. Self-Planned Professional Learning Among Public School Adult Education Directors: A Social Network Analysis." Proceedings of 24th annual Adult Education Research Conference, University of Montreal, Apr. 1983, 7–12.

Bejot, D. D. "The Degree of Self-Directedness and the Choice of Learning Methods as Related to a Co-operative Extension Program." Unpublished doctoral Dissertation, Iowa State

University, 1981. *(Dissertation Abstracts International, 42* (06A), 2434.)

Bellah, R. N., and others. *Habits of the Heart: Individualism and Commitment in American Life.* Berkeley: University of California Press, 1985.

Benn, S. I. "Freedom, Autonomy and the Concept of the Person." *Aristotelian Society Proceedings, new series,* 1976, *76* (6), 109–130.

Benson, F. B., Jr. "Learning Projects of Selected Administrators in Tennessee Colleges and Universities." Unpublished doctoral dissertation, School of Education, University of Tennessee, 1974. (*Dissertation Abstracts International, 35* (08A), 4958.)

Berger, P. L., and Luckmann, T. *The Social Construction of Reality.* Harmondsworth, England: Penguin Books, 1967.

Berkeley, G. *A Treatise Concerning the Principles of Human Knowledge.* Dublin: Papyat, 1710.

Bernard, D., and Papagiannis, G. J. "Educational Diversification in Less-Industrialized Countries: A Sociolinguistic Approach in the Study of Nonformal Education." In J. C. Bock and G. J. Papagiannis (eds.), *Nonformal Education and National Development: A Critical Assessment of Policy, Research, and Practice.* New York: Praeger, 1983.

Bernstein, B. *Class, Codes and Control.* Vol. 3. (2nd ed.) London: Routledge and Kegan Paul, 1977.

Biggs, J. B. "Individual Differences in Study Processes and the Quality of Learning Outcomes." *Higher Education,* 1979, *8* (4), 381–394.

Biggs, J. B. "The Role of Metacognition in Enhancing Learning Skills." Proceedings of the annual conference of the Australian Association for Research in Education, Hobart, Nov. 1985, 39–42.

Biggs, J. B. "Enhancing Learning Skills: The Role of Metacognition." In J. A. Bowden (ed.), *Student Learning: Research into Practice — The Marysville Symposium.* Parkville, Australia: Centre for the Study of Higher Education, University of Melbourne, 1986.

Biggs, J. B. *Student Approaches to Learning and Studying.* Melbourne: Australian Council for Educational Research, 1987.

Birge, L. E. "The Evolution of American Public Library Services to Adult Independent Learners." Unpublished doctoral dissertation, Arizona State University, 1979. (*Dissertation Abstracts International, 40* (03A), 1133.)

Birge, L. E. *Serving Adult Learners: A Public Library Tradition.* Chicago: American Library Association, 1981.

Birren, J. E., and Hedlund, B. "The Metaphors of Aging and the Self-Constructing Individual." In J. E. Thornton (ed.), *Aging as Metaphor.* Proceedings of a conference held at the University of British Columbia, Vancouver, July 1984.

Bivens, L. W., Campbell, V. N., and Terry, D. F. *Self-Direction in Programmed Instruction: Effects on Learning in Low Ability Students.* Final report of project no. AIR-DIO 7/63-TR. Washington, D.C.: Office of Education, U.S. Department of Health, Education, and Welfare, 1964.

Black, M. *Models and Metaphors: Studies in Language and Philosophy.* Ithaca, N.Y.: Cornell University Press, 1962.

Blackburn, D. J. "Method Orientations of Adults for Participation in Educative Activities." Unpublished doctoral dissertation, University of Wisconsin, 1967. (*Dissertation Abstracts International, 28* (08A), 2971–2972.)

Blaney, J. "Program Development and Curricular Authority." In J. Blaney, I. Housego, and G. McIntosh (eds.), *A Monograph on Program Development in Education.* Vancouver: Centre for Continuing Education, University of British Columbia, 1974.

Block, J. H. (ed.), *Mastery Learning.* New York: Holt, Rinehart & Winston, 1971.

Bock, J. "Institutionalization of Nonformal Education." *Comparative Education Review,* 1976, *20* (3), 346–367.

Bodi, S. "Critical Thinking and Bibliographic Instruction: The Relationship." *Journal of Academic Librarianship,* 1988, *14* (3), 150–153.

Bogdan, R., and Taylor, S. J. *Introduction to Qualitative Research Methods: A Phenomenological Approach to the Social Sciences.* New York: Wiley, 1975.

Bogenschneider, K. "Learning Patterns of Mothers of Young Children in a Rural Wisconsin County." Unpublished master's thesis, University of Wisconsin, 1977.

Bolton, E. B. "A Conceptual Analysis of the Mentor Relationship in the Career Development of Women." *Adult Education (U.S.),* 1980, *30* (4), 195–207.

Bonneau, C. "Les activités éducatives de femmes célibataires ou divorcées parents uniques" [The educational activities of unmarried or divorced women who are single parents]. Mémoire de maîtrise inédit. Université de Montreal, 1984.

Bonthius, R. H., Davis, F. J., and Drushal, J. G. *The Independent Study Program in the United States: A Report on an Undergraduate Instructional Method.* New York: Columbia University Press, 1957.

Boot, R., and Reynolds, M. "Learning and Experience—Themes and Issues." In R. Boot and M. Reynolds (eds.), *Learning and Experience in Formal Education.* Manchester, England: Department of Adult and Higher Education, University of Manchester, 1983.

Booth, N. "Information Resource Utilization and the Learning Efforts of Low Income Urban Adults." Unpublished doctoral dissertation, University of Maryland, 1979a. (*Dissertation Abstracts International, 40* (06A), 3048.)

Booth, N. "Information Resource Utilization and the Learning Efforts of Low Income Urban Adults." Paper presented at the 20th annual Adult Education Research Conference, Ann Arbor, Mich., Apr. 1979b, 100–105.

Borgström, L. "Self-Directed Learning and the Reproduction of Inequalities." Unpublished manuscript, Department of Educational Research, Stockholm Institute of Education, Stockholm, Sweden, 1985.

Borgström, L., and Olofsson, L.-E. "Participation in Study Circles and the Creation of Individual Resources." Proceedings of 24th annual Adult Education Research Conference, Montreal, Apr. 1983, 13–19.

Borko, H. "An Examination of Some Factors Contributing to Teachers' Preinstructional Classroom Organizational and Management Decisions." Paper presented at the 59th annual conference of the American Educational Research Association, Toronto, Mar. 1978.

Boshier, R. W. *Education Participation Scale.* Vancouver: Learning Press, 1982.

Boshier, R. W. "Adult Learning Projects Research: An Alchemist's Fantasy?" Invited address to 64th annual conference of the American Educational Research Association, Montreal, Apr. 1983.

Botkin, J., Elmandjra, M., and Malitza, M. *No Limits to Learning: Bridging the Human Gap.* Oxford: Pergamon Press, 1979.

Boucouvalas, M., and Pearse, P. "Self-Directed Learning in an Other-Directed Environment: The Role of Correctional Education in a Learning Society." *Journal of Correctional Education,* 1982, *32* (4), 31–35.

Boud, D. J. "Toward Student Responsibility for Learning." In D. J. Boud (ed.), *Developing Student Autonomy in Learning.* London: Kogan Page, 1981.

Boud, D. J. "Is Scientific Research an Appropriate Model for Research in Adult Education? A Search for Alternatives." *Studies in Continuing Education,* 1983, *9,* 41–55.

Boud, D. J., and Bridge, W. "Keller Plan: A Case Study in Individualised Learning." In Nuffield Foundation Group for Research and Innovation in Higher Education, *Towards Independence in Learning.* Paper no. 5.1. London: Nuffield Foundation, 1975.

Boud, D. J., and Griffin, V. *Appreciating Adults Learning: From the Learners' Perspective.* London: Kogan Page, 1987.

Boud, D. J., Keogh, R., and Walker, D. (eds.). *Reflection: Turning Experience into Learning.* London: Kogan Page, 1985.

Boud, D. J., and Prosser, M. T. "Sharing Responsibility: Staff-Student Cooperation in Learning." *British Journal of Educational Technology,* 1980, *11* (1), 24–35.

Bourdieu, P. "Cultural Reproduction and Social Reproduction." In R. Brown (ed.), *Knowledge, Education and Social Change.* London: Tavistock, 1973. (First published in French 1970.)

Bourdieu, P. *Outline of a Theory of Practice.* Cambridge: Cambridge University Press, 1977. (First published in French 1972.)

Bouwman, P. J. "Self-Education in Time Perspective Since the Ancient World (from 500 A. D.)." Unpublished doctoral dissertation, University of South Africa, 1982. (*Dissertation Abstracts International, 44* (08A), 2385.)

Bova, B. M., and Phillips, R. R. "Mentoring as a Learning

Experience for Adults." *Journal of Teacher Education,* 1984, *35* (3), 16–20.

Bova, B. M., and Phillips, R. R. "Adulthood: Definitions and Perspectives." Proceedings of the 26th annual Adult Education Research Conference, Arizona State University-Tempe, Mar. 1985, 38–41.

Bowers, J., and Fisher, E. A. la S. "The Search for a Terminology of Adult Education and for Better Statistics: Exploration in a Semantic Jungle." *Convergence: An International Journal of Adult Education,* 1972, *5* (4), 44–49.

Bowles, S., and Gintis, H. *Schooling in Capitalist America.* New York: Basic Books, 1976.

Box, B. J. "Self-Directed Learning Readiness of Students and Graduates of an Associate Degree Nursing Program." Unpublished doctoral dissertation, Oklahoma State University, 1982. (*Dissertation Abstracts International, 44* (03A), 679.)

Boyd, E. M., and Fales, A. W. "Reflective Learning: Key to Learning from Experience." *Journal of Humanistic Psychology,* 1983, *23* (2), 99–117.

Boyd, R. D., Apps, J. W., and Associates. *Redefining the Discipline of Adult Education.* San Francisce: Jossey-Bass, 1980.

Boyle, P. G. *Planning Better Programs.* New York: McGraw-Hill, 1981.

Brabner, G. *The Decline of Pedagocentricity.* The Educational Technology Review Series, no. 5: *Individualizing Instruction.* Englewood Cliffs, N. J.: Educational Technology Publications, 1973.

Bradwin, E. *The Bunkhouse Man.* New York: Columbia University Press, 1928. (Reissued with an introduction by J. Burnet, Toronto: University of Toronto Press, 1972.)

Bravay, F. "Étude de la formation extra-scolaire dispensée à des femmes en milieu rural camerounais." [Study of out-of-school learning undertaken by rural Cameroon women]. Thèse de doctorat inédite, Université de Montréal, 1983.

Brillinger, M. E. "Individuals' Intentional Changes Related to Marriage." Unpublished doctoral dissertation, University of Toronto, 1983. (*Dissertation Abstracts International, 44* (09A), 2651.)

Brockett, R. G. "Self-Directed Learning Readiness and Life Satisfaction Among Older Adults." Unpublished doctoral dissertation, Syracuse University, 1982. (*Dissertation Abstracts International, 44* (01A), 42.)

Brockett, R. G. "The Relationship Between Life Satisfaction and Self-Directedness Among Older Adults." Proceedings of the fifth Lifelong Learning Research Conference, University of Maryland, Feb. 1983a, 16–20. College Park: Department of Agriculture and Extension Education, University of Maryland. (ERIC Document Reproduction Service no. ED 226 228.)

Brockett, R. G. "Self-Directed Learning and the Hard-to-Reach Adult." *Lifelong Learning: The Adult Years,* 1983b, *6* (8), 16–18.

Brockett, R. G. "Methodological and Substantive Issues in the Measurement of Self-Directed Learning Readiness." *Adult Education Quarterly,* 1985a, *36* (1), 15–24.

Brockett, R. G. "The Relationship Between Self-Directed Learning Readiness and Life-Satisfaction Among Older Adults." *Adult Education Quarterly,* 1985b, *35* (4), 210–219.

Brockett, R. G. "A Response to Brookfield's Critical Paradigm of Self-Directed Adult Learning." *Adult Education Quarterly,* 1985c, *36* (1), 55–59.

Brookfield, S. D. "Supporting Autonomous Adult Learning Groups." *Adult Education (U. K.),* 1979, *51* (6), 366–369.

Brookfield, S. D. "Independent Adult Learning." Unpublished doctoral dissertation, University of Leicester, 1980a.

Brookfield, S. D. "The Nature of Independent Adult Learning." *Continuing Education (National Extension College, Cambridge),* 1980b, *3,* 2–3.

Brookfield, S. D. "The Adult Learning Iceberg: A Critical Review of the Work of Allen Tough." *Adult Education (U. K.),* 1981a, *54* (2), 110–118.

Brookfield, S. D. "Independent Adult Learning." *Studies in Adult Education,* 1981b, *13* (1), 15–27.

Brookfield, S. D. *Independent Adult Learning.* Adults: Psychological and Educational Perspectives, no. 7. Nottingham, England: Department of Adult Education, University of Nottingham, 1982a.

Brookfield, S. D. "Successful Independent Learning of Adults of Low Educational Attainment in Britain: A Parallel Educational Universe." Proceedings of 23rd annual Adult Educational Research Conference, University of Nebraska, Lincoln, Apr. 1982b, 48–53.

Brookfield, S. D. *Adult Learners, Adult Education and the Community.* Milton Keynes, England: Open University Press, 1983.

Brookfield, S. D. "Self-Directed Adult Learning: A Critical Paradigm." *Adult Education Quarterly,* 1984a, *35* (2), 59–71.

Brookfield, S. D. "Self-Directed Adult Learning: A Critique of Research and Theory." Proceedings of 25th annual Adult Education Research Conference, North Carolina State University, Raleigh, Apr. 1984b, 14–19.

Brookfield, S. D. "Analyzing a Critical Paradigm of Self-Directed Learning: A Response." *Adult Education Quarterly,* 1985a, *36* (1), 60–64.

Brookfield, S. D. (ed.) *Self-Directed Learning: From Theory to Practice.* New Directions for Continuing Education, no. 25, San Francisco: Jossey-Bass, 1985b.

Brookfield, S. D. "Self-Directed Learning: A Conceptual and Methodological Exploration." *Studies in the Education of Adults,* 1985c, *17* (1), 19–32.

Brookfield, S. D. "Decoding Television: Developing Media Literacy in Adults." Proceedings of 27th annual Adult Education Research Conference, Syracuse University, May 1986, 25–30.

Brookfield, S. D. *Developing Critical Thinkers: Challenging Adults to Explore Alternative Ways of Thinking and Acting.* San Francisco: Jossey-Bass, 1987.

Brown, C. "Confessions of an Autodidact." *Adult Education (U. K.),* 1983, *56* (3) 227–232.

Brown, J. S., Collins, A., and Duguid, P. "Situated Cognition and the Culture of Learning." *Educational Researcher,* 1989, *18* (1), 32–42.

Brown, M. J. "Adult Education Among Members of a North Vancouver Labour Union." Unpublished master's thesis, University of British Columbia, 1972.

Brown, R. K. "Increasing Competence in Self-Directed Learning: An Exploratory Study in the Teaching of Biology." Unpublished doctoral dissertation, University of Illinois–Urbana-Champaign, 1966. (*Dissertation Abstracts International, 27* (03A), 697.)

Brown, V. A. "The Self-Directed Learner: An Undiscovered Species?" In A. H. Miller (ed.), *Freedom and Control in Higher Education*. Research and Development in Higher Education, vol. 3. Sydney, Australia: Higher Education Research and Development Society of Australasia, 1980.

Bruner, J. S. "Going Beyond the Information Given." In J. S. Bruner and others (eds.), *Contemporary Approaches to Cognition: A Symposium Held at the University of Colorado.* Cambridge, Mass.: Harvard University Press, 1957.

Bruner, J. S. *Toward a Theory of Instruction.* New York: Norton, 1966.

Bryson, L. *Adult Education.* New York: American Book Company, 1936.

Burge, E. J. (Ed.). "Adult Learners, Learning and Public Libraries." *Library Trends,* 1983, *31* (4) (entire issue).

Burstow, B. "Adult Education: A Sartrean Based Perspective." *International Journal of Lifelong Education,* 1984, *3* (3), 193–202.

Buss, A. R. (ed.). *Psychology in Social Context.* New York: Irvington, 1979.

Butler, A. *Lifelong Education Revisited: Australia as a Learning Society.* Melbourne, Australia: Commission for the Future, 1989.

Buzan, T. *Use Your Head.* London: BBC Productions, 1978.

Cacères, B. *Regard neuf sur les autodidactes.* [A fresh look at autodidacts]. Paris: Seuil, 1967.

Caffarella, R. S. "Fostering Self-Directed Learning in Post-Secondary Education: The Use of Learning Contracts." *Lifelong Learning: An Omnibus of Practice and Research,* 1983, *7* (3), 7–10, 25–26.

Caffarella, R. S. "Self-Directed Adult Learning Abilities." Proceedings of 25th annual Adult Education Research Conference, North Carolina State University, Raleigh, Apr. 1984, 281–283.

Caffarella, R. S. "Qualitative Research on Self-Directed Learning." Paper presented at annual meeting of the American Association of Adult and Continuing Education, Tulsa, Okla., Nov. 1988.

Caffarella, R. S., and Caffarella, E. P. "The Learning Contract as a Tool for Developing Readiness and Competencies in Self-Directed Learning." Proceedings of 25th annual Adult Education Research Conference, North Carolina State University, Raleigh, Apr. 1984, 32–37.

Caffarella, R. S., and Caffarella, E. P. "Self-Directedness and Learning Contracts in Adult Education." *Adult Education Quarterly,* 1986, *36* (4), 226–234.

Caffarella, R. S., and O'Donnell, J. M. "Self-Directed Adult Learning: A Critical Paradigm Revisited." Paper presented at the Commission of Professors of Adult Education, Milwaukee, Wis., Nov. 1985.

Caffarella, R. S., and O'Donnell, J. M. "Self-Directed Adult Learning: A Critical Paradigm Revisited." Proceedings of 27th annual Adult Education Research Conference, Syracuse University, May 1986, 37–42.

Caffarella, R. S., and O'Donnell, J. M. "Self-Directed Adult Learning: A Critical Paradigm Revisited." *Adult Education Quarterly,* 1987, *37* (4), 199–211.

Caffarella, R. S. and O'Donnell, J. M. "Research in Self-Directed Learning: Past, Present, and Future Trends." In H. B. Long and Associates, *Self-Directed Learning: Application and Theory.* Athens: Department of Adult Education, University of Georgia, 1988.

Caffarella, R. S., and O'Donnell, J. M. *Self-Directed Learning.* Adults: Psychological and Educational Perspectives, no. 1. Nottingham, England: Department of Adult Education, University of Nottingham, 1990.

Cameron, S. W. "The Perry Scheme: A New Perspective on Adult Learners." Proceedings of 24th annual Adult Education Research Conference, University of Montreal, Apr. 1983, 38–43.

Cameron, W. B. *Informal Sociology: A Casual Introduction to Sociological Thinking.* New York: Random House, 1963.

Campbell, D. D. *Adult Education as a Field of Study and Practice: Strategies for Development.* Vancouver: Centre for Continuing

Education, University of British Columbia, and International Council for Adult Education, 1977.

Campbell, V. N. "Self-Direction and Programmed Instruction for Five Different Types of Learning Objectives." *Psychology in the Schools,* 1964, *1* (4), 348–359.

Campbell, V. N., and Chapman, M. A. "Learner Control vs. Program Control of Instruction." *Psychology in the Schools,* 1967, *4* (1), 121–130.

Candy, P. C. "Learning Styles and Strategies." *Icarus: The Journal of the Association of Independent Schools of Queensland,* 1980, *1* (1), 37–46.

Candy, P. C. *Good Intentions and Needs Assessment — Two Paths to Hell?"* Canberra Papers in Continuing Education, new series 3. Canberra: Centre for Continuing Education, Australian National University, 1983.

Candy, P. C. "The Ideology of Autonomous Learning: An Attempt to Cut the Gordian Knot." Proceedings of 4th annual conference of the Canadian Association for the Study of Adult Education, University of Montreal, May 1985, 59–76.

Candy, P. C. "The Eye of the Beholder: Metaphor in Adult Education Research." *International Journal of Lifelong Education,* 1986, *5* (2), 87–111.

Candy, P. C. "Reframing Research into 'Self-Direction' in Adult Education: A Constructivist Perspective." Unpublished doctoral dissertation, Department of Administrative, Adult, and Higher Education, University of British Columbia, 1987. (*Dissertation Abstracts International, 49* (05A), 1033.)

Candy, P. C. "On the Attainment of Subject-Matter Autonomy." In D. J. Boud (ed.), *Developing Student Autonomy in Learning.* (2nd ed.) London: Kogan Page, 1988.

Candy, P. C. "Repertory Grids: Playing Verbal Chess." In J. Mezirow, and Associates, *Fostering Critical Reflection in Adulthood: A Guide to Transformative and Emancipatory Learning.* San Francisco: Jossey-Bass, 1990.

Candy, P. C., Harri-Augstein, E. S., and Thomas, L. F. "Reflection and the Self-Organized Learner: A Model of

Learning Conversations." In D. J. Boud, R. Keough, and D. Walker (eds.), *Reflection: Turning Experience into Learning.* London: Kogan Page, 1985.

Cantor, N. *The Dynamics of Learning.* Buffalo, N.Y.: Foster and Stewart, 1946.

Carney, F. M. "An Exploratory Study of Learning Style Variables Related to Success or Failure in Self-Directed Independent Study Among Intellectually Gifted Students." Unpublished doctoral dissertation, Michigan State University, 1985. (*Dissertation Abstracts International, 46* (07A), 1873.)

Carr, D. W. "The Agent and the Learner: A Study of Critical Incidents and Contexts in Assisted Adult Library Learning." Unpublished doctoral dissertation, Rutgers University, 1979. (*Dissertation Abstracts International, 40* (10A), 5230–5231.)

Carr, D. W. "Self-Directed Learning in Cultural Institutions." In S. D. Brookfield (ed.), *Self-Directed Learning: From Theory to Practice.* New Directions for Continuing Education, no. 25. San Francisco: Jossey-Bass, 1985.

Carr, W., and Kemmis, S. *Becoming Critical: Knowing Through Action Research.* Highton, Australia: Deakin University Press, 1983.

Castle, E. B. *The Teacher.* Oxford: Oxford University Press, 1970.

Cawelti, J. G. *Apostles of the Self-Made Man.* Chicago: University of Chicago Press, 1965.

Cell, E. *Learning to Learn from Experience.* Albany: State University of New York Press, 1984.

Cembalo, M., and Gremmo, M. J. "Autonomie de l'apprentissage: Réalités et perspectives" [Autonomous Learning: Realities and Opinions]. *Mélanges Pédagogiques — 1974.* Nancy, France: Centre de Recherches et d'Applications Pédagogiques en Langues, Université de Nancy, 1974.

Cembalo, M., Holec, H. "Les langues aux adultes: Pour une pédagogie de l'autonomie" [Adult Language: Toward Autonomous Teaching Methods]. *Mélanges Pédagogiques — 1973.* Nancy, France: Centre de Recherches et d'Applications Pédagogiques en Langues, Université de Nancy, 1973.

Chall, J. S. "The Great Debate: Ten Years Later with a Modest Proposal For Reading Stages." In L. B. Resnick, and P. A. Weaver (eds.), *Theory and Practice of Early Readings,* Vol. 1. Hillsdale, N.J.: Erlbaum, 1979.

Chamberlain, M. N. "The Professional Adult Educator: An Examination of His Competencies and of the Programs of Graduate Study Which Prepare Him for Work in the Field." Unpublished doctoral dissertation, University of Chicago, 1961. (*Dissertation Abstracts International, 1861–1972,* X1961, 70.)

Champion, A. "Towards an Ontology of Adult Education." *Studies in Adult Education,* 1975, *7* (1), 16–33.

Channing, W. E. "Self-Culture: An Introductory to the Franklin Lectures, Delivered at Boston, September, 1838." In W. E. Channing, *The Works of William E. Channing, D. D.* (Rev. ed.). Boston: American Unitarian Association, 1883.

Chené, A. "The Concept of Autonomy in Adult Education: A Philosophical Discussion." *Adult Education Quarterly,* 1983, *34* (1), 38–47.

Cheren, M. I. "Facilitating the Transition from External Direction in Learning to Greater Self-Direction in Learning in Educational Institutions: A Case Study in Individualized Open System Post-Secondary Education." Unpublished doctoral dissertation, University of Massachusetts, 1978. (*Dissertation Abstracts International, 39* (03A), 1362.)

Cherin, M. I. "Helping Learners Achieve Greater Self-Direction." In R. M. Smith (ed.), *Helping Adults Learn How to Learn.* New Directions for Continuing Education, no. 19. San Francisco: Jossey-Bass, 1983.

Chickering, A. W. "Dimensions of Independence: The Findings of an Experiment at Goddard College." *Journal of Higher Education,* 1964, *35* (1), 38–41.

Chickering, A. W. *Education and Identity.* San Francisco: Jossey-Bass, 1969.

Christensen, R. S. "Dear Diary: A Learning Tool for Adults." *Lifelong Learning: The Adult Years,* 1981, *5* (2), 4–5, 31.

Clark, K. M. "Independent Learning: A Concept Analysis." In *Proceedings of a Conference on Independent Learning,* W. K. Kellogg Foundation Project Report No. 7. Vancouver: Adult Education Research Centre, University of British Columbia, 1973.

Clark, N. P. "The Effects of the Use of Self-Directed Learning Activities on Achievement and Retention Among College Students." Unpublished doctoral dissertation, Auburn University, 1969. (*Dissertation Abstracts International, 30* (09A), 3824.)

Clarke, J. F. *Self-Culture* Boston: Osgood, 1880.

Clarkson, S. "Home-Centered Learning Activities of Families with Teenager Children." Unpublished master's thesis, Michigan State University, 1975.

Clawson, J. G. "Superior-Subordinate Relationships in Managerial Development." Unpublished doctoral dissertation, Harvard University, 1979. (*Dissertation Abstracts International, 40* (04A), 2158.)

Clawson, J. G. "Mentoring in Managerial Careers." In C. B. Derr (ed.), *Work, Family, and the Career.* New York: Praeger, 1980.

Claxton, G. "School Science: Falling on Stony Ground or Choked by Thorns?" Unpublished paper. London: Centre for Science and Mathematics Education, Chelsea College, University of London, 1982.

Cobb, J. E. "Self-Directed Learning of Prospective Parents." Unpublished doctoral dissertation, Kansas State University, 1978. (*Dissertation Abstracts International, 39* (05A), 2684.)

Cohen, L., and Manion, L. *Research Methods in Education.* (2nd. ed.) London: Croom Helm, 1985.

Collard, S. "The Self-Directed Andragogue is Alive and Well and Inhabiting Discourse." Unpublished manuscript, Department of Adult Education, University of British Columbia, 1985.

Combs, A. W. "Fostering Self-Direction." In E. G. Talbert and L. E. Frase (eds.), *Individualized Instruction: A Book of Readings.* Columbus, Ohio: Merrill, 1972.

Cone, R. "Teachers' Decisions in Managing Student Behaviour: A Laboratory Simulation of Interactive Decision Making by Teachers." Paper presented at 59th annual conference of the American Educational Research Association, Toronto, Mar. 1978.

Connell, R. W., Ashenden, D. J., Kessler, S., and Dowsett, G. W. *Making the Difference: Schools, Families and Social Division.* Sydney, Australia: Allen & Unwin, 1982.

Conroy, B. *Lifelong Learning for Adults Through Libraries.* Report of the Task Force on Libraries and Lifelong Learning. Washington, D.C.: Adult Education Association of the USA, 1980. (ERIC Document Reproduction Service no. ED 194 785.)

Conti, G. J. "The Collaborative Mode in Adult Education: A Literature Review." In G. J. Conti, *Principles of Adult Learning Scale: An Instrument for Measuring Teacher Behavior Related to the Collaborative Teaching-Learning Mode.* Unpublished doctoral dissertation, Northern Illinois University, 1978a. (ERIC Document Reproduction Service no. ED 229 534.)

Conti, G. J. "Principles of Adult Learning Scale: An Instrument for Measuring Teacher Behavior Related to the Collaborative Teaching-Learning Mode." Unpublished doctoral dissertation, Northern Illinois University, 1978b. (*Dissertation Abstracts International, 39* (12A), 7111.)

Coolican, P. M. "The Learning Style of Mothers of Young Children." Unpublished doctoral dissertation, Syracuse University, 1973. (*Dissertation Abstracts International, 35* (02A), 783.)

Coolican, P. M. *Self-Planned Learning: Implications for the Future of Adult Education.* Technical Report no. 74-507. Syracuse, N.Y.: Syracuse University Research Corporation, 1974. (ERIC Document Reproduction Service no. ED 095 254.)

Coombs, P. H., Prosser, R. C., and Ahmed, M. *New Paths to Learning for Rural Children and Youth.* New York: International Council for Educational Development, 1973.

Cooper, H. M. *The Integrative Research Review: A Systematic Approach.* Applied Social Research Methods Series. vol. 2. Newbury Park, Calif.: Sage, 1984.

Cooper, J. F. *The American Democrat.* New York: Knopf, 1956.

Cornelius, S. "Without Teacher: A Different Learning." *Journal of Adult Education (U.S.),* 1941, *13* (2), 162–164.

Cornwall, M. G. "Putting it into Practice: Promoting Independent Learning in a Traditional Institution." In D. J. Boud (ed.), *Developing Student Autonomy.* London: Kogan Page, 1981.

Cottingham, L. A. "A Classification System for Independent Learning." Unpublished doctoral dissertation, University of New Mexico, 1977. (*Dissertation Abstracts International, 39* (01A), 247.)

Council of Europe. *The Integration of Adult Education within a Framework of Permanent Education: Trends Towards the Self-Management of Education.* Final report of a colloquy held at Lillehammer, Norway, May 1975. Strasbourg: Committee for Out-of-School Education and Cultural Development of the Council for Cultural Co-operation, Council of Europe, 1975.

Craik, G. L. *The Pursuit of Knowledge Under Difficulties.* (Rev. ed.) London: Bell and Daldy, 1866.

Cremin, L. *American Education: The Colonial Experience, 1607–1783.* New York: Harper & Row, 1970.

Crittenden, B. "Autonomy as an Aim of Education." In K. A. Strike and K. Egan (eds.), *Ethics and Educational Policy.* London: Routledge and Kegan Paul, 1978.

Crockett, W. H. "Cognitive Complexity and Impression Formation." In B. A. Maher (ed.), *Progress in Experimental Personality Research,* vol. 2. New York: Academic Press, 1965.

Cronbach, L. J., and Snow, R. E. *Aptitudes and Instructional Methods: A Handbook for Research on Interactions.* New York: Irvington, 1977.

Crooks, T. J. "The Impact of Classroom Evaluation Practices on Students." *Review of Educational Research,* 1988, *58* (4), 438–481.

Cropley, A. J. *Lifelong Education: A Psychological Analysis.* Oxford/Hamburg: Pergamon Press/Unesco Institute for Education, 1977.

Cropley, A. J. "Lifelong Education: Issues and Questions." In A. J. Cropley (ed.), *Lifelong Education: A Stocktaking.* Oxford/Hamburg: Pergamon Press/Unesco Institute for Education, 1979.

Cropley, A. J. *Towards a System of Lifelong Education: Some Practical Considerations.* Hamburg: Unesco Institute for Education, 1980.

Cropley, A. J., and Dave, R. H. *Lifelong Education and the Training of Teachers.* Oxford/Hamburg: Pergamon/Unesco Institute for Education, 1978.

Cross, K. P. *Accent on Learning: Improving Instruction and Reshaping the Curriculum.* San Francisco: Jossey-Bass, 1976.

Cross, K. P. *The Missing Link: Connecting Adult Learners to Learning Resources.* New York: College Entrance Examination Board, 1978.

Cross, K. P. *Adults as Learners: Increasing Participation and Facilitating Learning.* San Francisco: Jossey-Bass, 1981.

Cross, K. P., and Zusman, A. "The Needs of Nontraditional Learners and the Response of Nontraditional Programs." In C. B. Stalford (ed.), *An Evaluative Look at Nontraditional Postsecondary Education.* Washington, D.C.: National Institute of Education, 1979.

Cunningham, I. "Self-Managed Learning in Independent Study." In T. H. Boydell and M. Pedler (eds.), *Management Self-Development: Concepts and Practices.* Westmead, England: Gower, 1981.

Curran, C. A. *Counseling-Learning: A Whole Person Model for Education.* New York: Grune & Stratton, 1972.

Curran, C. A. *Counseling-Learning in Second Languages.* East Dubuque, Ill.: Counseling-Learning Publications, 1976.

Curry, C. A. "The Analysis of Self-Directed Learning Readiness Characteristics in Older Adults Engaged in Formal Learning Activities in Two Settings." Unpublished doctoral dissertation, Kansas State University, 1983. (*Dissertation Abstracts International, 44* (05A), 1293.)

Dadswell, G. "The Adult Independent Learner and Public Libraries: A New Perspective for Library Service." *Adult Education (U.K.),* 1978, *51* (1), 5–11.

Dale, S. M. "The Adult Independent Learning Project: Work with Adult Self-Directed Learners in Public Libraries." *Journal of Librarianship,* 1979, *11* (2), 83–106.

Dale, S. M. "Another Way Forward for Adult Learners: The Public Library and Independent Study." *Studies in Adult Education,* 1981, *12* (1), 29–38.

Daloz, L. A. "Mentors: Teachers Who Make a Difference." *Change: The Magazine of Higher Learning,* 1983, *15* (6), 24–27.

Daloz, L. A. *Effective Teaching and Mentoring: Realizing the Transformational Power of Adult Learning Experience.* San Francisco: Jossey-Bass, 1986.

Daniel, J. S. "Learning Styles and Strategies: The Work of Gordon Pask." In N. J. Entwistle and D. J. Hounsell (eds.), *How Students Learn.* Bailrigg, England: Institute for Research and Development in Post-Compulsory Education, University of Lancaster, 1975.

Danis, C., and Tremblay, N. "Critical Analysis of Adult Learning Principles from a Self-Directed Learner's Perspective." Proceedings of 26th annual Adult Education Research Conference, Arizona State University, Tempe, Mar. 1985a, 138–143.

Danis, C., and Tremblay, N. "The Self-Directed Learning Experience: Major Recurrent Tasks to Deal with." Proceedings of the 4th annual conference of the Canadian Association for the Study of Adult Education, Montreal, May 1985b, 285–301.

Danis, C., and Tremblay, N. A. "Propositions Regarding Autodidactic Learning and Their Implications for Teaching." *Lifelong Learning: An Omnibus of Practice and Research,* 1987, *10* (7), 4–7.

Darkenwald, G. G., and Merriam, S. B. *Adult Education: Foundations of Practice.* New York: Harper & Row, 1982.

Dave, R. H. *Lifelong Education and the School Curriculum. Unesco Institute for Education Monograph No. 1.* Hamburg: Unesco Institute for Education, 1973.

Dave, R. H. *Foundations for Lifelong Education.* Oxford/Hamburg: Pergamon Press/Unesco Institute for Education, 1976.

Dearden, R. F. "Autonomy and Education." In R. F. Dearden, P. H. Hirst, and R. S. Peters (eds.), *Education and the Development of Reason.* London: Routledge and Kegan Paul, 1972.

Dearden, R. F. "Autonomy as an Educational Ideal I." In S. C. Brown (ed.), *Philosophers Discuss Education.* London: Macmillan, 1975.

deCharms, R. "Personal Causation Training in the Schools." *Journal of Applied Social Psychology,* 1972, *2* (2), 95–113.

DeCoster, D. A., and Brown, R. D. "Mentoring Relationships and the Education Process." In D. A. DeCoster and R. D. Brown (eds.), *Mentoring-Transcript Systems for Promoting Student Growth.* New Directions for Student Services, no. 19. San Francisco: Jossey-Bass, 1982.

Della-Dora, D., and Blanchard, L. J. (eds.). *Moving Toward Self-Directed Learning: Highlights of Relevant Research and of Promising Practices.* Alexandria, Va.: Association for Supervision and Curriculum Development, 1979.

Denton, V. L. "Do Grades Sabotage Self-Direction in Adult Learning?" *Lifelong Learning: An Omnibus of Practice and Research,* 1986, *9* (7), 19–22, 28.

Denys, L. O. J. "The Major Learning Efforts of Two Groups of Accra Adults." Unpublished doctoral dissertation, University of Toronto, 1973. (*Dissertation Abstracts International, 35* (09A), 5759.)

Denzin, N. K. *The Research Act: A Theoretical Introduction to Sociological Methods.* (2nd ed.) New York: McGraw Hill, 1978.

De Roos, K. K. B. "Persistence of Adults in Independent Study." Proceedings of 23rd annual Adult Educational Research Conference, University of Nebraska, Lincoln, Apr. 1982a, 78–83.

De Roos, K. K. B. "Persistence of Adults in Independent Study." Unpublished doctoral dissertation, University of Minnesota, 1982b. (*Dissertation Abstracts International, 43* (01a), 47.)

Descartes, R. *Discourse on Method.* (D. Cress, trans.) Indianapolis: Hackett, 1981. (Originally published 1637.)

Dewey, J. *Democracy and Education.* New York: Macmillan, 1916.

Dewey, J. *Experience and Education.* New York: Collier, 1963. (Originally published 1938.)

Dickinson, G., and Clark, K. M. "Learning Orientations and Participation in Self-Education and Continuing Education." *Adult Education (U.S.),* 1975, *26* (1), 3–15.

Dill, W. R., Crowston, W.B.S., and Elton, E. J. "Strategies for Self-Education — to Counteract the Threat of Personal Obsolescence at all Levels." *Harvard Business Review,* 1965, *43* (6), 119–130.

Dittman, J. K. "Concomitant Learning in Home Economics Classrooms" Unpublished doctoral dissertation, Pennsylvania State University, 1974. (*Dissertation Abstracts International, 36* (03A), 1346.)

Dittman, J. K. "Individual Autonomy: The Magnificent Obsession." *Educational Leadership,* 1976, *33* (6), 463–467.

Dorsey, M., Manning, R., and Shindell, T. "Action Science as a Paradigm for a Critical Theory of Self-Directed Learning." Paper presented at 3rd North American symposium on

Adult Self-Directed Learning, Oklahoma Research Center for Continuing Professional and Higher Education, Norman, Feb. 1989.

Doyle, W. "Academic Work." *Review of Educational Research,* 1983, *53* (2), 159–199.

Dressel, P. L., and Thompson, M. M. *Independent Study.* San Francisco: Jossey-Bass, 1973.

Driver, R., and Erickson, G. L. "Theories in Action: Some Theoretical and Empirical Issues in the Study of Students' Conceptual Frameworks in Science." *Studies in Science Education,* 1983, *10,* 37–60.

Dubin, R., and Taveggia, T. C. *The Teaching-Learning Paradox: A Comparative Analysis of College Teaching Methods.* Eugene, Oreg.: Center for the Advanced Study of Educational Administration, University of Oregon, 1968.

Duke, C. *Australian Perspectives on Lifelong Education.* Hawthorn: Australian Council for Educational Research, 1976.

Dunbar, R., and Dutton, J. "Student Learning in a Restructured Environment." *Journal of Research and Development in Education,* 1972, *6* (1), 26–37.

Durkheim, E. *Moral Education.* New York: Free Press, 1925.

Ebersole, B. P. "Foreword." In D. Della-Dora and L. J. Blanchard (eds.), *Moving Toward Self-Directed Learning: Highlights of Relevant Research and of Promising Practices.* Alexandria, Va.: Association for Supervision and Curriculum Development, 1979.

Eglash, A. "A Group-Discussion Method of Teaching Psychology." *Journal of Educational Psychology,* 1954, *45* (5), 257–267.

Eichler, M., and Lapointe, J. *On the Treatment of the Sexes in Research.* Ottawa: Social Sciences and Humanities Research Council of Canada, 1985.

Einstein, A., and Infeld, L. *The Evolution of Physics.* New York: Simon & Schuster, 1952.

Eisenman, G. "Self-Directed Learning: A Growth Process?" Paper presented at 3rd North American symposium on Adult Self-Directed Learning, Okahoma Research Center for

Continuing Professional and Higher Education, Norman, Feb. 1989.

Eisner, E. W. "On the Differences Between Scientific and Artistic Approaches to Qualitative Research." *Educational Researcher,* 1981, *10* (4), 5–9.

Eizenberg, N. "Approaches to Learning Anatomy: Developing a Program for Preclinical Medical Students." In P. Ramsden (ed.), *Improving Learning: New Perspectives.* London: Kogan Page, 1988.

Elbaz, F. *Teaching Thinking: A Study of Practical Knowledge.* London: Croom Helm, 1983.

Elias, J. L., and Merriam, S. *Philosophical Foundations of Adult Education.* Malabar, Fla.: Krieger, 1980.

Elliot, J. "Developing Hypotheses About Classrooms From Teachers' Practical Constructs: An Account of the Work of the Ford Teaching Project." *Interchange,* 1976–77, *7* (2), 2–20.

Elsey, B. "Voluntary Organisations and Informal Adult Education." *Adult Education (U.K.),* 1974, *46* (6), 391–396.

Elton, L.R.B. "Motivation and Self Study." In C. F. Page and J. Gibson (eds.), "Motivation: Non-Cognitive Aspects of Student Performance." In *Papers Presented at the Eighth Annual Conference of the Society for Research into Higher Education, July 1973.* London: Society for Research into Higher Education, 1973.

Elton, L.R.B. "Conditions for Learner Autonomy at a Distance." *Programmed Learning and Education Technology,* 1988, *25* (3), 216–224.

Emery, M. "Introduction." In M. Emery (ed.), *Qualitative Research: Papers from a Symposium, May 22–23 1986.* Canberra, Australia: Research Network, Australian Association of Adult Education, 1986.

Ennis, R. H. "Critical Thinking and the Curriculum." *National Forum,* 1985, *65* (1), 28–31.

Entwistle, H. Antonio Gramsci: Conservative Schooling for Radical Politics. London: Routledge & Kegan Paul, 1979.

Entwistle, N. J., Hanley, M., and Hounsell, D. J. "Identifying Distinctive Approaches to Studying." *Higher Education,* 1979, *8* (4), 365–180.

Entwistle, N. J., and Hounsell, D. J. (eds.) *Higher Education,* 1979, *8* (4) (entire issue).

Entwistle, N. J., and Percy, K. A. "Critical Thinking or Conformity? An Investigation of the Aims and Outcomes of Higher Education." In C. Flood Page and J. Gibson (eds.) *Research into Higher Education — 1973: Papers Presented at the Ninth Annual Conference of the Society.* London: Society for Research into Higher Education, 1974.

Entwistle, N. J., and Ramsden, P. *Understanding Student Learning.* London: Croom Helm, 1983.

Eraut, M., MacKenzie, N., and Papps, I. "The Mythology of Educational Development: Reflections on a Three-Year Study of Economics Teaching." *British Journal of Educational Technology,* 1975, *6* (3), 20–34.

Erickson, G. L. "Constructivist Epistemology and the Professional Development of Teachers." Paper presented at the 68th annual meeting of the American Educational Research Association, Washington, D.C., Apr. 1987.

Esland, G. "Teaching and Learning as the Organisation of Knowledge." In M. Young (ed.), *Knowledge and Control: New Directions for the Sociology of Education.* London: Collier Macmillan, 1972.

Essert, P. *Creative Leadership of Adult Education.* Englewood Cliffs, N. J.: Prentice-Hall, 1951.

Even, M. J., Caffarella, R. S., Brockett, R. G., and Smith, R. M. "Symposium on Adults Learning Alone." Proceedings of 25th annual Adult Education Research Conference, North Carolina State University, Raleigh, Apr. 1984, 279–284.

Even, M. J. "Adult Classroom Locus of Control." Proceedings of 26th annual Adult Education Research Conference. Arizona State University, Tempe, Mar. 1985, 157–162.

Fair, J. W. "Teachers as Learners: The Learning Projects of Beginning Elementary-School Teachers." Unpublished doctoral dissertation, University of Toronto, 1973. (*Dissertation Abstracts International, 35* (09A), 5759.)

Farnes, N. "Student-Centered Learning." *Teaching at a Distance,* 1975, *3,* 2–6.

Farquharson, W.A.F. "Peers as Helpers: Personal Change in Members of Self-Help Groups in Metropolitan Toronto." Unpublished doctoral dissertation, University of Toronto, 1975. (*Dissertation Abstracts International, 38* (10A), 5848.)

Faure, E., and others. *Learning to Be: The World of Education Today and Tomorrow:* Report of the International Commission on the Development of Education. Paris/London: Unesco/Harrap, 1972.

Felder, B. D. " Characteristics of Independent Study Practices in Colleges and Universities of the United States." Unpublished doctoral dissertation, University of Texas, 1963. (*Dissertation Abstracts International, 24* (07A), 2807.)

Felder, B. D. "Independent-Study Practices in Colleges and Universities." *Journal of Higher Education,* 1964, *35* (6), 335–338.

Feldman, D. H. *Beyond Universals in Cognitive Development.* Norwood, N.J.: Ablex, 1980.

Feyerabend, P. *Against Method.* London: Verso, 1975.

Field, J. L. "The Learning Efforts of Jamaican Adults of Low Literacy Attainment." Unpublished doctoral dissertation. University of Toronto, 1977. (*Dissertation Abstracts International, 39* (07A), 3979.)

Field, L. D. "An Investigation into the Structure, Validity, and Reliability of Guglielmino's Self-Directed Learning Readiness Scale." *Adult Education Quarterly,* 1989, *39* (3), 125–139.

Finestone, P. M. "A Construct Validation of the Self-Directed Learning Readiness Scale with Labour Education Participants." Unpublished doctoral dissertation, University of Toronto, 1984. (*Dissertation Abstracts International, 46* (05A),1160.)

Fisher, K. M., and others. "Computer-Based Knowledge Representation as a Tool for Students and Teachers." Working paper. University of California–Davis, 1987.

Fitzpatrick, A. *The University in Overalls.* Toronto: Press of the Hunter-Rose Co., 1920

Flanagan, J. C. "The Psychologist's Role in Youth's Quest for Self-Fulfilment." Paper presented at 78th annual convention of the American Psychological Association. Miami Beach, Fla., Sept. 1970.

Flavell, J. H. "Metacognition and Cognitive Monitoring: A New

Area of Cognitive-Developmental Inquiry." *American Psychologist,* 1979, *34* (10), 906–911.

Flew, A. *Sociology, Equality and Education.* London: Macmillan, 1976.

Floden, R. E., and Klinzing, H. G. "What Can Research on Teacher Thinking Contribute to Teacher Preparation? A Second Opinion." *Educational Researcher,* 1990, *19* (5), 15–20.

Floyd, A. "Cognitive Styles." *Block 5, Second Level Course in Educational Studies: Personality and Learning.* Milton Keynes, England: Open University Press, 1976.

Foley, G. "Adult Education for the Long Haul." Paper presented at 27th national conference of the Australian Association of Adult Education, Institute of Technical and Adult Teacher Education, Sydney, Sept. 1987.

Ford, M. M. "A Framework for Adult Independent Study." Unpublished doctoral dissertation, Indiana University, 1971. (*Dissertation Abstracts International, 32* (10A), 5524.)

Forster, J. C. "Independent Study: A Philosohpical and Historical Analysis with Implications for the Technological Society." Unpublished doctoral dissertation, Catholic University of America, 1972. (*Dissertation Abstracts International, 33* (02A), 584.)

Fowler, O. S. *Self-Culture and Perfection of Character.* New York: Fowler and Wells, 1851.

Fransella, F., and Bannister, D. *A Manual for Repertory Grid Technique.* London: Academic Press, 1977.

Freire, P. *Pedagogy of the Oppressed.* Harmondsworth, England: Penguin, 1972.

French, D. "Development of a Model for Learner-Directed Instruction." Unpublished doctoral dissertation, University of Texas, 1974. (*Dissertation Abstracts International, 35* (08A), 4980.)

French, D. "History 213 or the Yearning to Be Free." *Liberal Education,* 1976, *62* (3), 472–487.

Frewin, C. C. "The Relationship of Educational Goal Setting Behavior to the Conceptual Level Model." Unpublished doctoral dissertation, University of Toronto, 1976. (*Dissertation Abstracts International, 39* (03A), 1259.)

Frewin, C. C. "The Relationship of Educational Goal Setting to the Conceptual Level Model." Paper presented at 18th annual Adult Education Research Conference, Minneapolis, Minn., Apr. 1977. (ERIC Document Reproduction Service no. ED 138 807.)

Frick, E. "Teaching Information Structure: Turning Dependent Researchers into Self-Teachers." In C. Oberman and K. Stranch (eds.), *Theories of Bibliographic Education.* New York: Bowker, 1982.

Fry, J. P. "Interactive Relationship Between Inquisitiveness and Student-Control of Instruction." *Journal of Educational Psychology,* 1972, *63* (5) 459–465.

Furedy, C., and Furedy, J. J. "Critical Thinking: Toward Research and Dialogue." In J. G. Donald and A. M. Sullivan (eds.), *Using Research to Improve Teaching.* New Directions for Teaching and Learning, no. 23. San Francisco: Jossey-Bass, 1985.

Gagnon, R. "The Personalized Education Project of the Montreal Catholic School Commission." *Adult Training,* 1978, *3* (2), 32–35.

Galtung, J. "Literacy, Education and Schooling — For What?" In L. Bataille (ed.), *A Turning Point for Literacy: Adult Education for Development.* Oxford: Pergamon Press, 1976.

Gardner, J. W. *Self Renewal.* New York: Harper & Row, 1963.

Garfinkel, A. *Forms of Explanation: Rethinking the Questions in Social Theory.* New Haven, Conn.: Yale University Press, 1981.

Garforth, F. W. *Educative Democracy: John Stuart Mill on Education in Society.* Oxford: Oxford University Press, 1980.

Garrison, D. R. "Self-Directed and Distance Learning: Facilitating Self-Directed Learning Beyond the Institutional Setting." *International Journal of Lifelong Education,* 1987, *6* (4), 309–318.

Garrison, D. R. "Facilitating Self-Directed Learning: Not a Contradiction in Terms." In H. B. Long and Associates, *Self-Directed Learning: Emerging Theory and Practice.* Norman: Oklahoma Research Center for Continuing Professional and Higher Education, 1989.

Gay, G. "Interaction of Learner-Control and Prior Understanding in Computer-Assisted Video Instruction." *Journal of Educational Psychology,* 1986, *78* (3), 225–227.

Geertz, C. *The Interpretation of Culture.* New York: Basic Books, 1973.

Geis, G. L. "Student Participation in Instruction: Student Choice." *Journal of Higher Education,* 1976, *47* (3), 249–273.

Geisler, K. K. "Learning Efforts of Adults Undertaken for Matriculating into a Community College." Unpublished doctoral dissertation, Texas A&M University, 1984. (*Dissertation Abstracts International, 45,* (09A), 2737.)

Gelpi, E. *A Future for Adult Education:* Vol. 1: *Lifelong Education: Principles, Policies and Practices.* Manchester Monograph No. 13. Manchester, England: Department of Adult and Higher Education, University of Manchester, 1979.

George, T. W. "An Investigation of Teacher- Versus Learner-Control of Learning Activities: Effects on Immediate Achievement, Progress Rate, Delayed Recall and Attitude." Unpublished doctoral dissertation, University of Tennessee, 1973. (*Dissertation Abstracts International, 34* (08A), 4865.)

George, T. W. "Student-Control of Learning: A Review of Research." *Programmed Learning and Educational Technology,* 1976, *13* (2), 55–57.

George, T. W. "Teacher- Versus Student-Choice of Learning Activities." *Educational Research Quarterly,* 1977, *2* (1), 22–29.

Gergen, K. J. "The Social Constructionist Movement in Modern Psychology.' *American Psychologist,* 1985, *40* (3), 266–275.

Gerstner, L. S. "On The Theme and Variations of Self-Directed Learning: An Exploration of the Literature." Unpublished doctoral dissertation, Teachers' College, Columbia University, 1987.

Gibbon, E. *Autobiography.* (Lord Sheffield, ed.) London: Oxford University Press, 1907. (First published 1796 as *Memoirs of My Life and Writings.*)

Gibbons, M., and Phillips, G. "Helping Students Through the Self-Education Crisis." *Phi Delta Kappan,* 1978, *60* (4), 296–300.

Gibbons, M., and Phillips, G. "Teaching for Self-Education: Promising New Professional Role." *Journal of Teacher Education,* 1979, *30* (5), 26–28.

Gibbons, M., and Phillips, G. "Self-Education: The Process of Lifelong Learning." *Canadian Journal of Education,* 1982, *7* (4), 67–86.

Gibbons, M., and others. "Toward a Theory of Self-Directed

Learning: A Study of Experts Without Formal Training." *Journal of Humanistic Psychology,* 1980, *20* (2), 41–56.

Gibbs, B. "Autonomy and Authority in Education." *Journal of Philosophy of Education,* 1979, *13,* 119–132.

Gibbs, G. "Changing Students' Approaches to Study Through Classroom Exercises." In R. M. Smith (ed.), *Helping Adults Learn How to Learn.* New Directions for Continuing Education, no. 19. San Francisco: Jossey-Bass, 1983.

Gibbs, G., Morgan, A., and Taylor, E. *Understanding Why Students Don't Learn.* Study Methods Group Report No. 5. Milton Keynes, England: Institute of Educational Technology, Open University, 1980.

Gibbs, G., Morgan, A., and Taylor, E. "A Review of the Research of Ference Marton and the Göteborg Group: A Phenomenological Research Perspective on Learning." *Higher Education,* 1982, *11* (2), 123–145.

Giroux, H. A. *Theory and Resistance in Education: A Pedagogy for the Opposition.* Hadley, Mass.: Bergin and Garvey, 1983.

Glaser, B. G., and Strauss, A. L. *The Discovery of Grounded Theory: Strategies for Qualitative Research.* Chicago: Aldine, 1967.

Gleason, G. T. (ed.), *Theory and Nature of Independent Learning.* Scranton, Pa.: International Textbook, 1967.

Godbey, G. C. *Applied Andragogy: A Practical Manual for the Continuing Education of Adults.* University Park: Pennsylvania State University, 1978.

Goodman, D. "The Influence of Self-Concept as Learner on Participation Patterns of Adult Learners." Proceedings of 26th annual Adult Education Research Conference, Arizona State University, Tempe, Mar. 1985, 177–181.

Goodman, K. S. "Reading: A Psycholinguistic Guessing Game." In H. Singer and R. Ruddell (eds.), *Theoretical Models and the Process of Reading.* (2nd ed.) Newark, Del.: International Reading Association, 1976.

Gooler, D. D. *The Education Utility: The Power to Revitalize Education and Society.* Englewood Cliffs, N.J.: Educational Technology Publications, 1986.

Gores, H. B. "A Place to Learn." *Prospects: Quarterly Review of Education,* 1972, *2* (1), 65–67.

Gould, S. B. "Independent Learning and the Future Role of Libraries." In *ALA Yearbook: A Review of Library Events — 1975.* Chicago: American Library Association, 1976.

Greenfield, P. M. "A Theory of the Teacher in the Learning Activities of Everyday Life." In B. Rogoff and J. Lave (eds.), *Everyday Cognition: Its Development in Social Context.* Cambridge, Mass.: Harvard University Press, 1984.

Grenier, P. "Les projets éducatifs de femmes agées: Objets d'apprentissage et moyens privilégiés [Learning projects of older women: Objects of study and means employed]. Mémoire de maîtrise inédit. Université de Montréal, 1980.

Griffin, C. "Ettore Gelpi." In P. Jarvis (ed.), *Twentieth Century Thinkers in Adult Education.* London: Croom Helm, 1987.

Griffin, V. R. "A Grass-Roots Movement." Paper presented at the Adult Educators' Lyceum, Pewaukee, Wis., July 1977.

Griffin, V. R. "Self-Directed Adult Learners and Learning: Part 1." *Learning,* 1978, *2* (1), 6–8.

Griffin, V. R. "Self-Directed Adult Learners and Learning: Part 2." *Learning,* 1979, *2* (2), 12–15.

Griffin, V. R. "Through a Glass Brightly: A New Image of Learners and Learning." Unpublished manuscript, Department of Adult Education, Ontario Institute for Studies in Education, 1981.

Gross, L. "An Experimental Study of the Validity of the Non-Directive Method of Teaching." *Journal of Psychology,* 1948, *26,* 243–248.

Gross, R. D. *The Lifelong Learner.* New York: Simon & Schuster, 1979.

Gross, R. D., and Gross, B. *Independent Scholarship: Promise, Problems, and Prospects.* New York: College Entrance Examination Board, 1983.

Groundwater-Smith, S. "The Concept of Collaborative Research: A Means of Breaking Down Divisions Between Researchers and Researched." In M. Emery (ed.), *Qualitative Research: Papers from a Symposium, May 22–23, 1986.* Canberra, Australia: Research Network, Australian Association of Adult Education, 1986.

Gruber, H. E. "The Future of Self-Directed Study." In W. R.

Hatch and A. L. Richards (eds.), *Approach to Independent Study.* New Dimensions in Higher Education, no. 13. Washington, D.C.: U.S. Department of Health, Education, and Welfare, 1965.

Gruber, H. E., and Weitman, M. *Self-Directed Study: Experiments in Higher Education.* Behavior Research Laboratory Report No. 19. Boulder: University of Colorado, 1962.

Gruber, H. E., and Weitman, M. "The Growth of Self-Reliance." *School and Society,* 1963, *91,* 222–223.

Guglielmino, L. M. "Development of the Self-Directed Learning Readiness Scale." Unpublished doctoral dissertation, University of Georgia, 1977. (*Dissertation Abstracts International, 38* (11A), 6467.)

Guglielmino, L. M. "Guglielmino Responds to Field's Investigation." *Adult Education Quarterly,* 1989, *39* (4), 235–240.

Guglielmino, L. M., and Guglielmino, P. J. *Learning Style Assessment (Self-Scoring Form).* Boca Raton, Fla.: Guglielmino and Associates, 1982.

Habermas, J. *Towards a Rational Society.* Boston: Beacon Press, 1970.

Habermas, J. *Knowledge and Human Interests.* (J. J. Shapiro, trans.) Boston: Beacon Press, 1971.

Hadley, H. N. "Development of an Instrument to Determine Adult Educators' Orientation: Andragogical or Pedagogical." Unpublished doctoral dissertation, School of Education, Boston University, 1975. (*Dissertation Abstracts International, 35* (12A), 7595.)

Halkes, A.R.J., and Olson, J. K. (eds.). "Teaching Thinking: A New Perspective on Persisting Problems in Education." *Proceedings of the First Symposium of the International Study Association on Teacher Thinking, Tilburg, The Netherlands, October 1983.* Lisse, The Netherlands: Swets and Zeitlinger, 1984.

Halverson, C. "Individual and Cultural Determinants of Self-Directed Learning Ability: Straddling an Instructional Dilemma." In D. Della-Dora and L. J. Blanchard (eds.), *Moving Toward Self-Directed Learning: Highlights of Relevant Research and of Promising Practices.* Alexandria, Va.: Association for Supervision and Curriculum Development, 1979.

Hamm, C. "Critique of Self-Education." *Canadian Journal of Education,* 1982, *7* (4), 82–106.

Hampden-Turner, C. *Maps of the Mind.* London: Beazley, 1982.

Hargreaves, D. H. "Deschoolers and New Romantics." In M. Flude and J. Ahier (eds.), *Educability, Schools and Ideology.* London: Croom Helm, 1974.

Hargeaves, D. H. "A Sociological Critique of Individualism in Education." *British Journal of Educational Studies,* 1980, *28* (3), 187–198.

Harker, R. K. "On Reproduction, Habitus and Education." *British Journal of Sociology of Education,* 1984, *5* (2), 117–127.

Harré, R. *Personal Being: A Theory for Individual Psychology.* Oxford: Blackwell, 1983.

Harri-Augstein, E. S., Smith, M., and Thomas, L. F. *Reading to Learn.* London: Methuen, 1982.

Harri-Augstein, E. S., and Thomas, L. F. "Tools for Raising Awareness of the Learning Process." Working paper, Centre for the Study of Human Learning, Brunel University, Uxbridge, England, 1976.

Harris, J., Legge, A., and Merriam, S. B. "From Banking to Gardening: The Use of Metaphors in Adult Education." *Lifelong Learning: The Adult Years,* 1981, *5* (3), 10–11.

Harris, R. McL. "Reflections on Self-Directed Adult Learning: Some Implications for Educators of Adults." *Studies in Continuing Education,* 1990, *11* (2), 102–116.

Harrison, J.F.C. *Learning and Living, 1790–1960.* London: Routledge and Kegan Paul, 1961.

Harrison, R. "How to Design and Conduct Self-Directed Learning Experiences." *Group & Organization Studies,* 1978, *3* (2), 149–167.

Hassan, A. M. "An Investigation of the Learning Projects Among Adults of High and Low Readiness for Self-Direction in Learning." Unpublished doctoral dissertation, Iowa State University, 1981. (*Dissertation Abstracts International, 42* (09A), 3838.)

Hatch, W. R., and Bennet, A. *Independent Study.* New Dimensions in Higher Education, no. 1. Washington, D.C.: U.S. Department of Health, Education, and Welfare, 1960.

Hausdorff, J. "Independent Study Experience of Baccalaureate Nursing Students and Perceived Autonomy." Unpublished doctoral dissertation, Columbia University, 1973. (*Dissertation Abstracts International, 34* (06A), 3023.)

Havighurst, R. J. "Changing Status and Roles During the Adult Life Cycle: Significance for Adult Education." In H. W. Burns (ed.), *Sociological Backgrounds of Adult Education: Papers Presented at a Syracuse University Conference, Sagamore, N.Y., October 1963.* Chicago: Center for the Study of Liberal Education for Adults, 1964.

Häyrynen, Y.-P., and Häyrynen, S.-L. "Aesthetic Activity and Cognitive Learning: Creativity and Orientation of Thinking in New Problem Situations." *Adult Education in Finland,* 1980, *17* (3), 5–16.

Heffernan, J. N. "Educational Brokering: New Services for Adult Learners." *Alternative Higher Education: The Journal of Non-Traditional Studies,* 1977, *1,* 111–123.

Heffernan, J. N., Macy, F. L., and Vickers, D. *Education Brokering: A New Service for Adult Learners.* Washington, D.C.: National Center for Educational Brokering, 1976.

Heider, F. *The Psychology of Interpersonal Relations.* New York: Wiley, 1958.

Heisenberg, W. *Physics and Beyond: Encounters and Conversations.* (A. J. Pomerans, trans.) New York: Harper & Row, 1971.

Henner-Stanchina, C. "Two Years of Autonomy: Practise and Outlook." *Mélanges pédagogiques — 1976.* Nancy, France: Centre de Recherches et d'Applications Pédagogiques en Langues, Université de Nancy, 1976.

Henner-Stanchina, C. and Holec, H. "Evaluation in an Autonomous Learning Scheme." *Mélanges pédagogiques — 1977.* Nancy, France: Centre de Recherches et d'Applications Pédagogiques en Langues, Université de Nancy, 1977.

Henney, M. "Facilitating Self-Directed Learning." *Improving College and University Teaching,* 1978, *26* (2), 128–130.

Herman, R. *The Design of Self-Directed Learning: A Handbook for Teachers and Administrators.* (Rev. ed.) Toronto: Ontario Institute for Studies in Education, 1980.

Herman, R. "Student Perceptions of Three Models of Self-Directed Learning in a Graduate Program of Adult Education." Proceedings of 3rd annual conference of the Canadian Association for the Study of Adult Education, Guelph, June 1984, 324–339.

Heron, J. *Experience and Method: An Inquiry into the Concept of Experiential Research.* Guildford, England: Human Potential Research Project, University of Surrey, 1971.

Heron, J. "Assessment Revisited." In D. J. Boud (ed.), *Developing Student Autonomy in Learning.* London: Kogan Page, 1981.

Hettich, P. "The Journal: An Autobiographical Approach to Learning." *Teaching of Psychology,* 1976, *3,* 60–63.

Hiemstra, R. *The Older Adult and Learning.* Lincoln: Department of Adult and Continuing Education, University of Nebraska, 1975. (ERIC Document Reproduction Service no. ED 117–317.)

Hiemstra, R. "The Older Adult's Learning Projects." *Educational Gerontology: An International Quarterly,* 1976, *1* (4), 331–341.

Hiemstra, R. (ed.). "Policy Recommendations Related to Self-Directed Learning." *Occasional Paper No. 1.* Syracuse, N.Y.: Division of Educational Development and Administrative Support, Syracuse University, 1980. (ERIC Document Reproduction Service no. ED 198 304.)

Hiemstra, R., and others. "Naturalistic Inquiry Methodologies Appropriate to Research on Adult Learning." Symposium presented at twenty-second annual Adult Education Research Conference, De Kalb, Ill., Apr. 1981, 279–285.

Higgs, J. "Program Structure and Self-Direction in Independent Learning Programs: Towards a Theory of Liberating Program Systems for Independent Learning Programs." Unpublished doctoral dissertation, University of New South Wales, 1989.

Hill, J. E. *The Educational Sciences.* Bloomfield Hills, Mich.: Institute for Educational Sciences, Oakland Community College, 1971.

Himmel, C. E. "A Critical Review and Analysis of Self-Directed Learning Methods Utilized in the Teaching of Undergraduate Psychology Courses." Unpublished doctoral dissertation,

University of Illinois—Urbana-Champaign, 1970. (*Dissertation Abstracts International, 31* (05A), 2182.)

Hirschfeld, S. "Intentional Learning Efforts: Learning Projects of Adults in Haifa." Unpublished doctoral dissertation, University of Toronto, 1981. (*Dissertation Abstracts International, 42* (10A), 4252.)

Hitchcock, D. *Critical Thinking: A Guide to Evaluating Information.* Toronto: Methuen, 1983.

Hofsess, K., and Burke, P. "Self-Directed Learning: Problem Solving and Trust-Building." In proceedings of the 3rd Lifelong Learning Research Conference, University of Maryland, Feb. 1981, 94–98. College Park: Department of Agriculture and Extension Education, University of Maryland. (ERIC Document Reproduction Service no. ED 197 198.)

Hoghielm, R., and Rubenson, K. *Adult Education for Social Change: Research on the Swedish Allocation Policy.* Lund, Sweden: C.W.K. Gleerup Liber, 1980.

Holland, J. G. "The Misplaced Adaptation to Individual Differences." Paper presented at 77th annual conference of the American Psychological Association, Washington, D.C., Sept. 1969. (ERIC Document Reproduction Service no. ED 040 754.)

Holmberg, B. *Adult Education: Students' Independence and Autonomy as Foundations and as Educational Outcomes.* ZIFF Papiere 49. Hagen, Germany: Zentrales Institut für Fernstudienforschung, Fern Universität, 1984.

Holmes, M. R. "Interpersonal Behaviors and Their Relationship to the Andragogical and Pedagogical Orientations of Adult Educators." *Adult Education (U.S.),* 1980, *31* (1), 18–29.

Holyoake, G. J. *Sixty Years of an Agitator's Life.* (2 vols.) London: Unwin, 1892.

Hood, J. L. "An Analysis of Job-Related Self-Learning Projects Performed by Civilian Procurement Personnel in the US Air Force." Unpublished doctoral dissertation, Ohio State University, 1975. (*Dissertation Abstracts International, 36* (08A), 4960.)

Hopkins, F. L. "Bibliographic Instruction: An Emerging Professional Discipline." In C. A. Kirkendall (ed.), *Directions for the Decade: Library Instruction in the 1980s.* Ann Arbor, Mich.: Pierian Press, 1981.

Hopper, E., and Osborn, M. *Adult Students: Education, Selection and Social Control.* London: Pinter, 1975.

Hostler, J. "The Aims of Adult Education." *Manchester Monograph No. 17.* Manchester, England: Department of Adult Education, University of Manchester, 1981.

Houle, C. O. *The Inquiring Mind: A Study of the Adult Who Continues to Learn.* Madison: University of Wisconsin Press, 1961. (Rpt. in facsimile, with an introduction by H. B. Long, Norman, Okla.: Oklahoma Research Center for Continuing Professional and Higher Education, 1988.)

Houle, C. O. *The Design of Education.* San Francisco: Jossey-Bass, 1972.

Houle, C. O. *Patterns of Learning: New Perspectives on Life-Span Education.* San Francisco: Jossey-Bass, 1984.

Hounsell, D. J. "Understanding Teaching and Teaching for Understanding." In F. Marton, D. J. Hounsell, and N. J. Entwistle (eds.), *The Experience of Learning.* Edinburgh: Scottish Academic Press, 1984.

Hovey, D. E., Gruber, H. E., and Terrell, G. "Effects of Self-Directed Study on Course Achievement, Retention and Curiosity." *Journal of Educational Research,* 1963, *56* (7), 346–351.

Hudson, J. W. *History of Adult Education.* London: Longmans, 1851.

Hudson, L. *Contrary Imaginations.* Harmondsworth, England: Penguin, 1966.

Huggins, K. B. "A Study of the Correlation Between Student-Teacher Self-Concept and the Fostering of Pupil Autonomy in the Classroom." Unpublished doctoral dissertation, University of Massachusetts, 1975. (*Dissertation Abstracts International, 36* (06A), 3604.)

Humphrey, F. C. "A Study of Adults' Preferences for Control of Molar Learning Activities." Unpublished doctoral dissertation, University of Wisconsin, 1973. (*Dissertation Abstracts International, 34* (05A), 2259.)

Humphrey, F. C. "A Study of Adults' Preferences for Control of Molar Learning Activities." Paper presented at 15th annual Adult Education Research Conference, Chicago, Apr, 1974. (ERIC Document Reproduction Service no. ED 094 103.)

Hunt, D. E. *Matching Models in Education: The Co-Ordination of Teaching Methods with Student Characteristics.* Toronto: Ontario Institute for Studies in Education, 1971.

Huntington, J. "Power and Social Influence in the Relationship Between Staff Member and Course Member." In B. Anderson, D. J. Boud, and G. McLeod (eds.), *Experience-Based Learning: How? Why?* Sydney: Australian Consortium on Experiential Education, 1980.

Husén, T. *The Learning Society.* London: Methuen, 1974.

Husserl, E. *Cartesian Meditations: An Introduction to Phenomenology.* (Dorian Cairns, trans.) The Hague: Nijhoff, 1960.

Hutchins, R. M. *The Learning Society.* Harmondsworth, England: Penguin, 1968.

Hynes, D. "Theory into Practice." In J. R. Baird and I. J. Mitchell (eds.), *Improving the Quality of Teaching and Learning: An Australian Case Study — The PEEL Project.* Melbourne, Australia: PEEL Group, Monash University, 1986.

Illich, I., and Verne, E. *Imprisoned in the Global Classroom.* London: Writers and Readers Publishing Cooperative, 1976.

Ingleby, D. "The Psychology of Child Psychology." In M.P.M. Richards (ed.), *The Integration of a Child into a Social World.* Cambridge: Cambridge University Press, 1974.

Ingram, J. B. *Curriculum Integration and Lifelong Education.* Oxford/Hamburg: Pergamon Press/Unesco Institute for Education, 1979.

Ingram, L. C. "Teaching the Sociology of Religion: The Student's Religious Autobiography." *Teaching Sociology,* 1979, *6,* 161–172.

Irish, G. H. "Critical Decision Making for More Effective Learning." In A. B. Knox (ed.), *Teaching Adults Effectively.* New Directions for Continuing Education, no. 6. San Francisco: Jossey-Bass, 1980.

Jackins, H. *The Human Side of Human Beings: The Theory of Re-Evaluation Counselling.* Seattle, Wash.: Rational Island, 1965.

Jackson, G. B. "Methods for Integrative Reviews." *Review of Educational Research,* 1980, *50* (3), 438–460.

Jackson, R. J. "The Learning Activities of Thirty Adults as Revealed by Selected Autobiographies." Unpublished doctoral dissertation, Northern Illinois University, 1979. (*Dissertation Abstracts International, 40* (08A), 4354.)

Jankovic, V., and others. *European Expert Meeting on the Forms of Autodidactic Learning — Paris, October 16–19, 1979.* Final report and recommendations. Paris: Division of Structures, Contents, Methods and Techniques, Unesco, 1979.

Jarvis, P. "Andragogy — A Sign of the Times." *Studies in the Education of Adults,* 1984, *16* (1), 32–38.

Jarvis, P. *Adult Learning in the Social Context.* London: Croom Helm, 1987a.

Jarvis, P. "Towards a Discipline of Adult Education." In P. Jarvis (ed.), *Twentieth Century Thinkers in Adult Education.* London: Croom Helm, 1987b.

Jenks, C. L., Murphy, C. J., and Simms, D. *Experience-Based Learning and the Facilitative Role of Teachers.* (Field version.) San Francisco: Far West Laboratory for Educational Research and Development, 1978.

Jennings, L. E. "Paradigmatic Choices in Adult Education: From the Empirical to the Critical." *Australian Journal of Adult Education,* 1985, *25* (2), 3–7.

Jennings, L. E. "Issues for Consideration by Case Study Workers." In M. Emery (ed.), *Qualitative Research: Papers from a Symposium, May 22–23, 1986.* Canberra: Research Network, Australian Association of Adult Education, 1986.

Jensen, G. E. "The Nature of Education as a Discipline." In G. E. Jensen (ed.), *Readings for Educational Researchers.* Ann Arbor, Mich.: Ann Arbor Publications, 1960.

Jensen, G. E., Liveright, A. A., and Hallenback, W. *Adult Education: Outlines of an Emerging Field of University Study.* Washington, D.C.: Adult Education Association of the United States, 1964.

Jessup, F. W. *Lifelong Learning: A Symposium on Continuing Education.* Oxford: Pergamon Press, 1969.

Joblin, D. "Self-Direction in Adult Education: An Analysis, Defence, Refutation and Assessment of the Notion that Adults Are More Self-Directed Than Children and Youth." *International Journal of Lifelong Education,* 1988, *7* (2), 115–125.

Johannson, L. *Utbildning: Resonerande del. Utkast till kap 7 i Betän-*

kande on Svenska Folkets Levnadsförhållanden [Education: Discursive section. Draft version of chapter 7 in the Report on the Living Conditions of the Swedish People]. Stockholm: Allmänna Förlaget, 1970.

Johns, W. E., Jr. "Selected Characteristics of the Learning Projects Pursued by Practicing Pharmacists." Unpublished doctoral dissertation, University of Georgia, 1973. (*Dissertation Abstracts International, 34* (08A), 4677.)

Johnson, A. A. "The Effects of an Individualized Mode of Instruction upon Pre-Service Teachers' Self-Reported Tendency to Facilitate Self-Directed Learning in the Classroom." Unpublished doctoral dissertation, Pennsylvania State University, 1973. (*Dissertation Abstracts International, 34* (10A), 6499.)

Johnson, E. A. "Selected Characteristics of the Learning Projects Pursued by Adults Who Have Earned a High School Diploma and/or High School Equivalency Certificate." Unpublished doctoral dissertation, University of Georgia, 1973. (*Dissertation Abstracts International, 34* (06A), 3004.)

Johnson, J. K. "Freshman Responses to Autonomous Learning: A Study of Intrinsic Versus Extrinsic Disposition to Learn." Unpublished doctoral dissertation, University of Minnesota, 1974. (*Dissertation Abstracts International, 35* (06A), 3458.)

Johnson, R. " 'Really Useful Knowledge': Radical Education and Working-Class Culture 1790–1848." In J. Clarke, G. Critcher, and R. Johnson (eds.), *Working-Class Culture: Studies in History and Theory*. London: Hutchinson in association with the Centre for Contemporary Cultural Studies, University of Birmingham, 1979.

Johnson, V., Levine, H., and Rosenthal, E. L. "Learning Projects of Unemployed Adults in New Jersey." Unpublished manuscript, Educational Advancement Project, Rutgers Labor Education Center, New Brunswick, N.J., 1977.

Johnstone, J.W.C., and Rivera, R. J. *Volunteers for Learning: A Study of the Educational Pursuits of American Adults*. Chicago: Aldine, 1965.

Jones, G. R. "Life History Methodology." In G. Morgan (ed.), *Beyond Method: Strategies for Social Research*. Newbury Park, Calif.: Sage, 1983.

Jordan, W. D. "Searching for Adulthood in America." In E. Erickson (ed.), *Adulthood.* New York: Norton, 1978.

Jourard, S. M. "Fascination: A Phenomenological Perspective on Independent Learning." In G. T. Gleason (ed.), *The Theory and Nature of Independent Learning.* Scranton, Pa.: International Textbook, 1967.

Joyce, B. R., and Weil, M. *Models of Teaching.* (2nd ed.) Englewood Cliffs, N.J.: Prentice-Hall, 1980.

Judd, R. S. "A Comparison of Self-directed Learning in Learning Projects in School and out of School." Unpublished master's thesis, Department of Professional Studies in Education, Iowa State University, 1981.

Judd, W. A. "Individual Differences in Learner-Controlled CAI." Paper presented at 56th annual meeting of the American Educational Research Association, Washington, D.C., Mar.-Apr. 1975.

Kallen, D. "Recurrent Education and Lifelong Learning: Definitions and Distinctions." In T. Schuller and J. Megarry (eds.), *Recurrent Education and Lifelong Learning.* London: Kogan Page, 1979.

Kallen, H. M. *Philosophical Issues in Adult Education.* Springfield, Ma.: Thomas, 1962.

Kamii, C. "Autonomy: The Aim of Education Envisioned by Piaget." *Phi Delta Kappan,* 1984, *65* (6), 410–415.

Karabel, J., and Halsey, A. H. (eds.), *Power and Ideology in Education.* New York: Oxford University Press, 1977.

Kasworm, C. E. "An Exploratory Study of the Development of Self-Directed Learning as an Instructional/Curriculum Strategy." Proceedings of 4th Lifelong Learning Research Conference, University of Maryland, Feb. 1982, 125–129. College Park, Md.: Department of Agriculture and Extension Education, University of Maryland. (ERIC Document Reproduction Service no. ED 215 198.)

Kasworm, C. E. "An Examination of Self-Directed Contract Learning as an Instructional Strategy." *Innovative Higher Education,* 1983a, *8* (1), 45–54.

Kasworm, C. E. "Self-Directed Learning and Lifespan Development." *International Journal of Lifelong Education,* 1983b, *2* (1), 29–46.

Kathrein, M. A. "A Study of Self-Directed Continued Professional Education of Members of the Illinois Nurses' Association: Content and Process." Unpublished doctoral dissertation, Northern Illinois University, 1981. (*Dissertation Abstracts International, 42* (05A), 1902.)

Keddie, N. "Adult Education: An Ideology of Individualism." In J. L. Thompson (ed.), *Adult Education for a Change.* London: Hutchinson, 1980.

Keller, F. S. "'Goodbye, Teacher . . .'" *Journal of Applied Behavioral Analysis,* 1968, *1* (1), 78–89.

Kelley, N. E. "A Comparative Study of Professionally Related Learning Projects of Secondary School Teachers." Unpublished master's thesis, Cornell University, 1976.

Kelly, G. A. *The Psychology of Personal Constructs.* 2 vols. New York: Norton, 1955.

Kelly, G. A. "Autobiography of a Theory." In B. Maher (ed.), *Clinical Psychology and Personality: The Selected Papers of George Kelly.* New York: Wiley, 1969.

Kelly, G. A. "A Brief Introduction to Personal Construct Theory." In D. Bannister (ed.), *Perspectives in Personal Construct Theory.* London: Academic Press, 1970.

Kelley, G. A. "The Psychology of the Unknown." In D. Bannister (ed.), *New Perspectives in Personal Construct Theory.* London: Academic Press, 1977.

Kelly, T. "Public Libraries in Adult Education." *Journal of Librarianship,* 1970, *2* (3), 145–159.

Kemmis, S. "Action Research in Retrospect and Prospect." In *The Action Research Reader.* Highton, Australia: Deakin University Press, 1982.

Kenny, V. (guest ed.). "Radical Constructivism, Autopoiesis & Psychotherapy." *The Irish Journal of Psychology,* 1988, *9* (1) (entire issue).

Kerlinger, F. N., and Kaya, E. "The Construction and Factor-Analytic Validation of Scales to Measure Attitudes Toward Education." *Education and Psychological Measurement,* 1959, *19* (1), 13–29.

Kessen, W. "Questions for a Theory of Cognitive Development." *Child Development Monograph,* 1966, *31* (5), 58–59.

Kidd, J. R. *The Implications of Continuous Learning*. Toronto: Gage, 1966.

Kidd, J. R. *How Adults Learn*. (Rev. ed.) New York: Association Press, 1973.

Kidd, J. R. "Learning and Libraries: Competencies for Full Participation." *Library Trends*, 1983, *31* (4), 525–542.

Kirschenbaum, D. S., and Perri, M. G. "Improving Academic Competence in Adults: A Review of Recent Research." *Journal of Counseling Psychology*, 1982, *29* (1), 76–94.

Klauss, R. "Formalized Mentor Relationships for Management and Executive Development Programs in the Federal Government." *Public Administration Review*, 1981, *41* (4), 489–496.

Knapper, C. K., and Cropley, A. J. "Lifelong Learning and Higher Education: Implications for Teaching." Paper presented at 6th international conference on Improving University Teaching, Lausanne, Switzerland, July 1980.

Knoepfli, H.E.B. "The Origins of Women's Autonomous Learning Groups." Unpublished doctoral dissertation, University of Toronto, 1971. (*Dissertation Abstracts International, 33* (01A), 136.)

Knowles, M. S. *The Modern Practice of Adult Education: Andragogy versus Pedagogy*. Chicago: Follett, 1970.

Knowles, M. S. *Self-Directed Learning: A Guide for Learners and Teachers*. New York: Association Press, 1975.

Knowles, M. S. *The Modern Practice of Adult Education: From Pedagogy to Andragogy*. (Rev. ed.) Chicago: Follett, 1980.

Knowles, M. S. "Andragogy: An Emerging Technology for Adult Learning." In M. Tight (ed.), *Adult Learning and Education*. London: Croom Helm, 1983a.

Knowles, M. S. "Creating Lifelong Learning Communities: Conceptualizing All Social Systems as Learning Resources." Unpublished manuscript, Unesco Institute for Education, Hamburg, 1983b.

Knowles, M. S. *The Adult Learner: A Neglected Species*. (3rd ed.) Houston, Tex.: Gulf, 1984.

Knox, A. B. "Lifelong Self-Directed Education." Unpublished manuscript, University of Illinois–Urbana-Champaign, 1973. (ERIC Document Reproduction Service no. ED 074 346.)

Knox, A. B. *Helping Adults Learn: A Guide to Planning, Implementing, and Conducting Programs.* San Francisco: Jossey-Bass, 1986.

Koetting, J. R. "Foundations of Naturalistic Inquiry: Developing a Theory Base for Understanding Individual Interpretations of Reality." *Media and Adult Learning,* 1984, *6* (2), 8–18.

Kolb, D. A. *Learning Style Inventory Technical Manual.* Boston: McBer, 1976a.

Kolb, D. A. "Management and the Learning Process." *California Management Review,* 1976b, *28* (3), 21–31.

Kondani, K. "Analyse des projets autodidactiques d'adultes analphabètes de Kinshasa" [Analysis of self-directed learning projects of illiterate adults in Kinshasa]. Thèse de doctorat inédite, Université de Montréal, 1982.

Kotaska, J. G. "The Effect of Guidance on Learning in Independent Study." Unpublished master's thesis, University of British Columbia, 1973.

Kotaska, J. G., and Dickinson, G. "Effects of a Study Guide on Independent Adult Learning." *Adult Education (U.S.),* 1975, *25* (3), 161–168.

Kratz, R. J. "The Effects of Programs Which Foster Self-Directed Learning on Dropout Rate, the Length of Stay, and the Preference for Self-Directed Learning of Adult Basic Education Students." Unpublished doctoral dissertation, State University of New York–Albany, 1978. (*Dissertation Abstracts International, 39* (04A), 1263.)

Kratz, R. J. "Implications of Self-Directed Learning for Functionally Illiterate Adults." Proceedings of 21st annual Adult Education Research Conference, Vancouver, May 1980, 134–137.

Kremer, L. "Teachers' Attitudes Toward Educational Goals as Reflected in Classroom Behavior." *Journal of Educational Psychology,* 1978, *78* (6), 993–997.

Krimerman, L. I. "Autonomy: A New Paradigm for Research." In L. G. Thomas (ed.), *Philosophical Redirections of Educational Research.* The Seventy-First Yearbook of the National Society for the Study of Education. Part 1. Chicago: National Society for the Study of Education, 1972.

Kuhn, D. "The Role of Self-Directed Activity in Cognitive Development." In I. E. Sigel, D. M. Brodzinsky, and R. M.

Golinkoff (eds.), *New Directions in Piagetian Theory and Practice.* Hillsdale, N.J: Erlbaum, 1981.

Kuhn, T. S. *The Structure of Scientific Revolutions.* (2nd ed.) Chicago: University of Chicago Press, 1970.

Kulich, J. "The Adult Self-Learner: An Historical Perspective." In J. R. Kidd and G. R. Selman (eds.), *Coming of Age: Canadian Adult Education in the 1960's.* Toronto: Canadian Association for Adult Education, 1978.

Laing, R. D. *Knots.* London: Tavistock, 1970.

Lakatos, I. "Falsification and the Methodology of Scientific Research Programmes." In I. Lakatos and A. Musgrove (eds.), *Criticism and the Growth of Knowledge.* Cambridge: Cambridge University Press, 1970.

Landvogt, P. L. "A Framework for Exploring the Adult Educator's Commitment Toward the Construct of 'Guided Learning.'" Unpublished master's thesis, University of Wisconsin, 1969.

Landvogt, P. L. "A Framework for Exploring the Adult Educator's Commitment Toward the Construct of 'Guided Learning.'" Paper presented at 11th annual Adult Education Research Conference, Minneapolis, Minn., Feb. 1970.

Langford, T. L. "Effects of a Course Designed to Encourage Student Self-Direction in Learning." Unpublished doctoral dissertation, University of Texas, 1974. (*Dissertation Abstracts International, 35* (01A), 322.)

Larsson, S., and Helmstad, G. "Factory Storemen's Ideas About Education." Paper presented at 1st annual conference of the International League for Social Commitment in Adult Education, Sånga-Säby, Sweden, July 1985.

Laudan, L. *Progress and Its Problems: Towards a Theory of Scientific Growth.* Berkeley: University of California Press, 1977.

Laurillard, D. M. "Computers and the Emancipation of Students: Giving Control to the Learner." In P. Ramsden (ed.), *Improving Learning: New Perspectives.* London: Kogan Page, 1988.

Lawson, K. H. "Avoiding the Ethical Issues." In K. H. Lawson, *Philosophical Concepts and Values in Adult Education.* (Rev. ed.) Milton Keynes, England: Open University Press, 1979.

Lawson, K. H. *Analysis and Ideology: Conceptual Essays on the Edu-*

cation of Adults. Nottingham, England: Department of Adult Education, University of Nottingham, 1982.

Leakey, R. E., and Lewin, R. *Origins: What New Discoveries Reveal About the Emergence of Our Species and Its Possible Future.* London: Macdonald and James, 1977.

Leclerc, G. J. "L'autodidaxie et l'autodidaxie assistée comme méthode d'éducation" [Autodidaxy and assisted autodidaxy as a method of education]. Unpublished manuscript, Département d'Andragogie, Université de Sherbrooke, Sherbrooke, Canada, 1973.

Lee, R. E. *Continuing Education for Adults Through the American Public Library, 1833–1964.* Chicago: American Library Association, 1966.

Leean, C., and Sisco, B. R. *Learning Projects and Self-Planned Learning Efforts Among Undereducated Adults in Rural Vermont.* Final report. Washington, D.C.: National Institute of Education, U.S. Department of Health, Education, and Welfare, 1981a.

Leean, C., and Sisco, B. R. "Naturalistic Inquiry Methodologies Appropriate to Research on Adult Learning." Proceedings of 22nd annual Adult Education Research Conference, Northern Illinois University, De Kalb, Apr. 1981b, 279–285.

Leeb, J. G. "Self-Directed Learning and Growth Toward Personality Responsibility: Implications for a Framework for Health Promotion." Unpublished doctoral dissertation, Syracuse University, 1983. (*Dissertation Abstracts International, 45* (03A), 724.)

Lefcourt, H. M. *Locus of Control: Current Trends in Theory and Research.* Hillsdale, N.J.: Erlbaum, 1976.

Lengrand, P. *An Introduction to Lifelong Education.* Paris: Unesco, 1970.

Lensch, O. H., III. "An Investigation of the Adult Learning Patterns in Montgomery County, Ohio." Unpublished doctoral dissertation, Union for Experimenting Colleges and Universities, 1980. (*Dissertation Abstracts International, 40* (12A), 6110.)

Lester, V., and Johnson, C. "The Learning Dialogue: Mentoring." In J. Fried (ed.), *Education for Student Development.* New

Directions for Student Services, no. 15. San Francisco: Jossey-Bass, 1981.

Levchuk, J. W. "Pharmacists' Self-Management of Self-Directed Learning Projects." Unpublished doctoral dissertation, University of Arizona, 1977. (*Dissertation Abstracts International, 38* (03B), 1148.)

Lévi-Strauss, C. *The Savage Mind.* Chicago: University of Chicago Press, 1962.

Levinson, D., and others. *The Seasons of a Man's Life.* New York: Ballentine, 1978.

Lewis, G. R. "A Comparative Study of Learning Networks in the United States." Unpublished doctoral dissertation, Northwestern University, 1978. (*Dissertation Abstracts International, 39* (08A), 4631.)

Lewis, H. A. "A Teacher's Reflections on Autonomy." *Studies in Higher Education,* 1978, *3* (2), 149–159.

Lincoln, Y. S., and Guba, E. G. *Naturalistic Inquiry.* Newbury Park, Calif.: Sage, 1985.

Lindeman, E. C. "What Is Adult Education?" Unpublished paper, box 4, Lindeman Archive, Butler Library, Columbia University, 1925.

Lindeman, E. C. *Worker's Education and the Public Libraries.* Workers' Education Pamphlet Series, no. 7. New York: Workers' Education Bureau of America, 1926a.

Lindeman, E. C. *The Meaning of Adult Education.* Montreal: Harvest House, 1926b. (Rpt. in facsimile, with an introduction by H. B. Long, Norman, Okla.: Oklahoma Research Center for Continuing Professional and Higher Education, 1989.)

Lindsay, P. H., and Norman, D. A. *Human Information Processing.* (2nd ed.) London: Academic Press, 1977.

Little, D. J. "Adult Learning and Education: A Concept Analysis." In *Yearbook of Adult and Continuing Education, 1979–80.* Chicago: Marquis Academic Media, 1979.

Little, D. J. "Self-Directed Education: A Conceptual Analysis." Proceedings of 26th annual Adult Education Research Conference, Arizona State University, Tempe, Mar. 1985, 189–194.

Livingstone, R. W. *The Future in Education.* Cambridge: Cambridge University Press, 1941.

Long, H. B. "Item Analysis of Gugliemino's Self-Directed Learning Readiness Scale." *International Journal of Lifelong Education,* 1987, *6* (4), 331–336.

Long, H. B. "Self-Directed Learning Reconsidered." In H. B. Long and Associates, *Self-Directed Learning: Application and Theory.* Athens: Department of Adult Education, University of Georgia, 1988.

Long, H. B. "Some Additional Criticisms of Field's Investigation." *Adult Education Quarterly,* 1989, *39* (4) 240–243.

Long, H. B., and Agyekum, S. K. "Guglielmino's Self-Directed Learning Readiness Scale: A Validation Study." *Higher Education,* 1983, *12* (1), 77–87.

Long, H. B., and Agyekum, S. K. "Multi-Trait, Multi-Method Validation of Guglielmino's Self-Directed Learning Readiness Scale." Proceedings of 25th annual Adult Education Research Conference, North Carolina State University, Raleigh, Apr. 1984, 272–278.

Long, H. B., and Agyekum, S. K. "Toward a Theory of Self-Directed Learning: An Appraisal of Gibbons' Principles and Strategies." Paper presented at 3rd North American symposium on Adult Self-Directed Learning, Oklahoma Research Center for Continuing Professional and Higher Education, Norman, Feb. 1989.

Long, H. B., and Ashford, M. L. "Self-Directed Inquiry as a Method of Continuing Education in Colonial America." *Journal of General Education,* 1976, *28* (3), 245–255.

Long, H. B., and Associates. *Self-Directed Learning: Application and Theory.* Athens: Department of Adult Education, University of Georgia, 1988.

Long, H. B., and Associates. *Self-Directed Learning: Emerging Theory and Practice.* Norman: Oklahoma Research Center for Continuing Professional and Higher Education, University of Oklahoma, 1989.

Long, H. B., and Associates. *Advances in Research and Practice in Self-Directed Learning.* Norman: Oklahoma Research Center for Continuing Professional and Higher Education, University of Oklahoma, 1990.

Lovett, W. *Life Struggles of William Lovett in Pursuit of Bread, Knowledge, and Freedom.* New York: Knopf, 1920.

Luikart, C. "Social Networks and Self-Planned Adult Learning." Unpublished doctoral dissertation, University of North Carolina, 1976. (*Dissertation Abstracts International, 37* (08A), 4782.)

Luikart, C. "Social Networks and Self-Planned Adult Learning." *University of North Carolina Extension Bulletin,* 1977, *61* (2) (entire issue).

Lukes, S. *Individualism.* Oxford: Blackwell, 1973.

Lukinsky, J. "Reflective Withdrawal Through Journal Writing." In J. Mezirow and Associates, *Fostering Critical Reflection in Adulthood: A Guide to Transformative and Emancipatory Learning.* San Francisco: Jossey-Bass, 1990.

McCatty, C.A.M. "Patterns of Learning Projects Among Professional Men." Unpublished doctoral dissertation, University of Toronto, 1973. (*Dissertation Abstracts International, 35* (01A), 323.)

McCatty, C.A.M. "Patterns of Learning Projects Among Professional Men." *Alberta Journal of Educational Research,* 1975, *21* (2), 116–129.

McCatty, C.A.M. "Patterns of Learning Projects Among Physical and Health Education Teachers." *Reporting Classroom Research (Ontario Educational Research Council),* 1976, *5* (2), 7–8.

McClintock, R. "Reaffirming a Great Tradition." In R. Gross (ed.), *Invitation to Lifelong Learning.* Chicago: Follett, 1982.

McCreary, E. K. "Use and Utility of Information Channels for Self-Help Advocacy Groups." Unpublished doctoral dissertation, Department of Administrative, Adult, and Higher Education, University of British Columbia, 1984. (*Dissertation Abstracts International, 46* (12A), 3570.)

McCune, S. K., and Austin, S. F. "A Statistical Critique of Field's Investigation." *Adult Education Quarterly,* 1989, *39* (4), 243–245.

McCune, S. K., Guglielmino, L. N., and Garcia, G. "Adult Self-Direction in Learning: A Meta-Analytic Study of Research Using the Self-Directed Learning Readiness Scale." Paper presented at 3rd North American symposium on Adult Self-Directed Learning, University of Oklahoma, Norman, Feb. 1989.

Macdonald, C. *Self-Learning*. Payneham, Australia: TAFE National Centre for Research and Development, 1984.

Macdonald, J. B. "Independent Learning: The Theme of the Conference." In G. T. Gleason (ed.), *Theory and Nature of Independent Learning*. Scranton, Pa.: International Textbook, 1967.

McGee, G. "The Effects of Collaborative Planning on Adult Learners." Unpublished M.A. thesis, Department of Administrative, Adult, and Higher Education, University of British Columbia, 1984.

McKeachie, W. J. "Student-Centered Versus Instructor-Centered Instruction." *Journal of Educational Psychology*, 1954, *45*, 143–150.

McKeachie, W. J. "The Improvement of Instruction." *Review of Education Research*, 1960, *30* (4), 351–360.

McKeachie, W. J. "Procedures and Techniques of Teaching: A Survey of Experimental Studies." In N. Sanford (ed.), *The American College: A Psychological and Social Interpretation of the Higher Learning*. New York: Wiley, 1962.

McKean, R. B. "Adult Learners' Pedagogical Expectations About Level of Formality and Type of Learning Experience." Unpublished doctoral dissertation, Michigan State University, 1977. (*Dissertation Abstracts International, 38* (10A), 5850.)

MacKenzie, N., Postgate, R., and Scupham, J. *Open Learning: Systems and Problems in Post-Secondary Education*. Paris: Unesco, 1975.

MacNeil, C. "A Comparative Study of Two Instructional Methods Employed in Teaching Nutrition: Lecture-Discussion and Self-Directed Study." Unpublished doctoral dissertation, University of Minnesota, 1967. (*Dissertation Abstracts International, 28* (11A), 4534.)

McPeck, J. E. *Critical Thinking and Education*. Oxford: Robinson, 1981.

Mager, R. F., and Clark, C. "Explorations in Student-Controlled Instruction." *Psychological Reports*, 1963, *13*, 71–76.

Mager, R. F., and McCann, J. *Learner-Controlled Instruction*. Palo Alto, Calif.: Varian Associates, 1961.

Magoon, A. J. "Constructivist Approaches in Educational Research." *Review of Educational Research*, 1977, *47* (4), 651–693.

Mair, J.M.M. "Metaphors for Living." In J. K. Cole (ed.), *Personal Construct Psychology: Nebraska Symposium on Motivation*. Lincoln: University of Nebraska Press, 1977.

Maloney, D. C. "Effects of Psychological and Demographic Characteristics of External Degree Students on Achievement in a Teacher-Directed Versus Self-Directed General Psychology Course." Unpublished doctoral dissertation, Clark University, 1978. (*Dissertation Abstracts International, 39* (06A), 3405.)

Mandl, H., Stein, N. L., and Trabasso, T. (eds.). *Learning and Comprehension of Text*. Hillsdale, N.J.: Erlbaum, 1984.

Manicas, P. T., and Secord, P. F. "Implications of the New Philosophy of Science." *American Psychologist*, 1983, *38* (4), 399–413.

Maras, R. J. "The Autonomous Learner." Unpublished doctoral dissertation, Clark University, 1978. (*Dissertation Abstracts International, 39* (12A), 7247.)

Marbeau, V. "Autonomous Study by Pupils in Secondary Schools. *Education and Culture*, 1976, *31*, 14–21.

Margarones, J. J. "Critical Requirements of Independent Study Based Upon an Analysis of Critical Incidents as Observed and Reported by Students and Instructor." Unpublished doctoral dissertation, Boston University, 1961. (*Dissertation Abstracts International, 22* (09A), 3119.)

Margarones, J. J. "Independent Study: An Operational Definition." *Teacher Education Quarterly*, 1965, *23*, 28–37.

Markman, E. M. "Comprehension Monitoring." In P. Dickinson (ed.), *Children's Oral Communication Skills*. New York: Academic Press, 1981.

Martin, J. R. "Technicality and Abstraction: Language for the Creation of Specialized Texts." In F. Christie, R. Maclean, D. Morris, and P. Williams (eds.), *Writing in Schools: Reader*. Highton, Australia: Deakin University Press, 1989.

Marton, F. "What Does It Take to Learn?" In N. J. Entwistle and D. J. Hounsell (eds.), *How Students Learn*. Bailrigg, England: Institute for Research and Development in Post-Compulsory Education, University of Lancaster, 1975.

Marton, F. *Describing Conceptions of the World Around Us*. Reports of the Institute of Education, University of Göteborg, Sweden: Institute of Education, University of Göteborg, 1978.

Marton, F. "Phenomenography—Describing Conceptions of the World Around Us." *Instructional Science,* 1981, *10* (2), 177–200.

Marton, F., Hounsell, D. J., and Entwistle, N. H., (eds.). *The Experience of Learning.* Edinburgh: Scottish Academic Press, 1984.

Marton, F., and Säljö, R. "On Qualitative Differences in Learning: I—Outcome and Process." *British Journal of Educational Psychology,* 1976a, *46,* 4–11.

Marton, F., and Säljö, R. "On Qualitative Differences in Learning: II—Outcome as a Function of the Learner's Conception of the Task." *British Journal of Educational Psychology,* 1976b, *46,* 115–127.

Maslow, A. H. *Toward a Psychology of Being.* (2nd ed.) New York: Van Nostrand, 1968.

Maslow, A. H. "Existential Psychology: What's in It for Us?" In R. May (ed.), *Existential Psychology.* (2nd ed.) New York: Random House, 1969.

Maslow, A. H. *Motivation and Personality.* (2nd. ed.) New York: Harper and Row, 1970.

Maslow, A. H. *The Farther Reaches of Human Nature.* New York: Viking, 1971.

Maudsley, D. B. "A Theory of Meta-Learning and Principles of Facilitation." Unpublished doctoral dissertation, Department of Educational Theory, University of Toronto, 1979. (*Dissertation Abstracts International, 40* (08A), 4354–4355.)

Maurice, F. D. *Learning and Working.* London: Oxford University Press, 1968. (Originally published 1855.)

Mavor, A. S., Toro, J. A., and DeProspo, E. R. *The Role of the Public Libraries in Adult Independent Learning.* Part II—final report. New York: College Entrance Examination Board, 1976. (ERIC Document Reproduction Service no. ED 149 773.)

Mead, M. "Thinking Ahead: Why is Education Obsolete?" *Harvard Business Review,* 1958, *36* (6), 23–24, 26–28, 30, 34, 36–37, 164, 166–168, 170.

Means, R. P. "Information Seeking Behavior of Michigan Family Physicians." Unpublished doctoral dissertation, University of Illinois–Urbana-Champaign, 1979. (*Dissertation Abstracts International, 40* (08A), 4355.)

Meisler, R. *Trying Freedom: The Case for Liberating Education.* San Diego, Calif.: Harcourt Brace Jovanovich, 1984.

Merriam, S. B., and Simpson, E. *A Guide to Research for Educators and Trainers of Adults.* Malabar, Fla.: Krieger, 1984.

Merriam, S. B., Beder, H., and Ewart, M. "The Use of Ethnography, Case Study and Grounded Theory in Adult Education Research." Symposium presented at 24th annual Adult Education Research Conference, Montreal, Apr. 1983.

Messick, S., and Associates. *Individuality in Learning.* San Francisco: Jossey-Bass, 1976.

Meyer, G. R. *Cognitive Mapping — Matching the Styles of Teaching and Learning.* Minicourse Manual No. 45. North Ryde, Australia: Centre for the Advancement of Teaching, Macquarie University, 1978.

Mezirow, J. D. "A Critical Theory of Adult Learning and Education." *Adult Education,* 1981, *31* (1), 3–24. (Also in M. Tight [ed.], *Adult Learning and Education.* London: Croom Helm, 1983.)

Mezirow, J. D. "A Critical Theory of Self-Directed Learning." In S. D. Brookfield (ed.), *Self-Directed Learning: From Theory to Practice.* New Directions for Continuing Education, no. 25. San Francisco: Jossey-Bass, 1985.

Mezirow, J. D., and Associates. *Fostering Critical Reflection in Adulthood: A Guide to Transformative and Emancipatory Learning.* San Francisco: Jossey-Bass, 1990.

Millar, C. J., Morphet, A. R., and Saddington, J. A. "Case Study: Curriculum Negotiation in Professional Adult Education." *Journal of Curriculum Studies,* 1986, *18* (4), 429–442.

Miller, C., and Parlett, M. *Up to the Mark: A Study of the Examination Game.* London: Society for Research into Higher Education, 1974.

Miller, H. L. *Teaching and Learning in Adult Education.* London: Macmillan, 1964.

Miller, N. "Teachers and Non-Teaching Professionals as Self-Directed Learners." Unpublished master's thesis, Cornell University, 1977.

Miller, N. L., and Botsman, P. B. " Continuing Education for Extension Agents." *Human Ecology Forum,* 1975, *6* (2), 14–17.

Missirian, A. K. "The Process of Mentoring in the Career Development of Female Managers." Unpublished doctoral dissertation, University of Massachusetts, 1980. (*Dissertation Abstracts International, 41* (08A), 3654.)

Mocker, D. W., and Spear, G. E. *Lifelong Learning: Formal, Nonformal, Informal, and Self-Directed.* Information series, no. 241. ERIC Clearinghouse on Adult, Career, and Vocational Education. Columbus: National Center for Research in Vocational Education, Ohio State University, 1982.

Moorcraft, R. "The Origins of Women's Learning Projects." Unpublished master's thesis, University of Toronto, 1975.

Moore, M. G. "Learner Autonomy: The Second Dimension of Independent Learning." *Convergence: An International Journal of Adult Education,* 1972, *5* (2), 76–87.

Moore, M. G. "Speculations on a Definition of Independent Study." In *Proceedings of a Conference on Independent Learning,* W. K. Kellog Foundation Project Report No. 7. Vancouver: Adult Education Research Centre, University of British Columbia, 1973a.

Moore, M. G. "Toward a Theory of Independent Learning and Teaching." *Journal of Higher Education,* 1973b, *44* (12), 661–679.

Moore, M. G. "Investigation of the Interaction Between the Cognitive Style of Field Independence and Attitudes to Independent Study Among Adult Learners Who Use Correspondence Independent Study and Self-Directed Independent Study." Unpublished doctoral dissertation, University of Wisconsin, 1976. (*Dissertation Abstracts International. 37* (06A), 3344.)

Moore, M. G. "A Model of Independent Study." *Epistolodidactika,* 1977, *1,* 6–40.

Moore, M. G. "Independent Study." In R. D. Boyd, J. W. Apps, and Associates, *Redefining the Discipline of Adult Education.* San Francisco: Jossey Bass, 1980.

Moore, M. G. "The Individual Adult Learner." In M. Tight (ed.), *Education for Adults,* Vol. 1: *Adult Learning and Education.* London: Croom Helm, 1983.

Moore, M. G. "Self-Directed Learning and Distance Education." *Journal of Distance Education,* 1986, *1* (1), 7–24.

More, W. S. *Emotions and Adult Learning.* Westmead, England: Saxon House, 1974.

Morris, A., and Stewart-Dore, N. *Learning to Learn from Text: Effective Reading in the Content Areas.* North Ryde, Australia: Addison-Wesley, 1984.

Morris, J. F. "The Planning Behavior and Conceptual Complexity of Selected Clergymen in Self-Directed Learning Projects Related to Their Continuing Professional Education." Unpublished doctoral dissertation, University of Toronto, 1977. (*Dissertation Abstracts International, 39* (04A), 1994-5.)

Mourad, S. A. "Relationship of Grade Level, Sex and Creativity to Readiness for Self-Directed Learning Among Intellectually Gifted Students." Unpublished doctoral dissertation, University of Georgia, 1979. (*Dissertation Abstracts International, 40* (04A), 2002.)

Murphy, J. "The Voice of Memory: History, Autobiography and Oral Memory." *Historical Studies,* 1986, *22* (87), 157-175.

Naisbitt, N. *Megatrends: Ten New Directions Transforming Our Lives.* London: Macdonald, 1984.

Neehall, J. *Degree of Intentionality of Adult Change.* Toronto: University of Toronto Press, 1983.

Neel, A. F. "The Relationship of Authoritarian Personality to Learning: F Scale Scores Compared to Classroom Performance." *Journal of Educational Psychology,* 1959, *50,* 195-199.

Neimeyer, R. A. *The Development of Personal Construct Psychology.* Lincoln: University of Nebraska Press, 1985.

Nelson-Jones, R. *The Theory and Practice of Counselling Psychology.* London: Holt, Rinehart & Winston, 1982.

Newman, J. H. *Discourses on the Scope and Nature of University Education.* Dublin: Duffy, 1852.

Newman, S. E. "Student- Versus Instructor-Design of Study Method." *Journal of Educational Psychology,* 1957, *48* (6), 328-333.

Newsom, R. "Lifelong Learning in London: 1558-1640." *Lifelong Learning: The Adult Years,* 1977, *1* (4), 4-5, 19-21.

Nolan, R. E. "Autonomy Versus Dependency in Adult Second Language Learning." Unpublished doctoral dissertation, Northern Illinois University, 1981a. (*Dissertation Abstracts International, 42* (10A), 4253.)

Nolan, R. E. "Dependency Versus Autonomy in Adult Second Language Learning." Proceedings of 22nd annual Adult Education Research Conference, Northern Illinois. University, De Kalb, Apr. 1981b, 140–145.

Novak, J. D., and Gowin, D. B. *Learning How to Learn.* New York: Cambridge University Press, 1984.

Nuffield Foundation Group for Research and Innovation in Higher Education. *Towards Independence in Learning.* London: Nuffield Foundation, 1975.

Nunney, D. N. "Educational Cognitive Style: A Basis for Personalizing Instruction." *Educational Scientist: Journal of the American Educational Sciences Association,* 1975, *1* (1), 13–26.

Nystedt, L., and Magnusson, D. "Construction of Experience." In J. Mancuso and J. Adams-Webber (eds.), *The Construing Person.* New York: Praeger, 1982.

Oakeshott, M. "Learning and Teaching." In R. S. Peters (ed.), *The Concept of Education.* London: Routledge and Kegan Paul, 1967.

Oberg A. "Uncovering Teacher Images: An Exploratory Study." Paper presented at fifth conference on Curriculum Theory and Practice, Dayton, Ohio, Oct. 1983.

Ochoa, A. M., and Rodriguez, A. M. "Forces Which Affect Self-Responsibility of Students." In D. Della-Dora and L. J. Blanchard (eds.), *Moving Toward Self-Directed Learning: Highlights of Relevant Research and of Promising Practices.* Alexandria, Va.: Association for Supervision and Curriculum Development, 1979.

Oddi, L. F. "Development of an Instrument to Measure Self-Directed Continuing Learning." Unpublished doctoral dissertation, Northern Illinois University, 1984. (*Dissertation Abstracts International, 46* (01A), 49.)

Oddi, L. F. "Development and Validation of an Instrument to Identify Self-Directed Continuing Learners." Proceedings of twenty-sixth annual Adult Education Research Conference, Arizona State University, Tempe, Mar. 1985, 230–235.

Oddi, L. F. "Development and Validation of an Instrument to Identify Self-Directed Continuing Learners." *Adult Education Quarterly,* 1986, *36* (2), 97–107.

Oddi, L. F. "Perspectives on Self-Directed Learning." *Adult Education Quarterly,* 1987, *38* (1), 21–31.

O'Gorman, J. D. "Philosophical and Educational Orientations

of Adult Basic Education Teachers." Unpublished doctoral dissertation, Fordham University, 1981. (*Dissertation Abstracts International, 42* (03A), 963.)

Ohliger, J. D. "Is Lifelong Education a Guarantee of Permanent Inadequacy?" *Convergence,* 1974, *7* (2), 47–58.

Olson, W. C. "Self-Selection as a Principle of Curriculum and Method." *University of Michigan School Education Bulletin,* 1945, *16,* 52–55.

Ordos, D. G. "Models of Motivation for Participation in Adult Education." Proceedings of 21st annual Adult Education Research Conference, University of British Columbia, Vancouver, May 1980, 150–156.

Orlando, A. J. "The Learning Patterns of Parents of Teenagers in a Suburban Community." Unpublished doctoral dissertation, Teachers' College, Columbia University, 1977. (*Dissertation Abstracts International, 38* (10A), 5850.)

Overstreet, H. A. *The Mature Mind.* London: Gollancz, 1950.

Parer, M. S. *Students' Experience of External Study.* Churchill, Australia: Centre for Distance Learning, Gippsland Institute, 1988.

Parkyn, G. W. *Towards a Conceptual Model of Lifelong Education.* Paris: Unesco, 1973.

Parlett, M. R. "The Syllabus-Bound Student." In L. Hudson (ed.), *Ecology of Human Intelligence.* Harmondsworth, England: Penguin Books, 1970.

Parlett, M. R., and Hamilton, D. "Evaluation as Illumination: A New Approach to the Study of Innovatory Programs." In D. Hamilton and Associates, *Beyond the Numbers Game.* Basingstoke, England: Macmillan, 1977.

Partridge, Y. M. "Personal Autonomy and Compulsory Liberal Education." Unpublished doctoral dissertation, University of British Columbia, 1979. (*Dissertation Abstracts International, 41* (11A), 4641.)

Pask, G. "Styles and Strategies of Learning." *British Journal of Educational Psychology,* 1976, *46,* 128–148.

Pask, G., and Scott, B.C.E. "Learning Strategies and Individual Competence." *International Journal of Man-Machine Studies,* 1972, *4,* 217–253.

Pask, G., Scott, B.C.E., and Kallikourdis, D. "The Theory of Conversations and Individuals." *International Journal of Man-Machine Studies,* 1973, *5,* 443–566.

Passmore, J. A., and others. *Teaching Methods in Australian Universities.* Report based on a survey conducted by a committee appointed by the Australian Vice-Chancellors' Committee. Melbourne: Australian Vice-Chancellors' Committee, 1963.

Paterson, R.W.K. *Values, Education and the Adult.* London: Routledge and Kegan Paul, 1979.

Patton, J. A. "A Study of the Effects of Student Acceptance of Responsibility and Motivation on Course Behavior." Unpublished doctoral dissertation, University of Michigan, 1955. (*Dissertation Abstracts International, 15* (04), 637.)

Paul, R. "Teaching Critical Thinking in the 'Strong' Sense: A Focus on Self-Deception, World News, and a Dialectical Mode of Analysis." *Informal Logic,* 1982, *4,* 3–7.

Pedler, M. "Teaching Students to Learn." *Adult Education (U.K.),* 1972, *45* (2), 87–91.

Penland, P. R. *Self-Planned Learning in America.* Final report of project no. 475AH60058, Office of Libraries and Learning Resources, U.S. Department of Health, Education, and Welfare. Pittsburgh, Pa.: Graduate School of Library and Information Sciences, University of Pittsburgh, 1977. (ERIC Document Reproduction Service no. ED 183 589.)

Penland, P. R. "Self-Initiated Learning." *Adult Education (U.S.),* 1979, *29* (3), 170–179.

Penland, P. R. "Individual Self-Planned Learning in America: A Summary Report." In *Yearbook of Adult and Continuing Education, 1979–80,* Chicago: Marquis Academic Media, 1979.

Penland, P. R. *Towards Self-Directed Learning Theory.* Washington, D.C.: National Institute of Education, U.S. Department of Health, Education, and Welfare, 1981. (ERIC Document Reproduction Service no. ED 209 475.)

Pepper, S. C. *World Hypotheses.* Berkeley: University of California Press, 1942.

Percy, K. A. "Provision; Inter-Relationships; Policy: A Survey of Formal and Informal Adult Education in the North West of England." Proceedings of twenty-second annual Adult

Education Research Conference, Northern Illinois University, De Kalb, Apr. 1981, 152–158.

Percy, K. A., and Ramsden, P. *Independent Study: Two Examples from English Higher Education.* Guildford, England: Society for Research into Higher Education, 1980.

Perkins, A. T. "The Learning Exchange Network: An Evolutionary Step in Providing Support for Self-Directed Learning." *Lifelong Learning: An Omnibus of Practice and Research,* 1985, *8* (4), 9–11, 28.

Perkins, D. N., and Salomon, G. "Are Cognitive Skills Context-Bound?" *Educational Researcher,* 1989, *18* (1), 16–25.

Perry, R. P., and Dickens, W. J. "Perceived Control in the College Classroom: Response-Outcome Contingency Training and Instructor Expressiveness Effects on Student Achievement and Causal Attributions." *Journal of Educational Psychology,* 1984, *76* (5), 966–981.

Perry, W. G. *Forms of Intellectual and Ethical Development in the College Years: A Scheme.* New York: Holt, Rinehart & Winston, 1970.

Perry, W. G. "Cognitive and Ethical Growth: The Making of Meaning." In A. W. Chickering and Associates, *The Modern American College: Responding to the New Realities of Diverse Students and a Changing Society.* San Francisco: Jossey-Bass, 1981.

Perry, W. G. "Different Worlds in the Same Classroom." In P. Ramsden (ed.), *Improving Learning: New Perspectives.* London: Kogan Page, 1988.

Peters, J. M. "Toward a New Procedure for Learning Project Research." Paper presented at joint meeting of the Adult Education Research Conference and the Standing Committee on University Teaching and Research in the Education of Adults, University of Leeds, July 1988.

Peters, J. M., and Gordon, S. *Adult Learning Projects: A Study of Adult Learning in Urban and Rural Tennessee.* Knoxville: University of Tennessee, 1974. (ERIC Document Reproduction Service no. ED 102 431.)

Peters, J. M., Johnson, M., and Lazzara, P. "Adult Problem Solving and Learning." Paper presented at 62nd annual conference of the American Educational Research Association,

Los Angeles, Apr. 1981. (ERIC Document Reproduction Service no. ED 200 758.)

Peters, R. S. "Freedom and the Development of the Free Man." In J. F. Doyle (ed.), *Educational Judgements*. London: Routledge and Kegan Paul, 1973.

Peterson, D. A., and Eden, D. Z. "Cognitive Styles and the Older Learner." *Educational Gerontology*, 1981, *7* (1), 57–66.

Phillips, D. C. "The Anatomy of Autonomy." *Educational Philosophy and Theory*, 1975, *7* (2), 1–12.

Phillips, D. C. "After the Wake: Postpositivistic Educational Thought." *Educational Researcher*, 1983, *12* (5), 4–12.

Phillips, D. Z. "Democratization: Some Themes in Unexamined Talk." *British Journal of Educational Studies*, 1973, *21* (2), 133–148.

Phillips, E. M. "Education for Research: The Changing Constructs of the Postgraduate." *International Journal of Man-Machine Studies*, 1980, *13*, 39–48.

Phillips, E. M. "Gridding the Grad." Paper presented at the fourth international conference on Personal Construct Psychology, St. Catharine's, Ontario, Canada, Aug. 1981.

Phillips-Jones, L. *Mentors and Protégés*. New York: Arbor House, 1982.

Piaget, J. *The Moral Judgment of the Child*. London: Routledge & Kegan Paul, 1932.

Piaget, J. *The Principles of Genetic Epistemology*. New York: Viking, 1972.

Pineau, L. *Les possibilités de l'auto-formation* [*The Potential for Self-Development*]. Montréal: Bureau de la Recherche, Faculté de l'Education Permanente, Université de Montréal, 1978.

Pipke, I. "Institution Related Motivation Predictors of the Penchant for Learning in the Natural Societal Setting." Proceedings of 24th annual Adult Education Research Conference, University of Montreal, Apr. 1983, 181–186.

Plutarch. *Plutarch's Lives: Translated from the Original Greek with Notes, Critical and Historical*. (J. Langhorne and W. Langhorne, trans.) London: William Tegg, 1878. (Originally written 1st century A.D.)

Polanyi, M. *The Tacit Dimension*. London: Routledge and Kegan Paul, 1967.

Pole, T. *A History of the Origin and Progress of Adult Schools with an Account of Some of the Beneficial Effects Already Produced on the Moral Character of the Labouring Poor* . . . (Rev. ed.) Bristol: McDowal, 1816 (Rpt. in facsimile, with an introduction by C. Verner, Washington, D.C.: Adult Education Association of the U.S.A., 1967.)

Pope, M. L. "Personal Construction of Formal Knowledge." *Interchange: A Journal of Educational Policy*, 1982, *13* (4), 3–14.

Pope, M. L. "Personal Experience and the Construction of Knowledge in Science." In R. Boot and M. Reynolds (eds.), *Learning and Experience in Formal Education*. Manchester, England: Department of Adult and Higher Education, University of Manchester, 1983.

Pope, M. L. "Constructivist Goggles: Implications for Process in Teaching and Learning." Paper presented at the British Educational Research Association conference, Sheffield, Aug. 1985.

Pope, M. L., and Keen, T. R. *Personal Construct Psychology and Education*. London: Academic Press, 1981.

Pope, M. L., and Shaw M.L.G. "Negotiation in Learning." Paper presented at third international congress on Personal Construct Psychology, Breukelen, The Netherlands, July 1979.

Popkewitz, T. S. *Paradigm and Ideology in Educational Research: The Social Functions of the Intellectual*. London: Falmer Press, 1984.

Popper, K. R. *Conjectures and Refutations*. London: Routledge and Kegan Paul, 1963.

Postman, N., and Weingartner, C. *Teaching as a Subversive Activity*. Harmondsworth, England: Penguin Books, 1971.

Powell, J. P. "Autobiographical Learning." In D. J. Boud, R. Keogh, and D. Walker (eds.), *Reflection: Turning Experience into Learning*. London: Kogan Page, 1985.

Powell, M. C. "The Relationship of Cognitive Style, Achievement, and Self-Concept to an Indicated Preference for Self-Directed Study." Unpublished doctoral dissertation, Memphis State University, 1976. (*Dissertation Abstracts International*, *37* (06A), 3383.)

Pratt, D. D. "Andragogy as a Relational Construct." *Adult Education Quarterly*, 1988, *38* (3), 160–172.

Quine, W. V., and Ullian, J. S. *Web of Belief.* New York: Random House, 1978.

Quinton, A. M. "Authority and Autonomy in Knowledge." *Proceedings of the Annual Conference of the Philosophy of Education Society of Great Britain,* 1971, *5* (2) (suppl.), 201–215.

Raiskii, B. F. "Preparing Pupils for Continuing Education: An Urgent Task of the School." *Soviet Education,* 1979, *21* (5), 70–76.

Ramsden, P. "Student Learning and Perceptions of the Academic Environment." *Higher Education,* 1979, *8* (4), 411–427.

Ramsden, P. "The Context of Learning." In F. Marton, D. J. Hounsell, and N. J. Entwistle (eds.), *The Experience of Learning.* Edinburgh: Scottish Academic Press, 1984.

Ramsden, P. "Student Learning Research: Retrospect and Prospect." *Higher Education Research and Development,* 1985, *4* (1), 51–69.

Ramsden, P. "Improving Teaching and Learning in Higher Education: The Case for a Relational Perspective." *Studies in Higher Education,* 1987, *12* (3), 275–286.

Ramsden, P. "Studying Learning: Improving Teaching." In P. Ramsden (ed.), *Improving Learning: New Perspectives.* London: Kogan Page, 1988.

Ramsden, P., Beswick, D., and Bowden, J. "Learning Processes and Learning Skills." In J.T.E. Richardson, M. W. Eysenck, and D. Warren Piper (eds.), *Student Learning: Research in Educational Cognitive Psychology.* London: Society for Research into Higher Education and Open University Press, 1987.

Ranger, P. "L'éducation des adultes comme rite nocturne" [Adult education as a nocturnal rite]. Proceedings of 4th annual conference of the Canadian Association for the Study of Adult Education, University of Montreal, May 1985, 47–58.

Rathbone, C. H. "The Implicit Rationale of the Open Education Classroom." In C. H. Rathbone (ed.), *Open Education: The Informal Classroom.* New York: Citation Press, 1971.

Ravid, G. "Self-Directed Learning in Industry." In V. J. Marsick (ed.), *Learning in the Workplace.* London: Croom Helm, 1987.

Redditt, R. S. "A Quasi-Experimental Comparison of a Group Lecture Method and a Self-Directed Method in Teaching

Basic Electricity at the College Level." Unpublished doctoral dissertation, University of Tennessee, 1973. (*Dissertation Abstracts International, 34* (09A), 5599.)

Reilly, J. A. "The Public Librarian as Learners' Advisor: A Developing Trend in Adult Human Services." Unpublished doctoral dissertation, Union for Experimenting Colleges/University Without Walls and Union Graduate School, 1978. (*Dissertation Abstracts International, 39* (11A), 6382.)

Reilly, J. A. *The Public Librarian as Adult Learners' Advisor: An Innovation in Human Services.* Westport, Conn.: Greenwood Press, 1981.

Reinhart, E. "A Study of the Effects of the Learning Contract on Cognitive Gains and Attitudes of Practicing Registered Nurses in Self-Directed Learning." Unpublished doctoral dissertation, Kansas State University, 1976. (*Dissertation Abstracts International, 37* (09A), 5533.)

Reinhart, E. "Independent Study: An Option in Continuing Education." *Journal of Continuing Education in Nursing,* 1977, *8* (1), 38–42.

Reisser, L. J. "A Facilitation Process for Self-Directed Learning." Unpublished doctoral dissertation, University of Massachusetts, 1973. (*Dissertation Abstracts International, 34* (10A), 6418.)

Resnick, D. P., and Resnick, L. B. "The Nature of Literacy: An Historical Exploration." *Harvard Educational Review,* 1977, *47* (3), 370–385.

Resnick, L. B. *Education and Learning to Think.* Washington, D.C.: National Academy Press, 1987a.

Resnick, L. B. "Learning in School and Out." *Educational Researcher,* 1987b, *16* (9), 13–20.

Rex, J. (ed.). *Approaches to Sociology: An Introduction to Major Trends in British Sociology.* London: Routledge and Kegan Paul, 1974.

Ricard, V. R. *Self-Directed Learning: Exploring the Fears,* 1982. (ERIC Document Reproduction Service no. ED 234 141.)

Richards, J. "Epistemology and Mathematical Proof." In C. D. Smock and E. von Glasersfeld (eds.), *Epistemology and Education: The Implications of Radical Constructivism for Knowledge Acquisition.* Mathemagenic Activities Program—Follow Through, Research Report No. 14. Athens: University of Georgia, 1974.

Riesman, D. *The Lonely Crowd.* New Haven, Conn.: Yale University Press, 1950.

Rist, R. C. "On the Relations Among Educational Research Paradigms: From Disdain to Detente." *Anthropology and Education Quarterly,* 1977, *8* (2), 42–49.

Rix, E.A.H. "Towards a Reflective Epistemology of Practice: Canadian Educational Applications of Personal Construct Psychology." Paper presented at 5th international congress on Personal Construct Psychology, Chestnut Hill, Mass., July 1983.

Robbins, D. *The Rise of Independent Study: The Politics and Philosophy of an Educational Innovation, 1970–1987.* London: Society for Research in Higher Education and Open University Press, 1988.

Robertson, G. "How 'Self' Directed is Self-Directed Learning?" *Management Education and Development,* 1987, *18* (2), 75–87.

Robinson, A. W. "A Study of Tasks and Assistance During Adult Self-Planned Learning Projects." Unpublished doctoral dissertation, University of Alabama, 1983. (*Dissertation Abstracts International, 44* (02A), 359.)

Rodriguez, C. "Lifelong Education." *Educational Documentation and Information: Bulletin of the International Bureau of Education,* 1972, *46* (185) (entire issue).

Rogers, C. R. *Freedom to Learn: A View of What Education Might Become.* Columbus, Ohio: Merrill, 1969.

Rogers, J. "Independent Learning in the Post-Compulsory Sector in the United Kingdom." In *Learning Opportunities for Adults.* Vol. 2: *New Structures, Programmes and Methods.* Paris: Organisation for Economic Cooperation and Development, 1979.

Rogge, W. M. "Independent Study is Self-Directed Learning." In D. W. Beggs and E. G. Buffie (eds.), *Independent Study: Bold New Venture.* Bloomington: Indiana University Press, 1965.

Rogoff, B. "Introduction: Thinking and Learning in Social Context." In B. Rogoff and J. Lave (eds.), *Everyday Cognition: Its Development in Social Context.* Cambridge, Mass.: Harvard University Press, 1984.

Rogoff, B., and Lave, J. *Everyday Cognition: Its Development in Social Context.* Cambridge, Mass.: Harvard University Press, 1984.

Rosenblatt, R. "The Rugged Individual Rides Again." *Time,* Oct. 15, 1984, p. 94.

Rosenblum, S., and Darkenwald, G. G. "Effects of Adult Learner Participation in Course Planning on Achievement and Satisfaction." *Adult Education Quarterly,* 1983, *33* (3), 147–153.

Rosenthal, R., and Jacobson, L. *Pygmalion in the Classroom: Teacher Expectation and Pupils' Intellectual Development.* New York: Holt, Rinehart & Winston, 1968.

Ross, R. G. "Self-Help Groups as Education." In H. B. Reed and E. L. Loughran, (eds.), *Beyond Schools: Education for Economic, Social, and Personal Development.* Amherst: Citizen Involvement Training Program, Community Education Resource Center, School of Education, University of Massachusetts, 1984.

Roth, S. "A Revised Model of Learned Helplessness in Humans." *Journal of Personality,* 1980, *48,* 103–133.

Rothkopf, E. Z. "Writing to Teach and Reading to Learn: A Perspective on the Psychology of Written Instruction." In N. L. Gage (ed.), *The Psychology of Teaching Methods.* The seventy-fifth yearbook of the National Society for the Study of Education. Part 1. Chicago: University of Chicago Press, 1976.

Rotter, J. B. *Generalized Expectancies for Internal Versus External Control of Reinforcement.* Psychological Monographs, no. 80, 1966.

Rousseau, J. J. *Emile.* London: Dent, 1911. (B. Foxley, trans.) (Originally published in 1762 in French as *Emile ou de l'éducation.*)

Rubenson, K. "Adult Education Research: In Search of a Map of the Territory." *Adult Education (U.S.),* 1982, *32* (2), 57–74.

Rubenson, K., and Borgström, L. "Equality in the Context of Lifelong Education: Consequences for Policy and Research." In B. Harvey, J. Daines, D. Jones, and J. Wallis (eds.), *Policy and Research in Adult Education: The First Nottingham International Colloquium—1981.* Nottingham, England: Department of Adult Education, University of Nottingham, 1981.

Rugg, E. A., and Norris, R. C. "Student Ratings of Individualized Faculty Supervision: Description and Evaluation." *American Education Research Journal,* 1975, *12* (1), 41–53.

Rumelhart, D. E. *An Introduction to Human Information Processing.* New York: Wiley, 1977.

Russo, N. "Capturing Teachers' Decision Policies: An Investigation of Strategies for Teaching Reading and Mathematics." Paper presented at the 59th annual conference of the American Educational Research Association, Toronto, March 1978.

Ruth, B., and Frey, B. *Mentoring: An Annotated Bibliography.* Buffalo, N.Y.: Bearly, 1983.

Ryerson, E. "A Lecture on the Social Advancement of Canada." *Journal of Education for Upper Canada,* 1849, *2* (12), 177–184.

Ryle, A. *Frames and Cages: The Repertory Grid Approach to Human Understanding.* London: University of Sussex Press, 1975.

Rymell, R. G. "Learning Projects Pursued by Adult Degreed Engineers." Unpublished doctoral dissertation, North Texas State University, 1981. (*Dissertation Abstracts International, 42* (03A), 964.)

Sabbaghian, Z. "Adult Self-Directedness and Self-Concept: An Exploration of Relationship." Unpublished doctoral dissertation, Iowa State University, 1979. (*Dissertation Abstracts International, 40* (07A), 3701.)

Säljö, R. *Qualitative Differences in Learning as a Function of the Learner's Conception of the Task.* Göteborg Studies in Educational Sciences, no. 14. Göteborg, Sweden: University of Göteborg, 1975.

Säljö, R. "Learning About Learning." *Higher Education,* 1979a, *8* (4), 443–451.

Säljö, R. *Learning in the Learner's Perspective II: Differences in Awareness.* Report of the Institute of Education, no. 77. Göteborg, Sweden: Institute of Education, University of Göteborg, 1979b.

Sanders, D. P., and McCutcheon, G. "On the Evolution of Teachers' Theories of Action Through Action Research." Paper presented at the 65th annual conference of the American Educational Research Association, New Orleans, Apr. 1984.

Sarbin, T. R. "Contextualism: A World View for Modern Psychology." In A. W. Landfield (ed.), *Nebraska Symposium on Motivation, Current Theory and Research in Motivation.* Vol. 24. Lincoln: University of Nebraska, 1977.

Savićević, D. "Self-Directed Education for Lifelong Education." *International Journal of Lifelong Education,* 1985, *4* (4), 285–294.

Savoie, M. L. "Continuing Education for Nurses: Predictors of Success in Courses Requiring a Degree of Learner Self-Direction." Unpublished doctoral dissertation, University of Toronto, 1979. (*Dissertation Abstracts International, 40* (12A), 6114.)

Schleiderer, A. I. "The Development of Self-Directed Learning: A Systematic Approach Utilizing Human Relations Skills in the Classroom." Unpublished doctoral dissertation, University of Massachusetts, 1979. (*Dissertation Abstracts International, 39* (12A), 7168.)

Schön, D. A. *The Reflective Practitioner: How Professionals Think in Action.* New York: Basic Books, 1983.

Schön, D. A. *Educating the Reflective Practitioner: Toward a New Design for Teaching and Learning in the Professions.* San Francisco: Jossey-Bass, 1987.

Schroeder, W. L. "Adult Education Defined and Described." In R. M. Smith, G. F. Aker, and J. R. Kidd (eds.), *Handbook of Adult Education.* New York: Macmillan, 1970.

Schuttenberg, E. M., and Tracy, S. J. "The Role of the Adult Educator in Fostering Self-Directed Learning." *Lifelong Learning: An Omnibus of Practice and Research,* 1987, *10* (5), 4–6, 9.

Schutz, A. *The Phenomenology of the Social World.* (George Walsh and Frederick Lehnert, trans.) Evanston, Ill.: Northwestern University Press, 1967.

Selby, D. "Towards Self-Education." *Adult Education (U.K.),* 1973, *46* (4), 245–249.

Seligman, M.E.P. *Helplessness: On Depression, Development, and Death.* San Francisco: Freeman, 1975.

Selman, G., and Kulich, J. "Between Social Movement and Profession: An Historical Perspective on Canadian Adult Education." *Studies in Adult Education,* 1980, *12* (2), 109–116.

Serdahely, W., and Adams, M. "Students' Feelings About Themselves as Self-Directed Learners." *Improving College and University Teaching,* 1979, *27* (4), 178–181.

Serré, F. "L'importance d'apprendre seul, ou les objets et les processus des projets éducatifs et autodidactes des adultes de la classe dite défavourisée" [The importance of learning alone: The objectives and processes of self-directed learning projects undertaken by disadvantaged adults]. Thèse de doctorat inédite, Université de Montréal, 1977.

Serré, F. "The Importance of Learning Alone: A Study of Self-Planned Learning Projects." *Adult Learning,* 1978, *3* (2) 16–20.

Sexton-Hesse, C. A. "Assuming Responsibility for Self-Directed Learning in Professional Practice: The Contributions of Psycho-Social Factors." Proceedings of 25th annual Adult Education Research Conference. North Carolina State University, Raleigh, Apr. 1984, 202–207.

Shackelford, R. A. "Self-Directed Learning Projects Among Black Adults in Havana, Florida." Unpublished doctoral dissertation, Florida State University, 1983. (*Dissertation Abstracts International, 44* (03A), 647.)

Shapiro, H. S. "Ideology, Hegemony, and the Individualizing of Instruction: The Incorporation of 'Progressive Education.'" *Journal of Curriculum Studies,* 1984, *16* (4), 367–378.

Sheckley, B. G. "Effects of Individual Differences on Learning Projects Completed by Adults Enrolled in Community College Courses." *Community College Review,* 1988, *16* (1), 27–33.

Shipton, J., and Steltenpohl, E. "Self-Directedness of the Learner as a Key to Quality Assurance." In M. Keeton (ed.), *Defining and Assuring Quality in Experiential Learning.* New Directions for Experiential Learning, no. 9. San Francisco: Jossey-Bass, 1980.

Shirk, J. C. "Relevance Attributed to Urban Public Libraries by Adult Learners: A Case Study and Content Analysis of 81 Interviews." Unpublished doctoral dissertation, Texas A & M University, 1983. (*Dissertation Abstracts International, 45* (01A), 53.)

Shores, W. L. "Study of Interactions of Adult Learners with Learning Situations." Unpublished doctoral dissertation, Department of Administrative, Adult, and Higher Education, University of British Columbia, 1986. (*Dissertation Abstracts International 48* (09A), 2223.)

Siegel, H. "Critical Thinking as an Educational Ideal." *Educational Forum,* 1980, *45* (1), 7–23.

Sigel, I. E., Brodzinsky, D. M., and Golinkoff, R. M. (eds.). *New Directions in Piagetian Theory and Practice.* Hillsdale, N.J.: Erlbaum, 1981.

Simkins, T. J. "Non-Formal Education and Development: Some Critical Issues." *Manchester Monograph No. 8.* Manchester, England: Department of Adult and Higher Education, University of Manchester, 1977.

Simons, G. L. *Is Man a Robot?* Chichester: Wiley, 1986.

Sinnett, W. E. "Toward a Philosophical Framework for Conceptualizing Adult Education." Proceedings of 4th annual conference of the Canadian Association for the Study of Adult Education, University of Montreal, May 1985, 251–266.

Sizemore, B. A. "Forces Which Affect Self-Direction and Self-Responsibility of Students." In D. Della-Dora and L. J. Blanchard (eds.), *Moving Toward Self-Directed Learning: Highlights of Relevant Research and of Promising Practices.* Alexandria, Va.: Association for Supervision and Curriculum Development, 1979.

Skager, R. W. *Lifelong Learning and Evaluation Practice.* Oxford/ Hamburg: Pergamon Press/Unesco Institute for Education, 1978.

Skager, R. W. "Self-Directed Learning and Schooling: Identifying Pertinent Theories and Illustrative Research." *International Review of Education,* 1979, *25,* 517–543.

Skager, R. W. *Organizing Schools to Encourage Self-Direction in Learners.* Oxford/Hamburg: Pergamon Press/Unesco Institute for Education, 1984.

Skager, R. W., and Dave, R. H. *Curriculum Evaluation for Lifelong Education.* Oxford/Hamburg: Pergamon Press/Unesco Institute for Education, 1977.

Skaggs, B. J. "The Relationship Between Involvement of Professional Nurses in Self-Directed Learning Activities, Loci of Control, and Readiness for Self-Directed Learning Activities." Unpublished doctoral dissertation, University of Texas, 1981. (*Dissertation Abstracts International, 42* (05A), 1906.)

Skinner, B. F. *Beyond Freedom and Dignity.* New York: Bantam Books, 1971.

Skruber, R. "Designing Learning Environments for the Enhancement of Self-Directed Learning: A Personal Approach to Integrating Theory and Practice." Paper presented at National Adult Education Conference, San Antonio, Tex., Nov. 1982. (ERIC Document Reproduction Service no. ED 239 028.)

Smiles, S. *Self Help.* London: John Murray, 1859. (Reissued with a centenary introduction by Asa Briggs, London: Murray, 1958.)

Smith, J. C. "Librarians and Self-Directed Learners." Proceedings of 27th annual Adult Education Research Conference, Syracuse University, May 1986, 249–254.

Smith, M.L.H. "The Facilitation of Student Self-Directed Learning as Perceived by Teachers with High and Low Levels of Self-Actualization and Dogmatism." Unpublished doctoral dissertation, Pennsylvania State University, 1968. (*Dissertation Abstracts International, 29* (05A), 1467.)

Smith, R. M. "Learning How to Learn in Adult Education." *Information Series No. 10.* DeKalb, Ill.: ERIC Clearinghouse in Career Education, 1976.

Smith, R. M. *Learning How to Learn: Applied Theory for Adults.* New York: Cambridge, 1982.

Smith, R. M. "Adult Instructional Processes and Self-Directedness: Some Research Issues." In M. J. Even and others, *Symposium on Adults Learning Alone.* Proceedings of 25th annual Adult Education Research Conference, North Carolina State University, Raleigh, Apr. 1984, 279–284.

Smith, R. M. *Learning How to Learn for Lifelong Education.* Course Notes for LEAC-533. De Kalb: Department of Adult Education, Northern Illinois University, 1986.

Smith, R. M. *Theory Building for Learning How to Learn.* Chicago: Educational Studies Press, 1987.

Sneddon, D. "Self-Education: A Needed Emphasis in Current Proposals for Adult Education." *Journal of Adult Education,* 1930, *2* (1), 32–37.

Snow, R. E. "Aptitude, Learner-Control and Adaptive Instruction." *Educational Psychologist,* 1980, *15* (3), 151–158.

Snyder, B. R. *The Hidden Curriculum.* New York: Knopf, 1971.

Solomon, D. (ed.). *The Continuing Learner.* Chicago: Center for the Study of Liberal Education for Adults, 1964.

Soltis, J. F. "On the Nature of Educational Research." *Educational Researcher,* 1984, *13* (10), 5-10.

Sorenson, G., and Kagan, D. "Conflicts Between Doctoral Candidates and Their Sponsors: A Contrast in Expectations." *Journal of Higher Education,* 1967, *38* (1), 17-27.

Southern, A. M. "Attitudes Found Among Students in University Courses on Adult Education When Given Increased Opportunities for Self-Direction." Unpublished doctoral dissertation, Ohio State University, 1971. (*Dissertation Abstracts International, 32* (05A), 2394.)

Spath, B. K. "Lifelong Learning in Voluntary Organizations: A Review of the Literature." Proceedings of fourth Lifelong Learning Research Conference, University of Maryland, Feb. 1982, 220-224. College Park: Department of Agriculture and Extension Education, University of Maryland. (ERIC Document Reproduction Service no. ED 215 198.)

Spear, G. E. "Beyond the Organizing Circumstance: A Search for Methodology for the Study of Self-Directed Learning." In H. B. Long and Associates, *Self-Directed Learning: Application and Theory.* Athens: Department of Adult Education, University of Georgia, 1988.

Spear, G. E., and Mocker, D. W. *The Organizing Circumstance: Environmental Determinants in Self-Directed Learning.* Kansas City: Center for Resource Development in Adult Education, University of Missouri–Kansas City, 1981.

Spear, G. E., and Mocker, D. W. "The Organizing Circumstance: Environmental Determinants in Self-Directed Learning." *Adult Education Quarterly,* 1984, *35* (1), 1-10.

Spearman, C. *The Nature of Intelligence and Principles of Cognition.* London: Macmillan, 1923.

Spence, J. T. "Achievement American Style: The Rewards and Costs of Individualism." *American Psychologist,* 1985, *40* (12), 1285-1295.

Stalker-Costin, A. J. "Adult Education and Educational Equality: A Study of the Interrelationships Between the Role of Adult Education and Obstacles to Educational Equality." Proceedings of 26th annual Adult Education Research Conference, Arizona State University, Tempe, Mar. 1985, 123-129.

Stalker-Costin, A. J. "Threatening the Priesthood: The Potential for Social Transformation Through Nonformal Education." Proceedings of 27th annual Adult Education Research Conference, Syracuse University, Syracuse, N.Y., May 1986, 273–278.

Stein, C. W. "An Historical Survey of Independent Study Plans in American Colleges with Specific Reference to the Development of Honors Programs." Unpublished doctoral dissertation, State University of New York–Buffalo, 1954. (*Doctoral Dissertations Accepted by American Universities, 1953–54,* 180.)

Stephens, M. D., and Roderick, G. W. (eds.). *Samuel Smiles and Nineteenth Century Self-Help in Education.* Nottingham Studies in the History of Adult Education, no. 1. Nottingham, England: Department of Adult Education, University of Nottingham, 1983.

Stern, G. G. "Environments for Learning." In N. Sanford (ed.), *The American College: A Psychological and Social Interpretation of the Higher Learning.* New York: Wiley, 1962.

Stipek, D. J., and Weisz, J. R. "Perceived Personal Control and Academic Achievement." *Review of Educational Research,* 1981, *51* (1), 101–137.

Strike, K. A. *Liberty and Learning.* Oxford: Martin Robertson, 1982.

Strong, M. "The Autonomous Adult Learner: The Idea of Autonomous Learning, the Capabilities and Perceived Needs of the Autonomous Learner." Unpublished master's thesis, University of Nottingham, 1977.

Sullivan, E. V. *A Critical Psychology: Interpretation of the Personal World.* New York: Plenum, 1984.

Sutton, C. "Introduction: Making Sense of New Ideas." In C. Sutton (ed.), *Communicating in the Classroom: A Guide for Subject Teachers on the More Effective Use of Reading, Writing and Talk.* London: Hodder and Stoughton, 1981.

Svensson, L. "Study Skill and Learning." *Göteborg Studies in Educational Sciences, no. 19,* University of Göteborg, 1976.

Svensson, L. "Skill in Learning." In F. Marton, D. Hounsell, and N. Entwistle (eds.), *The Experience of Learning.* Edinburgh: Scottish Academic Press, 1984.

Svensson, L. "Autodidactics." Paper presented at 3rd European conference for Research on Learning and Instruction, Madrid, Sept. 1989.

Taylor, M. M. "Adult Learning in an Emergent Learning Group: Toward a Theory of Learning from the Learner's Perspective." Unpublished doctoral dissertation, Department of Educational Theory, University of Toronto, 1979. (Canadian Theses on Microfiche, no. 40968.)

Taylor, M. M. "A Conceptual Representation of Learning from the Learner's Point of View." Proceedings of 21st annual Adult Education Research Conference, University of British Columbia, Vancouver, May 1980, 193–198.

Taylor, M. M. "Learning for Self-Direction in the Classroom: The Pattern of a Transition Process." *Studies in Higher Education,* 1986, *11* (1), 55–72.

Taylor, M. M. "Self-Directed Learning: More Than Meets the Observer's Eye." In D. J. Boud and V. Griffin (eds.), *Appreciating Adults Learning: From the Learners' Perspective.* London: Kogan Page, 1987.

Telfer, E. "Autonomy as an Educational Ideal II." In S. C. Brown (ed.), *Philosophers Discuss Education.* London: Macmillan, 1975.

Tennant, M. *Psychology and Adult Learning.* London: Routledge, 1988.

Ternent, W. A. "Planning for a Student-Directed, Student-Evaluated Learning Situation." Paper presented at the convention of the International Communication Association, Atlanta, Ga., Apr. 1972. (ERIC Document Reproduction Service no. ED 067 716.)

Theil, J.-P. "Les styles d'apprentissage d'adultes autodidactes" [Learning styles of adult self-directed learners]. Mémoire de maîtrise inédit, Université de Montréal, 1984a.

Theil, J.-P. "Successful Self-Directed Learners' Learning Styles." Proceedings of twenty-fifth annual Adult Education Research Conference, North Carolina State University, Raleigh, Apr. 1984b, 237–242.

Theil, J.-P., and Tzuk, T. R. "Typical and Specific Stylistic Learning Approaches of Self-Directed Learners." Proceedings of 4th annual conference of the Canadian Association for the Study of Adult Education, University of Montreal, May 1985, 317–337.

Thelen, H. A. *Education and the Human Quest.* Chicago: University of Chicago Press, 1972.

Thomas, A. M. "Studentship and Membership: A Study of Roles in Learning." *Journal of Educational Thought,* 1967, *1* (1), 65–76.

Thomas, J. W. "Agency and Achievement: Self-Management and Self-Regard." *Review of Educational Research,* 1980, *50* (2), 213–240.

Thomas, L. F., and Harri-Augstein, E. S. *Learning to Learn: The Personal Construction and Exchange of Meaning.* Uxbridge, England: Centre for the Study of Human Learning, Brunel University, 1976.

Thomas, L. F., and Harri-Augstein, E. S. "The Development of Self-Organised Learners: The C.S.H.L.'s Conversational Technology for Reflecting on Behaviour and Experience." Working paper, Centre for the Study of Human Learning, Brunel University, Uxbridge, England, 1982.

Thomas, L. F., and Harri-Augstein, E. S. *The Self-Organised Learner and Computer-Aided Learning Systems: An Exploratory Study with the Air Intercept Control Skills Trainer.* Final report of project no. 2066/020, Admiralty Marine Technology Establishment, Applied Psychology Unit. Uxbridge, England: Centre for the Study of Human Learning, Brunel University, 1983.

Thomas, L. F., and Harri-Augstein, E. S. *Self-Organised Learning: Foundations of a Conversational Science for Psychology.* London: Routledge and Kegan Paul, 1985.

Thompson, J. L. (ed.). *Adult Education for a Change.* London: Hutchinson, 1980.

Tight, M. *Education for Adults.* Vol. 1: *Adult Learning and Education.* London: Croom Helm, 1983.

Todd, F. "Developing Teaching Skills for Collaborative Learning." *Studies in Higher Education,* 1981, *6* (1), 91–96.

Toppins, A. D. "Teaching Students to Teach Themselves." *College Teaching,* 1987, *35* (3), 95–99.

Torbert, W. R. *Creating a Community of Inquiry: Conflict, Collaboration, Transformation.* London: Wiley, 1976.

Torbert, W. R. "Educating Toward Shared Purpose, Self-

Direction and Quality Work: The Theory and Practice of Liberating Structure." *Journal of Higher Education,* 1978, *49* (2), 109–135.

Torrance, E. P., and Mourad, S. A. "Some Creativity and Style of Learning and Thinking Correlates of Guglielmino's Self-Directed Learning Readiness Scale." *Psychological Reports,* 1978, *43,* 1167–1171.

Tough, A. M. "The Assistance Obtained by Adult Self-Teachers." *Adult Education (U.S.),* 1966a, *17* (1), 30–37.

Tough, A. M. "The Teaching Tasks Performed by Adult Self-Teachers." Unpublished doctoral dissertation, University of Chicago, 1966b. (*Dissertation Abstracts International, 1861–1972,* X1966, 58.)

Tough, A. M. *Learning Without a Teacher: A Study of Tasks and Assistance During Adult Self-Teaching Projects.* Educational Research Series, no. 3. Toronto: Ontario Institute for Studies in Education, 1967.

Tough, A. M. *Why Adults Learn: A Study of the Major Reasons for Beginning and Continuing a Learning Project.* Toronto: Ontario Institute for Studies in Education, 1968.

Tough, A. M. "Self-Planned Learning and Major Personal Change." In R. M. Smith (ed.), *Adult Learning: Issues and Innovations.* Information Series, no. 8. ERIC Clearinghouse in Career Education. De Kalb: Department of Secondary and Adult Education, Northern Illinois University, 1976.

Tough, A. M. "Major Learning Efforts: Recent Research and Future Directions." *Adult Education (U.S.),* 1978, *28* (4), 250–263.

Tough, A. M. *The Adult's Learning Projects: A Fresh Approach to Theory and Practice in Adult Learning.* (Rev. ed.) Toronto: Ontario Institute for Studies in Education, 1979a.

Tough, A. M. "Choosing to Learn." In G. M. Healy and W. L. Ziegler (eds.), *The Learning Stance: Essays in Celebration of Human Learning.* Final report of a Syracuse Research Corporation project. Syracuse, N.Y.: Syracuse Research Corporation, Syracuse University, 1979b.

Tough, A. M. "Finding Resources on Self-Planned Learning." In J. N. Robbins (ed.), *1979 Directory of Resources for the Education of Adults.* Information Series, no. 174. Columbus: National Center for Research in Vocational Education, Ohio State University, 1979c.

Tough, A. M. "Fostering Self-Planned Learning." In *Learning Opportunities for Adults*. Vol. 2: *New Structures, Programmes and Methods*. Paris: Organisation for Economic Cooperation and Development, 1979d.

Tough, A. M. "Individual Learning." In R. D. Boyd, J. W. Apps, and Associates (eds.), *Redefining the Discipline of Adult Education*. San Francisco: Jossey Bass, 1980.

Tough, A. M. "Interests of Adult Learners." In A. W. Chickering and Associates, *The Modern American College: Responding to the New Realities of Diverse Students and a Changing Society*. San Francisco: Jossey-Bass, 1981.

Toulmin, S. (ed.). *Physical Reality*. New York: Harper & Row, 1970.

Tremblay, N. "L'aide à l'apprentissage en situation d'autodidaxie" [Help with learning in situations of autodidaxy]. Thèse de doctorat inédite, Université de Montréal, 1981.

Tremblay, N. "L'aide à l'apprentissage chez les autodidactes." [Help with autodidactic learning]. Proceedings of 24th annual Adult Education Research Conference, Montreal, Apr. 1983, 231–236.

Tremblay, N., and Danis, C. "Manifestations de méta-apprentissage en situation d'autodidaxie" [Manifestations of meta-learning in situations of autodidaxy]. Proceedings of 3rd annual conference of the Canadian Association for the Study of Adult Education, Guelph, June 1984, 151–166.

Tzuk, R. "The Relationship Between Readiness to [sic] Self-Directed Learning and Field–Dependence Independence Among Adult Students: Preliminary Findings and Tentative Conclusions." Proceedings of 4th annual conference of the Canadian Association for the Study of Adult Education, Montreal, May 1985a, 135–154.

Tzuk, R. "The Relationship of Self-Directedness in Learning Among Adults to Field Dependence–Independence: An Exploratory Investigation." Unpublished master's thesis, Concordia University, 1985b.

Umoren, A. P. "Learning Projects: An Exploratory Study of Learning Activities of Adults in a Select Socio-Economic Group." Unpublished doctoral dissertation, University of Nebraska, 1977. (*Dissertation Abstracts International, 38* (05A), 2490.)

Umstattd, J. G. "The Prevalence and Practice of Independent Study: A Survey of Independent-Study Plans in Higher Educational Institutions." *Journal of Higher Education,* 1935, *6* (7), 364–367.

Underwood, C. A. "The Learning Efforts and Learning Strategies of Extension Officers." Unpublished master's thesis, University of Melbourne, 1980.

Unesco. *International Standard Classification of Education.* Paris: Division of Statistics on Education, Unesco, 1986.

Unesco Principal Regional Office for Asia and the Pacific. *APPEAL Training Materials for Literacy Personnel.* Vol. 10: *Post-Literacy Activities and Continuing Education.* Bangkok: Unesco Principal Office for Asia and the Pacific, 1990.

Usher, R., and Johnston, R. "Exploring Problems of Self-Directed Learning Within Practice and Discourse." *Studies in Continuing Education,* 1988, *10* (2), 137–151.

Verner, C. "Definition of Terms." In G. Jensen, A. A. Liveright, and W. Hallenbeck (eds.), *Adult Education: Outlines of An Emerging Field of University Study.* Washington, D.C.: Adult Education Association of the U.S.A., 1964.

Vico, G. *De antiquissima italorum sapientia* [Concerning the most ancient Italian wisdom]. Naples: Stamperia de'classici, 1858. (Originally published 1710.)

Vladislavlev, A. P. "Continuing Education in Developed Soviet Society." *Soviet Education,* 1979, *21* (5), 6–25.

von Foerster, H. "On Constructing a Reality." In P. Watzlawick (ed.), *The Invented Reality: How Do We Know What We Believe We Know? Contributions to Constructivism.* New York: Norton, 1984.

von Glasersfeld, E. "Piaget and the Radical Constructivist Epistemology." In C. D. Smock and E. von Glasersfeld (eds.), *Epistemology and Education: The Implications of Radical Constructivism for Knowledge Acquisition.* Mathemagenic Activities Program — Follow Through, Research Report No. 14. Athens: University of Georgia, 1974.

von Glasersfeld, E. "An Introduction to Radical Constructivism." In P. Watzlawick (ed.), *The Invented Reality: How Do We Know*

What We Believe We Know? Contributions to Constructivism. New York: Norton, 1984.

von Glasersfeld, E., and Smock, C. D. "Introduction." In C. D. Smock and E. von Glasersfeld (eds.), *Epistemology and Education: The Implications of Radical Constructivism for Knowledge Acquisition.* Mathemagenic Activities Program — Follow Through, Research Report No. 14. Athens: University of Georgia, 1974.

Vukadinović, G. Z. "Training for Self-Instruction: An Ongoing Experiment." *Prospects: Quarterly Review of Education,* 1988, *18* (1), 27–39.

Wain, K. *Philosophy of Lifelong Education.* London: Croom Helm, 1987.

Walker, G. A. "Written with Invisible Ink: Women in the Adult Education Knowledge Base." Unpublished manuscript, School of Social Work, Carleton University, Ottawa, Canada, 1984.

Wallace, M. J. "Personalizing Instruction Using Hill's Cognitive Mapping Techniques." In S. N. Postlethwaite and Associates (eds.), *Examining Teaching Alternatives.* Minneapolis, Minn.: Burgess, 1977.

Wang, M. C. "Adaptive Instruction: Building on Diversity." *Theory into Practice,* 1980, *19* (2), 122–128.

Wang, M. C. "Development and Consequences of Students' Sense of Personal Control." In J. M. Levine and M. C. Wang (eds.), *Teacher and Student Perceptions: Implications for Learning.* Hillsdale, N.J.: Erlbaum, 1983.

Washburne, C. W. "Adapting the Schools to Individual Differences." In C. W. Washburne (ed.), *The Twenty-Fourth Yearbook of the National Society for the Study of Education,* Part 2. Chicago: National Society for the Study of Education, 1925.

Watt, J. *Individualism and Educational Theory.* Dordrecht, Netherlands: Kluwer Academic Publishers, 1989.

Watzlawick, P. (ed.). *The Invented Reality: How Do We Know What We Believe We Know? Contributions to Constructivism.* New York: Norton, 1984.

Weber, B. "Authority of the Adult Educator: Clarifying our Role." Paper presented at the North West Adult Education Association Conference, Ashland, Oreg., Apr. 1985.

Wedemeyer, C. A. "Independent Study." In L. C. Deighton

(ed.), *The Encyclopedia of Education,* Vol. 4. New York: Macmillan, 1971.

Wedemeyer, C. A. "Independent Learning and the Distant Independent Learner." In *Proceedings of a Conference on Independent Learning,* W. K. Kellogg Foundation Project Report No. 7. Vancouver: Adult Education Research Centre, University of British Columbia, 1973.

Wedemeyer, C. A. "Implications of Open Learning for Independent Study." In G. W. Granholm (ed.), *The System of Distance Education,* Vol. 2. Papers and proceedings of the 10th ICCE International Conference, Brighton, England, May 1975.

Wedemeyer, C. A. *Learning at the Back-Door: Reflections on Non-Traditional Learning in the Lifespan.* Madison: University of Wisconsin Press, 1981.

Weinstein, C. E., and Rogers, B. T. "Comprehension Monitoring as a Learning Strategy." In G. d'Ydewalle (ed.), *Proceedings of the Twenty-Third International Congress of Psychology of the International Union of Psychological Science, Acapulco Mexico, September 2-7, 1984.* Vol. 3: *Cognition, Information Processing and Motivation.* Amsterdam: North Holland, 1985.

Welton, M. R. "'Vivisecting the Nightingale': Reflections on Adult Education as an Object of Study." *Studies in the Education of Adults,* 1987, *19* (1), 46–68.

West, R., and Bentley, E. "Structural Analysis of the Self-Directed Learning Readiness Scale: A Confirmatory Factor Analysis Using LISREL Modeling." Paper presented at the 3rd North American Symposium on Adult Self-Directed Learning, University of Oklahoma, Feb. 1989.

Wexler, P. *Critical Social Psychology.* Boston: Routledge and Kegan Paul, 1983.

Whipple, E. P. *Success and Its Conditions.* Boston: Houghton Mifflin, 1888.

White, J. P. *The Aims of Education Restated.* London: Routledge and Kegan Paul, 1982.

White, T. H. *The Sword in the Stone.* London: Collins, 1938.

Wickett, R.E.Y. "Adult Learning Projects Related to Spiritual Growth." Unpublished doctoral dissertation, University of Toronto, 1978a. (*Dissertation Abstracts International, 39* (07A), 3987.)

Wickett, R.E.Y. "Adult Learning Projects Related to Spiritual Growth." Paper presented at 19th annual Adult Education Research Conference, San Antonio, Tex., Apr. 1978b. (ERIC Document Reproduction Service no. ED 152 983.)

Wight, A. R. "Participative Education and the Inevitable Revolution." *The Journal of Creative Behavior,* 1970, *4* (4), 234–282.

Wilenius, R. "Lifelong General and Cultural Education: A Critical Commentary." *Adult Education in Finland,* 1979, *16* (2), 25–28.

Wiley, K. R. "Effects of a Self-Directed Learning Project and Preference for Structure on the Self-Directed Learning Readiness of Baccalaureate Nursing Students." Unpublished doctoral dissertation, Northern Illinois University, 1981. (*Dissertation Abstracts International, 43* (01A), 49.)

Wiley, K. R. "Effects of a Self-Directed Learning Project and Preference for Structure on Self-Directed Learning Readiness." Proceedings of twenty-third annual Adult Education Research Conference, University of Nebraska, Lincoln, Apr. 1982, 227–232.

Williams, A., and Delahaye, B. "Student Transition to Self-Directed Learning in Economics." Paper presented to the Australian and New Zealand Association of Management Educators, Perth, Australia, Nov. 1988.

Wilson, G. D. (ed.), *The Psychology of Conservatism.* London: Academic Press, 1973.

Wispe, L. G. "Evaluating Section Teaching Methods in the Introductory Course." *Journal of Educational Research,* 1951, *45* (3), 161–186.

Witkin, H. A., Moore, C. A., Goodenough, D. R., and Cox, P. W. "Field-Dependent and Field-Independent Cognitive Styles and Their Educational Implications." *Review of Educational Research,* 1977, *47* (1), 1–64.

Wolf, R. L., and Tymitz, B. L. "Ethnography and Reading: Matching Inquiry Modes to Process." *Reading Research Quarterly,* 1976–77, *12* (1), 5–11.

Woodlands Group. "Management Development Roles: Coach, Sponsor and Mentor." *Personnel Journal,* 1980, *59* (11), 918–921.

Woolfe, R., Murgatroyd, S., and Rhys, S. *Guidance and Coun-*

selling in Adult and Continuing Education: A Developmental Perspective. Milton Keynes, England: Open University Press, 1987.

Yeaxlee, B. A. *Lifelong Education: A Sketch of the Range and Significance of the Adult Education Movement.* London: Cassell, 1929.

Young, L. D. "The Relationship of Race, Sex and Locus of Control to Self-Directed Learning." Unpublished doctoral dissertation, University of Georgia, 1985. (*Dissertation Abstracts International, 46* (07A), 1886.)

Zabari, P. L. "The Role of Self-Directed Learning in the Continuing Education of Gerontological Practitioners." Unpublished doctoral dissertation, Teachers' College, Columbia University, 1985. (*Dissertation Abstracts International, 46* (04A) 1060.)

Zangari, D. J. "Learning Projects of Adult Educators in Nebraska Post-Secondary Institutions." Unpublished doctoral dissertation, University of Nebraska, 1977. (*Dissertation Abstracts International, 38* (12A), 7086.)

Ziegler, W. L. *The Future of Adult Education and Learning in the United States.* Final report of project no. OEG-0-73-5232, Division of Adult Education, Office of Education, U.S. Department of Health, Education, and Welfare. Syracuse, N.Y.: Educational Policy Research Center, Syracuse Research Corporation, 1977.

Zinn, L. M. "Development of a Valid and Reliable Instrument to Identify a Personal Philosophy of Adult Education." Unpublished doctoral dissertation, Florida State University, 1983. (*Dissertation Abstracts International, 44* (06A), 1667–1668.)

Zottoli, J. V. "Self-Directed Learning in Public Management Masters' Programs." Unpublished doctoral dissertation, University of Southern California, 1984. (*Dissertation Abstracts International, 45* (08A), 2649.)

Zubir, R. "The Impact of Individualised Learning and Lecturing on Student Learning in a Malaysian Context: Perspectives of Lecturers and Students." Unpublished doctoral dissertation, University of Surrey, 1983.

NAME INDEX

SUBJECT INDEX

A

Activities Preference Inventory, 146
Adult education: aim of, 425; and democratic responsibilities, 34–35; differentiating, 43–44; function of, 391; goals of, 19–22, 317, 331; iceberg image of, 194–195, 196; instrumental and expressive, 289–290; and interest in self-direction, 24–26; and learner-control, 211–215; and librarians, 191–193; motives for, 28–29; and personal autonomy, 120–124, 126; self-direction as goal of, 19–22; and self-improvement, 28, 128; social contexts for, 22, 42, 81, 88–89, 121–122, 123; universality of, 27–28
Adult Education Research Conference, 212
Adulthood, construct of, and self-directed learning, 42–46, 60, 118
Africa: autodidaxy in, 161, 163; independent learning in primitive, 157; learner-control studies in, 372
Age, and adulthood constructs, 45
American Association of School Administrators, 74
American Education Research Association, 270, 305, 338
American Psychological Association, 132
Andragogy, emergence of, 213
Anticipatory scheme: and constructivism, 272–273; development of, 356–357; and subject matter learning, 353–357

Athens, ancient, as learning society, 78
Attitude Toward Evaluation Scale, 234
Attributions of success and failure, and learner-control, 388–389
Australia: autodidaxy in, 161, 195–196; historical development of adult education in, 28, 192; individual differences in, 82; levels of independence in, 12–13; research on learning in, 249; thinking questions in, 328
Autodidaxy: and adult constructs, 44; aspects of, 157–201; background on, 157–158; concept of, 411; counseling relationship in, 189–191; criticisms of studies of, 162–165; and depth of learning, 289; distinguishing, 402–410; enhancing, 142–149; generalizations on, 31–32; 199–200; gray area between learner-control and, 407–410; group context for, 197–198; helpers for, 180–194; heuristic nature of, 176–177; implications of, 200–201; incidence of, 159–161; and independence, 87–88; and independent study, 13; and individual differences, 74–75, 81–83, 371–373; information sources for, 178–180; and instruction, 86–87; learner-control and development of, 17–19, 56–58, 71–73, 223, 375; learner's view of, 448–449; in learning journals and diaries, 172–174; and learning society, 77–79, 87–91; and levels of assistance, 16–17; librarian-client relationship in, 191–193; and lifelong education, 75–77,

559

M